A COMPANION TO YOUR STUDY OF THE NEW TESTAMENT

THE FOUR GOSPELS

Daniel H. Ludlow

DESERET
BOOK

SALT LAKE CITY, UTAH

Visit us at www.deseretbook.com
First published in hardbound 1982
First published in paperbound 2002

ISBN 0-87747-945-3 (hardbound)
ISBN 1-57008-881-0 (paperbound)

Printed in the United States of America   72706-300205B

Publisher's Printing, Salt Lake City, Utah

10   9   8   7   6   5   4   3

CONTENTS

PREFACE

The New Testament is the most widely accepted testament of the divinity of Jesus Christ, and the four accounts of the gospel written by Matthew, Mark, Luke, and John form the basis of the New Testament.

One purpose of this work, *A Companion to Your Study of the New Testament: The Four Gospels,* is to help the reader of the New Testament better appreciate and understand the many contributions of the four writers of the gospel message. Numerous commentaries on various scriptural passages by inspired prophets of this dispensation and by other scriptural scholars have been included to help achieve this purpose.

The basic scriptural text referred to by this book is the King James Version of the New Testament. The many other study aids referred to are in the Latter-day Saint edition of the King James Version of the Bible, published in 1979 by The Church of Jesus Christ of Latter-day Saints, including chapter headings, footnotes, maps, and entries in the Topical Guide (TG), Bible Dictionary (BD), and Gazetteer.

The following publications have been particularly helpful and are quoted quite extensively in this book. Students of the New Testament are encouraged to study these books in their entirety:

Doctrinal New Testament Commentary, volume 1, by Elder Bruce R. McConkie of the Council of the Twelve Apostles of The Church of Jesus Christ of Latter-day Saints. (Salt Lake City: Bookcraft, 1965–73.)

Jesus the Christ, by Elder James E. Talmage, an earlier apostle in the Church. (12th ed. Salt Lake City: The Church of Jesus Christ of Latter-day Saints, 1924.)

Life and Teachings of Jesus, prepared by the Church Educational System. (Salt Lake City, 1978.)

The author of this book is fully aware of the admonition of Peter: "Knowing this first, that no prophecy of the scripture is of any private interpretation. For the prophecy came not in old time by the will of man: but holy men of God spake

as they were moved by the Holy Ghost." (2 Pet. 1:20–21.)
Thus, specific interpretations of scriptural passages have
been left largely to those who have been called, ordained,
and set apart to speak for the Lord in these latter days: the
prophets, seers, and revelators of The Church of Jesus Christ
of Latter-day Saints.

In section 1, a list of key words and terms from the New
Testament, "BD" indicates that the Bible Dictionary contains
an entry for that word. Section 1 also contains definitions of
many of these words and terms. This should prove very
helpful to students of the New Testament, as the English language has changed a great deal since the King James Version
of the Bible was prepared in 1611. The definitions given in
section 1 have been carefully checked with standard Bible
dictionaries and with a 1737 edition of *An Universal
Etymological English Dictionary* published by N. Bailey
publishers in England. Section 1 also includes many cross-
references to the scriptures, so that if the reader has a question
on a certain topic during his reading, he can turn to section 1
and find other scriptures covering that topic.

In section 2, some scripture references are in large italics, for example, *1:1– 17.* Such references indicate major
sections within chapters.

Because of the many contributions of the articles in the
Bible Dictionary and because other books and manuals on
the New Testament are readily available, it was not felt necessary to include in this volume a section pertaining to the
origin of the New Testament itself nor to the background of
the four writers of the gospels. Thus, after section 1, this
book begins directly with commentaries on the writings of
Matthew.

ACKNOWLEDGMENTS

Several persons have assisted in the preparation and publication of this book and deserve special thanks and appreciation:

My wife, Luene, for her support and numerous contributions in so many ways.

Our two daughters, Kathy and Michelle, for many hours of checking references, quotations, and footnotes. Special thanks to Kathy for her research and typing assistance; for her special insights, perspectives, and helpful suggestions; and for helping to see the proofs through to final publication.

Gary Gillespie, a gifted friend with a special spirit, for his assistance in editing the manuscript for delivery to the publishers.

Merle Romer and Diane Chrysler for typing some of the early copy and for being such fine and loyal friends.

Eleanor Knowles and Jack Lyon, editors at Deseret Book, for their efficient and effective editorial assistance, which was appreciated particularly because of the many miles that separated us physically.

And, as always, sincere and humble thanks to our Heavenly Father and to his Divine Son for making the New Testament available to the world.

My prayer is that this book might serve in some small way to help us all appreciate this important book of scripture and come to a better understanding of it.

KEY TO ABBREVIATIONS

AF   *Articles of Faith*, James E. Talmage

AGQ *Answers to Gospel Questions*, Joseph Fielding Smith

BD   Bible Dictionary, Latter-day Saint edition of the King James Version of the Bible

COT *A Companion to Your Study of the Old Testament*, Daniel H. Ludlow

CR   Conference Report

DNTC *Doctrinal New Testament Commentary*, Bruce R. McConkie

DS   *Doctrines of Salvation*, Joseph Fielding Smith

Dummelow   *A Commentary on the Whole Bible*, edited by J.R. Dummelow

GD   *Gospel Doctrine*, Joseph F. Smith

HC   *History of the Church*, Joseph Smith

JB   Jerusalem Bible

JD   *Journal of Discourses*

JST   Joseph Smith Translation of the Bible

JTC   *Jesus the Christ*, James E. Talmage

KIT   Kingdom Interlinear Translation of the Greek Scriptures

LB   Living Bible

LTJA *Life and Teachings of Jesus and the Apostles*, Church Educational System

MD   *Mormon Doctrine*, Bruce R. McConkie

MF   *The Miracle of Forgiveness*, Spencer W. Kimball

NEB New English Bible

NIV   New International Version of the Bible

PME Phillips Modern English Bible

RSV   Revised Standard Version of the Bible

TEV   Today's English Version of the Bible

TG   Topical Guide, Latter-day Saint edition of the King James Version of the Bible

TPJS   *Teachings of the Prophet Joseph Smith*, selected by
        Joseph Fielding Smith
WP   *The Way to Perfection*, Joseph Fielding Smith

Note: Some of the sources quoted in this book refer to
Teachings of the Prophet Joseph Smith as *Teachings*, to the
Joseph Smith Translation as the Inspired Version or I. V., and
to *History of the Church* as Jos. Smith

SECTION 1
KEY WORDS
AND TERMS

KEY WORDS AND TERMS

Aaronic Priesthood BD
Abased humbled; lowered; brought
down
Abba BD; transliteration of the
Hebrew *father;* Mark 14:36
Abide continue; tarry; stay
Me wait for me
Abilene BD
Abominable abhorred; hated
Abomination of Desolation BD; Matt.
24:15–22
Abraham BD; Matt. 3:9
Children raised up to Matt. 3:9;
Luke 3:8
Covenant of BD; John 8:37–40
Abraham's Bosom BD; Luke 16:22
Abstinence fasting; refraining one's
self
Accounting considering; reckoning;
reputing
Aceldama BD
Adam, no men before Luke 3:38
Addicted devoted; appointed; to give
up one's self wholly to a thing
Adjure charge you under oath; cause
you to swear; implore; charge in
God's name; strictly or earnestly
Ado uproar; tumult; affair
Adulterous generation Matt. 12:39
Adultery BD; Matt. 5:27–28
Woman taken in John 8:1–11
Advocate BD; intercessor; helper;
comforter; supporter; one that lays
to heart, takes care of, or secures
the interest of another
Aenon BD; John 3:23–24
Affirm strongly assert; assure; ratify;
confirm
Affrighted amazed; astonished; put
into a fright or fear; scared
Aforehand beforehand

Aforetime beforetime
Against, if not with Matt. 12:30
Against (opposite) Matt. 27:61
Alexander BD
Alleluia BD; praise ye Jehovah, praise
ye the Lord
Allow give or grant; approve of; permit
Allure entice; entrap; decoy; draw to
the lure or bait
Alms righteousness; acts of religious
devotion
Almsgiving BD; Matt. 6:1–4
Alpha BD; the first letter in the Greek
alphabet
Alphaeus BD
Altar BD
Amazement dismay; consternation;
astonishment; daunted; surprised
Amen BD; a transliteration of a
Hebrew word meaning "thus it is"
or "so be it"
Anathema renounced or given up; a
solemn curse; sentence of
excommunication
Andrew BD
Angels BD; messengers
Ministered to John the Baptist
Matt. 4:12
Anger wrath
Anise BD; dill
Anna BD; Luke 2:36
Annas BD; John 18:13–14
Annunciation BD; Luke 1:26–38
Anoint BD; Matt. 26:6–13; Mark 6:13
Anointed One BD
Anon BD; readily; immediately; by
and by; Matt. 13:20
Antichrist BD
Apostasy Matt. 24:23–27

Apostle BD; Mark 3:14; Luke 6:13

Apostles, calling of Matt. 10:1–4; Luke 5:1–11; 6:13

Apt fit; convenient; meet; proper

Archangel chief angel

Archelaus BD

Arimathaea BD; Mark 15:43

Ascension BD; Mark 16:19–20

Ask John 16:24

Assayed tried; attempted

Asunder divided; separated; in two parts

Atonement BD; reconciliation; appeasing of anger; Matt. 26:36–46

Augustus BD; Luke 2:1

Austere harsh; ungenerous; severe; stern; sour; crabbed

Babblings empty soundings; fruitless discussion; idle talk; pratings

Backbiting talking against; evil speaking; speaking ill of behind one's back

Baptism BD; Mark 1:4; Luke 7:30
of Jesus Matt. 3:15–16; Luke 3:21
Jesus practiced Matt. 9:15–16; John 3:22; 4:1–2
of Spirit Mark 1:8; John 20:22

Bar BD; son of

Barabbas BD; Matt. 27:15–26; Mark 15:6

Bar-jona BD

Barley BD

Barn storehouse; repository for any sort of grain or hay

Bartholomew BD

Bartimaeus BD; Mark 10:46–52

Base low; humble; mean; vile; cowardly; dishonest; stingy

Beam a great piece of timber used in building

Beatitudes BD; Matt. 5:1–12; 5:3–11; Luke 6:24–26

Becometh is fitting for us; to be made or done

Beelzebub BD; Matt. 12:24–26

Begat became father to; produced; generated

Beguile deceive

Behoved was necessary for; was proper for; was the duty of

Believe exercise faith; give credit to

Believeth not disbelieve; disobey; uncompliant to

Beseech exhort

Beside himself out of his senses

Besought entreated; requested; earnestly urged

Beth BD

Bethabara BD; John 1:28

Bethany BD

Bethesda BD; John 5:4

Bethlehem BD; Luke 2:4

Bethphage BD

Bethsaida BD

Betrayal of Jesus Matt. 26:47–56

Bewrayeth reveals (from Middle English *bewraien:* to declare or discover)

Bible BD

Bidden invited; offered

Bishop a chief officer in the church

Blasphemies slanderous statements

Blasphemy BD; falsely assuming or claiming; cursing; reviling; speaking evil of God or holy things; John 10:31–33
Against the Holy Ghost Matt. 12:33

Blaze abroad spread widely

Blessed happy

Blindness BD; Mark 7:32–37; John 9:1–41

Blood BD
And water John 19:34

Bond slaves; an obligation; persons who bind themselves to serve

Border coast; Mark 5:17

Borne carried; brought

Bottles BD; leather or skin bags; waterskins; wineskins; vessels to contain liquids; Matt. 9:17; Mark 2:22

Bowels At one point in history the bowels were considered to be the location of feeling; the meaning of the word might include affections, compassion, commiseration.

Brawler quarrelsome; wrangler; scolder

Bread of Life John 6:28–59

Brethren of the Lord BD; Matt. 12:46–50; John 7:2–9

Brimstone sulfur; combustible material; burning of fire and stone

Bruise crush; grind; injure or spoil the form of by hard compression

Buffet treat roughly; strike on the ear with a fist; slap on the face

Burial BD

Burning Bush BD

Busybodies meddlers

By and by BD; at once; immediately

Caesar BD
    Render to Matt. 22:15–22; Mark 12:17

Caesarea Philippi BD; Matt. 16:13–20; Mark 8:27–30

Caiaphas BD; Matt. 26:3; John 11:49–52; 18:13–14

Calendar BD

Calvary BD

Camel BD

Camel's hair BD

Cana of Galilee BD; John 2:1–11

Canaanite BD

Canon BD

Capernaum BD

Captain of the Temple BD

Carcass, eagles gather to Matt. 24:28

Carnal temporal; material; belonging to the flesh; fleshy; sensual

Cedron BD

Celestial heavenly; above the sky

Censer BD; incense vessel; perfuming pan

Centurion BD; captain over 100 foot soldiers; Matt. 8:8–9

Cephas BD; John 1:38–42

Chalcedony copperlike; a sort of onyx stone

Chambering whoredoms; lewdness; cohabitation; debauchery; riotousness

Charge command; direct; enjoin; order

Charged them straitly strongly warned them

Charger BD; platter; large dish or plate; Matt. 14:8

Chasten instruct; admonish; correct; punish

Chastening correction; instruction; discipline

Children
    Inherit heaven Matt. 18:1–5; 19:13; Mark 10:14; Luke 18:16
    No baptism Matt. 18:1–5; 19:13; Mark 1:4; 10:14

Choked drowned; stopped up

Chorazin BD; Matt. 11:20–24

Christ BD; Greek term meaning "Anointed One"; essentially the same as the Hebrew *Messiah;* Matt. 1:16
    Names of BD; Matt. 1:16

Christs, false BD

Circumcision BD; Luke 1:57–66

Clamour cry; outcry; make a noise; complain; cry out against

Clave past tense of cleave: cut in pieces

Clean BD, "Clean and unclean"; pure

Clemency equity; mildness; gentleness; meekness; courtesy

Clement merciful; meek; gentle

Cleopas BD

Closet private room; small apartment in a room

Cloth, shrunk and unshrunk Matt. 9:16

Clothing BD

Cloud BD

Coasts borders; surrounding regions; lands

Coat/cloke Matt. 5:38–41

Codex BD

Comely becoming; proper; fitting; handsome; beautiful; graceful

Comforter BD; John 14:16

Comforters John 14:15–26

Coming of Jesus Christ BD

Commandment, the great Matt. 22:34–40

Commandments, the Ten BD
Commendation recommendation; praising or setting forth
Commending setting together; approving; standing with
Common customary
    People accepted Christ Mark 8:1–10
Communed talked; conferred
Concision cutting down; mutilation; circumcision
Concupiscence longing for that which is forbidden; desire; lust
Confess acknowledge; praise; testify; witness; own, declare
    Me solemnly covenant with me; promise me
Confession BD; Matt. 18:17
Confirm establish; make; secure; strengthen; give new assurance of the truth
Confirmation BD; holy rite by which one becomes a member of the Church
Considered not did not understand
Consolation comfort; easing of grief
Consorted partook of the same condition
Constrained persuaded
Contrariwise absolutely different
Conversation BD
Conversion BD
Conversion of Peter Luke 22:32
Convince BD
Corban BD; a gift or offering made on the altar, properly the treasure kept for the use of the temple or priests at Jerusalem; Matt. 15:3–6; Mark 7:11
Corn BD; grain; grain of wheat, barley, rice, oats, etc.
    Of wheat kernel, grain, or seed of wheat
Corrupt decayed; rotten; stale; tainted; naught; Matt. 7:17
Covet lust for; set the heart upon; desire eagerly
Crave request; beseech; desire earnestly; ask for (Note: in Luke 23:52 translated as "begged")

Cross, take up Matt. 16:24
Crucifixion BD; Matt. 27:32; 27:35
Crucify impale; fasten or nail to a cross; kill or mortify
Cubit BD
Cumbered laden down
Cummin BD; Matt. 23:23–24
Cup, to drink of, of Christ Matt. 20:21, 23; Mark 10:39
Cyrene BD; Matt. 27:32
Cyrenius BD

Dalmanutha BD; Mark 8:10
Damnation BD; the punishment of the dammed. The Greek word frequently translated "damnation" could sometimes have been translated "punishment" or "condemnation."
Damned Mark 16:16
Damsel servant girl; young maiden
Danger of the judgment subject to condemnation
Darkness BD
Daughters of Jerusalem Luke 23:27–31
David, city of Luke 2:11
Dayspring BD; dawn; Luke 1:78
Deacon BD; "ministry"; an office in the priesthood; a minister or servant; one whose office is to assist the priest. The meanings of the word in the Greek include the ideas of serving, attending, ministering, supporting.
Dead
    Bury dead Matt. 8:22; Luke 9:60
    If one raised from, people still would not believe Luke 16:31
    Raised to life Luke 7:11–17
Dead Sea BD
Dead Sea Scrolls BD
Dearth famine; great scarcity of provisions or victuals
Death BD
Death of Jesus Matt. 27:50; Luke 23:46
Debt (can't get God in) Matt. 19:27–29

Debts sins; trespasses; offenses; faults
Decapolis BD; Matt. 4:25; Mark 7:31
Defile spoil; corrupt; deprave; pollute
Deny disown; not to admit of or grant; gainsay or disown; Matt. 10:33; 26:34–35
Desert solitary places; desolate places; wilderness; Mark 6:31
Despite insult; envy; malice; spite
Determined appointed; decreed; purposed; designed
Devil BD
Devils
>   **Also believe** Matt. 8:29
>   **Are spirits** Mark 1:26
>   **Possess bodies** Matt. 8:28–34; 12:28; Mark 1:21–28; 1:32
>   **Power to cast out** Matt. 12:28; Luke 11:14–15
Diaspora BD
Didymus BD; John 11:16
Die the death he shall surely die
Disciple BD
Disciples slept in Gethsemane Mark 14:41
Dispensations BD
Dispersion BD
Dissimulation hypocrisy; counterfeiting; pretending to one thing and designing quite the contrary
Ditch pit; well; cistern; trench around a field
Divers many; some; various; sundry; several
Diverse in different places; one place after another; divers; various; contrary
Divine Sonship of Jesus John 10:17–21
Divorce BD; Matt. 19:1–12; Mark 10:4
Doctrine, strong, people reject John 6:60–65
Doctrines, some of men Matt. 15:9
Dogs, little Matt. 15:26
Doting hankering after; fond of
Doubletongued telling a different story

Dove BD; Matt. 10:16
>   **Sign of** BD; John 1:32–34; Matt. 3:16
Draught catch; haul; place of sitting apart; privy (sewer)
Dreams BD; sometimes means "visions"
Dresser vine worker or pruner
Dropsy "looking watery"; the settlement of a watery humour either through the whole body or some part of it
Dumb speechless
Dung refuse (garbage); ordure; filth
Durst dared

Easter BD; the Passover
Edify build up; profit by instruction
Education BD
Effectual active; operative; efficient; powerful; forcible; producing an effect
Egypt BD
>   **Jesus in** Matt. 2:13–15
El BD
Elders BD
Elect of God Matt. 24:25
Eli BD
Eliakim BD
Elias BD; Matt. 17:10–13
>   **John an** Matt. 11:13–15; John 1:20–21
Eliezer BD
Elijah BD; Matt. 16:14
Elijah at transfiguration Matt. 17:3–4
Elisabeth BD
Eliseus BD; Luke 4:27
Eloi BD; Mark 15:34
Emmanuel BD, "Immanuel"; "God with us"
Emmaus BD; Luke 24:13
Emulation striving to excel or go beyond another; envying or disdaining
Endowment Luke 24:49
Endued clothed; invested; endowed; furnished with
Engrafted grafted; implanted

Enjoin accomplish; do; finish; bid; charge; order

Ensamples types; examples; patterns

Ensue pursue; follow eagerly

Entangle ensnare; involve in difficulties; perplex

Enticing persuasive; alluring; tempting

Epaphroditus BD

Ephphatha BD; Mark 7:34

Ephraim BD; a city

Epistles BD

Esaias BD

Eschew turn away from; avoid; shun

Espousal Matt. 1:18–24; Luke 1:27

Espoused betrothed

Essenes BD

Estate condition of things or affairs; revenue; property

Eternal life, what to gain Matt. 19:16; John 17:3

Eunuch BD; courtier; official; officer; unmarried man; gelded man; Matt. 19:12

Evangelist BD; preacher of the gospel; messenger of good tidings

Evidently clearly; distinctly; apparently; clearly

Evil bad; spoiled; degenerate; ill; mischief

Exalt raise; lift up; praise highly; extol

Excommunication Matt. 18:8–9

Exhort call; invite; invoke; beseech; encourage; incite

Expedient beneficial; profitable; advantageous; fit; convenient; necessary

Experiment experience; proof; trial; essay

Eyes and hands (members of family) Matt. 5:29–30

Eyesalve poultice; plaster

Ezekias BD

Fable tale of fiction; story devised for the sake of instruction; feigned tale; falsehood

Fain desire; covet; set the heart upon; glad

Faith BD; Mark 9:24; Luke 17:5–6; John 14:12–14

Faithful, be Matt. 10:23–28

Fall of Adam BD

Family BD

Members will not all accept Matt. 5:29–30; Luke 12:50; 12:53

Fan BD; Luke 3:17

Farthing

Of gold a coin in ancient times; the fourth part of a noble

Of land a certain considerable quantity

Fasting Matt. 6:16–18

Fasts BD

Father, God as John 5:17–24

Fear caution; reverence; apprehension of evil; dread; fright

Feast

Of Dedication John 10:22–39

Of Tabernacles John 7:2–9

Feasts BD

Fellowship sharing; company; partnership

Fig tree BD

Cursed Matt. 21:18–22; Mark 11:12–14

Figure type; pattern; similitude; fashion; shape; representation

Fire BD

Firkin John 2:6

First/last Matt. 20:1–16; Mark 7:27

Fish BD

Fishers of men Matt. 4:18–22

Flax, smoking Matt. 12:20

Flesh BD

Flux dysentery; flood or tide; looseness of the belly

Follow come after; imitate

Followers The Greek word frequently translated "followers" could have been translated "imitators."

Forasmuch since

Foreknowledge knowledge; understanding; acquaintance with

Foreordained defined before; designed before

Forgive

Sins, Jesus can Mark 2:6–12

Them (the soldiers) Luke 23:34

Forgiveness Matt. 9:1–8; Luke 23:34; John 20:23

    Till 70 x 7 Matt. 18:23–35

For my name's sake because of my name

For my sake on account of me

Fornication The Greek word frequently translated "fornication" could also have been translated "immorality." Sexual immorality between single persons

Forsook left

Forswear thyself break your oath; perjure yourself; swear falsely

Forthwith immediately; suddenly; presently; quickly

Frankincense BD; Matt. 2:11

Frontlets, or phylacteries BD; Matt. 23:5

Froward crooked; wicked; deceitful; perverse; peevish; fretful; surly

Fruit product of the earth, trees, plants, etc.; also, profits of goods, rent, revenue, etc. The Greek word frequently translated "fruit" sometimes could have been translated as "benefit," "reward."

Fulfill all righteousness Matt. 3:15–16

Fuller BD; one who fulls, mills, or scours cloth; Mark 9:3

Furlong eighth of a mile; John 6:19

Furniture BD

Gabriel BD

Gadara BD; Mark 5:1

Gainsay oppose; contradict; speak against; deny

Gainsayers those who deny; contradict

Gainsaying contradicting; opposing

Galilee BD

Galilee, Sea of BD; Matt. 4:18; Luke 5:1

Gall BD; Matt. 27:34

Games BD

Garner storehouse; granary; barn

Garnished Matt. 12:44; Luke 11:25

Gate BD

Gehenna BD

Genealogies of Jesus BD, "Genealogy"; Luke 3:23–38

Genealogy BD

General Epistles BD

Generation offspring; the production of something in a natural way; lineage; race; descent; Matt. 24:34

Gennesaret(h), land of BD; Mark 6:53

Gentile BD; Mark 7:28–30

Gentiles, times of Luke 21:24–25

Gergesenes BD

Gethsemane BD; "place of the olive press"; garden on the Mount of Olives; Matt. 26:36–46; Mark 14:32–42; Luke 22:40–46

    Agony in Luke 22:40–46

Gihon (spring) BD

Girdest bind about; tie up close

Glistering radiant; brilliant; glistening; shining; bright; sparkling

Glory not do not assume superiority over; not to brag or boast

Glorified, Son and Father John 13:31

Glory wealth; honor; boast; renown; reputation

Glory of the Lord BD

Glorying boasting

Goats BD

God BD

    No man hath seen John 1:18

    Forbid May it not be!; Luke 20:16

Gold BD; Matt. 2:11

Golden rule Matt. 7:12

Golgotha BD; place of burial; has been interpreted as "place of a skull"; was at Jerusalem, on the North side of Mount Sion; a place full of the bones of malefactors; Matt. 27:33; Mark 15:22

Gomorrah BD

Good, why callest me Matt. 19:17

Gospels BD

Gospel

    Preached in the beginning John 1:1–5

    To be preached in latter days Matt. 24:14

Grace BD; undeserved kindness; the mercy of God in supplying redemption for mankind; disposition of mind or power to yield obedience to divine laws

Grave, gravity The Greek word referring to a personal characteristic that is frequently translated "grave" could also have been translated "dignified," "respectful," "honorable."

Greatness Luke 22:24

Greece BD

Greeks, Jesus taught John 12:20–26

Green tree (Christ) Luke 23:27–31

Guile deceit, fraud

Hagiographa BD

Hair of head not lost Matt. 10:30

Hallel BD

Hallowed be thy name let thy name be sanctified

Halt lame; crippled

[at] Hand has come; has arrived

Handkerchief utensil for wiping the face

Haply perhaps; perchance; fortunately; happily

Hard strict; close; compacted; difficult

Hardly enter enter only with great difficulty

Hardness of heart insensibility; dullness

Harmless innocent; guileless

Hasidaeans BD

Hasmonaean BD

Hate, not literal Luke 14:25–26

Haven harbor; an entrance of a sea at the mouth of a river; a harbor for ships

Healing Matt. 4:24; Luke 4:40–44; John 4:46–54

　　Extended Mark 8:22–26

　　On Sabbath Matt. 12:10–13; Luke 13:10–17; 14:1–6

Hear understand; learn; receive; listen; examine a cause

Heaven BD

Hebrew BD

Hell BD; Matt. 5:22

Hem of garment BD; Matt. 14:36

Herb vegetable; plant whose stalk dies away every year

Hereafter from now on; after this time

Heretick a schismatic; one who holds an opinion contrary to a religion

Hermon BD

Herod BD; Matt. 2:1; 2:19; 14:1–2; 14:1–12; Luke 23:6–12

Herodians BD; Matt. 22:16

Herodias BD

High Priest BD

High Priestly Prayer John 17:1–26

Hill country BD; Luke 1:39

Hold me not detain me not; keep me not

Holden restrained

Holiness BD

Holpen helped; succored; supported

Holy Ghost BD; John 7:39; 14:15–26; 16:5–15

　　Not the father of Jesus Matt. 1:18

Holy of Holies BD

Holy One of Israel BD

Holy Spirit, temporary gift of Luke 24:45

Honor John 5:41

Hosanna BD; Matt. 21:1–11; 21:9

Hospitality BD

Hour BD

House, my Matt. 23:38

Husbandman farmer; cultivator; manager of expenses; one employed in husbandry

Husbandry farm; cultivated field; the art of tilling and improving land; management of expenses

Husks BD; Luke 15:16

Hymns BD; religious ode; spiritual song or psalm; Matt. 26:30; Mark 14:26

Hypocrisy condemned Matt. 23:1–22

Hypocrite BD; Matt. 6:2

Hyssop BD; John 19:29

I AM John 8:58
Idol BD
Idumea BD; Mark 3:8
If on the cross Matt. 27:39– 44
Immanuel BD; Matt. 1:23
Implacable truceless; truce-breaker;
not to be appeased or pacified
Implead call in question; bring to
account; sue or prosecute by court
of law
Importunity impudence; eager
pressing or urging
Impute attribute or ascribe the merit or
blame
Incense BD
Incontinent excess; want of
self-restraint; without self-control;
unchaste; unstayed; intemperate;
loose
Inexcusable indefensible; without
excuse; not to be excused
Infidel unbeliever; without faith;
disbeliever; heathen; one who
believes nothing of the Christian
religion
Iniquity lawlessness; want of equity;
injustice; wickedness
Instant urgent; earnest; eager; press-
ing; present; near at hand
Instantly sometimes used as *earnestly,
intently*
Intercessor, Christ as John 17:1–26
In the way by the road
Intreaty entreaty; imploring;
submissive asking; supplication
Isaiah BD
Is it I? Matt. 26:22; 26:25
Israel BD
Issue of blood hemorrhage
Italics BD
It had been good it would have been
good

Jacob's Well BD
Jairus BD; Mark 5:22
James BD
    Epistle of BD
Jangling babble; random talk
Jehovah BD; John 8:58

Jericho BD
Jerusalem BD; Matt. 23:37–39; Luke
19:41
    **To be destroyed, but righteous
saved** Mark 11:11
Jesting witticism; ribaldry
Jesus BD; Matt. 1:21; Luke 1:31
    As head of corner Matt. 21:46
    As the Bridegroom Matt. 9:15;
25:1–13
    Birthdate of Luke 2:7
    Called prophet of Galilee Matt.
21:11
    Childhood of Luke 2:39– 40; 2:52
    Death of Matt. 27:50; Luke 23:46
    Distinguishes *me* and *thee* Matt.
17:27
    In temple at age 12 Luke 2:42
    Offered drugged wine Matt.
27:34; Mark 15:23
    Power of, over death John
10:17–21
    Trial of Matt. 26:57–68
Jew BD
Joanna BD
John BD
John
    Epistles of BD
    Gospel of BD
John the Baptist BD; Matt. 3:1–6;
Luke 1:57–66; 1:80
    Escaped the slaughter Matt.
2:16–18; 23:35
    Greatest Prophet Matt. 11:9;
11:11; Luke 7:28
    On Mount of Transfiguration
Matt. 17:10–13; Mark 9:4
    Sent disciples to question Jesus
Matt. 11:2–6
    Taught against Herod Matt.
14:1–2
Jona or Jonas BD
Jonah, reference to Matt. 12:40; Mark
8:12
Jordan River BD; Matt. 3:5–6
Joseph, son of Heli BD
    Not real father of Jesus Matt.
2:22

Joseph of Arimathaea BD
Joseph Smith Translation BD
Joses BD
Jot the tenth letter of the Hebrew
  alphabet; a very small part of
  anything
Joy might be full John 15:8
Juda BD
Judas BD; Matt. 26:47–56; 27:4–5;
  John 13:18
  Did Satan actually enter? Luke
  22:3
  Son of perdition? Matt. 26:24;
  John 17:12
Jude BD
  Epistle of BD
Judea BD, "Judaea"
Judgment Matt. 7:1–2
Judgment hall BD; John 18:28
Just righteous; reasonable; fit
Justified declared righteous; to make
  or declare innocent

Key instrument to open a lock;
  guardian; warden
Keys of kingdom Matt. 16:19; 18:18;
  Luke 3:4–5
Kill murder; deprive of life; Matt. 5:21
**King, followers wanted to make
  Christ** John 6:15
Kingdom of God within Luke
  17:20–21
**Kingdom of heaven or Kingdom of
  God** BD; Matt. 3:2; 6:10; 10:7;
  John 3:5
**Kingdoms sometimes obtained
  elsewhere** Luke 19:14
Kiss, sign of betrayal Matt. 26:50;
  Luke 22:48
Knew, I never, you Matt. 7:23
Know thee John 17:3
Know recognize; detect; understand
Knowledge BD

Lamb of God BD; John 1:29
Lamp BD; Matt. 25:7

Lasciviousness licentiousness; loose
  conduct; filthiness; wantonness
Laud applaud; commend; praise
Laughed him to scorn ridiculed him
Law of Moses BD
Lawyer BD
Laying await plot; conspiracy
Laying on of hands BD
Lazarus BD; John 11:1–46
Leaven BD; yeast; piece of dough
  salted and soured; to ferment and
  relish the whole lump; Matt. 13:33
  Of Pharisees Matt. 16:6–12
Legion BD; Roman regiment consist-
  ing of about 6,000 men; Mark 5:9
Leper BD; Matt. 8:1–4; Luke 17:11–19
Leprosy BD; Matt. 8:1–4
Let BD
Levirate marriage BD; Matt. 22:23
Levites BD; Luke 10:32
Lewd wicked; evil; dissolute; wanton;
  riotous
Lewdness crime
Life, lose to save Matt. 10:39
Light of Christ BD; John 1:9
Light of the World John 8:12–20
Listed desired; willed; chose; intended
Listeth intend; be disposed
Lively living; brisk; vivacious
Locusts BD
Lodge dwell; live
Lord's Prayer BD; Matt. 6:9–13;
  Luke 11:4–5
Lord's Supper BD
Lost books BD
Love, gospel of Matt. 5:43–47;
  22:37–40; John 13:34
Lowring dark; gloomy; overcast with
  clouds
Lucifer BD; Luke 10:18
Luke BD
Lunatick crazy; moonstruck; one with
  distemper that makes eyes seem
  covered with white
Lust desire; long for; have an

inclination to; unlawful passion or desire; natural desire

Lusts violent desires

Magdalene BD; inhabitant of Magdala

Magi BD; Matt. 2:11–12

Magnificat Luke 1:55

Malefactors criminals; evildoers; wrongdoers; offenders; Luke 23:32–33,

Malignity mischievousness; bad character; hurtfulness; grudge; ill-will

Mammon BD; Matt. 6:24–25; Luke 16:9

Manger stall; crib for fodder

Manna BD; John 6:30–31

Manner fashion; way; custom; usage

Mansions, many John 14:2

Mark BD

Mark them watch them; beware of them

Marriage BD; Matt. 19:4–6; 22:23–33

Martha BD

Martyrdom not necessary Luke 9:24–25

Marvelled Matt. 22:22

Mary BD; John 19:25–27

Mary and Martha Luke 10:38–42

Mary Magdalene BD

Master teacher

Matthew BD; Matt. 9:9; Luke 5:27

May be may become

Meat BD; food; meal; flesh; provisions of any sort; Matt. 6:25–26; Mark 8:8; Luke 9:13; John 4:8

Mediator reconciler; go-between; arbitrator; intercessor

Meek gentle; forgiving; benevolent; kind; mild; quiet; not easily provoked

Meet BD; suitable for; appropriate to; worthy of; fit; apt

Melchizedek Priesthood BD

Messiah BD; Hebrew term for the Anointed One; essentially the

same as the Greek *Christ;* anointed; the name and title of our Lord and Savior Jesus Christ; John 4:26

Mete reckon; calculate; figure

Miles, go two Matt. 5:41

Millstone BD

Minister The Greek word often translated "minister" could also be translated "servant"

Mint where the King's coin is made; coin money

Miracles BD; Matt. 4:24; John 2:1–11
    Fed 5,000 Matt. 14:13–21; John 6:5–14
    Fed 4,000 Matt. 15:32–39
    Healing man blind from birth John 9
    Healing of nobleman's son John 4:46–54
    Raising of Lazarus John 11:1–46
    Stilled storm Luke 8:22–25
    Walked on water Matt. 14:22–23
    Water into wine John 2:1–11

Mischief hurt; damage

Mite small coin; a fourteenth of a grain in weight

Mocked deceived; derided; flouted

Money BD

Moneychangers from temple Matt. 21:12–17; John 2:13–17

Mortify subdue; deaden; conquer

Moses BD

Mote speck; chip; splinter; Matt. 7:3; Luke 6:41–42

Mother, behold thy John 19:25–27

Murder BD; Matt. 5:21

Muse deliberate; consider; reason; think; pause; study

Music BD

Mustard BD; Matt. 13:31

Myrrh BD

Mysteries BD, "Mystery"; sacred secrets; secret truths; great truths; things concealed; secrets not easy to be comprehended; Matt. 13:11; Mark 4:11

Nain BD
Names of Persons BD
Napkin towel for wiping perspiration from the face; handkerchief
Nathanael BD; John 1:43–51
Nazarene BD; inhabitant of Nazareth; Matt. 2:23
Nazareth BD; Matt. 2:23
    Jesus rejected at Luke 4:16–30
Nazarite BD; Matt. 3:4–5
Needle, eye of Matt. 19:24; Luke 18:25
Neighbor Luke 10:25–37
Nephew descendant; grandchild; son of a brother or sister
Neutrals, no Matt. 12:30
Nicodemus BD; John 3:1–8
Nigh near at hand; hard by
Noised abroad discussed
Noisome bad; evil; loathsome; stinking; nasty
Nurture instruction; disciplinary correction; nourishing, instructing, or bringing up in good manners

Oaths Matt. 5:33; 23:16–22
Offend cause to stumble
Offended stumbled
Offense stumbling block
Olive tree BD
Olives, Mount of BD
Omega BD; the last letter in the Greek alphabet; metaphorically, the end of anything
Omnipotent all powerful; the all-ruling Almighty; the absolute and universal sovereign
Oneness John 17:20–26
Oracles ambiguous and obscure answers heathen priests gave about things to come, making people believe that God spoke through them
Oration a discourse or speech pronounced in public
Ordain order; prescribe; command; appoint; confer Holy Orders
Ordained prepared; built; John 15:16
Ordinance John 15:16

Ought anything; somewhat; owed
Over against on the other side of; above; beyond; in front of

Palestine BD
Palm trees John 11:13
Palsy stroke; paralysis; Matt. 8:5–13
Paps breasts; teats; nipples; Luke 23:29
Parable BD; illustration; continued similitude or comparison; Matt. 13:1–58; 13:1–3; 13:11; 13:34–35
    Abraham's bosom Luke 16:19–31
    Fig tree Matt. 24:32–33; Luke 13:6–9
    Friend at midnight Luke 11:5–8
    Great supper Luke 14:12–24
    Householder at Second Coming Luke 12:35–48
    King forgives debtor Matt. 18:23–35
    Laborers in vineyard Matt. 20:1–16
    Lazarus and rich man Luke 16:19–31
    Lost coin Luke 15:8–10
    Lost sheep Matt. 18:11–14; Luke 15:1–7
    Meal, three measures Matt. 13:33
    Mustard seed (kingdom of heaven) Matt. 13:31–32; 13:31
    Pharisee and publican Luke 18:9–14
    Pounds Luke 19:11–28
    Prodigal son Luke 15:11–32
    Rich young fool Luke 12:13–21
    Royal marriage feast Matt. 22:1–14
    Samaritan, the good Luke 10:25–37
    Seed Matt. 13:19
    Soils Matt. 13:3–9; 13:19
    Sower Matt. 13:3–9; 13:19
    Talents Matt. 25:14–30
    Ten virgins Matt. 25:1–13

Treasure in field Matt. 13:44
Two sons Matt. 21:28–32
Unjust steward Luke 16:1–13
Unmerciful servant Matt. 18:23–35
Vineyard, husbandmen Matt. 21:33–46
Wedding guests Luke 14:7–11
Wheat and tares Matt. 13:24–30
Paraclete BD; John 14:16
Paradise BD; place of future happiness; park; place of pleasure; Garden of Eden
Parousia BD
Passover Matt. 26:17–20; 26:26–29; John 2:13–14
Pastoral epistles BD
Patience endurance; ability to bear afflictions and pains with calmness of mind
Patriarch BD; a progenitor; chief father; first father of a family or nation
Pattern model or plan
Paul BD
Pauline epistles BD
Peace of Christ John 14:27
Peculiar BD; precious; rare; purchased; preserved; particular; singular; private; proper
Pella BD
Penury poverty; want; extreme want of necessities
Peradventure perchance; it may be
Perdition lost; ruin; damnation; destruction; utter ruin
Perfect complete; whole; finished; fully developed; entire; accomplished; excellent
Perfectness Matt. 5:48; Luke 6:36
Pernicious ruining; wasting; destructive; mischievous; very harmful
Perverse corrupt; froward (peevish, fretful, surly); cross-grained
Peter BD
    Appearance of resurrected Christ to Luke 24:33–35
    Denial of Matt. 26:69–75; Luke 22:34

    Epistles of BD
    Marriage of Matt. 8:14–15
    Rebuked by Jesus Matt. 16:23
    Testimony of Matt. 16:16
    Walked on water Matt. 14:28–33
Peter, James, and John, a presidency Matt. 17:1–9
Pharisees BD; Matt. 3:7
    Were money lovers Luke 16:14; 16:15
Philip BD
Phylacteries BD; a case for wearing strips of scripture texts worn by Pharisees on their foreheads, arms, and hem of their garments; Matt. 23:5
Physician
    Not needed Matt. 9:10–12
    Heal thyself Luke 4:23
Piece of silver BD; Matt. 26:14–16; 27:9
Pierced by spear Matt. 27:49; Luke 2:35; John 19:34–37
Pilate BD; Matt. 27:24–25
    Trial before Matt. 27:1–2
Pilgrim resident alien; sojourner; one who travels through foreign countries
Pinnacle BD, "Pinnacle of the Temple"; top corner; extremity; wing; battlement; highest top of a building or spire; figuratively, eminence or height
Pit hole in the ground; well
Pitched fixed; set up; pave
Pitiful tenderhearted; compassionate; inclined to pity
Pity compassion; concern of mind
Plaiting elaborate braiding of the hair
Platted woven; twined; braided; Matt. 27:29; Mark 15:17
Plucked asunder broken; taken apart
Pontius BD
Potter's Field BD
Power ability; authority; force; natural faculty; sovereign prince or state
Praetorium BD; governor's court;

judgment hall; Matt. 27:27; Mark 15:16; John 18:28

Prayer BD; Matt. 6:5–8; Luke 11:1–5; 18:1–8

Value in persistence Luke 18:1–8

Prayer, Lord's Matt. 6:9–13

Predestinated foreordained

Pre-earthly existence John 9:2

Presbytery eldership; priesthood; government of a church by elders

Presently BD; immediately; at once; in the present

Press crowd; multitude; throng

Pressed upon him impetuously rushed at him

Prevent BD

Pricked in their heart cut to the heart; deeply troubled; moved deeply

Prick BD, "Goad"; point; goad; sting; wound with a pointed weapon

Priesthood keys Matt. 16:19; 18:18

Priests BD

Prince one who governs a state; a principal, chief, or excellent person

Of the world John 14:30

Privily secretly

Privy having an interest in an action or thing

Profane abuse holy things; pollute or unhallow; unholy; ungodly

Property gift; own; belonging to certain persons or things

Prophet BD

Christ also a John 7:40–41

Dead Matt. 23:29–33

False Matt. 24:10–13

To be received Matt. 10:41

Sent by Jesus Matt. 23:34–36

Prophetess Luke 2:36

Propitiation atonement

Proselyte BD; convert; one from a foreign country; a stranger converted to a religion

Proverb figurative discourse; comparison; similitude; common or old pithy saying

Publican BD; tax collector; a farmer of public rents and revenues; Matt. 9:9

Purgeth purifies; cleanses; clears oneself

Purification BD

Purloining rob; misappropriate; pilfer

Purse and scrip Matt. 10:9–10; Luke 22:36

Put away separated from

Quaternion BD; squad of four Roman soldiers; the number four

Quick BD; living; agile; nimble; brisk

Quicken make alive; become alive; hasten

Quit you behave; give over

Quotations from the Old Testament found in the New Testament BD

Rabbi BD; Matt. 23:7–8; John 6:25

Rabboni BD; Lord

Raca a term of utter vilification; "thou worthless one"; "O empty one"; Matt. 5:22

Rail blaspheme; reproach; scold; use harsh words; Mark 15:29

Raiment clothing; attire; garments; Matt. 6:25–26

Ravening plunder; spoil; vapacious; extortion; rapine; greedy

Receipt of custom tax office; tax collector's place of business

Receiveth not, you lose Matt. 13:12; Mark 4:24–25

Reckoneth settle accounts; count

Reconcile make those friends again who were at variance; make to agree what seems contrary; Matt. 18:15

Record witness; testimony; evidence

Redeem ransom; purchase; buy; recover

Reed, bruised Matt. 12:20

Refrain keep one's self from; forbear

Regeneration BD; spiritual rebirth; new birth

Reins BD; desires and thoughts;
kidneys

Remit send back; return; abate; grow
less; forgive

Render give back; recompense;
restore; return; yield; give up

Repent turn around; be sorry for what
one has done or omitted; Matt. 3:2;
7:6

Repentance BD; Matt. 7:6; Mark 6:12

Reprove check; chide

Requite reward; make amends for

Resemble compare

Residue remainder

Restitution BD; restoration;
reconstitution
Part of repentance Luke 19:8

Restoration Matt. 24:14

Resurrected being
Appearances of Jesus as Matt.
28:1–10; 28:9–10; 28:16–20; John
21:14
Can eat Luke 24:36–44

Resurrection BD; Mark 8:38; 16:5–6
Difficulty of believing Luke 24:11
Lie to discredit Matt. 28:11–15
Of just and unjust John 5:29–30
Taught early Matt. 16:21–23;
20:17–19; 26:1–5
Women at Matt. 28:1–8; Mark
16:9

Retaliation BD

Return come back; answer or
acknowledge

Revelation BD; a discovering; laying
open
Of John BD
Rock of Matt. 16:18

Revenge BD

Reward recompence

Rich toward God Luke 12:21

Rich young man Matt. 19:16–22

Righteous just; upright; equitable;
reasonable

Robe of Jesus Matt. 27:35

Roman Empire BD

Room place

Sabachthani a cry of distress

Sabaoth BD; armies; hosts

Sabbath BD; Matt. 12:1; Luke 6:9
Jesus Lord of Matt. 12:3–6; Mark
2:27

Sabbaths of the resurrection Matt.
28:1

Sacrament Matt. 26:26–29; Mark
14:22; Luke 22:19–20
Feeds spiritual hunger John
6:53–54

Sacrifice offer up; devote or give one's
self to

Sadducees BD; Matt. 3:7

Saint BD; a holy or godly person

Salim BD

Salome BD

Salt Luke 14:34–35
Of the earth Matt. 5:13–16

Salute greet; show respect and civility
in words or ceremonies

Samaritan, Parable of the Good Luke
10:25–37

Samaritans BD; Luke 17:11–19; John
4:9; 8:48

Sanhedrin BD; Matt. 26:57–68; Mark
15:1

Satan the adversary; the devil; Luke
10:18

Saved, who is? Luke 13:22–30

Savor odor; scent; smell

Savour taste; relish; Matt. 5:13

Savourest not do not consider or
cherish

Scarlet bright red

Scorpion BD; a venomous insect; a fish

Scourge a whip made of thongs; Matt.
10:17; 7:27–32

Scribe BD; Matt. 2:4

Scrip BD; traveling bag; beggar's bag;
food pouch; Matt. 10:9–10; Luke
9:3

Scripture BD
Devil hates Luke 11:53
Search diligently John 5:39

Sealing keys of priesthood Matt.
16:19; 18:18
Second Coming
Conditions of Matt. 16:27
No definite date for Matt. 24:36;
24:42–51
Signs of Matt. 24:3; 24:6–8; 24:28
Seer BD; one who sees (see-er); John
1:38–42
Senate BD; eldership; Jewish
Sanhedrin
Sent them away bid them farewell
Sermon on the Mount BD; Matt. 5–7
Serpents, be wise as Matt. 10:16
Seventies, call and mission of Luke
10:1–11
Sever divide; separate; part asunder
Several many; divers; sundry
Sheep BD
Other John 10:16
Sheepfold John 10:1
Shepherd, the Good John 10:1–16
Shew proclaim; announce; show;
declare; let see; discover; make
known; prove; make appear
Shewbread BD; Matt. 12:3–6
Sidon BD
Signs Matt. 12:39; Mark 16:17
Follow John 12:37–43
Silly simple; foolish
Siloam BD
Simon BD
Lovest thou me John 21:1–17
Simon, the Cyrenian Luke 23:26
Simple innocent; guileless
Single sincere; without guile; healthy
Sion BD
Smite strike; hit; slay
Sober moderate; temperate; modest;
grave; serious
Solitary place a deserted area
Solomon's Porch BD; John 10:23
Sometime formerly
Son of David Matt. 12:23; 22:41–46;
Luke 1:32
Son of God BD; Matt. 16:13; John
10:36
Son of Man BD; Matt. 16:13; John
1:51
Sons, two (one went) Matt. 21:28–32

Sop morsel; mouthful; crumb; bread
soaked in broth, gravy, or another
liquid; John 13:26–27,
Sore greatly; much
Sorrow uneasiness of mind; grief
Sorrowful distressed; troubled; grieved
Soul the immortal part of man
Fear those who can destroy
Matt. 10:28
Worth of Matt. 16:25–26
Spikenard BD; genuine; unadulter-
ated; sweet-smelling plant; Matt.
26:6–13; Mark 14:3
Spirit BD
The Holy BD
Enters body Luke 1:41
Has body Luke 24:36–44
Spoil plunder; rob; mar; damage
Stablish keep; strengthen; protect
Stanch cease; stop; hold up
Star at Bethlehem Matt. 2:2
Staves boards
Stay detain; delay; stop; let; hinder
Stock trunk or stem of a tree; race or
family; fowl; drawers; stockings;
supply; furnish
Stoning, Jews practiced John 8:6
Straightway immediately; at once;
without delay; suddenly; at that
moment; directly; Mark 1:30
Strait narrow; restricted; Matt. 7:13–14
Strait betwixt two hard pressed to
choose
Straitened distressed; hard pressed
Straitly charged them sternly warned
them
Strake let down; struck
Stranger BD; one who is not privy or
party to an act
Straw scatter; stretch out
Stricken in years advanced in age
Suborn throw in stealthily; introduce
by collusion; send one privately
and instruct what to do or say;
obtain perjured testimony or
unlawful acts
Subvert pervert; change; overturn;
overthrow; ruin
Succour help; relieve; supply;
strengthen; make firm

Suffer BD; permit; allow; let; give leave; bear; Matt. 3:15–16

Sundry piecemeal; variously as to time and agency; divers

Supererogation Matt. 25:8–12

Superfluity superabundance; overabundance; overplus; excess

Superstitious more religious than others; addicted to superstition (mistaken devotion)

Surfeit debauchery; excess in eating or drinking

Swaddling clothes cloth bands wrapped around infants

Swine BD; Mark 5:13

Symbolism BD

Synagogue BD

Syria BD

Syrophenician BD; Matt. 15:22; Mark 7:26

Take no thought do not be unduly or anxiously concerned; do not worry

Talents, parable of Matt. 25:14–30

Tares BD; weeds; Matt. 13:25

Teachings of Jesus Luke 4:15

Teareth lacerate; convulse; dash on the ground

Temple BD
    Cleansed Mark 11:17; John 2:13–17
    Destroyed Matt. 24:1–2
    Of Herod BD
    Of His body John 2:19–21

Tempt BD; test; prove; try; allure; entice; Matt. 22:18; 22:34–40

Temptation trial; affliction; test
    At pinnacle of temple Matt. 4:5–7
    Being led into Matt. 6:13

Temptations of Jesus Matt. 4:1–11; Luke 4:1–13

Ten Virgins Matt. 25:1–13

Terrestrial earthly; belonging to the the earth

Testament covenant

Testator one who witnesses, covenants, or makes his last will

Testimony against them witness to them

Tetrarch BD; ruler of fourth of a country; governor of four provinces; Luke 3:1

Thaddaeus BD

Thankworthy pleasing; gracious

Theophilus BD

Thirty pieces of silver BD, "Piece of silver"; Matt. 26:14–16; 27:9

Thomas BD

Thomas, doubting John 20:24–29

Thought, take no Matt. 10:19

Three days will rise Matt. 27:63; John 20:1

Tiberias BD

Tiberias, Sea of BD

Tithe BD; tenth part; Matt. 23:23–24

Token sign; mark; small part

Tombs opened Matt. 27:52

Touch me not John 20:17

Trachonitis BD

Traditions can be harmful Mark 7:3

Transfiguration, Mount of BD; Matt. 17:1–9

Transgressors, Jesus numbered with Luke 22:37

Translated transferred; changed; carried over; Matt. 16:28; John 21:20–24

Transubstantiation, no John 6:52–58

Treasures in heaven Matt. 6:19–21

Treatise discourse upon some particular subject

Trench fortification; rampart

Trespasses Matt. 6:14–15

Tribute tax; toll; Matt. 17:24–27
    To Caesar? Matt. 22:15–22

Trinity, no Matt. 3:16–17; Luke 10:22; John 14:7–11

Triumphant entry Matt. 21:1–11; John 12:15

Troubled frightened

Trow think; suppose; seem; believe; trust

Truth
    Can be determined by doing John 7:17

Freedom John 8:33–34
What is? John 18:38
Try test; put to proof; essay; examine
Twinkling of an eye wink of the eye;
an instant; quickly
Two together at Second Coming
Luke 17:34–37
Tyre BD

Unbelief lack of faith
Uncorruptible incorruptible; immortal
Unction anointing
Unleavened bread unfermented cakes
Unpardonable sin Matt. 12:31–32;
Mark 3:28–30
Unreasonable unsuitable; absurd;
improper; unjust
Unruly untamable; uncontrollable; not
to be ruled or governed
Unseemly indecently; unbecomingly;
not decent
Untoward crooked; perverse; corrupt;
wicked
Upbraideth reproaches; denounces
Usury BD; interest; the gain of
anything above the principal; Matt.
25:27

Vain deceptive; fruitless; useless;
ineffective; erroneous; empty;
frivolous; foolish
Veil of the temple rent Matt. 27:51
Vexed oppressed; afflicted; teased;
troubled; tormented
Vial bowl; small, thin, glass bottle
Victuals food; things to eat; provisions
Vine BD; Matt. 21:33–46
The true John 15:1–11
Vinegar offered Matt. 27:34
Virgin Matt. 1:23; 12:46–50
Virgin birth Luke 1:28
Virtue power; strength; force; quality;
Mark 5:30; Luke 8:46
Vision sometimes "dream"; revelation
in a dream

Vocation calling; employ; course of
life to which one is appointed

War in heaven and on earth BD,
"War in Heaven"; John 15:18–27
Washing of feet John 13:1–17
Washing of hands by Jews Matt.
15:2; Mark 7:3
Watch of the night BD, "Watches";
Matt. 14:25
Water, living John 4:10
Water changed to wine John 2:1–11
Wavering doubting; hesitating;
uncertain as to what to do
Waxed became; grew
Wedding garment Matt. 22:11
Weights and measures BD
Whale BD; the greatest of fishes
What have ye to do with us? What
business do you have with us?
Whence how; from where
Wherefore? why?
Wherewith soever however so many
Whether of these two which one?
Widow's mite Mark 12:41–44
Wilderness desert
Will be desire to be
Will have desire
Will not do not desire
Winebibber drunkard
Winefat, winepress BD
Wise discreet; Matt. 25:2, 4, 8–9
Who think they are Luke 10:21
Wise men of the east BD; Matt. 2:1–12
Wist knew
Without outside
Without spot blameless
Witness of Jesus by himself John 5:31
Witnessed testified
Woman John 2:4
Touching hem Matt. 9:21–22;
Mark 5:30
Wondered marvelled; Matt. 15:31
Wont accustomed; be used to
World, end of Matt. 13:39–43; 13:49;
24:3; 24:23–27; 24:51
Worthy deserving

Wot know
Would I have I have desired
Would not come did not desire to
come
Wrest twist; distort; turn about
Writing BD
Writing of divorcement certificate of
divorce making the divorce legal
Written, what I have Mark 15:26;
John 19:19–22
Wrought performed; worked; did work

Yokefellow associate; colleague; one
who bears the fame, yoke, or
burden with another, especially a
wife or husband

Zacchaeus BD; Luke 19:2–10
Zacharias BD; Luke 1:5–25
Zebedee BD; Mark 1:19
Zebulun and Naphtali BD,
"Zebulun," "Naphtali"; Matt. 4:13
Zelotes BD; Luke 6:15
Zion BD

SECTION 2
A COMPANION TO
YOUR STUDY OF
THE NEW TESTAMENT:
THE FOUR GOSPELS

MATTHEW

The Joseph Smith Translation entitles this book "The Testimony of St. Matthew." For background information on this book, see BD, "Gospels," "Harmony of the Gospels," and "Matthew."

1:1–17 (Read Luke 3:23–38.) The phrase "book of the generation of Jesus Christ" (v. 1) refers to the following seventeen verses, which trace the genealogy of the Savior from Abraham to David and from David to the time of Jesus; this phrase does not pertain to the entire book of Matthew, only to verses 2–17. A similar phrase is used in verse 1 in Genesis 5, which contains "the book of the generations of Adam" down to the sons of Noah.

The genealogical information provided by Matthew is not identical with that provided in Luke 3:23–38. Matthew's testimony is directed primarily toward the Jews; he traces the Savior's lineage through Abraham and David, inasmuch as the Jewish scriptures contained promises that the Messiah would come from their lineage. (See Gen. 12:3; Ps. 132; Isa. 11; Jer. 25:5. See also Gal. 3:16 and D&C 113:1.) Luke's testimony is directed primarily toward the Gentiles and thus traces Christ's lineage from Adam. (See BD, "Joseph, Son of Heli.")

1:9–10 See BD, "Ezekias."

1:13 See BD, "Eliakim."

1:16 The footnote indicates that "the Greek title 'Christ' and the Hebrew title 'Messiah' are synonymous, meaning 'Anointed One.'"

Christ is a sacred title, and not an ordinary appellation or common name; it is of Greek derivation, and in meaning is identical with its Hebrew equivalent *Messiah* or *Messias,* signifying the *Anointed One.* Other titles, each possessing a definitive meaning, such as *Emmanuel, Savior, Redeemer, Only Begotten Son, Lord, Son of God, Son of Man,* and many more, are of scriptural occurrence; the fact of main present importance to us is that these several titles are expressive of our Lord's divine origin and Godship. (JTC, pp. 35–36.)

(See section 1, "Christ"; BD, "Christ, Names of.")

1:18–24 (Read Luke 1:26–38.) "Mary was espoused to Joseph" (v. 18) could have been translated "Mary was promised (engaged, betrothed) in marriage to Joseph." (See section 1, "Espousal.")

Verse 19 could also have been translated somewhat differently: "However, Joseph, her husband, because he was righteous and did not want to make her a public spectacle, intended to release her secretly."

According to Jewish law, marriage took place in two steps, first came the espousal or betrothal, later the formal marriage ceremony. Both formalities preceded assumption of the full privileges and responsibilities of the marital state. In a sense, espoused persons were viewed as already married, so that the angel in counseling Joseph to fulfill his marriage plans properly referred to Mary as his "wife." Espoused persons were considered bound to each other so that their betrothal could only be broken by a formal action akin to divorce. This is what Joseph had contemplated prior to receiving direction from the angelic visitant. (DNTC 1:83.)

Betrothal, or espousal, in that time was in some respects as binding as the marriage vow, and could only be set aside by a ceremonial separation akin to divorce; yet an espousal was but an engagement to marry, not a marriage. (JTC, p. 84.)

1:18 "She was found with child of the Holy Ghost" should *not* be interpreted to mean that the Holy Ghost is the father of Jesus Christ. As clarified by other scriptures, Mary conceived by the *power* of the Holy Ghost, but that which was born of her was "of God." (See Alma 7:10.)

Just as Jesus is literally the Son of Mary, so he is the personal and literal offspring of God the Eternal Father, who himself is an exalted personage having a tangible body of flesh and bones. (D&C 130:22.) Apostate religionists — unable to distinguish between the Father, Son, and Holy Ghost — falsely suppose that the Holy Ghost was the Father of our Lord. Matthew's statement, "she was found with child of the Holy Ghost," properly translated should say, 'she was found with child *by the power of the Holy Ghost.*' (Matt. 1:18.) Luke's account (Luke 1:35) accurately records what took place. Alma perfectly describes our Lord's conception and birth by prophesying: Christ "shall be born of Mary, . . . she being a virgin, a precious and chosen vessel, who shall be overshadowed and *conceive by the power of the Holy Ghost,* and bring forth a son, yea even *the Son of God."* (Alma 7:10.) Nephi spoke similarly when he said that at the time of her conception, Mary "was carried away in the Spirit," with the result that the child born of her was "the Lamb of God, yea, even the Son of the Eternal Father." (1 Ne. 11:19–21.) As Gabriel told Luke, he was the "Son of the Highest" (Luke 1:32), and "the Highest" is the first member of the godhead, not the third. (DNTC 1:82–83.)

1:20 The angel's salutation was significant; "Joseph, thou son of David," was the form of address; and the use of that royal title must have meant to Joseph that, though he was of kingly lineage, marriage with Mary would cast no shadow upon his family status. (JTC, p. 85.)

(See BD, "Angels," "Dreams.")

1:21 The name *Jesus* is the Greek form of the Old Testament Hebrew name *Joshua* or *Jeshua,* meaning "God is savior" or "God is help." Thus, Matthew notes that the Savior's name shall be Jesus, "for he shall save his people from their sins." (See section 1, "Jesus.")

1:22 The phrase "which was spoken of the Lord by the prophet" could have been translated "which was spoken by Jehovah through his prophet." This phrase means that the words of the prophet are really the words of the Lord as revealed *to* the prophet.

1:23 The promise that the mother of Jesus would be "a virgin" at the time of the birth of Jesus should *not* be interpreted to mean that she would remain a virgin throughout her life. The false doctrine of the "perpetual virginity" of Mary is not substantiated from the scriptures. Indeed, "brothers and sisters" of Jesus are specifically mentioned later in the record. (See Matt. 12:46–50 and commentary. See also Mark 3:31–35; Luke 8:19–21; section 1, "Virgin.")

The last clause in this verse could have been translated "With Us Is God." The name-title Emmanuel is spelled this way only in this reference, but is the same word used in Isaiah 7:14 and 8:8. (See BD, "Immanuel.")

1:24 Mary was espoused to Joseph. They were not married but were promised to each other under the strictest terms. Mary was virtually regarded as the wife of Joseph, and unfaithfulness on her part during the espousal period was punishable by death (Deuteronomy 22:23, 24). During the espousal period, the bride-elect lived with her family or friends, and all communication between herself and her promised husband was carried on through a friend. When Joseph learned of Mary's prospective maternity and knew he was not the father, he had two alternatives: (1) he could demand that Mary submit to a public trial and judgment, which even at that late point in Jewish history may have resulted in Mary's death; or (2) he could privately sever the espousal contract before witnesses. Joseph obviously chose the most merciful of the two alternatives. He *could* have reacted selfishly and with bitterness when he learned that Mary was expecting, and it is a profound witness to Joseph's character that he chose to annul the espousal privately. Of this, Elder James E. Talmage has written:

"Joseph was a just man, a strict observer of the law, yet no harsh extremist; moreover he loved Mary and would save her all unnecessary humiliation, whatever might be his own sorrow and suffering. For Mary's sake he dreaded the thought of publicity; and therefore determined to have the espousal annulled with such privacy as the law allowed." (*Jesus the Christ*, p. 84.) It may be that the Lord designed such an experience to test Joseph, and if that be the case, Joseph proved faithful. *After* Joseph had made his decision, *then* the angel visited him and directed that he should proceed and take Mary as his wife. Mary's high station was known before she was born (Mosiah 3:8; Alma 7:10; 1 Ne. 11:15, 18–21; Isaiah 7:14), and Joseph no doubt was foreordained to the honored station that he held, for the Prophet Joseph Smith taught that "*every man who has a calling to minister to the inhabitants of the world was ordained to that very purpose in the Grand Council of heaven before this world was.*" (*Teachings*, p. 365. Italics added.) Surely Joseph was a noble soul in premortality to be blessed with the signal honor of coming to earth and acting as the legal guardian of the Son of the Eternal Father in the flesh. (LTJA, p. 22.)

1:25 (Read Luke 2:21.) The Joseph Smith Translation replaces "he" with "they," indicating that both Joseph and Mary agreed on the name.

2:1–12 Our Heavenly Father has testified that his word would be established "in the mouth of two or three witnesses." (2 Cor. 13:1; see also Deut. 19:15.) Several types of witnesses are provided concerning the birth of the Son of God, including the annunciations to Mary (Luke 1:26–28) and Joseph (Matt. 1:20–25), the humble shepherds (Luke 2:8–17), the devout Simeon (Luke 2:22–35), and the faithful Anna (Luke 2:36–38). Matthew recounts the visit of "wise men from the east" (Matt. 2:1) but does not give the number of the wise men or the lands of their origin. These wise men may have been witnesses from the rich and powerful, as indicated by their costly gifts of "gold, frankincense, and myrrh." (V. 11.) (See Micah 5:2 and BD, "Bethlehem," "Magi," "Wise Men of the East.")

2:1 The Herod mentioned here is identified, with some of his infamous relatives, in the genealogical charts provided in the Bible Dictionary entry "Herod."

Herod was professedly an adherent of the religion of Judah, though by birth an Idumean, by descent an Edomite or one of the posterity of Esau, all of whom the Jews hated; and of all Edomites not one was more bitterly detested than was Herod the king. He was tyrannical and merciless, sparing neither foe nor friend who came under suspicion of being a possible hindrance to his ambitious designs. He had his wife and several of his sons, as well as others of his blood kindred, cruelly murdered; and he put to death nearly all of the great national council, the Sanhedrin. His reign was one of revolting cruelty and unbridled oppression. Only when in danger of inciting a national revolt or in fear of incurring the displeasure of his imperial master, the Roman emperor, did he stay his hand in any undertaking. (JTC, pp. 97–98.)

(See section 1, "Herod.")

2:2 Where is *the child* that is born, *the Messiah* of the Jews? (JST; italics added.)

The statement of the wise men "We have seen his star in the east" is extremely interesting inasmuch as the star as a sign at the birth of Jesus is not mentioned in the present Old Testament. However, reference to the sign of a star was mentioned by Samuel the Lamanite in the Book of Mormon some five years before the birth of Jesus. (Hel. 14:1–5; see also 3 Ne. 1:21.) The definiteness of the language used by the wise men would indicate that other groups besides the Lehites were aware that a new star would bear record of the birth of the Son of God.

Attempts have been made to identify the star whose appearance in their eastern sky had assured the magi that the King was born; but astronomy furnishes no satisfactory confirmation. The recorded appearance of the star has been associated by both ancient and modern interpreters with the prophecy of Balaam, who, though not an Israelite had blessed Israel, and under divine inspiration had predicted: "there shall come a Star out of Jacob, and a Sceptre shall rise out of Israel." [Num. 24:17.] Moreover, as already shown, the appearance of a new star was a predicted sign recognized and acknowledged among the people of the western world as witness of Messiah's birth. [Hel. 14:5; 3 Ne. 1:21.] (JTC, p. 99.)

2:4 This is the first use of the word *scribes* in the New Testament, although it appears several times in the Old Testament. (See BD, "Scribe.")

A foremost actor in a New Testament list of characters is the scribe. He is found in Jerusalem, Judea, and Galilee and is not new to Jewish life and culture. Present in Babylon and also throughout the dispersion, he is spokesman of the people; he is the sage; he is the man of wisdom, the rabbi who received his ordination by the laying on of hands. His ability to cross-examine and to question is renowned. Dignified and important, he is an aristocrat among the common people who have no knowledge of the law. Regarding faith and religious practice, he is the authority and the last word; and as a teacher of the law, as a judge in ecclesiastical courts, is the learned one who must be respected, whose judgment is infallible. He travels in the company of the Pharisees, yet he is not necessarily a member of this religious party. He holds office and has status. His worth is beyond that of all the common folk and they must honor him, for he is to be praised by God and by angels in heaven. In fact, so revered are his words regarding law and practice that he must be believed though his state-ments contradict all common sense, or though he pronounce that the sun does not shine at noon day when in fact it is visible to the naked eye. (See Edersheim, *The Life and Times of Jesus the Messiah,* 1:93–94.) (LTJA, p. 96.)

2:4 "Demanded of them" means "began to inquire of them."

He demanded of them, saying, Where is the place that is written of by the prophets, in which Christ should be born? For he greatly feared, yet he believed not the prophets. (JST.)

2:6 This verse could have been translated "And you, O Bethlehem of the land of Judah, are by no means the most insignificant city among the governors of Judah; for out of you will come forth a governing one, who will shepherd my people, Israel." (See BD, "Judah, Kingdom of.")

For out of thee shall come *the Messiah, who* shall *save* my people Israel. (JST; italics added.)

The prophet quoted here is Micah, as recorded in Micah 5:2.

2:7 "Herod, when he had privily called" could have been translated "Herod secretly summoned."

2:11–12 Many modern nativity scenes and pageants depict the wise men as coming to visit and worship Jesus on the night of his birth. The New Testament record, however, indicates that their visit was probably some time after the Savior's birth.

The wise men arrived in Jerusalem when Jesus was a young child. They were directed by Herod's court to Bethlehem. "And when they were come into the *house* [Jesus was no longer in a stable], they saw the *young child* [no longer a babe] . . . and fell down, and worshipped him." (LTJA, pp. 22–23.)

It is worthy of note that the wise men found Jesus in a house, not a stable, inn, or temporary abiding place; that he is called a "young child," not a baby, a total of seven times in the course of fourteen consecutive verses; that Matthew makes two pointed references to the diligent nature of Herod's inquiry as to the actual time of the birth; and that a child is two years of age until the time of his third birthday. Now assuming that Herod would order the massacre of all young children in the general age bracket involved, still the presumption arises that a number of months or even one or two years may have elapsed before the arrival of the eastern visitors. (DNTC 1:107.)

That Herod subsequently ordered the killing of all the children "from two years old and under" (v. 16) would also indicate that Jesus was no longer a newborn babe when the wise men came.

The number and identity of the wise men are also in question:

> Much has been written, beyond all possible warrant of scriptural authority, concerning the visit of the magi, or wise men, who thus sought and found the infant Christ. As a matter of fact, we are left without information as to their country, nation, or tribal relationship; we are not even told how many they were, though unauthenticated tradition has designated them as "the three wise men," and has even given them names; whereas they are left unnamed in the scriptures, the only true record of them extant, and may have numbered but two or many. (JTC, p. 99.)

> To suppose they were members of the apostate religious cult of the *Magi* or ancient Media and Persia is probably false. Rather, it would appear they were true prophets, righteous persons like Simeon, Anna, and the shepherds, to whom Deity revealed that the promised Messiah had been born among men. Obviously they were in possession of ancient prophecies telling of the rise of a new star at his birth. That they did receive revelation for their personal guidance is seen from the inspired dream in which they were warned not to return to Herod after they had found and worshiped the Son of Mary. (DNTC 1:103.)

2:11 No special significance should be placed on the nature of the gifts presented by the wise men, other than as indicated in the scriptures:

> The offering of gifts to a superior in rank, either as to worldly status or recognized spiritual endowment, was a custom of early days and still prevails in many oriental lands. It is worthy of note that we have no record of these men from the east offering gifts to Herod in his palace; they did, however, impart of their treasure to the lowly Infant, in whom they recognized the King they had come to seek. The tendency to ascribe occult significance to even trifling details mentioned in scripture, and particularly as regards the life of Christ, has led to many fanciful suggestions concerning the gold and frankincense and myrrh specified in the incident. Some have supposed a half-hidden symbolism therein—gold a tribute to His royal estate, frankincense an offering in recognition of His priesthood, and myrrh for His burial. The sacred record offers no basis for such conjecture. Myrrh and frankincense are aromatic resins derived from plants indigenous to eastern lands, and they have been used from very early times in medicine and in the preparation of perfumes and incense mixtures. They were presumably among the natural productions of the lands from which the magi came, though probably even there they were costly and highly esteemed. Such, together with gold, which is of value among all nations, were most appropriate as gifts for a king. Any mystical significance

one may choose to attach to the presents must be remembered as his own supposition or fancy, and not as based on scriptural warrant. (JTC, p. 108.)

(See BD, "Frankincense," "Gold," "Myrrh.")

2:13–15 Anciently Israel had been called out of Egypt by the Lord, and now the young "King of Israel," the Son of God, lived in and was called forth from that land. The prophecy of Hosea "When Israel was a child, then I loved him, and called my son out of Egypt" (Hosea 11:1) might be one of the many prophecies with dual meaning and fulfillment.

It is not clear from the New Testament how long Joseph, Mary, and the child Jesus remained in Egypt, but it was probably for only a few months. The record seems to indicate that Jesus spent most of his childhood in Nazareth.

2:14 The Joseph Smith Translation makes it clear that Joseph took "the *child's* mother," rather than Joseph's own mother, into Egypt.

2:15 See the commentary for Matthew 1:22.

2:16–18 Some have wondered how John the Baptist escaped Herod's slaughter. Joseph Smith taught:

When Herod's edict went forth to destroy the young children, John was about six months older than Jesus, and came under this hellish edict, and Zacharias caused his mother to take him into the mountains, where he was raised on locusts and wild honey. When his father refused to disclose his hiding place, and being the officiating high priest at the Temple that year, was slain by Herod's order, between the porch and the altar, as Jesus said. (TPJS, p. 261.)

(See Jer. 31:15; section 1, "John the Baptist: Escaped the slaughter.")

2:16 "Children" really means "male children" or "boys."

2:17 Jeremiah. (See Jer. 31:15.)

2:19–23 Read Luke 2:39–40.

2:19 "Appeareth in a dream" could be translated "appeared in a vision." (JST.)

Elder James E. Talmage wrote of the death of Herod:

The mortal end of the tyrant and multi-murderer is thus treated by Farrar in his *Life of Christ,* pp. 54–55: "It must have been very shortly after the murder of the innocents that Herod died. Only five days before his death he had made a frantic attempt at suicide, and had ordered the execution of his eldest son Antipater. His deathbed . . . was accompanied by circumstances of peculiar horror; and it has been asserted that he died of a loathsome disease, which is hardly mentioned in history, except in the case of men who have been rendered infamous by an atrocity of persecuting zeal. On his bed of intolerable anguish, in that splendid and luxurious palace which he had built for himself, under the palms of Jericho, swollen with disease and scorched by thirst, ulcerated externally and glowing inwardly with a soft slow fire, surrounded by plotting sons and plundering slaves, detesting all and detested by all, longing for death as a release from his tortures yet dreading it as the beginning of worse terrors, stung by remorse yet still unslaked with murder, a horror to all around him yet in his guilty conscience a worse terror to himself, devoured by the premature corruption of an anticipated grave, eaten of worms as though visibly smitten by the finger of God's wrath after seventy years of successful villainy, the wretched old man, whom men had called the Great, lay in savage frenzy awaiting his last hour. As he knew that none would shed one tear for him, he determined that they should shed many for themselves, and issued an order that, under pain of death, the principal families of the kingdom and the chiefs of the tribes should come to Jericho. They came, and then, shutting them in the hippodrome, he secretly commanded his sister Salome that at the moment of his death they should all be massacred. And so, choking as it were with blood, devising massacres in its very delirium, the soul of Herod passed forth into the night." (JTC, pp. 107–8.)

2:22 "Being warned of God in a dream, he turned aside into the parts of Galilee" might read, "being warned of God in a vision, he went into the eastern part of Galilee." (JST.)

"Notwithstanding" could have been translated "moreover" or "in addition to." (See BD, "Archelaus.")

2:23 The statement "by the prophets" that "He shall be called a Nazarene" is not found in our present Old Testament. Evidently this prophecy has been lost.

Joseph had to receive a second message from the Lord that he was to return to Nazareth (vv. 22–23); at first he was simply instructed to "go into the land of Israel" (v. 20).

Nazareth was the abode of Jesus until He was about thirty years of age; and, in accordance with the custom of designating individuals by the names of their home towns as additions to their personal names, our Lord came to be generally known as Jesus of Nazareth. He is also referred to as a Nazarene, or a native of Nazareth. . . . That Nazareth was an obscure village, of little honor or renown, is evidenced by the almost contemptuous question of Nathanael, who, on being informed that the Messiah had been found in Jesus of Nazareth, asked: "Can there any good thing come out of Nazareth?" The incredulous query had passed into a proverb current even today as expressive of any unpopular or unpromising source of good. Nathanael lived in Cana, but a few miles from Nazareth, and his surprise at the tidings brought by Philip concerning the Messiah incidentally affords evidence of the seclusion in which Jesus had lived. (JTC, pp. 117–18.)

(See BD, "Nazarene," "Nazareth.")

Elder Bruce R. McConkie has provided this possible chronology of the places where Jesus lived:

Although the chronological order of the travels and sojournings of our Lord's early years is not entirely clear, the following seems reasonably certain:

(1) At the time of their espousement and marriage, Joseph and Mary lived in Nazareth in the eastern part of the province of Galilee. (Luke 1:26–35; 1 Ne. 11:13.)

(2) Guided by divine providence, they traveled to Bethlehem, the city of David, where Jesus was born in a stable. (Luke 2:1–7.)

(3) On the eighth day, while the couple was still in Bethlehem, Jesus was circumcised. (Luke 2:21.)

(4) Following the days of Mary's purification, a forty-day period (Lev. 12), the holy family traveled to Jerusalem where Jesus was presented in the temple, with Simeon and Anna then bearing record of his divine Sonship. (Luke 2:22–38.)

(5) Thus, having "performed all things according to the law of the Lord," they then went immediately to Nazareth. (Luke 2:39.) Obviously the wise men had not yet come to worship their King, because following their visit comes the flight of Egypt. That they could not have gone to Egypt and returned to Bethlehem within the forty-day period is clear (a) because they were in Egypt at the time of Herod's death which did not occur until about two years after the nativity, and (b) because they returned from Egypt to Nazareth, not Bethlehem.

(6) Next, for some unknown and unrecorded reason, Joseph and Mary and the child returned to Bethlehem, obtained a house there, and were part of the community life when the wise men came. (Matt. 2:1–12.)

(7) Warned of God, the holy family now fled to Egypt for a sojourn of unknown length, possibly one of only a few weeks or months. (Matt. 2:13–15.)

(8) After Herod's death they returned with obvious purpose of settling again in Bethlehem, where they must have had an adequate place to live. But fearing Archelaus, son of Herod, they forsook the Judean province for the greater security of the Galilean. Hence their return to and abode in Nazareth. (Matt. 2:19–23.)

(9) From then until his formal ministry began, a period of perhaps twenty-seven or twenty-eight years, our Lord continued to live in Nazareth. (Luke 2:51–52; I.V. Matt. 3:22–26.) (DNTC 1:108–9.)

The Joseph Smith Translation adds the following after Matthew 2:23:

And it came to pass that Jesus grew up with his brethren, and waxed strong, and waited upon the Lord for the time of his ministry to come.

And he served under his father, and he spake not as other men, neither could he be taught; for he needed not that any man should teach him.

And after many years, the hour of his ministry drew nigh. (JST.)

Although the word *father* in [the Joseph Smith Translation] perhaps refers to Joseph, yet the content of the passage certainly shows that Jesus was taught by his real father, God the Father.

It is, however, possible that Jesus attended the Jewish synagogues and was taught in the learning of the Jews by the rabbis. If so, much of what Jesus heard would have been a perversion of truth, for Judaism was in a state of apostasy. His most significant education, therefore, came through the Spirit from his Heavenly Father. Jesus testified of himself: "I do nothing of myself; but as my Father hath taught me, I speak these things." (John 8:28.) And again: "The Father which sent me, he gave me a commandment, what I should say, and what I should speak." (John 12:49.) Who taught Jesus what he knew? His Father, God the Father, taught him. That he was taught by wiser than mortal men is evident, and that he learned his lessons well, for the Prophet Joseph Smith said of him: "When still a boy, He had all the intelligence necessary to enable Him to rule and govern the kingdom of the Jews, and could reason with the wisest and most profound doctors of law and divinity, and make their theories and practice to appear like folly compared with the wisdom He possessed; but He was a boy only, and lacked physical strength even to defend His own person; and was subject to cold, to hunger, and to death." (LTJA, p. 24.)

3:1–6 (Read Mark 1:1–8; Luke 3:1–18; John 1:6–37.) The following commentaries have been written concerning the calling and mission of John the Baptist:

Few prophets rank with *John the Baptist*. Among other things, his ministry was foretold by Lehi (1 Ne. 10:7–10), Nephi (1 Ne. 11:27; 2 Ne. 31:4–18), and Isaiah (Isa. 40:3); Gabriel came down from the courts of glory to announce John's coming birth (Luke 1:5–44); he was the last legal administrator, holding keys and authority under the Mosaic dispensation (D&C 84:26–28); his mission was to prepare the way before, baptize, and acclaim the divine Sonship of Christ (John 1); and in modern times, on the 15th of May, 1829, he returned to earth as a resurrected being to confer the Aaronic Priesthood upon Joseph Smith and Oliver Cowdery. [JS–H 1:66–75; D&C 13.] (MD, p. 393.)

This miraculously-born son of Zacharias was the last legal administrator of the old dispensation, the first of the new; he was the last of the old prophets, the first of the new. With him ended the old law, and with him began the new era of promise. He is the one man who stood, literally, at the crossroads of history; with him the past died and the future was born. He was the herald of the Messianic age, the messenger, forerunner, and Elias who began the great restoration in the meridian of time and on whose secure foundation the Son of Man himself built the eternal gospel structure. His ministry ended the preparatory gospel; Messiah's commenced again the era of gospel fulness. (DNTC 1:113.)

The spirit of Elias was a going before to prepare the way for the greater, which was the case with John the Baptist. He came crying through the wilderness, "Prepare ye the way of the Lord, make his paths straight." And they were informed, if they could receive it, it was the spirit of Elias;

and John was very particular to tell the people, he was not that Light, but was sent to bear witness of that Light.

He told the people that his mission was to preach repentance and baptize with water; but it was He that should come after him that should baptize with fire and the Holy Ghost.

If he had been an impostor, he might have gone to work beyond his bounds, and undertook to have performed ordinances which did not belong to that office and calling, under the spirit of Elias.

The spirit of Elias is to prepare the way for a greater revelation of God, which is the Priesthood of Elias, or the Priesthood that Aaron was ordained unto. And when God sends a man into the world to prepare for a greater work, holding the keys of the power of Elias, it was called the doctrine of Elias, even from the early ages of the world.

John's mission was limited to preaching and baptizing; but what he did was legal; and when Jesus Christ came to any of John's disciples, He baptized them with fire and the Holy Ghost. (TPJS, pp. 335–36.)

(See section 1, "John the Baptist.")

3:2 The first recorded word in John's ministry was "Repent." When this same John the Baptist, as a resurrected being, restored the Aaronic Priesthood in this dispensation, he indicated that he was restoring, among other things, "the keys of the . . . gospel of repentance."

The Lord has also counseled in this dispensation that we are to "say nothing but repentance unto this generation." (D&C 6:9; see also 11:9; 14:8; 19:21.) (See section 1, "Repent.")

"Is at hand" could more literally have been translated "has drawn near." Other translations are "is coming soon," "has arrived," "is close at hand," "is near," and "is upon you."

The kingdom of God on earth, the one true Church, the sole organization through which salvation is administered, the very Church and kingdom is here. "John came preaching the Gospel for the remission of sins," the Prophet [Joseph Smith] taught. "He had his authority from God, and the oracles of God were with him, and the kingdom of God for a season seemed to rest with John alone. . . . But, says one, the kingdom of God could not be set up in the days of John, for John said the kingdom was at hand. But I would ask if it could be any nearer to them than to be in the hands of John. The people need not wait for the days of Pentecost to find the kingdom of God, for John had it with him, and he came forth from the wilderness crying out, 'Repent ye, for the kingdom of heaven is nigh at hand,' as much as to say, 'Out here I have got the kingdom of God, and you can get it, and I am coming after you; and if you don't receive it, you will be damned'; and the scriptures represent that all Jerusalem went out unto John's baptism. There was a legal administrator, and those that were baptized were subjects for a king; and also the laws and oracles of God were there; therefore the kingdom of God was there; for no man could have better authority to administer than John; and our Savior submitted to that authority himself, by being baptized by John; therefore the kingdom of God was set up on the earth, even in the days of John." (*Teachings,* pp. 272–73.) (DNTC 1:114.)

While the expressions "Kingdom of God" and "Kingdom of Heaven" are used in the Bible synonymously or interchangeably, later revelation gives to each a distinctive meaning. The Kingdom of God is the Church established by divine authority upon the earth; this institution asserts no claim to temporal rule over nations; its sceptre of power is that of the Holy Priesthood, to be used in the preaching of the gospel and in administering its ordinances for the salvation of mankind living and dead. The Kingdom of Heaven is the divinely ordained system of government and dominion in all matters, temporal and spiritual; this will be established on earth only when its rightful Head, the King of kings, Jesus the Christ, comes to reign. His administration will be one of order, operated through the agency of His commissioned representatives invested with the Holy Priesthood. When Christ appears in His glory, and not before, will be realized a complete fulfilment of the supplication: "Thy kingdom come. Thy will be done in earth, as it is in heaven."

The Kingdom of God has been established among men to prepare them for the Kingdom of Heaven which shall come; and in the blessed reign of Christ the King shall the two be made one. (JTC, pp. 788–89.)

(See BD, "Kingdom of Heaven.")

3:3 "This is he" might be translated "I am he." (JST.)

3:4–5 The nature of John's existence in the wilderness of Judea has prompted some scholars to conclude he was a Nazarite, although the term is never used in the scriptures to refer to him.

Nazarites are not named in the New Testament, though of specific record in the earlier scriptures; and from sources other than scriptural we learn of their existence at and after the time of Christ. The Nazarite was one of either sex who was bound to abstinence and sacrifice by a voluntary vow for special service to God; the period of the vow might be limited or for life. (JTC, pp. 67–68.)

(See BD, "Nazarite," "Locusts.")

3:5 See BD, "Jordan River."

3:6 "Confessing" means "openly confessing."

3:7–12 Read Mark 1:4–8; Luke 3:7–18; John 1:19–28.

3:7–8 The literal translation of "O generation of vipers" is "generated ones of vipers." It could also have been translated "you offspring of vipers," "you sons of snakes," "you serpent's brood," or "you brood of vipers."

The obvious meaning of the expression is that these wicked people were poisoning the people with their false teachings and bad examples. The Lord used the same expression to refer to persecutors of the Saints in Joseph Smith's day. (D&C 121:23.)

The Joseph Smith Translation adds the following between these two verses: "Why is it that ye receive not the preaching of him whom God hath sent? If ye receive not this in your hearts, ye receive not me; and if ye receive not me, ye receive not him of whom I am sent to bear record; and for your sins ye have no cloak."

"Bring forth therefore fruits meet for repentance" (v. 8) should read "Repent, therefore, and bring forth fruits meet for repentance," according to the Joseph Smith Translation.

3:7 This is the first occurrence of the terms *Pharisees* and *Sadducees* in the New Testament.

> The origin of the Pharisees is not fixed by undisputed authority as to either time or circumstance; though it is probable that the sect or party had a beginning in connection with the return of the Jews from the Babylonian captivity. New ideas and added conceptions of the meaning of the law were promulgated by Jews who had imbibed of the spirit of Babylon; and the resulting innovations were accepted by some and rejected by others. The name "Pharisee" does not occur in the Old Testament, nor in the Apocrypha, though it is probable that the Assideans mentioned in the books of the Maccabees were the original Pharisees. By derivation the name expressed the thought of separatism; the Pharisee, in estimation of his class, was distinctively set apart from the common people, to whom he considered himself as truly superior as the Jews regarded themselves in contrast with other nations. Pharisees and scribes were one in all essentials of profession, and rabbinism was specifically their doctrine. . . .
>
> The Sadducees came into existence as a reactionary organization during the second century B.C., in connection with an insurgent movement against the Maccabean party. Their platform was that of opposition to the ever-increasing mass of traditional lore, with which the law was not merely being fenced or hedged about for safety, but under which it was being buried. The Sadducees stood for the sanctity of the law as written and preserved, while they rejected the whole mass of rabbinical precept both as orally transmitted and as collated and codified in the records of the scribes. The Pharisees formed the more popular party; the Sadducees figured as the aristocratic minority. . . .
>
> Pharisees and Sadducees differed on many important if not fundamental matters of belief and practice, including the preexistence of spirits, the reality of the future state involving reward and punishment, the necessity for individual self-denial, the immortality of the soul, and the resurrection from the dead; in each of which the Pharisees stood for the affirmative while the Sadducees denied. Josephus avers—the doctrine of the Sadducees is that the soul and body perish together; the law is all that they are concerned to observe. They were "a skeptical school of aristocratic traditionalists; adhering only to the Mosaic law." (JTC, pp. 65–67.)

Two of the most influential apostate sects among the Jews. The *Pharisees* were a zealous, devoted sect who accepted both the law of Moses and the traditions of the elders. They were pious and puritanical in conduct, glorying in frequent fasts and public prayers. Intensely patriotic and nationalistic, they believed in spirits, angels, revelation, immortality, eternal judgment, the resurrection from the dead, and rewards and punishments in the life to come.

The *Sadducees,* on the other hand, categorically rejected and believed in none of these things. They were a sect composed of skeptical, worldly, wealthy people—a selfish group finding their most powerful adherents among the chief priests. Though the Sadducees professed belief in the law, they rejected the traditions of the elders, and made no pretentions of piety or devout worship. The Pharisees were far more powerful and influential in Jewish political and religious life than were the Sadducees. (DNTC 1:119.)

(See section 1, "Pharisees," "Sadducees.")

3:9 Judaism held that the posterity of Abraham had an assured place in the kingdom of the expected Messiah, and that no proselyte from among the Gentiles could possibly attain the rank and distinction of which the "children" were sure. John's forceful assertion that God could raise up, from the stones on the river bank, children to Abraham, meant to those who heard that even the lowest of the human family might be preferred before themselves unless they repented and reformed. (JTC, p. 123.)

(See section 1, "Meet"; BD, "Abraham"; commentary for Luke 3:8.)

3:11–12 I indeed baptize you with water, *upon your* repentance; and when he of *whom I bear record* cometh, who is mightier than I, whose shoes I am not worthy to bear, (*or whose place I am not able to fill,*) *as I said, I indeed baptize you before he cometh, that when he cometh* he may baptize you with the Holy Ghost and fire. And it is *he of whom I shall bear record,* whose fan shall be in his hand, and he will thoroughly purge his floor, and gather his wheat into the garner; but *in the fulness of his own time* will burn up the chaff with unquenchable fire. (JST; italics added.)

Elder Bruce R. McConkie has commented on the phrase "in the fulness of his own time":

Wicked men do not suffer the torments of unquenchable fire until they are cast into the spirit prison which is hell; and the earth itself will not be burned until the Second Coming, the great and dreadful day, the day of burning and desolation. (DNTC 1:22.)

3:12 This verse could have been translated, "His winnowing shovel is in his hand, and he will completely clean up his threshing floor, and will gather his wheat into the storehouse, but the chaff he will burn up with fire that cannot be put out."

And it is he of whom I shall bear record, whose fan *shall be* in his hand, and he will thoroughly purge his floor, and gather his wheat into the garner; but in the fulness of his own time will burn up the chaff with unquenchable fire. (JST; italics added.)

Christ is the great Judge. He shall reap the earth and harvest the ripened sheaves. With the winnowing fan of judgment, he shall separate the wicked chaff from the righteous wheat, gathering the wheat into the celestial garner and burning the chaff in the depths of hell; his threshing-floor is the whole earth. (DNTC 1:121.)

3:13–17 Read Mark 1:9–11; Luke 3:21–22; John 1:32–34. See BD, "Jordan River."

3:13 The Joseph Smith Translation adds the following between verses 12 and 13: "Thus came John, preaching and baptizing in the river Jordan; bearing record, that he who was coming after him had power to baptize with the Holy Ghost and fire."

3:14 "But John forbad him" might be translated "But John refused him." (JST.)

3:16 "Then he suffered him" could have been translated "Then he quit preventing him." Other translations are "So then John baptized him"; "Then he consented"; "At this, John gave in to him"; and "John then allowed him to come." (See section 1, "Suffer," "Baptism of Jesus.")

Why was Jesus baptized? Not for the remission of sins, for he was the one sinless person, the one person whose thoughts were pure, whose heart knew no guile, whose lips gave forth no improper words, and whose every act was in perfect harmony with the divine will of his Father. Yet baptism was required of him. Why?

Nephi gives four reasons as to how our Lord fulfilled all righteousness in being baptized: (1) He humbled himself before the Father; (2) He covenanted to be obedient and keep the Father's commandments; (3) He had to be baptized to gain admission to the celestial kingdom; and (4) He set an example for all men to follow. (2 Ne. 31:4–11.) To fulfill all righteousness is to perform every ordinance, keep every commandment, and do every act necessary to the attainment of eternal life. (DNTC 1:123.)

As every informed person knows, Jesus was baptized by immersion. Baptism means immersion. There was no thought of any other mode or form of baptism in the Church of our Lord set up until after that holy organization had fallen prey to the doctrine of men and of devils. (DNTC 1:124.)

All four gospel authors record that the Spirit descended "like a dove"; Luke adds that he also came in "bodily shape"; and the Book of Mormon accounts say he came "in the form of a dove." (1 Ne. 11:27; 2 Ne. 31:8.)

Joseph Smith said that John "led the Son of God into the waters of baptism, and had the privilege of beholding the Holy Ghost descend in the form of a dove, or rather in the *sign of the dove,* in witness of that administration."

Then [Joseph Smith] gives this explanation: "The sign of the dove was instituted before the creation of the world, a witness for the Holy Ghost, and the devil cannot come in the sign of a dove. *The Holy Ghost is a personage, and is in the form of a personage.* It does not confine itself to the *form* of the dove, but in sign of the dove. The Holy Ghost cannot be transformed into a dove; but the sign of a dove was given to John to signify the truth of the deed, as the dove is an emblem or token of truth and innocence." (Smith, *Teachings,* pp. 275–76. Italics added.) It thus appears that John witnessed the sign of the dove, that he saw the Holy Ghost descend in the "bodily shape" of the personage that he is, and that the descent was "like a dove." (DNTC 1:123–24.)

(See section 1, "Dove, sign of.")

The Joseph Smith Translation gives the following between verses 15 and 16: "And John went down into the water and baptized him."

3:16–17 And Jesus when he was baptized, went up straightway out of the water; and *John saw,* and lo, the heavens were opened unto him, and he saw the Spirit of God descending like a dove and lighting upon *Jesus*. And lo, *he heard* a voice from heaven, saying. This is my beloved Son, in whom I am well pleased. *Hear ye him*. (JST; italics added.)

This makes it clear that it was John who saw the heavens open and beheld the manifestation of the Holy Ghost. And it was John who heard the voice of the Father testifying of the divinity of his Son. The record is not clear whether any of the multitude also saw and heard these things.

This incident is a clear manifestation of the three separate beings in the Godhead:

The four Gospel-writers record the descent of the Holy Ghost upon the baptized Jesus as accompanied by a visible manifestation "like a dove"; and this sign had been indicated to John as the foreappointed means by which the Messiah should be made known to him; and to that sign, before specified, was now added the supreme testimony of the Father as to the literal Sonship of Jesus. Matthew records the Father's acknowledgment as given in the third person, "This is my beloved Son"; while both Mark and Luke give the more direct address, "Thou art my beloved Son." The variation, slight and essentially unimportant as it is though bearing on so momentous a subject, affords evidence of independent authorship and discredits any insinuation of collusion among the writers.

The incidents attending the emergence of Jesus from the baptismal grave demonstrate the distinct individuality of the three Personages of the Godhead. On that solemn occasion Jesus the Son was present in the flesh;

the presence of the Holy Ghost was manifest through the accompanying sign of the dove, and the voice of the Eternal Father was heard from heaven. Had we no other evidence of the separate personality of each member of the Holy Trinity, this instance should be conclusive. (JTC, pp. 126–27.)

(See section 1, "Trinity, no.")

4:1–11 Read Mark 1:12–13; Luke 4:1–13.

Now, nearly every temptation that comes to you and me comes in one of those forms. Classify them, and you will find that under one of those three nearly every given temptation that makes you and me spotted, ever so little maybe, comes to us as (1) *a temptation of the appetite; (2) a yielding to the pride and fashion and vanity of those alienated from the things of God; or (3) a gratifying of the passion, or a desire for the riches of the world, or power among men.* (David O. McKay, Conference Report, Oct. 1911, p. 59.)

The importance of not accommodating temptation in the least degree is underlined by the Savior's example. Did not he recognize the danger when he was on the mountain with his fallen brother, Lucifer, being sorely tempted by that master tempter? He could have opened the door and flirted with danger by saying, "All right, Satan, I'll listen to your proposition. I need not succumb, I need not yield, I need not accept—but I'll listen."

Christ did not so rationalize. He positively and promptly closed the discussion, and commanded: "Get thee hence Satan," meaning, likely, "Get out of my sight—get out of my presence—I will not listen—I will have nothing to do with you." Then, we read, "the devil leaveth him." (MF, p. 216.)

(See section 1, "Temptations of Jesus.")

Because the Greek word often translated as "tempt" also has the basic meanings of "test," "try," and "prove," some scholars have wondered whether or not it was even possible for Christ to be "tempted."

A question deserving some attention in this connection is that of the peccability or impeccability of Christ—the question as to whether He was capable of sinning. Had there been no possibility of His yielding to the lures of Satan, there would have been no real test in the temptations, no genuine victory in the result. Our Lord was sinless yet peccable; He had the capacity, the ability to sin had He willed so to do. Had He been bereft of the faculty to sin, He would have been shorn of His free agency; and it was to safeguard and insure the agency of man that He had offered Himself, before the world was, as a redeeming sacrifice. To say that He could not sin because He was the embodiment of righteousness is no denial of His agency of choice between evil and good. (JTC, p. 134.)

President Harold B. Lee has indicated that all who are given positions of leadership in the kingdom of God will be tested:

It is my conviction that every man who will be called to a high place in this Church will have to pass . . . tests not devised by human hands, by which our Father numbers them as a united group of leaders willing to follow the prophets of the Living God and be loyal and true as witnesses and exemplars of the truths they teach." (Conference Report, Apr. 1950, p. 101; italics added.)

4:1–2 Then Jesus was led up of the Spirit, into the wilderness, *to be with God.*

And when he had fasted forty days and forty nights, *and had communed with God,* he was *afterwards* an hungered, *and was left to be tempted of the devil.* (JST; italics added.)

Jesus did not go into the wilderness to be tempted of the devil; righteous men do not seek out temptation. He went "to be with God." Probably he was visited by the Father; without question he received transcendent spiritual manifestations. The temptations came after he "had communed with God," "after forty days." The same was true in the case of Moses. He communed with God, saw the visions of eternity, and was then left unto himself to be tempted of the devil. After resisting temptation he again communed with Deity, gaining further light and revelation. (DNTC 1:28; see also Mosiah 3:7.)

4:5–6, 8–9 Then *Jesus was taken* up into the holy city, and *the Spirit* setteth him on the pinnacle of the temple.

Then the devil came unto him and said, If thou be the Son of God, cast thyself down, for it is written, He shall give his angels charge concerning thee, and in their hands they shall bear thee up, lest at any time thou dash thy foot against a stone.

And again, Jesus was in the Spirit, and it taketh him up into an exceeding high mountain, and showed him all the kingdoms of the world and the glory of them.

And the devil came unto him again, and said, All these things will I give unto thee, if thou wilt fall down and worship me. (JST; italics added.)

Lucifer did not transport Jesus to the pinnacle of the temple or into a high mountain. Such is not his power or prerogative. In each instance Jesus was taken to these locales by the Spirit, and then the devil came to tempt him. Nor did Lucifer show him all the kingdoms of the world; such was done by the Spirit; it was after he had seen the vision that the devil made his false offer. (DNTC 1:128.)

4:5–7 "Pinnacle" has also been translated "parapet" and "highest point." (See BD, "Pinnacle of the Temple.")

"Thou shalt not tempt the Lord the God" could have been translated more literally as "You must not put Jehovah your God to the test."

The devil tried to support his suggestion by scripture. . . . Our Lord met and answered the devil's quotation with another, saying: "It is written again, Thou shalt not tempt the Lord thy God."

The glaring sophistry of Satan's citation of scripture was unworthy a categorical reply; his doctrine deserved neither logic nor argument; his misapplication of the written word was nullified by scripture that was germane; the lines of the psalmist were met by the binding fiat of the prophet of the exodus, in which he had commanded Israel that they should not provoke nor tempt the Lord to work miracles among them. Satan tempted Jesus to tempt the Father. It is as truly a blasphemous interference with the prerogatives of Deity to set limitations or make fixations of time or place at which the divine power shall be made manifest as it is to attempt to usurp that power. God alone must decide when and how His wonders shall be wrought. (JTC, pp. 130–31.)

4:10 "Him only shalt thou serve" could have been translated as "It is to him alone you must render sacred service."

4:11 "Then the devil leaveth him" should not be interpreted to mean that the devil did not attempt to test or try Jesus later:

It is not to be supposed that Christ's victorious emergence from the dark clouds of the three specified temptations exempted Him from further assaults by Satan, or insured Him against later trials of faith, trust, and endurance. Luke closes his account of the temptations following the forty-day fast as follows: "And when the devil had ended all the temptation, he departed from him for a season." This victory over the devil and his wiles, this triumph over the cravings of the flesh, the harassing doubts of the mind, the suggested reaching out for fame and material wealth, were great but not final successes in the struggle between Jesus, the embodied God, and Satan, the fallen angel of light. . . . It is not given to the rest of us, nor was it given to Jesus, to meet the foe, to fight and overcome in a single encounter, once for all time. The strife between the immortal spirit and the flesh, between the offspring of God on the one hand, the world and the devil on the other, is persistent through life. (JTC, p. 133.)

4:12 (Read Mark 6:17–20; Luke 3:19–20.) The King James Version suggests that the angel came to minister unto Jesus, and then the Savior also learned that John had been cast into prison. The Joseph Smith Translation makes a significant contribution to these events: *"And now Jesus knew that John was cast into prison, and he sent angels, and, behold, they came and ministered unto him."* (JST; italics added.)

Though in mortality ministering among men, Jesus was still the King of angels. He did not ask his Father to send angels to comfort John; Jesus himself sent them. (DNTC 1:149.)

4:13–16 Read Luke 4:16–32.

4:13 "In the borders" has also been translated "in the territory," "in the area," and "in the district."

The Joseph Smith Translation clarifies the locations of the places mentioned: "*And Jesus departed into Galilee,* and leaving Nazareth, *in Zebulun,* he came and dwelt in Capernaum, which is upon the sea coast, in the borders of Nephthalim." (JST; italics added.)

Isaiah had foretold that the Messiah would be sent to those in "the land of Zebulun and the land of Naphtali" (Isa. 9:1–2), and Matthew obviously sees the various living places of the Savior as fulfilling this prophecy. Nazareth was in the area assigned to Zebulun; Capernaum was in the land of Naphtali near the border of the land of Zebulun. (See Map 5 in the Latter-day Saint edition of the King James Version of the Bible.)

4:15 [Galilee of the Gentiles is] so called because of its position as a frontier province, one standing as a buffer state between Samaria, Perea, and Judea and the heathen kingdoms of the north. Many Gentiles inhabited the northern portions of Galilee. This association, coupled with their trade with outside nations, made the Galileans somewhat more independent than their southern neighbors. Even their language had its distinctive dialect so that it could be said of them, "Thy speech bewrayeth thee." (Matt. 26:73; Luke 22:54–60.) (DNTC 1:163.)

4:17 (Read Mark 1:14–15; Luke 4:14–15; John 4:43–46.) "Repent" was the first recorded word of the Savior's ministry, just as it was the first recorded word of John's ministry. (See commentary for Matt. 3:2.)

4:18–22 (Read Mark 1:16–20; Luke 5:1–11.)

The process by which leaders become spiritual as those disciples were is set forth in a very simple admonition of the Master. The Savior called fishermen, and he called tax collectors and others in various occupations to constitute his chosen twelve. He gave to each of them the same simple promise: "Follow me, and I will make you fishers of men," or as another writer puts it, "I will make you to become fishers of men." (Matt. 4:19; Mark 1:17.)

To "come after him" is another way of saying, "Keep my commandments," for thus he had explained it when he said to the Nephites: "Therefore, what manner of men ought ye to be?" And then he answered his own question, "Verily I say unto you, even as I am." (3 Ne. 27:27.)

To become "fishers of men" is just another way of saying "become leaders of men." So in today's language we would say to those who are so to teach: "If you will keep my commandments, I will make you leaders among men." (Harold B. Lee, Conference Report, Oct. 1960, p. 15.)

4:19–20 And he *said* unto them, *I am he of whom it is written by the prophets;* follow me, and I will make you fishers of men.

And they, *believing on his words,* left their *net,* and *straightway* followed him. (JST; italics added.)

Only after Jesus testifies that he is the Messiah does he challenge Simon (Peter) and Andrew to follow him. Because the two brethren believed on his words, they immediately left their nets and followed him. (See BD, "Andrew," "Peter.")

4:23–25 (Read Mark 1:32–34; Luke 4:40–44.) The Joseph Smith Translation adds the clause "which believed on his name" at the end of verse 23, indicating that "healings were not showered upon people promiscuously; they were reserved solely and exlusively for those who had faith in Christ." (DNTC 1:171.) (See text and commentaries for Matt. 8:16–17.)

4:24 "Lunatick" has also been translated as "insane" and "epileptic."

"Palsy" is translated as "paralyzed" in virtually all modern translations.

Concerning the miracles of Jesus, Elder James E. Talmage has written:

> Miracles cannot be in contravention of natural law, but are wrought through the operation of laws not universally or commonly recognized.
>
> In the contemplation of the miracles wrought by Christ, we must of necessity recognize the operation of a power transcending our present human understanding. In this field, science has not yet advanced far enough to analyze and explain. To deny the actuality of miracles on the ground that, because we cannot comprehend the means, the reported results are fictitious, is to arrogate to the human mind the attribute of omniscience, by implying that what man cannot comprehend cannot be, and that therefore he is able to comprehend all that is.
>
> To comprehend the works of Christ, one must know Him as the Son of God; to the man who has not yet learned to know, to the honest soul who would inquire after the Lord, the invitation is ready; let him "Come and see." (JTC pp. 148–49.)

President Harold B. Lee wrote:

> *The greatest miracles I see today are not necessarily the healing of sick bodies, but the greatest miracles I see are the healing of sick souls,* those who are sick in soul and spirit and are downhearted and distraught, on the verge of nervous breakdowns. We are reaching out to all such, because they are precious in the sight of the Lord, and we want no one to feel that they are forgotten. ("Stand Ye in Holy Places," p. 123; italics added.)

(See BD, "Syria"; section 1, "Healing.")

4:25 "From beyond Jordan" could have been translated "from the other side of the Jordan."

The word *Decapolis* ("ten cities") appears only three times in the Bible (Matt. 4:25; Mark 5:20 and 7:31).

> The name means "the ten cities," and was applied to a region of indefinite boundaries lying mostly on the east of Jordan and southerly from the sea of Galilee. Scythopolis, which Josephus (Wars of the Jews, iii, 9:7) refers to as the largest of the ten cities, was on the west side of the river. There is lack of agreement among historians as to the cities comprized under the name. Biblical mention (Matt 4:25; Mark 5:20; 7:31) implies a general region rather than a definite area. (JTC, p. 367.)

(See section 1, "Decapolis.")

5–7 Many Christians consider the Sermon on the Mount to be one of the greatest discourses ever given. However, in recent years some scholars and Bible critics have listed the following concerns about this sermon:

1. To whom was the sermon directed? The first two verses of Matthew 5 indicate two possible audiences: "the multitudes" and "his disciples." A third possible audience would be the multitude *and* the disciples.

2. The doctrinal implication of some of the Beatitudes. Is it really blessed to be "poor in spirit" or to "mourn"? Also, with what will "they which do hunger and thirst after righteousness" be filled?

3. The consistency with some of the other teachings of Jesus. In this sermon the Savior admonished "Take . . . no thought for the morrow." However, in other teachings the Savior counsels his hearers to "lay up treasures in heaven," which would require taking thought for the morrow.

4. The Lord's Prayer in this sermon includes the clause, "And lead us not into temptation." Does the Lord really lead us into temptation?

The Joseph Smith Translation of this sermon and its counterpart in 3 Nephi answer all of these concerns:

1. Part of the sermon was directed to the multitude and another part was meant only for the apostles.

2. The beatitudes were conditional upon obedience to the principles of faith, repentance, baptism, and receiving the Holy Ghost. The Joseph Smith Translation makes it clear that being poor in spirit or mourning are not blessed conditions in and of themselves, but *if* one is poor in spirit or is called upon to mourn he will be blessed if he comes unto Christ. This

changes the entire emphasis of the beatitudes. Also, each beatitude in the Joseph Smith Translation is joined by a coordinating conjunction to the preceding conditional verse.

3. The Joseph Smith Translation makes it clear that when the Savior counseled "take no thought for the morrow" concerning temporal reeds, he was speaking only to the twelve apostles. This counsel was not intended for the multitude nor the world in general.

4. The Lord's Prayer in the Joseph Smith Translation includes, "And suffer us not to be led into temptation." This wording indicates that the Lord does not lead us into temptation.

(See BD, "Beatitudes"; section 1, "Beatitudes.")

5:1–12 Read Luke 6:17–26.

5:1 These two verses from the Joseph Smith Translation follow Matthew 5:1:

> Blessed are they who shall believe on me; and again, more blessed are they who shall believe on your words, when ye shall testify that ye have seen me and that I am. Yea, blessed are they who shall believe on your words, and come down into the depth of humility, and be baptized in my name; for they shall be visited with fire and the Holy Ghost, and shall receive a remission of their sins.

> **5:3** *Yea,* blessed are the poor in spirit, *who come unto me;* for theirs is the kingdom of heaven. (JST; italics added.)

5:8 The Joseph Smith Translation clarifies this verse: "And blessed are all they that do hunger and thirst after righteousness; for they shall be filled with the Holy Ghost."

5:10–11 The Joseph Smith Translation adds the word *all* to both of these verses so that they read "all the pure in heart" and "all the peacemakers."

5:11 "And shall say all manner of evil against you falsely" could have been translated "and lyingly say every sort of wicked thing against you."

5:13–16 Read Luke 8:16; 11:33; 14:34–35.

> *Verily, verily, I say unto you, I give unto you to be* the salt of the earth; but if the salt *shall lose its savour,* wherewith shall *the earth* be salted? *the salt shall* thenceforth *be* good for nothing, but to be cast out, and to be trodden under foot of men.
>
> *Verily, verily, I say unto you, I give unto you to be* the light of the world; a city that is set on a hill cannot be hid.
>
> *Behold,* do men light a candle and put it under a bushel? *Nay,* but on a candlestick; and it giveth light to all that are in house.

Therefore, let your light so shine before *this world,* that they may see your good works, and glorify your Father who is in heaven. (JST; italics added.)

People are not automatically "the salt of the earth" or "the light of the world," but if they accept and live the gospel, they can become the "salt" and the "light."

5:13 "If the salt have lost his savour, wherewith shall it be salted?" could have been translated "If the salt loses its strength, how will its saltness be restored?"

Elder James E. Talmage quoted from Dummelow to explain this verse:

Dummelow's *Commentary,* on Matt. 5:13, states: "Salt in Palestine, being gathered in an impure state, often undergoes chemical changes by which its flavor is destroyed while its appearance remains." Perhaps a reasonable interpretation of the expression, "if the salt have lost his savor," may be suggested by the fact that salt mixed with insoluble impurities may be dissolved out by moisture, leaving the insoluble residue but slightly salty. The lesson of the Lord's illustration is that spoiled salt is of no use as a preservative. The corresponding passage in the sermon delivered by Jesus to the Nephites after His resurrection reads: "Verily, verily, I say unto you, I give unto you to be the salt of the earth; but if the salt shall lose its savor, wherewith shall the earth be salted? The salt shall be thenceforth good for nothing, but to be cast out, and to be trodden under foot of men." (3 Nephi 12:13.) (JTC, p. 248.)

(See section 1, "Savour.")

5:15 "Candle" and "candlestick" could also have been translated "lamp" and "lampstand."

5:17–20 Read Luke 16:17.

5:18 "One jot or one tittle" could have been translated "one smallest letter or one particle of a letter."

5:19 The same shall be called great, and shall be saved in the kingdom of heaven. (JST.)

5:20 "Your righteousness shall exceed the righteousness of the scribes and Pharisees" could have been translated "if your righteousness does not abound more than that of the scribes and Pharisees."

5:21–26 Read Luke 12:58–59.

5:21 The Greek word translated "kill" really means "murder." This meaning is consistent with the Hebrew word used in the Ten Commandments. (See BD, "Murder.")

5:22 "Without a cause" is deleted in the Joseph Smith Translation, indicating that unrighteous anger is evil whether or not it is provoked.

The Joseph Smith Translation also indicates that one should not say to his brother "Raca" or "Rabcha." These words show contempt, and undoubtedly the Savior meant to condemn any language that conveys improper feelings for another.

The word *Raca* has several possible definitions, but all of them suggest derision or contempt. "Idiot" would be a close equivalent. (See section 1, "Raca.")

The Greek word translated "fool" near the end of the verse has a stronger meaning, such as "despicable fool."

Whereas the law forbade murder, and provided a just penalty for the crime, Christ taught that one's giving way to anger, which might possibly lead to violence or even murder, was of itself a sin. To maliciously use an offensive epithet such as "Raca" laid one liable to punishment under the decree of the council, and to call another a fool placed one "in danger of hell fire." These objectionable designations were regarded at that time as especially opprobrious and were therefore expressive of hateful intent. The murderer's hand is impelled by the hatred in his heart. The law provided penalty for the deed; the gospel rebuked the evil passion in its incipiency. To emphasize this principle, the Master showed that hatred was not to be atoned by a material sacrifice; and that if one came to make an offering at the altar, and remembered that he was at enmity with his brother, he should first go to that brother and be reconciled, even though such a course involved the interruption of the ceremonial, which was a particularly grievous incident according to the judgment of the priests. Differences and contentions were to be adjusted without delay. (JTC, p. 234.)

In all our daily pursuits in life, of whatever nature and kind, Latter-day Saints, and especially those who hold important positions in the kingdom of God, should maintain a uniform and even temper, both when at home and when abroad. They should not suffer reverses and unpleasant circumstances to sour their natures and render them fretful and unsocial at home, speaking words full of bitterness and biting acrimony to their wives and children, creating gloom and sorrow in their habitations, making themselves feared rather than beloved by their families. Anger should never be permitted to rise in our bosoms, and words suggested by angry feelings should never be permitted to pass our lips. "A soft answer turneth away wrath, but grievous words stir up anger." "Wrath is cruel, and anger is outrageous," but "the discretion of a man deferreth his anger; and it is his glory to pass over a transgression." (Brigham Young, JD 11:136.)

Verse 22 contains the first reference to hell in the New Testament.

The Church does teach that there is a place called hell. Of course we do not believe that all those who do not receive the gospel will eventually be cast into hell. We *do not* believe that hell is a place where the wicked are being burned forever. The Lord has prepared a place, however, for all those who are to be eternally punished for the violation of his laws. . . .

A place where those who cannot be redeemed and who are called the sons of Perdition will go into outer darkness. This is the real hell where those who once knew the truth and had the testimony of it and then turned away and blasphemed the name of Jesus Christ, will go. These are they who have sinned against the Holy Ghost. For them there is no forgiveness, and the Lord said he had prepared a place for them. (D&C 76:31–37; 88:32–33.)

All those who enter the telestial kingdom, which will be a place, as each of these kingdoms will be, will be punished for their sins. Satan for a time will have dominion over them until they have paid the price of their sinning, before they can enter into that telestial kingdom.

This earth will become a celestial kingdom when it is sanctified. Those who enter the terrestrial kingdom will have to go to some other sphere which will be prepared for them. Those who enter the telestial kingdom, likewise will have to go to some earth which is prepared for them, and there will be another place which is hell where the devil and those who are punished to go with him will dwell. Of course, those who enter the telestial kingdom, and those who enter the terrestrial kingdom will have the eternal punishment which will come to them in knowing that they might, if they had kept the commandments of the Lord, have returned to his presence as his sons and his daughters. This will be a torment to them, and in that sense it will be hell. (AGQ 2:208–10.)

5:23–24 Therefore, if ye shall come unto me, or shall desire to come unto me, or if thou bring thy gift to the altar, and there rememberest that thy brother hath aught against thee,

Leave *thou* thy gift before *the altar,* and go thy way *unto thy brother, and* first be reconciled to thy brother, and then come and offer thy gift. (JST; italics added.)

5:24 Elder Bruce R. McConkie has provided valuable insight into the phrase "thy brother hath aught against thee":

Not a remembrance that you are angry with your brother, for it is assumed that the true saint will have overcome his own ill feelings, but a remembrance that your brother hath aught against you! The command: 'Go to him; do not wait for him to come to you, simply because you are the one who has been wronged.' How often one person supposes he has been wronged, or imagines another is offended at him, when a simple brotherly explanation would remove the source of all possible ill feeling. Or, how often are actual cases of resentment and antagonism cleared up when the hand of fellowship, literally and verbally, is extended. (DNTC 1:223.)

5:25 "Agree with thine adversary quickly" could have been translated more literally as "quickly settle matters with the one complaining against you."

5:26 The Greek words translated "the uttermost farthing" have the basic meaning of "the last coin of very little value."

Elder Bruce R. McConkie has suggested that the counsel in verses 25–26 pertains primarily to missionaries and general Church leaders:

Counsel to avoid lawsuits and entangling legal difficulties, lest fine and imprisonment result, is directed particularly to the apostles and missionaries as they go forth to carry the gospel message to a wicked world. It is more important that they suffer legal wrongs than that their ministries be hindered or halted by legal processes. (DNTC 1:223.)

5:27–32 Read Luke 16:18.

5:27–28 The Joseph Smith Translation of these verses begins, "Behold, it is written by them of old time, that thou shalt not commit adultery."

There are no grosser personal crimes than adultery, except murder and the commission of the unpardonable sin. (Alma 39:5–6.) Adulterous acts are committed mentally before the physical debauchery ever takes place, and sensual and evil thoughts are in themselves a debasing evil. (MD, pp. 23–24, 638–39.)

Many acknowledge the vice of physical adultery, but still rationalize that anything short of that heinous sin may *not* be condemned too harshly; however, the Lord has said many times: "Ye have heard that it was said by them of old times, Thou shalt not commit adultery:

"But I say unto you, That whosoever looketh on a woman to lust after her hath committed adultery with her in his heart." (Matt. 5:27–28.)

And to paraphrase and give the modern version: "And she that looketh upon a man to lust after him shall deny the faith, and shall not have the Spirit; and if she repents not she shall be cast out [or excommunicated]." (See D&C 42:23.) The commands of the Lord apply to women with equal force as to their husbands, and those scriptures come with the same sharpness and exactness to both sexes, for he has but a single standard of morality. It is not always the man who is the aggressor. Often it is the pursuing, coveting woman, and note that for both, *all* is lost if there is not true, sustained, and real repentance.

Home-breaking is sin, and any thought, act, or association which will tend to destroy another's home is a grievous transgression. (Spencer W. Kimball, Conference Report, Oct. 1962, p. 58.)

(See BD, "Adultery.")

5:28 The Joseph Smith Translation includes this additional verse after Matthew 5:28: "Behold, I give unto you a commandment, that ye suffer none of these things to enter into your heart, for it is better that ye should deny yourselves of these things, wherein ye will take up your cross, than that ye should be cast into hell."

5:29–30 These verses have been greatly misunderstood, but are made clear in the Joseph Smith Translation:

Behold, I give unto you a commandment, that ye suffer none of these things to enter into your heart, for it is better that ye should deny yourselves of these things, wherein ye will take up your cross, than that ye should be cast into hell.

Therefore, if thy right eye offend thee, pluck it out and cast it from thee; for it is profitable for thee that one of thy members should perish, and not that thy whole body should be cast into hell.

Or if thy right hand offend thee, cut it off and cast it from thee; for it is profitable for thee that one of thy members should perish, and not that thy whole body should be cast into hell.

And now this I speak, a parable concerning your sins; wherefore, cast them from you, that you may not be hewn down and cast into the fire. (JST; italics added.)

(See BD, "Gehenna.")

Elder Bruce R. McConkie has offered the following commentary:

In a figurative manner of speaking various organs of the body are said to commit sin when what is actually meant is that the person himself is guilty of the evil deed. We refer to someone as having a lying *tongue,* meaning he is a liar. We speak of *"hands* that shed innocent blood," *hearts* that devise "wicked imaginations, *feet* that be swift in running to mischief" (Prov. 6:16–18), *eyes* guilty of lust (1 John 2:16), and so forth. And this is the type and kind of expression used by Jesus in his parable about destroying offending members of the body as a means of casting one's sins away.

If thy right eye offend thee, pluck it out and cast it from thee—that is, if a situation or circumstance exists which might might lead to sin, avoid it, lest continued association therewith lead to sin. If thy neighbor's wife is unduly attractive to you, stay away from her. If you have an urge to gamble, don't associate with gamblers or go where gambling is found. If you love money and the riches of men, consecrate your properties to the Welfare Plan, and ask your bishop to recommend you for a mission. (Matt. 19:16–26.) If you have an urge to steal, lock yourself in your closet until it passes. If the smell of coffee is enticing, don't go where it is being prepared.

If thy right hand offend thee, cut it off and cast it from thee—that is, get away from the environment of sin. Forsake the world, including father and mother, brothers and sisters, if need be. Do not let evil thoughts enter your mind, lest they become your master. Live a life of severe spiritual discipline. If it is more difficult for you to keep the commandments than it is for your neighbor, avoid the enticements which have no pulling power on him. (DNTC 1:224–25.)

Joseph Fielding Smith commented that the Savior was referring to close friends and relatives:

When the Lord spoke of parts of the body, it is evident that he had in mind close friends or relatives who endeavored to lead us from the path of rectitude and humble obedience to the divine commandments we receive from the Lord.

If any friend or relative endeavors to lead a person away from the commandments, it is better to dispense with his friendship and association rather than to follow him in evil practices to destruction. This use of comparison or illustration was as common in ancient days as it is in the present age. We should not, in reading these ancient expressions in the New Testament, take such a statement as this referred to in the words of the Savior recorded by Mark in the literal interpretation. When properly understood it becomes a very impressive figure of speech. (AGQ 5:79.)

(See section 1, "Family members will not all accept.")

"It is profitable" has the basic meaning of "it is advantageous." Thus, the term could have been translated "it is more beneficial."

5:33–37 See also 3 Nephi 12:33–37; Deuteronomy 23:21; Psalm 139:20; Isaiah 66:1.

5:33 "Thou shalt not forswear thyself" could have been translated more literally "You must not swear without performing." Other translations are "You shall not break your vows"; "You shall not swear falsely"; "Do not break your promise"; and "Do not break your oath."

In ancient dispensations, particularly the Mosaic, the taking of oaths was an approved and formal part of the religious lives of the people. These oaths were solemn appeals to Deity, or to some sacred object or thing, in attestation of the truth of a statement or of a sworn determination to keep a promise. These statements, usually made in the name of the Lord, by people who valued their religion and their word above their lives, could be and were relied upon with absolute assurance. (MD, pp. 486–88.)

Beginning in the meridian of time, Jesus revealed a higher standard relative to truthfulness in conversation. It was simply that Yea meant Yea, and Nay meant Nay, and that no oath was required to establish the verity of any promise or thing. Every man's every word was to be as true and accurate as if it had been spoken with an oath. (DNTC 1:226.)

(See section 1, "Oaths.")

5:38–42 Read Luke 6:29–30; see 3 Ne. 12:38–42.

5:38–41 The Greek words translated "coat" and "cloke" in verse 40 have the basic meaning of "inner garment" and "outer garment," respectively. Other translations of the word translated as "coat" are "shirt" and "tunic."

Concerning the principles taught in these verses, Elder James E. Talmage has observed:

Christ taught that men should rather suffer than do evil, even to the extent of submission without resistance under certain implied conditions. His forceful illustrations—that if one were smitten on one cheek he should turn the other to the smiter; that if a man took another's coat by process of law, the loser should allow his cloak to be taken also; that if one was pressed into service to carry another's burden a mile, he should willingly go two miles; that one should readily give or lend as asked—are not to be construed as commanding abject subserviency to unjust demands, nor as an abrogation to the principle of self-protection. These instructions were directed primarily to the apostles, who would be professedly devoted to the work of the kingdom to the exclusion of all other interests. In their ministry it would be better to suffer material loss or personal indignity and imposition at the hands of wicked oppressors, than to bring about an impairment of efficiency and a hindrance in work through resistance and contention. To such as these the Beatitudes were particularly applicable—Blessed are the meek, the peace-makers, and they that are persecuted for righteousness' sake. (JTC, pp. 235–36.)

(See BD, "Retaliation," "Revenge.")

5:39 "Resist not evil" could have been translated "do not resist him that is wicked."

5:41 The Joseph Smith Translation adds significantly to this verse: "And whosoever shall compel thee to go a mile, go with him a mile; and whosoever shall compel thee to go with him twain, thou shalt go with him twain."

Apparently Jesus had reference to the Roman law which authorized troops passing a district to commandeer the people and compel them to carry their luggage. To comply with this law often resulted in great inconvenience. The principle involved is that the saints should pay their taxes, abide by the laws of the land, and submit to those public burdens attendant upon citizenship. (DNTC 1:228–29.)

5:43–47 Read Luke 6:27–35; see 3 Nephi 12:43–45.

Jesus is here restoring the perfect gospel law of love. To those subject to the Mosaic standard it was a new doctrine. Never before had they been required to love their foes; indeed, they had grown to look upon Israel's enemies as God's enemies. But now the gospel of love was to extend to all man, not just to those of the chosen seed. (DNTC 1:230.)

(See section 1, "Love, gospel of.")

5:48 Read Luke 6:36; see 3 Nephi 12:48.

Ye are therefore commanded to be perfect, even as your Father *who* is in heaven is perfect." (JST; italics added.)

This commandment was given by Jesus Christ in New Testament times before he had completed his atonement; thus, he had one example of perfectness to recommend to us. After his resurrection and glorification, however, the Savior could offer himself as an example also, as indicated in 3 Nephi 12:48: "Therefore I would that ye should be perfect even as I, or your Father who is in heaven is perfect."

Perfection is of two kinds—finite or mortal, and infinite or eternal. Finite perfection may be gained by the righteous saints in this life. It consists in living a godfearing life of devotion to the truth, of walking in complete submission to the will of the Lord, and of putting first in one's life the things of the kingdom of God. Infinite perfection is reserved for those who overcome all things and inherit the fulness of the Father in the mansions hereafter. It consists in gaining eternal life, the kind of life which God has in the highest heaven within the celestial world. (MD, pp. 512–14.)

6:1–4 (See also 3 Nephi 13:1–4.) Taking care of the poor and needy has been part of the gospel of Jesus Christ in every dispensation. When the Savior was on the earth, almsgiving was an important part of Jewish custom and practice. Evidently, however, much of the almsgiving was done in public where the donors expected to gain recognition and popularity. Such people have already received their reward when they "are seen of men" and should expect no other reward or blessing from our Heavenly Father. (See BD, "Almsgiving.")

To give to the needy is praiseworthy; but to give for the purpose of winning the praise of men is rank hypocrisy. The tossing of alms to a beggar, the pouring of offerings into the temple treasure chests, to be seen of men, and similar displays of affected liberality, were fashionable among certain classes in the time of Christ; and the same spirit is manifest today. Some there be now who cause a trumpet to be sounded, through the columns of the press perchance, or by other means of publicity, to call attention to their giving, that they may have glory of men—to win political favor, to increase their trade or influence, to get what in their estimation is worth more than that from which they part. With logical incisiveness the Master demonstrated that such givers have their reward. They have received what they bid for; what more can such men demand or consistently expect? (JTC, p. 237.)

6:1 This portion of the Sermon on the Mount is given to the disciples, as shown by the Joseph Smith Translation: "And it came to pass that, as Jesus taught his disciples he said unto them, . . ."

6:2, 5, 16 The phrase "in full" could be added to these verses, according to the Greek. The last clause in each verse would thus read, "They have their reward in full."

6:2 The Greek word translated here as "hypocrites" essentially means "excessive exaggeration."

6:5–15 (Read Mark 11:25–26; Luke 11:1–8; see 3 Nephi 13:5–15.) If our prayers are offered only so that others can see and hear us pray, we should not expect to receive any other reward. If we pray in secret, however, we receive the Lord's blessings. (See BD, "Prayer"; section 1, "Prayer.")

Among the Jews, when praying, it was the custom to stand, face Jerusalem, cover one's head, and cast one's eyes downward. Certain hours of the day were set aside for prayers, and those desiring to make an ostentatious show of piety would arrange to be in the streets and public places at these hours. Those desiring to make a show of devoutness would also say their own prayers out loud during the synagogue services. This type of conduct, symbolical of all hypocrisy in prayer, was what Jesus condemned. (DNTC 1:235.)

Go where you can be alone, go where you can think, go where you can kneel, go where you can speak out loud to him. The bedroom, the bathroom, or the closet will do. Now, picture him in your mind's eye. Think to whom you are speaking, control your thoughts—don't let them wander, address him as your Father and your friend. Now tell him things you really feel to tell him—not trite phrases that have little meaning, but have a sincere, heartfelt conversation with him. Confide in him, ask him for forgiveness, plead with him, enjoy him, thank him, express your love to him, and then listen for his answers. Listening is an essential part of praying. Answers from the Lord come quietly—ever so quietly. In fact, few hear his answers audibly with their ears. We must be listening so carefully or we will never recognize them. Most answers from the Lord are felt in our heart as a warm comfortable expression, or they may come as thoughts to our mind., They come to those who are prepared and who are patient. (H. Burke Peterson, "Adversity and Prayer," *Ensign,* Jan. 1974, p. 19.)

6:7 This verse could have been translated "But when praying, do not say the same things over and over again, just as the people of the nations do, for they imagine they will get a hearing for their use of many words."

6:9–13 "After this manner therefore pray ye" suggests that Jesus is giving a sample of prayer only; he is not giving a prayer to be repeated verbatim.

This is not the final word in prayer, nor is it designed for verbatim repetition by the saints in their private or public prayers. Rather the disciples were receiving from Jesus instruction in prayer in the same way that revelation comes in all fields; it was coming line upon line, precept upon precept, with the assurance that greater understanding and direction would be given as rapidly as the spiritual progression of the saints permitted. The Lord's Prayer, for instance, does not conclude in the name of Christ, as all complete and proper prayers should. Later Jesus was to command his disciples to pray in his name (John 14:13–14; 15:16; 16:23), explaining that though they had "hitherto . . . asked nothing" in his name, yet that should be the order from thenceforth. (John 16:24.)

But this prayer was given as a sample or illustration of how Deity might appropriately be addressed in prayer, of the praise and adoration that should be extended to him, and of the type and kind of petitions men should make to him. As far as it goes it is one of the most concise, expressive, and beautiful statements found in the scriptures. (DNTC 1:235.)

(See section 1, "Lord's Prayer.")

6:10 Jesus Christ presently rules over his kingdom (the Church). When he comes in power to rule as King of kings and Lord of lords, then his will truly will be done on earth as it is in heaven.

Elder Talmage has written concerning how we can help to bring forth this blessed condition:

The kingdom of God is to be a kingdom of order, in which toleration and the recognition of individual rights shall prevail. One who really prays that this kingdom come will strive to hasten its coming by living according to the law of God. His effort will be to keep himself in harmony with the order of the kingdom, to subject the flesh to the spirit, selfishness to altruism, and to learn to love the things that God loves. To make the will of God supreme on earth as it is in heaven is to be allied with God in the affairs of life. There are many who profess belief that as God is omnipotent, all that is is according to His will. Such a supposition is unscriptural, unreasonable, and untrue. Wickedness is not in harmony with His will; falsehood, hypocrisy, vice and crime are not God's gifts to man. By His will these monstrosities that have developed as hideous deformities in human nature and life shall be abolished, and this blessed consummation shall be reached when by choice, without surrender or abrogation of their free agency, men shall do the will of God. (JTC, p. 239.)

(See section 1, "Kingdom of Heaven or Kingdom of God.")

6:11 Even though we store food for future needs, we should still remember to thank our Heavenly Father for our "daily bread." Elder Talmage explains:

We are taught to pray day by day for the food we need. . . . Israel in the desert received manna as a daily supply, and were kept in mind of their reliance upon Him who gave. The man with much finds it easier to forget his dependence than he who must ask with each succeeding day of need. (JTC, p. 240.)

6:13 The Joseph Smith Translation of the first part of this verse reads, "And suffer us not to be led into temptation." This agrees with the Syriac, which reads "Do not let us enter into temptation."

God does not lead men into temptation except in the sense that he has placed them here on earth where temptation is found so they can be tried and tested in accordance with the terms and provisions of the eternal plan of salvation. Rather, this is a plea to be able to avoid greater temptation than we can successfully withstand. It is a request to be delivered from entice-ments and seductions which are so great as to overcome the normal powers of resistance. Obviously it would be nothing short of hypocrisy to utter this prayer and then go out where sin and lust and evil are found. Implicit in the prayer to avoid being led into temptation is the promise on the petitioner's part to avoid the places where sin and evil are found. (DNTC 1:237.)

The closing clause of this verse, "For thine is the king-dom, and the power, and the glory, for ever" has been trans-lated from some late Greek manuscripts. Many modern translations do not include this expression, although it is found in the Joseph Smith Translation.

6:14–15 The Greek word translated "trespasses" has also been translated "wrongs," "sins," "failings," and "failures."

The Joseph Smith Translation indicates that "trespass" is a good translation which might also have been used in verse 12 in place of "debts":

And forgive us our *trespasses,* as we forgive *those who trespass against us. . . .*

For if ye forgive men their trespasses, *who trespass against you,* your heavenly Father will also forgive you; but if ye forgive not men their tres-passes, neither will your *heavenly* Father forgive you your trespasses. (JST; italics added.)

6:16–18 See 3 Nephi 13:16–18; Zechariah 7:5–6.

As the Church views it, fasting consists in the complete abstinence from food and drink. Fasting, with prayer as its companion, is designed to increase spirituality; to foster a spirit of devotion and love of God; to increase faith in the hearts of men, thus assuring divine favor; to encourage humility and contrition of soul; to aid in the acquirement of righteousness; to teach man his nothingness and dependence upon God; and to hasten those who properly comply with the law of fasting along the path to salvation. (MD, pp. 256–57.)

Self-righteous zealots in Jesus' day made great outward display of their fasting. It is the showy display, not the fasting itself, which is to be shunned by the true saint. While engaged in fasting and prayer it is proper to go about one's normal and usual affairs, without attempting to advertise an assumed status of piety. (DNTC 1:238.)

6:16 See commentary for Matthew 6:2, 5, 16.

6:19–34 Read Luke 11:33–36; 12:22–32; 16:9–13; see 3 Nephi 13:19–34.

6:19–21 "Treasures in heaven" could have two meanings: (1) the things we must do to inherit heaven, and (2) the things we do or acquire on this earth that can be taken with us into heaven.

One lays up treasures in heaven when he is baptized, receives the gift of the Holy Ghost, and remains faithful to the end. Knowledge and righteous attributes (honesty, dependability, mercy, love, etc.) are also "treasures in heaven," for we have been told, "Whatever principle of intelligence we attain unto in this life, it will rise with us in the resurrection." (D&C 130:18.)

> Many there were and many there are whose principal effort in life has been that of amassing treasures of earth, the mere possession of which entails responsibility, care, and disturbing anxiety. Some kinds of wealth are endangered by the ravages of moths, such as silks and velvets, satins and furs; some are destroyed by corrosion and rust—silver and copper and steel; while these and others are not infrequently made the booty of thieves. Infinitely more precious are the treasures of a life well spent, and wealth of good deeds, the account of which is kept in heaven, where the riches of righteous achievement are safe from moth, rust, and robbers. Then followed the trenchant lesson: *"For where your treasure is, there will your heart be also."* (JTC, p. 242.)

6:19 The Greek term translated "break through" means to dig through, as through an earthen wall.

6:22 The Joseph Smith Translation adds an important clause: "if therefore thine eye be single *to the glory of God.*" (Italics added.)

6:24–25 The Greek word translated here as "mammon" means "riches" or "money," but also has the connotation of "worldliness." (See section 1, "Mammon.")

The Joseph Smith Translation adds three additional verses between verses 24 and 25:

> And, again, I say unto you, go ye into the world, and care not for the world; for the world will hate you, and will persecute you, and will turn you out of their synagogues.
>
> Nevertheless, ye shall go forth from house to house, teaching the people; and I will go before you.
>
> And your heavenly Father will provide for you, whatsoever things ye need for food, what ye shall eat; and for raiment, what ye shall wear or put on.

6:25, 27–28, 31, 34 The Greek term translated "take no thought" means "do not be overly anxious."

6:25–26 The Greek words translated "meat" and "raiment"

literally mean "food" and "clothing." (See section 1, "Meat," "Raiment.")

The Joseph Smith Translation makes it clear that this portion of the sermon is directed only to the disciples; it is not intended for the world: "As Jesus taught his disciples, he said unto them. . . ." (JST.)

This portion of the Sermon on the Mount was delivered to the apostles and such of the disciples as were called to forsake their temporal pursuits and carry the message of salvation to the world. There is not now and never has been a call to the saints generally to "sell that ye have" (Luke 12:33), give alms to the poor, and then to take no thought for the temporal needs of the present or future. Rather, as part of their mortal probation, the true followers of the Master are expected by him to provide for themselves and their families. (D&C 75.)

However, a special rule applies to those who are called to go into the world without purse or scrip and preach the gospel. For the time and season of their missionary service they are to have no concern about business enterprises or temporal pursuits. They are to be free of the encumbering obligations that always attend those who manage temporal affairs. Their whole attention and all of their strength and talents are to be centered on the work of the ministry, and they have the Father's promise that he will look after their daily needs. (DNTC 1:243.)

6:26 The Joseph Smith Translation adds the following sentence and additional verse:

How much more will he not feed you? Wherefore take no thought for these things, but keep my commandments wherewith I have commanded you.

6:30 The end of this verse reads, "if ye are not of little faith," according to the Joseph Smith Translation.

6:32 Why is it that ye murmur among yourselves, saying, We cannot obey the word because ye have not all these things, and seek to excuse yourselves, saying that, After all these things do the Gentiles seek. (JST.)

6:33 *Wherefore, seek not the things of this world* but seek ye first to build up the kingdom of God, and *to establish* his righteousness, and all these things shall be added unto you. (JST; italics added.)

It is common to quote this command as one directing men to seek, through righteousness, the things of the celestial world. Counsel so to do is never inappropriate. But, actually, as seen from the Inspired Version accounts of Matthew and Luke, Jesus is directing his ministers "to build up the kingdom of God" (I. V. Matt. 6:38), and to seek "to bring forth the kingdom of God" (I. V. Luke 12:34), meaning the Church of Jesus Christ, which is the kingdom of God on earth. They were being sent forth, as are the missionaries in this day, to preach the gospel so that converts might come into the Church or kingdom, thereby building it up in strength and power. (DNTC 1:244.)

6:34 The final sentence could be translated "Sufficient for each day is its own evil." Other translations are "Live one day at a time"; "One day's trouble is enough for one day"; "Let the day's own trouble be sufficient for the day"; "There is no need to add to the troubles each day brings"; "Each day has enough trouble of its own"; "Each day has troubles enough of its own."

7:1–5 Read Luke 6:37–42. See also 3 Nephi 14:1–5.

7:1–2 The Joseph Smith Translation indicates that in these verses the Lord is teaching the disciples what "they should say unto the people": "Now these are the words which Jesus taught his disciples that they should say unto the people, Judge not unrighteously, that ye be not judged; but judge righteous judgment."

> The reason . . . that we cannot judge is obvious. We cannot see what is in the heart. We do not know motives, although we impute motives to every action we see. They may be pure while we think they are improper.
>
> It is not possible to judge another fairly unless you know his desires, his faith, and his goals. Because of a different environment, unequal opportunity, and many other things, people are not in the same position. One may start at the top and the other at the bottom, and they may meet as they are going in opposite directions. Someone has said that it is not where you are but the direction in which you are going that counts; not how close you are to failure or success but which way you are headed. How can we, with all our weaknesses and frailties, dare to arrogate to ourselves the position of a judge? At best, man can judge only what he sees: he cannot judge the heart or the intention, or begin to judge the potential of his neighbor.
>
> When we try to judge people, which we should not do, we have a great tendency to look for and take pride in finding weaknesses and faults, such as vanity, dishonesty, immorality, and intrigue. As a result, we see only the worst side of those being judged. (N. Eldon Tanner, "Judge Not, That Ye Be Not Judged," *Ensign,* July 1972, p. 35.)

> This is not a prohibition against sitting in judgment either on one's fellowmen or upon principles of right and wrong, for the saints are commanded to do these very things. The sense and meaning of our Lord's utterance is, "Condemn not, that ye be not condemned." It is, "Judge wisely and righteously, so that ye may be judged in like manner." (DNTC 1:245.)

7:2 The Greek word translated "mete" means "measure out."

7:3 The Greek words translated as "mote" and "beam" have been translated as "straw" and "rafter," "speck" and "board," "speck" and "plank," and "speck" and "log." (See section 1, "Mote.")

7:4–5 The Joseph Smith Translation adds the following between these two verses:

And Jesus said unto his disciples, Beholdest thou the scribes, and the Pharisees, and the Priests, and the Levites? They teach in their synagogues, but do not observe the law, nor the commandments; and all have gone out of the way, and are under sin.

Go thou and say unto them, Why teach ye men the law and the commandments, when ye yourselves are the children of corruption?

Say unto them, Ye hypocrites, . . .

7:6 (See also 3 Ne. 14:6.) The Joseph Smith Translation adds considerably to this verse:

Go ye into the world, saying unto all, Repent, for the kingdom of heaven has come nigh unto you.

And the mysteries of the kingdom ye shall keep within yourselves; for it is not meet to give that which is holy unto the dogs; neither cast ye your pearls unto swine, lest they trample them under their feet.

For the world cannot receive that which ye, yourselves, are not able to bear; wherefore ye shall not give your pearls unto them, lest they turn again and rend you. (JST; italics added.)

The Joseph Smith Translation emphasizes that the basic message of the gospel is "Repent." The meaning of this word is "to change" or "to turn around." Thus, it can be used as pertaining to both positive and negative situations. If a person is *doing* something *bad* or *wrong,* he repents by ceasing to do the bad thing. If a person is *not doing* something *good* or *right,* then he repents by doing the good thing. (See section 1, "Repent," "Repentance.")

Elder McConkie has emphasized why missionaries and other teachers of the gospel should teach these basic principles:

Missionaries ordinarily confine their teachings to such things as the nature and kind of being that God is, the atonement of our Lord, the apostasy from and restoration of the gospel, and the plan of salvation. After people are converted and have the gift of the Holy Ghost to enlighten their minds it is time enough for them to learn the deeper things pertaining to exaltation in the eternal worlds. The sacred teachings revealed in temple ordinances, for instance, are mysteries reserved for selected and faithful members of the kingdom who have attained sufficient stability and background to understand them. (DNTC 1:248–49.)

7:7–12 Read Luke 11:9–13; see also 3 Nephi 14:7–12.

7:7 The Joseph Smith Translation of this verse begins with the admonition "Ask of God."

How will those in the world be able to recognize the gospel and receive its truths? How can they learn the mysteries of the kingdom? Jesus answers: "Ask of God." True conversion is not born of contention or debate. The things of God are known only by revelation from the Spirit of God. (1 Cor. 2:11.) To gain a knowledge of the truth men must abide the law which enables them to gain personal revelation from the Lord. They must desire to know of the divinity of the message, must learn what is being taught, must practice its principles, and must pray in faith for guidance and direction from on high. (DNTC 1:249.)

7:8–9 The Joseph Smith Translation adds the following between these two verses:

And then said his disciples unto him, they will say unto us, We ourselves are righteous, and need not that any man should teach us. God, we know, heard Moses and some of the prophets; but us he will not hear. And they will say, We have the law for our salvation, and that is sufficient for us. Then Jesus answered, and said unto his disciples, thus shall ye say unto them, What man among you, having a son, and he shall be standing out, and shall say, Father, open thy house that I may come in and sup with thee, will not say, Come in, my son; for mine is thine, and thine is mine?

7:12 Other translations of this famous verse are:

Do for others what you want them to do for you. This is the teaching of the laws of Moses in a nutshell. (LB.)

Treat other people exactly as you would like to be treated by them—this is the meaning of the Law of the Prophets. (PME.)

So whatever you wish that men would do to you, do so to them; for this is the law and the prophets. (RSV.)

Do for others what you want them to do for you: this is the meaning of the Law of Moses and the teaching of the prophets. (TEV.)

In everything do to others what you would have them do to you, for this sums up the Law and the Prophets. (NIV.)

So always treat others as you would like them to treat you; that is the meaning of the Law and the Prophets. (JB.)

Always treat others as you would like them to treat you: that is the law and the prophets. (NEB.)

7:13–14 (Read Luke 13:23–24. See also 3 Ne. 14:13–14.) These verses could have been translated "Go in through the narrow gate; because broad and spacious is the road leading off into destruction, and many are the ones going in through it; whereas narrow is the gate and cramped the road leading off into life, and few are the ones finding it."

The Greek word translated "strait" is translated "narrow" in virtually all modern translations.

Not *straight,* but s-t-r-a-i-t, meaning narrow, restricted, limited. By entering the strait gate men get on the path which is both strait and which leads to eternal reward hereafter. Baptism is the strait gate which puts men on the path leading to the celestial world; the new and everlasting covenant of marriage is the strait gate which starts men and women out in the direction of exaltation in the highest heaven of that world. (DNTC 1:250.)

The course leading to eternal life is both *strait* and *straight.* It is *straight* because it has an invariable direction—always it is the same. There are no diversions, crooked paths, or tangents leading to the kingdom of God. It is *strait* because it is narrow and restricted, a course where full obedience to the full law is required. Straightness has reference to direction, straitness to width. The gate is *strait;* the path is both strait and straight. (MD, p. 769.)

The Joseph Smith Translation of verse 13 begins "Repent, therefore, and enter. . . ."

7:15–20 Read Luke 6:43–44. See also 3 Nephi 14:15–20.

7:15 The Greek word translated "ravening" has also been translated "ferocious," "greedy, "savage," and "wild."

7:17 "A corrupt tree bringeth forth evil fruit" could have been translated "every rotten tree produces worthless fruit." The Greek word translated "corrupt" has also been translated "bad" and "poor." (See section 1, "Corrupt fruit.")

7:21–23 Read Luke 6:46; 13:25–30. See also 3 Nephi 14:21–27.

7:21–22 The Joseph Smith Translation adds the following between these two verses: "For the day soon cometh, that men shall come before me to judgment, to be judged according to their works."

7:21 Elder Bruce R. McConkie has listed some of the things that might be included in doing the will of the Father:

Salvation does not come to those who merely confess Christ with their lips, or even to those who go about doing good works (as men generally view good works). It is reserved for those who do the very things which constitute the will of the Father, namely: (1) Accept and believe the true gospel, thus gaining faith in Christ, and thus believing in the prophets sent by Christ to reveal his truths, Joseph Smith being the greatest of these in this dispensation; (2) Repent; (3) Be baptized by a legal administrator who has power from God to bind on earth and seal in heaven; (4) Receive the gift of the Holy Ghost, also by the authorized act of a duly appointed priesthood bearer; and (5) Endure in righteousness and devotion to the truth, keeping every standard of personal righteousness that appertains to the gospel, until the end of one's mortal probation. (DNTC 1:254.)

7:22 The "many [who] will say" what they have done for the cause of Jesus Christ includes various types of people:

These fall into two categories: (1) False ministers, those who have professed to teach the gospel, but who have acted without authority from God. Included in this group are all teachers of religion—whether pagan, Jewish, Christian, or of whatever classification—who have not been "called of God, by prophecy, and by the laying on of hands, by those who are in authority, to preach the Gospel and administer in the ordinances thereof." (Fifth Article of Faith.) Some of these are ministers who have so completely sold themselves to Satan that they have worked miracles by his power. (Matt. 24:24; 2 Thess. 2:9; Rev. 13:13–14; 16:13–14; 19:20.)

(2) Those of the elders of Israel who are true ministers and prophets; who have been on missions for the Church, for instance; who have healed the sick and performed great miracles; but who did not magnify their callings all their lives and thereby endure in righteousness to the end. Some miracles, as the casting out of devils, are performed only by the true ministers who actually hold the power and authority of the priesthood. (Matt. 12:24–30.) (DNTC 1:255.)

7:23 "I never knew you" is changed to "Ye never knew me" in the Joseph Smith Translation.

These two expressions convey substantially the same general thought. Jesus is saying: "I never knew you as true disciples, for you never received the fulness of my gospel and came into my Church, and hence, Ye never knew me"; Or, "Ye never knew me so fully as to be sealed up unto eternal life with your callings and elections made sure, and since you did not magnify your callings in the priesthood, you shall be cast out and be made as though I never knew you." (DNTC 1:255.)

"Depart from me, ye that work iniquity" could have been translated more literally, "get away from me, you workers of lawlessness."

7:24–29 Read Luke 6:46–49; 13:25–30. See also 3 Nephi 14:21–27; D&C 11:16–25.

7:28–29

Joseph Smith Translation	King James Version
And it came to pass when Jesus had ended these sayings *with his disciples,* the people were astonished at his doctrine;	And it came to pass, when Jesus had ended these sayings, the people were astonished at his doctrine:
For he taught them as one having authority *from God,* and not as having authority from the scribes.	For he taught them as one having authority, not as the scribes.

8:1–4 (Read Mark 1:40–45; Luke 5:12–16.) The miracle of the cleansing of the leper would have made a great impact on the multitude:

Scarcely is there a more loathsome, defiling, and hopeless disease than leprosy. Even to this day it remains incurable except through divine intercession. Typical language describing the leprosy of Biblical times is cited in *Jesus the Christ,* pp. 199–201. For instance: "Leprosy was nothing short of a living death, a corrupting of all the humors, a poisoning of the very springs, of life; a dissolution, little by little, of the whole body, so that one limb after another actually decayed and fell away. Aaron exactly describes the appearance which the leper presented to the eyes of the beholders, when, pleading for Miriam, he says, 'Let her not be as one dead, of whom the flesh is half consumed when he cometh out of his mother's womb.' (Num. 12:12.) The disease, moreover, was incurable by the art and skill of man; not that the leper might not return to health; for, however rare, such cases are contemplated in the Levitical law." (Trench, *Notes on the Miracles,* pp. 165–68, cited, *Talmage,* pp. 200–201.)

Also: "The symptoms and the effects of this disease are very loathsome. There comes a white swelling or scab, with a change of the color of the hair . . . from its natural hue to yellow; then the appearance of a taint going deeper than the skin, or raw flesh appearing in the swelling. Then it spreads and attacks the cartilaginous portions of the body. The nails loosen and drop off, the gums are absorbed, and the teeth decay and fall out; the breath is a stench, the nose decays; fingers, hands, feet, may be lost, or the eyes eaten out. The human beauty has gone into corruption, and the patient feels that he is being eaten as by a fiend, who consumes him slowly in a long remorseless meal that will not end until he be destroyed. He is shut out from his fellows. As they approach he must cry, 'Unclean! unclean!' that all humanity may be warned from his precincts. He must abandon wife and child. He must go to live with other lepers, in disheartening view of miseries similar to his own. He must dwell in dismantled houses or in the tombs." (Deems, *Light of the Nations,* p. 185, cited, *Talmage,* p. 199.) (DNTC 1:173–74.)

(See section 1, "Leper," "Leprosy.")

8:5–13 (Read Luke 7:1–10.) The Greek word translated "palsy" is translated "paralyzed" in virtually all modern translations. (See section 1, "Palsy.")

8:8–9 Faith, righteousness, and the hope of eternal salvation are not confined to members of the chosen race. Manifesting faith greater than any theretofore exhibited to Jesus by Israel, this Gentile centurion prevailed upon the Master to heal a beloved servant without so much as having our Lord come to the sick bed.

The centurion's reasoning—profound in logic, perfect in showing forth faith—was to this effect: If I, a mere officer in the Roman army, must obey my superiors, and also have power myself to send others forth at my command, then surely the Lord of all needs but speak and his will shall be done.

No better setting could have been arranged to give our Lord opportunity to teach the eternal gospel truth that salvation is for the righteous of all nations, all of whom shall sit down with Abraham and his fellow prophets in the everlasting kingdom of the Father. See Luke 13:22–30. (DNTC 1:258.)

8:10

Joseph Smith Translation	King James Version
And when they that followed him, heard this, they marvelled. And when Jesus heard this, he said unto them that followed, . . .	When Jesus heard it, he marvelled, and said to them that followed, . . .

The significance of the praise of a Gentile by the Savior has been noted by Elder Talmage:

> This remark may have caused some of the listeners to wonder; the Jews were unaccustomed to hear the faith of a Gentile so extolled, for, according to the traditionalism of the day, a Gentile, even though an earnest proselyte to Judaism, was accounted essentially inferior to even the least worthy of the chosen people. Our Lord's comment plainly indicated that Gentiles would be preferred in the kingdom of God if they excelled in worthiness. (JTC, pp. 250–51.)

8:12 The Joseph Smith Translation begins this verse: "But the children of the wicked . . ."

8:13 This verse could have been translated "Then Jesus said to the army officer: 'Go. Just as it has been your faith, so let it come to pass for you.' And the manservant was healed in that hour."

(See BD, "Centurion"; section 1, "Centurion.")

8:14–15 (Read Mark 1:29–31; Luke 4:38–39.) These verses make it clear that Peter was married. This has presented some problems for Catholics, who believe that their popes should be celibate (unmarried) and yet maintain that Peter was the first pope ("papa bishop").

8:16–17 Read Matthew 4:23–25; Mark 1:32–34; Luke 4:40–44; compare 2 Nephi 9:21; Alma 7:11; D&C 18:11; 19:15–20.

8:16 The Joseph Smith Translation makes it clear that the spirits were evil: " . . . and he cast out the *evil* spirits with the word, and healed all that were sick."

8:17 "Himself took our infirmities, and bare our sicknesses" could have been translated "He himself took our sicknesses and carried our diseases."

8:18–22 Read Luke 9:57–62.

8:20 "Holes" and "nests" could have been translated "dens" and "roosts."

8:21 The Greek word translated "suffer" has the basic meaning of "permit."

8:22 "Let the dead bury their dead" has also been translated "Let those who are spiritually dead care for their own dead." (LB.)

Some readers have felt that this injunction was harsh, though such an inference is scarcely justified. While it would be manifestly unfilial for a son to absent himself from his father's funeral under ordinary conditions, nevertheless, if that son had been set apart to service of importance transcending all personal or family obligations, his ministerial duty would of right take precedence. Moreover, the requirement expressed by Jesus was no greater than that made of every priest during his term of active service, nor was it more afflicting than the obligation of the Nazarite vow, under which many voluntarily placed themselves. The duties of ministry in the kingdom pertained to spiritual life; one dedicated thereto might well allow those who were negligent of spiritual things, and figuratively speaking, spiritually dead, to bury their dead. (JTC, p. 306.)

(See section 1, "Dead bury dead.")

8:23–27 Read Mark 4:35–41; Luke 8:22–25.

8:25 "We perish" gives the idea that the action is still going on. A more literal translation would have been "we are about to perish."

8:28–34 (Read Mark 5:1–20; Luke 8:26–39.) The Joseph Smith Translation verifies that only one man was possessed of evil spirits, not two. Elder Bruce R. McConkie mentions several lessons that might be learned from this incident:

This particular instance of ejecting spirit beings from a stolen tenement is set forth in detail by the gospel authors to show:

(1) That evil spirits, actual beings from Lucifer's realm, gain literal entrance into mortal bodies;

(2) That they then have such power over those bodies as to control the physical acts performed, even to the framing of the very words spoken by the mouth of those so possessed;

(3) That persons possessed by evil spirits are subjected to the severest mental and physical sufferings and to the basest sort of degradation—all symbolical of the eternal torment to be imposed upon those who fall under Satan's control in the world to come;

(4) That devils remember Jesus from pre-existence, recognize him as the One who was then foreordained to be the Redeemer, and know that he came into mortality as the Son of God;

(5) That the desire to gain bodies is so great among Lucifer's minions as to cause them, not only to steal the mortal tabernacles of men, but to enter the bodies of animals;

(6) That the devils know their eventual destiny is to be cast out into an eternal hell from whence there is no return;

(7) That rebellious and worldly people are not converted to the truth by observing miracles; and

(8) That those cleansed from evil spirits can then be used on the Lord's errand to testify of his grace and goodness so that receptive persons may be led to believe in him. (DNTC 1:311.)

(See BD, "Gergesenes"; section 1, "Devils possess bodies.")

8:29 Conviction that Jesus is the Christ is not enough; one must also be converted to the gospel and must live its teachings. As indicated here and in other scriptures, the devils "also believe" (see James 2:19; Luke 8:27–28; Mark 5:7) because they remember the Savior from the premortal existence:

Our Lord's true identity is known to unclean spirits. Mortal men may profess not to know of his divinity, but there is no doubt in the minds of the devils in hell. They remember him from their pre-existent association. They know he was foreordained to be the Redeemer, that he was born into the world as the literal offspring of the Father, and that their course in opposing him is one in open rebellion against Deity. (Moses 4:1–4; Abra. 3:26–28; Rev. 12; D&C 29:36–40; 76:25–29.) (DNTC 1:312.)

"What have we to do with thee" is usually translated in most modern versions as "What do you want with us?"

Elder Bruce R. McConkie explains the meaning of the phrase "before the time":

There is a set time appointed when devils shall have no more power over mortal men and when they shall be cast out into that eternal hell prepared for them. This fact is known to them, in consequence of which they labor with inordinate zeal to overthrow the work of God during the "short time" allotted to them. (Rev. 12:12.) (DNTC 1:311–12.)

8:34 "Besought" and "coasts" could have been translated "entreated" and "districts."

9:1–8 Read Mark 2:1–12; Luke 5:17–26. See BD, "Capernaum"; section 1, "Forgiveness."

9:2 The Joseph Smith Translation concludes this verse, " . . . thy sins be forgiven thee: go thy way and sin no more."

Forgiveness of sins comes only by compliance with that law of forgiveness which the Lord has ordained. That the paralytic here healed had compiled with that law is evident; otherwise the Lord Jesus, whose law it is, would not have pronounced the heartening benediction, "Thy sins be forgiven thee." Our Lord's ministry was in conformity, not in opposition, to his own laws.

For nonmembers of the Church, forgiveness is gained through repentance and baptism for the remission of sins under the hands of a legal administrator. Sins committed after baptism are forgiven through repentance and renewing the covenant made in the waters of baptism. Godly sorrow, abandonment of sin, confession, restitution, and renewed obedience are part of the process of cleansing oneself from sin. (*MD*, pp. 271–274.)

The overwhelming probability is that the paralytic here restored to health and vigor was a member of the Church who had already been baptized for the remission of sins. It is not logical to suppose that a man who believed in Jesus as the Christ, who had grown in faith to the point that he had power to rise from his bed of palsy at the Master's word, who had lived in Capernaum where for months Jesus and his disciples had been baptizing converts, it is not reasonable to believe that such a person would have remained outside the sheepfold of the Good Shepherd.

If the man cured of palsy was a member of the Church, then the forgiving of his sins would have been comparable to the gracious cleansing extended to Joseph Smith and many of the early elders in this dispensation, a cleansing and forgiveness bestowed upon them by the Lord after their baptisms. (D&C 29:3; 36:1; 50:36; 60:7; 62:3; 64:3; 108:1; 110:5.) If, however, the subject of Jesus' healing power was not a baptized convert, then the forgiveness of sins here given must be understood to be predicated upon the subsequent keeping of the commandments of Jesus, including the direct and express command to repent and join the Church through the waters of baptism. Such would be the only way whereby the penitent nonmember of the kingdom could retain a remission of his sins.

Where members of the Church are concerned, there is a very close connection between manifestations of healing grace and the forgiveness of sins. When the elders administer to faithful saints, the promise is: "And the prayer of faith shall save the sick, and the Lord shall raise him up; and if he have committed sins, they shall be forgiven him." (Jas. 5:15.) The very fact that a member of the kingdom has matured in the gospel to the point that he has power through faith in Christ to be healed, means that he also has so lived that he is entitled to have his sins remitted. Since all men repeatedly sin they must all gain successive remissions of their sins, otherwise none would eventually stand pure and spotless before the Lord and thus be worthy of a celestial inheritance. (DNTC 1:178–79.)

9:3 See BD, "Blasphemy."

9:5–6 For is it not easier to say, Thy sins be forgiven thee, than to say, Arise and walk?

But I said this that ye may know that the Son of Man hath power on earth to forgive sins. (JST.)

9:7 And he *immediately* arose, and departed to his house. (JST; italics added.)

9:9–13 Read Mark 2:13–17; Luke 5:27–32.

9:9 And as Jesus passed forth from thence, he saw a man named Matthew, sitting at the *place where they received tribute, as was customary in those days,* and he said unto him, Follow me. And he arose and followed him. (JST; italics added.)

Matthew, the new convert, was a publican, one of the most hated groups within the Jewish culture:

Publicans were tax collectors, representatives of an alien power which held the Jews in subjection, and as such they formed a hated, despised, and derided social group. No doubt it was particularly offensive to the Jews for one of their own race, such as Matthew, to accept such employment.

Publicans were customarily classed with and considered to be sinners. The rabbis ranked them as cutthroats and robbers, as social outcasts, as religiously half-excommunicated. They were forbidden to serve as judges or to give evidence, and it was common to say of them: "A religious man who becomes a publican, is to be driven out of the society of religion. It is not lawful to use the riches of such men, of whom it is presumed that all their wealth was gotten by rapine, and that all their business was the business of extortioners, such as publicans and robbers are." (*Dummelow,* p. 657.)

Matthew was one of these social outcasts; his friends and associates obviously belonged to the same group; and when he gave a feast (a sort of a reception) for Jesus, it was publicans and sinners who assembled to meet the Master. (DNTC 1:181–82.)

(See section 1, "Matthew.")

"Receipt of custom" is translated from a Greek term meaning "tax office." Other translations are "tax collection booth," "tax collector's office," and "customs house."

9:12 Citing one of the common aphorisms of the day, [Jesus] said: "They that be whole need not a physician, but they that are sick." To this He added: "I am not come to call the righteous, but sinners to repentance." The hypercritical Pharisees were left to make their own application of the rejoinder, which some may have understood to mean that their self-righteousness was arraigned and their claims to superiority derided. Aside from the veiled sarcasm in the Master's words, they ought to have perceived the wisdom enshrined in His answer and to have profited thereby. Is not the physician's place among the afflicted ones? Would he be justified in keeping aloof from the sick and the suffering? His profession is that of combating disease, preventing when possible, curing when necessary, to the full extent of his ability. If the festive assembly at Matthew's house really did comprise a number of sinners, was not the occasion one of rare opportunity for the ministrations of the Physician of Souls? The righteous need no call to repentance; but are the sinners to be left in sin, because those who profess to be spiritual teachers will not condescend to extend a helping hand? (JTC, pp. 195.)

9:13 The full text of Hosea 6:6, which is alluded to here by the Savior, is: "For I desired mercy, and not sacrifice; and the knowledge of God more than burnt offerings." Jesus emphasized that acquiring such attributes as love and mercy is much more important than keeping ceremonies and sacrifices.

9:14–17 Read Mark 2:18–22; Luke 5:33–39.

9:14 The Joseph Smith Translation adds the clause, "while he was thus teaching."

9:15–16 The Joseph Smith Translation inserts the following material between these two verses:

> Then said the Pharisees unto him, Why will ye not receive us with our baptism, seeing we keep the whole law?
>
> But Jesus said unto them, Ye keep not the law. If ye had kept the law, ye would have received me, for I am he who gave the law.
>
> I receive not you with your baptism, because it profiteth you nothing.
>
> For when that which is new is come, the old is ready to be put away.

The deletion of these verses removes evidence that the Jews were practicing baptism at the time of Jesus. However, the following facts confirm the likelihood of their baptizing at that time:

1. Whenever Jesus did anything not required by Jewish practices, customs, or beliefs, he was criticized by the Pharisees, Sadducees, or scribes.

2. There is not a single word of criticism in the New Testament concerning the baptisms of Jesus.

The Dead Sea Scrolls and other recent manuscript discoveries provide strong evidence that the Jews were baptizing at the time of Jesus. (See section 1, "Baptism: Jesus practiced.")

> Baptism in the power and authority of the Aaronic Priesthood was the accepted order among the Pharisees; from time immemorial they and their forbears had been immersed in water by legal administrators; and not only that, but from their ritualistic standpoint, they had kept the whole law of Moses. Why then should Jesus reject their baptisms and command them to be baptized again in his name by his disciples?
>
> In reply, Jesus taught: "The old order changeth; the law is fulfilled; it is superceded by the gospel. Messiah has come; look to him for salvation. Your baptism, good and legal in former days, now 'profiteth you nothing.'"
>
> An analogous situation arose in the early days of this dispensation. So-called Christian churches on every hand were going through the formality of baptism, and some persons who had previously been baptized desired to unite with the restored kingdom without a new baptism. Thereupon the Lord revealed: "Behold, I say unto you that all old covenants have I caused to be done away in this thing; and this is a new and an everlasting covenant, even that which was from the beginning. Wherefore, although a man should be baptized an hundred times it availeth him nothing, for you cannot enter in at the strait gate by the law of Moses, neither by your dead works. For it is because of your dead works that I have caused this last covenant and this church to be built up unto me, even

as in days of old. Wherefore, enter ye in at the gate, as I have commanded, and seek not to counsel your God." (D&C 22.)

Both Jesus and Joseph Smith were restoring the gospel in their respective days. All organizations except the restored kingdom were false. And reformation is not restoration. Who ever heard of adding live branches to a dead tree? (DNTC 1:185–86.)

9:15 John 3:25–29 makes clear that John the Baptist identified Jesus as the "bridegroom," but referred to himself only as the "friend" of the bridegroom. In this instance, Jesus used John's analogy to teach John's disciples an important principle: after the bridegroom would be crucified, the children of the bridechamber would mourn and fast. (See section 1, "Jesus: Bridegroom, the.")

9:16 This verse could have been translated more literally "Nobody sews a patch of unshrunk cloth upon an old outer garment: for its full strength would pull the outer garment and the tear would become worse." The Revised Standard Version gives this verse as follows: "And no one puts a piece of unshrunk cloth on an old garment, for the patch tears away from the garment, and a worse tear is made."

9:17 "Bottles," which appears four times in this one verse, is a translation of a Greek term meaning "wineskins" (skin bags). Virtually all modern translations use the word *skins or wineskins* for this Greek term.

The bottles here referred to were really bags, made of the skins of animals, and of course they deteriorated with age. Just as old leather splits or tears under even slight strain, so the old bottle-skins would burst from the pressure of fermenting juice, and the good wine would be lost. The gospel taught by Christ was a new revelation, superseding the past, and marking the fulfilment of the law; it was no mere addendum, nor was it a reenactment of past requirements; it embodied a new and an everlasting covenant. Attempts to patch the Judaistic robe of traditionalism with the new fabric of the covenant could result in nothing more sightly than a rending of the fabric. The new wine of the gospel could not be held in the old time-worn containers of Mosaic liberations. Judaism would be belittled and Christianity perverted by any such incongruous association. (JTC, p. 197.)

(See section 1, "Bottles.")

9:18–26 Read Mark 5:21–43; Luke 8:40–56.

9:18 The Greek words translated as "is even now dead" do not necessarily mean that the girl was dead. They have also been translated: "By now my daughter must be dead; but

come and lay your hand upon her and she will come to life."
(KIT.)

> According to Luke (8:42) the daughter of Jairus "lay a dying" when the
> grief-stricken father sought help of the Lord; Mark (5:23) reports the man
> as stating that the girl lay "at the point of death." These two accounts agree;
> but Matthew (9:18) represents the father as saying: "My daughter is even
> now dead." Unbelieving critics have dwelt at length on what they designate
> an inconsistency if not a contradiction in these versions; and yet both
> accounts embodied in the three records are plainly true. The maid was seem-
> ingly breathing her last, she was in the very throes of death, when the father
> hurried away. Before he met Jesus he felt that the end had probably come;
> nevertheless his faith endured. His words attest his trust, that even had his
> daughter actually died since he left her side, the Master could recall her to
> life. He was in a state of frenzied grief, and still his faith held true. (JTC,
> p. 324.)

(See BD, "Laying on of hands.")

9:19 The Joseph Smith Translation adds at the end of
this verse: "and much people thronged him."

9:21–22 The word "whole" used three times in these
verses is a translation from a Greek word meaning "saved"
or "well."

Concerning the possible significance of the woman's trying to touch the hem of Jesus' garment, Elder James E.
Talmage has written:

> The faith of those who believed that if they could but touch the border
> of the Lord's garment they would be healed is in line with that of the woman
> who was healed of her long-standing malady by so touching His robe (see
> Matt. 9:21; Mark 5:27, 28; Luke 8:44). The Jews regarded the border or hem
> of their outer robes as of particular importance, because of the requirement
> made of Israel in earlier days (Numb. 15:38, 39) that the border be fringed
> and supplied with a band of blue, as a reminder to them of their obligations
> as the covenant people. The desire to touch the hem of Christ's robe may
> have been associated with this thought of sanctity attaching to the hem or
> border. (JTC, pp. 346–47.)

It was the implicit faith of this sister that resulted in her
healing, rather than any special significance attached to the
garment of Jesus. This was affirmed by Jesus and is discussed by Elder Bruce R. McConkie:

> It is unwarranted and false to suppose this woman was healed
> through a superstitious belief that some special virtue attached to the
> clothes worn by Jesus. Rather, as the Master affirmed, she had faith to be
> healed; and such faith is based on truth and knowledge, not superstition
> and fantasy. It is a perversion of the truth to suppose that special healing

powers are attached to so called relics or items once owned or possessed by either real or presumed prophets and holy men. In this instance, it was as though the woman had said: 'If I may have any contact at all with this great Healer, even if it be but to touch the hem of his garment, then I shall be healed.' Such a thought shows the greatness and perfection of her faith, not that she was a superstitious and ignorant person attempting to be healed of her plague by believing a false principle. (DNTC 1:318.)

(See section 1, "Woman, touching hem.")

9:23–26 "Minstrels" could have been translated "flute players." The presence of these and the hired mourners indicates the certainty of those present that the maid was indeed dead, as they were all part of the orthodox mourning ritual for the dead.

9:24–25 The command "Give place" (v. 24) could have been translated "Leave the place." This meaning is consistent with verse 25, where the basic meaning of "the people were put forth" is "the crowd had been sent outside."

9:24 From an eternal perspective, the dead maid was indeed sleeping, for her spirit continued to live. But as men view death, she was indeed dead. "And they laughed him to scorn" has also been translated "But they laughed at him" and "They all started making fun of him."

9:25 The Joseph Smith Translation adds the comment "and much people thronged him" at the end of this verse.

9:26 "Hereof" is replaced by "of Jesus" in the Joseph Smith Translation.

9:27–34 (Read Luke 11:14–15.) Although Jesus touched the eyes of the blind men and "their eyes were opening," the physical act of touching was not necessary as part of the healing:

Frequently in opening the eyes of the blind, Jesus, as here, coupled his spoken command with some physical act. On this and other occasions he touched the sightless eyes. (Matt. 20:30–34.) In healing the man in Jerusalem who was blind from birth, he anointed the man's eyes with clay made with spittle and then had the man wash in the pool of Siloam. (John 9:6–7.) The blind man of Bethsaida was healed by application of saliva to his eyes. (Mark 8:22–26.) Similarly, in healing a deaf man with a speech impediment, Jesus both touched the man's tongue and put his own fingers into the man's ears. (Mark 7:32–37.)

None of these unusual and dissimilar acts are essential to the exercise of healing power. Healing miracles are performed by the power of faith and in the authority of the priesthood. By doing these physical acts, however, the Master's apparent purpose was to strengthen the faith of the blind or deaf person, persons who were denied the ability to gain increased assurance and resultant faith by seeing his countenance or hearing his words. (DNTC 1:320.)

9:30 And their eyes were opened; and straitly he charged them, saying, *Keep my commandments, and see ye* tell no man *in this place,* that no man know it. (JST; italics added.)

"Straitly" is usually translated "sternly" in most modern translations.

Healed persons are obligated to repay Deity for his beneficent goodness to them, insofar as they can, by devoted service in his cause. They have no right to turn again to evil practices or former false beliefs. Such would make a mockery of the sacred power exercised in their behalf. Jesus was not going about healing people and leaving them free to continue in the ungodly practices and beliefs of the Jews. After being made whole by the Master Physician, the healed persons were obligated to keep the commandments, to join the Church of Jesus Christ, if they had not already done so, and to endure in righteousness to the end so that an eventual celestial inheritance would be assured. (DNTC 1:321.)

9:35–38 Read Matthew 10:5–15; Mark 6:7–13; Luke 9:1–6.

9:36 The Greek words translated as "they fainted" literally mean "skinned ones." Evidently, the essential meaning is that they were "picked upon," "taken advantage of," or "harassed." Other translations of these words are: "they were harassed and helpless" and "they were worried and helpless."

10:1–4 (Read Mark 3:13–21; Luke 6:13–16. Compare 1 Ne. 13:24–26, 39–41; D&C 95:4.) The calling of twelve special witnesses by Jesus was evidently in accord with previous practice among the Jewish people, for there is no criticism of this action by either the Pharisees, Sadducees, or scribes, all of whom were quick to criticize the Master whenever he deviated from their practices and customs. The Dead Sea Scrolls clearly indicate that a "Council of Twelve" was not something new at the time of Jesus; it was evidently a practice handed down from the time of the establishment of the twelve tribes of Israel.

Concerning the calling of the twelve apostles by Jesus, President Spencer W. Kimball has written:

The first apostles were called by the Lord: "Come follow me," he said, "and I will make you fishers of men." This was more than a *casual* statement. It was a definite call.

"And they straightway left their nets, and followed him." (See Matt.

4:19–20.) "For he taught them as one having authority." (*Ibid.*, 7:29.) "And when he had called unto him his twelve disciples, he gave them power. . . ." (*Ibid.*, 10:1.) This included their commission to preach and perform ordinances. It included the *setting apart*, the *charge*, the *blessing*. The promise given these leaders was most spectacular. Full authority was given them as the Redeemer said: "He that receiveth you receiveth me." (*Ibid.*, 10:40.) "All power is given unto me in heaven and in earth: Go . . . teach all nations . . . to observe all things whatsoever I have commanded you." (*Ibid.*, 28:18–20.) (Conference Report, Oct. 1958, pp. 53–54.)

Elder Bruce R. McConkie connects this calling with having the gift of revelation:

Anyone who knows by personal revelation that Jesus Christ is the Son of God is, in a general sense, an apostle, but those called to serve in the Twelve are in addition ordained to the apostolic office in the higher priesthood. In such a position they have not only apostolic insight and the call to serve as witnesses of the truth, but they are also given the administrative responsibility of regulating all of the Lord's affairs on earth. (MD, p. 44.)

10:2 This is the first use of the word *apostles* in the New Testament and the only time it is used by Matthew.

The word "apostle" is an Anglicized form derived from the Greek *apostolos,* meaning literally "one who is sent," and connoting an envoy or official messenger, who speaks and acts by the authority of one superior to himself In this sense Paul afterward applied the title to Christ as one specially sent and commissioned of the Father. [Heb. 3:1.] (JTC, p. 228.)

10:3 A publican is a tax collector. (See BD, "Alphaeus," "Bartholomew," "Thaddeus," "Thomas.")

10:4 See BD, "Canaanite," "Judas."

10:5–15 Read text and commentaries for Matthew 9:35–38. Read also Mark 6:7–13; Luke 9:1–6.

10:6 In context it is evident the Savior included as "the lost sheep of the house of Israel" the Jews of his day who were not converted. The term should not be restricted to mean the "lost" ten tribes of Israel only. In the preceding verse the Savior had counseled not to go to the Gentiles nor the Samaritans. (See BD, "Samaritans.") In this verse he is essentially saying, "You are to go to the house of Israel who have been lost from the covenant."

[The apostles] were directed to confine their ministrations for the time being "to the lost sheep of the house of Israel," and not to open a propaganda among the Gentiles, nor even in Samaritan cities. This was a temporary restriction, imposed in wisdom and prudence; later, . . . they were directed to preach among all nations, with the world for their field. (JTC, p. 328.)

10:7 "The kingdom of heaven is at hand" could have been translated more literally "the kingdom of heaven has drawn near." Other translations are "the kingdom of heaven is near," "the kingdom of heaven has arrived," and "the kingdom of heaven is upon you."

The Lord has used the same terminology in this dispensation: "Ye shall go forth baptizing with water, saying: Repent ye, repent ye, for the kingdom of heaven is at hand." (D&C 42:7; 33:9–11; 39:19–20.) (See section 1, "Kingdom of heaven or Kingdom of God.")

10:9–10 In keeping with the social customs of the day, Jesus sent his disciples out without purse or scrip. They were to dress modestly, carry no money, food, or extra clothing, have only one staff, and rely on the hospitality of the people for food, clothing, and shelter. Shoes (made in that day of soft leather) were forbidden as too luxurious; sandals (of more rugged construction) were approved. A *purse* was a girdle in which money was carried; *scrip* was a small bag or wallet used to carry provisions. Later Jesus revoked the requirement to rely on the hospitality of the people and commanded instead, "Now he that hath a purse, let him take it, and likewise his scrip." (Luke 22:35–36.)

Acting through his duly appointed representatives on earth, the Lord has now withdrawn this requirement that all modern missionary work should be done by laborers who go forth without purse or scrip. Legal requirements, and different social, economic, and industrial circumstances, have made such a change necessary—a fact which illustrates the need for continuous revelation so that the Lord's affairs on earth always may be conducted as befit the existing circumstances. Instead of relying for food, clothing, and shelter upon those to whom they are sent, missionaries are now expected to support themselves or be supported by their family or friends. There is, of course, no paid missionary force in the Lord's true Church. (DNTC 1:325–26.)

(See section 1, "Purse and scrip"; "Scrip.")

10:10 The Greek word translated "scrip" has also been translated "duffle bag," "knapsack," "bag," "haversack," and "pack." (See BD, "Scrip.")

10:11, 13 The Greek word translated "worthy" has the basic meaning of "deserving."

10:12 The Greek words translated "salute it" have also been translated "give it your blessing," "let your peace come upon it," "give it your greeting," and "Wish the house peace as you enter it."

10:14 "Shake off the dust of your feet" has "for a testimony against them" added to it in the Joseph Smith Translation.

To ceremonially shake the dust from one's feet as a testimony against another was understood by the Jews to symbolize a cessation of fellowship and a renunciation of all responsibility for consequences that might follow. It became an ordinance of accusation and testimony by the Lord's instructions to His apostles as cited in the text. In the current dispensation, the Lord has similarly directed His authorized servants to so testify against those who willfully and maliciously oppose the truth when authoritatively presented (see Doc. and Cov. 24:15; 60:15; 75:20; 84:92; 99:4). The responsibility of testifying before the Lord by this accusing symbol is so great that the means may be employed only under unusual and extreme conditions, as the Spirit of the Lord may direct. (JTC, p. 345.)

For other New Testament references to this procedure, see Mark 10:14; Luke 9:5, and Acts 13:51. For instructions from the Lord concerning this matter in our day, see D&C 24:15; 75:18–22; 84:92–96.

10:15 "Tolerable" has the basic meaning of "endurable." (See BD, "Gomorrah.")

10:16–31 Read Luke 6:40; 12:1–7, 11–12.

10:16 "Be ye therefore wise as serpents, and harmless as doves" could have been translated more literally "therefore prove yourselves cautious as serpents and yet innocent as doves." Other translations are "be wary as serpents, innocent as doves," "be shrewd as snakes and as innocent as doves," and "be as cautious as snakes and as gentle as doves."

The Joseph Smith Translation adds a new element: "be ye therefore wise *servants*. . . ." (Italics added.) (See BD, "Dove.")

10:17 Although some scourging was actually carried out in the synagogues, the term "to be scourged in the synagogues" could also have been used as a figure of speech:

In Jesus' day the synagogues were literally houses of scourging. Three Jewish elders, sitting as a court, heard both secular and religious cases. Condemned persons were ofttimes scourged in the synagogue itself to the singing accompaniment of a Psalm. Thus, to be scourged in the synagogue is a figure of speech meaning to be persecuted by and at the instigation of false ministers of religion. Indeed, hypocritical priests, their satanic craft endangered by the spread of revealed truth, are at the root of nearly all persecution of the saints. Jesus and his apostles were scourged and slain at the instigation of Jewish priests whose corrupt beliefs they so vocally exposed. Sectarian ministers were and are the instigators and promoters of most of the mob violence against the saints in this day. (DNTC 1:330.)

10:18 The testimonies of prophets and apostles, whether oral or written, will be used at the day of judgment against the wicked.

Though men may reject the teachings of the apostles and prophets concerning Jesus Christ and his gospel, yet those very teachings shall rise to condemn the unbelievers in the day of judgment. That is, the words of the apostles and prophets shall stand as a testimony against unbelievers at the judgment bar of Christ. (2 Ne. 33:10–14; Moro. 10:27–29, 34.) For instance, speaking of the divinity of the Book of Mormon, Moroni wrote: "And in the mouth of three witnesses shall these things be established; and the testimony of three, and this work, in the which shall be shown forth the power of God and also his word, of which the Father, and the Son, and the Holy Ghost bear record—*and all this shall stand as a testimony against the world at the last day. . . .* And now, if I have no authority for these things, judge ye; for ye shall know that I have authority when ye shall see me, and we shall stand before God at the last day." (Ether 5:4, 6.) (DNTC 1:330.)

10:19 Whether preaching the gospel while in bonds before kings and rulers, while in the congregations of the wicked, while assembled with the saints of God, or wherever the Lord's true ministers may be, they are subject to this decree: *"Neither take ye thought beforehand what ye shall say; but treasure up in your minds continually the words of life, and it shall be given you in the very hour that portion that shall be meted unto every man."* (D&C 84:85.) One of the chief identifying characteristics of the Lord's true servants is that they speak forth divine truths "as they are moved upon by the Holy Ghost." (D&C 68:2–4.) False ministers, on the other hand, "teach with their learning, and deny the Holy Ghost, which giveth utterance." (2 Ne. 28:4.) (DNTC 1:331–32.)

10:22 The Greek words translated "for my name's sake" have also been translated "for your allegiance to me," "on account of my name," and "because of me."

10:23–28 Elder Bruce R. McConkie has provided the following thoughts on the importance of being faithful in bearing witness of Jesus Christ and the gospel:

Missionaries should expect hatred, persecution, revilings, opposition. If the Lord himself, whose every act manifested the power of God, was hated and reviled, what can his servants of lesser power and ability expect?

Those who preach the gospel are to do so boldly, without timidity or trepidation, not fearing the face of man, but with the courage of their convictions and in the fervor of their testimonies. "Use boldness, but not overbearance," Alma said. (Alma 38:10–12.) Truths learned in the day of preparation and schooling are to be broadcast from the housetops, even though these teachings reveal the wickedness of the secret acts of men. "For verily the voice of the Lord is unto all men, and there is none to escape; and there is no eye that shall not see, neither ear that shall not hear, neither heart that shall not be penetrated. And the rebellious shall be pierced with much sorrow; for their iniquities shall be spoken upon the housetops, and their secret acts shall be revealed." (D&C 1:2–3; 88:108–110.)

True, some of the Lord's agents shall be slain for their testimonies, but even so, why fear the wicked? They can only kill the body, not the soul. "And whose layeth down his life in my cause, for my name's sake, shall find it again, even life eternal. Therefore, be not afraid of your enemies, for I have decreed in my heart, saith the Lord, that I will prove you in all things, whether you will abide in my covenant, even unto death, that you may be found worthy." (D&C 98:13–14.) (DNTC 1:333–34.)

10:23 "Ye shall not have gone over the cities of Israel, till the Son of man be come" has also been translated "before you have gone through all the towns of Israel the Son of Man will have come" and as "you will not finish your work in all the towns of Israel before the Son of Man comes." Many of the translations capitalize the first letter of the word "Man" in this verse.

As revealed in Moses 6:57, the title "Son of Man" is a sacred title referring to the "Only Begotten" of God, one of whose titles is "Man of Holiness."

10:27 The last clause could have been translated "and what you hear whispered, preach from the housetops."

10:28 David O. McKay admonishes us to beware of those who seek to destroy the soul:

There are those . . . who act as though they do not believe in eternity or a resurrection. They cower at the thought of nuclear war, and to save their own bodies they would have peace at any price. Yet the best assurance of peace and life is to be strong morally and militarily. But they want life at the sacrifice of principles. Rather than choose liberty or death, they prefer life with slavery. But they overlook a crucial scripture " . . . fear not them which kill the body but are not able to kill the soul; but rather fear him which is able to destroy both soul and body in hell." (Matt. 10:28.) *The Lord could, I suppose, have avoided the war in heaven over free agency. All he needed to do was to compromise with the devil, but had he done so he would have ceased to be God.*

While it is more difficult to live the truth, such as standing for free agency, some of us may in the not-too-distant future be required to die for the truth. But the best preparation for eternal life is to be prepared at all times to die—fully prepared by a valiant fight for right. (CR. Apr. 1964, p. 20; italics added.)

President Spencer W. Kimball has indicated that false teachers might also be listed among those who seek to destroy the soul:

Apparently there were in the early church those who taught for doctrines the sophistries of men. There are those today who seem to take pride in disagreeing with the orthodox teachings of the Church and who present their own opinions which are at variance with the revealed truth. Some may be partially innocent in the matter; others are feeding their own egotism; and some seem to be deliberate. Men may think as they please, but they have no right to impose upon others their unorthodox views. Such persons should realize that their own souls are in jeopardy. . . .

The great objective of all our work is to build character and increase faith in the lives of those whom we serve. If one cannot accept and teach the program of the Church in an orthodox way without reservations, *he should not teach*. It would be the part of honor to resign his position. Not only would he be dishonest and deceitful, but he is also actually under condemnation, for the Savior said that it were better that a millstone were hanged about his neck and he be cast into the sea than that he should lead astray doctrinally or betray the cause or give offense, destroying the faith of one of "these little ones" who believe in him. And remember that this means not only the small children, it includes even adults who believe and trust in God. (CR, Apr. 1948, pp. 109–10.)

10:29 The Joseph Smith Translation clarifies the end of this verse: "without your Father *knoweth it.*" (Italics added.)

10:30 According to Elder Bruce R. McConkie, the expression "the hairs of your head are numbered" is "not a mere figurative expression, but a literal actual fact. So scientific and accurate is the divine accounting that in the resurrection 'even a hair of the head shall not be lost.'" (DNTC 1:334.)

10:32–33 For additional information about how forgiveness and pardoning grace operate, read Matthew 12:31–37, 43–45; Mark 3:28–30; Luke 6:45; 11:24–26; 12:8–10.

10:33 The Greek word translated "deny" has the basic meaning of "disown." (See section 1, "Deny.")

10:34–42 Read Mark 9:41; Luke 11:16, 29–32; 12:49–53.

10:34–36 When honest truth seekers accept the gospel, they forsake the world and gain its hatred. The sword of persecution, of domestic dissension, and of family bitterness is often unsheathed by their closest relatives. Thousands of devout converts, in this dispensation alone, have been driven from their homes and denied their temporal inheritances, for accepting Joseph Smith and the pure, primitive gospel restored through his instrumentality.

False churches have frequently sought to justify their ungodly courses by reference to our Lord's statement that he came not to bring peace, but a sword. It is, for instance, a wicked heresy to suppose such things as:

(1) That war is approved of God because only through war can lasting peace come;

(2) That Deity, as a means of bringing to pass his purposes by force, approves so-called "holy wars" (as the crusades of the middle ages); and

(3) That the true gospel can be spread by the sword (as Cortez falsely supposed he was doing when he enforced Catholicism upon the natives of Mexico). (DNTC 1:335.)

10:39 "He that findeth his life shall lose it" has been changed to "He who seeketh to save his life shall lose it" in the Joseph Smith Translation. Joseph Fielding Smith explains how we can save our lives by losing them:

To say that his disciples must *hate* all *that* is dear to them is surely a hard saying. But we discover from other interpretations of the doctrine (Matt. 10:37–38) that the meaning is that anyone who *loves* his father, mother, wife, and all that is dear to him, even his own life, *more* than he loves Christ, is not worthy of him and cannot be his disciple. The thought is very clear in this instruction that all who seek eternal life are required to come to Christ willing to give up all that they possess, if necessary. Should they be unwilling to do so, even to the laying down of life in his cause, then they are not worthy of his kingdom. This is reasonable; no unjust demand is made by our Savior, for he came and laid down his life for us that we might have life everlasting. He suffered for us; should we not love him more than we love our own lives? (WP, pp. 272–73.)

10:40–41 This statement is worth emphasizing. "He that receiveth my servants receiveth me." *Who are his servants? They are his representatives in the offices of the Priesthood*—the General, Stake, Priesthood Quorum, and Ward officers. It behooves us to keep this in mind when we are tempted to disregard our presiding authorities, bishops, quorum and stake presidents, etc., when, within the jurisdiction of their callings, they give us counsel and advice. (Marion G. Romney, CR, Oct. 1960, p. 73; italics added.)

10:41 This verse could have been translated more literally "He that receives a prophet because he is a prophet will get a prophet's reward, and he that receives a righteous man because he is a righteous man will get a righteous man's reward." Other translations are:

Anyone who welcomes a prophet because he is a prophet will have a prophet's reward; and anyone who welcomes a holy man because he is a holy man will have a holy man's reward. (JB.)

Whosoever welcomes God's messenger because he is God's messenger will share in his reward; and whoever welcomes a truly good man, because he is that, will share in his reward. (TEV.)

10:42 The Greek words translated "only in the name of a disciple" have also been translated "because he is my disciple" and "because he is my follower."

11:1–19 Read Luke 7:18–35; 16:16.

11:2–6 No one should conclude that John the Baptist was questioning whether or not Jesus Christ was the promised Messiah simply because he sent two of his disciples to Jesus. John sent his disciples to Jesus so they would become converted to Jesus as the Messiah, rather than to reinforce his own testimony concerning Jesus as the Messiah:

> The question often arises why John would send his disciples to ask such a question of Jesus. Many have wondered if it was possible that John himself was not sure of Christ's identity and divine calling. However, we must remember that John's last recorded testimony was to his disciples when they were concerned about the growing popularity of Jesus. John reminded them that he himself was not the Messiah, and that they should leave him and follow Jesus. That was several months prior to the present event under discussion. It appears that one of the difficulties experienced by John was successfully persuading his disciples to forsake him and become the disciples of Jesus Christ, of whom he had borne witness. Now, months after the baptism of Jesus and after John's repeated efforts to persuade them, John found some of his disciples still reluctant to detach themselves from him and to follow their true Master. It seems most consistent to identify John's motive in sending the two disciples to Jesus as one of persuasion for them, rather than of reassurance for himself. *The question they were to put to Jesus was for their edification, not for his own.* John knew, as no one else knew, who Jesus was, and he had known it for a long time. He had had revelation from heaven to this effect: he had seen with his eyes, he had heard with his ears, and he had the testimony of the Holy Ghost. He even had received the ministry of angels while in the prison. The most satisfactory answer seems to be that John sent his disciples to question Jesus about his identity so that they themselves would at long last realize the truth of what John had been testifying for these many months. (Robert J. Matthews, *A Burning Light: The Life and Ministry of John the Baptist,* p. 92.)

11:3–7 The Joseph Smith Translation makes several significant contributions to some of these verses: "Art thou he of whom it is written in the prophets that he should come, or do we look for another?"

11:4 "Go and *tell* John," according to the Joseph Smith Translation. (Italics added.)

11:6–7 The Joseph Smith Translation reads: "And blessed is *John,* and whosoever shall not be offended in me." (V. 6; italics added.) "And they answered him, No" is added at the end of verse 7.

11:9 There are greater callings than those which constitute men prophets of God. "A seer is greater than a prophet," for instance, for "a seer is a revelator and a prophet also; and a gift which is greater can no man have." (Mosiah 8:15–16.) John was a prophet and something more in addition. He was a prophet because he had the testimony of Jesus, meaning that he knew by personal revelation from the Holy Ghost that Jesus was the Christ. (Rev. 19:10.) But in addition to standing as a prophet, he performed the mighty work which enabled the Lord himself to come and restore the fulness of the gospel. (DNTC 1:262.)

(See section 1, "John the Baptist, greatest prophet.")

11:11 How is it that John was considered one of the greatest prophets? His miracles could not have constituted his greatness.

First, He was entrusted with a divine mission of preparing the way before the face of the Lord. Whoever had such a trust committed to him before or since? No man.

Secondly, He was entrusted with the important mission, and it was required at his hands, to baptize the Son of Man. Whoever had the honor of doing that? Whoever had so great a privilege and glory?

Thirdly, John, at that time, was the only legal administrator in the affairs of the kingdom there was then on the earth, and holding the keys of power. The Jews had to obey his instructions or be damned, by their own law; and Christ Himself fulfilled all righteousness in becoming obedient to the law which he had given to Moses on the mount, and thereby magnified it and made it honorable, instead of destroying it. The son of Zacharias wrested the keys, the kingdom, the power, the glory from the Jews, by the holy anointing and decree of heaven, and these three reasons constitute him the greatest prophet born of a woman. (TPJS, pp. 275–76.)

Whom did Jesus have reference to as being the least? Jesus was looked upon as having the least claim in God's kingdom, and [seemingly] was least entitled to their credulity as a prophet; as though He had said—"He that is considered the least among you is greater than John—that is I myself." (TPJS, p. 276.)

11:12 "The violent take it by force" essentially means "those who are pressing forward are seizing control of it, or plundering it."

11:13–15 *But the days will come, when the violent shall have no power;* for all the prophets and the law prophesied *that it should be thus* until John.

Yea, as many as have prophesied have foretold of these days.

And if ye will receive it, verily, he was the Elias, who was for to come and prepare all things. (JST; italics added.)

John was the Elias who was to *prepare* all things. (See section 1, "Elias, John an.")

It is important to know that the designation, Elias, here applied by Jesus to the Baptist, is a title rather than a personal name, and that it has no reference to Elijah, the ancient prophet called the Tishbite. (JTC, p. 257.)

11:16 "But whereunto shall I liken this generation?" has also been translated "But to what shall I compare this generation?" and "Now, to what can I compare the people of this day?"

11:19 See BD, "Son of Man."

11:20–24 (Read Luke 10:12–15.) The cities mentioned in these verses might be identified as follows:

Chorazin: located near the northern shore of the Sea of Galilee, supposedly about two miles from Capernaum.

Bethsaida: the city of Peter, Andrew, and Philip (John 1:44; 12:21), probably located where the Jordan River enters the Sea of Galilee.

Capernaum: a major city on the shore of the Sea of Galilee. It was evidently a center for trade and commerce during the days of Jesus.

Tyre and Sidon: famous Phoenician seaports to the west, on the shore of the Mediterranean Sea.

Sodom: a wicked city of earlier days that had been destroyed because of its wickedness. (Gen. 14:2; 19:24–25.)

(Look up each of these cities in the Bible Dictionary.)

President Spencer W. Kimball described his visit to the sites of the triplet cities of Chorazin, Bethsaida, and Capernaum:

> We ask [our guide] for the cities in which [Jesus] lived and performed so many miracles, for we remember that in this area of but a few miles much of his work was done, much of his ministry was accomplished. We would like to walk through the triplet cities so often visited: Bethsaida, Chorazin, and Capernaum. We see no spires nor towers, nor walls. We ask our guide: "Where is Chorazin?" He shakes his head. There is no Chorazin. We conclude it must have been on those hills above where now are sprouting grain and vegetables and dry weeds.
>
> "Then where is Bethsaida?" we ask. "Where is that noted city where so many sick were healed and the lame were made to walk; where deaf could hear and lepers lost their curse? Where is his favorite place he often lodged, the home of Andrew, Peter, and Philip, his dearest friends? Where is Bethsaida, the house of fishers, the place of miracles, the seat of gospel teachings, where fishermen became apostles?" In these very few miles much of interest happened. "Where is Bethsaida?" Our guide shakes his head again. There is no Bethsaida. "Capernaum, then?" we ask. "Where is that important place, the port where fish were loaded, traded, marketed?" He shakes his head again, then smiles as he thinks it through and changes the accent, and "Oh, you mean CaperNAUM." He shows us the ruins of a large synagogue.
>
> If this was of the Messianic period, it is the sole survivor. A back wall, great stones tumbled in disarray, some olive presses are mute

reminders of long ago. But that can't be Capernaum, his own city, the great Capernaum, the haughty, wicked, rebellious, Capernaum!

Now we realize that we should not have expected to see these cities, for were they not doomed 1,900 years ago? Have we forgotten the prophetic curse of the Master? In their unrepentant attitudes toward the Savior of the world and his exalting message, Christ warned: "Woe unto thee, Chorazin! Woe unto thee, Bethsaida! for if the mighty works, which were done in you, had been in Tyre and Sidon, they would have repented long ago in sackcloth and ashes.

"But I say unto you. It shall be more tolerable for Tyre and Sidon at the day of judgment, than for you." We found that Tyre and Sidon still exist on the Mediterranean coast.

"And thou, Capernaum, which art exalted unto heaven, shalt be brought down to hell: for if the mighty works, which have been done in thee, had been done in Sodom, it would have remained until this day. But I say unto you, That it shall be more tolerable for the land of Sodom in the day of judgment, than for thee." (Matt. 11:21–24.)

And then we remember that only prophets and angels had visited Sodom to call that people to repentance, but for these tri-cities the Creator, the Lord, the Christ had come in person and for nearly three years had dwelt among them and performed the miracles and taught the gospel. They had ignored and rejected him. (We cannot remember ever reading about any Church branches in these cities.) Sodom and Gomorrah went up in smoke "as the smoke of a furnace." If these cities were more rebellious than Tyre and Sidon, more corrupt than Sodom, and more wicked than Gomorrah, we think we understand. (CR, Apr. 1961, pp. 77–78.)

11:20 "Upbraid" means "reproach" or "denounce."

11:21 The Joseph Smith Translation inserts "since" in place of "ago." (See BD, "Bethsaida," "Chorazin," "Sidon.")

11:22 See BD, "Tyre."

11:25–30 Read Luke 10:21–22.

11:25–27 Three great truths are contained in the solemn affirmation of the Lord in these verses:

(1) Spiritual realities, gospel truths, the doctrines and principles of salvation, come only by revelation; they are only known to and understood by the spiritually literate, those who so live as to attune their souls to the spirit of revelation; they are withheld from and remain unknown to the worldly wise and those who trust in the arm of the flesh.

(2) All things which the Father hath are committed unto the Son. See Luke 10:22.

(3) The Father and the Son, perfectly united as one in the eternal Godhead, reveal and manifest each other to those prepared by righteousness to know God. And only those so qualified do or can see or know the Gods of heaven. (DNTC 1:466.)

11:25 The Joseph Smith Translation begins this verse with some additional insights: "And at that time, there came a voice out of heaven, and Jesus answered and said, . . ."

11:27 The final part of this verse is changed in the Joseph Smith Translation to read "and they to whom the Son will reveal himself; they shall see the Father also."

Two principles are here taught: (1) Without revelation from the Father by means of the Holy Ghost no man can know the Son; and (2) No man can know the Father unless the Son reveals him. This latter truth is inherent in the general law of intercession which provides that since the fall of Adam all the dealings of God with man have been through the Son rather than coming directly from the Father. (DNTC 1:467.)

11:28–30 This solemn pronouncement by Jesus should be considered from two aspects: (1) The doctrine, teaching, and message it contains; and (2) The authoritative manner in which the message is presented.

As to the message: It is a call to repentance, to forsake the world, to come unto Christ, to believe his gospel, to conform to his teachings—with the sure promise that in such a course will be found spiritual rest and peace.

As to the mode of expression chosen: It is one that in its nature affirms the divine status and Sonship of Jesus. He did not say, "Come unto Christ, and be perfected in him" (Moro. 10:32), as Moroni did; nor did he follow Isaiah's pattern: "Seek ye the Lord, . . . return unto the Lord, . . . and to our God, for he will abundantly pardon." (Isa. 55:6–7.) His language was not that of a prophet speaking for Deity; rather, as Deity, he was speaking for himself. He did not say, "Come unto God and find salvation," but instead, "Come unto me and find salvation, for I am God, the very Messiah in whom salvation centers." (DNTC 1:469.)

11:30 "Easy" could also have been translated "kindly."
12:1–9 Read Mark 2:23–28; Luke 6:1–5.

12:1 "Corn" and "ears of corn" could have been more literally translated "grainfields" and "heads of grain" or "heads of wheat" or even "barley." (See section 1, "Sabbath.")

12:2 The Joseph Smith Translation replaces "it" with "them." Elder Bruce R. McConkie offers the following explanation of the term "not lawful":

Their act violated, not the Mosiac law forbidding servile work on the Sabbath, but the rabbinical interpretations prevailing in that darkened era. To rub ears of grain together in the hands was considered to be threshing, to blow away the chaff, winnowing. When the Lord revealed the law of Sabbath observance in this dispensation, he expressly authorized such servile work as was required to prepare necessary food. (D&C 59:13.) (DNTC 1:204.)

12:3–6 The incident mentioned here is recorded in 1 Samuel 21:3–6. Of this event, Elder Talmage has written:

Jesus defended the disciples by citing a precedent applicable to the case, and of much greater import. The instance was that of David, who with a small company of men had asked bread of the priest Ahimelech; for they were hungry and in haste. The priest had none but consecrated bread, the loaves of shewbread which were placed in the sanctuary at intervals, and which none but the priests were allowed to eat. In view of the condition of urgent need the priest had given the shewbread to the hungry men. Jesus also reminded the critical Pharisees that the priests in the temple regularly did much work on the Sabbath in the slaughtering of sacrificial victims and in altar service generally, yet were held blameless because of the higher requirements of worship which rendered such labor necessary; and added with solemn emphasis: "But I say unto you, That in this place is one greater than the temple." He cited the word of God spoken through Hosea, "I will have mercy, and not sacrifice," and reproved at once their ignorance and their unrighteous zeal by telling them that had they known what that scripture meant they would not have condemned the guiltless. Be it remembered, "The sabbath was made for man, and not man for the sabbath."

His reproof was followed by the affirmation of His personal supremacy: *"For the Son of man is Lord even of the sabbath day."* What can we gather from the declaration but that He, Jesus, there present in the flesh, was the Being through whom the Sabbath had been ordained, that it was He who had given and written in stone the decalog, including "Remember the sabbath day, to keep it holy," and, "the seventh day is the sabbath of the Lord thy God"? (JTC, pp. 213–14.)

(See section 1, "Sabbath, Jesus Lord of"; BD, "Shewbread.")

12:5 "Profane the sabbath" could have been translated "treat the sabbath as not sacred."

Or have ye not read in the law, how that on the Sabbath *day* the priests of the temple profane the Sabbath, and *ye say they are* blameless? (JST; italics added.)

12:6–8 The one "greater than the temple" is Jesus Christ himself, for he is the "Son of Man" who is "Lord even of the sabbath day." In these verses, Jesus is clearly declaring himself to be the Messiah or Anointed One.

12:9 The Joseph Smith Translation renders the last word plural: "synagogues."

12:10–13 (Read Mark 3:1–6; Luke 6:6–11.) This is only one of several healings performed by Jesus on the Sabbath, indicating that it is indeed "lawful to do well on the sabbath days."

By their religious forms and practices men reveal whether they have pure religion in their souls or not. These Jews bore record of their own apostasy by exhibiting their false and fanatical views about Sabbath observance. To them the Sabbath had become a day of restrictions and petty prohibitions. In large measure their very religion was the rabbinical interpretations surrounding it. The formalities of Sabbath observance had come to outweigh the basic virtues of revealed religion—faith, charity, love, integrity, mercy, healings, and gifts of the spirit.

But it is difficult to see how even these Jews could have construed this healing to be a Sabbath violation. Jesus had performed no physical labor, administered no medicine, and required no exertion on the part of the healed person, except that of stretching forth his hand. That Jesus totally discomfited his detractors but added to their hatred and madness.

From the account we gain a reaffirmation of the eternal truth that *it is lawful to do good on the Sabbath,* that as a day of worship it is one on which men lawfully and properly should glorify God by doing his work. (DNTC 1:206.)

(See section 1, "Healing on Sabbath.")

12:13 "Whole" could also have been translated "sound."

12:14–21 Read Mark 3:6–12.

12:14 "And held a council" has also been translated "called a meeting," "made plans," and "laid a plot."

12:15 But Jesus knew when they took counsel . . . (JST.)

12:18 The Greek word translated "servant" literally means "boy"; thus, it could also mean "son." In context it probably means the Messiah or Son of God.

12:20 "Bruised reed" and "smoking flax" are figurative expressions, evidently used here to indicate the loving, tender, merciful nature of the Lord as explained by Jamieson:

"Whereas one rough touch will break a bruised reed, and quench the flickering, smoking flax, His it should be, with matchless tenderness, love, and skill, to lift up the meek, to strengthen the weak hands and confirm the feeble knees, to comfort all that mourn, to say to them that are of a fearful heart, Be strong, fear not." (Robert Jamieson et al., *Commentary on the Whole Bible,* p. 40.)

12:22–30 (Read Mark 3:22–27; Luke 14:23.) Elder Talmage has written concerning this event:

At this triumph over the powers of evil the people were the more amazed and said: "Is not this the son of David?" in other words, Can this be any other than the Christ we have been so long expecting? The popular judgment so voiced maddened the Pharisees, and they told the almost adoring people: "This fellow doth not cast out devils, but by Beelzebub the prince of devils." Jesus took up the malicious charge and replied thereto, not in anger but in terms of calm reason and sound logic. He laid the foundation of His defense by stating the evident truth that a kingdom divided against itself cannot endure but must surely suffer disruption. If their assumption were in the least degree founded on truth, Satan through Jesus would be opposing Satan. Then, referring to the superstitious practices and exorcisms of the time, by which some such effects as we class today under mind cures were obtained, He asked: "If I by Beelzebub cast out devils, by whom do your children cast them out? therefore they shall by your judges." And to make the demonstration plainer by contrast, He continued: "But if I cast out devils by the Spirit of God, then the kingdom of God is come unto you." By the acceptance of either proposition, and surely one was true, for the fact that Jesus did cast out devils was known throughout the land and was conceded in the very terms of the charge now brought against Him, the accusing Pharisees stood defeated and condemned. (JTC, pp. 267–68.)

12:23 "Is not this the son of David?" could have been translated more literally "May this not perhaps be the Son of David?"

The Joseph Smith Translation drops the word "not": "Is this the Son of David?" (See section 1, "Son of David.")

12:24–26 *Beelzebub* is a name-title of the devil, and is also used to refer to a heathen god. (See 2 Kings 1:3; BD, "Beelzebub.") *Satan* is a formal Hebrew name for the devil.

But when the Pharisees heard *that he had cast out the devil,* they said, This *man* doth not cast out devils, but by Beelzebub the prince of devils. (JST; italics added.)

12:27 "Therefore they shall be your judges" has also been translated "They can settle that question for you," "they themselves will refute you," and "Your own followers prove that you are wrong!"

12:28 But if I cast out devils by the Spirit of God, then the kingdom of God is come unto you. *For they also cast out devils by the Spirit of God, for unto them is given power over devils, that they may cast them out.* (JST; italics added.)

Sectarian commentators, almost universally, have assumed that by exorcism, magic, or incantation of some sort the false religionists of Christ's day were able to cast out devils. With nothing but the King James Version before them it should be evident that this conclusion is absurd and illogical, for the whole tenor of this passage is that Satan cannot cast out Satan. But from the Inspired Version we learn that those others of the Jews who were casting out devils were persons who had gained the Spirit of God, that is they had been baptized, were members of the Church, held the priesthood, and were walking uprightly and faithfully before the Father. False ministers have not, do not, will not, and cannot cast out devils. (DNTC 1:269.)

(See section 1, "Devils possess bodies," "Devils, power to cast out.")

12:30 As he went about in his ministry, Jesus was met with varied reactions. There were some who gladly accepted him, followed him wherever he went and tried to live his teachings. There were some who were indifferent, and then there were others who openly opposed him. So the people of that day had before them a clear working example of the law of opposition in all things. On the one hand was Jesus preaching the way of life; on the other were the Scribes and the Pharisees who fought him at every step. Then there were the indifferent ones. Can we say that they were for the Lord or against him, or were they merely, as we say, indifferent? I call to your mind that the indifferent ones did not keep the commandments, and by their indifference they encouraged others to be indifferent, and as the others became indifferent, they also refused to obey the commandments of the Lord their God.

These indifferent ones built up a barrier against the Christ, and as they spread the example of disobedience they became a hindrance to him in his work, and for that reason the Lord said: "He that is not with me is against me: and he that gathereth not with me scattereth abroad." (Matt. 12:30.) (Mark E. Petersen, CR, Apr. 1945, pp. 41–42.)

12:31–37 Read text and commentaries for Matthew 10:32–33. Read also Mark 3:28–30; Luke 12:8–10.

12:31–32 The Joseph Smith Translation adds the clause "who receive me and repent" to verse 31, so it reads as follows: "Wherefore I say unto you, All manner of sin and blasphemy shall be forgiven unto men *who receive me and repent;* but the blasphemy against the Holy Ghost shall not be forgiven unto men." (Italics added.)

Concerning this "unpardonable sin" mentioned in these verses, Joseph Smith declared:

What must a man do to commit the unpardonable sin? He must receive the Holy Ghost, have the heavens opened unto him, and know God, and then sin against him. After a man has sinned against the Holy Ghost, there is no repentance for him. He has got to say that the sun does not shine while he sees it; he has got to deny Jesus Christ when the heavens have been opened unto him, and to deny the plan of salvation with his eyes open to the truth of it; and from that time he begins to be an enemy. This is the case with many apostates of the Church of Jesus Christ of Latter-day Saints. (TPJS, p. 358.)

(See section 1, "Unpardonable sin," "Blasphemy against the Holy Ghost.")

President Joseph Fielding Smith has indicated why this sin is so serious:

The testimony of the Spirit is so great, and the impressions and revelations of divine truth so forcefully revealed that there comes to the recipient a conviction of the truth that he cannot forget. Therefore, when a person once enlightened by the Spirit so that he receives knowledge that Jesus Christ is the Only Begotten Son of God in the flesh, then turns away and fights the Lord and his work, he does so against the light and testimony he has received by the power of God. Therefore, he has resigned himself to evil knowingly. Therefore Jesus said there is no forgiveness for such a person.

The testimony of the Holy Ghost is the strongest testimony that a man can receive. (AGQ 4:92.)

12:34 Another possible translation for this first sentence is "Offspring of vipers, how can you speak good things, when you are wicked?" (See commentary for Matt. 3:7.)

12:36 "Idle word" could have been translated "unprofitable saying." The Joseph Smith Translation replaces "but" with "and again."

12:38–42 Read Luke 11:16, 29–32.

12:39 Elder Bruce R. McConkie has observed concerning the statement "An evil and adulterous generation seeketh after a sign":

Some sins cannot be separated; they are inseparably welded together. There never was a sign seeker who was not an adulterer, just as there never was an adulterer who was not also a liar. Once Lucifer gets a firm hold over one human weakness, he also applies his power to kindred weaknesses.

"When I was preaching in Philadelphia," the Prophet said, "a Quaker called out for a sign. I told him to be still. After the sermon, he again asked for a sign. I told the congregation the man was an adulterer; that a wicked and adulterous generation seeketh after a sign; and that *the Lord had said to me in a revelation, that any man who wanted a sign was an adulterous person.* 'It is true,' cried one, 'for I caught him in the very act,' which the man afterwards confessed when he was baptized." (*Teachings,* p. 278) (DNTC 1:277–78.)

Elder James E. Talmage indicated that the Savior referred to the sign-seeking Jews as "an evil and adulterous generation" and explains why:

The severity of the accusation as applied by Jesus, however, was intensified by the fact that the older scriptures represented the covenant between Jehovah and Israel as a marriage bond (Isa. 54:5–7; Jer. 3:14; 31:32; Hos. 2:19, 20); even as the later scriptures typify the Church as a bride, and Christ as the husband (2 Cor. 11:2; compare Rev. 21:2). To be spiritually adulterous, as the rabbis construed the utterances of the prophets, was to be false to the covenant by which the Jewish nations claimed distinction, as the worshipers of Jehovah, and to be wholly recreant and reprobate. Convicted on such a charge those sign-seeking Pharisees and scribes understood that Jesus classed them as worse than the idolatrous heathen. The words "adultery" and "idolatry" are of related origin, each connoting the act of unfaithfulness and the turning away after false objects of affection or worship. (JTC, p. 279.)

(See section 1, "Signs.")

12:40 That the Savior would refer to Jonah's being in the belly of a whale for "three days and three nights" as a sign of his own death and resurrection clearly establishes the historicity of the story of Jonah.

The Greek word translated as "whale" means "huge fish."

12:42 The Joseph Smith Translation adds the following between the equivalent of verses 42 and 43: "Then came some of the scribes and said unto him, Master, it is written that, Every sin shall be forgiven; but ye say, Whosoever speaketh against the Holy Ghost shall not be forgiven. And they asked him, saying, How can these things be?"

12:43–45 (Read Luke 11:24–26.) The Joseph Smith Translation adds the words in italics:

And he said unto them, When the unclean spirit is gone out of a man, he walketh through dry places, seeking rest and findeth none; but *when a man speaketh against the Holy Ghost,* then he saith, I will return into my house from whence I came out; and when he is come, he findeth him empty, swept and garnished; *for the good spirit leaveth him unto himself.*

Then goeth *the evil spirit,* and taketh with himself seven other spirits more wicked than himself; and they enter in and dwell there; and the last end of that man is worse than the first. Even so shall it be also unto this wicked generation.

Without these clarifying words from the Joseph Smith Translation, this passage still has significance:

In this weird example is typified the condition of those who have received the truth, and thereby have been freed from the unclean influences of error and sin, so that in mind and spirit and body they are as a house swept and garnished and set in cleanly order, but who afterward renounce the good, open their souls to the demons of falsehood and deceit, and become more corrupt than before. "Even so," declared the Lord, "shall it be also unto this wicked generation." (JTC, p. 271.)

12:44 "Garnished" has also been translated "put in

order," "tidy," and "all fixed up." The basic meaning of the word is that the house was put in order.

12:45 "Last state" could have been translated "final circumstance."

12:46–50 (Read Mark 3:31–35; Luke 8:19–21; 11:27–28.) These verses have proven troublesome to churches and groups that have maintained that Mary was not only a virgin when she gave birth to Jesus but all of her life. This false doctrine of the "perpetual virginity" of Mary is not substantiated from the scriptures:

> Jesus had brothers and sisters who were the offspring of Joseph and Mary. False teachings about Mary and her supposed perpetual virginity have caused the Catholics and others to go to great lengths to make it appear that those specifically named as his brothers and sisters were cousins or kinsmen of some other degree. They hold it to be irreverent to think that Mary, the wife of Joseph, could have lived a normal life with him and been the mother of his children. In reality, of course, motherhood is the crowning glory of womanhood, and God himself has ordained the manner in which children shall be brought into the world.
>
> In Mary's case, the plain meaning of a host of scriptures is that she bore Joseph's children, children who were the half-brothers and half-sisters of the Son of God. Jesus had more than one sister and at least four brothers — James, Joses (Joseph), Simon, and Judas. (Matt. 13:55.) These children lived with Mary and were regarded by the people as members of her family. (John 2:12; 7:3.) They seem to have been jealous of Jesus and may not have believed in his divine Sonship until after the resurrection. (Mark 3:21; 6:3–4; John 7:5.) None of his brothers were included in the original Twelve, but they seem to have been converted after the resurrection by his appearance to James. (1 Cor. 15:7.) Thereafter they associated themselves with the disciples. (Acts 1:14; 1 Cor. 9:5.) One of them, James, was later called to the apostleship. (Gal. 1:19.) (DNTC 1:280–81.)

(See section 1, "Brethren of the Lord," "Virgin.")

12:46–47 "Without" could have been translated more literally "outside."

12:49–50 The Joseph Smith Translation tells of the Savior's delegation of responsibility to the disciples: "Behold my mother and my brethren! And he gave them charge concerning her, saying, I go my way, for my Father hath sent me."

> Jesus here comments that Mary and his brothers are members of his literal earthly family, and he, as the eldest son, gives directions as to what the others should do in caring for their mother. The clear inference is that Joseph was dead and hence the sons of Mary were attending to her needs.

Then he reminds them that though they have the same mother, yet God is his Father and that he must continue about his Father's business. (DNTC 1:281.)

13:1–58 (Read Mark 4:1–34; Luke 8:4–18; HC 2:264–72.) Some have wondered why the Savior did not teach all his doctrines in plainness and simplicity rather than veil some of the meanings through the use of parables and allegories:

> When opposition to his message became bitter and intense, the master Teacher chose to present many of the truths of salvation in parables in order to hide his doctrine from those not prepared to receive it. It was not his purpose to cast pearls before swine. (*Mormon Doctrine,* p. 500.)
>
> Parables seldom clarify a truth; rather, they obscure and hide the doctrine involved so that none but those already enlightened and informed, on the very point presented, are able to grasp the full meaning. Nowhere is this better illustrated than in the parable of the wheat and the tares. When Jesus first gave this parable, even the disciples did not understand it. They asked for the interpretation, and he gave it, partially at least. And then with both the parable and the interpretation before the world, the Lord still had to give a special revelation in latter-days so that the full meaning of this marvelous parable might sink into the hearts of men. (D&C 86.) . . .
>
> But had Jesus taught all of his doctrine in plainness, such would have added to the condemnation of his hearers. (D&C 82:2–4.) His use of parables to hide the full and deep import of portions of his message was an act of mercy on his part. Should any of his hearers later come to a knowledge of the truth, they would then remember his simple stories and gain from them the message he intended. On the other hand, those already spiritually enlightened receive recurring flashes of knowledge by recalling the stories involved. As they continue their temporal pursuits of sowing, planting, harvesting, fishing, and mixing bread, they are reminded continually of eternal truths. (DNTC 1:283–84.)

(See section 1, "Parables.")

13:1–3 Read text and commentaries for Matthew 13:10–17, 34–35. Read also Mark 4:1–2, 10–13, 33–34; Luke 8:4, 9–10.

13:3 "Parables" could also have been translated "illustrations."

13:3–9 (Read text and commentaries for Matthew 13:18–23. Read also Mark 4:3–9, 14–20; Luke 8:5–8, 11–15.) The teachings in these verses have been referred to as "the parable of the sower" (see v. 18); however, Elder Bruce R. McConkie has suggested that it might also be called "the parable of the four kinds of soil":

Jesus in this parable teaches that to reap the harvest of eternal life men must: (1) Plow, harrow, fertilize, and in all respects prepare the soil of their hearts to receive the word of God; and (2) Nurture, cultivate, and care for the sown seed so that the sprouting plant will mature and bring forth an hundred fold.

Our Lord's emphasis is not on the sower or the seed, but on the soil. The seed is the word of God, the gospel, the truths of salvation, and all these are ever the same. But whether the seed sprouts depends upon proper planting in prepared soil; whether it matures depends upon the continued care given the growing plant. Thus, in view of the message taught, this parable aptly may be considered as the *Parable of the Four Kinds of Soil*. (DNTC 1:288.)

The Prophet Joseph Smith has indicated the major purpose of this parable:

This parable was spoken to demonstrate the effects that are produced by the preaching of the word; and we believe that *it has an allusion directly, to the commencement, or the setting up of the Kingdom in that age*. (TPJS, p. 97; italics added.)

Elder James E. Talmage offers this commentary:

Observe the grades of soil, given in the increasing order of their fertility: (1) the compacted highway, the wayside path, on which, save by a combination of fortuitous circumstances practically amounting to a miracle, no seed can possibly strike root or grow; (2) the thin layer of soil covering an impenetrable bed-rock, wherein seed may sprout yet can never mature; (3) the weed-encumbered field, capable of producing a rich crop but for the jungle of thistles and thorns; and (4) the clean rich mold receptive and fertile. Yet even soils classed as good are of varying degrees of productiveness, yielding an increase of thirty, sixty, or even a hundred fold, with many intergradations. (JTC, pp. 284–85.)

(See section 1, "Soils," Sower.")

13:5–6 The first part of verse 5 could also have been translated "Others fell upon the rocky places where they did not have much soil."

The King James Version suggests that the seeds "sprung up *because* they had no deepness of earth," whereas the Joseph Smith Translation clarifies that the young plants "were *scorched* because they had no deepness of earth." (Italics added.)

King James Version	*Joseph Smith Translation*
Some fell upon stony places, where they had not much earth: and forthwith they sprung up, because they had no deepness of earth:	Some fell upon stony places, where they had not much earth; and forthwith they sprung up; and when the sun was up, they were scorched, because they had no deepness of
And when the sun was up, they were scorched: . . .	earth; . . .

13:9 This verse could also have been translated "Let him that has ears listen." Other translations are "The man who has ears to hear should use them" and "Listen, anyone who has ears."

The condemnation which rested upon the multitude that received not His saying, was *because they were not willing to see* with their eyes, and hear with their ears; not because they could not, and were not privileged to see and hear, but *because their hearts were full of iniquity and abominations;* "as your fathers did, so do ye." . . .

We draw the conclusion, then, that the very reason why the multitude, or the world, as they were designated by the Savior, did not receive an explanation upon His parables, was because of unbelief. To you, He says (speaking to His disciples) it is given to know the mysteries of the Kingdom of God. And why? Because of the faith and confidence they had in Him. (TPJS, pp. 96–97; italics added.)

13:10–17 Read text and commentaries for Matthew 13:1–3, 34–35. Read also Mark 4:1–2, 10–13, 33–34; Luke 8:4, 9–10.

13:11 The Savior makes it clear that the "mysteries of the kingdom" can be known only by those who are spiritually enlightened. Elder Bruce R. McConkie has suggested that the mysteries of the kingdom "are doctrines that are beyond the comprehension of the spiritually untutored; when a person is enlightened by the Spirit so as to understand the doctrine, it is no longer a mystery to him." (MD, pp. 473–74.) (See section 1, "Mysteries," "Parables.")

13:12

King James Version	Joseph Smith Translation
. . . but whosoever hath not, from him shall be taken away even that he hath.	But whosoever continueth not to receive, from him shall be taken away even that he hath.

(See Alma 12:9–11; section 1, "Receiveth not, you lose.")

13:13–17 Isaiah not only foresaw the apostate conditions at the time of Jesus, but throughout history. (See Isaiah 6:9–10.)

13:13 This verse could also have been translated "This is why I speak to them by the use of illustrations, because, looking, they look in vain, and hearing, they hear in vain, neither do they get the sense of it." The basic meaning of the Greek term is that the people listen but they do not hear nor understand. (See also commentary for Matt. 13:9.)

The Joseph Smith Translation adds "concerning them" after "Esaias."

13:16 The Joseph Smith Translation adds, "And blessed are you because these things are come unto you, that you might understand them."

13:18–23 Read text and commentaries for Matthew 13:3–9. Read also Mark 4:3–9, 14:20; Luke 8:5–8, 11:15.

13:19 "Catcheth away" also could have been translated "snatches away."

The Prophet Joseph Smith has explained why the "wicked one . . . catcheth away that which was sown in his heart":

> Men who have no principle of righteousness in themselves, and whose hearts are full of iniquity, and have no desire for the principles of truth, do not understand the word of truth when they hear it. The devil taketh away the word of truth out of their hearts, *because there is no desire for righteousness* in them. (TPJS, p. 96.)

(See section 1, "Soils," "Sower.")

13:20 "Anon" means "at once." In the Joseph Smith Translation it reads "readily." (See section 1, "Anon.")

13:21 An important message from this parable is that a person must have "root in himself" or else he will not be able to endure "tribulation or persecution" when it comes. Concerning this principle, President Heber C. Kimball has said:

> Let me say to you, that many of you will see the time when you will have all the trouble, trial and persecution that you can stand, and plenty of opportunities to show that you are true to God and his work. This Church has before it many close places through which it will have to pass before the work of God is crowned with victory. To meet the difficulties that are coming, it will be necessary for you to have a knowledge of the truth of this work for yourselves. The difficulties will be of such a character that the man or woman who does not possess this personal knowledge or witness will fall. If you have not got the testimony, live right and call upon the Lord and cease not till you obtain it. If you do not you will not stand.
>
> Remember these sayings, for many of you will live to see them fulfilled. The time will come when no man nor woman will be able to endure on borrowed light. Each will have to be guided by the light within himself. If you do not have it, how can you stand? (Quoted by Harold B. Lee, Conference Report, Oct. 1965, p. 128; see also Orson F. Whitney, *Life of Heber C. Kimball,* pp. 446, 449–50.)

The essential meaning of "dureth for a while" is that it will last only a little while. (See BD, "By and by.")

13:23 The Joseph Smith Translation adds "and endureth" to "understandeth."

13:24–30 Read commentaries for Matthew 13:36–43. See D&C 86:4–7.

We learn by this parable not only the setting up of the kingdom in the days of the Savior (which is represented by the good seed which produced fruit), but also the corruptions of the Church (which are represented by the tares which were sown by the enemy), which his disciples would fain have plucked up, or cleansed the Church of, if their views had been favored by the Savior. But he, knowing all things, says, Not so. As much as to say, Your views are not correct; the Church is in its infancy, and if you take this rash step, you will destroy the wheat, or the Church, with the tares; therefore it is better to let them grow together until the harvest, or the end of the world, which means the destruction of the wicked, which is not yet fulfilled. . . .

The harvest and the end of the world have an allusion directly to the human family in the last days. . . . As, therefore, the tares are gathered and burned in the fire, so shall it be in the end of the world; that is, *as the servants of God go forth warning the nations, both priests and people, and as they harden their hearts and reject the light of truth*—these first being delivered over to the buffetings of Satan, and the law and the testimony being closed up, as it was in the case of the Jews—*they are left in darkness, and delivered over unto the day of burning.* Thus, being *bound up by their creeds, and their bands being made strong by their priests,* [they] are prepared for the fulfillment of the saying of the Savior—"The Son of Man shall send forth his angels, and they shall gather out of his kingdom all things that offend, and them which do iniquity; And shall cast them into the furnace of fire: there shall be wailing and gnashing of teeth."

We understand that the work of gathering together of the wheat into barns, or garners, is to take place while the tares are being bound over, and [incident to] preparing for the day of burning, [and] that after the day of burnings, the righteous shall shine forth like the sun, in the kingdom of their Father. (TPJS, pp. 97–98, 101; italics added.)

13:25 The writer of the article "Tares" in Smith's Dictionary says: "Critics and expositors are agreed that the Greek plural *zizania,* A. V. 'tares,' of the parable (Matt. 13:25) denotes the weed called 'bearded darnel' (Lolium temulentum), a widely-distributed grass, and the only species of the order that has deleterious properties. The bearded darnel before it comes into ear is very similar in appearance to wheat, and the roots of the two are often intertwined; hence the command that the 'tares' should be left in till the harvest, lest while men plucked up the tares 'they should root up also the wheat with them.' This darnel is easily distinguishable from the wheat and barley when headed out, but when both are less developed, the closet scrutiny will often fail to detect it. Even the farmers, who in this country generally weed their fields, do not attempt to separate the one from the other. . . . The taste is bitter, and, when eaten separately, or even when diffused in ordinary bread, it causes dizziness, and often acts as a violent emetic." The secondary quotation is from

Thompson's *The Land and the Book,* ii. 111, 112. It has been asserted that the darnel is a degenerated kind of wheat; and attempts have been made to give additional significance to our Lord's instructive parable by injecting this thought; there is no scientific warrant for the strained conception, however, and earnest students will not be misled thereby. (JTC, p. 301.)

(See BD, "Tares.")

13:30 In the King James Version the tares are gathered first, whereas the Joseph Smith Translation indicates that first the wheat will be gathered and secured:

King James Version	*Joseph Smith Translation*
Gather ye together first the tares, and bind them in bundles to burn them: but gather the wheat into my barn.	Gather ye together first the wheat into my barn; and the tares are bound in bundles to be burned.

The meaning of "barn" is "storehouse."
13:31–32 Read Mark 4:30–32; Luke 13:18–19.

And again, another parable put He forth unto them, having an allusion to the Kingdom that should be set up, just previous to or at the time of the harvest, which reads as follows—"The Kingdom of Heaven is like a grain of mustard seed. . . ." Now we can discover plainly that this figure is given to represent the Church as it shall come forth in the last days.

Let us take the Book of Mormon, which a man took and hid in his field, securing it by his faith, to spring up in the last days, or in due time; let us behold it coming forth out of the ground, which is indeed accounted the least of all seeds, but behold it branching forth, yea, even towering, with lofty branches, and God-like majesty, until it, like the mustard seed, becomes the greatest of all herbs. And it is truth, and it has sprouted and come forth out of the earth, and righteousness begins to look down from heaven, and God is sending down His powers, gifts and angels, to lodge in the branches thereof. (TPJS, p. 98.)

The Kingdom of Heaven is like a *grain of mustard* seed. The mustard seed is small, but brings forth a large tree, and the fowls lodge in the branches. The fowls are the angels. Thus angels come down, combine together to gather their children, and gather them. We cannot be made perfect without them, nor they without us; when these things are done, the Son of Man will descend, the Ancient of Days sit; we may come to an innumerable company of angels, have communion with and receive instruction from them. (TPJS, p. 159.)

13:31 To make the illustration more effective He specified that the seed spoken of was "the least of all seeds." This superlative expression was made in a relative sense; for there were and are smaller seeds than the mustard, even among garden plants, among which rue and poppy have been named; but each of these plants is very small in maturity, while the well-cultivated mustard plant is one of the greatest among common herbs, and presents a strong contrast of growth from tiny seed to spreading shrub. (JTC, p. 290.)

It should be known that the mustard plant attains in Palestine a larger growth than in more northerly climes. The lesson of the parable is easy to read. The seed is a living entity. When rightly planted it absorbs and assimilates the nutritive matters of soil and atmosphere, grows, and in time is capable of affording lodgment and food to the birds. So the seed of truth is vital, living, and capable of such development as to furnish spiritual food and shelter to all who come seeking. In both conceptions, the plant at maturity produces seed in abundance, and so from a single grain a whole field may be covered. (JTC, p. 291.)

(See BD, "Mustard.")

13:32 "The least of all seeds" means "the tiniest of all seeds." Also, "herbs" could have been translated "vegetables."

13:33 (Read Luke 13:20–21.) The Greek wording indicates that this verse refers to "three *large* measures of meal [flour]."

This brief parable undoubtedly has many applications, one of which pertains to the three witnesses of the Book of Mormon:

It may be understood that the Church of the Latter-day Saints has taken its rise from a little leaven that was put into three witnesses. Behold, how much this is like the parable! It is fast leavening the lump, and will soon leaven the whole. (TPJS, p. 100.)

(See section 1, "Leaven.")

Elder Bruce R. McConkie has made the following comparison between this parable and the parable of the mustard seed:

Whereas the *Parable of the Mustard Seed* points to the growth and stability of the kingdom, as such is seen by viewing the outward organization of the Church, this *Parable of the Leaven* calls attention to the inward spiritual influence which make this growth possible. The leaven or yeast of eternal truth is "kneaded" into the souls of men; then its spreading, penetrating, life-giving effect enlarges the soul and "raises" sinners into saints. (DNTC 1:299.)

Elder James E. Talmage makes a similar comparison:

Points of both similarity and contrast between this parable and the last are easily discerned. In each the inherent vitality and capacity for development, so essentially characteristic of the kingdom of God, are illustrated. The mustard seed, however, typifies the effect of vital growth in gathering the substance of value from without; while the leaven or

yeast disseminates and diffuses outward its influence throughout the mass
of otherwise dense and sodden dough. Each of the processes represents a
means whereby the Spirit of Truth is made effective. Yeast is no less truly a
living organism than a mustard seed. As the microscopic yeast plant develops
and multiplies within the dough, its myriad living cells permeate the lump,
and every bit of the leavened mass is capable of affecting likewise another
batch of properly prepared meal. The process of leavening, or causing dough
"to rise," by the fermentation of the yeast placed in the mass, is a slow one,
and moreover as quiet and seemingly secret as that of the planted seed growing without the sower's further attention or concern. (JTC, pp. 291–92.)

13:34–35 (Read text and commentaries for Matt. 13:1–3,
10–17. Read also Mark 4:1–2, 10–13, 33–34; Luke 8:4,
9–10.) The last clause could have been translated "I will
publish things hidden since the founding." (See section 1,
"Parables.")

13:36–43 Read commentaries for Matthew 13:24–30.

13:39–43 The harvest is the end of the world, *or the destruction of
the wicked.*

The reapers are the angels, *or the messengers sent of heaven.*

As, therefore, the tares are gathered and burned in the fire, so shall it be
in the end of this world, *or the destruction of the wicked.*

For in that day, before the Son of Man *shall come, he* shall send forth
his angels *and messengers of heaven.*

And they shall gather out of his kingdom all things *which* offend, and
them which do iniquity and shall cast them *out among the wicked; and* there
shall be wailing and gnashing of teeth.

For the world shall be burned with fire. (JST; italics added.)

(See section 1, "World, end of.")

13:41 Another translation of this verse is "The Son of
Man will send out his angels, and they will weed out of his
kingdom everything that causes sin and all who do evil."
(NIV.)

13:44–53 Compare Joseph Smith Translation Matthew
13:46, 50. (See commentaries for vv. 44, 49.)

13:44 Again, the kingdom of heaven is like unto a treasure hid in a
field. *And* when a man hath found *a treasure which is hid,* he *secureth it, and
straightway,* for joy thereof, goeth and selleth all that he hath, and buyeth
that field. (JST; italics added.)

In the context of the latter days, the following meanings
might be applied to the major symbols in the parable:

Kingdom of heaven: The Church of Jesus Christ of
Latter-day Saints together with its saving ordinances and
truths.

Treasure: the gospel of Jesus Christ in its fulness.

Field: the world; even today the gospel is largely "hid" in the world because relatively few people have accepted it; the treasures of the gospel are hidden from the spiritually illiterate because "the things of God knoweth no man, but the Spirit of God." (1 Cor. 2:11.)

Selleth all that he hath: the person who has discovered the truths of the gospel should "secure" the treasure (become converted and live the principles) and should be willing to put the gospel and the Church first in his life.

By seeming accident a man sometimes discovers the gospel treasure. Unaware of the saving grace of our Lord, devoid of true religious understanding, overburdened with the cares of the world, hardened by sin, walking in an ungodly and carnal course—he suddenly stumbles onto Christ and the pure Christianity found in his true Church. Immediately all else seems as dross. Temporal wealth becomes but glittering tinsel as compared to the eternal riches of Christ. Then worldly things are forsaken; then no sacrifice is too great for the new convert, as he seeks a valid title to the treasures of the kingdom.

In addition to showing the comparative worth of temporal and eternal treasures, this parable has an allusion to the gathering of Israel in the last days. "The saints work after this pattern," the Prophet said, after quoting the parable. "See the Church of the Latter-day Saints, selling all that they have, and gathering themselves together unto a place that they may purchase for an inheritance, that they may be together and bear each other's afflictions in the day of calamity." (*Teachings,* p. 101.) (DNTC 1:300.)

13:45–46 The "pearl of great price" in this parable is similar to the "treasure" of the preceding parable (see commentary for Matt. 13:44).

This parable is the story of the devout and devoted investigator. The treasure hidden in the field was found by chance; the finder suddenly had his eyes opened to the gospel which had been in plain view all along. But here we see the inquiring mind at work. The truth seeker finds the cherished pearl after long and diligent search; he has compared the conflicting claims of the various sects which are crying, Lo, here is Christ, Lo, there. Perhaps he joins one church and then another, but he is never quite satisfied with what the various branches of Christendom have to offer.

Finally he gives ear to the Elders of Israel, learns of Joseph Smith and the restoration, reads the Book of Mormon, prays to the Father in faith and with real intent to learn whether it is true, seeks to conform his life to the newly learned high gospel standards—and Lo, the Lord reveals to him by the power of the Holy Ghost that the great latter-day kingdom has been set up on earth for the last time. Then he has found the pearl of great price, and as with the man who chanced upon the hidden treasure, he sells all that he has to obtain the blessings of the gospel. (DNTC 1:301.)

Observe that in this parable as in that of the hidden treasure, the price of possession is one's all. No man can become a citizen of the kingdom by partial surrender of his earlier allegiances; he must renounce everything foreign to the kingdom or he can never be numbered therein. If he willingly sacrifices all that he has, he shall find that he has enough. The cost of the hidden treasure, and of the pearl, is not a fixed amount, alike for all; it is all one has. Even the poorest may come into enduring possession; his all is a sufficient purchase price. (JTC, p. 294.)

13:45 "Merchant man" means "traveling merchant."

13:47–50 When those whom God hath chosen to be "fishers of men" (Matt. 4:19; Jer. 16:16) go forth preaching the gospel, they catch men of all sorts in the gospel net. Rich and poor, bond and free, Jew and Gentile, learned and ignorant, sincere and hypocritical, stable and wavering—men of all races, cultures, and backgrounds accept the gospel and seek its blessings. But all who are caught in the gospel net are not saved in the celestial kingdom; church membership alone gives no unconditional assurance of eternal life. (2 Ne. 31:16–21.) Rather, there will be a day of judgment, a day of sorting and dividing, a day when the wicked shall be cast out of the Church, "out into the world to be burned." For those then living the Second Coming will be an initial day of burning, sorting, and judgment (Matt. 25:31–46; D&C 63:54); for all men of all ages the ultimate day of sorting and dividing will occur, after all men have been raised from the dead, at the final great day of judgment. (2 Ne. 9:15–16.)

Joseph Smith, in applying this parable to latter-day conditions, wrote: "Behold the seed of Joseph, spreading forth the gospel net upon the face of the earth, gathering of every kind, that the good may be saved in vessels prepared for that purpose, and the angels will take care of the bad. So shall it be at the end of the world—the angels shall come forth and sever the wicked from among the just, and cast them into the furnace of fire, and there shall be wailing and gnashing of teeth." (*Teachings,* p. 102.) (DNTC 1:302–3.)

13:48 "Bad" could have been translated "unsuitable [rotten ones]."

13:49 So shall it be at the end of the world. *And the world is the children of the wicked* . . . (JST; italics added.)

"Sever" is frequently translated "separate." (See section 1, "World, end of.")

13:52 Joseph Smith has offered the following interpretation of the phrase "things new and old":

For the works of this example, see the Book of Mormon coming forth out of the treasure of the heart. Also the covenants given to the Latter-day Saints, also the translation of the Bible—thus bringing forth out of the heart things new and old, thus answering to three measures of meal undergoing the purifying touch by a revelation of Jesus Christ, and the ministering of angels, who have already commenced this work in the last days, which will answer to the leaven which leavened the whole lump. (TPJS, p. 102.)

(See BD, "Scribe.")

13:54–58 Read Mark 6:1–6.

13:54 "Whence hath this man this wisdom, and these mighty works?" could have been translated "Where did this man get this wisdom and these powerful works?"

By acknowledging that Jesus and his teachings and works were far beyond anything they had witnessed or imagined, the Nazarenes were witnesses against themselves when they failed to accept him as the Messiah and rejected his teachings.

13:55 See BD, "Brethren of the Lord," "Joses," "Simon."

13:57 "Own country" has the basic meaning of "father place." Thus, this famous statement could have been translated "A prophet is not unhonored except in his home territory and in his own house."

14:1–12 (Read Mark 6:14–29; Luke 9:7–9.) Some of the major characters in this story are:

Herod: Herod Antipas, tetrarch of Galilee and Perea; son of Herod the Great.

Herodias: Niece of Herod Antipas; she previously had been the wife of Herod Antipas's half-brother Herod Philip.

Philip: Herod Philip, son of Herod the Great and half-brother of Herod Antipas; previous husband of Herodias.

The Mosaic law clearly taught, "If a man shall take his brother's wife, it is an unclean thing." (Lev. 20:21; see also Lev. 18:16.) The marriage of Herod Antipas and Herodias was in direct violation of this law, and thus was strongly opposed by John the Baptist.

14:1–2 Robert J. Matthews has provided the following insights of Herod the tetrarch, the self-proclaimed king of the Jews:

The record states that the king was "exceeding sorry" to issue an order for the death of John. The sorrow was probably genuine, for he feared that John was a prophet and he knew that John was very popular among the people. That Herod could not forget the deed is reflected in his later mistaking Jesus for John and thinking that John had risen from the dead. His conscience must have bothered and even haunted him to think that John had returned from the dead and that "mighty works" were now manifest in him. John had done no miracles in his ministry (John 10:41), but as a man raised from the dead (as Herod supposed), he would quite possibly have had miraculous powers. This is probably why the emphasis is given to Herod's statement that "therefore mighty works do shew forth themselves in him" (Matthew 14:2). Herod's apprehension in this instance is an illustration of the principle that the "wicked flee when no man pursueth: but the righteous are bold as a lion" (Proverbs 28:1). (*A Burning Light: The Life and Ministry of John the Baptist*, p. 96.)

Elder James E. Talmage has provided background on this particular Herod:

> Herod Antipas, the degenerate son of his infamous sire, Herod the Great, was at this time tetrarch of Galilee and Perea, and by popular usage, though without imperial sanction, was flatteringly called king. He it was who, in fulfilment of an unholy vow inspired by a woman's voluptuous blandishments, had ordered the murder of John the Baptist. He ruled as a Roman vassal, and professed to be orthodox in the observances of Judaism. He had come up to Jerusalem, in state, to keep the feast of the Passover. Herod was pleased to have Jesus sent to him by Pilate; for, not only was the action a gracious one on the part of the procurator, constituting as after events proved a preliminary to reconciliation between the two rulers, but it was a means of gratifying Herod's curiosity to see Jesus, of whom he had heard so much, whose fame had terrified him, and by whom he now hoped to see some interesting miracle wrought. (JTC, p. 635.)

(See section 1, "Herod.")

14:3 "For Herodias' sake, his brother Philip's wife" could have been translated "on account of Herodias, the wife of Philip his brother."

14:5 "And when he would have put him to death" could have more literally been translated "And being willing to kill him." "Counted" has also been translated "believed," "thought," "considered," and "regarded."

14:6 See BD, "Herodias."

14:8 This verse could have been translated "Then she, under her mother's coaching, said: 'Give me here upon a platter the head of John the Baptist.'" "Charger" has been translated "tray," "dish," and "platter."

> So ended the life of the prophet-priest, the direct precursor of the Christ; thus was stilled the mortal voice of him who had cried so mightily in the wilderness: "Prepare ye the way of the Lord." After many centuries his voice has been heard again, as the voice of one redeemed and resurrected; and the touch of his hand has again been felt, in this the dispensation of restoration and fulness. In May, 1829, a resurrected personage appeared to Joseph Smith and Oliver Cowdery, announced himself as John, known of old as the Baptist, laid his hands upon the two young men, and conferred upon them the priesthood of Aaron, which comprises authority to preach and minister the gospel of repentance and of baptism by immersion for the remission of sins. (JTC, p. 260.)

(See section 1, "Charger.")

14:13–21 For other accounts of this miracle, see Mark 6:30–44, Luke 9:10–17, and John 6:1–14.

Why did Jesus feed the five thousand?

(1) For the obvious reason that they were hungry, fainting for want of temporal food, and there was none available for them. They had left their camps and villages to hear his word, and now it was his design to supply their temporal needs also. On this same basis, if the servants of God, while on the Lord's errand, have done all they can to supply their own wants, they are entitled, in faith, to expect their Lord to supply them manna from heaven or whatever else their straightened circumstances may require.

(2) As a testimony and witness that he was the Son of God, the promised Messiah, the Lord Omnipotent, the Creator of all things from the beginning. That the assembled hosts so understood his beneficent act is evidenced by their acclamation, "This is of a truth that prophet that should come into the world." (John 6:14.) Because there is not and cannot be a natural explanation of this act of pure creation, this miracle not only bears record of our Lord's divinity, but is considered by many to be a miracle of transcendent significance. And so, perhaps, it is. But why should it be deemed a thing incredible that he whose words caused worlds to come rolling into existence should speak to the elements and cause loaves and fishes to multiply?

(3) Further, Jesus performed this miracle as a setting for one of his strongest and deepest recorded discourses—the Sermon on the Bread of Life. The providing of temporal food to sustain mortal life was but prelude to teaching that men must eat spiritual bread to gain eternal life. (DNTC 1:343–44.)

(See section 1, "Miracles: Fed 5,000.")

14:13 "Desert place" means "lonely" or "isolated" place.

"He departed thence by ship into a desert place apart" means "he went by boat to a remote area to be by himself."

The Joseph Smith Translation begins this verse: "When Jesus heard that John was beheaded . . ."

14:15 "Victuals" means "things to eat."

14:20 This verse could have been translated "So all ate and were satisfied, and they took up the surplus of fragments, twelve baskets full."

14:22–33 For other accounts of this miracle, see Mark 6:45–52 and John 6:16–21.

Why did Jesus walk on the water and then quell the storm?

(1) To reach the boat, keep a planned rendezvous with the apostles, and save them in their hour of despair and physical exhaustion.

(2) To teach again by concrete means, under circumstances where no natural explanation could spiritualize the miracle away, that faith is a principle of power by which natural forces are controlled. (*Mormon Doctrine*, pp. 242–248.)

(3) To bear testimony that he was indeed the promised Messiah, the Son of God, the Incarnate Word, who though made flesh to fulfil the

Father's purposes, yet had resident in him the powers of divinity. Here in the boat with weak mortals was he "who hath gathered the wind in his fists, who hath bound the waters in a garment" (Prov. 30:4), he who "spreadeth out the heavens, and treadeth upon the waves of the sea." (Job 9:8.) And that the disciples knew him for what he was, and saw in this renewed manifestation of his power the proof of his eternal godhood, is evident from the fact that they then worshiped him and acclaimed, "Of a truth thou art the Son of God." (Matt. 14:33.) (DNTC 1:347.)

Aside from the marvelous circumstances of its literal occurrence, the miracle is rich in symbolism and suggestion. By what law or principle the effect of gravitation was superseded, so that a human body could be supported upon the watery surface, man is unable to affirm. The phenomenon is a concrete demonstration of the great truth that faith is a principle of power, whereby natural forces may be conditioned and controlled. Into every adult human life come experiences like unto the battling of the storm-tossed voyagers with contrary winds and threatening seas; ofttimes the night of struggle and danger is far advanced before succor appears; and then, too frequently the saving aid is mistaken for a greater terror. As came unto Peter and his terrified companions in the midst of the turbulent waters, so comes to all who toil in faith, the voice of the Deliverer—"It is I; be not afraid." (JTC, p. 337.)

14:25 According to the Roman practice of dividing the night into "watches" rather than hours, the "fourth watch" of the night would be from 3 to 6 A.M., having been preceded by the first watch (6 to 9 P.M.), second watch (9 P.M. to midnight), and third watch (midnight to 3 A.M.).

During the greater part of Old Testament time, the people of Israel divided the night into three watches, each of four hours, such a period being that of individual sentinel duty. Before the beginning of the Christian era, however, the Jews adopted the Roman order of four night-watches, each lasting three hours. These were designated numerically, e.g. the fourth watch mentioned in the text (see Matt. 14:25), or as even, midnight, cock-crowing, and morning (see Mark 13:35). The fourth watch was the last of the three-hour periods between sunset and sunrise, or between 6 P.M. and 6 A.M. and therefore extended from 3 to 6 o'clock in the morning. (JTC, p. 346.)

(See BD, "Watches.")

14:27 This verse could have been translated "At once Jesus spoke to them with the words: 'Take courage, it is I; have no fear.'"

14:28–33 This event clearly demonstrates that if we have the faith of Jesus, we can perform some of his works.

The comparison the Lord makes between the wavering soul and the wave of the sea driven with the winds and tossed has touched the lives of many. Most of us have seen the calm seas, and at other times the damage

caused when the winds become intense and the waves rise and become powerful, destructive forces. A parallel can be drawn to the buffetings of Satan.
When we are serene and on the Lord's side, Satan's influence is not felt; but
when we cross over and are deceived by the winds of false doctrine, by the
waves of man-made philosophies and sophistries, we can be drenched, sub-
merged, and even drowned in the depths of disbelief, and the Spirit of the
Lord driven completely from our lives. These deceived and wavering souls
cannot, because of their incontinence, expect to receive anything of the Lord.
(Delbert L. Stapley, CR, Apr. 1970, p. 74.)

From Peter's remarkable experience, we learn that the power by which
Christ was able to walk the waves could be made operative in others, provided only their faith was enduring. It was on Peter's own request that he
was permitted to attempt the feat. Had Jesus forbidden him, the man's faith
might have suffered a check; his attempt, though attended by partial failure,
was a demonstration of the efficacy of faith in the Lord, such as no verbal
teaching could ever have conveyed. (JTC, pp. 336–37.)

14:33 This is the first time in the book of Matthew that
someone has specifically referred to Jesus as the Son of
God, although John's record contains an earlier usage of this
term. (See John 1:49.)

14:34–36 Read Mark 6:53–56; John 6:22–27. See BD,
"Gennesaret(h), land of."

14:35 "Had knowledge of him" means "recognized
him."

14:36 The Savior and his disciples came into the land of Gennesaret,
where "all that were diseased" were brought to the Lord "that they might
only touch the hem of his garment: and as many as touched were made perfectly whole."

Perhaps they had knowledge of the woman who, plagued for twelve
years with an issue of blood, had been healed by touching the hem of his
garment (Mark 5:25–34); perhaps they considered the garment fringe as holy
because of the divine command that garments be bordered in blue so that all
Israel might "look upon it, and remember all the commandments of the Lord,
and do them" (Num. 15:37–41); or perhaps, overpowered in the divine presence, they sought even the slightest and least physical contact with him. But
in any event, so great was their faith that all partook of his infinite goodness
and were healed. (DNTC 1:350–51.)

(See BD, "Hem of garment.")

"Besought" means "entreated" or "requested earnestly."

15:1–20 Read Mark 7:1–23; Luke 6:39.

15:1–2 "They wash not their hands when they eat bread"
has also been translated "They don't wash their hands in the
proper way before they eat!" and "[They] eat their food
without washing their hands properly first." The basic idea is

that the Jewish people required the washing of the hands in a particular ceremonial way, and evidently the disciples were not following these regulations precisely.

The numerous washings required by Jewish custom in the time of Christ were admittedly incident to rabbinism and "the tradition of the elders" and not in compliance with the Mosaic law. Under certain conditions, successive washings were prescribed, in connection with which we find mention of "first," "second" and "other" waters, the "second water" being necessary to wash away the "first water," which had become defiled by contact with the "common" hands; and so further with the later waters. Sometimes the hands had to be dipped or immersed; at other times they were to be cleansed by pouring, it being necessary that the water be allowed to run to the wrist or the elbow according to the degree of supposed defilement; then again, as the disciples of Rabbi Shammai held, only the finger tips, or the fingers up to the knuckles, needed to be wetted under particular circumstances. Rules for the cleansing of vessels and furniture were detailed and exacting; distinct methods applied respectively to vessels of clay, wood, and metal. Fear of unwittingly defiling the hands led to many extreme precautions. It being known that the Roll of the Law, the Roll of the Prophets, and other scriptures, when laid away were sometimes touched, scratched, or even gnawed by mice, there was issued a rabbinical decree, that the Holy Scriptures, or any part thereof comprising as many as eighty-five letters (the shortest section in the law having just that number), defiled the hands by mere contact. Thus the hands had to be ceremonially cleansed after touching a copy of the scriptures, or even a written passage therefrom.

Emancipation from these and "many such like things" must have been relief indeed. (JTC, p. 366; see also Mark 7:1–23.)

15:3–6 "Corban" is used in Mark 7:11 to describe this tradition, which is described by Elder James E. Talmage:

The law of Moses prescribed rules relating to vows (Lev. 27; Numb. 30). "Upon these rules," says the writer in Smith's *Bible Dict.,* "the traditionalists enlarged, and laid down that a man might interdict himself by vow, not only from using for himself, but from giving to another or receiving from him, some particular object whether of food or any other kind whatsoever. The thing thus interdicted was considered as corban. A person might thus exempt himself from any inconvenient obligation under plea of corban. Our Lord denounced practices of this sort (Matt. 15:5; Mark 7:11), as annulling the spirit of the law."

The revised version, Matt. 15:5 is made to read "But ye say, Whosoever shall say to his father or his mother, That wherewith thou mightest have been profited by me is given to God; he shall not honor his father (or, his mother)." The following account of this pernicious custom appears in the *Commentary on The Holy Bible* edited by Dummelow, "'Corban,' meaning originally a sacrifice or a gift to God, was used in New Testament times as a mere word of vowing, without implying that the thing vowed would actually be offered or given to God. Thus a man would say 'Corban to me is wine for such a time,' meaning that he took a vow to abstain from wine. Or a man would say to a friend 'Corban to me for such a time is whatsoever I might be profited by thee,' meaning that for such a time he vowed that he would receive neither hospitality nor any other benefit from his friend. Similarly, if a son said to his father or mother, 'Corban is whatsoever thou mightest have profited by me' he took a vow not to assist his father or mother in any way, however much they might require it. A vow of this kind was held by the scribes to excuse a man from the duty of supporting his parents, and thus by their tradition they made void the word of God." (JTC, pp. 366–67.)

(See section 1, "Corban.")

15:4 The Joseph Smith Translation adds "which Moses shall appoint."

15:5 This verse could have been translated "Whoever says to his father or mother: 'Whatever I have by which you might get benefit from me is a gift dedicated to God.'"

The Joseph Smith Translation adds "it is a gift from me and honour not his father or mother, it is well."

15:6 Jesus' accusation against the scribes and Pharisees that they had "made the commandment of God of none effect" by their traditions is explained by Elder James E. Talmage:

> This accusing affirmation was followed by the citing of an undeniable instance: Moses had voiced the direct commandment of God in saying: "Honour thy father and thy mother," and had proclaimed the ordained penalty in extreme cases of unfilial conduct thus: "Whoso curseth father or mother, let him die; but this law, though given of God direct to Israel, had been so completely superseded that any ungrateful and wicked son could find ready means, which their traditions had made lawful, of escaping all filial obligations, even though his parents were destitute. (JTC, pp. 351–52.)

15:7–9 This quotation from Isaiah (Isa. 29:13) was not only used by the Savior in this instance to refer to the apostates of his day, but at the time of the First Vision to refer to the apostates in this dispensation. (See JS-H 2:19.)

15:9 "Teaching for doctrines the commandments of men" could have been translated "they teach commands of men as doctrines." Today's English Version reads "they teach man-made commandments as though they were God's rules!"

The Joseph Smith Translation phraseology is "teaching the doctrines and the commandments of men."

15:12–14 It is as though Jesus had said: "If these false ministers are offended because I preach the truth, let them take offense. I have more important things to do than worry about their feelings. They are corrupt and apostate, and in due course shall be rooted out by the very truths which I now declare."

There is no profit in debating or quarreling with false ministers who are steeped in tradition, whose deeds are evil, and who are affirmatively trying to prevent the spread of gospel truth. (DNTC 1:368–69.)

15:14 "Ditch" could have been translated "pit."

15:21–28 Read Mark 7:24–30.

15:21 "Coasts" can also mean "border," "area," "region," "district," "vicinity," or "parts."

15:22 Elder James E. Talmage identified the "woman of Canaan":

> Mark tells us she was a Greek, or more literally a Gentile who spoke Greek, and by nationality a Syro-Phoenician; Matthew says she was "a woman of Canaan"; these statements are in harmony, since the Phoenicians were of Canaanite descent. The Gospel-historians make clear the fact that this woman was of pagan or heathen birth; and we know that among the peoples so classed the Canaanites were held in particular disrepute by the Jews. (JTC, p. 354.)

Elder Bruce R. McConkie adds that this Canaanitish woman was "a member of a pagan-heathen nation despised and hated by the Jews. The Phoenicians were of Canaanite descent. Though a Gentile, this Canaanitish woman believed in the ancient prophets, recognizing the Jews as a chosen race, and accepted Jesus as the promised Messiah." (DNTC 1:371.) (See section 1, "Syrophenician.")

15:24 In this instance Jesus clearly included the Jews as part of "the lost sheep of the house of Israel." Later he appeared to other branches of these "lost sheep." (See John 10:16; 3 Ne. 15:11–24; 16:1–3; D&C 10:59.)

15:25 "Worshipped" is translated as "knelt" in most modern translations.

15:26 The Greek word which is translated as "dogs" here is *kunariois* which is the diminutive of the word and is better translated as "little dogs." One commentator notes the significance of this.

The rabbis often spoke of the Gentiles as dogs. . . .

"[Jesus] says not 'dogs,' but 'little dogs,' i.e. household, favourite dogs, and the woman cleverly catches at the expression, arguing that if the Gentiles arc household dogs, then it is only right that they should be fed with the crumbs that fall from their master's table." (Dummelow, *Commentary,* pp. 678–79.) (LTJA, p. 97.)

15:28 "Be it unto thee even as thou wilt" could have been translated "let it happen to you as you wish."

15:29–31 Read Mark 7:31–37.

15:31 "Wondered" has also been translated "marveled," "were amazed," and "were astonished."

15:32–39 (Read Mark 8:1–10.) There are significant differences between the feeding of the four thousand as recorded here and the feeding of the five thousand recorded earlier. (See Matt. 14:15–21.)

This miraculous feeding of the four thousand is not a mere duplication or repetition of the feeding of the five thousand which took place a short time before near Bethsaida. Then our Lord was mingling with his own kindred of Israel; now he is teaching other hosts who in substantial part, being inhabitants of Decapolis, are presumed to be Gentile. Then he was laying the foundation for his incomparable sermon on the Bread of Life; now he is prefiguring the future presentation of the living bread to the Gentile nations. And significantly, this mixed multitude from the east of the Jordan were more receptive, and took a more sane and sound view of the matchless miracle of feeding thousands by use of the creative powers resident in him, than did the members of the chosen seed. (DNTC 1:375.)

16:1–12 Read Mark 8:11–21; Luke 12:54–57.

16:1 Strange bedfellows these—Sadducees and Pharisees, bitter religious enemies of each other, now uniting in an unholy alliance to fight Jesus and his doctrines. But such is ever the case with the various branches of the devil's Church. One thing always unites warring sects of religionists—their common fear and hatred of the pure truths of salvation. Sects of modern Christendom fight each other on nearly all fronts save one-—on that they unite to oppose Joseph Smith and the gospel restored through his instrumentality. (DNTC 1:378.)

16:3 The Joseph Smith Translation ends this verse, "but ye cannot tell the signs of the times."

Those events and wonders—prophetically foretold and then occurring—which identified Jesus as the Messiah. Similarly, "the signs of the times for our age or dispensation are the marvelous events—differing in kind, extent, or magnitude from events of past times—which identify the dispensation of the fulness of times and presage the Second Advent of our Lord." (*Mormon Doctrine*, pp. 645–63.) (DNTC 1:378.)

16:4 Several Greek texts do not include the words "the prophet."

"A wicked and adulterous generation seeketh after a sign" has also been translated "A wicked and unfaithful age insists on a sign."

16:6–12 Literally, leaven is a substance that produces fermentation, as for instance yeast which causes bread to rise. Figuratively, leaven is any element which, by its fermenting, spreading influence, affects groups of people so that they believe and act in particular ways. Thus to beware of the leaven of the Pharisees and Sadducees is to shun their false doctrines, their concept that the Messiah must prove his claim to divinity by signs, for instance, Similarly, today, the warning is to beware of the leaven of any group whose false doctrines and antichrist philosophies work to keep men from accepting the truths of the restored gospel. (DNTC 1:379.)

(See BD, "Leaven.")

16:8 "Which when Jesus perceived" could be interpreted to mean that Jesus learned of this matter later. However, the Greek word suggests that Jesus knew this while the action was taking place; thus, another translation of this construction would be "Knowing this, Jesus said . . ."

And when they reasoned among themselves, Jesus perceived it. (JST.)

16:12 "Doctrine" also means "teaching." (See commentary for Matt. 15:9.)

16:13–20 Read Mark 8:27–30; Luke 9:18–22. See commentary for Matthew 15:21.

Caesarea Philippi, a town located, . . . near Mount Hermon at the source of the Jordan, had been enlarged and beautified by Philip the tetrarch, and by him was named Caesarea in honor of the Roman emperor. It was called Caesarea Philippi to distinguish it from the already existing Caesarea, which was situated on the Mediterranean shore of Samaria, and which in later literature came to be known as Caesarea Palestina. Caesarea Philippi is believed to be identical with the ancient Baal Gad (Josh. 11:17) and Baal Hermon (Judg. 3:30). It was known as a place of idolatrous worship, and while under Greek sovereignty was called Paneas in recognition of the mythological deity Pan. See Josephus, Ant. xviii, 2:1; this designation persists in the present Arabic name of the place, Banias. (JTC, p. 368.)

Not a coastal but an inland area, located some distance north of the Sea of Galilee, near Mount Hermon and the source of the Jordan River. *Coasts* frequently means territory or region according to the usage of the King James translators. Mark designates the area as "the towns of Caesarea Philippi." (Mark 8:27.) (DNTC 1:381.)

(See section 1, "Caesarea Philippi," "Son of God," "Son of Man"; BD, "Hermon.")

16:13 The Savior very seldom referred to himself as the "Son of Man," but the title "Son of God" means the same thing:

The name-titles *Son of God* and *Son of Man* are synonymous; they are as identical in meaning as two phrases containing different words can be. In the pure Adamic language, the name of Elohim, the Father, is *Man of Holiness* (signifying that God is a *Holy Man*), and the name of Christ, the Son, is *Son of Man of Holiness* or *Son of Man*. (DNTC 1:381.)

16:14 Apparently others in addition to Herod believed that John the Baptist might have risen from the dead (see Matt. 14:1–2) as is indicated by the answer that some considered Jesus to be John the Baptist.

Elias (Elijah) and Jeremias (Jeremiah) are also mentioned in this verse. The prophet Malachi had foretold a future role for Elijah (Mal. 4:5–6; D&C 110:13–16), and according to the Jewish legends Jeremiah was also to be associated with an event pertaining to the coming of the Messiah. Dummelow has written:

> [Jeremiah] was said to have hidden the ark when Jerusalem was captured by the Babylonians, and to have called Abraham, Isaac, Jacob, and Moses from their tombs to assist him in mourning for the destruction of the Temple. In the days of the Messiah it was said that he and Elijah would dig up the ark from the cave on Mt. Nebo in which it was concealed, and replace it in the Holy of Holies. (*Dummelow,* p. 680.) (Quoted in DNTC 1:382.)

(See BD, "Elijah.")

16:16 Peter's affirmation that Jesus was "the Christ, the Son of the living God" was a strong and definite declaration, but it was not the first time that man had so declared:

> Peter spoke as the Holy Ghost gave him utterance, bearing his own personal testimony and acting as mouth for his brethren of the Twelve. But great and majestic as Peter's confession was, it brought forth no new or novel doctrine; it was not forthcoming as the climax of a long period of training and schooling which convinced the apostles that their Master was the Messiah, as some have falsely supposed. Rather, it was the spoken averment of what had long been in the hearts of each of them; it was a plain and inspired restatement of the same testimony the true disciples had been bearing from the very time of Jesus' birth.
>
> Shepherds to whom his birth was announced (Luke 2:7–20), Simon and Anna in the temple (Luke 2:25–39), wise men from the east (Matt. 2:1–12), John the Baptist (John 1:1–36; 3:22–36; Matt. 3), Elizabeth (Luke 1:41–45), Andrew (John 1:37–42), Phillip (John 1:43–45), Nathanael (John 1:46–51), the Samaritan woman (John 4:28–29, 39), the apostles as a group (Matt. 14:33), mortal men possessed with devils (Luke 4:33–37), the people generally (Matt. 9:27; 12:23; 15:22)—all these on previous occasions, using language having exactly the same sense and meaning as Peter's, had born testimony of our Lord's divine Sonship. And for that matter, he himself had taken frequent opportunity, both in plain language and by symbols which were clearly understood by his Jewish hearers, to bear testimony of his own divinity. (Luke 2:41–50; 4:16–32; John 2:13–22; 3:13–21; 4:4–45; 5:17–47; Matt. 12:1–8.) (DNTC 1:382.)

Mortal man was not the source of Peter's knowledge that Jesus was "the Christ, the Son of the living God." He had learned it by personal revelation from the Father who had sent the Holy Ghost to Peter to testify of the Son. The Holy Ghost is a Revelator; one of his chief assigned missions is to bear testimony to receptive mortals that Jesus is the Christ. Peter had received such a revelation on previous occasions (John 6:69), and here we find the Holy Ghost speaking to him again, certifying anew of the divinity of his Lord.

It is a false notion to suppose that the apostles and other righteous men did not receive revelation from the Holy Ghost while Christ was with them in the flesh. It is true that (with the apparent exception of John the Baptist) they did not enjoy the gift of the Holy Ghost, meaning the constant companionship of that member of the Godhead, until after the day of Pentecost. But they did receive flashes of revelation from time to time from the Holy Ghost, as Peter did in this instance. Simeon's testimony, for instance, "was revealed unto him by the Holy Ghost." (Luke 2:26); and so it was with the testimonies of all the disciples. John the Baptist, however—because of his position as the Lord's forerunner, and possibly because he did not enjoy the close personal relationship with Jesus that the other disciples had—was "filled with the Holy Ghost from his mother's womb." (D&C 84:27.) Jesus himself, of course, had the Holy Ghost with him at all times and operated in all that he did in conformity with that member of the Godhead. (DNTC 1:384.)

16:17 See BD, "Bar-jona."

16:18 This verse is one of the most widely misunderstood verses in all the scriptures. One difficulty is that people try to interpret it without reference to the preceding verse, which contains some of the words referred to in verse 18.

The Roman Catholic Church and most traditional Christian churches have maintained that the essential meaning of the verse is: "Thou art Peter, and upon this rock [Peter] I will build my church; and the gates of hell shall not prevail against it [the church]."

Thus, Peter is declared to be the first Pope ("Papa Bishop") of the Roman Catholic Church. Further, the Catholics maintain, there could not have been an apostasy, for the Lord himself said the gates of hell shall not prevail against the church.

When the preceding verse is taken into consideration, however, it is evident that *revelation* is the rock referred to by the Lord. Thus, an entirely different meaning is possible: "Thou art Peter, and upon this rock [revelation] I will build my church; and the gates of hell shall not prevail against it [the rock of revelation]."

That this is the intended meaning of the verse is made clear in the Greek manuscripts, which comprise the earliest known manuscripts of the New Testament. In the Greek account, the word for "rock" is neuter in gender rather than masculine as would be required if the rock referred to Peter.

The Lord uses the same term in several latter-day revelations (D&C 11:16, 24; 18:4–5, 17; 33:12–13), and it is abundantly clear that he is speaking of the gospel or of a principle of the gospel (revelation) rather than of the man Peter. When the word *rock* is used to refer to a person, it usually refers to Jesus Christ. (See D&C 50:44.)

The Prophet Joseph Smith explained, "Jesus says, 'Upon this rock I will build my Church and the gates of hell shall not prevail against it.' What rock? Revelation." (HC 5:258.)

It is fruitless for uninspired scriptural exegesists to argue and debate about this passage in an attempt to sustain the particular leanings with which they chance to have encumbered themselves. What does it matter that the name Peter in Greek happens to mean a rock or a stone? What difference does it make that Peter was promised the gift of seership, or anything else for that matter? And what bearing does it have on the problem to show that all of the Twelve held all of the keys of the kingdom? None of these things establish the divinity of any false church.

But suppose it were true that the wholly untenable apostate view were correct, and that the Lord had set up his kingdom with Peter as the rock, still any church claiming to trace its authority back to Peter would be a false church unless it believed in and operated on the principles of modern revelation. Why? Simply because conditions are so different in the world today that a church without daily revelation cannot make the change necessary to meet those new conditions. How would the modern church know what stand to take with reference to the use of tobacco, or coffee, or the atomic bomb, or motion pictures, or television, or a thousand things that were not so much as known to men in Peter's day?

Clearly it is only by revelation that the Lord establishes his work among men. In the final analysis, no person can have conclusive knowledge as to the true meaning of this passage without revelation from that God who is no respecter of persons and who giveth wisdom liberally to all who ask of him in faith. And how can those who deny the very existence of revelation for this age, and who deliberately refrain from seeking such for themselves, how can they, in their uninspired state, ever come to a sure knowledge of this or any other eternal, spiritual truth? (DNTC 1:387.)

Through direct revelation from God Peter knew that Jesus was the Christ; and upon revelation, as a rock of secure foundation, the Church of Christ was to be built. Though torrents should fall, floods roll, winds rage, and all beat together upon that structure, it would not, could not, fall, for it was founded upon a rock; and even the powers of hell would be impotent to prevail against it. By revelation alone could or can the Church of Jesus Christ be builded and maintained; and revelation of necessity implies revelators, through whom the will of God may be made known respecting His Church. (JTC, p. 362.)

That Jesus said "I will build my church" clearly indicates that there could be only one church established by him (he didn't say "my church*es*"). Thus, how could all the various churches today be this one true church?

There is and can be only one true Church, even as there is only one true science of mathematics or chemistry. Two different churches, teaching conflicting doctrines, cannot both be true. If one group of religionists affirms that God is a personal being in whose image man is created, and that he has a body of flesh and bones which is as tangible as man's; and if another assembly of so-called believers professes to think that Deity is a spirit essence which fills the immensity of space, an immaterial nothingness that is everywhere and nowhere in particular present, a spirit that is incorporeal, uncreated, immaterial and unknowable (all of which is found in the false creeds of Christendom)—then both of these concepts cannot be true. Two and two cannot be four and also three.

Christ's Church is the one true Church. In this dispensation it is the Church of Jesus Christ of Latter-day Saints, "the only true and living church upon the face of the whole earth." (D&C 1:30.) And since truth is eternal, this one true Church, founded as it is upon the rock of revelation, has every key, power, priesthood, grace, and authority, that was enjoyed by the saints of God in any past age. Further, such of the doctrines and principles of salvation as have been revealed in this age are identical with and constitute the same concepts and views that were revealed anciently to men of faith and devotion. (DNTC 1:388.)

16:19 Peter, holding the keys of the kingdom, was as much the president of the High Priesthood in his day as Joseph Smith and his successors, to whom also these "keys" were given in our day, are the presidents of the High Priesthood, and the earthly heads of the Church and kingdom of God on the earth. (Harold B. Lee, Conference Report, Oct. 1953, p. 25.)

Keys are the right of the presidency, the directing, controlling, governing power. The keys of the kingdom are the power, right, and authority to preside over the kingdom of God on earth (which is the Church) and to direct all of its affairs. (MD, pp. 377–79.)

These keys include the *sealing power,* that is, the power to bind and seal on earth, in the Lord's name and by his authorization, and to have the act ratified in heaven. Thus if Peter performed a baptism by the authority of the sealing power here promised him, that ordinance would be of full force and validity when the person for whom it was performed went into the eternal worlds, and it would then admit him to the celestial heaven. Again, if Peter used these sealing keys to perform a marriage, then those so united in eternal marriage would continue as husband and wife forever. When they attained their future heaven, they would find themselves bound together in the family unit the same as they were on earth. (MD, pp. 615–16.)

(See section 1, "Keys of kingdom," "Priesthood keys.")

16:20 The Greek word translated "charged" has a stronger meaning, such as "gave rebuke" or "sternly charged." Other translations are "warned," "ordered," and "impressed on."

16:21–23 (Read Mark 8:31–33; Luke 9:21–22.) In these verses the Lord clearly teaches his disciples of his coming atonement and resurrection:

On previous occasions Jesus had spoken of the Bridegroom being taken from the children of the bride chamber (Matt. 9:15); of the Son of Man spending three days in the earth, as Jonah spent a like period in the whale's belly (Matt. 12:40); of raising up the temple of his body after three days (John 2:19); of the Son of Man being lifted up, even as Moses lifted up the serpent in the wilderness (John 3:14); and of the need to eat his flesh as the living bread in order to inherit eternal life (John 6:50–57)—all referring to his atoning sacrifice, death, burial, and resurrection. But now, openly and in plainness, in language devoid of symbolism or figurative expression, he told his apostles of these things. (DNTC 1:391.)

(See section 1, "Resurrection: Taught early.")

16:22 A more literal translation is "At this Peter took him aside and commenced rebuking him, saying: 'Be kind to yourself, Lord; you will not have this [destiny] at all.'"

16:23 In addressing Peter as "Satan," Jesus was obviously using a forceful figure of speech, and not a literal designation; for Satan is a distinct personage, Lucifer, that fallen, unembodied son of the morning . . . ; and certainly Peter was not he. In his remonstrance or "rebuke" addressed to Jesus, Peter was really counseling what Satan had before attempted to induce Christ to do, or tempting, as Satan himself had tempted. The command, "Get thee behind me, Satan," as directed to Peter, is rendered in English by some authorities "Get thee behind me, tempter." The essential meaning attached to both Hebrew and Greek originals for our word "Satan" is that of an adversary, or "one who places himself in another's way and thus opposes him." (Zenos.) The expression "Thou art an offense unto me" is admittedly a less literal translation than "Thou art a stumbling-block unto me." The man whom Jesus had addressed as Peter—"the rock," was now likened to a stone in the path, over which the unwary might stumble. (JTC, pp. 368–69.)

16:24–26 Read Mark 8:34–37; Luke 9:23–25.

16:24 The term *take up your cross* is found in both ancient and modern scripture, including at least three references in the Doctrine and Covenants (23:6; 56:2; 112:12). In Matthew 16:24 the Savior says, "If any man will come after me, let him deny himself, and take up his cross, and follow me." The Inspired Version of the Bible provides the meaning of this term as given by Jesus Christ himself: "And now for a man to take up his cross, is to deny himself all ungodliness, and every worldly lust, and keep my commandments." (Matt. 16:25–26.)

The meaning of this term is also clarified in other scriptures. For example, the Lord in 3 Nephi 12:30 states: "It is better that ye should deny yourself of these things, wherein ye will take up your cross, than that ye should be cast into hell."

Each person has areas of weakness where he or she must strive diligently to overcome that weakness and turn it into a strength. The term "take up your cross" has to do with this strengthening process by denying yourself "all ungodliness" and by keeping the commandments of God. (CSDC, pp. 56–57.)

And now for a man to take up his cross, *is to* deny himself *all ungodliness, and every worldly lust, and keep my commandments.* (JST; italics added.)

16:25–26 *Break not my commandments for to save your lives;* for whosoever will save his life *in this world,* shall lose it *in the world to come.*

And whosoever will lose his life *in this world,* for my sake, shall find it *in the world to come.*

Therefore, forsake the world, and save your souls; for what is a man profited, if he shall gain the whole world, and lose his own soul? Or what shall a man give in exchange for his soul? (JST; italics added.)

What value is to be placed on a human soul? How can we determine its worth? Two things will give some indication of the priceless value of the souls of men: (1) What these souls have cost up to this point—the labor, material and struggle that has gone into their creation and development; and (2) The effective use to which they can be put—the benefits that result when souls fill the full measure of their creation and take their rightful place in the eternal scheme of things.

To use these standards of judgment it is necessary to view human souls in their relationship to the eternal plan of creation, progression, and salvation. Souls had their beginning, as conscious identities, when they were born as the spirit offspring of Deity. There then followed an infinitely long period of training, schooling, and preparation, so that these spirits might go on and attain their exaltation. "God himself," as the Prophet Joseph Smith expressed it, "finding he was in the midst of spirits and glory, because he was more intelligent, saw proper to institute laws whereby the rest could have a privilege to advance like himself." (*Teachings,* p. 354.)

As part of this schooling process this earth was created; spirits were given temporal bodies; gospel dispensations were vouchsafed to men; prophets were sent forth to labor and preach; oftentimes they were persecuted, tormented, and slain; and even the Son of God taught and served among mortals, climaxing his ministry by suffering beyond mortal endurance in working out the infinite and eternal atonement. All this is included in the price already paid toward the purchase of human souls.

Such of these souls as keep all the commandments shall attain eternal life. They shall go on to exaltation and glory in all things, becoming like the Father, begetting spirit offspring, creating worlds without number, and forever and endlessly rolling forth the eternal purposes of the Infinite God. (DNTC 1:393.)

16:27–28 Read Mark 8:38–9:1; Luke 9:26–27.

16:27 "Shall come" could have been translated "is destined to come."

16:28 The Lord's promise "There be some standing here, which shall not taste of death, till they see the Son of man coming in his kingdom" was at least partially fulfilled in the subsequent translation of John the Apostle. (Read John 21:20–24; D&C 7:3–4. See commentary for John 21:20–24.)

17:1–9 (Read Mark 9:2–10; Luke 9:28–36.) The Lord counseled his three special apostles that they were to tell no man of this experience "until the Son of Man be risen again from the dead." (Verse 9.) And even the account in our present New Testament is very sketchy.

President Joseph Fielding Smith has indicated that Peter, James, and John were given the keys of presidency, which entitled them to preside over the Church after the ascension of the resurrected Jesus into heaven:

In the days of Christ's ministry he called the first apostles who were ever ordained to that office so far as we have any knowledge. He conferred upon them all the power and authority of the priesthood. He also appointed three of these Twelve to take the keys of presidency. *Peter, James, and John acted as the First Presidency of the Church in their day.* (DS 3:152.)

(See BD, "Elias," "Transfiguration, Mount of.")

Elder Bruce R. McConkie has reviewed some of the salient features of the Transfiguration:

Until men attain a higher status of spiritual understanding than they now enjoy, they can learn only in part what took place upon the Mount of Transfiguration. From the New Testament accounts and from the added light revealed through Joseph Smith it appears evident that:

(1) Jesus singled out Peter, James, and John from the rest of the Twelve; took them upon an unnamed mountain; there he was transfigured before them, and they beheld his glory. Testifying later, John said, "We beheld his glory, the glory as of the only begotten of the Father" (John 1:14); and Peter, speaking of the same event, said they "were eyewitnesses of his majesty." (2 Pet. 1:16.)

(2) Peter, James, and John, were themselves "transfigured before him" (*Teachings*, p. 158), even as Moses, the Three Nephites, Joseph Smith, and many prophets of all ages have been transfigured, thus enabling them to entertain angels, see visions and comprehend the things of God. (*Mormon Doctrine*, pp. 725–726.)

(3) Moses and Elijah—two ancient prophets who were translated and taken to heaven without tasting death, so they could return with tangible bodies on this very occasion, an occasion preceding the day of resurrection—appeared on the mountain; and they and Jesus gave the keys of the kingdom to Peter, James, and John. (*Teachings*, p. 158.)

(4) John the Baptist, previously beheaded by Herod, apparently was also present. It may well be that other unnamed prophets, either coming as translated beings or as spirits from paradise, were also present.

(5) Peter, James, and John saw in vision the transfiguration of the earth, that is, they saw it renewed and returned to its paradisiacal state—an event that is to take place at the Second Coming when the millennial era is ushered in. (D&C 63:20–21; *Mormon Doctrine*, pp. 718–719.)

(6) It appears that Peter, James, and John received their own endowments while on the mountain. (*Doctrines of Salvation*, vol. 2, p. 165.) Peter says that while there, they "received from God the Father honour and glory," seemingly bearing out this conclusion. It also appears that it was while on the mount that they received the more sure word of prophecy, it then being revealed to them that they were sealed up unto eternal life. (2 Pet. 1:16–19; D&C 131:5.)

(7) Apparently Jesus himself was strengthened and encouraged by Moses and Elijah so as to be prepared for the infinite sufferings and agony ahead of him in connection with working out the infinite and eternal atonement. (*Jesus the Christ*, p. 373.) Similar comfort had been given him by angelic visitants following his forty-day fast and its attendant temptations (Matt. 4:11), and an angel from heaven was yet to strengthen him when he would sweat great drops of blood in the Garden of Gethsemane. (Luke 22:42–44.)

(8) Certainly the three chosen apostles were taught in plainness "of his death and also his resurrection" (I. V. Luke 9:31), teachings which would be of inestimable value to them in the trying days ahead.

(9) It should also have been apparent to them that the old dispensations of the past had faded away, that the law (of which Moses was the symbol) and the prophets (of whom Elijah was the typifying representative) were subject to Him whom they were now commanded to hear.

(10) Apparently God the Father, overshadowed and hidden by a cloud, was present on the mountain, although our Lord's three associates, as far as the record stipulates, heard only his voice and did not see his form. (DNTC 1:399–401.)

17:1 The Greek word translated "apart" could refer to the mountain or to the Savior and His apostles. It is frequently translated "by themselves," referring to the persons involved rather than the place.

Concerning the time and place of the Transfiguration, Elder Bruce R. McConkie has written:

Mark agrees that it was six days; Luke says it was eight. In other words, one week elapsed between Jesus' promise to Peter, to give him the keys of the kingdom, and that glorious day of transfiguration when the keys were actually conferred upon Peter and his two associates. Two of the synoptists are excluding the two terminal days from their count, the other is including them. (DNTC 1:401.)

Long held by tradition to have been Mt. Tabor, a less than eighteen hundred foot plateau in southern Galilee, which in that day was capped by a fortress and upon which, in the sixth century, three churches were erected, presumably to commemorate Peter's desire to erect three tabernacles. Later a monastery was built on Mt. Tabor. But more probably the site of the transfiguration was Mt. Hermon, a nine thousand foot eminence north of Caesarea Philippi, where Jesus had been the week before. Mt. Hermon is north of Galilee, and the record shows that after Jesus departed from the mount he then went through Galilee. (Mark 9:30.)(DNTC 1:402.)

17:3 Moses, the great prophet-statesman whose name symbolized the law, and Elijah the Tishbite, a prophet of so great fame that his name had come to typify and symbolize the collective wisdom and insight of all the prophets. Moses held the keys of the gathering of Israel and the leading of the ten tribes from the land of the north; Elijah, the keys of the sealing power. These are the keys which they conferred upon Peter, James, and John upon the mount, and which they also conferred upon Joseph Smith and Oliver Cowdery in the Kirtland Temple nearly two thousand years later. (D&C 110:11–16.) Both of them were translated beings and had bodies of flesh and bones, a status they apparently enjoyed so that they could confer keys upon mortal men. We have a detailed scriptural account of Elijah's translation (2 Kings 2) and a number of scriptural references concerning Moses which can only be interpreted to mean that he too was taken to heaven without tasting death. (Alma 45:18–19; *Mormon Doctrine,* pp. 726–730; *Doctrines of Salvation,* vol. 2, pp. 107–111.) When these two holy men appeared in this dispensation to restore again their keys and powers, they came as resurrected personages. (D&C 133:55.) (DNTC 1:402–3.)

(See BD, "Moses.")
17:4 "If thou wilt" means "if you wish."

These words appear to have been spoken in response to some unrecorded statements of Moses and Elijah. Since the record is so fragmentary it is not possible to tell their exact meaning. In this connection, it should be noted that at the annual feast of Tabernacles, it is customary for worshipers to erect small booths in which they retired for private devotions. (DNTC 1:403.)

17:5 Aside from the proclamation of the Son's divine nature, the Father's words were otherwise decisive and portentous. Moses, the promulgator of the law, and Elijah the representative of the prophets and especially distinguished among them as the one who had not died, had been seen ministering unto Jesus and subservient to Him. The fulfilment of the law and the superseding of the prophets by the Messiah was attested in the command—Hear ye *Him*. A new dispensation had been established, that of the gospel, for which the law and the prophets had been but preparatory. The apostles were to be guided neither by Moses nor Elijah, but by *Him,* their Lord, Jesus the Christ. (JTC, pp. 373–74.)

17:6 "Sore afraid" is translated in the Revised Standard Version as "filled with awe." The Joseph Smith Translation inserts "the voice" to clarify the meaning of "it."

17:9 "Charged" could also have been translated "commanded" or "enjoined." (See commentary for Matt. 16:20.)

Elder Bruce R. McConkie has commented on the "bright cloud" that overshadowed them:

> Not a watery cloud, but what the Jews called the *Shekinah or Dwelling* cloud, the cloud which manifested the presence and glory of God. This cloud had rested upon the tabernacle in the wilderness (Num. 9:15–22), had covered Jehovah when he visited his people (Ex. 33:9–11; Num. 11:25), and is the one which enveloped Jesus, after his resurrection, when he ascended to his Father. (Acts 1:9.) (DNTC 1:403.)

17:10–13 Read Mark 9:11–13.

> And Jesus answered and said unto them, Elias truly shall first come, and restore all things, *as the prophets have written.*
> *And again* I say unto you that Elias *has* come already, *concerning whom it is written, Behold, I will send my messenger, and he shall prepare the way before me;* and they knew him not, *and* have done unto him, whatsoever they listed.
> Likewise shall the Son of Man suffer of them.
> *But I say unto you, Who is Elias? Behold, this is Elias, whom I sent to prepare the way before me.*
> Then the disciples understood that he spake unto them of John the Baptist, *and also of another who should come and restore all things, as it is written by the prophets.* (JST; italics added.)

(See section 1, "John the Baptist: On Mount of Transfiguration.")

The three selected apostles, "the Man of Rock and the Sons of Thunder" had seen the Lord in glory; and they marveled that such a thing could be at that time, since as they had interpreted the scriptures, it had been predicted that Elijah should precede the Messiah's triumphal advent. As they wended their way down the mountain-side, they asked the Master: "Why then say the scribes that Elias must first come?" Jesus confirmed the prophecy that Elias should first come, that is, before the Lord's advent in glory, which event they had in mind: "But," He added, "I say unto you, That Elias is come already, and they knew him not, but have done unto him whatsoever they listed. Likewise shall also the Son of man suffer of them. Then the disciples understood that he spake unto them of John the Baptist." That John the Baptist would officiate "in the spirit and power of

Elias," as the forerunner of the Christ, had been announced by the angel Gabriel to Zacharias, before the Baptist's birth; and that John was *that* particular Elias had been shown by Jesus in His memorable tribute to the Baptist's fidelity and greatness. That His words would not be generally accepted with understanding is evidenced by the context; Jesus, on that occasion, had said: "And if ye will receive it, this is Elias, which was for to come." [Matt. 11:14.]

It is not possible that Jesus could have meant that John was the same individual as Elijah; nor could the people have so understood His words, since the false doctrine of transmigration or reincarnation of spirits was repudiated by the Jews. The seeming difficulty is removed when we consider that, as the name appears in the New Testament, "Elias" is used for "Elijah," with no attempt at distinction between Elijah the Tishbite, and any other person known as Elias. Gabriel's declaration that the then unborn John should manifest "the spirit and power of Elias" indicates that "Elias" is a title of office; every restorer, forerunner, or one sent of God to prepare the way for greater developments in the gospel plan, is an Elias. The appellative "Elias" is in fact both a personal name and a title. (JTC, pp. 374–75.)

17:14–21 (Read Mark 9:14–29; Luke 9:37–43.) In these verses the Lord indicates that different men have varying degrees of faith. The Prophet Joseph Smith taught this same principle: "If a man has not faith enough to do one thing, he may have faith to do another; if he cannot remove a mountain, he may heal the sick." (HC 5:355.)

17:15 The Greek word translated "lunatick [moonstruck]" is sometimes translated "epileptic."

17:17 The basic meaning of the Greek word translated "perverse" is "twisted."

17:20 The Greek word translated "unbelief" means "little faith."

"Remove hence to yonder place" could also have been translated "Transfer from here to there."

The example used here by the Lord was not only a promise capable of future fulfilment but was reflective of at least two earlier prophets who had literally moved mountains: Enoch (Moses 7:13) and the Brother of Jared (Ether 12:30).

17:21 This verse is missing in many of the ancient manuscripts. Today's English Version translates the verse, "But only prayer and fasting can drive this kind out; nothing else can."

The Savior's statement concerning the evil spirit that the apostles were unable to subdue—"Howbeit this kind goeth not out but by prayer and fasting"—indicates gradation in the malignity and evil power of demons, and gradation also in the results of varying degrees of faith. The apostles who failed on the occasion referred to had been able to cast out demons at other times. Fasting, when practised in prudence, and genuine prayer are conducive to the development of faith with its accompanying power for good. Individual application of this principle may be made with profit. Have you some besetting weakness, some sinful indulgence that you have vainly tried to overcome? Like the malignant demon that Christ rebuked in the boy, your sin may be of a kind that goeth out only through prayer and fasting. (JTC, p. 395.)

17:22–23 (Read Mark 9:30–32; Luke 9:43–45.) This is one of many statements from the Savior concerning his forthcoming atonement and resurrection.

17:24–27 See Exodus 30:13; 38:26; D&C 58:21–22.

The annual capitation tax here referred to amounted to half a shekel or a didrachm, corresponding to about thirty-three cents in our money; and this had been required of every male adult in Israel since the days of the exodus; though, during the period of captivity the requirement had been modified. This tribute, as prescribed through Moses, was originally known as "atone-ment money," and its payment was in the nature of a sacrifice to accompany supplication for ransom from the effects of individual sin. . . . Peter must have seen the inconsistency of expecting Jesus, the acknowledged Messiah, to pay atonement money, or a tax for temple maintenance, inasmuch as the temple was the House of God, and Jesus was the Son of God, and particu-larly since even earthly princes were exempted from capitation dues. (JTC, pp. 383–84.)

17:24 "Master" could also have been translated "teacher." Also, "tribute" is frequently translated "tax" or "temple-tax."

This was not a civil, but an ecclesiastical tax. It consisted of an annual payment of a half shekel or didrachma and was levied upon all males twenty years of age and older for the maintenance of the temple. As originally announced by Moses, it was an offering whereby men made an atonement for their sins; that is, the payment was in the nature of a sacrifice designed to accompany prayers beseeching forgiveness from personal sins. (Ex. 30:11–16.) Jesus, of course, was without sin and needed to offer no such supplications. Indeed, in his days, rabbis and priests generally claimed exemption from this tax. (DNTC 1:412.)

17:25 "Jesus prevented him" could have been translated "Jesus got ahead of him" or "Jesus spoke to him first." (See BD, "Prevent.") The Joseph Smith Translation reads, "Jesus rebuked him." Elder Bruce R. McConkie explains why:

Peter had erred; Jesus was not obligated to pay the atonement money. As Jesus then explained, even earthly princes were free from capitation taxes; why then should it be supposed that the Son of God was obligated to pay for the upkeep of the house of his Father? (DNTC 1:412.)

17:26 The word "free" could have been expanded to "tax-free."

17:27 "Notwithstanding" has also been translated "however" and "but."

The Lord's careful distinction "for me and thee" suggests that although he did not need to pay the tax as the Son of God, yet he would pay both for himself and for Peter.

It is significant that Jesus did not say *us* but *me and thee*. Such careful choice of words was in keeping with his invarying custom of maintaining a distinction between himself and other men. He was the Son of God, literally; other men had mortal fathers. Thus, for instance, he was careful to say, "I ascend unto my Father, and your Father; and to my God and your God" (John 20:17), not unto *our Father* and *our God*. (DNTC 1:413.)

The "piece of money," which Jesus said Peter would find in the mouth of the first fish that took his bait, is more correctly designated by the literal translation "stater," indicating a silver coin equivalent to a shekel, or two didrachms, and therefore the exact amount of the tax for two persons. While the circumstances of the finding of the stater in the fish are not detailed, and the actual accomplishment of the miracle is not positively recorded, we cannot doubt that what Jesus had promised was realized, as otherwise there would appear no reason for introducing the incident into the Gospel narrative. The miracle is without a parallel or even a remotely analogous instance. We need not assume that the stater was other than an ordinary coin that had fallen into the water, nor that it had been taken by the fish in any unusual way. Nevertheless, the knowledge that there was in the lake a fish having a coin in its gullet, that the coin was of the denomination specified, and that that particular fish would rise, and be the first to rise to Peter's hook, is as incomprehensible to man's finite understanding as are the means by which any of Christ's miracles were wrought. The Lord Jesus held and holds dominion over the earth, the sea, and all that in them is, for by His word and power were they made. (JTC, pp. 384–85.)

18:1–5 (Read Mark 9:33–37; Luke 9:46–48.) The Lord did not qualify his statement that little children should inherit "the kingdom of heaven." Nothing in these verses would indicate that children need to be baptized, although it is clear that adults must "be converted" and become *as* little children in order to "enter into the kingdom of heaven."

The Lord has reiterated this doctrine in this dispensation: "Little children are redeemed from the foundation of the world through mine Only Begotten; Wherefore, they cannot sin, for power is not given unto Satan to tempt little children, until they begin to become accountable before me." (D&C 29:46–47.)

Christ would not have had His chosen representatives become childish; far from it, they had to be men of courage, fortitude, and force; but He would have them become childlike. The distinction is important. Those who belong to Christ must become like little children in obedience, truthfulness, trustfulness, purity, humility, and faith. The child is an artless, natural, trusting believer; the childish one is careless, foolish, and neglectful. In contrasting these characteristics, note the counsel of Paul: "Brethren, be not children in understanding: howbeit in malice be ye children, but in understanding be men." (JTC, pp. 387–88.)

(See section 1, "Children: No baptism," "Children: Inherit heaven.")

18:3 The Greek word translated "converted" means literally to "turn around."

18:4 True greatness in the Lord's earthly kingdom is measured, not by positions held, not by pre-eminence attained, not by honors bestowed by mortals, but by intrinsic merit and goodness. Those who become as little children and acquire the attributes of godliness for themselves, regardless of the capacity in which they may be called to serve, are the "greatest in the kingdom of heaven." (DNTC 1:415.)

18:6–10 (Read Mark 9:42–50; Luke 17:1–2.) The Lord taught that "it must needs be that offenses come," and perhaps one reason for this is clarified in the Book of Mormon statement "It must needs be, that there is an opposition in all things." (2 Ne. 2:11.)

18:6 The Greek translated "offend" has the basic meaning of "cause to stumble." The Book of Mormon also teaches the serious situation of those who attempt to lead others astray through the preaching of false doctrine: "All those who preach false doctrines, and all those who commit whoredoms, and pervert the right way of the Lord, wo, wo, wo be unto them, saith the Lord God Almighty, for they shall be thrust down to hell!" (2 Ne. 28:15.) (See BD, "Millstone.")

18:8–9 Elder Bruce R. McConkie has applied "cutting off" and "plucking out" to excommunication:

Iniquity within the Church and kingdom of God on earth cannot be condoned; unrepentant members of the Church must be cast out, even though their severance from the body of the saints is as grievous an operation as cutting off a hand or foot or plucking out an eye. False doctrines and evil practices originating with those outside the Church are easily identified, both because of their nature and their source. But the same doctrines and practices when espoused and promulgated by those within the fold of Christ, who are presumed to be in harmony with the truth, may more easily lead the unwary astray. Indeed, one of the major factors contributing to the great apostasy in the early part of the Christian Era was the failure to cut off the dead, decaying, and corrupt branches of the gospel tree. (DNTC 1:419.)

18:9–10 The Joseph Smith Translation adds the following between the equivalent of these two verses: "And a man's hand is his friend, and his foot also; and a man's eye, are they of his own household."

18:10 This verse could have been translated, "See to it that you men do not despise one of these little ones; for I tell you that their angels in heaven always behold the face of my Father who is in heaven." The term "their angels" might refer to the spirits of children in heaven, and thus be considered evidence for premortal existence.

18:11–14 (Read Luke 15:1–7 and its commentary.) A careful reading of these two accounts (one in Matthew, the other in Luke) suggests that the Savior may have given some of the parables more than once in different situations:

This parable was given twice. Indeed, it may be that all of the parables were given numerous times to different groups of hearers and with differing purposes and applications.

As recorded by Matthew, the *Parable of the Lost Sheep* was given in Capernaum of Galilee in response to claims of pre-eminence by those who wanted to be first in the kingdom of God. In it Jesus is the Shepherd who has come to save the "little ones" who otherwise would be lost. The emphasis is on keeping the sheep from getting lost, on showing how precious the sheep are, and on how reluctant the Shepherd is to lose even one.

Luke's account tells what happened more than a year later in Perea. There the parable was given in response to the murmurings of the Pharisees and scribes that Jesus ate with sinners. This time the Master Teacher places the emphasis on finding that which is lost; he shows the length the Shepherd will go to find the sheep and the rejoicing that takes place when the lost is found. This time, in applying the parable, the complaining religious leaders, who considered themselves as just men needing no repentance, become the shepherds who should have been doing what the Chief Shepherd was doing—seeking to find and save that which was lost.

In further interpretation of Luke's account, the Prophet said: "The hundred sheep represent one hundred Sadducees and Pharisees, as though Jesus had said, 'If you Sadducees and Pharisees, are in the sheepfold, I have no mission for you; I am sent to look up sheep that are lost; and when I have found them, I will back them up and make joy in heaven.' This represents hunting after a few individuals, or one poor publican, which the Pharisees and Sadducees despised." (*Teachings,* p. 277.) (DNTC 1:508–9.)

18:11 For the Son of Man is come to save that which was lost, and to call sinners to repentance; but these little ones have no need of repentance, and I will save them. (JST.)

18:12–14 In this effective analogy the saving purpose of Christ's mission is made prominent. He is verily the Savior. The shepherd is portrayed as leaving the ninety and nine, pastured or folded in safety we cannot doubt, while he goes alone into the mountains to seek the one that has strayed. In finding and bringing back the wayward sheep, he has more joy than that of knowing the others are yet safe. (JTC, p. 389.)

18:13 The Joseph Smith Translation replaces "of that sheep" with "over that which was lost."

18:15–22 Read Luke 17:3–4.

18:15 The rule of the rabbis was that the offender must make the first advance; but Jesus taught that the injured one should not wait for his brother to come to him, but go himself, and seek to adjust the difficulty; by so doing he might be the means of saving his brother's soul. If the offender proved to be obdurate, the brother who had suffered the trespass was to take two or three others with him, and again try to bring the transgressor to repentant acknowledgment of his offense; such a course provided for witnesses, by whose presence later misrepresentation would be guarded against. (JTC, p. 391.)

(See section 1, "Reconciliation.")

It is not the sinner, the trespasser, the offender, who is to take the initiative in restoring peace and unity among brethren. If perchance he should do so, well and good. But the Lord commands the innocent person, the one without fault, the one who has been offended, to search out his brother and seek to repair the breach. Thus: "If thy brother trespass against thee, wait not for him to repent and make restitution; he is already somewhat hardened in spirit because of the trespass itself; rather, go to him, extend the hand of fellowship, shower him with love, and perchance 'thou hast gained thy brother.'" (DNTC 1:422–23.)

18:17 The Lord's instruction to "tell it unto the church" should not be interpreted to mean that confessions should be made openly before Church congregations:

Not the congregation in general, for such would spread the knowledge of sin and might create gossip, but tell it unto the church officers who are appointed to handle such matters. "And if thy brother or sister offend thee, thou shalt take him or her between him or her and thee alone; and if he or she confess thou shalt be reconciled. And if he or she confess not thou shalt deliver him or her up unto the church, not to the members, but to the elders. And it shall be done in a meeting, and that not before the world." (D&C 42:88–89.) (DNTC 1:423.)

President Spencer W. Kimball has explained the responsibility of Church leaders:

The function of proper Church leaders in the matter of forgiveness is two-fold: (1) to exact proper penalty—for example, to initiate official action in regard to the sinner in cases which warrant either disfellowshipment or excommunication; (2) to waive penalties and extend the hand of fellowship to the one in transgression. Whichever of the two steps is taken, either forgiveness or Church disciplinary action, it must be done in the light of all the facts and the inspiration which can come to those making the decision. Hence the importance of the repentant transgressor making full confession to the appropriate authority. (MF, pp. 325–26.)

(See BD, "Confession.")

"If he shall neglect to hear them" means "if he refuses to listen."

18:18 Earlier, the Lord had given the sealing keys of the priesthood to Peter (Matt. 16:13–20) and to James and John (Matt. 17:1–3; TPJS, p. 158). Here these powers are extended to the other apostles:

Now we find our Lord announcing that all of the Twelve possessed these same sealing powers and keys; either the remaining nine apostles had received them sometime between the Transfiguration and the occasion of this sermon or they received them at this time. After his resurrection, we shall find Jesus again specifying that all the Twelve held these keys. (John 20:21–23.) . . .

It should be noted that Peter's position in the primitive Church bore no resemblance to that of a modern pope. No key, power, grace, or authority was conferred upon Peter that was not enjoyed by each of his associates in the apostolic quorum. (Matt. 19:28; Rev. 21:14.) True, as the senior apostle of God on earth, Peter presided over the other members of his quorum so long as he lived. But the priesthood, keys, powers, graces, and prerogatives with which he was endowed were identically the same as those vested in each member of the supreme apostolic quorum. Accordingly, after Peter and James had departed this life, the beloved John, not the Bishop of Rome or of any other locality, served as the presiding officer of the Lord's earthly kingdom, using the same keys and sealing powers which Peter himself had exercised in the days of his presidency.

In the meridian of time, the Church was built, not upon Peter or upon any special powers given him, nor for that matter upon any one or even all of the Twelve, or any special powers given them, but upon the rock of revelation. Since all the Twelve—as prophets, seers, and revelators to the Church—held the keys whereby revelation comes from God to man, it follows that any of them could have presided over the Church had the occasion required. Because they, as apostles and prophets, following in the footsteps of their Master, were the agents appointed to receive revelation for the Church, thus keeping the kingdom in the course charted by the Lord himself, Paul properly concluded that the Church was "built upon the foundation of the apostles and prophets, Jesus Christ being the chief corner stone." (Eph. 2:20.)

Since keys include the right of presidency, and there can never be two equal heads at the same time, it follows that the keys of the kingdom can be exercised in their fulness only by one man at a time on earth. (D&C 132:7.) Thus, as far as their full and unlimited exercise was concerned, the keys lay dormant in each of the Twelve as long as Peter lived. Peter's pre-eminence lay in the fact that as the senior apostle who presided over all others, he could direct all of the affairs of the kingdom including the labors of his fellow special witnesses of the Lord. (DNTC 1:424–25.)

(See section 1, "Keys of kingdom," "Priesthood keys.")

18:19 Again, I say unto you, that if two of you shall agree on earth as touching any thing that they shall ask, *that they may not ask amiss,* it shall be done for them of my Father *who is in heaven.* (JST; italics added.)

James also taught that we should not ask amiss: "Ye ask, and receive not, because ye ask amiss, that ye may consume it upon your lusts." (James 4:3.)

18:20 The Savior's statement that he will be "in the midst of them" pertains to his presence by the power of the Spirit:

> Not literally but by the power of the Spirit. Speaking similarly, Paul said to the members of the Church, "Jesus Christ is in you, except ye be reprobates." (2 Cor. 13:5.) In other words, the saints have the gift of the Holy Ghost which reveals to them "the mind of Christ" (1 Cor. 2:9–16), so that Christ in effect dwells in each righteous member of the Church and reigns in the midst of their congregations. (DNTC 1:427.)

18:21 Peter here broke in with a question: "Lord, how oft shall my brother sin against me, and I forgive him? till seven times?" He would fain have some definite limit set, and he probably considered the tentative suggestion of seven times as a very liberal measure, inasmuch as the rabbis prescribed a triple forgiveness only. They based this limitation on Amos 1:3 and Job 33:29. In the latter passage, as it appears in the authorized version, the word "oftentimes" is an erroneous rendering of the original, which really signified "twice and thrice." (JTC, p. 392.)

18:23–35 (See 2 Kgs. 4:1.) A major point of this parable, given immediately after the Lord's statement to Peter that we should forgive each other until "seventy times seven" offenses, is that surely we should forgive our fellowmen their relatively slight transgressions against us, inasmuch as God forgives us an immeasurably greater debt. The "lord" in the parable forgave his servant ten thousand talents, whereas the servant in turn was not willing to forgive his fellowman even the hundred pence owed to him.

Concerning any possible implications of the approval of slavery in this story, Elder James E. Talmage has written:

> Some readers have assumed that they find in the Parable of the Unmerciful Servant an implied approval of the institution of slavery. The greater debtor, who figures in the story, was to be sold, together with his wife and children and all that he had. A rational consideration of the story as a whole is likely to find at most, in the particular incident of the king's command that the debtor and his family be sold, that the system of buying and selling bondservants, serfs, or slaves, was legally recognized at the

time. The purpose of the parable was not even remotely to endorse or condemn slavery or any other social institution. The Mosaic law is explicit in matters relating to bondservants. The "angel of the Lord" who brought to Hagar a message of encouragement and blessing respected the authority of her mistress (Gen. 16:8, 9). In the apostolic epoch, instruction was directed toward right living under the secular law, not rebellion against the system (Eph. 6:5; Col. 3:22; 1 Tim. 6:1–3; 1 Pet. 2:18). Recognition of established customs, institutions, and laws, and proper obedience thereto, do not necessarily imply individual approval. The gospel of Jesus Christ, which shall yet regenerate the world, is to prevail—not by revolutionary assaults upon existing governments, nor through anarchy and violence—but by the teaching of individual duty and by the spread of the spirit of love. When the love of God shall be given a place in the hearts of mankind, when men shall unselfishly love their neighbors, then social systems and governments shall be formed and operated to the securing of the greatest good to the greatest number. Until men open their hearts to the reception of the gospel of Jesus Christ, injustice and oppression, servitude and slavery, in some form or other, are sure to exist. Attempts to extirpate social conditions that spring from individual selfishness cannot be otherwise than futile so long as selfishness is left to thrive and propagate. (JTC, p. 397.)

18:23–27 Concerning the state of the servant who was in debt, Elder Talmage has noted:

The man was in arrears for debt. He did not come before his lord voluntarily but had to be brought. So in the affairs of our individual lives periodical reckonings are inevitable; and while some debtors report of their own accord, others have to be cited to appear. The messengers who serve the summons may be adversity, illness, the approach of death; but, whatever, whoever they are, they enforce a rendering of our accounts. (JTC, p. 394.)

18:25 "But forasmuch as he had not to pay" has the essential meaning of "Since he was not able to pay."

18:26–27 The Joseph Smith Translation transposes some of the elements in these two verses and adds new information:

King James Version	*Joseph Smith Translation*
The servant therefore fell down, and worshipped him, saying, Lord, have patience with me, and I will pay thee all.	And the servant besought him, saying, Lord, have patience with me, and I will pay thee all.
Then the lord of that servant was moved with compassion, and loosed him, and forgave him the debt.	Then the lord of that servant was moved with compassion, and loosed him, and forgave him the debt. The servant, therefore, fell down and worshipped him.

18:29 See commentary for Matthew 14:36.

18:31 The word translated "sorry" more literally means "grieved" or "distressed."

18:33 The words translated "compassion" and "pity" have the basic meaning of "mercy."

18:34 "Wroth" has been translated "angry" in most modern translations. Also, "tormentors" is frequently translated "jailers."

Concerning the judgment that came upon the man, Elder James E. Talmage has noted:

> The man came under condemnation, not primarily for defalcation and debt, but for lack of mercy after having received of mercy so abundantly. He, as an unjust plaintiff, had invoked the law; as a convicted transgressor he was to be dealt with according to the law. Mercy is for the merciful. As a heavenly jewel it is to be received with thankfulness and used with sanctity, not to be cast into the mire of undeservedness. Justice may demand retribution and punishment: "With what measure ye mete, it shall be measured to you again." The conditions under which we may confidently implore pardon are set forth in the form of prayer prescribed by the Lord: "Forgive us our debts, as we forgive our debtors." (JTC, pp. 394–95.)

Elder Bruce R. McConkie has observed concerning the phrase "all that was due":

> If men repent and obey the gospel law, they are forgiven of their sins; they inherit mercy from the Lord's hands, Christ himself through the infinite and eternal atonement bearing their burdens and paying the penalty for their transgressions. But if men do not repent and keep the commandments, if they continue to transgress against their brethren and to walk after the manner of the world, they are denied the full mercies of the atonement and instead are required to pay the penalty for their own sins. (D&C 19:4–20.) (DNTC 1:430.)

19:1–12 (Read Mark 10:1–12. Compare John 8:6.) "Tempting is usually translated in modern versions as "testing." Also, "put away" really means "divorce."

> Legal justification for divorce today varies from almost the mere whim of the parties on the one hand to adultery on the other, depending upon the laws of the state or nation involved. This same divergence of opinion existed among the Jews, and Jesus was being asked to decide one of the burning issues of the day.
>
> "Among the questions of the day fiercely debated between the great rival schools of Hillel and Shammai, no one was more so than that of divorce. The school of Hillel contended that a man had a right to divorce his wife for any cause he might assign, if it were no more than his having ceased to love her, or his having seen one he liked better, or her having cooked a dinner badly. The school of Shammai, on the contrary, held that

divorce could be issued only for the crime of adultery, and offences against chastity. If it were possible to get Jesus to pronounce in favor of either school, the hostility of the other would be roused, and hence, it seemed a favorable chance for compromising him." (*Geikie,* vol. 2, pp. 347–348, cited, *Talmage,* p. 484.) (DNTC 1:547–48.)

(See section 1, "Divorce.")

19:2 Belief is necessary to be healed, as shown in the Joseph Smith Translation: "And great multitudes followed him; *and many believed on him,* and he healed them there." (Italics added.)

19:3–9 Elder James E. Talmage quotes Geikie concerning this incident:

Geikie thus paraphrases part of Christ's reply to the Pharisee's question concerning divorce, and comments thereon. "'I say, therefore, that whoever puts away his wife, except for fornication, which destroys the very essence of marriage by dissolving the oneness it had formed, and shall marry another, commits adultery; and whoever marries her who is put away for any other cause commits adultery, because the woman is still, in God's sight, wife of him who had divorced her.' This statement was of far deeper moment than the mere silencing of malignant spies. It was designed to set forth for all ages the law of His New Kingdom in the supreme matter of family life. It swept away for ever from His Society the conception of woman as a mere toy or slave of man, and based true relations of the sexes on the eternal foundation of truth, right, honor, and love. To ennoble the House and the Family by raising woman to her true position was essential to the future stability of His Kingdom, as one of purity and spiritual worth. By making marriage indissoluble, He proclaimed the equal rights of woman and man within the limits of the family, and, in this, gave their charter of nobility to the mothers of the world. For her nobler position in the Christian era, compared with that granted her in antiquity, woman is indebted to Jesus Christ." — *Life and Words of Christ,* vol. ii, p. 349. (JTC, p. 484.)

Elder Bruce R. McConkie has provided pertinent commentary on the true concepts of marriage and divorce:

Divorce is not part of the gospel plan no matter what kind of marriage is involved. But because men in practice do not always live in harmony with gospel standards, the Lord permits divorce for one reason or another, depending upon the spiritual stability of the people involved. In ancient Israel men had power to divorce their wives for relatively insignificant reasons. (Deut. 24:1–4.) Under the most perfect conditions there would be no divorce permitted except where sex sin was involved. In this day divorces are permitted in accordance with civil statutes, and the divorced persons are permitted by the Church to marry again without the stain of immorality which under a higher system would attend such a course. (DNTC 1:547.)

19:4–6 "At the beginning" is a reference to the marriage of Adam and Eve:

As he so often did in answering their questions, Jesus simply went back to basic principles. He referred them to the marriage of Adam and Eve which occurred before death entered the world and while the first man and the first woman were still in the Garden of Eden. He cited the divine decree itself, thus making this first marriage a pattern for all others and said that God himself had joined the parties together, and that man, therefore, did not have power to tear them asunder. In other words, Jesus is here preaching a sermon on celestial or eternal marriage, marriage that is to last forever, in this life and in the next, marriage that does not countenance divorce, except, as he then amplified, when sex sin occurs. (DNTC 1:548.)

(See section 1, "Marriage.")

19:7 "Writing of divorcement" could have been translated "certificate of dismissal." The Greek words clearly differentiate between the "putting away of a wife," which does not require legal action, and the "writing of divorcement [certificate of dismissal]," which makes the action legal.

19:11 The Greek word translated "receive" has the basic meaning of "make room." Thus, this statement could have been translated "Not all men make room for the saying, but only those who have the gift."

But he said unto them, *it is not for them* save to whom it is given. (JST; italics added.)

This strict law governing divorce was not given to the Pharisees, nor to the world in general, but to the disciples only, "in the house," at a later time as Mark explains. Further, Jesus expressly limited its application. All men could not live such a high standard; it applied only to those "to whom it is given."

Earlier in his ministry the Master had given it to some of his Jewish disciples (Matt. 5:31–32), and after his resurrection he would yet give it to the Nephites. (3 Ne. 12:31–32.) Presumably it prevailed among them during the near two-hundred-year period following his ministry on the American continent. We can suppose it prevailed in the City of Enoch and that it will be the law during the millennium. It may have been in force at various times and among various people, but the Church is not bound by it today. At this time divorces are permitted in the Church for a number of reasons other than sex immorality, and divorced persons are permitted to marry again and enjoy all of the blessings of the gospel. If every divorced person who remarried were guilty of adultery, the Church would be obligated to expel such from membership and to deny them the blessings of the gospel and the temple. (DNTC 1:548–49.)

19:12 The Greek word translated several times in this verse as "eunuchs" means one who "cannot marry." (See section 1, "Eunuchs.")

This verse has been quite freely paraphrased: "Some are born without the ability to marry, and some are disabled by men, and some refuse to marry for the sake of the Kingdom of Heaven. Let anyone who can, accept my statement." (LB.)

Some added background and additional information is needed to understand fully what is meant by this teaching about eunuchs. In the true Church and among normal people, there is no place for the practice of celibacy. "Apparently those who made themselves eunuchs were men who in false pagan worship had deliberately mutilated themselves in the apostate notion that such would further their salvation. It is clear that such was not a true gospel requirement of any sort. There is no such thing in the gospel as wilful emasculation; such a notion violates every true principle of procreation and celestial marriage." (*Mormon Doctrine*, p. 223.) (DNTC 1:549.)

In the Joseph Smith Translation, the last sentence in this verse reads: "He that is able to receive, let him receive my sayings."

19:13–15 Read Mark 10:13–16; Luke 18:15–17.

19:13 Then were there brought unto him little children, that he should put his hands on them and pray. And the disciples rebuked them saying, There is no need, for Jesus hath said, Such shall be saved. (JST.)

When did he say it? Nowhere is it recorded in the gospels as we have them, and it was even lost from this passage until restored by the spirit of inspiration. If it had been preserved, what a blow it would strike against the heresies of infant baptism and original sin. One wonders how many other lost statements would overthrow other false doctrines. What would happen to the creeds of the day if it were sometime discovered that Paul wrote such a sentence as this, "God is an exalted man"? How little we have, comparatively speaking, of the teachings of Jesus! (DNTC 1:551.)

(See section 1, "Children: No baptism," "Children: Inherit heaven.")

19:16–26 Read Mark 10:17–27; Luke 18:18–27. Compare 1 Nephi 12:7–10.

19:16–22 As you know, the young man went away sorrowful, "for he had great possessions." (Matt. 19:16–22.) And we are left to wonder what intimacies he might have shared with the Son of God, what fellowship he might have enjoyed with the apostles, what revelations and visions he might have received, if he had been *able* to live the law of a celestial kingdom. As it is he remains nameless; as it might have been, his name could have been had in honorable remembrance among the saints forever.

Now I think it is perfectly clear that the Lord expects far more of us than we sometimes render in response. We are not as other men. We are the saints of God and have the revelations of heaven. Where much is given much is expected. We are to put first in our lives the things of his kingdom. (Bruce R. McConkie, CR, Apr. 1975, pp. 75–76.)

19:16 The question "What good thing shall I do, that I may have eternal life?" is one that we all might well ask.

To gain eternal life a man must do five things:

(1) Have faith in Christ, a true and living faith, a faith based on knowledge, a faith that accepts him as the Son of God and recognizes that God his Father is a personal being in whose image man was created.

(2) Repent and forsake the world.

(3) Submit to baptism under the hands of a legal administrator.

(4) Receive the gift of the Holy Ghost by the laying on of hands by one having authority so to act. This gift is the right to the constant companionship of the Holy Ghost, a gift which if actually enjoyed enables a person to walk in paths of righteousness at all times.

(5) Endure in faith, devotion, and obedience to the whole gospel law to the end of life. Included in this requirement is entrance into the order of celestial marriage and conformity to the whole program of the Church. Special acts of sacrifice and devotion may be involved in particular instances, depending upon the special circumstances which face various individuals. The rich young ruler was commanded to forsake his worldly possessions, the early Latter-day Saints their homes, those called on missions to devote themselves to that work for the time and season involved, and so forth. . . .

It would appear that the inquiring rich man had lived in strict conformity to the laws known to him, that he saw in Jesus a teacher who could direct him to the fulness of reward in the mansions on high, and that he erroneously supposed he would receive direction to conform to some ritualistic requirement of the law. He had not learned that the Lord requires the whole soul and that those who gain salvation must love and serve God with an eye single to his glory. Rather, good as he was, his heart was still set on the things of this world in preference to the riches of eternity. (DNTC 1:554–55.)

(See section 1, "Eternal life, what to gain.")

19:17 It should be noted that Jesus does not say that he is not good. He merely asks why he is being so designated when it is Deity that is known to be good. Perhaps the meaning is this: "Why callest thou me good without accepting me as the Son of God, for none is good but God; and if I am good, as thou sayest, then I am God and should be accepted as such." (DNTC 1:555.)

19:18 The Joseph Smith Translation changes "do no murder" to "not kill."

19:23 The statement by Jesus could have been translated "Truly I say to you that it will be a difficult thing for a rich man to get into the kingdom of heaven."

Elder Bruce R. McConkie suggests conditions that must be met:

> Rich men who are otherwise worthy can be saved provided: (1) They forsake or are willing to forsake their riches in the cause of Christ; and (2) Their love of wealth does not cause them to trust in riches. (DNTC 1:556.)

19:24 In comparing the difficulty of a rich man entering the kingdom with that of a camel passing through the eye of a needle, Jesus used a rhetorical figure, which, strong and prohibitory as it appears in our translation, was of a type familiar to those who heard the remark. There was a "common Jewish proverb, that a man did not even in his dreams see an elephant pass through the eye of a needle" (Edersheim). Some interpreters insist that a rope, not a camel, was mentioned by Jesus, and these base their contention on the fact that the Greek word *kamelos* (camel) differs in but a single letter from *kamilos* (rope), and that the alleged error of substituting "camel" for "rope" in the scriptural text is chargeable to the early copyists. Farrar (p. 476) rejects this possible interpretation on the ground that proverbs involving comparisons of a kind with that of a camel passing through the eye of needle are common in the Talmud.

It has been asserted that the term "needle's eye" was applied to a small door or wicket set in or alongside the great gates in the walls of cities; and the assumption has been raised that Jesus had such a wicket in mind when He spoke of the seeming impossibility of a camel passing through a needle's eye. It would be possible though very difficult for a camel to squeeze its way through the little gate, and it could in no wise do so except when relieved of its load and stripped of all its harness. If this conception be correct, we may find additional similitude between the fact that the camel must first be unloaded and stripped, however costly its burden or rich its accoutrement, and the necessity of the rich young ruler, and so of any man divesting himself of the burden and trappings of wealth, if he would enter by the narrow way that leadeth into the kingdom. The Lord's exposition of His saying is all-sufficient for the purposes of the lesson: "With men this is impossible, but with God all things are possible." (Matt. 19:26.) (JTC, pp. 485–86.)

(See section 1, "Needle, eye of"; BD, "Camel.")

19:25 "Exceedingly amazed" could have been translated "greatly surprised" or "astounded."

19:26 But Jesus beheld *their thoughts,* and said unto them, With men this is impossible; *but if they will forsake all things for my sake,* with God whatsoever things I speak are possible. (JST; italics added.)

19:27–30 Read Matthew 20:1–16; Mark 10:28–31; Luke 18:28–30.

19:27–29 In reality, a man cannot get God into his debt. As King Benjamin explained in the Book of Mormon, our Heavenly Father gave us life in the first place, and his only requirement is that we keep his commandments, which, when we do, he immediately blesses us, and thus we continue to be indebted to him for life itself and will be "forever and ever." (See Mosiah 2:21–24.)

19:28 The Joseph Smith Translation changes "regeneration" to "resurrection." (See BD, "Regeneration.")

19:29 Many Greek texts do not include the equivalent of "or wife" in this verse, although the term is included in Luke 18:29.

19:30 Read commentaries for Matthew 20:1–16.

But many of the first shall be last, and the last first. (JST.)

20:1–16 (Read Matt. 19:27–30 and its commentaries; Mark 10:28–31; Luke 18:28–30. See also 1 Ne. 12:7–10.) This parable actually begins with the last verses of chapter 19, which conclude with the statement "But many of the first shall be last, and the last first." (JST Matt. 19:30.) This same idea closes the parable in Matthew 20:16.

This difficult parable is closely linked with what goes before, and can only be understood in connection with it. It rebukes the spirit of Peter's enquiry (Matt. 19:27), "We have left all and followed thee; what shall we have?" The Twelve through Peter had demanded a superlatively great reward, because they had been called first and had labored longest. Such a reward had been promised them, should they prove worthy of it (Matt. 18:28), though at the same time it was darkly hinted, that some outside the apostolic circle would prove in the end more worthy than some of the apostles. (Matt. 19:30.)

In principle the *Parable of the Laborers in the Vineyard* applies to all who are called into the ministry of the Master. When the Melchizedek Priesthood is conferred upon them and they are ordained to offices therein, they make a covenant with the Lord to magnify their callings in the priesthood. On his part the Lord promises that if they do magnify their callings, he will give them "all that my Father hath" which, of course, is exaltation in the kingdom of God. (D&C 84:33–41.)

This promise is to all; all are promised the same wages. The bargaining spirit has no place in the gospel. If every elder who magnifies his calling is assured of that eternal life which consists in attaining all that the Father hath, how can any receive more than the "penny" appointed? For those who gain exaltation the promise is: "And he makes them equal in power, and in might, and in dominion." (D&C 76:95; 88:107.) And though the laborers may not comprehend the full significance of all this while they are yet laboring in the vineyard, yet trusting in the Lord they know that "whatsoever is right" shall be given them. (DNTC 1:560–61.)

(See section 1, "First/last.")

20:1–15 The procedure of a householder going into the marketplace to hire laborers was common to the time and place, and is still an ordinary occurrence in many lands. The first to be hired in the course of the story made a definite bargain as to wages. Those who were employed at nine, twelve, and three o'clock respectively went willingly without agreement as to what they were to receive; so glad were they to find a chance to work that they lost no time in specifying terms. At five o'clock in the afternoon or evening, when but a single hour of the working day remained, the last band of laborers went to work, trusting to the master's word that whatever was right they should receive. That they had not found work earlier in the day was no fault of theirs; they had been ready and willing, and had waited at the place where employment was most likely to be secured. At the close of the day, the laborers came for their wages; this was in accordance with law and custom, for it had been established by statute in Israel that the employer should pay the servant, hired by the day, before the sun went down. Under instructions, the steward who acted as paymaster began with those who had been engaged at the eleventh hour; and to each of them he gave a denarius, or Roman penny, worth about fifteen cents in our money, and the usual wage for a day's work. This was the amount for which those who began earliest had severally bargained; and as these saw their fellow-workers, who had served but an hour, receive each a penny, they probably exulted in the expectation of receiving a wage proportionately larger, notwithstanding their stipulation. But each of them received a penny and no more. Then they complained; not because they had been underpaid, but because the others had received a full day's pay for but part of a day's work. The master answered in all kindness, reminding them of their agreement. Could he not be just to them and charitable to the rest if he so chose? His money was his own, and he could give of it as he liked. Were those grumblers justified in their evil displeasure because their master was charitable and good? "So," said Jesus, passing directly from the story to one of the lessons it was designed to teach, "the last shall be first, and the first last: for many be called, but few chosen." (JTC, pp. 480–81.)

20:3, 6 "Standing idle" means "unemployed."

20:8 This verse could have been translated "When it became evening, the master of the vineyard said to his man in charge, 'Call the workers and pay them their wages, proceeding from the last to the first.'"

20:9 The Joseph Smith Translation uses "began" rather than "were hired."

20:16 In this dispensation the Lord has given further explanation as to why "many are called but few are chosen." (See D&C 121:34–40.)

20:17–19 (Read Mark 10:32–34; Luke 18:31–34.) This was not the first time the Savior had told his disciples of his impending crucifixion and forthcoming resurrection. (See also Matt. 16:21–23; 17:22–23; Mark 8:31–33; 9:30–32; Luke 9:43–45.) Here, however, he makes it clear that the "chief priests and . . . the scribes" are the ones who will deliver him "to the Gentiles to mock, and to scourge, and to crucify."

(See section 1, "Resurrection: Taught early.")

20:18 The Greek words translated "shall be betrayed" have the basic meaning of "will be given over" or "will be delivered up."

20:20–28 (Read Mark 10:35–45; Luke 22:24–27.) It is quite evident "the mother of Zebedee's children" had not heard the parable of the laborers in the vineyard, which is also recorded in this chapter (verses 1–16) but was probably given sometime before.

Elder Bruce R. McConkie has observed concerning the request of the mother of James and John:

> What does it matter whether a man is a ward teacher, priesthood quorum president, bishop, stake president, or general authority? It is not where a man serves, but how. There is as great personal satisfaction through faithful service in one position as another. And, as Jesus had before explained, the final reward of exaltation is the same for all who obtain it. It is eternal increase, the fulness of the kingdom of the Father, all power in heaven and on earth; it is all that the Father hath. (DNTC 1:556.)

20:20 "Worshipping" is frequently translated "kneeling before" or "bowing down."

20:21, 23 The Joseph Smith Translation makes the following contributions to verse 21: "What wilt thou *that I should do?*" (Italics added.)

> And he *said* unto them, Ye shall drink indeed of my cup, and be baptized with the baptism that I am baptized with; but to sit on my right hand, and on my left, is *for whom it is prepared of my Father, but not mine to give.* (JST; italics added.)

Elder Bruce R. McConkie has suggested that the phrase "to drink of the cup" is a metaphorical expression meaning, "to do the things which my lot in life requires of me," while the phrase "to be baptized with the baptism that I am baptized with" essentially means "to follow my course, suffer persecution, be rejected of men, and finally be slain for the truth's sake." (DNTC 1:566.) (See section 1, "Cup, to drink of, of Christ.")

20:26 This verse could have been translated, "This is not the way among you; but whoever wants to become great among you must be your minister."

20:29–34 Similar, but not identical, accounts of this healing of the blind are contained in Mark 10:46–52 and

Luke 18:35– 43. Undoubtedly the conflicts in the accounts could be resolved if we had the original records.

Elder James E. Talmage has written concerning this incident:

> In the course of His journey Jesus came to Jericho, at or near which city He again exerted His wondrous power in opening the eyes of the blind. Matthew states that two sightless men were made to see, and that the miracle was enacted as Jesus was leaving Jericho; Mark mentions but one blind man, whom he names Bartimeus or the son of Timeus, and agrees with Matthew in saying that the healing was effected when Jesus was departing from the city; Luke specifies but one subject of the Lord's healing mercy, "a certain blind man," and chronicles the miracle as an incident of Christ's approach to Jericho. These slight variations attest the independent authorship of each of the records, and the apparent discrepancies have no direct bearing upon the main facts, nor do they detract from the instructional value of the Lord's work. As we have found to be the case on an earlier occasion, two men were mentioned though but one figures in the circumstantial account. (JTC, pp. 504–5.)

> Christ was not a physician who relied upon curative substances, nor a surgeon to perform physical operations; His healings were the natural results of the application of a power of his own: It is conceivable that confidence, which is a stepping-stone to belief, as that in turn is to faith, may have been encouraged by these physical ministrations, strengthened, and advanced to a higher and more abiding trust in Christ, on the part of the afflicted who had not sight to look upon the Master's face and derive inspiration therefrom, nor hearing to hear His uplifting words. There is apparent not alone an entire absence of formula and formalism in His ministration, but a lack of uniformity of procedure quite as impressive. (JTC, p. 321.)

20:31 "Rebuked them, because they should hold their peace" has the essential meaning of "scolded them and told them sharply to be quiet."

20:32 The statement of the Savior could have been translated, "What do you want me to do for you?"

21:1–11 (Read Mark 11:1–11; Luke 19:29– 40; John 12:12–19.) Although these accounts are very similar, there are some unresolved minor conflicts. The Joseph Smith Translation makes it clear that there was only one, not two animals.

The following explanation of words and terms might also be helpful:

1. The Greek word designating the animal referred to as an ass could also have been translated "beast of burden."

2. The word "strawed" in verse 8 could have been translated "spread."

3. "Hosanna" is a transliteration of a Hebrew word with the essential meaning of "grant us salvation." Other possible meanings are "save now," "save, we pray," and "save, we beseech thee."

4. "Son of David" is a sacred title reserved for the Messiah. It is derived from the numerous Old Testament prophecies that the Messiah would be of the loins of David.

5. The Joseph Smith Translation of the last sentence is "This is Jesus of Nazareth, the prophet of Galilee."

(See section 1, "Triumphant entry"; BD, "Bethphage," "Olives, Mount of.")

21:5 See BD, "Sion."

21:7–11 The purpose of Christ in thus yielding Himself for the day to the desires of the people and accepting their homage with kingly grace may not be fully comprehended by us of finite mind. That the occasion was no accidental or fortuitous happening, of which He took advantage without pre- conceived intention, is evident. He knew beforehand what would be, and what He would do. It was no meaningless pageantry; but the actual advent of the King into His royal city, and His entry into the temple, the house of the King of kings. He came riding on an ass, in token of peace, acclaimed by the Hosanna shouts of multitudes; not on a caparisoned steed with the panoply of combat and the accompaniment of bugle blasts and fanfare of trumpets. That the joyous occasion was in no sense suggestive of physical hostility or of seditious disturbance is sufficiently demonstrated by the indul- gent unconcern with which it was viewed by the Roman officials, who were usually prompt to send their legionaries swooping down from the fortress of Antonia at the first evidence of an outbreak; and they were particularly vig- ilant in suppressing all Messianic pretenders, for false Messiahs had arisen already, and much blood had been shed in the forcible dispelling of their delusive claims. But the Romans saw nothing to fear, perhaps much to smile at, in the spectacle of a King mounted upon an ass, and attended by subjects, who, though numerous, brandished no weapons but waved instead palm branches and myrtle sprigs. The ass has been designated in literature as "the ancient symbol of Jewish royalty," and one riding upon an ass as the type of peaceful progress. (JTC, pp. 516–17.)

(See section 1, "Hosanna.")

21:11 Concerning the Joseph Smith Translation contri- bution ("This is Jesus of Nazareth, the prophet of Galilee"), Elder Bruce R. McConkie has commented:

Debate raged in all Jewry. Was Jesus of Nazareth, the prophet of Galilee, indeed the Messiah? Had he in truth done the works and taught the doctrines of Israel's promised Deliverer? Should the people follow him or wait for another?

In the midst of all this uncertainty, at the time of the Passover, when the question on every lip was, "Will he come to the feast and make further claim of his divinity?" Jesus, as though to place the capstone on all the testimony of Messiahship which he had previously borne, arranged to fulfil in detail one of the great Messianic prophecies.

As was known and understood among the people, Zechariah had prophesied: "Rejoice greatly, O daughter of Zion; shout, O daughter of Jerusalem: behold, thy King cometh unto thee: he is just, and having salvation; lowly, and riding upon an ass, and upon a colt the foal of an ass." (Zech. 9:9.) Now as we see our Lord's triumphal entry into Jerusalem, amid waving palm branches, riding over the careful placed clothing of the people, and accepting their acclamations of praise and divinity, it is as though Zechariah had viewed the scene and written, not prophecy, but history.

Every detail of this unique episode joined in testifying of the identity of the central figure in the picture. It was as though Jesus had said: "Many times I have told you in plain words and by necessary implication that I am the Messiah. My disciples also bear the same witness. Now I come unto you as the King of Israel in the very way that the prophet of old said I would; and your participation in this event is itself a witness that I am he who should come to redeem my people." (DNTC 1:577–78.)

21:12–17 (Read Mark 11:15–19; Luke 19:45–48.) Some three years before the Savior had driven the money changers out of "his Father's house." (See John 2:13–17.) On this occasion, he quoted from Isaiah 56:7, "My house shall be called the house of prayer; but ye have made it a den of thieves." Later in the week, after being largely rejected by the people and their apostate religious leaders, the Savior referred to the same building as "your house": "I leave your house unto you desolate."

The use of the different possessive pronouns is of particular interest; three years before, the Savior was just beginning his ministry, while at this time he was at the very height of his ministry. The last statement was made as he closed his ministry.

(See section 1, "Money changers from temple.")

21:12 "Seats" could have been translated "benches."

21:13 "Den" could also be translated "cave."

21:15 "They were sore displeased" could have been translated "they became indignant."

The Joseph Smith Translation reads, " . . . and the children *of the kingdom* crying in the temple, . . ." (Italics added.)

The following commentary has been prepared as to why the "chief priests and scribes" were "sore displeased":

The chief priests were the guardians of the temple and, in fact, guardians (as they supposed) of the whole structure of Jewish religion. They glutted themselves on the profits from temple business, and so the temple was not just the source of their favored social position (which they coveted so jealously) but also the source of their incomes—more, their fortunes. . . . The anger of the chief priests and scribes was raging against Him; but it was impotent. They had decreed His death, and had made repeated efforts to take him, and there he sat within the very area over which they claimed supreme jurisdiction, and they were afraid to touch Him because of the common people, whom they professed to despise yet heartily feared—"for all the people were very attentive to hear him." (JTC, pp. 528–29.)

21:17 "He lodged there" means "he passed the night there." (See BD, "Bethany.")

21:18–22 (Read Mark 11:12–14, 20–26. Compare Luke 13:6–9.) The Joseph Smith Translation adds the clause "there was not any fruit on it" to this incident of the fig tree.

Why did Jesus curse the fruitless fig tree? Unique among our Lord's miracles, this manifestation of divine power teaches a number of great truths:

(1) By exercising his power over nature, Jesus was testifying in language written in the earth itself that he was Lord of all. As the Lord Jehovah he had in times past created all things in heaven and on earth; now, though tabernacled in mortal clay, he possessed the same eternal powers over life, death, and the forces of nature. By using these powers—as he had before done in calming the tempest, multiplying loaves and fishes, walking on the water, healing multitudes, and raising the dead—he was leaving a visible and tangible witness of his own divine Sonship.

(2) Though Jesus had come to bless and save, yet he had the power to smite, destroy, and curse. "It must needs be, that there is an opposition in all things" (2 Ne. 2:11); if blessings are born of righteousness, their opposite, curses, must come from wickedness. True gospel ministers seek always to bless, yet curses attend rejection of their message. "Whomsoever you bless I will bless, and whomsoever you curse I will curse, saith the Lord." (D&C 132:47.) It is fitting that Jesus should leave a manifestation of his power to curse, and the fact that he chose, not a person, but a tree, is an evident act of mercy.

(3) Withering and dying at Jesus' command, the fruitless fig tree stands as a type and a shadow of what shall befall hypocrites. On fig trees the fruit grows first and then the leaves. But here was a precocious tree, holding itself out as bearing fruit because its leaves were now grown, but in fact being deceptively barren. "Were it reasonable to regard the tree as possessed of moral agency, we would have to pronounce it a hypocrite; its utter barrenness coupled with its abundance of foliage made of it a type of human hypocrisy." (*Talmage*, p. 527.)

(4) Also: "The leafy, fruitless tree was a symbol of Judaism, which loudly proclaimed itself as the only true religion of the age, and condescendingly invited all the world to come and partake of its rich ripe fruit; when in truth it was but an unnatural growth of leaves, with no fruit of the season, nor even an edible bulb held over from earlier years, for such as it

had of former fruitage was dried to worthlessness and made repulsive in its worm-eaten decay. The religion of Israel had degenerated into an artificial religionism, which in pretentious show and empty profession outclassed the abominations of heathendom." (*Talmage,* p. 527.)

(5) Perhaps the most obvious lessons to be drawn from this unusual display of divine power are that by faith all things are possible and that faith is a principle of power which operates in the temporal as well as the spiritual realm. (DNTC 1:582–83.)

(See section 1, "Fig tree, cursed.")

21:19–20 The same Greek word is translated in verse 19 as "presently" and in verse 20 as "soon." The basic meaning is "instantly" or "in the present." (See BD, "Presently.")

21:22 The necessity of faith is shown in the Joseph Smith Translation: "And all things, whatsoever ye shall ask in prayer, in faith believing, ye shall receive."

21:23–27 (Read Mark 11:27–33; Luke 20:1–8.) The apostate Jewish leaders who controlled the temple mount felt their authority had been usurped by Jesus when he had driven the money changers out of "their" temple. Still incensed over that act, they now challenge the authority of the Savior to do "these things." It is interesting that they recognize that authority is necessary and that they don't ask him for a sign as they had done earlier when he had cleansed the temple. (See John 2:13–18.)

21:28–32 (See also Jacob 5:70–71.) Some of the standard Greek texts indicate that the first son is the one who said "I will" and then went not. Thus, in these texts, the crowd selected the latter as the son having done the will of the father. For example, the New English Bible records the account as:

But what do you think about this? A man had two sons. He went to the first, and said, "My boy, go and work today in the vineyard." "I will, sir," the boy replied; but he never went. The father came to the second and said the same. "I will not," he replied, but afterwards he changed his mind and went. Which of these two did as his father wished? "The second," they said.

Elder James E. Talmage sees in these two sons some interesting parallels with the Pharisees and the publicans and sinners:

The opening sentence, "But what think ye?" was a call to close attention. It implied a question soon to follow; and that proved to be: Which of the two sons was the obedient one? There was but one consistent answer, and they had to give it, however loath. The application of the parable followed with convicting promptness. They, the chief priests, scribes, Pharisees and elders of the people, were typified by the second son, who, when told to labor in the vineyard answered so assuringly, but went not, though the vines were running to wild growth for want of pruning, and such poor fruit as might mature would be left to fall and rot upon the ground. The publicans and sinners upon whom they vented their contempt, whose touch was defilement, were like unto the first son, who in rude though frank refusal ignored the father's call, but afterward relented and set to work, repentantly hoping to make amends for the time he had lost and for the unfilial spirit he had shown. (JTC, p. 532.)

21:31 In this statement Jesus does two things: (1) He testifies that the ministry of John was of God, that the Baptist was a legal administrator whose teachings and priestly performances did in fact prepare men for salvation in the kingdom of God; and (2) He teaches in forceful and plain language that repentance is a living, abiding principle which actually works. "Christ Jesus came into the world to save sinners." (1 Tim. 1:15.) What, publicans and harlots in the kingdom of God! Yes, and even the chief priests, scribes, and elders—if they also repent and keep the commandments. (DNTC 1:589–90.)

21:32 The Joseph Smith Translation adds the following after this verse:

For he that believed not John concerning me, cannot believe me, except he first repent.

And except ye repent, the preaching of John shall condemn you in the day of judgment.

Christ and his prophets cannot be separated from each other. Men cannot believe in one and not the other. John was a true prophet who bore record that Jesus was the Messiah. Accordingly no one could accept John as a prophet without believing in Christ; and conversely, no one could believe in the divine Sonship of Jesus without accepting the Baptist as his forerunner and witness.

Similarly, Joseph Smith is the prophet through whom the divinity of Christ is revealed to the modern world. Accordingly, for this day, a belief in the divine mission of either presupposes an acceptance of the legality and divinity of the ministry of the other. (DNTC 1:590.)

21:33–46 (Read Mark 12:1–12; Luke 20:9–19.) The interpretation of the major symbols helps to make this parable more understandable:

the householder: God

the vineyard: the earth and its inhabitants

the husbandmen: the priests and teachers of Israel

the servants: prophets, teachers, and missionaries

the son and heir: Jesus Christ

Deity's dealings with men from the creation of Adam down to the Second Coming of the Son of Man are summarized in the *Parable of the Wicked Husbandmen*.

God himself is the householder; his vineyard is the earth and its inhabitants; and the husbandmen appointed to work in the vineyard are the spiritual overseers of the people. Those who are stoned, beaten, persecuted, and killed are the prophets and seers sent to minister among men; and the Son and Heir, slain and cast out of the vineyard at the instigation of the wicked husbandmen, is of course Jesus.

For rejecting the Stone of Israel, the Church and kingdom was to be taken from the Jews and given to the Gentiles. Those Jews who rejected and slew the Heir were to be destroyed, as was also later to be the case with the Gentiles in the day of their apostasy and rejection of the "head of the corner." Finally, "in the last days," the vineyard was to be let out to other husbandmen preparatory to the return of the Lord to "reign in his vineyard." (DNTC 1:593–94.)

(See BD, "Vine.")

21:34 For examples of prophets who had been persecuted by Israel's religious leaders, see Jeremiah 26:20–24; 37:15–21; 38:6; 2 Chronicles 24:18–22; Nehemiah 9:26. According to tradition, Isaiah was sawn in two.

21:37 "Reverence" could have been translated "respect."

21:46 (See JST Matt. 21:47–56.) This verse could have been translated, "But, although they were seeking to seize him, they feared the crowds, because these held him to be a prophet."

22:1–14 (Compare Luke 14:16–24. See also D&C 121:34–40.) This parable has been called both the "Parable of the Royal Marriage Feast" and the "Parable of the King's Son."

The king in the parable is God; the son whose marriage was the occasion of the feast is Jesus, the Son of God; the guests who were bidden early, yet who refused to come when the feast was ready, are the covenant people who rejected their Lord, the Christ; the later guests, who were brought in from the streets and the roads, are the Gentile nations, to whom the gospel has been carried since its rejection by the Jews; the marriage feast is symbolical of the glorious consummation of the Messiah's mission. (JTC, pp. 537–38.)

22:2 This glorious event, still future, has reference to the ushering in of Messiah's millennial reign, the day when he shall reign in triumph and glory over all the earth. By their preaching in this present dispensation, the "servants" of the King are inviting guests to come to the marriage supper of the Lamb. "For this cause I have sent you," the Lord says to his modern missionaries, "that a feast of fat things might be prepared for the poor; yea, a feast of fat things, of wine on the lees well refined, that the earth may know that the mouths of the prophets shall not fail; Yea, a supper of the house of the Lord, well prepared, unto which *all nations shall be invited*. First, the rich and the learned, the wise and the noble; And after that cometh the day of my power; then shall the poor, the lame, and the blind, and the deaf, come in unto the marriage of the Lamb, and partake of the supper of the Lord, prepared for the great day to come." (D&C 58:6–11; 65:3.)

That a royal marriage feast would signal the beginning of the Messiah's triumphant reign had been revealed to the prophets of old. (Zeph. 1:7–8.) Among the Jews of Jesus' day, however, the doctrine had been diluted and distorted. According to rabbinical tradition, only the seed of Abraham would be invited while the Gentile peoples would remain hungry and unfed. (DNTC 1:597.)

22:3–4 The Joseph Smith Translation of verse 3 begins, "And when the marriage was ready . . ."

"Bidden" could have been translated either "invited" or "called."

The Joseph Smith Translation adds information to the ending of verse 4: "Behold, I have prepared my oxen, and my fatlings have been killed, and my dinner is ready, and all things are prepared; therefore come unto the marriage."

22:5 The Greek term translated "But they made light of it" has the basic meaning of "having not cared." Thus, this phrase could have been translated "But unconcerned they went off."

22:7 The "city" of the people to whom Jesus was then speaking was literally destroyed within forty years by the Romans.

But when the king heard *that his servants were dead,* he was wroth; and he sent forth his armies, and destroyed those murderers, and burned up their city. (JST; Italics added.)

22:9 "Into the highways" has frequently been translated "to the street corners" and "main streets."

22:10 "Bad" could more literally have been translated "wicked."

22:11 The "wedding garment" has reference to "robes of righteousness":

[This guest] had accepted the invitation (the gospel); joined with the true worshipers (come into the true Church); but had not put on the robes of righteousness (that is, had not worked out his salvation after baptism).

In using this figure Jesus was harking back to what Zephaniah had said about the Second Coming: "Hold thy peace at the presence of the Lord God: for the day of the Lord is at hand: for the Lord hath prepared a sacrifice, *he hath bid his guests*. And it shall come to pass in that day of the Lord's sacrifice, that I will punish the princes, and the king's children, and *all such as are clothed with strange apparel*." (Zeph. 1:7–8.)

Similar imagery was used by the angelic ministrant who, speaking in the Lord's name, told the Revelator, John, of these same events: "Let us be glad and rejoice, and give honour to him: for the marriage of the Lamb is come, and his wife hath made herself ready. And to her was granted that she should be arrayed in fine linen, clean and white; for the fine linen is the righteousness of saints. And he saith unto me, Write, Blessed are they which are called unto the marriage supper of the Lamb." (Rev. 19:7–9.) (DNTC 1:598–99.)

22:14 The Joseph Smith Translation adds, "wherefore all do not have on the wedding garment."

22:15–22 (Read Mark 12:13–17; Luke 20:20–26.) If Jesus had answered yes, he would have enabled the Pharisees to turn the people against him, for the Jews hated the Romans and did not want to be subject to them. If he had answered no, the Herodians could have taken him for trial before the Roman courts for treason, or, at the very least, for sedition and rebellion.

The wisdom of this answer defines the limitations of dual sovereigns and defines the jurisdiction of the two empires of heaven and earth. The image of monarchs stamped on coins denotes that temporal things belong to the temporal sovereign. The image of God stamped on the heart and soul of a man denotes that all its facilities and powers belong to God and should be employed in his service. . . .

In the present day of unrest, the question might appropriately be asked, what do we owe to Caesar? To the country in which we live? We owe allegiance, respect, and honor. Laws enacted to promote the welfare of the whole and suppress evil doing are to be strictly obeyed. We must pay tribute to sustain the government in the necessary expense incurred in the protection of life, liberty, property, and in promoting the welfare of all persons. (Howard W. Hunter, CR, Apr. 1968, p. 65.)

22:15 The Jewish authorities continued unceasingly active in their determined efforts to tempt or beguile Jesus into some act or utterance on which they could base a charge of offense, under either their own or Roman law. The Pharisees counseled together as to "how they might entangle him in his talk"; and then, laying aside their partisan prejudices, they conspired to this end with the Herodians, a political faction whose chief characteristic was the purpose of maintaining in power the family of the Herods, which policy of necessity entailed the upholding of the Roman power, upon which the Herods depended for their delegated authority. The same incongruous association had been entered into before in an attempt to provoke Jesus to overt speech or action in Galilee; and the Lord had coupled the parties together in His warning to the disciples to beware of the leaven of both. So, on the last day of our Lord's teaching in public, Pharisees and Herodians joined forces against Him; the one watchful for the smallest technical infringement of the Mosiac law, the other alert to seize upon the slightest excuse for charging Him with disloyalty to the secular powers. Their plans were conceived in treachery, and put into operation as the living embodiment of a lie. (JTC, p. 544.)

22:16 The Herodians constituted a politico-religious party who favored the plans of the Herods under the professed belief that through that dynasty alone could the status of the Jewish people be maintained and a reestablishment of the nation be secured. We find mention of the Herodians laying aside their partisan antipathies and acting in concert with the Pharisees in the effort to convict the Lord Jesus and bring Him to death. (JTC, p. 68.)

22:17 The Greek term translated "tribute" has the basic meaning of "head tax." Virtually all modern versions translate the term as "tax." (See BD, "Caesar.")

22:18 The question of the Savior could have been translated "Why do you put me to the test, hypocrites?"

22:20–21 Every human soul is stamped with the image and superscription of God, however blurred and indistinct the lines may have become through the corrosion or attrition of sin; and as unto Caesar should be rendered the coins upon which his effigy appeared, so unto God should be given the souls that bear his image. Render unto the world the stamped pieces that are made legally current by the insignia of worldly powers, and give unto God and his service, yourselves—the divine mintage of his eternal realm. (JTC, pp. 546–47.)

22:22 "Marvelled" has also been translated "were amazed." The basic meaning is that the reply of Jesus took the people by surprise and they were baffled at it.

Pharisees and Herodians were silenced by the unanswerable wisdom of the Lord's reply to their crafty question. Try as they would, they could not "take hold of his words," and they were put to shame before the people who were witnesses to their humiliation. Marveling at His answer, and unwilling to take the chance of further and possibly greater embarrassment, they "left him, and went their way." Nevertheless these perverted Jews persisted in their base and treacherous purpose, as appears nowhere more glaringly evident than in their utterly false accusation before Pilate—that Jesus was guilty of "forbidding to give tribute to Caesar, saying that he himself is Christ a King." [Luke 23:2] (JTC, p. 547.)

22:23–33 (Read Mark 12:18–27; Luke 20:27–40.) The teaching of Moses to which the Sadducees referred is found in Deuteronomy 25:5–6, and an application of it is in Ruth 4 in the marriage of Boaz and Ruth. Unfortunately, the answer by Jesus has been misinterpreted to mean that there are no family or marriage relationships in heaven after the resurrection:

This colloquy between Jesus and his Saducean detractors does not question or throw doubt, in proper cases, on the eternal verity that the family unit continues in the resurrection. Jesus had previously taught the eternal nature of the marriage union. "What therefore God [not man!] hath joined together, let no man put asunder." That is, when a marriage is performed by God's authority—not man's!—it is eternal. See Matt. 19:1–12. "Whatsoever God doeth, it shall be for ever." (Eccles. 3:14.) . . .

The Saducean effort here is based on the assumption that Jesus and the Jews generally believe in marriage in heaven. They are using this commonly accepted concept to ridicule and belittle the fact of the resurrection itself. They are saying: "How absurd to believe in a resurrection (and therefore in the fact that there is marriage in heaven) when everybody knows that a woman who has had seven husbands could not have them all at once in the life to come."

A most instructive passage showing that the Jews believed there should be marriage in heaven is found in *Dummelow*. "There was some division of opinion among the rabbis as to whether resurrection would be to a natural or to a supernatural (spiritual) life," he says. "A few took the spiritual view, e.g. Rabbi Raf is reported to have often said, 'In the world to come they shall neither eat, nor drink, nor beget children, nor trade. There is neither envy nor strife, but the just shall sit with crowns on their heads, and shall enjoy the splendor of the Divine Majesty.' But the majority inclined to a materialistic view of the resurrection. The pre-Christian book of Enoch says that *the righteous after the resurrection shall live so long that they shall beget thousands*. The received doctrine is laid down by Rabbi Saadia, who says, 'As the son of the widow of Sarepton, and the son of the Shunamite, *ate and drank, and doubtless married wives, so shall it be in the resurrection'*; and by Maimonides, who says, *'Men after the resurrection will use meat and drink, and will beget children, because since the Wise Architect makes nothing in vain, it follows of necessity that the members of the body are not useless, but fulfill their functions.'* The point raised by the Sadducees was often debated by the Jewish doctors, who decided that *'a woman who married two husbands in this world is restored to the first in the next." (Dummelow,* p. 698.) (DNTC 1:604–5.)

(See section 1, "Marriage"; BD, "Levirate marriage.")

22:24 This verse could have been translated "Teacher, Moses said, If any man dies without having children, his brother must take his wife in marriage and raise up offspring for his brother."

22:29 This verse could have been translated "In reply Jesus said to them: You are mistaken, because you know neither the scriptures nor the power of God."

President Joseph F. Smith has made it clear that these people did not understand the principle of eternal marriage or at least did not believe it:

They did not understand the principle of sealing for time and for all eternity; that what God hath joined together neither man nor death can put asunder. (Matt. 19:6.) They had wandered from that principle. It had fallen into disuse among them; they had ceased to understand it; and consequently they did not comprehend the truth; but Christ did. She could only be the wife in eternity of the man to whom she was united by the power of God for eternity, as well as for time; and Christ understood the principle, but he did not cast his pearls before the swine that tempted him. (GD, p. 280.)

22:30 For additional teachings of the Lord concerning the eternity of the marriage covenant under certain conditions met by the righteous, read D&C 131:1–4 and 132:5–17. These scriptures also further explain the term "angels of God in heaven."

What then is the Master Teacher affirming by saying, "in the resurrection *they* neither marry, nor are given in marriage, but are as the angels of God in heaven"?

He is not *denying* but *limiting* the prevailing concept that there will be marrying and giving in marriage in heaven. He is saying that as far as "they" (the Sadducees) are concerned, that as far as "they" ("the children of this world") are concerned, the family unit does not and will not continue in the resurrection. Because he does not choose to cast his pearls before swine, and because the point at issue is not *marriage* but *resurrection* anyway, Jesus does not here amplify his teaching to explain that there is marrying and giving of marriage in heaven only for those who live the fulness of gospel law—a requirement which excludes *worldly* people. (DNTC 1:605–6.)

22:32 The combining of these two concepts by the Savior indicates clearly that a person cannot honestly say he believes the scriptures and yet does not believe in life after death. Why? Because the scriptures teach that God is the God of Abraham, Isaac, and Jacob; and the scriptures teach that God is God of the living. Both of these concepts are taught in the scriptures *after* the physical deaths of Abraham, Isaac, and Jacob; therefore these patriarchs must *still be living,* even though their physical bodies might still be in the tombs. No wonder "when the multitude heard this, they were astonished at his doctrine." (V. 33.)

Elder Bruce R. McConkie has effectively paraphrased these verses:

"You say Jehovah is the God of Abraham, Isaac, and Jacob, and at the same time claim there is no resurrection. But you know that God is not the God of the dead but of the living, and therefore Abraham, Isaac, and Jacob live and will rise in the resurrection; hence, your doctrine that life ceases with death is false" Or: "You believe there is a God; you deny there is a resurrection. Is God the God only of the dead? Is he a failure? Is there no purpose in creation? Or could it be that you have erred and that there is in reality a resurrection?" (DNTC 1:608.)

22:33 "Doctrine" is frequently translated "teaching."

22:34–40 (Read Mark 12:28–34. Compare Luke 10:5–37.) The Greek word translated "tempting" in verse 35 has the basic meaning of "testing." (See section 1, "Tempt.") Evidently the Pharisees were ready to bring all the other laws against the one the Savior would select as the "great commandment." However, Jesus did not select one of the ten commandments; rather he reiterated the basic teaching that provides the undergirding for "all the law and the teachings of the prophets," which teaching he himself had given earlier as Jehovah to Moses. (See Deut. 6:4–5; Lev. 19:18. Also, review D&C 42:29; 59:5–6; John 14:15; and 1 John 4:20–21.)

Concerning the multitudinous laws of the Jews, Farrar has written in his *Life of Christ,* chapter 52:

> The Rabbinical schools, in their meddling, carnal, superficial spirit of word-weaving and letter-worship, had spun large accumulations of worthless subtlety all over the Mosaic law. Among other things they had wasted their idleness in fantastic attempts to count, and classify, and weigh, and measure all the separate commandments of the ceremonial and moral law. They had come to the sapient conclusion that there were 248 affirmative precepts, being as many as the members in the human body, and 365 negative precepts, being as many as the arteries and veins, or the days of the year; the total being 613, which was also the number of letters in the decalog. They arrived at the same result from the fact that the Jews were commanded (Numb. 15:38) to wear fringes (*tsitsith*) on the corners of their *tallith,* bound with a thread of blue; and as each fringe had eight threads and five knots, and the letters of the word *tsitsith* make 600, the total number of commandments was, as before 613. Now surely, out of such a large number of precepts and prohibitions, *all* could not be of quite the same value; some were 'light' (*kal*), and some were 'heavy' (*kobhed*). But which? and what was the greatest commandment of all? According to some Rabbis, the most important of all is that about the *tephillin* and the *tsitsith,* the fingers and phylacteries; and "he who diligently observes it is regarded in the same light as if he had kept the whole Law."
>
> Some thought the omission of ablutions as bad as homicide; some that the precepts of the Mishna were all "heavy"; those of the Law were some "heavy" and some "light." Others considered the *third* to be the greatest commandment. None of them had realized the great principle, that the wilful violation of one commandment is the transgression of all (James 2:10), because the object of the entire Law is the spirit of *obedience to God.* (Quoted in JTC, pp. 564–65.)

22:35 See BD, "Lawyer."

22:37–40 One eternal command!—supreme above all others; comprehending all lesser requirements; embracing the whole law of the whole gospel; blazing forth like the sun with a brilliance beyond compare—one divine decree! "Thou shalt love thy God and thy neighbor."

In every age the counsel of God has been to worship, love, and serve the living God and to feel after the welfare of one's fellowmen with solicitude and charity. (Moses 6:33; Luke 4:8.) When Jesus here selected the chief commands of importance to man, he was but quoting, first, what Moses had said as the climax of his restatement of the law to Israel (Deut. 6:4–5), and, then, what he himself as the Lord Jehovah had said to that same people. (Lev. 19:18.) The genius of his organization lay in the insight with which he picked out from among all the revelations the two requirements which exceed in importance all others. (DNTC 1:609.)

(See section 1, "Love, gospel of.")

22:41–46 (Read Mark 12:34–37; Luke 20:41–44.) The statement of David quoted by Jesus is found in Psalm 110:1: "The Lord said unto my Lord."

Many scriptures indicate that the Messiah would be of the loins of David and thus would rightfully be called the Son of David. However, Jesus Christ as the pre-earthly Jehovah and as the Only Begotten Son of God in the flesh presides over David, even though through His earthly mother, Mary, He might also be called a son of David. (See section 1, "Son of David.")

23:1–22 For similar denunciations of hypocrisy by Jesus, read Mark 12:38–40; Luke 11:37–54; 20:45–47. See BD, "Pharisees."

How scathingly Jesus condemns false teachers, apostate ministers, priestly administrators devoid of divine authority—all who teach anything except revealed truth. The scribes and rabbis of his day are but types and shadows of the blind guides of any age. Religious leaders must teach the truth or face for themselves the same excoriating and damning condemnation as that heaped by an indignant Lord upon the blind guides of his day. (DNTC 1:615.)

As God condemns immorality, so he denounces hypocrisy, which is one of the worst forms of dishonesty. When he describes the hell of the world to come, he specifies that dishonest persons will go there. As no unclean thing can enter the presence of the Lord, so no liar nor cheat nor hypocrite can abide in his kingdom.

Dishonesty is directly related to selfishness, which is its origin and source. Selfishness is at the root of nearly all the disorders that afflict us, and man's inhumanity to man continues to make countless thousands mourn. (Mark E. Petersen, CR, Oct. 1971, pp. 63–64.)

23:3 This verse could have been translated "Therefore all the things they tell you, do and observe, but do not do according to their deeds, for they say but do not perform."

The Joseph Smith Translation is: "All, therefore, whatsoever they bid you observe, *they will make you* observe and do; *for they are ministers of the law, and they make themselves your judges.* But do not ye after their works; for they say, and do not." (JST; italics added.)

23:5 The first clause could have been translated "All the works they do, they do to be viewed by men."

As a phylactery is a small box made to contain copies of selected scriptures, the Greek clause could have been literally translated "for they broaden the scripture-containing cases that they wear as safeguards, and enlarge the fringes of their garments." The Living Bible refers to phylacteries as "little prayer boxes with Scripture verses inside."

The use of phylacteries had developed in ancient Israel, apparently in response to their interpretation of Exodus 13:9, 16 and Deuteronomy 6:8 and 11:18.

Through a traditional interpretation of Exo. 13:9 and Deut. 6:8, the Hebrews adopted the custom of wearing phylacteries, which consisted essentially of strips of parchment on which were inscribed in whole or in part the following texts: Exo. 13:2–10 and 11–17; Deut. 6:4–9, and 11:13–21. Phylacteries were worn on the head and arm. The parchment strips for the head were four, on each of which one of the texts cited above was written. These were placed in a cubical box of leather measuring from 1/2 inch to 1 1/2 inches along the edge; the box was divided into four compartments and one of the little parchment rolls was placed in each. Thongs held the box in place on the forehead between the eyes of the wearer. The arm phylactery comprized but a single roll of parchment on which the four prescribed texts were written; this was placed in a little box which was bound by thongs to the inside of the left arm so as to be brought close to the heart when the hands were placed together in the attitude of devotion. The Pharisees wore the arm phylactery above the elbow, while their rivals, the Sadducees, fastened it to the palm on the hand (see Exo. 13:9). The common people wore phylacteries only at prayer time; but the Pharisees were said to display them throughout the day. Our Lord's reference to the Pharisees' custom of making broad their phylacteries had reference to the enlarging of the containing box, particularly the frontlet. The size of the parchment strips was fixed by rigid rule.

The Lord had required of Israel through Moses (Numb. 15:38) that the people attach to the border of their garment a fringe with a ribbon of blue. In ostentatious display of assumed piety, the scribes and Pharisees delighted to wear enlarged borders to attract public attention. It was another manifestation of hypocritical sanctimoniousness. (JTC, pp. 565–66.)

(See section 1, "Phylacteries.")

23:7–8 The Joseph Smith Translation adds "which is master" at the end of verse 7.

There are many titles of respect that are appropriate at certain times. The Savior is not condemning their use, but is more concerned about the vanity that results.

Such titles of respect as Brother, Elder, Bishop, or Rabbi, are appropriate and proper when used discreetly and with respect for the office or status involved. What Jesus here condemns is not the use of titles as such, but the vainglory and presumptuous self-adulation which called forth their excessive and patronizing use. Indeed, it would appear . . . that these religious leaders were so wrapped up in their own conceit that they ranked themselves along with Deity in importance. "The rabbis really did put themselves in the place of God, and almost on an equality with him. Their traditions were more binding than the Law, and were regarded as in a sense binding upon God." (*Dummelow,* p. 700.) (DNTC 1:617.)

(See section 1, "Rabbi.")

Elder James E. Talmage discusses the use of ecclesiastical titles and provides background on the title *Rabbi:*

Our Lord severely condemned the seeking after titles as insignia of rank in His service. Nevertheless He named the Twelve whom He chose, Apostles; and in the Church founded by Himself the offices of Evangelist, High Priest, Pastor, Elder, Bishop, Priest, Teacher, and Deacon were established (see *Articles of Faith,* xi:1–4). It was the empty man-made title that attached to the individual, not the authorized title of office to which men were called through authoritative ordination, to which the Lord affixed the seal of His disapproval. Titles of office in the Holy Priesthood are of too sacred a character to be used as marks of distinction among men. In the restored Church in the current dispensation, men are ordained to the Priesthood and to the several offices comprized within both the Lesser or Aaronic, and the Higher or Melchizedek Priesthood; but though one be thus made an Elder, a Seventy, a High Priest, a Patriarch or an Apostle, he should not court the usage of the title as a mere embellishment of his name. (JTC, p. 566.)

The title Rabbi is equivalent to our distinctive appellations Doctor, Master, or Teacher. By derivation it means Master or my Master, thus connoting dignity and rank associated with politeness of address. A definite explanation of the term is given by John (1:38), and the same meaning attaches by implication to its use as recorded by Matthew (23:8). It was applied as a title of respect to Jesus on several occasions (Matt. 23:7, 8; 26:25, 49; Mark 9:5; 11:21; 14:45; John 1:38, 49; 3:2, 26; 4:31; 6:25; 9:2; 11:8). The title was of comparatively recent usage in the time of Christ, as it appears to have first come into general use during the reign of Herod the Great, though the earlier teachers, of the class without the name of Rabbis, were generally reverenced, and the title was carried back to them by later usage. Rab was an inferior title and Rabban a superior one to Rabbi. Rabboni was expressive of most profound respect, love and honor (see John 20:16). At the time of our Lord's ministry the Rabbis were held in high esteem, and rejoiced in the afflations of precedence and honor among men. They were almost exclusively of the powerful Pharisaic party. (JTC, p. 71.)

Scribes and rabbis were exalted to the highest rank in the estimation of the people, higher than that of the Levitical or priestly orders; and rabbinical sayings were given precedence over the utterances of the prophets, since the latter were regarded as but messengers or spokesmen, whereas the living scholars were of themselves sources of wisdom and authority. Such secular powers as Roman suzerainty permitted the Jews to retain were vested in the hierarchy, whose members were able thus to gather unto themselves practically all official and professional honors. As a natural result of this condition, there was practically no distinction between Jewish civil and ecclesiastical law, either as to the code or its administration. Rabbinism comprized as an essential element the doctrine of the equal authority of oral rabbinical tradition with the written word of the law. The aggrandizement implied in the application of the title "Rabbi" and the self-pride manifest in welcoming such adulation were especially forbidden by the Lord, who proclaimed Himself the one Master; and, as touching the interpretation of the title held by some as "father," Jesus proclaimed but one Father and He in heaven; "But be not ye called Rabbi: for one is your Master, even Christ; and all ye are brethren. And call no man your father upon the earth: for one is your Father, which is in heaven. Neither be ye called masters: for one is your Master, even Christ." [Matt. 23:8–10; see also John 1:38; 3:2.] (JTC, p. 64.)

23:9–10 And call no *one your creator* upon the earth, *or your heavenly Father;* for one is your *creator and heavenly Father, even he who* is in heaven.

Neither be ye called Master; for one is your master, *even he whom your heavenly Father sent, which* is Christ; *for he* hath *sent him among you that ye might have life.* (JST; italics added.)

23:12 "Abased" could have been translated "humbled."

23:14 This verse is omitted in the Westcott and Hort Greek text and thus in many modern translations.

"Ye devour widows' houses" has been translated "while you are evicting widows from their homes" and "You take advantage of widows and rob them of their homes."

"Damnation" is changed to "punishment" in the Joseph Smith Translation.

23:15 "Compass sea" means "go about the sea," and in this context could have been translated "traverse the sea."

One Ethiopic version reads, "to baptize one proselyte,"

which would indicate along with Joseph Smith Translation Matthew 9:18 that the Pharisees were baptizing at the time of Jesus: "Then said the Pharisees unto him, Why will ye not receive us with our baptism, seeing we keep the whole law?"

The end of this verse in the Joseph Smith Translation is "ye make him twofold more the child of hell *than he was before, like unto yourselves*." (Italics added.)

23:16–22 In the Sermon on the Mount, Jesus had earlier given instructions against the use of oaths. (See Matt. 5:31–37.) Here he is denouncing particular oaths used by these apostate leaders:

> Thus did the Lord condemn the infamous enactments of the schools and the Sanhedrin concerning oaths and vows; for they had established or endorsed a code of rules, inconsistent and unjust, as to technical trifles by which a vow could be enforced or invalidated. If a man swore by the temple, the House of Jehovah, he could obtain an indulgence for breaking his oath; but if he vowed by the gold and treasure of the Holy House, he was bound by the unbreakable bonds of priestly dictum. Though one should swear by the altar of God, his oath could be annulled; but if he vowed by the corban gift or by the gold upon the altar, his obligation was imperative. To what depths of unreason and hopeless depravity had men fallen, how sinfully foolish and how wilfully blind were they, who saw not that the temple was greater than its gold, and the altar than the gift that lay upon it! (JTC, p. 556.)

(See section 1, "Oaths.")

23:17 "For whether is greater" could have been translated "Which, in fact, is greater."

23:18, 20 The Joseph Smith Translation begins verse 18 with "And ye say" and verse 20 with "Verily I say unto you." Thus, the sayings in verses 18 and 19 are from the "fools and blind," whereas verse 20 begins the statement by Jesus.

23:23–24 (Read Luke 11:42.) The law of tithing, which has been defined as one-tenth of a person's increase annually, has apparently been required of the faithful from earliest times. (See Malachi 3:8 and D&C 119.) Here the Savior reaffirms that law, but also teaches another principle, according to Elder McConkie:

> Charitable contributions for other worthy causes, whether ecclesiastical or otherwise, are commendable and soul enlarging, but tithing is a payment of a tenth as tithing and for tithing purposes. (*Mormon Doctrine*, pp. 719–721.)

Observance of the law of tithing is one of the essential identifying characteristics of the true Church. Where the true Church is, there the law of tithing will be preached and practiced. Where such a course is not pursued, there the true Church is not found.

According to Mosaic requirements, flocks and herds, fruits and grains, all should be tithed. (Lev. 27:30–34; Deut. 14:22–28.) Here we find Jesus endorsing such a course, even as it applied to the herbs and small items grown in the garden.

The sin of those false religious leaders lay in their ostentatious display of paying tithing on every grain of sand and blade of grass, as it were, while they transgressed the "whole law."

Self-righteous religionists might also learn from the passage that it is easier to pay an honest tithing than to manifest in one's soul the godly attributes of justice, mercy, and faith; the one, comparatively speaking, is lesser in importance; the others are "the weightier matters of the law." (DNTC 1:618–19.)

The law of the tithe had been a characteristic feature of the theocratic requirements in Israel from the days of Moses; and the practice really long antedated the exodus. As literally construed, the law required the tithing of flocks and herds, fruit and grain, but by traditional extension all products of the soil had been included. The conscientious tithing of all one's possessions, even potherbs and other garden produce, was approved by the Lord; but He denounced as rank hypocrisy the observance of such requirements as an excuse for neglecting the other duties of true religion. The reference to "the weightier matters of the law" may have been an allusion to the rabbinical classification of "light" and "heavy" requirements under the law; though it is certain the Lord approved no such arbitrary distinctions. To omit the tithing of small things, such as mint leaves, and sprigs of anise and cummin, was to fall short in dutiful observance; but to ignore the claims of judgment, mercy, and faith, was to forfeit one's claim to blessing as a covenant child of God. By a strong simile, the Lord stigmatized such inconsistency as comparable to one's scrupulous straining at the gnat while figuratively willing to gulp down a camel. (JTC, p. 557.)

(See BD, "Anise," "Cummin," "Tithe.")

23:24 This verse could have been translated "Blind guides, who strain out the gnat but gulp down the camel!"

The Joseph Smith Translation completes this verse "who make yourselves appear unto men that ye would not commit the least sin, and yet you yourselves transgress the whole law."

23:25–28 (Read Luke 11:37–44.) The two examples mentioned by Jesus are concerned with the outward appearance being one thing while the inner actuality is another.

It has seemed to me that the one sin that the Savior condemned as much as any other was the sin of hypocrisy—the living of the double life, the life we let our friends and sometimes our wives believe, and the life we actually live. (J. Reuben Clark, Jr., *Church News,* 2 Feb. 1963, p. 16.)

"Whited sepulchres" means "whitewashed graves" or "whitewashed tombs." (See BD, "Burial.")

23:29–33 (Read Luke 11:45–48.) "Garnish the sepulchres of the righteous" has been translated "lay flowers on the graves of the godly men," "decorate monuments for good men of the past," "embellish the monuments of the saints," and "decorate the monuments of those who lived good lives."

The wicked have always found it easier to believe in and claim to follow the dead prophets than to follow those who are living, according to Elder Bruce R. McConkie:

> "Dead prophets, Yes; living prophets, No!" Such is the pious feeling of sanctimonious though worldly religionists in every age. Almost all men, Christians and Jews alike, revere dead prophets; almost none cleave unto the Lord's living representatives. Today men build houses of worship to Peter and Paul while they persecute and kill Joseph Smith and the living oracles. There seems to be a conscience soothing comfort in acclaiming a dead prophet while slaying a living one. . . .
>
> What pure, unadulterated hypocrisy it is for those who reject the living prophets to say: "If we had lived in former days, we would have accepted the prophets whom others rejected." Prophets are prophets, truth is truth, and rebellion is rebellion. The spirit which leads men to fight God in one age is the same that operates in every age. Those who reject the Lord's anointed today would have done so anciently. (DNTC 1:621–22.)

23:32 The Joseph Smith Translation explains how they will fill up the measure of their fathers: "And will fill up the measure of your fathers; *for ye, yourselves, kill the prophets like unto your fathers.*" (Italics added.)

23:33 "How can ye escape the damnation of hell" has also been translated "how are you to escape being sentenced to hell" and "How do you expect to escape from being condemned to hell."

23:34–36 (Read Luke 11:49–51.) "I send unto your prophets" clearly indicates that Jesus Christ, as the preearthly Jehovah, was the one who sent prophets to earlier Israel, as he is also the one who sends prophets in any dispensation.

After quoting Matthew 23:36, Joseph Smith explained:

> Hence as they possessed greater privileges than any other generation, not only pertaining to themselves, but to their dead, their sin was greater, as they not only neglected their own salvation but that of their progenitors, and hence their blood [that of the progenitors] was required at their hands. (TPJS pp. 222–23.)

23:35 The reference to "Zacharias son of Barachias, whom ye slew between the temple and the altar" has generally been considered by Bible scholars to refer to the death of Zechariah son of Jehoiada whose death is recorded in 2 Chronicles 24:15–24. However, "whom ye slew" seems to indicate that Jesus was referring to an event that might have directly involved some of his listeners at that time:

> When Herod's edict went forth to destroy the young children, John was about six months older than Jesus, and came under this hellish edict, and Zacharias caused his mother to take him into the mountains, where he was raised on locusts and wild honey. When his father refused to disclose his hiding place, and being the officiating high priest at the Temple that year, was slain by Herod's order, between the porch and the altar, as Jesus said. (TPJS, p. 261.)

(See commentary for Matt. 2:16–18; section 1, "John the Baptist: Escaped the slaughter.")

23:36 The Joseph Smith Translation adds the following after this verse:

> Ye bear testimony against your fathers, when ye, yourselves, are partakers of the same wickedness.
>
> Behold your fathers did it through ignorance, but ye do not; wherefore, their sins shall be upon your heads.
>
> Then Jesus began to weep over Jerusalem, saying, . . .

23:37–39 (Read Luke 13:34–35.) "Ye would not" in verse 37 means "you people did not want it."

Jesus' desire to gather his people together in righteousness is a sign of his divine Sonship and of his role as the God of the Old Testament. In modern times, he has repeated this lament concerning the peoples of today. (See D&C 43:24.)

23:38 "Your house" could refer to the temple, to the city of Jerusalem, to the land of Israel, or to any combination of these.

Elder James E. Talmage related this term to the temple:

> The stupendous temple, which but a day before the Lord had called "My house," was now no longer specifically His; "Your house," said He, "is left unto you desolate." He was about to withdraw from both temple and nation; and by the Jews His face was not again to be seen, until, through the discipline of centuries of suffering they shall be prepared to acclaim in accents of abiding faith, as some of them had shouted but the Sunday before under the impulse of an erroneous conception, "Blessed is he that cometh in the name of the Lord." (JTC, pp. 560–61.)

23:39 The Joseph Smith Translation alters this verse and includes two additional verses. It also includes another affirmation that Jesus Christ is the promised Messiah, the son of God: "I am he of whom it is written by the prophets."

For I say unto you, *that* ye shall not see me henceforth, *and know that I am he of whom it is written by the prophets, until* ye shall say,

Blessed is he *who* cometh in the name of the Lord, *in the clouds of heaven, and all the holy angels with him.*

Then understood his disciples that he should come again on the earth, after that he was glorified and crowned on the right hand of God. (Italics added.)

24:1–51 (Read Mark 13:1–37; Luke 12:37–48; 17:20–37; 21:5–38: JS–M 1:1–55; HC 5:336.) Latter-day Saints should know more about the contents of this stirring chapter than any other people because of modern scriptures dealing with the same subject. President Harold B. Lee has referred to some of these scriptures and has indicated the importance of the subject:

There are among us many loose writings predicting the calamities which are about to overtake us. Some of these have been publicized as though they were necessary to wake up the world to the horrors about to overtake us. Many of these are from sources upon which there cannot be unquestioned reliance.

Are you priesthood bearers aware of the fact that we need no such publications to be forewarned, if we were only conversant with what the scriptures have already spoken to us in plainness?

Let me give you the sure word of prophecy on which you should rely for your guide instead of these strange sources which may have great political implications.

Read the 24th chapter of Matthew—particularly that inspired version as contained in the Pearl of Great Price. [Joseph Smith–Matthew.]

Then read the 45th section of the Doctrine and Covenants where the Lord, not man, has documented the signs of the times.

Now turn to section 101 and section 133 of the Doctrine and Covenants and hear the step-by-step recounting of events leading up to the coming of the Savior.

Finally, turn to the promises the Lord makes to those who keep the commandments when these judgments descend upon the wicked, as set forth in the Doctrine and Covenants, section 38.

Brethren, these are some of the writings with which you should concern yourselves, rather than commentaries that may come from those whose information may not be the most reliable and whose motives may be subject to question. And may I say, parenthetically, most of such writers are not handicapped by having any authentic information on their writings. (CR, Oct. 1972, p. 128.)

This chapter contains some of the greatest truths revealed about the signs of the Second Coming. The importance of these teachings is evident when the context is considered:

1. The teachings were given directly by Jesus Christ.

2. The teachings were given during the Savior's last week

upon the earth, just before his atonement, death, and resurrection.

3. The teachings were given in response to earnest questions by some of the apostles.

4. The teachings were given in private conversation with four of the Lord's most trusted apostles—Peter, James, John, and Andrew (the two sets of brothers among the Twelve).

24:1–2 Read Mark 13:1–2; Luke 21:5–6.

How aptly Jesus chooses his illustrations. To those who saw the stones, to say that not one should be left upon another, symbolized the destruction of a once stable and securely built nation. Some single stones were about 67¹/₂ feet long, 7¹/₂ feet high, and 9 feet broad; the pillars supporting the porches, all one stone, were some 37¹/₂ feet tall. It is said that when the Romans destroyed and ploughed Jerusalem, six days battering of the walls failed to dislodge these mighty stones. The temple was, of course, finally leveled to the ground, and as the stones were rooted out and scattered elsewhere so was a once secure and great nation. (DNTC 1:637.)

The prophetic announcement of the desolation and destruction of the temple was thus more than the death knell of a building, even of a sacred building that was the "Father's house." It was in fact a prediction of gloom and doom upon a nation. It was the announcement of the final end of a dispensation, the end of a kingdom, the end of the Lord's people as a distinct nation.

With the passing of the temple the Jews, as a distinct nation, also ceased. Without the symbol of all that was sacred to them, without the holy of holies where God was found, there was no longer a rallying point for them as a nation. They were ready for and in fact were scattered among all nations. (DNTC 1:637.)

24:1 According to the Joseph Smith Translation, it was Jesus who was to show the disciples concerning the buildings of the temple, not the other way around: " . . . his disciples came to him for to hear him, saying, Master, show us concerning the buildings of the temple; as thou hast said; They shall be thrown down and left unto you desolate."

24:3–5 Read Mark 13:3–6; Luke 21:7–8.

24:3 Joseph Smith explained the term "end of the world":

Now men cannot have any possible grounds to say that this is figurative, or that it does not mean what it says: for [Jesus] is now explaining what He had previously spoken in parables; and according to this language, the end of the world is the destruction of the wicked, the harvest and the end of the world have an allusion directly to the human family in the last days, instead of the earth, as many have imagined; and that which shall precede the coming of the Son of Man, and the restitution of all things spoken of by the mouth of all the holy prophets since the world began; and the angels are to have something to do in this great work, for they are the reapers. As, therefore, the tares are gathered and burned in the fire, so shall it be in the end of the world; that is, as the servants of God go forth warning the nations, both priests and people, and as they harden their hearts and reject the light of truth, these first being delivered over to the buffetings of Satan, and the law and the testimony being closed up, as it was in the case of the Jews, they are left in darkness, and delivered over unto the day of burning; thus being bound up by their creeds, and their bands being made strong by their priests, are prepared for the fulfillment of the saying of the Savior— "The Son of Man shall send forth His angels, and gather out of His Kingdom all things that offend, and them which do iniquity, and shall cast them into a furnace of fire, there shall be wailing and gnashing of teeth." We understand that the work of gathering together of the wheat into barns, or garners, is to take place while the tares are being bound over, and preparing for the day of burning; that after the day of burnings, the righteous shall shine forth like the sun, in the Kingdom of their Father. Who hath ears to hear, let him hear. (TPJS, pp. 100–101.)

The inquiry referred specifically to time—when were these things to be? The reply dealt not with dates, but with events; and the spirit of the subsequent discourse was that of warning against misapprehension, and admonition to ceaseless vigilance. (JTC, p. 570.)

Two questions are asked by the disciples: (1) "Tell us concerning the destruction of the temple and the scattering of the Jews"; and (2) "Tell us of the signs of thy Second Coming and of the end of the world."

Apparently the disciples thought these two events would be closely related in time. In reply Jesus will speak of *events* and not of *time,* and the key to understanding the whole discourse is to know which statements of our Lord pertain to the day of the ancient apostles and which to those ages following their ministries. (DNTC 1:640.)

(See section 1, "Second Coming: Signs of," "World, end of"; BD, "Christs, false," "Parousia," "Second Coming.")

24:6–8 (Read Mark 13:7–8; Luke 21:9–11.) Concerning some of the calamities prophesied in these verses, Elder Bruce R. McConkie has written:

Many revelations summarize the signs and world conditions, the wars, perils, and commotions of the last days. Preceding our Lord's return, the prophetic word tells of plagues, pestilence, famine, and disease such as the world has never before seen; of scourges, tribulation, calamities, and disasters without parallel; or strife, wars, rumors of wars, blood, carnage, and desolation which overshadow anything of past ages; of the elements being in commotion with resultant floods, storms, fires, whirlwinds, earthquakes—all of a proportion and intensity unknown to men of former days; of evil, iniquity, wickedness, turmoil, rapine, murder, crime, and commotion among men almost beyond comprehension. (MD, p. 623.)

24:7 "In divers places" means "in one place after another."

24:8 "The beginning of sorrows" has to do with "pangs of birth." Thus this verse has been translated "All these things are like the first pains of childbirth," "All this is but the beginning of the birth-pangs," and "With all these things the birth-pangs of the new age begin."

> How sobering it is to realize that the wars and desolations which precede our Lord's return are but "the beginning of sorrows." World wars, with their attendant evils; communistic conspiracy, reminiscent of Gadianton and his band; earthquakes and pestilences which desolate whole regions — all these are but "the beginning." The sorrows incident to Jesus' actual return in "the day of vengeance" (D&C 133:51) shall surpass them all. (DNTC 1:654.)

24:9 Read Mark 13:9, 11–13; Luke 21:12–19.

> If ever there was a dispensation of persecution, it was the apostolic era of old. Volumes tell of the hate and venom, of the scourgings and slayings, of the betrayals and court trials, of the murders and martyrdom, that began in Jerusalem and continued in the gladitorial arenas of Rome, until pure Christianity was no longer found among men. (DNTC 1:641.)

24:10–13 Read Mark 13:13.

24:11 That there will be "false prophets" should not be construed to mean there will not be true prophets. The importance of the warning of impending destruction suggests that God would send prophets to warn his children and that the adversary would also send forth those under his power to deceive and mislead.

> **24:12** Jesus is here speaking to and of the saints. Because of sin their love of God (which is shown by service in his Cause) will fade away; there will be apostasy from the Church. (DNTC 1:641.)

> **24:13** But he that *remaineth steadfast, and is not overcome,* the same shall be saved. (JST; italics added.)

24:14 (Read Mark 13:10.) "*This* gospel of the kingdom" and the word "again" in the Joseph Smith Translation (Matt. 24:32) suggest that the gospel taught by Jesus and his apostles would be taught again in the last days "in all the world for a witness unto all nations." Only then would "the end come."

Jesus is here announcing the restoration of the gospel in the last days. "This gospel of the kingdom" was to be preached "again" among men before the Second Coming of the Son of Man. After the great apostasy—the era during which "darkness covereth the earth, and gross darkness the minds of the people" (D&C 112:23)—a gracious God was to restore the glorious gospel anew.

This latter-day restoration of the same gospel taught by Jesus and his apostles is the most important of all the signs of the times. It is the greatest of all the events destined to occur before the end of the world, and of it many prophets have borne record. Peter said Jesus "must" remain in "heaven" until the great era of restoration—an age in which God would reveal anew "all things . . . spoken by the mouth of his holy prophets since the world began." (Acts 3:19–21.) Paul said that in this final "dispensation" God would "gather together in one all things in Christ." (Eph. 1:10.) John recorded that the restoration would come to pass through angelic ministration; that "the everlasting gospel" so restored would be preached to all the inhabitants of the earth; and that all this would transpire just before the Second Coming. (Rev. 14:6–8.) (DNTC 1:649–50.)

24:15–22 Read Mark 13:14–20; Luke 17:31–37; 21:20–24.

24:15 When you, therefore, shall see the abomination of desolation, spoken of by Daniel the prophet, *concerning the destruction of Jerusalem, then you shall* stand in the holy place; whoso readeth let him understand. (JST; italics added.)

A later verse in the Joseph Smith Translation refers to a later fulfillment of Daniel's words concerning the abomination of desolation: "And again shall the abomination of desolation, spoken by Daniel the prophet, be fulfilled."

Thus, there are two different periods of the fulfillment of the "abomination of desolation, spoken of by Daniel the prophet": the first shortly after Jesus spoke to his disciples on the Mount of Olives; the second in the latter days after the gospel shall be preached again in all the world.

Elder Bruce R. McConkie wrote of the first "abomination of desolation":

And now the ax was laid at the root of the rotted tree. Jerusalem was to pay the price. Daniel had foretold this hour when desolation, born of abomination and wickedness, would sweep the city. (Dan. 9:27; 11:31; 12:11.) Moses had said the siege would be so severe women would eat their own children. (Deut. 28.) Jesus specified the destruction would come in the days of the disciples.

And come it did, in vengeance, without restraint. Hunger exceeded human endurance; blood flowed in the streets; destruction made desolate the temple; 1,100,000 Jews were slaughtered; Jerusalem was ploughed as a field; and a remnant of a once mighty nation was scattered to the ends of the earth. The Jewish nation died, impaled on Roman spears, at the hands of Gentile overlords.

But what of the saints who dwelt in Jerusalem in that gloomy day? They heeded Jesus' warning and fled in haste. Guided by revelation, as true saints always are, they fled to Pella in Perea and were spared. (DNTC 1:644–45.)

He wrote of the second "abomination of desolation":

All the desolation and waste which attended the former destruction of Jerusalem is but prelude to the coming siege. Titus and his legions slaughtered 1,100,000 Jews, destroyed the temple and ploughed the city. In the coming reenactment of this "abomination of desolation," the whole world will be at war, Jerusalem will be the center of the conflict, every modern weapon will be used, and in the midst of the siege the Son of Man shall come, setting his foot upon the mount of Olives and fighting the battle of his saints. (Zech. 12:1–9.)

Speaking of these final battles which shall accompany his return, the Lord says: "I will gather all nations against Jerusalem to battle; and the city shall be taken, and the houses rifled, and the women ravished; and half of the city shall go forth into captivity, and the residue of the people shall not be cut off from the city." However, the final end of the conflict shall be different this time than it was anciently. "Then shall the Lord go forth," the prophetic record says, "and fight against those nations, as when he fought in the day of battle. And his feet shall stand in that day upon the mount of Olives, . . . and the Lord shall be king over all the earth." (Zech. 14.) (DNTC 1:659–60.)

(See BD, "Abomination of Desolation."
24:18 "Clothes" means "outer garment."
24:21–22

King James Version	Joseph Smith Translation
21 For then shall be great tribulation, such as was not since the beginning of the world to this time, no, nor ever shall be.	18 For then, in those days, shall be great tribulations on the Jews, and upon the inhabitants of Jerusalem; such as was not before sent upon Israel, of God, since the beginning of their kingdom until this time; no, nor ever shall be sent again upon Israel.
8 All these are the beginning of sorrows.	19 All things which have befallen them, are only the beginning of the sorrows which shall come upon them; and except those days should be shortened, there should none of their flesh be saved.
22 And except those days should be shortened, there should not flesh be saved: but for the elect's sake those days shall be shortened.	

Joseph Smith Translation
20 But for the elect's sake,
according to the covenant,
those days shall be shortened.
21 Behold these things I
have spoken unto you
concerning the Jews.

24:22 "For the elect's sake" means "for the sake of God's chosen people."

24:23–27 (Read Mark 13:21–23; Luke 17:22–25.) The Joseph Smith Translation indicates that verse 22 essentially ends the prophecies of Jesus concerning the destruction of Jerusalem and the scattering of the Jews. Beginning with verse 23, he answers the other questions asked by the apostles concerning the "sign of thy coming and of the end of the world." (See Matt. 24:3.)

And again, after the tribulation of those days which shall come upon Jerusalem, if any man shall say unto you, Lo, here is Christ, or there, believe him not;

For *in those days,* there shall *also* arise false Christs, and false prophets, and shall *show* great signs and wonders, insomuch, that, if possible, they shall deceive the very elect, *who are the elect according to the covenant.*

Behold, I speak these things unto you for the elect's sake;

And ye also shall hear of wars, and rumors of wars; see that ye be not *troubled, for all I have told you must come to pass; but the end is not yet.* (JST; italics added.)

Elder Bruce R. McConkie notes that the warnings of the Lord in verses 22–24 of the Joseph Smith Translation have to do with apostasy:

After the destruction of Jerusalem and the scattering of the Jews, and after the establishment of the primitive Church, an era of false religions is to commence, an era of division, disunity, discord and disagreement, an era of change and apostasy, so that among those who profess to follow Christ, some will advocate one doctrine of salvation and some another. Perfect Christianity will be lost; and Jesus' warning is to beware of all false and conflicting claims made in his name. (DNTC 1:647.)

24:24 The Prophet Joseph Smith, in his inspired version of that same scripture, added these significant words: *"who are the elect, according to the covenant."* This is what has been said, in effect, in this conference: Unless every member of this Church gains for himself an unshakable testimony of the divinity of this Church, he will be among those who will be deceived in this day when the "elect according to the covenant" are going to be tried and tested. Only those will survive who have gained for themselves that testimony. (Harold B. Lee, CR, Oct. 1950, p. 129.)

Only the saints, the elect of God, those who walk in light and truth, can read the signs of the times; it is to them, not the world, that Jesus speaks when telling the events which shall precede his return. Worldly people will suppose that the wars and desolations of the last days are simply the normal and continuing course of history. They will fail to see in them the promised but destructive prelude to that millennial peace which will be possible only through the personal reign of the Prince of Peace. (DNTC 1:654.)

(See section 1, "World, end of.")

24:28 (Read Luke 17:37.) The Joseph Smith Translation provides the interpretation of this parable:

And now I show unto you a parable. Behold, wheresoever the carcass is, there will the eagles be gathered together; so *likewise shall mine elect be gathered from the four quarters of the earth.* (Italics added.)

If the "elect" includes those of Israel gathered in the last days, then the "carcass" could refer to the land of Israel where the blood descendants of Judah will gather, and it could also refer to the true Church where covenant Israel will gather.

In the parable, as here given, the carcass is the body of the Church to which the eagles, who are Israel, shall fly to find nourishment. "The gathering of Israel is first *spiritual* and second *temporal*. It is spiritual in that the lost sheep of Israel are first 'restored to the true church and fold of God,' meaning that they come to a true knowledge of the God of Israel, accept the gospel which he has restored in latter-days, and join the Church of Jesus Christ of Latter-day Saints. It is temporal in that these converts are then 'gathered home to the lands of their inheritance, and . . . established in all their lands of promise.' (2 Ne. 9:2; 25:15–18; Jer. 16:14–21), meaning that the house of Joseph will be established in America, the house of Judah in Palestine, and that the Lost Tribes will come to Ephraim in America to receive their blessings in due course. (D&C 133.)" (*Mormon Doctrine,* p. 280.) (DNTC 1:648–49.)

24:29–31 Read Mark 13:24–27; Luke 21:25–28.

Judah must return, Jerusalem must be rebuilt, and the temple, and water come out from under the temple, and the waters of the Dead Sea be healed. It will take some time to rebuild the walls of the city and the temple, &c.; and all this must be done before the Son of Man will make His appearance. There will be wars and rumors of wars, signs in the heavens above and on the earth beneath, the sun turned into darkness and the moon to blood, earthquakes in divers places, the seas heaving beyond their bounds; then will appear one grand sign of the Son of Man in heaven. But what will the world do? They will say it is a planet, a comet, etc. But the Son of man will come as the sign of the coming of the Son of Man, which will be as the light of the morning cometh out of the east. (TPJS, pp. 286–87.)

24:30–31 *And, as I said before, after the tribulation of those days, and the powers of the heavens shall be shaken,* then shall appear the sign of the Son of Man in heaven, and then shall all the tribes of the earth mourn;

And they shall see the Son of Man coming in the clouds of heaven, with power and great glory. *And whoso treasureth up my words, shall not be deceived.* (JST; italics added.)

Not *read,* not *study,* not *search,* but *treasure up* the Lord's word. *Possess* it, *own* it, *make it yours* by both believing it and living it. For instance: the voice of the Lord *says* that if men have faith, repent, and are baptized, they shall receive the Holy Ghost. It is not sufficient merely to *know* what the scripture *says.* One must *treasure it up,* meaning take it into his possession so affirmatively that it becomes a part of his very being; as a consequence, in the illustration given, one actually receives the companionship of the Spirit. Obviously such persons will not be deceived where the signs of the times and the Second Coming of the Messiah are concerned. (DNTC 1:662.)

24:31 The Joseph Smith Translation reveals that only the remainder of the elect will be saved: "They shall gather together the remainder of his elect . . ."

24:32–41 Read Mark 13:28–32; Luke 21:29–33.

24:32–33 Many commentaries have noted the special characteristic of the fig tree; it puts forth leaves and develops fruit at the same time, and it doesn't begin to leaf until "summer is nigh."

In giving the *Parable of the Fig Tree,* Jesus both reveals and keeps hidden the time of his coming. The parable is perfect for his purposes. It announces that he will most assuredly return in the "season" when the promised signs are shown. But it refrains from specifying the day or the hour when the figs will be harvested, thus leaving men in a state of expectant hope, ever keeping themselves ready for the coming harvest. (DNTC 1:664.)

(See section 1, "Fig tree.")

24:33 The Greek reads *"he* is near" rather than *"it* is near."

24:34 Verily I say unto you, this generation, *in which these things shall be shown forth,* shall not pass away until all I have told you shall be fulfilled.

Although the days will come that heaven and earth shall pass away, yet my word shall not pass away; but all shall be fulfilled.

And as I said before, after the tribulation of those days, and the powers of the heavens shall be shaken, then shall appear the sign of the Son of Man in heaven; and then shall all the tribes of the earth mourn. (JST; italics added.)

Consult any reliable unabridged dictionary of the English language for evidence of the fact that the term "generation," as connoting a period of time, has many meanings, among which are "race, kind, class." The term is not confined to a body of people living at one time. Fausett's *Bible Cyclopedia, Critical and Expository,* after citing many meanings attached to the word, says: "In Matthew 24:34 'this generation shall not pass (viz. the Jewish race, of which the generation in Christ's days was a sample in character: compare Christ's address to the "generation," 24:35, 36, in proof that "generation" means at times the whole Jewish race) till all these things be fulfilled' — a prophecy that the Jews shall be a distinct people still when He shall come again." (JTC, p. 590.)

24:36 Question: Does or will anyone know when the Lord will come? Answer: As to the day and hour, No; as to the generation, Yes.

Question: Who shall know the generation? Answer: The saints, the children of light, those who can read the signs of the times, those who treasure up the Lord's word so they will not be deceived.

Paul told the Thessalonians that "the coming of the Lord" would be "as travail upon a woman with child"; that where people of the world are concerned Jesus would come "as a thief in the night," that is unexpectedly and without warning; but that where "the children of light" are concerned, the Lord would not come as "a thief in the night," for they are aware of the "times and seasons" connected with his return. (1 Thess. 4:13–18; 5:1–7.) Thus, though the saints do not know the day, they are aware of the season. As a woman in travail feels the pains of the approaching birth, so the saints read the signs of the times; neither knows the exact moment of the anticipated happening, but both know the approximate time. (DNTC 1:665–66.)

(See section 1, "Second Coming: No definite date.")

24:39–40 The Joseph Smith Translation adds the following between these two verses: "Then shall be fulfilled that which is written, that, In the last days, . . ."

24:40 Elder Bruce R. McConkie explains why one is destroyed and the other left alone when the Lord returns.

Those who shall abide the day, who shall remain on the earth when it is transfigured (D&C 63:20–21), are those who are honest and upright and who are living at least the law which would take them to the terrestrial kingdom of glory in the resurrection. Anyone living by telestial standards can no longer remain on earth and so cannot abide the day.

Hence we find Malachi listing among those who shall not abide the day the following: sorcerers; adulterers; false swearers; those who oppress the hireling, the widow, and the fatherless in their wages; those who lead men away from the truth; those who do not fear God; members of the true Church who do not pay an honest tithing; they that work wickedness;

and the proud. All these, he says, shall be as stubble when the day comes that shall burn as an oven. (Mal. 3:4; D&C 64:23–25.) (DNTC 1:669.)

24:42–51 (Read Mark 13:33–37; Luke 12:35–48; 21:34–36.) Our Heavenly Father has a definite purpose in not revealing the exact time of the Second Coming of the Lord in glory:

Deliberately and advisedly the actual time of his coming has been left uncertain and unspecified, so that men of each succeeding age shall be led to prepare for it as though it would be in their mortal lives. And for those who pass on before the promised day, none of their preparation will be wasted, for both the living and the dead, speaking in the eternal sense, must prepare to abide the day. (DNTC 1:674–75.)

24:42 The Greek words translated "what hour" actually mean "what sort of day."

24:44 "Be ye also ready" could have been more literally translated "prove yourselves ready."

24:45–46 "To give them meat in due season" (v. 45) means "to give them their food at the proper time."

Who will be the "faithful and wise servants" to whom the Lord refers in these verses of Matthew?

Jesus speaks here of his ministers, his servants, the holders of his holy priesthood. They are the ones whom he has made rulers in the household of God to teach and perfect his saints. Theirs is the responsibility to be so engaged when the Master returns. If they are so serving when the Lord comes, he will give them exaltation. But if the rulers in the Lord's house think the Second Coming is far distant, if they forget their charge, contend with their fellow ministers, and begin to live after the manner of the world, then the vengeance of their rejected Lord shall, in justice, fall upon them when he comes again. (DNTC 1:675.)

Those who are found faithful when the Savior comes in power and glory will be caught up to meet him:

The face of the Lord shall be unveiled; And the saints that are upon the earth, who are alive, shall be quickened and be caught up to meet him. And they who have slept in their graves shall come forth, for their graves shall be opened; and they also shall be caught up to meet him in the midst of the pillar of heaven—They are Christ's, the first fruits, they who shall descend with him first, and they who are on the earth and in their graves, who are first caught up to meet him. (D&C 88:95–98.)

24:51 "And shall cut him asunder" means "will punish him with the greatest severity." The Joseph Smith Translation concludes this extremely interesting chapter with the following words: "And thus cometh the end of the wicked, according to the prophecy of Moses, saying: They should be cut off from among the people; but the end of the earth is not yet; but by and by."

25:1–13 (Compare Luke 12:35–36. Read D&C 45: 56–59.) The Joseph Smith Translation sheds new light on the parable of the ten virgins by adding the following to verse 1: "And then, *at that day, before the Son of Man comes,* the kingdom of heaven shall be likened unto ten virgins . . ." (Italics added.)

This precious parable pertains to the last days; it is now beginning to be fulfilled and will be finally consummated when the Bridegroom comes. Already the invitations have been issued to the marriage feast (meaning, the gospel is being preached), and the cry is going forth inviting men to come and meet the Bridegroom.

Early in this dispensation the Lord said to Joseph Smith: "Yea, let the cry go forth among all people: Awake and arise and go forth to meet the Bridegroom; behold and lo, the Bridegroom cometh; go ye out to meet him. Prepare yourselves for the great day of the Lord." (D&C 133:10.) "And at that day, when I shall come in my glory," the Lord said in another revelation, "shall the parable be fulfilled which I spake concerning the ten virgins." (D&C 45:56.) (DNTC 1:685.)

The story itself is based on oriental marriage customs, with which the Lord's attentive listeners were familiar. It was and yet is common in those lands, particularly in connection with marriage festivities among the wealthy classes, for the bridegroom to go to the home of the bride, accompanied by his friends in processional array, and later to conduct the bride to her new home with a larger body of attendants composed of groomsmen, brides-maids, relatives and friends. As the bridal party progressed, to the accompaniment of gladsome music, it was increased by little groups who had gathered in waiting at convenient places along the route, and particu-larly near the end of the course where organized companies came forth to meet the advancing procession. Wedding ceremonies were appointed for the evening and night hours; and the necessary use of torches and lamps gave brilliancy and added beauty to the scene. (JTC, p. 577.)

The purpose of this lesson was to impress upon those called to the min-istry and upon his followers and upon the world that there should be an unceasing watchfulness and preparation for the day which he had predicted when the Lord would come again in judgment upon the earth.

The bridegroom of the parable was the Master, the Savior of mankind. The marriage feast symbolized the second coming of the Savior to receive his Church unto himself. The virgins were those who were professed believers in Christ, because they were expectantly waiting for the coming of the bridegroom to the marriage feast, or they were connected with the Church and the events which were to transpire with reference to it.

That this parable did refer particularly to the believers in Christ with a warning to them is further indicated by what the Lord has told us in modern revelation in which he said:

"These things are the things that ye must look for; . . . even in the day of the coming of the Son of Man.

"And until that hour there will be foolish virgins among the wise; and at that hour cometh an entire separation of the righteous and the wicked. (D&C 63:53–54.)" [This] undoubtedly mean[s] a separation of the wicked from the righteous among the professing believers in the Lord Jesus Christ.

The Lord defines the wise virgins of his parable in still another revelation in which he said.

"For they that are wise and have received the truth, and have taken the Holy Spirit for their guide, and have not been deceived—verily I say unto you, they shall not be hewn down and cast into the fire, but shall abide the day. (*ibid., 45:57.*)"

Here is clearly indicated a truth we must all recognize, that among the people of God, the believers in the Savior of the world, there are those who are wise and keep the commandments, and yet there are those who are foolish, who are disobedient, and who neglect their duties. (Harold B. Lee, CR, Oct. 1951, pp. 26–27.)

(See section 1, "Jesus: As the Bridegroom.")

25:2, 4, 8–9 "Wise" means "discreet." It is also frequently translated "sensible."

> Not good and bad, not righteous and wicked, but wise and foolish. That is, all of them have accepted the invitation to meet the Bridegroom; all are members of the Church; the contrast is not between the wicked and the worthy. Instead, five are zealous and devoted, while five are inactive and lukewarm; ten have the testimony of Jesus, but only five are valiant therein. Hence, five shall enter into the house where Jesus is and five shall remain without—all of which raises the question: What portion of the Church shall be saved? Surely this parable is not intended to divide half the saints into one group and half into another. But it does teach, pointedly and plainly, that there are foolish saints who shall fail to gain the promised rewards. (DNTC 1:685.)

25:7 "Trimmed their lamps" means "put their lamps in order." (See BD, "Lamp.")

25:8–12 That the wise virgins were not able to supply the needs of the foolish virgins indicates that each person will be judged by his own merits.

25:8 The Greek term translated "our lamps are gone out" suggests that the lamps are still burning but "are about to go out."

25:10 For an explanation of those who will be ready, see D&C 45:57–59.

25:12 The people did not know Jesus, according to the

Joseph Smith Translation: "Verily I say unto you, *Ye knew me not.*" (Italics added.)

25:14–30 (Read D&C 52:13; 60:2–3, 13; 72:3–5; 82:3, 18.) The Joseph Smith Translation makes it clear that this is a parable: "Now I will liken these things unto a parable. For it is like as a man travelling . . ."

You know, brethren, that when the Master in the Savior's parable of the stewards called his servants before him he gave them several talents to improve on while he should tarry abroad for a little season, and when he returned he called for an accounting. So it is now. Our Master is absent only for a little season, and at the end of it He will call each to render an account; and where the five talents were bestowed, ten will be required; and he that has made no improvement will be cast out as an unprofitable servant, while the faithful will enjoy everlasting honors. Therefore we earnestly implore the grace of our Father to rest upon you, through Jesus Christ His Son, that you may not faint in the hour of temptation, nor be overcome in the time of persecution. (TPJS, p. 68.)

In the *Parable of the Talents* we find the Lord Jesus counseling his apostles, his ministers, those called into his divine service, to use every talent, ability, strength, energy, and capacity in the Master's service. "O ye that embark in the service of God, see that ye serve him with all your heart, might, mind and strength." (D&C 4:2.) In the similar, though distinct, *Parable of the Pounds* (Luke 19:11–28), Jesus taught the multitudes that men will be judged according to their works and rewarded with much or little in eternity. Here, however, the emphasis is on using the diverse and varying endowments which all men have, with the assurance that all who work and minister according to their own abilities and capacities will be rewarded eternally. Even those with lesser talents, if they use them to the full, are to become rulers in the Master's house. (DNTC 1:687–88.)

25:15 "Every man according to his several ability" could have been translated more literally "each one according to his own ability."

Men are not born equal. Each person in this life is endowed with those talents and capacities which his pre-earth life entitle him to receive. Some by obedience to law acquired one talent and some another in pre-existence, and all bring with them into mortality the talents and capacities acquired there. (Abra. 3:22–23.) (DNTC 1:688.)

25:20 "Deliveredst" could have been translated "committed."

25:21–23 Elder Bruce R. McConkie has mentioned a few of the "many things" the faithful might receive:

Glories promised the faithful saints hereafter are described in terms of kingdoms and thrones, of principalities and powers, of being rulers in

God's house, of ascending the throne of eternal power—all such heights being beyond even the comprehension of finite men. In this mortal sphere those called to the Lord's ministry labor in limited spheres only—as quorum presidents, as bishops, as apostles (for it was they to whom this parable was more particularly directed), or in other capacities. How gratifying it is to learn, therefore, the eternal principle that those servants who are faithful over a few things shall be made rulers over many in the realms to be. (DNTC 1:688.)

25:24, 26 "Strawed" could have been translated "scattered" or "winnowed." The Joseph Smith Translation renders it "scattered."

25:25 And I was afraid, and went and hid thy talent in the earth; and lo, *here is thy talent; take it from me as thou hast from thine other servants, for it is thine.* (JST; italics added.)

The unfaithful servant prefaced his report with a grumbling excuse, which involved the imputation of unrighteousness in the Master. The honest, diligent, faithful servants saw and reverenced in their Lord the perfection of the good qualities which they possessed in measured degree; the lazy and unprofitable serf, afflicted by distorted vision, professed to see in the Master his own base defects. The story in this particular, as in the other features relating to human acts and tendencies, is psychologically true; in a peculiar sense men are prone to conceive of the attributes of God as comprising in augmented degree the dominant traits of their own nature. (JTC, p. 582.)

25:27 The Joseph Smith Translation begins this verse "Having known this, therefore . . ." "With usury" means "with interest." (See section 1, "Usury.")

25:28 "I will take" begins this verse in the Joseph Smith Translation.

25:29 For unto every one *who* hath *obtained other talents,* shall be given, and he shall have *in* abundance.

But from him that hath not *obtained other talents,* shall be taken away even that which he hath *received.* (JST; italics added.)

Every man must use such talents as he may have or they will be lost. If a man cannot compose music, perhaps he can sing in the choir; if he cannot write books, at least he can read them; if he cannot paint pictures, he can learn to appreciate the artistry of others; if he cannot achieve preeminence in one specific field, so be it, he still can succeed in his own field; for each man has some talent, and he will be judged on the basis of how he uses what he has.

It is an eternal law of life that men either progress or retrogress; they either increase their talents and abilities, or those they have wither and die. No one stands still; there is no such thing as pure neutrality. (DNTC 1:689.)

25:30 "Unprofitable" could have been translated "useless" or "good-for-nothing."

Elder James E. Talmage has noted several parallels between this parable and the one immediately preceding it on the ten virgins, including similar fates for the "unprofitable servant" and the "foolish virgins":

Viewing as one discourse the two parables and the teaching that directly followed, we find in it such unity of subject and thoroughness of treatment as to give to the whole both beauty and worth beyond the sum of these qualities exhibited in the several parts. Vigilant waiting in the Lord's cause, and the dangers of unreadiness are exemplified in the story of the virgins; diligence in work and the calamitous results of sloth are prominent features of the tale of the talents. These two phases of service are of reciprocal and complementary import; it is as necessary at times to wait as at others to work. The lapse of a long period, as while the Bridegroom tarried, and as during the Master's absence in "a far country," is made plain throughout as intervening between the Lord's departure and His return in glory. The absolute certainty of the Christ coming to execute judgment upon the earth, in the which every soul shall receive according to his deserts, is the sublime summary of this unparalleled discourse. (JTC, pp. 585–86.)

25:31–46 (Read Prov. 14:31; Mosiah 2:17; D&C 29:27–28; 42:38.) From time immemorial, the Saints have been counseled "to bear one another's burdens, that they may be light . . . to comfort those that stand in need of comfort." (Mosiah 18:8–9.) Ancient and modern scriptures that might be reviewed on this subject include Mosiah 4:14–26; D&C 52:40; 56:14–16; 104:11–18; 121:45; 1 Timothy 5:8.

25:33 The Joseph Smith Translation of the end of this verse reads, "And he shall sit upon his throne, and the twelve apostles with him."

25:35 "Ye took me in" means "you received me in your homes."

25:36 The Greek word translated "visited" has a broader meaning of "looked after" or "took care of."

25:40, 45 "Inasmuch" means "to the extent."

25:43 "Ye took me not in" means "you did not receive me hospitably."

26:1–5 (Read Mark 14:1–2; Luke 22:1–2.) The Savior had already prophesied several times concerning his coming betrayal and crucifixion. (John 2:18–22; Luke 9:21–22; Mark 9:30–32; 10:32–34.) Elder James E. Talmage has explained

why the Jewish leaders were so careful concerning the time
they selected to have Jesus put to death:

> The rulers feared especially an outbreak by the Galileans, who had a
> provincial pride in the prominence of Jesus as one of their countrymen, and
> many of whom were then in Jerusalem. It was further concluded and for the
> same reasons, that the Jewish custom of making impressive examples of
> notable offenders by executing public punishment upon them at times of
> great general assemblages, be set aside in the case of Jesus; therefore the
> conspirators said: "Not on the feast day, lest there be an uproar among the
> people." (JTC, p. 591.)

26:3 This is the first mention in Matthew of Caiaphas,
who, although called a high priest, had been appointed to his
position by political power.

> Rule in God's earthly kingdom is by legal administrators appointed by
> the Lord. Church officers are chosen by other church officers as the Holy
> Spirit directs. One of the many sure signs of total apostasy is the appoint-
> ment of religious leaders by civil authorities, as often has been and now is
> the case among branches and sects of Christendom. This, also, was the fallen
> spiritual state into which the once divinely approved Jewish religion had
> slipped. Accordingly, Joseph Caiaphas, son-in-law of Annas, appointed high
> priest by the Roman procurator Valerius Gratus (Pilate's predecessor), found
> himself in the priestly office at this dread time in history when the Creator of
> men was to be taken by sinful men and hung on the cross. Under the Jewish
> law the presiding priest in the Aaronic Priesthood was called the high priest;
> it was, to them, a position of administration and spiritual supremacy. (DNTC
> 1:696–97.)

(See section 1, "Caiaphas.")

26:4 "Subtilty" could also be translated "crafty device."
"And consulted that they might take Jesus by subtilty, and
kill him" has been translated "and made plans to arrest Jesus
secretly and put him to death."

This verse could also have been translated "and took
counsel together to seize Jesus by crafty device and kill
him."

26:6–13 Read Mark 14:3–9; John 12:2–8. Compare
Luke 7:37–50.

> To understand this solemn scene one must both know and feel the reli-
> gious significance of Mary's act. Here sat the Lord of Heaven, in the house
> of his friends, as the hour of his greatest trials approached, with those who
> loved him knowing he was soon to face betrayal and crucifixion. What act of
> love, of devotion, of adoration, of worship, could a mere mortal perform for
> him who is eternal? Could a loved one do more than David had said the
> Good Shepherd himself would do in conferring honor and blessing upon
> another, that is: "Thou anointest my head with oil"? (Ps. 23:5.) (DNTC
> 1:700.)

To anoint the head of a guest with ordinary oil was to do him honor; to anoint his feet also was to show unusual and signal regard; but the anointing of the head and feet with spikenard, and in such abundance, was an act of reverential homage rarely rendered even to kings. Mary's act was an expression of adoration; it was the fragrant outwelling of a heart overflowing with worship and affection. (JTC, p. 512.)

(See section 1, "Spikenard"; commentary for Mark 6:13; BD, "Anoint.")

26:6 The location of the house of Simon the leper (Bethany) was about two miles from Jerusalem beyond the Mount of Olives (see also John 11:18 and Mark 11:1), but additional facts concerning the man or his household are scanty:

This means of identifying the place of the feast gives rise to many interesting speculations. Who was Simon? If living and present he was obviously no longer afflicted with leprosy. Was he, then, one who had been healed by Jesus? And since Martha served and Lazarus sat at the table, while Mary anointed the Master, was this also their Bethany home? Was Simon their father? The gospel authors seem to have drawn a reverent curtain over many of the details of Jesus' private life and friendships, revealing only those things needed to give proper testimony of his ministry and mission. (DNTC 1:699.)

26:10 The Joseph Smith Translation alters this verse as follows: "When they had said thus, Jesus understood them, and he said unto them . . ."

26:12 "For my burial" could have been translated "to prepare me for my burial."

26:13 The Joseph Smith Translation begins this verse: "And in this thing that she hath done, she shall be blessed; for verily I say unto you . . ."

26:14–16 (Read Mark 14:10–11; Luke 22:1–6.) The "chief priests" set as the price of the life of their God the exact amount that their law fixed for the price of a slave. (See Ex. 21:28–32.) This price fulfilled the prophecy contained in Zechariah: "So they weighed for my price thirty pieces of silver." (Zech. 11:12.)

Judas took the initiative. He sought out the chief priests; he chose to betray his Lord; he asked for the money. It was a wilful, deliberate, premeditated act; and it is useless to speculate (as so many commentators do) as to why he did it. Such speculation usually seeks to excuse Judas for an act which the scriptural account in no way mitigates. The revealed record lays the onus for the deed on Judas and stops there. (DNTC 1:702.)

(See section 1, "Thirty pieces of silver.")

26:17–20 Read Mark 14:12–17; Luke 22:7–14.

Ancient Israel, in the day of Moses, was freed from temporal bondage in Egypt by the Lord Jehovah. To commemorate this deliverance, they were commanded to keep the Feast of the Passover. This feast was designed to bring two things to their remembrance: (1) That the angel of death passed over the houses and flocks of Israel, while slaying the firstborn among the men and beasts of the Egyptians; and (2) That Jehovah was their Deliverer, the same holy being who in due course would come into the world as King-Messiah to work out the infinite and eternal atonement. . . .

Arrangements for this final Passover of our Lord's ministry, a Passover to be known ever after to the Church as the Last Supper, were made by Peter and John as directed by the seeric vision of Jesus. The Supper itself must have been in the home of a disciple, for the two apostles had but to mention the Master's desires and the upper room was made available.

This was the final approved Passover. Following the sacrifice of Christ as a Paschal Lamb this old ordinance was to cease and other symbols (those shown forth in the sacrament of the Lord's Supper) were to find approved usage among the Lord's people. Now the only proper celebration of the Passover is in the spiritual sense of which Paul speaks: "For even Christ our passover is sacrificed for us: Therefore let us keep the feast, not with old leaven, neither with the leaven of malice and wickedness; but with the unleavened bread of sincerity and truth." (1 Cor. 5:7–8.) (DNTC 1:704–5.)

(See section 1, "Passover.")

26:17 Closely associated with the passover was the Feast of Unleavened Bread. As the ancient Israelites made their hasty preparations to leave Egypt and its unwelcome hardships, they did not have sufficient time to permit their bread to rise as was the custom. Instead they baked in haste and vacated their homes as quickly as possible. The festival of Unleavened Bread was held to commemorate this fact. Where Passover lasted one day originally, the Feast of Unleavened Bread lasted seven. In process of time, both festivals were combined into one, making the entire Passover period eight days in length. (LTJA, p. 160.)

26:18 "My time is at hand" could have been translated "My appointed time is near."

26:19 "Had appointed them" has also been translated "had instructed them" and "had directed them."

26:21–25 Read Mark 14:18–21; Luke 22:21–30; John 13:18–30.

26:22 "Lord, is it I?" could have been translated "Lord, it is not I, is it?"

I remind you that these men were apostles. They were of apostolic stature. It has always been interesting to me that they did not on that occasion, nudge one another and say, "I'll bet that is old Judas. He has surely been acting queer lately." It reflects something of their stature. . . .

Would you, I plead, overrule the tendency to disregard counsel and assume for just a moment something apostolic in attitude at least, and ask yourself these questions: Do I need to improve myself? Should I take this counsel to heart and act upon it? If there is one weak or failing, unwilling to follow the brethren, Lord, is it I? (Boyd K. Packer, "Follow the Brethren," *Speeches of the Year,* 1965, p. 3.)

(See section 1, "Is it I?")

26:24 The Greek word translated "good" has the basic meaning of "better" and is so translated in most modern versions.

In what sense would it have been better for Judas never to have been born?

This statement, which should be taken literally, can be understood only in the light of pre-existence. All men earned the right to pass by birth from a pre-existent first estate into this life, to come from the personal presence of God into a life where trials and tests await. Those who fail the tests of mortality go eventually to a telestial sphere of which the revealed word says: "Where God and Christ dwell they cannot come, worlds without end." (D&C 76:112.)

Thus, in the sense here spoken, they would have been better off never to have been born, never to have left their pre-existent home, the home where the Eternal Father presides in glorious immortality. The Book of Mormon presentation of this doctrine is in these words: "And wo be unto him that will not hearken unto the words of Jesus, and also to them whom he hath chosen and sent among them; for whoso receiveth not the words of Jesus and the words of those whom he hath sent receiveth not him; and therefore he will not receive them at the last day; And it would be better for them if they had not been born. For do ye suppose that ye can get rid of the justice of an offended God, who hath been trampled under feet of men, that thereby salvation might come?" (3 Ne. 28:34–35.) (DNTC 1:714.)

(See section 1, "Judas: Son of perdition"; commentary for John 17:12.)

26:25 "Thou hast said" means "You yourself said it."

In their innocence, not even deigning to impute so dastardly a deed to another, eleven of the Twelve ask: "Is it I?" Judas, however—already the greedy possessor of thirty pieces of silver (the price of a slave!), and knowing his own evil heart—waited till last; then, lest his silence be construed as confession, he too is forced to ask the fateful query: "Is it I?" (DNTC 1:712.)

26:26–29 (Read Mark 14:22–25; Luke 22:15–20.) It has been observed by many that this final Passover was, in reality, two separate and distinct events (the Passover and the sacrament), although joined in symbolism. The Passover formalities were:

(1) The first cup was blessed and drunk. (2) The hands were washed while a blessing was said. (3) Bitter herbs, emblematic of the sojourn in Egypt, were partaken of, dipped in sour broth made of vinegar and bruised fruit. (4) The son of the house asked his father to explain the origin of the observance. (5) The lamb and the flesh of the thank offerings (*chagigah*) were placed on the table, and the first part of the Hallel sung (Psalms 113, 114). (6) The second cup was blessed and drunk. (7) Unleavened bread was blessed and broken, a fragment of it was eaten, then a fragment of the thank offerings, then a fragment of the lamb. (8) Preliminaries being thus ended, the feast proceeded at leisure till all was consumed. (9) The lamb being quite finished, the third cup, the cup of blessing, was blessed and drunk. (10) The fourth cup was drunk, and meanwhile the second part of the Hallel (Psalms 115–118) was sung.

Those who partook of the Passover were required to be ceremonially clean, and to have been fasting from the time of the evening sacrifice, which on this day was offered early, about 1:30 P.M. All male Israelites above the age of fourteen were required to partake of it. (Dummelow, p. 710.)

(See section 1, "Passover," "Sacrament.")

The word translated "is" has the basic meaning of "means." Thus, in effect, Jesus was saying, "Take, eat. This means my body."

And as they were eating, Jesus took bread *and brake it, and blessed it,* and gave to *his* disciples, and said, Take, eat; *this is in remembrance of* my body *which I give a ransom for you.*

And he took the cup, and gave thanks, and gave it to them, saying, Drink ye all of it.

For this is *in remembrance of* my blood of the new testament, which is shed for *as* many *as shall believe on my name,* for the remission of *their* sins.

And I give unto you a commandment, that ye shall observe to do the things which ye have seen me do, and bear record of me even unto the end. (JST; italics added.)

26:27 "Drink ye all of it" does not mean that all of the liquid was to be drunk. Rather, it means that all of the people were to drink of it. Thus, it could have been translated: "Drink of it, all of you."

26:30 (Read Mark 14:26; Luke 22:39; John 14:27–31.) If this hymn was in keeping with the prescribed Passover procedures, It would have been Psalms 115–18. (See section 1, "Hymns"; BD, "Hallel.")

26:31–35 (Read Mark 14:27–31; Luke 22:31–38; John 13:36–38.) Although the gospel writers do not agree as to the precise place of this conversation, they do agree on the particulars and on the important principles. When considering the Savior's statement "All ye shall be offended because of me this night," it should be remembered that the apostles had not yet received the strengthening power of the gift of the Holy Ghost. This gift was not fully received until the day of Pentecost.

26:31 The scripture Jesus quoted is from Zechariah 13:7:

Awake, O sword, against my shepherd, and against the man that is my fellow, saith the Lord of hosts: smite the shepherd, and the sheep shall be scattered: and I will turn mine hand upon the little ones.

26:34–35 The word translated "deny" actually means "disown." A more accurate translation might be "you will disown me three times." (See section 1, "Deny.")

26:36–46 (Read Mark 14:32–42; Luke 22:40–46; John 18:1–2. Compare 2 Ne. 9:21–22; Mosiah 3:5–12; D&C 19:1–24.) The Garden of Gethsemane was located on the Mount of Olives, just east of Jerusalem.

Gethsemane.—The name means "oil-press" and probably has reference to a mill maintained at the place for the extraction of oil from the olives there cultivated. John refers to the spot as a garden, from which designation we may regard it as an enclosed space of private ownership. That it was a place frequented by Jesus when He sought retirement for prayer, or opportunity for confidential converse with the disciples, is indicated by the same writer (John 18:1, 2). (JTC, p. 620.)

Christ's agony in the garden is unfathomable by the finite mind, both as to intensity and cause. The thought that He suffered through fear of death is untenable. Death to Him was preliminary to resurrection and triumphal return to the Father from whom He had come, and to a state of glory even beyond what He had before possessed; and, moreover, it was within His power to lay down His life voluntarily. [John 5:26–27; 10:17–18.] He struggled and groaned under a burden such as no other being who has lived on earth might even conceive as possible. It was not physical pain, nor mental anguish alone, that caused Him to suffer such torture as to produce an extrusion of blood from every pore; but a spiritual agony of soul such as only God was capable of experiencing. No other man, however great his powers of physical or mental endurance, could have suffered so; for his human organism would have succumbed, and syncope would have produced unconsciousness and welcome oblivion. In that hour of anguish Christ met and overcame all the horrors that Satan, "the prince of this world" could inflict. The frightful struggle incident to the temptations immediately following the Lord's baptism was surpassed and overshadowed by this supreme contest with the powers of evil.

In some manner, actual and terribly real though to man incomprehensible, the Savior took upon Himself the burden of the sins of mankind from Adam to the end of the world. Modern revelation assists us to a partial understanding of the awful experience. In March 1830, the glorified Lord, Jesus Christ, thus spake: "For behold, I, God, have suffered these things for all, that they might not suffer if they would repent, but if they would not repent, they must suffer even as I, which suffering caused myself, even God, the greatest of all, to tremble because of pain, and to bleed at every pore, and to suffer both body and spirit: and would that I might not drink the bitter cup and shrink—nevertheless, glory be to the Father, and I partook and finished my preparations unto the children of men." (JTC, pp. 613–14.)

(See section 1, "Atonement," "Gethsemane.")

26:37 The last few words could have been translated "grieved and to be sorely troubled."

26:45– 46 It is evident that something is wrong in the King James translation. In verse 45 the Savior commands his disciples, "Sleep on now, and take your rest." However, in verse 46 Jesus says, "Rise, let us be going."

The Greek indicates that in verse 45 Jesus is chiding his apostles because of their sleeping at this important time. Thus, the sentence could have been translated "At such a time as this you are sleeping and taking your rest!"

Most modern versions express this idea in the form of a question:

"Are you still sleeping and taking your ease?" (PME.)

"Are you still sleeping and taking your rest?" (RSV; TEV; NIV.)

"Still sleeping? Still taking your ease?" (NEB.)

The Joseph Smith Translation indicates that the disciples slept for a short time: *"And after they had slept, he said unto them, Arise,* and let us be going." (Italics added.)

26:47–56 Read Mark 14:43– 42; Luke 22:47–53; John 18:3–11. See section 1, "Judas."

26:48 "Hold him fast" could have been translated "seize him" or "take him into custody." It has also been translated "Arrest him."

26:50 The Joseph Smith Translation clarifies how the betrayal would take place: " . . . wherefore art thou come *to betray me with a kiss?"* (Italics added.) (See section 1, "Kiss, sign of betrayal.")

26:54 This verse could have been translated "In that case, how would the Scriptures be fulfilled that it must take place this way?"

26:55 "Ye laid not hold on me" could have been translated "you did not take me into custody." (See commentary for Matt. 26:48.)

26:57–68 Read Mark 14:53–65; Luke 22:54–65; John 18:13–24.

The vile and demeaning indignities heaped upon the Son of God this night were planned in the courts of hell and executed by human demons who had surrendered their wills to Satan. Betrayed with a traitor's kiss, arrested and bound by an armed mob, he was taken first before Annas, a former high priest who dominated Caiaphas and the Jewish political scene. There can be no claim of legality or justice in arraigning Christ as it were before a private citizen; the act, designed to create inquisatorial opportunities, merely gratified the pride and dramatized the power of that evil conspirator.

Annas sent Jesus to Caiaphas, the official high priest, with whom were assembled the chief priests, elders, and scribes. Annas himself was probably present also, and included in the mob-type group were enough at least of the Sanhedrin to form a quorum. Through long hours they questioned, smote, and spit upon their King. How much of this inquisition was part of the formal trial before the Sanhedrin is not clear. But when the morning came that body of Jewish jurists took formal action against Jesus and sent him to Pilate to have their death decree ratified. (DNTC 1:787–88.)

(See section 1, "Sanhedrin.")

26:58 "Sat with the servants, to see the end" could also have been translated "sitting with the house attendants [subordinates] to see the outcome."

26:59–60 As presently worded, these two verses appear to be contradictory: the chief priests and elders "sought false witness against Jesus," and "though many false witnesses came, yet found they none."

The Joseph Smith Translation clarifies the situation: "Yea, though many false witnesses came, they found none *that could accuse him.*" (Italics added.)

The testimony of the false witnesses was not substantiated by the facts:

The nearest even false witnesses could come to testifying against Jesus was to hark back some three and a half years to his statement: "Destroy this temple, and in three days I will raise it up." (John 2:19.) That the chief priests and scribes knew he meant the temple of his body and not "the temple of God," as the false witnesses testified, is evident from their own subsequent statement to Pilate about Jesus rising again the third day. (Matt. 27:62–66.) Thus, despite all their search for at least two liars and perjurers who would agree on some one point, they found none; their verdict of guilty was to be left without even a false witness to support it. (DNTC 1:791.)

26:59 The "council" of the chief priests and elders is undoubtedly the Sanhedrin.

Comprised of an assembly of seventy-one ordained scholars, including Levites, priests, scribes, Pharisees, Sadducees, and those of other political persuasion, in the time of the Savior the Great Sanhedrin was the highest Jewish court of justice and the supreme legislative council at Jerusalem. Its main function was to serve as a supreme court when Jewish law was interpreted. The Sanhedrin met in the temple collonade in the impressive chambers of hewn stone, where members of the council sat in a semicircle. An accused prisoner, dressed in garments of mourning, was arraigned in front of the council; and if evidence against the prisoner warranted, the Sanhedrin had authority to decree capital punishment for offenses which violated major Jewish laws. However, the council was not authorized to carry out its sentence and execute the prisoner, for Roman law forbade them from putting an individual to death without the sanction of the Roman procurator. Jurisdiction of the Sanhedrin in the time of Jesus extended only throughout Judea; and as long as Jesus preached in Galilee and Perea, the council was unable to arrest him. When Jesus entered Jerusalem for his last Passover, however, he was within the jurisdiction of the Sanhedrin, where evil and unscrupulous leaders of the council were able to take him, arrange a charge of blasphemy against him, and then manipulate Pilate, the Roman procurator, to bring about the crucifixion. (LTJA, p. 182.)

26:63 "Jesus held his peace" could have been translated more literally "Jesus kept silent."

The court had found nothing for which they could sentence Jesus, so apparently they were hoping he would say something they could interpret as being incriminating.

There was nothing to answer. No consistent or valid testimony had been presented against Him; therefore He stood in dignified silence. Then Caiaphas, in violation of the legal proscription against requiring any person to testify in his own case except voluntarily and on his own initiative, not only demanded an answer from the Prisoner, but exercised the potent prerogative of the high-priestly office, to put the accused under oath, as a witness before the sacerdotal court. "And the high priest answered and said unto him, I adjure thee by the living, God, that thou tell us whether thou be the Christ, the Son of God." The fact of the distinct specification of "the Christ" and "the Son of God" is significant, in that it implies the Jewish expectation of a Messiah, but does not acknowledge that He was to be distinctively of divine origin. Nothing that had gone before can be construed as a proper foundation for this inquiry. The charge of sedition was about to be superseded by one of greater enormity—that of blasphemy. (JTC, p. 625.)

The demand "I adjure thee by the living God" required a response, as suggested in Leviticus 5:1. Only then did Jesus answer them.

26:66 "He is guilty of death" could have been translated "He is liable to death." (See Luke 23:15.)

The Joseph Smith Translation reads, "He is guilty, *and worthy* of death." (Italics added.)

Thus the judges in Israel, comprising the high priest, the chief priests, the scribes and elders of the people, the Great Sanhedrin, unlawfully assembled, decreed that the Son of God was deserving of death, on no evidence save that of His own acknowledgment. By express provision the Jewish code forbade the conviction, specifically on a capital charge, of any person on his own confession, unless that was amply supported by the testimony of trustworthy witnesses. As in the Garden of Gethsemane Jesus had voluntarily surrendered Himself, so before the judges did He personally and voluntarily furnish the evidence upon which they unrighteously declared Him deserving of death. There could be no crime in the claim of Messiahship or divine Sonship, except that claim was false. We vainly search the record for even an intimation that inquiry was made or suggested as to the grounds upon which Jesus based His exalted claims. The action of the high priest in rending his garments was a dramatic affectation of pious horror at the blasphemy with which his ears had been assailed. It was expressly forbidden in the law that the high priest rend his clothes; but from extra-scriptural writings we learn that the rending of garments as an attestation of most grievous guilt, such as that of blasphemy, was allowable under traditional rule. There is no indication that the vote of the judges was taken and recorded in the precise and orderly manner required by the law. . . .

In strict accuracy we cannot say that the Sanhedrists sentenced Christ to death, inasmuch as the power to authoritatively pronounce capital sentences had been taken from the Jewish council by Roman decree. The highpriestly court, however, decided that Jesus was worthy of death, and so certified when they handed Him over to Pilate. . . .

The law and the practice of the time required that any person found guilty of a capital offense, after due trial before a Jewish tribunal, should be given a second trial on the following day; and at this later hearing any or all of the judges who had before voted for conviction could reverse themselves; but no one who had once voted for acquittal could change his ballot. A bare majority was sufficient for acquittal, but more than a majority was required for conviction. By a provision that must appear to us most unusual, if all the judges voted for conviction on a capital charge the verdict was not to stand and the accused had to be set at liberty; for, it was argued, a unanimous vote against a prisoner indicated that he had no friend or defender in court, and that the judges might have been in conspiracy against Him. Under this rule in Hebrew jurisprudence the verdict against Jesus, rendered at the illegal night session of the Sanhedrists, was void, for we are specifically told that "they all condemned him to be guilty of death." [Mark 14:64.] (JTC, pp. 626–28.)

26:69–75 (Read Mark 14:66–72; Luke 22:54–62; John 18:15–18, 25–27. Review Matt. 26:33–35, Mark 14:29–31, Luke 22:33–34, John 13:36–38.) In this well-known account of Peter's denial or "disowning," note that he never denied the divinity of Jesus Christ; he rather denied *knowing* the man Jesus. (See section 1, "Peter: Denial of.")

Much of the criticism of Simon Peter is centered in his denial of his acquaintance with the Master. This has been labeled "cowardice." Are we sure of his motive in that recorded denial? He had already given up his occupation and placed all worldly goods on the altar for the cause. If we admit that he was cowardly and denied the Lord through timidity, we can still find a great lesson. Has anyone more completely overcome mortal selfishness and weakness? Has anyone repented more sincerely? Peter has been accused of being harsh, indiscreet, impetuous, and fearful. If all these were true, then we still ask, Has any man ever more completely triumphed over his weaknesses? (Spencer W. Kimball, *Speeches of the Year,* 1971.)

26:69 "Damsel" actually means "servant girl."

26:71 The Greek word translated "porch" also means "gatehouse."

26:73 The men's accusation could have been translated "Certainly you also are one of them, for your dialect gives you away."

26:74 "The cock crew" simply means "the rooster crowed."

"To curse" and "to swear" should not be understood in this context as being profane or vulgar. Rather, they are used in the sense of taking a solemn oath.

27:1–2 Read Mark 15:1; Luke 22:66; 23:1; John 18:28. See commentary for Matthew 26:59.

These titles as held by officials of the Jewish hierarchy in the time of Christ must not be confused with the same designations as applied to holders of the Higher or Melchizedek Priesthood. The high priest of the Jews was the presiding priest; he had to be of Aaronic descent to be a priest at all; he became high priest by Roman appointment. The elders, as the name indicates, were men of mature years and experience, who were appointed to act as magistrates in the towns, and as judges in the ecclesiastical tribunals, either in the Lesser Sanhedrins of the provinces, or in the Great Sanhedrin at Jerusalem. The term "elder" as commonly used among the Jews in the days of Jesus had no closer relation to eldership in the Melchizedek Priesthood than had the title "scribe." The duties of Jewish high priests and elders combined both ecclesiastical and secular functions; indeed both offices had come to be in large measure political perquisites. (JTC, p. 644.)

27:2 No Jewish tribunal had authority to inflict the death penalty; imperial Rome had reserved this prerogative as her own. The united acclaim of the Sanhedrists, that Jesus was deserving of death, would be ineffective until sanctioned by the emperor's deputy, who at that time was Pontius Pilate, the governor, or more properly, procurator, of Judea, Samaria, and Idumea. Pilate maintained his official residence at Caesarea, on the Mediterranean shore; but it was his custom to be present in Jerusalem at the times of the great Hebrew feasts, probably in the interest of preserving order, or of promptly quelling any disturbance amongst the vast and heterogeneous multitudes by which the city was thronged on these festive occasions. The governor with his attendants was in Jerusalem at this momentous Passover season. Early on Friday morning, the "whole council," that is to say, the Sanhedrin, led Jesus, bound, to the judgment hall of Pontius Pilate; but with strict scrupulosity they refrained from entering the hall lest they become defiled; for the judgment chamber was part of the house of a Gentile, and somewhere therein might be leavened bread, even to be near which would render them ceremonially unclean. Let every one designate for himself the character of men afraid of the mere proximity of leaven, while thirsting for innocent blood! (JTC, pp. 631–32.)

27:3–10 Read Acts 1:15–20.

27:3 "Repented himself" could have been translated more literally "felt remorse." The approximate value of the "thirty pieces of silver" has been given by Elder James E. Talmage:

> This amount, approximately seventeen dollars in our money, but of many times greater purchasing power with the Jews in that day than now with us, was the price fixed by the law as that of a slave; it was also the foreseen sum of the blood-money to be paid for the Lord's betrayal. That the silver was actually paid to Judas, either at this first interview or at some later meeting between the traitor and the priests, is demonstrated by after events. (JTC, p. 592.)

(See BD, "Aceldama," "Potter's Field.")

27:4–5 And they said unto him, What is that to us? See thou to *it; thy sins be upon thee.*

And he cast down the pieces of silver in the temple, and departed, and went, and hanged himself *on a tree. And straightway he fell down, and his bowels gushed out, and he died.* (JST; italics added.)

(See section 1, "Judas.")

27:4 "See thou to that" could have been translated "You must see to that!" This idea has also been translated "That's your problem"; "That's your affair"; "That is your business"; "That's your responsibility"; and "That is your concern."

27:5 There is an apparent discrepancy between the account of Judas Iscariot's death given by Matthew (27:3–10) and that in Acts (1:16–20). According to the first, Judas hanged himself; the second states that he fell headlong, "and all his bowels gushed out." If both records be accurate, the wretched man probably hanged himself, and afterward fell, possibly through the breaking of the cord or the branch to which it was attached. Matthew says the Jewish rulers purchased the "field of blood"; the writer of the Acts quotes Peter as saying that Judas bought the field with the money he had received from the priests. As the ground was bought with the money that had belonged to Iscariot, and as this money had never been formally taken back by the temple officials, the field bought therewith belonged technically to the estate of Judas. The variations are of importance mainly as showing independence of authorship. The accounts agree in the essential feature, that Judas died a miserable suicide. (JTC, p. 650.)

27:9 This verse has been translated "Then what was spoken by Jeremiah the prophet was fulfilled: "They took the thirty silver coins, the price set on him by the people of Israel.'" (NIV.)

This prophecy of Jeremiah ("Jeremy") is not found in our present Bible. (See section 1, "Thirty pieces of silver.")

27:10 *And therefore they took the pieces of silver,* and gave them for the potter's field, as the Lord appointed *by the mouth of Jeremy.* (JST; italics added.)

27:11–14 Read Mark 15:2–5; Luke 23:2–5; John 18:28–39.

27:12 And Jesus said unto him, Thou sayest *truly; for thus it is written of me.* (JST; italics added.)

27:14 The Joseph Smith Translation begins this verse: "And he answered him not to his questions; yea, never a word . . ."

27:15–26 (Read Mark 15:6–15; Luke 23:13–25; John 18:39–40.) These scriptures are usually considered to cover the "second hearing before Pilate," including the release of Barabbas, whereas most students of the scriptures feel the "first hearing before Pilate" was covered in Matthew 27:2–11, Mark 15:1–5, Luke 23:1–6, and John 18:28–38.

Jesus is now back before Pilate, who with a rude sense of justice is desirous of releasing him. The attempt to transfer jurisdiction and responsibility to Herod has failed. Calling together the chief priests and rulers, Pilate announces again that Jesus is innocent and tells them that Herod also confirms this finding. But to appease the Jews, Pilate offers to do two things: (1) To chastise Jesus for crimes he did not commit; and (2) To pardon him for offenses of which he was not convicted.

According to custom, Pilate could release at Passover time a convicted criminal. If, he reasoned, Jesus could be chosen as the culprit to free, such an act would have the effect of approving the conviction and death sentence imposed by the Sanhedrin, but of superseding it with an official pardon. Hence, Pilate asks, "Shall I pardon Jesus who has done nothing worthy of death anyway, or shall I release this insurrectionist Barabbas, who is also a robber and a murderer?"

Mingling with the mob-multitude are those friendly to the Master's Cause; they see the practical wisdom of Pilate's suggestions and so call for Jesus' release. But the chief priests spue forth their poisonous venom and persuade the multitude to ask for the life of Barabbas and the death of Jesus. The chorus chanted by the multitude becomes one of, "Crucify him. Crucify him."

And so it was to be—Christ crucified, Barabbas freed; and how often is the scene repeated wherever mob rule is found. Justice is crucified on a cross of hate; evil is freed to canker the souls of hate-filled persons. (DNTC 1:805–6.)

(See section 1, "Barabbas.")

27:15 The statement "the governor was wont [accustomed] to release unto the people a prisoner" would indicate that this procedure was an established custom. This verse could have been translated more literally "Now from festival to festival it was the custom of the governor to release a prisoner to the crowd, the one they wanted."

27:19 The Joseph Smith Translation replaces "dream" with "vision."

Concerning the wife of Pilate, Dummelow has written:

In tradition her name is given as Procla, or Claudia Procula, and she is said to have been inclined to Judaism, or even to have been a proselyte, and afterwards to have become a Christian. In the Greek Church she is canonized. (*Dummelow,* p. 716.)

27:20 The Greek text indicates that the word *for* should be inserted: "that they should ask *for* Barabbas."

27:24–25 Wherein lay the cause of Pilate's weakness? He was the emperor's representative, the imperial procurator with power to crucify or to save; officially he was an autocrat. His conviction of Christ's blamelessness and his desire to save Him from the cross are beyond question. Why did Pilate waver, hesitate, vacillate, and at length yield contrary to his conscience and his will? Because, after all, he was more slave than freeman. He was in servitude of his past. He knew that should complaint be made of him at Rome, his corruption and cruelties, his extortions and the unjustifiable slaughter he had caused would all be brought against him. He was the Roman ruler, but the people over whom he exercised official dominion delighted in seeing him cringe, when they cracked, with vicious snap above his head, the whip of a threatened report about him to his imperial master, Tiberius. (JTC, p. 641.)

(See BD, "Pilate.")

27:24 "A tumult was made" could have been translated more literally "an uproar was arising [occurring]."

"See ye to it" has been translated "The responsibility is yours"; "You must see to that yourselves"; "It is your concern."

The Joseph Smith Translation reads, " . . . see that ye do nothing unto him."

The meaning of Pilate's washing his hands before the Jews is given by Elder Bruce R. McConkie:

> At this point (or perhaps earlier, as the Inspired Version account indicates) Pilate, following the Jewish practice in such cases (Deut. 21:1–9), performed the ritualistic ceremony designed to free him from responsibility for Jesus' death. (DNTC 1:810.)

27:27–32 (Read Mark 15:15–21; Luke 23:26; John 19:1–16.) Prior to crucifixion a scourging or whipping takes place so that the victim will not suffer for an extended time on the cross.

> Scourging was a frightful preliminary to death on the cross. The instrument of punishment was a whip of many thongs, loaded with metal and edged with jagged pieces of bone. Instances are of record in which the condemned died under the lash and so escaped the horrors of living crucifixion. In accordance with the brutal customs of the time, Jesus, weak and bleeding from the fearful scourging He had undergone, was given over to the half-savage soldiers for their amusement. He was no ordinary victim, so the whole band came together in the Pretorium, or great hall of the palace, to take part in the diabolical sport. They stripped Jesus of His outer raiment, and placed upon Him a purple robe. Then with a sense of fiendish realism they platted a crown of thorns, and placed it about the Sufferer's brows; a reed was put into His right hand as a royal scepter; and, as they bowed in a mockery of homage, they saluted Him with: "Hail, King of the Jews!" Snatching away the reed or rod, they brutally smote Him with it upon the head, driving the cruel thorns into His quivering flesh; they slapped Him with their hands, and spat upon Him in vile and vicious abandonment. (JTC, pp. 638–39.)

(See section 1, "Scourge.")

27:27 "Common hall" has been translated "armory," "governor's palace," and "praetorium."

(See section 1, "Praetorium.")

27:29 "Platted" could have been translated "braided," "woven," or "twisted." (See section 1, "Platted.")

27:31 "And after that they had mocked him" has been translated "And when they had finished their fun"; "When they had finished making fun of him"; and "When they had finished their mockery."

27:32 The cross consisted of two parts, a strong stake or pole 8 or 9 ft. high, which was fixed in the ground, and a movable cross-piece (patibulum), which was carried by the criminal to the place of execution. Sometimes the patibulum was a single beam of wood, but more often it consisted of two parallel beams fastened together, between which the neck of the criminal was inserted. Before him went a herald bearing a tablet on which the offense was inscribed, or the criminal himself bore it suspended by a cord round his neck. At the place of execution the criminal was stripped and laid on his back, and his hands were nailed to the patibulum; the patibulum, with the criminal hanging from it, was then hoisted into position and fastened by nails or ropes to the upright pole. The victim's body was supported not only by the nails through the hands, but by a small piece of wood projecting at right angles (sedile), on which he sat as on a saddle. Sometimes there was also a support for the feet, to which the feet were nailed. The protracted agony of crucifixion sometimes lasted for days, death being caused by pain, hunger, and thirst. *(Dummelow,* pp. 716–17.)

Elder James E. Talmage has prepared commentary on the conscription of Simon to help carry the cross:

> Jesus started on the way bearing His cross. The terrible strain of the preceding hours, the agony in Gethsemane, the barbarous treatment He had suffered in the palace of the high priest, the humiliation and cruel usage to which He had been subjected before Herod, the frightful scourging under Pilate's order, the brutal treatment by the inhuman soldiery, together with the extreme humiliation and the mental agony of it all, had so weakened His physical organism that He moved but slowly under the burden of the cross. The soldiers, impatient at the delay, peremptorily impressed into service a man whom they met coming into Jerusalem from the country, and him they compelled to carry the cross of Jesus. No Roman or Jew would have voluntarily incurred the ignominy of bearing such a gruesome burden; for every detail connected with the carrying out of a sentence of crucifixion was regarded as degrading. The man so forced to walk in the footsteps of Jesus, bearing the cross upon which the Savior of the world was to consummate His glorious mission, was Simon, a native of Cyrene. From Mark's statement that Simon was the father of Alexander and Rufus we infer that the two sons were known to the evangelist's readers as members of the early Church, and there is some indication that the household of Simon the Cyrenian came to be numbered with the believers. (JTC, pp. 652–53.)

(See section 1, "Crucifixion," "Cyrene.")

27:33 (Read Mark 15:22; Luke 23:33; John 19:17.) The Joseph Smith Translation replaces "skull" with "burial." Elder James E. Talmage provides background on the possible meaning of the word, but also points out, "It is probable that the bodies of executed convicts were *buried* near the place of death." (Italics added.)

> "The Place of a Skull"—The Aramaic Hebrew name "Golgotha," the Greek "Kranion," and the Latin "Calvaria" or, as Anglicized, "Calvary," have the same meaning, and connote "a skull." The name may have been applied with reference to topographical features, as we speak of the brow of a hill; or, if the spot was the usual place of execution, it may have been

so called as expressive of death, just as we call a skull a death's head. It is probable that the bodies of executed convicts were buried near the place of death; and if Golgotha or Calvary was the appointed site for execution, the exposure of skulls and other human bones through the ravages of beasts and by other means, would not be surprising; though the leaving of bodies or any of their parts unburied was contrary to Jewish law and sentiment. The origin of the name is of as little importance as are the many divergent suppositions concerning the exact location of the spot. (JTC, p. 667.)

(See section 1, "Golgotha.")

27:34 (Read Mark 15:23; compare Luke 23:36; see Ps. 69:21.) The offering of vinegar was in direct fulfillment of the Messianic prophecy of Psalm 69:21: "And in my thirst they gave me vinegar to drink."

Preparatory to affixing the condemned to the cross, it was the custom to offer each a narcotic draught of sour wine or vinegar mingled with myrrh and possibly containing other anodyne ingredients, for the merciful purpose of deadening the sensibility of the victim. This was no Roman practice, but was allowed as a concession to Jewish sentiment. When the drugged cup was presented to Jesus He put it to His lips, but having ascertained the nature of its contents refused to drink, and so demonstrated His determination to meet death with faculties alert and mind unclouded. (JTC, pp. 654–55.)

(See BD, "Gall.")

27:35 (Read Mark 15:24; Luke 23:34; John 19:23–24. See Ps. 22:18.) Elder James E. Talmage quoted a description of crucifixion from Smith's *Bible Dictionary:*

"[Crucifixion] was unanimously considered the most horrible form of death. Among the Romans also the degradation was a part of the infliction, and the punishment if applied to freemen was only used in the case of the vilest criminals. . . . The criminal carried his own cross, or at any rate a part of it. Hence, figuratively *to take, to take up or bear one's cross is to endure suffering, affliction, or shame,* like a criminal on his way to the place of crucifixion (Matt. 10:38; 16:24; Luke 14:27, etc.). The place of execution was outside the city (Kings 21:13; Acts 7:58; Heb. 13:12), often in some public road or other conspicuous place. Arrived at the place of execution, the sufferer was stripped naked, the dress being the perquisite of the soldiers (Matt. 27:35). The cross was then driven into the ground, so that the feet of the condemned were a foot or two above the earth, and he was lifted upon it; or else stretched upon it on the ground and then he was lifted up with it." It was the custom to station soldiers to watch the cross, so as to prevent the removal of the sufferer while yet alive. "This was necessary from the lingering character of the death, which sometimes did not supervene even for three days, and was at last the result of gradual benumbing and starvation. But for this guard, the persons might have been taken down and recovered, as was actually done in the case of a friend of Josephus. . . . In most cases the body was suffered to rot on the cross by the action of sun and rain, or to be devoured by birds and beasts. Sepulture was generally therefore forbidden; but in consequence of Deut. 21:22, 23, an express national exception was made in favor of the Jews (Matt. 27:58). This accursed and awful mode of punishment was happily abolished by Constantine." (JTC, pp. 667–68.)

The "casting of lots" for some of Jesus" garments was a fulfillment of prophecy:

The Messianic prophecy—"They part my garments among them, and cast lots upon my vesture" (Psalm 22:18)—contains two parts: (1) His garments are to be divided among them; and (2) For his vesture or robe they are to cast lots.

Jewish men wore five articles of clothing: A headdress, shoes, an inner garment, an outer garment, and a girdle. These items, according to Roman custom, became the property of the soldiers who performed the crucifixion. There were four soldiers and each took one article of clothing. In the case of Jesus, the robe, woven of a single piece of cloth, apparently was of excellent workmanship, and for this the soldiers elected to cast lots. (DNTC 1:820.)

27:36–37 Read Mark 15:26; Luke 23:38; John 19:19–22.

27:37 And Pilate wrote a title, and put it on the cross, and the writing was,

JESUS OF NAZARETH, THE KING OF THE JEWS, in letters of Greek, and Latin, and Hebrew.

And the chief priests said unto Pilate, It should be written and set up over his head, his accusation, This is he that said he was Jesus, the King of the Jews.

But Pilate answered and said, What I have written, I have written; let it alone. (JST)

"His accusation written" could have been translated "the written notice of the accusation."

27:38 Read text and commentary for Mark 15:27–28. Read also Luke 23:32–33; John 19:18.

27:39–44 Read Mark 15:29–32; Luke 23:35–43. See Psalm 22:8.

The dominant note in all the railings and revilings, the ribaldry and mockery, with which the patient and submissive Christ was assailed while He hung, "lifted up" as He had said He would be, was that awful "If" hurled at Him by the devil's emissaries in the time of mortal agony; as in the season of the temptations immediately after His baptism it had been most insidiously pressed upon Him by the devil himself. That "If" was Satan's last shaft, keenly barbed and doubly envenomed, and it sped as with the fierce hiss of a viper. Was it possible in this the final and most dreadful stage of Christ's mission, to make Him doubt His divine Sonship, or, failing such, to taunt or anger the dying Savior into the use of His super-human powers for personal relief or as an act of vengeance upon His tor-mentors? To achieve such a victory was Satan's desperate purpose. The shaft failed. Through taunts and derision, through blasphemous challenge and dia-bolical goading, the agonized Christ was silent. (JTC, pp. 658–59.)

With evil intent and purpose, as he hung in agony on the cross, Jesus was mocked and derided by the spectator-multitude, whose members were pleased to see him die; by the chief priests, who caused his death; by the Roman soldiers, to whom slaughter and death were common occurrences; and by one of the thieves, who was crucified with him. (Luke 23:39–43.) And out of it all came added testimony of his divine Sonship.

(1) The railings of the multitude fulfilled the Messianic prophecy: "All they that see me laugh me to scorn: . . . They gaped upon me with their mouths, as a ravening and a roaring lion." (Psalm 22:7, 13.)

(2) Again the people are reminded of his promise to raise the temple of his body after three days.

(3) From the chief priests, scribes, and elders came the testimony that he saved others; that is, they knew and are certifying that Jesus healed the sick and raised the dead.

(4) With their words of scorn these same chief priests, scribes, and elders also fulfill the Messianic prophecy which foretold the very words of ridicule they would use as he hung before them: "He trusted on the Lord that he would deliver him: let him deliver him, seeing he delighted in him." (Psalm 22:8.)

(5) This very admission that Jesus trusted in God is itself a pronounce-ment that his enemies knew he had lived a righteous life and had walked in a pious path.

(6) They also certify that they knew and understood his claim to divine Sonship, and that his express teaching had been that he was the Son of God. (DNTC 1:821–22.)

27:39 "Reviled him" could have been translated "blas-pheming him" or "speaking abusively of him." Other trans-lations are "hurled abuse," "derided," "hurled insults," and "jeered."

27:43 The Joseph Smith Translation changes the clause "if he will have him" to "if he will save him, let him save him." (See BD, "Son of God.")

27:44 "Cast the same in his teeth" could have been translated more literally "began reproaching him." The basic idea is that they were insulting Jesus. Other translations are "insulted him in the same way," "taunted him in the same way," and "heaped insults on him."

One of the thieves also, which were crucified with him, cast the same in his teeth. *But the other rebuked him, saying, Dost thou not fear God, seeing thou art under the same condemnation; and this man is just, and hath not sinned; and he cried unto the Lord that he would save him.*

And the Lord said unto him, This day thou shalt be with me in Paradise. (JST; italics added.)

27:45 Read Mark 15:33; Luke 23:44–45. Compare John 19:14.

The darkness was brought about by miraculous operation of natural laws directed by divine power. It was a fitting sign of the earth's deep mourning over the impending death of her Creator. (JTC, p. 660.)

27:46–49 Read Mark 15:34–36; John 19:28–29. See Psalm 22:1.

27:46 Identical wording is found in Psalm 22:1: "My God, my God, why hast thou forsaken me?"

What mind of man can fathom the significance of that awful cry? It seems, that in addition to the fearful suffering incident to crucifixion, the agony of Gethsemane had recurred, intensified beyond human power to endure. In that bitterest hour the dying Christ was alone, alone in the most terrible reality. That the supreme sacrifice of the Son might be consummated in all its fulness, the Father seems to have withdrawn the support of his immediate Presence, leaving to the Savior of men the glory of complete victory over the forces of sin and death. (JTC, p. 661.)

(See BD, "Eli.")

27:49 Some Greek texts include the following idea at the end of this verse: "Another man took a spear and pierced his side, and blood and water came out." This would be consistent with John 19:34. (See section 1, "Pierced by spear.")

27:50–51 Read Mark 15:37–38; Luke 23:45–46; John 19:30.

27:50 "Yielded up the ghost" has also been translated "gave up his spirit," "breathed his last," and "dismissed his spirit and died."

Jesus when he had cried again with a loud voice, *saying, Father, it is finished, thy will is done*, yielded up the ghost. (JST; italics added.)

While . . . the yielding up of life was voluntary on the part of Jesus Christ, for He had life in Himself and no man could take His life except as He willed to allow it to be taken, (John 1:4; 5:26; 10:15–18) there was of necessity a direct physical cause of dissolution. As stated also the crucified sometimes lived for days upon the cross, and death resulted, not from the infliction of mortal wounds, but from internal congestion, inflammations, organic disturbances, and consequent exhaustion of vital energy. Jesus, though weakened by long torture during the preceding night and early morning, by the shock of the crucifixion itself, as also by intense mental agony, and particularly through spiritual suffering such as no other man has ever endured, manifested surprising vigor, both of mind and body, to the last. The strong, loud utterance, immediately following which He bowed His head and "gave up the ghost," when considered in connection with other recorded details, points to a physical rupture of the heart as the direct cause of death. . . . The present writer believes that the Lord Jesus died of a broken heart. The psalmist sang in dolorous measure according to his inspired prevision of the Lord's passion: "Reproach hath broken my heart: and I am full of heaviness; and I looked for some to take pity, but there was none; and for comforters, but I found none. They gave me also gall for my meat; and in my thirst they gave me vinegar to drink." (Psalm 69:20, 21; see also 22:14.) (JTC, pp. 668–69.)

(See section 1, "Death of Jesus.")

27:51 But Christ is now sacrificed; the law is fulfilled; the Mosaic dispensation is dead; the fulness of the gospel has come with all its light and power; and so—to dramatize, in a way which all Jewry would recognize, that the kingdom had been taken from them and given to others—Deity rent the veil of the temple "from the top to the bottom." The Holy of Holies is now open to all, and all, through the atoning blood of the Lamb, can now enter into the highest and holiest of all places, that kingdom where eternal life is found. Paul, in expressive language (Heb. 9 and 10), shows how the ordinances performed through the veil of the ancient temple were in similitude of what Christ was to do, which he now having done, all men become eligible to pass through the veil into the presence of the Lord to inherit full exaltation. (DNTC 1:830.)

27:52–53 Compare Helaman 14:25; 3 Nephi 23:7–13.

27:52 The word *saints* appears only this one time in the four gospels.

This verse could have been translated "And the memorial tombs were opened and many bodies of the holy ones that had fallen asleep were raised up."

The Joseph Smith Translation adds the clause "who were many."

Earlier prophets had foreseen the resurrection of Christ

and some of the things immediately associated with it. (See Isa. 26:19, Moses 7:55–56, Hel. 14:25, 3 Ne. 23:7–13.)

27:54–56 Read Mark 15:39–41; Luke 23:47–49.

27:55 The Joseph Smith Translation adds the phrase "for his burial" at the end of this verse.

27:56 See BD, "Salome."

27:57–60 Read text and commentaries for Mark 15:42–46. Read also Luke 23:50–54; John 19:38–42. See BD, "Arimathaea," "Joseph of Arimathaea."

27:61 (Read Mark 15:47; Luke 23:55–56.) "Sitting over against the sepulchre" means "sitting *opposite* the grave." Sometimes it has been translated "sitting before the grave." Other translations are "facing the grave" and "sitting in front of the tomb."

27:62–66 See Joseph Smith Translation Matthew 27:65.

27:63 By quoting the earlier words of the Savior ("After three days I will rise again") the enemies of Jesus became witnesses of his claim of the power of resurrection. Jesus had taught this doctrine not only to his disciples (Matt. 16:21; 17:22–23; 20:18–19) but also to the public (Matt. 12:40; John 2:19). (See section 1, "Three days will rise.")

27:64–66 "Sure" could also have been translated "secure."

27:64 "Error" could have been translated "fraud," or "deception." The Joseph Smith Translation uses the word "imposture."

28:1–10 (Read text and commentaries for Mark 16:1–8. Read also Luke 23:55–56; 24:1–11.) The Joseph Smith Translation makes several contributions to these verses: verse 1: "week, *early in the morning,* came"; verse 2: *"two angels";* verse 3: *"their* countenance . . . *their* raiment . . . fear of *them* . . . became *as though* they were dead"; verse 4: *"angels . . . we."* (Italics added.) (See section 1, "Resurrected being: Appearances of Jesus as.")

28:1–8 How much there is incident to the death, burial, and resurrection of our Lord which ennobles and exalts faithful women. They wept at the cross, sought to care for his wounded and lifeless body, and came to his tomb to weep and worship for their friend and Master. And so it is not strange that we find a woman, Mary of Magdala, chosen and singled out from all the disciples, even including the apostles, to be the first mortal to see and bow in the presence of a resurrected being. Mary, who had been healed of much and who loved much, saw the risen Christ! . . .

Jesus appeared first to Mary Magdalene and then to other women. To Mary the mother of Joses, to Joanna, to Salome the mother of James and John, and to other unnamed women, the two angels announced the resurrection, and sent them to tell Peter and the other disciples. As they went, Jesus appeared and greeted them with the familiar "All hail." And so again it was women who were honored with a visitation from their friend the resurrected Lord. (DNTC 1:843, 846.)

(See section 1, "Resurrection: Women at.")

28:1–4 Many people have questioned the exact time of the resurrection and have wondered when the Savior emerged from the tomb.

Our Lord definitely predicted His resurrection from the dead on the third day, (Matt. 16:21; 17:23; 20:19; Mark 9:31; 10:34; Luke 9:22; 13:32; 18:33), and the angels at the tomb (Luke 24:7), and the risen Lord in Person (Luke 24:46) verified the fulfillment of the prophecies; and apostles so testified in later years (Acts 10:40; 1 Cor. 15:4). This specification of the third day must not be understood as meaning after three full days. The Jews began their counting of the daily hours with sunset; therefore the hour before sunset and the hour following belonged to different days. Jesus died and was interred during Friday afternoon. His body lay in the tomb, dead, during part of Friday (first day), throughout Saturday, or as we divide the days, from sunset Friday to sunset Saturday, (second day), and part of Sunday (third day). We know not at what hour between Saturday sunset and Sunday dawn He rose. (JTC, p. 697.)

28:1 The Greek text of this verse clearly indicates the plural for "sabbath." According to the texts the first phrase of the verse should read "After the sabbaths." Some New Testament scholars have maintained that there were two sabbaths during the week of the atonement of Jesus Christ. They then theorize that the body of Jesus was in the tomb for one day more than is accounted for in the traditional position held by the Catholic Church.

28:2–4 See verses 11–15.

Saturday, the Jewish Sabbath, had passed, and the night preceding the dawn of the most memorable Sunday in history was well nigh spent, while the Roman guard kept watch over the sealed sepulchre wherein lay the body of the Lord Jesus. While it was yet dark, the earth began to quake; an angel of the Lord descended in glory, rolled back the massive stone from the portal of the tomb, and sat upon it. His countenance was brilliant as the lightning, and his raiment was as the driven snow for whiteness. The soldiers, paralyzed with fear, fell to the earth as dead men. When they had partially recovered from their fright, they fled from the place in terror. Even the rigor of Roman discipline, which decreed summary death to every soldier who deserted his post, could not deter them. Moreover, there was nothing left for them to guard; the seal of authority had been broken, the sepulchre was open, and empty. (JTC, p. 678.)

28:5–7 The darkness and the despair of Friday were changed into the light and joy of the day when the Savior was resurrected from the dead, breaking forever the bands of physical death and guaranteeing every person life after death.

> Here was the greatest miracle of human history. Earlier he had told them, "I am the resurrection and the life." (John 11:25.) But they had not understood. Now they knew. He had died in misery and pain and loneliness. Now, on the third day, he arose in power and beauty and life, the first fruits of all who slept, the assurance for men of all ages that "as in Adam all die, even so in Christ shall all be made alive." (1 Cor. 15:22.)
>
> On Calvary he was the dying Jesus. From the tomb he emerged the living Christ. The cross had been the bitter fruit of Judas' betrayal, the summary of Peter's denial. The empty tomb now became the testimony of His divinity, the assurance of eternal life, the answer to Job's unanswered question: "If a man die, shall he live again?" (Job 14:14.)
>
> Having died, he might have been been forgotten, or, at best, remembered as one of many great teachers whose lives are epitomized in a few lines in the books of history. Now, having been resurrected, he became the Master of Life. Now, with Isaiah, his disciples could sing with certain faith: "His name shall be called Wonderful, Counsellor, The mighty God, The everlasting Father, The Prince of Peace." (Isa. 9:6.) (Gordon B. Hinckley, *Ensign,* May 1975, p. 94.)

(See section 1, "Resurrected being" and "Resurrection.")

28:7 (See text and commentary for Matt. 28:16–20.) "I have told you" could have been translated "That is what I had to tell you."

28:8 "Fear" has also been translated "awe."

28:9–10 "All hail" means "Be you rejoicing." It could have been translated "Good day!"

Although this first appearance of the resurrected Jesus Christ as recorded by Matthew is very brief and sketchy, the New Testament carefully documents several other appearances:

> 1. To Mary Magdalene, near the sepulchre (Mark 16:9, 10; John 20:14).
> 2. To other women, somewhere between the sepulchre and Jerusalem (Matt. 28:9).
> 3. To two disciples on the road to Emmaus (Mark 16:12; Luke 24:13).
> 4. To Peter, in or near Jerusalem (Luke 24:34; 1 Cor. 15:5).
> 5. To ten of the apostles and others at Jerusalem (Luke 24:36; John 20:19).
> 6. To the eleven apostles at Jerusalem (Mark 16:14; John 20:26).

7. To the apostles at the Sea of Tiberias, Galilee (John 21).

8. To the eleven apostles on a mountain in Galilee (Matt. 28:16).

9. To five hundred brethren at once (1 Cor. 15:6); locality not specified, but probably in Galilee.

10. To James (1 Cor. 15:7). Note that no record of this manifestation is made by the Gospel-writers.

11. To the eleven apostles at the time of the ascension, Mount of Olives, near Bethany (Mark 16:19; Luke 24:50, 51). (JTC, p. 699.)

(See section 1, "Resurrected being: Appearances of Jesus as.")

28:11–15 (Compare Matt. 27:62–66.) "The inconsistent assertion that Christ had not risen but that his body had been stolen from the tomb by the disciples" is a falsehood that has its own refutation, claims Elder James E. Talmage.

Unbelievers of later date, recognizing the palpable absurdity of this gross attempt at misrepresentation, have not hesitated to suggest other hypotheses, each of which is conclusively untenable, Thus, the theory based upon the impossible assumption that Christ was not dead when taken from the cross, but was in a state of coma or swoon, and that He was afterward resuscitated, disproves itself when considered in connection with recorded facts. The spear-thrust of the Roman soldier would have been fatal, even if death had not already occurred. The body was taken down, handled, wrapped and buried by members of the Jewish council, who cannot be thought of as actors in the burial of a living man; and so far as subsequent resuscitation is concerned, Edersheim (vol. 2, p. 626) trenchantly remarks: "Not to speak of the many absurdities which this theory involves, it really shifts—if we acquit the disciples of complicity—the fraud upon Christ Himself." A crucified person, removed from the cross before death and subsequently revived, could not have walked with pierced and mangled feet on the very day of his resuscitation, as Jesus did on the road to Emmaus. Another theory that has had its day is that of unconscious deception on the part of those who claimed to have seen the resurrected Christ, such persons having been victims of subjective but unreal visions conjured up by their own excited and imaginative condition. The independence and marked individuality of the several recorded appearings of the Lord disprove the vision theory. Such subjective visual illusions as are predicated by this hypothesis, presuppose a state of expectancy on the part of those who think they see; but all the incidents connected with the manifestations of Jesus after His resurrection were directly opposed to the expectations of those who were made witnesses of His resurrected state.

The foregoing instances of false and untenable theories regarding the resurrection of our Lord are cited as examples of the numerous abortive attempts to explain away the greatest miracle and the most glorious fact of history. The resurrection of Jesus Christ is attested by evidence more conclusive than that upon which rests our acceptance of historical events in general. Yet the testimony of our Lord's rising from the dead is not founded on written pages. To him who seeks in faith and sincerity shall be given an individual conviction which shall enable him to reverently confess as exclaimed the enlightened apostle of old: "Thou art the Christ, the Son of the living God." Jesus, who is God the Son, is not dead. "I know that my Redeemer liveth." (Job 19:25.) (JTC, pp. 698–99.)

The recorder adds that until the day of his writing, the falsehood of Christ's body having been stolen from the tomb by the disciples was current among the Jews. The utter untenability of the false report is apparent. If all the soldiers were asleep—a most unlikely occurrence inasmuch as such neglect was a capital offense—how could they possibly know that any one had approached the tomb? And, more particularly, how could they substantiate their statement even if it were true, that the body was stolen and that the disciples were the grave-robbers? The mendacious fiction was framed by the chief priests and elders of the people. Not all the priestly circle were parties to it however. Some, who perhaps had been among the secret disciples of Jesus before His death, were not afraid to openly ally themselves with the Church, when, through the evidence of the Lord's resurrection, they had become thoroughly converted. We read that but a few months later "a great company of the priests were obedient to the faith." [Acts 6:7; compare John 12:42.] (JTC, pp. 684–85.)

28:12 "Large money" comes from a Greek term meaning "a sufficient number of silver pieces."

28:14 "Secure you" could have been translated "will set you free from worry." Other translations include "keep you out of trouble" and "see that you do not suffer."

28:16–20 Read Mark 16:15–18. Compare Mormon 9:22–24.

Of all the recorded appearances of the risen Christ to his disciples in Palestine, this one is paramount; and yet of it the present Bible preserves only a most fragmentary account. This was an appearance by appointment, by prearrangement, to which probably a great multitude of disciples was invited. It is likely the occasion of which, as Paul wrote later, "he was seen of above five hundred brethren at once." (1 Cor. 15:6.) If so, the seventies and leading brethren of the Church would have been present, as also perhaps the faithful women who are inheritors of like rewards with obedient priesthood holders.

We do not know when Jesus specified the location of the meeting, but on the night of his betrayal and arrest, he gave this promise: "After I am risen again, I will go before you into Galilee." (Matt. 26:32.) Then the angels at the tomb, as part of their announcement to the women that "he is risen," commanded them to tell his disciples: "He goeth before you into Galilee; there shall ye see him." (Matt. 28:7; Mark 16:7.) And then to confirm again their previously made appointment, and in so doing to reemphasize its importance, the risen Jesus himself said to the women, as they held him by the feet, and worshipped him: "Go tell my brethren that they go into Galilee, and there shall they see me." (Matt. 28:9–10.)

We may suppose that great preparation preceded this meeting; that it dealt with many things, perhaps being similar to his resurrected ministry to multitudes of Nephites; and that from it, by the mouths of many witnesses, the sure testimony of his divine Sonship went forth to the world. (DNTC 1:866–67.)

Concerning the expression "some doubted," Elder Bruce R. McConkie observes:

Not the apostles; they as a group, including Thomas, had come to know of the actual corporeity of his body. But others present, though they recognized him as the risen Lord, had yet (meaning, no doubt, only when he first appeared) to learn that he had a literal tangible body which ate food and could be handled and felt. These who at first doubted the literal nature of the resurrection would, like Thomas, have soon believed and acclaimed, each speaking from the depths of a grateful soul: "My Lord and my God." (John 20:28.) (DNTC 1:867.)

28:16–18 Jesus had designated a mountain in Galilee whereon He would meet the apostles; and thither the Eleven went. When they saw Him at the appointed place, they worshiped Him. The record adds "but some doubted," by which may be implied that others beside the apostles were present, among whom were some who were unconvinced of the actual corporeity of the resurrected Christ. This occasion may have been that of which Paul wrote a quarter of a century later, concerning which he affirms that Christ "was seen of above five hundred brethren at once," of whom, though some had died, the majority remained at the time of Paul's writing, living witnesses to his testimony. [1 Cor. 15:6.] (JTC, p. 694.)

28:19–20 Earlier the Savior had instructed his disciples to restrict their missionary activities to the house of Israel (Matt. 10:5–6), but now he instructed them to "go . . . and teach all nations."

Also earlier Jesus had counseled that prayers to the Father should be "in the name of Jesus Christ." However, as revealed here and in modern times, baptism should be performed "in the name of the Father, and of the Son, and of the Holy Ghost."

MARK

For background information on this book, see BD, "Gospels," "Harmony of the Gospels," and "Mark."

1:1–8 Read text and commentaries for Matthew 3:1–6, 7–12. Read also Luke 3:1–18. Compare John 1:6–34. See also 1 Nephi 10:7–10; D&C 35:4; 84:27–28.

1:1 "Beginning of the gospel" is used by Mark to indicate he is about to tell the story of Jesus Christ and the "good news" of the Atonement. It is not used to refer to the beginning of the gospel on this earth.

The "beginning" of that gospel is that men must repent, be baptized, and receive the Holy Ghost. (D&C 39:6.) This "beginning" merely puts them on the path leading to eternal life; to gain salvation they must thereafter "press forward with a steadfastness in Christ, having a perfect brightness of hope, and a love of God and of all men, . . . feasting upon the word of Christ, and endure to the end." (2 Ne. 31:20.) (DNTC 1:114.)

1:2 At least one of the prophets referred to in this verse is Malachi. (See Mal. 3:1.)

In two dispensations, before both the first and second comings of our Lord, John has come as a messenger before the Lord's face. Malachi's promise that the Lord would send a messenger to prepare the way of his coming, though properly here quoted by Mark, also refers to the Lord's coming in glory, to the day few can "abide," the day he shall sit in "judgment," "the great and dreadful day of the Lord." (Mal. 3:4.) In the full and complete sense, however, the latter-day messenger is the Prophet Joseph Smith; and the everlasting gospel, restored through his instrumentality, is the revealed message. (D&C 45:9.) John came to Joseph Smith and Oliver Cowdery on May 15th, 1829, as a messenger, to commence the actual restoration of the latter-day kingdom, he being the first to bring actual priesthood and keys back to earth again. (D&C 13.) (DNTC 1:115.)

1:8 The Joseph Smith Translation reads, "He shall *not only* baptize you with *water, but with fire, and* the Holy Ghost." (Italics added.) These significant additions make it clear that the baptism of fire is the baptism of the Holy Ghost. The baptism by the Spirit cleanses a person from the corruption of sin as though he had been cleansed by fire. (See section 1, "Baptism: of Spirit.")

1:9–11 Read text and commentaries for Matthew 3:13–17. Read also Luke 3:21–22; John 1:32–34. See also 1 Nephi 10:7–10; 2 Nephi 31:4–21.

1:11 And there came a voice from heaven, saying, Thou art my beloved Son, in whom I am well pleased. *And John bare record of it.* (JST; italics added.)

1:12–13 Read text and commentaries for Matthew 4:1–11. Read also Luke 4:1–13.

1:12 "And immediately the Spirit driveth him into the wilderness" has also been translated "At once the Spirit made him go into the desert." The Joseph Smith Translation simply reads, "The Spirit *took* him into the wilderness." (Italics added.)

1:13 The Joseph Smith Translation indicates that Jesus was not "tempted of Satan," but rather that Satan was "seeking to tempt him."

1:14–15 Read text and commentary for Matthew 4:17. Read also Luke 4:14–15. Compare John 4:43–46.

1:15 This sentence could have been translated "And saying: The appointed time has been fulfilled, and the kingdom of God has drawn near. Be repentant, you people, and have faith in the good news."

1:16–20 Read text and commentaries for Matthew 4:18–22. Read also Luke 5:1–11.

1:19 For further information on Zebedee, see BD, "Zebedee."

1:20 "Straightway" means "without delay," "immediately," or "at once."

The Joseph Smith Translation alters this verse slightly: "And he called them; and straightway they left their father Zebedee . . ."

1:21–28 (Read Luke 4:31–37.) Concerning whether or not evil spirits can enter into a person's body and take possession, Elder Bruce R. McConkie has written:

Before we can understand the casting out of devils, we must have a knowledge of pre-existence and of the personal Fatherhood of God. As revealed in the gospel, God is an exalted and holy Man, a personal being in whose image man is created, a being for whom the family unit continues in the state of immortality. He is the personal Father of the spirits of all men; his spirit children began life as men and women whose bodies were composed of spirit rather than temporal element.

These spirit offspring of Deity, endowed with agency and subject to law, had every opportunity to advance, progress, and gain the privilege of undergoing the probationary experiences of mortality. Two-thirds of them passed the tests of the pre-existent sphere and are now in process of being born into this world as mortal beings. The other one-third, failing to keep their first estate, finally came out in open rebellion against God and his laws. As a result there was war in heaven, and the devil and his followers were cast down to earth. Those so rejected are denied, eternally, the right to have bodies of their own. In this dejected and damnable state they seek to house themselves unlawfully in the bodies of mortal men.

Manifestly, as in all things, there are laws and conditions under which devils have power to force entry into human bodies. And of course in the power and majesty of their priesthood, both Jesus and the legal administrators sent from him have cast these usurping and unclean spirits out of their stolen habitations. On the numerous occasions that our Lord exercised his power over devils, he was fulfilling the Messianic promise: "And he shall cast out devils, or the evil spirits which dwell in the hearts of the children of men." (Mosiah 3:6.) (DNTC 1:167–68.)

(See section 1, "Devils: Possess bodies.")

1:23 The "crying out" is essentially being done by the evil spirit, not by the man possessed of the evil spirit:

When a devil manages to enter the body of a mortal person, such person loses his free agency, and his acts then become and are those of the devil by whom he is possessed. Thus when the devil speaks it is by the mouth of the person whose tabernacle he has stolen. (DNTC 1:168.)

1:24–25 Though Jesus was known to the devils because of his dealings with them in the pre-existent sphere, he consistently refused to permit them to bear record of his divinity. Converting testimony comes from God, not from Lucifer. Had Jesus let unclean spirits go unrebuked, or had he acquiesced in their testimony of him (though in fact it was true), the Jews would have claimed greater justification for their false charge against him, "He hath a devil, and is mad; why hear ye him?" (John 10:20.) (DNTC 1:168.)

1:26 Evil spirits have bodily shape, even though they do not have bodies of "flesh and bones." Thus, an evil spirit actually "steps out" of the physical body it has unrightfully possessed:

The evil spirit who had possessed the man stepped, literally, out of his body. Similarly, in April 1830, when Joseph Smith cast a devil out of Newell Knight, Brother Knight "saw the evil spirit leave him and vanish from his sight." (Joseph Fielding Smith, *Essentials in Church History,* pp. 95–96.) (DNTC 1:168.)

1:27 That the people felt that the teachings and actions of Jesus comprised a "new doctrine" is another indication of their apostate condition. Their scriptures contained accounts of earlier prophets having cured diseases, cast out devils, and even raised the dead. Unbelief among a people always causes such miracles to cease. (See Moro. 7:27–38.)

1:29–39 Read text and commentaries for Matthew 4:23–25; 8:14–15, 16–17. Read also Mark 1:21–22; Luke 4:38–44.

1:30 The Greek word translated "anon" is the same word translated "straightway" in Mark 1:20. The basic meaning of the word is "immediately," "at once," or "without delay." (See section 1, "Straightway.")

The Joseph Smith Translation changes "anon they tell him of her" to read "and they *besought* him *for* her." (Italics added.)

Since administrations and healings follow the exercise of faith, and since the condition of the sick person sometimes precludes a personal request for the blessings of the priesthood, it is proper for friends and loved ones to make such requests and use their faith for the ailing person. (DNTC 1:172.)

1:32 The Joseph Smith Translation of this verse begins: "And at evening after sunset . . ."

Many modern writers have attempted to explain the phenomenon of demoniacal possession; and beside these there are not a few who deny the possibility of actual domination of the victim by spirit personages. Yet the scriptures are explicit in showing the contrary. Our Lord distinguished between this form of affliction and that of simple bodily disease in His instructions to the Twelve: "Heal the sick, cleanse the lepers, raise the dead, cast out devils." In the account of the incidents under consideration, the evangelist Mark observes the same distinction, thus: "They brought unto him all that were diseased, and them that were possessed with devils." In several instances, Christ, in rebuking demons, addressed them as individuals distinct from the human being afflicted, [Matt. 8:32; Mark 1:25; Luke 4:35] and in one such instance commanded the demon to "come out of him, and enter no more into him." [Mark 9:35.] (JTC, pp. 182–83.)

(See section 1, "Devils: Possess bodies.")

1:34 The last part of this sentence could have been translated more literally "but he would not let the demons speak, because they knew him to be Christ." The Greek clearly indicates that the phrase "to be Christ" should be included.

1:40–45 Read text and commentary for Matthew 8:1–4. Read also Luke 5:12–16.

1:45 "And to blaze abroad the matter" has also been

translated "and began to spread the news everywhere" and "and began to talk freely about it, and to spread the news."

The Joseph Smith Translation indicates that "desert places" could have been translated "solitary places."

2:1–12 (Read text and commentaries for Matt. 9:1–8. Read also Luke 5:17–26.) Although Matthew and Luke both give accounts of this healing, Mark includes a few details not included in the other writings. Some scholars believe this man was healed in Peter's home in Capernaum, and Mark might have learned these additional details directly from Peter.

2:1 The Joseph Smith Translation notes that "after *many* days" it was "noised *abroad*." (Italics added.)

2:2 The Joseph Smith Translation replaces "them" with "the multitude." Again, the record indicates that wherever Jesus went "he preached the word unto them."

2:3 This verse could have been translated "And men came bringing him a paralytic carried by four." The Joseph Smith Translation adds "persons" to the end of the verse.

2:6–12 The Savior's acknowledgment that he has power to forgive sins is also an acknowledgment that he is the Son of God.

Both Jesus and the "doctors of the law" who were then present knew that none but God can forgive sins. Accordingly, as a pointed and dramatic witness that the power of God was resident in him, Jesus took (perhaps sought) this appropriate occasion to forgive sins. Being then called in question by the scripturalists who knew (and that rightly) that the false assumption of the power to forgive sins was blasphemy, Jesus did what no imposter could have done—he proved his divine power by healing the forgiven man. To his query, "Does it require more power to forgive sins than to make the sick rise up and walk?" there could be only one answer! They are as one; he that can do the one can do the other. (DNTC 1:177–78.)

2:12 In the Joseph Smith Translation, the last sentence reads, "We never saw the power of God after this manner." This is another acknowledgment that they were in an apostate condition. (See commentary for Mark 1:27.)

2:13–17 Read text and commentaries for Matthew 9:9–13. Read also Luke 5:27–32.

2:14 And as he passed by, he saw Levi the son of Alpheus, sitting at the *place where they receive tribute, as was customary in those days,* and *he* said unto him, Follow me; and he arose and followed him. (JST; italics added.)

2:18–22 Read text and commentaries for Matthew 9:14–17. Read also Luke 5:33–39.

2:18 And they *came* and *said* unto him, *The disciples of John and of the Pharisees used to fast; and* why do the disciples of John and of the Pharisees fast, but thy disciples fast not? (JST; italics added.)

2:20 According to the Greek, the last phrase should have been translated "in that day" rather than "in those days."

2:21 "A piece of new cloth on an old garment" could have been translated more literally "a patch of unshrunk cloth upon an old outer garment."

2:22 The gospel taught by Christ was a new revelation, superseding the past, and marking the fulfilment of the law; it was no mere addendum, nor was it a reenactment of past requirements; it embodied a new and an everlasting covenant. Attempts to patch the Judaistic robe of traditionalism with the new fabric of the covenant could result in nothing more sightly than a rending of the fabric. The new wine of the gospel could not be held in the old time-worn containers of Mosaic libations. Judaism would be belittled and Christianity perverted by any such incongruous association. (JTC, p. 197.)

(See section 1, "Bottles.")

2:23–28 Read text and commentaries for Matthew 12:1–9. Read also Luke 6:1–5.

2:23 "Ears of corn" means "heads of grain."

2:27 This verse could have been translated "The sabbath came into existence for the sake of man, and not man for the sake of the sabbath."

The Joseph Smith Translation adds significant material:

Wherefore the Sabbath was given unto man for a day of rest; and also that man should glorify God, and not that man should not eat;
For the Son of man made the Sabbath day, therefore the Son of Man is Lord also of the Sabbath. (Italics added.)

Elder Bruce R. McConkie explains:

Sabbath observance is not wholly a negative thing; it does not consist entirely in simply resting from one's labors. The Sabbath is a day of worship, a day for man to "glorify God," to pay his devotions to the Most High. (D&C 59:9–17.)

By announcing himself to the Jews as the Lord of the Sabbath, Jesus was in effect saying: "I am the God of Israel, the great Jehovah, your Messiah, the one who made the Sabbath day, giving it to Moses on Sinai; therefore, I am Lord also of the Sabbath and can specify in my own name what constitutes proper Sabbath observance." (DNTC 1:205.)

(See section 1, "Sabbath: Jesus Lord of.")

3:1–6 Read text and commentaries for Matthew 12:10–13. Read also Luke 6:6–11.

3:3 The Greek text indicates that Jesus invited the man with the withered hand to get up and come to the center of the group. It is evident from the text that Jesus wanted all watching him to be able to see what eventually happened.

3:4 "Held their peace" means "kept silent."

3:6–12 Read text and commentaries for Matthew 12:14–21.

3:6 The Herodians were the party followers of Herod. (See BD, "Herodians.")

3:8 "Idumea" appears only five times in the Bible, this being the only appearance in the New Testament. It also appears in D&C 1:36. (See BD and Gazetteer, "Idumea.")

Tyre and Sidon can be located on several of the maps in the Latter-day Saint edition of the King James version of the Bible, including Map 9, grids C/1 and D/1.

3:9 "Lest they should throng him" has also been translated "lest they should crush him."

3:13–21 Read text and commentaries for Matthew 10:1–4. Read also Luke 6:13–16. See 1 Nephi 13:24–26, 39–41; D&C 95:4.

3:14 The Greek text includes the word for *apostles.* Thus, the first part of this verse could have been translated "And he formed a group of twelve, whom he also named 'apostles.'" (See commentary for Luke 6:13; BD, "Apostle.")

3:19 The Greek text indicates that Judas Iscariot was to betray Jesus *later.*

3:21 The Joseph Smith Translation begins this verse: "And when his friends heard *him speak . . .*" (Italics added.)

So zealous and untiring was Jesus in his ministerial labors, not even stopping to eat or rest, that his friends were concerned over his physical well-being; driven by an unstoppable compulsion, he seemed to them as one "beside himself." (DNTC 1:211.)

3:22–27 Read text and commentaries for Matthew 12:22–30. Read also Luke 11:14–23.

3:23–26 *Now Jesus knew this,* and he called them, and said unto them in parables, How can Satan cast out Satan? And if a kingdom be divided against itself, *how can that kingdom stand?*

And if a house be divided against itself, that house cannot stand. And if Satan rise up against himself and be divided, he cannot stand; but *speedily* hath an end. (JST; italics added.)

3:28–30 (Read text and commentaries for Matthew 10:32–33; 12:31–37, 43– 45; Luke 6:45; 11:24–26; 12:8–10.) According to the Joseph Smith Translation, those who commit this unforgiveable sin shall *"inherit* eternal damnation," not just be "in danger" of it. In other words, they will become sons of perdition. (See section 1, "Unpardonable sin.")

And then came certain men unto him, accusing him, saying, Why do ye receive sinners, seeing thou makest thyself the Son of God.

But he answered them and said, Verily I say unto you, All sins *which men have committed, when they repent,* shall be forgiven *them; for I came to preach repentance unto the sons of men.*

And blasphemies, wherewith soever they shall blaspheme, *shall be forgiven them that come unto me, and do the works which they see me do.*

But there is a sin which shall not be forgiven. He that shall blaspheme against the Holy Ghost, hath never forgiveness; but is in danger of *being cut down out of the world. And they shall inherit* eternal damnation.

And this said he unto them because they said, He hath an unclean spirit. (JST; italics added.)

3:29 "Eternal damnation" could have been translated "everlasting sin."

3:31–35 Read text and commentaries for Matthew 12:46–50. Read also Luke 8:19–21; 11:27–28.

3:31 The Joseph Smith Translation begins this verse: "While he was yet with them, and while he was yet speaking, there came there some of his brethren, and his mother . . ."

4:1–2 Read text and commentaries for Matthew 13:1–3, 10–17, 34–35. Read also Mark 4:10–13, 33–34; Luke 8:4, 9–10.

4:3–9 Read text and commentaries for Matthew 13:3–9, 18–23. Read also Mark 4:14–20; Luke 8:5–8, 11–15.

4:3 The first two words in this verse could have been translated "Listen. Look!"

4:10–13 Read text and commentaries for Matthew 13:1–3, 10–17, 34–35. Read also Mark 4:1–2, 33–34; Luke 8:4, 9–10.

4:10 The Joseph Smith Translation reads, "And when he was alone with the twelve, and they that believed on him . . ." This shows that only the disciples learned why Jesus taught in parables and that only they learned the interpretation of the parable directly from him.

4:11 The Greek word and its plural that are translated *mystery* (or *mysteries*) appears twenty-seven times in the New Testament, but only three times in the four gospels: Matthew 13:11, Mark 4:11, and Luke 8:10. The basic meaning of the word is "sacred secret," and it has to do with *silence*. The entry "Mystery" in the Bible Dictionary indicates that the word "denotes in the N.T. a spiritual truth that was once hidden but now is revealed, and that, without special revelation, would have remained unknown. . . . The modern meaning of something incomprehensible forms no part of the significance of the word as it occurs in the N.T." (See section 1, "Mysteries.")

4:12 The Greek word translated as *converted* has the essential meaning of "turn back." (See commentary for Matt. 18:3.)

4:14–20 Read text and commentaries for Matthew 13:3–9, 18–23. Read also Mark 4:3–9; Luke 8:5–8, 11–15.

4:16, 18, 20 The Joseph Smith Translation alters a few words in each of these verses:

16. And these are they likewise *which receive the word* on stony . . .

18. And these are they *who receive the word* among thorns; . . .

20. And these are they *who receive the word* on good ground . . . (Italics added.)

4:18–20 Though Jesus used parables to hide the full meaning of his teachings from the Jews, yet those rebellious hearers could have understood if they had sought the light, and their failure to believe and understand rose to condemn them. Jesus here tells them, in effect, that gospel light does not burst upon men in full noonday splendor, but that it arises in their hearts gradually, line upon line, precept upon precept, here a little and there a little. "He that receiveth light, and continueth in God, receiveth more light; and that light groweth brighter and brighter until the perfect day." (D&C 50:24.) Eventually the faithful, having continued to grow in light and truth, shall have all things revealed to them and shall know all things. (D&C 76:5–10; 93:26–28; 101:32–34; 121:26–29.) (DNTC 1:291.)

4:21–25 Read text and commentaries for Matthew 13:9. Read also Luke 8:16–18.

4:21 The Greek word translated "candle" is often translated "lamp."

The Joseph Smith Translation adds to the end of this verse "I say unto you, Nay."

4:24–25 The Joseph Smith Translation adds to these two verses: " . . . and unto you that *continue to receive,* shall more be given; for he that *receiveth,* to him shall be given; *but* he that *continueth not to receive,* from him shall be taken even that which he hath." (Italics added.)

4:26–29 Compare Matthew 13:24–30. See also D&C 86:1–7; 101:65–66.

> This parable is addressed primarily to those called to carry the message of salvation to the world. Their obligation is to preach the gospel, to plant the seeds of truth in the hearts of men, and then to leave the event in the hands of Deity. Conversion cannot be forced upon a person anymore than man can require a seed to grow. The harvest of converted souls is not gained by the power of the minister who plants the seed. Paul plants, Apollos waters, but it is God who giveth the increase. (1 Cor. 3:6.)
>
> True it is that the soil should be cultivated, that the planted seeds should be watered, fertilized, and given every opportunity for growth. But the ultimate sprouting and growth depends upon a power beyond that of the sower. The earth brings forth of herself; seeds grow by the power of God. And so the minister continues on the Lord's errand, preaching to others, planting more seeds, raising the warning voice, offering salvation to others of the Father's children, and later returns to thrust in his sickle and harvest the original field. (DNTC 1:292.)

This interesting parable is contained only in Mark.

4:30–32 Read text and commentaries for Matthew 13:31–32. Read also Luke 13:18–19.

4:33–34 Read text and commentaries for Matthew 13:1–3, 10–17, 34–35. Read also Mark 4:1–2, 10–13; Luke 8:4, 9–10.

4:33 The last line of this verse is altered in the Joseph Smith Translation: " . . . as they were able to bear."

4:34 "When they were alone, he expounded all things to his disciples" indicates that the doctrines contained in these parables were explained in plainness only to the select few.

4:35–41 Read text and commentaries for Matthew 8:23–27. Read also Luke 8:22–25.

4:37–38 "So that it was now full" indicates that the boat "was getting filled [was nearly swamped]." However, the boat was not yet completely full of water. The Joseph Smith Translation deletes this idea entirely.

"In the hinder part of the ship" (v. 38) has also been translated "in the back of the boat" and "was in the stern."

5:1–20 Read text and commentaries for Matthew 8:28–34. Read also Luke 8:26–39.

5:1 The Gadarenes are the people of Gadara. The term is used only three times in the Bible: Mark 5:1 and Luke 8:26 and 37. (See BD, "Gadara.")

5:4 "The chains had been plucked asunder by him, and the fetters broken in pieces: neither could any man tame him" could have been translated "the chains were snapped apart by him and the fetters were actually smashed; and nobody had the strength to subdue him."

> Evil spirits can completely transform a person physically and mentally. Here we see a demoniac whose mind is deranged and whose physical strength is such as to break chains and fetters at will. From all outward appearances he would be classed by doctors as violently insane. (DNTC 1:312.)

5:7 Devils now suffer eternal torment because of the realization they cannot gain bodies. Even the momentary possession of stolen bodies seemingly gives them some satisfaction and lessens the sting of their torment. Eventually, following the day of final judgment, "the devil and his angels . . . shall go away into everlasting fire; prepared for them; and their torment is as a lake of fire and brimstone, whose flame ascendeth up forever and ever and has no end." (2 Ne. 9:16.) (DNTC 1:312.)

"Adjure" ("implore," "charge under oath") appears in the New Testament only here and in Matthew 26:63 and Acts 19:13.

5:9 The Joseph Smith Translation indicates Jesus did not *ask* the devil to give his name, he commanded him.

The name "Legion" has been described by Elder Bruce R. McConkie:

> Names used by Gods, angels, and devils have specific meanings which connote to the mind something about the personalities, attributes, or missions of the bearers. And what is more apt than for a host of evil spirits to be named *Legion!* Mortal man cannot calculate the total number of rebel spirits who followed Lucifer when one-third of the hosts of heaven assembled under his banner, but certainly their number and name is *Legion*. Some idea of their number may be seen by estimating how many people have and do live on earth and by speculating how many more will live before the final winding up scene. Presumably the earth's millennial population will so far exceed that of any past comparable age that there will be no comparison.
>
> In this instance it is evident that a great host of spirits had taken up unlawful tenancy in the body of one man. Literally, a legion in the Roman army amounted to some six thousand men; figuratively, a legion is an indefinitely large number. The number here was so great as to cause some two thousand swine to career crazily down a steep slope and drown themselves in the sea. (DNTC 1:312.)

5:13 "Jesus gave them leave" means "Jesus permitted them [gave permission to them] to leave."

"Choked" could have been translated "drowned."

Skeptics criticize Jesus for the supposed wanton destruction of the property of others because he commanded or allowed the devils to enter the swine, thus, in effect causing their death. "How can we justify the destruction of the swine?" they ask, as though any of the acts of him whose very course of conduct identifies what is right and wrong need justifying! Jesus did it; therefore, it was right. As well might we condemn Deity for sending or permitting hailstorms to destroy our crops, or for sending drouths upon the earth, or for creating desert land where crops will not grow, as to question the right of the giver of all to take back all or part of what he has given.

In the instant case, if the swine were owned by Jews, they drove an illegal trade; if the hog farm belonged to Gentiles, its very existence was an insult to the national religion. In either event, even according to the local customs and laws, the destruction of the swine was justified. (DNTC 1:312–13.)

5:16 And they that saw *the miracle,* told them *that came out,* how it befell him that was possessed with the devil, *and how the devil was cast out,* and concerning the swine. (JST; italics added.)

5:17 Why did the people request ("pray") Jesus to depart from their borders ("coasts")?

A dramatic miracle had come to their personal knowledge, and it created fear rather than faith in the hearts of the people. Why? Some few, perhaps, were fearful and angry because of the loss of their property. But the real reason was far more basic. These people, worldly and carnal by nature, actually preferred their way of life to that which they would have been obligated to pursue, had they accepted the gospel. Millions of people in the world today have a similar outlook. Such persons are not converted to the truth by miracles; they prefer to gratify their own sensual appetites rather than forsake the world. People whose whole hearts and desires are set on the things of the world would not accept the gospel, "though one rose from the dead" and taught it to them. (Luke 16:31.) Similarly they would not believe the Book of Mormon even if they had a view of the Gold Plates and the Urim and Thummim. (D&C 5:8–10.) Men, in the ultimate analysis, are controlled and governed by the desires of their hearts. When they desire and love darkness rather than light, neither miracles nor any thing else is sufficient to convert their benighted souls. Rather they rebel against the truth, reject the prophets, and pray Jesus "to depart out of their coasts." (DNTC 1:313.)

5:18 The Joseph Smith Translation indicates that the man out of whom the devil had been cast *"spoke to Jesus, and prayed him that he might be with him."* (Italics added.)

5:19 "Howbeit Jesus suffered him not" has also been translated "But Jesus would not let him."

Note that Jesus requested the man to "tell his friends" what had happened to him:

> Even people whose bodies have housed unclean spirits may be cleansed by the power of God, and may be called to serve as witnesses of his divine power. Frequently the great Healer commanded the recipients of his blessings to remain silent, lest their repeated recital of his goodness to them should bring persecution upon him. After each healing Jesus gave such instructions as applied to the particular case. No doubt this healed demoniac was commanded to testify in Decapolis, the region of ten cities, of his miraculous return to normality, because the bitterness against Jesus was not so great in that area, and some, perchance, hearing of the miracle would be led to investigate and believe the truth. (DNTC 1:313–14.)

5:20 The area and some of the cities of the Decapolis can be located on maps 14, 15, 16, and 18 of the Latter-day Saint edition of the King James Version of the Bible.

"And all men did marvel" could have been translated more literally "and all the people began to wonder." The Joseph Smith Translation reads: "and all *that heard him* did marvel." (Italics added.)

5:21–43 Read text and commentaries for Matthew 9:18–26. Read also Luke 8:40–56.

5:22 See BD, "Jairus."

5:24 "Thronged him" means "pressed against him."

5:26 This verse could have been translated more literally "and she had been put to many pains [or had much suffering] by many physicians and had spent all her resources and had not been benefited but, rather, had got worse."

5:30 The Greek word translated as "virtue" could more literally have been translated "power."

> Our Lord's inquiry as to who had touched Him in the throng affords us another example of His asking questions in pursuance of a purpose, when He could readily have determined the facts directly and without aid from others. There was a special purpose in the question, as every teacher finds a means of instruction in questioning his pupils. But there is in Christ's question, "Who touched me?" a deeper significance than could inhere in a simple inquiry as to the identity of an individual; and this is implied in the Lord's further words: "Somebody *hath* touched me: for I perceive that virtue is gone out of me." The usual external act by which His miracles were wrought was a word or a command, sometimes accompanied by the laying on of hands, or by some other physical ministration as in anointing the eyes of a blind man. That there was an actual giving of His own strength to the afflicted whom He healed is evident from the present instance. Passive belief on the part of a would-be recipient of blessing is insufficient; only when it is vitalized into active faith is it a power; so also of one who ministers in the authority given of God, mental

and spiritual energy must be operative if the service is to be effective. (JTC, p. 319.)

(See section 1, "Woman touching hem.")

5:34 The statement of the Savior could have been translated "Daughter, your faith has made you well. Go in peace, and be in good health from your grievous sickness."

> Jesus deliberately publicized this healing miracle. Rather than permit a story to go forth, from which spiritually illiterate persons might falsely suppose that the woman was healed by some virtue attaching to his clothing, or even his own person, Jesus required the woman to tell what she had done, to testify of the blessing received, and to receive from his lips the assurance that the healing grace had come to her because of her faith. (DNTC 1:318–19.)

5:35 "Certain which said" reads as "a man who said" in the Joseph Smith Translation.

5:36 "Believe" could more literally have been translated "exercise faith."

5:41 "Which is, being interpreted" could have been translated "which, translated, means."

Mark's preservation of the exact Aramaic words suggests he had been told these words directly by Peter.

5:42 The last sentence could have been translated more literally "And at once they were beside themselves with great ecstasy."

6:1–6 Read text and commentaries for Matthew 13:54–58.

6:3 The reference to Jesus as "the carpenter" would indicate that Jesus had followed the trade of his foster father, Joseph.

6:4 Another possible translation is "A prophet is not unhonored except in his home territory [father place] and among his relatives and in his own house."

> **6:5** According to the eternal laws which Jesus himself ordained in eternity, miracles are the fruit of faith. Where there is faith, there will be signs, miracles, and gifts of the Spirit. Where there is no faith, these things cannot occur (*Mormon Doctrine,* pp. 242–248, 459–461.) The Master could not and would not violate his own law, and therefore most of his own townsmen were denied the blessings of his healing ministry. On the same basis men cannot be saved in their sins (Alma 11:37); the Lord has ordained the laws by which salvation and all good things come, and until obedience prepares the way, the promised blessings are withheld. (D&C 88:21–24; 130:20–21; 132:5.) Men can no more be saved without obedience than they can be healed without faith. All things operate by law; blessings result from obedience to law and are withheld when there is no obedience. (DNTC 1:322.)

6:6 The first sentence could more literally have been translated "Indeed, he wondered at their lack of faith."

6:7–13 Read text and commentaries for Matthew 9:35–38; 10:5–15. Read also Luke 9:1–6.

6:8 This verse could have been translated more literally "Also, he gave them orders to carry nothing for the trip except a staff alone, no bread, no food pouch, no copper money in their girdle purses."

6:9 In the Joseph Smith Translation, the last clause reads " . . . and not *take* two coats." (Italics added.)

6:11 "Under your feet" is changed to "of your feet" in the Joseph Smith Translation.

6:12 The disciples followed the pattern already established by John the Baptist and by Jesus of commanding the people to *repent*.

To preach repentance is to preach the gospel in its fulness, for it is through repentance that men accept the gospel, have their sins washed away, and get on the path leading to eternal life. The latter-day command, "Say nothing but repentance unto this generation" (D&C 6:9; 11:9), is tantamount to saying, "Preach my gospel to this generation." (DNTC 1:328.)

6:13 Usually James 5:14–16 is quoted to show that the sick should be anointed with oil, and the disciples of Jesus followed this pattern.

According to the revealed pattern, part of the ordinance of administering to the sick consists in anointing with consecrated oil. (Jas. 5:14–16; D&C 42:43–44; *Mormon Doctrine,* pp. 21–22.) In sending the apostles forth they were expressly commanded to conform to the proper form of the ordinance, as well as to exercise the faith needed for the successful performance of healings. (DNTC 1:328.)

(See commentary for Matt. 26:6–13; BD, "Anoint.")

6:14–29 Read text and commentaries for Matthew 14:1–12. Read also Luke 9:7–9.

6:17–20 Read text and commentaries for Matthew 4:12; 14:3–5. Read also Luke 3:19–20.

6:20 The last sentence could have been translated "And after hearing him he was at a great loss what to do, yet he continued to hear him gladly."

For Herod feared John, knowing that he was a just man, and a holy man, and *one who feared God* and observed to *worship* him; and when he heard him he did many things *for him,* and heard him gladly. (JST; italics added.)

6:21 "Chief *estates* of Galilee" could have been translated more literally as "the foremost ones of Galilee."

But when Herod's birth-day was come, *he* made a supper *for* his lords, high captains, and *the* chief *priests* of Galilee. (JST; italics added.)

6:23 Herod's promise to give "unto the half of my kingdom" should not be taken literally. This rhetorical expression is used three times in the book of Esther: 5:3, 6; 7:2.

6:25 "Charger" means a large plate or platter.

6:30–44 Read text and commentaries for Matthew 14:13–21. Read also Luke 9:10–17; John 6:1–14.

6:31 The Greek word frequently translated "deseret place" means a lonely, private, or isolated place. It does not mean an area void of vegetation. The Joseph Smith Translation replaces "desert" with "solitary" in verses 31–32, 35. (See section 1, "Desert places.")

6:35 See commentary for Mark 6:31.

6:37 "Two hundred pennyworth" is derived from the Greek *denarii*. One denarius was equal to the daily wage of a working man

As used in the New Testament, the words *penny* and *pennyworth* mean the same thing. The coinage in use was that of Rome, and the penny, or *denarius,* was the chief Roman silver coin. It was worth about fifteen to seventeen of our cents. Two hundred pennyworth of bread would have cost approximately thirty-two dollars. (LTJA, p. 89.)

6:44 The Greek word translated as "men" literally means male persons. Thus, the word "men" in this verse may not be interpreted generically to include women and children. It is thus possible that *more* than five thousand people were involved in this miracle.

6:45–52 Read text and commentaries for Matthew 14:22–33. Read also John 6:16–21.

6:48 In the Joseph Smith Translation, the last clause reads " . . . *as if he* would have passed by them." (Italics added.)

6:51 "They were sore amazed in themselves beyond measure" could have been translated "in this they were very much amazed within themselves."

Why were the hearts of the apostles hardened with unbelief, wonder, and amazement to see Jesus walk on the sea and again calm the raging storm? Had they not just seen five loaves and two fishes feed five thousand men besides women and children? The answer is found in the fact that the chosen disciples had not yet received the gift of the Holy Ghost. Though they were all pillars of spiritual strength and righteousness, save Judas only, yet "the things of God knoweth no man, but the Spirit of God." (1 Cor. 2:11.) Until the natural man becomes a new creature of the Holy Ghost, until man is born again, until his stony heart is touched by the Spirit of the living God, he cannot, by any power of his own, stand sure and steadfast in the cause of truth. (DNTC 1:348–49.)

6:53–56 Read text and commentaries for Matthew 14:34–36. Read also John 6:22–27.

6:53 This region—a rich, fertile, and productive plain—extended southward along the western shore of the Sea of Galilee from Capernaum on the north to the region around Magdala and Tiberias. Though having set out for Capernaum, apparently because of the storm, Jesus and the apostles landed somewhat south of that city. It was while traveling northward to Capernaum that the sick and diseased from the cities, villages, and whole region of Gennesaret were brought to him to be healed. This day his grace and goodness were bounteously manifested. Truly but few of his healings and miracles find place in recorded writ. (DNTC 1:350.)

This area can be located on map 15 (grid D/3) of the Latter-day Saint edition of the King James Version of the Bible.

7:1–23 Read text and commentaries for Matthew 15:1–20. Read also Luke 6:39.

7:1 The account in John (John 7:1) indicates that during this time "the Jews sought to kill" Jesus. Because Jesus was not then going to Jerusalem, the apostate religious leaders sent a delegation of "Pharisees and scribes" to watch Jesus, follow him around, and find fault with the things he taught and did.

7:3 Some Greek texts indicate that the customary washing of the hands by the Pharisees included the idea that their hands were to be washed "up to the elbows."

In both ancient and modern scriptures, the Lord has counseled against undue emphasis on the "traditions" of the fathers. Obviously if only traditions were followed, even though they might be right, no progress could be made. When traditions are wrong, they not only impede progress but tend to close the mind to truth.

Rabbinical ordinances and interpretations were added to the Mosaic law by the scribes and teachers over the years. These traditions were actually and formally deemed to be more important and have greater binding force than the law itself. Among them, as supposed guards against ceremonial uncleanness, were the ritualistic washings which Jesus and his disciples had ignored.

This same process of transforming truth into traditions—of changing the law of God into "the doctrines and commandments of men" (I. V. Mark 7:7), by the interpretations and additions of uninspired teachers—is precisely what took place in the great apostasy of the Christian Era. To the pure and simple doctrines of Christ, the scribes and priests of early Christendom added such things as: selling indulgences, which freed the wicked from past sins and authorized them to commit future crimes without divine penalty; forgiving sins (supposedly) through repeated and perfunctory confessions; praying departed persons out of purgatory; burning candles for the dead; praying to Mary or other so-called saints, rather than to the Lord; worshiping of images; turning of sacramental emblems into the literal flesh and blood of Jesus (transubstantiation); laying up a reservoir of good works in heaven which the so-called Church can sell to those who need them (supererogation); sacrificing Jesus over again in the mass; forbidding priests and other church officials to marry; doing penance to gain forgiveness of sins; adorning houses of worship with costly materials; wearing of expensive robes and costumes by priests and other church officers; using elaborate ministerial titles; augmenting the church treasury by gambling; and so forth.

All these, and many other like traditions, are counted of more importance by some than the law of God as originally given by the Master. Indeed, the so-called Christian Church today is founded in large part on the traditions of the "elders" rather than on the revelations of heaven. (DNTC 1:366–67.)

(See section 1, "Washing of hands by Jews.")

7:4 In the Joseph Smith Translation, the last clause reads " . . . except they wash *their bodies,* they eat not." (Italics added.)

7:6–7 He answered and said unto them, Well hath Esaias prophesied of you hypocrites, as it is written, This people honoureth me with their lips, but their heart is far from me. Howbeit, in vain do they worship me, teaching *the* doctrines *and* commandments of men. (JST; italics added.)

7:9–10 And he said unto them, *Yea, altogether* ye reject the commandment of God, that ye may keep your own *traditions.*

Full well is it written of you, by the prophets whom ye have rejected.

They testified these things of a truth, and their blood shall be upon you.

Ye have kept not the ordinances of God; for Moses said, *Honor* thy father and thy mother; and whoso curseth father or mother, let him die the death *of the transgressor, as it is written in your law; but ye keep not the law.* (JST; italics added.)

By professing to believe in the prophets, while in practice rejecting their teachings, the Jews were in reality rejecting the prophets. Thus, those Jews were placing themselves in the same position which their fathers occupied when those fathers slew the prophets; and so the blood of the prophets would be required at the hands of the Jews and their fathers, for both rejected them. Similarly, some today, by rejecting the teachings of the ancient apostles and prophets, are classifying themselves as people who would have slain the holy men of old, and so the blood of the true martyrs of religion shall be upon them. (DNTC 1:368.)

7:11 "Corban" appears only in this one verse of scripture.

The word *Corban* means a gift, or sacrifice, to God. Its use permitted a man to take a vow to avoid or accept any obligation. Thus, a man would say, "I take a vow to God, or rather, Corban to me is, to abstain from wine for a certain length of time." He might say, "Corban to me is this or that man's hospitality." He could decline to assist his parents by saying. "Corban to me for a time is to not assist my parents." (See Dummelow, *A Commentary on the Holy Bible,* p. 678; see also Matthew 15:3–6.) In this way the intent of such laws as "honor thy father and thy mother" was frustrated. The Savior recognized this and chastised the Pharisees and scribes for avoiding legitimate obligations in this manner. (LTJA, p. 96.)

The Joseph Smith Translation reads, "he is of age" rather than "he shall be free."

(See section 1, "Corban.")

7:12 "And ye suffer him no more to do ought" could have been translated "you men no longer let him do a single thing," "you do not let him do anything," or "you let him do nothing."

7:15 There is nothing from without, that entering into *a man,* can defile him, *which is food;* but the things which come out of him; those are they that defile the man, *that proceedeth forth out of the heart.* (JST; italics added.)

7:19 Elder Bruce R. McConkie has offered commentary on the term "purging all meats":

Or, as per the marginal reading, "This he said, making all meats clean." In other words, Peter—who received the divine command to eat meat which had been unclean according to Mosaic standards (Acts 10)—speaking through Mark, his scribe, is showing that Jesus here revealed that the old prohibitions as to eating certain meats was ended. (DNTC 1:369.)

"Draught" appears five times in the Bible with three different meanings. Here it means "privy."

7:22 The eye is not evil in and of itself, but what the person thinks about what he sees may be evil.

7:24–30 Read text and commentaries for Matthew 15:21–28.

7:24 In the Joseph Smith Translation, the last part of this verse reads " . . . and would *that no man should come*

unto him. But he could not *deny them; for he had compassion upon all men.*" (Italics added.)

The references to Tyre and Sidon indicate that Jesus and his disciples had traveled from Capernaum north to the coastal areas of what is now known as the Mediterranean Sea, to the Gentile cities of Syrophenicia.

7:26 This background information on the woman indicates that she is a Gentile (not a Jew) who spoke Greek but by race was a Syrian living in Phoenicia. (See commentary for Matt. 15:21–28. See BD, "Syrophenician.")

7:27 "Let the children first be filled" is changed in the Joseph Smith Translation to "Let the children *of the kingdom* first be filled." (Italics added.)

> This is a clear statement that gospel blessings should go *first* to the chosen seed and *later* to others. In a manner of speaking, this principle applies today also. That is, the children of the kingdom—those who belong to the Church, those who love the Lord and are seeking to keep his commandments—are the ones who are entitled to the healing power of the priesthood; while those who are without and who have not yet covenanted in the waters of baptism to devote themselves to righteousness, are entitled to healing graces only on conditions of unusual faith and desire, a faith and desire which should lead them to join the Church when their petitions are granted. (DNTC 1:371.)

(See section 1, "First/last.")

The Greek word translated as "meet" means "right" or "proper." The basic meaning of the text is "It is not fair to take the bread of the children and throw it to the little dogs." The Jews sometimes referred to the Gentiles in this manner.

7:28–30 The Joseph Smith Translation adds to the answer of the woman "thou sayest truly," indicating that she accepted the explanation given by Jesus.

> Why did Jesus delay the granting of this Gentile woman's petition? For the very reason apparently, that she was a Gentile and not a Jew, for the gospel (with all its healing powers and graces) was to be offered to the Jews before it went to the Gentiles. Jesus mortal ministry was with Israel, not with other nations. His healing of this or any Gentile person came by special dispensation because of great faith. Previously he had commanded the apostles to go only to the lost sheep of the house of Israel and not to preach the message of salvation to the Gentiles. (Matt. 10:5–6.) Certainly the course he followed in this instance was instructive to his disciples, tested the faith of the Gentile woman, taught that persistence and importunity in prayer will bring reward, and showed that greater faith is sometimes found among heathens than in the chosen lineage of Israel. (DNTC 1:371.)

7:31–37 Read text and commentaries for Matthew 15:29–31.

7:31 For a further identification of the cities and area included in the Decapolis (ten cities located in an area south and east of the Sea of Galilee) see the commentary for Matthew 4:25 and section 1, "Decapolis."

7:32–37 The procedures used by Jesus in healing the blind are not always identical. (See commentaries for Matt. 9:27–34; section 1, "Blindness.")

In this account of the healing of a deaf person whose speech also was impaired, we find Jesus adapting his procedures to the need of the individual. As in some other cases, the need existed to strengthen the faith of the physically handicapped person. With the same purpose in mind, Jesus had once asked an impotent man, "Wilt thou be made whole?" (John 5:6); before opening the eyes of two blind men, he had engendered faith in their souls by asking, "Believe ye that I am able to do this?" (Matt. 9:28); and to two other blind men, on a coming occasion, he would ask, "What will ye that I shall do unto you?" (Matt. 20:32.)

But now the Lord is dealing with a believing soul who cannot hear his words or give fluent answer to them. And so what is more natural than to make use of common signs, known to and understood by the deaf and speech-inhibited man, to indicate what the Master could and would do in accordance with the law of faith? Thus we find Jesus putting his own fingers in the man's ears, to indicate that by faith the hearing obstruction would be pierced; we find the Master spitting and placing his own saliva on the man's tongue (a practice commonly believed by the rabbis and Jews to be one having healing virtue), to indicate that the tongue would be loosed and gain fluency; and finally, our Lord, looking up to heaven, spoke the divine command, "Ephphatha, that is, Be opened," to signify to the man that the power of God was opening his ears and loosing his tongue. (DNTC 1:373.)

7:34 See BD, "Ephphatha."

7:36 On some occasions a knowledge of healing miracles may engender faith, on others it fosters unbelief and persecution. Accordingly, Jesus sought either to advertise or keep secret his miraculous healings, depending upon the needs of the ministry at the particular time and place. On a previous occasion, when he was leaving this very region, he had commanded the man out of whom a legion of devils was cast to publish the miracle through all Decapolis. (Mark 5:19–20.) But now, sojourning, for a season in the area, the Master Healer sought to keep secret the dramatic nature of this particular miracle. (DNTC 1:373.)

7:37 The Greek word translated "dumb" means "speechless."

8:1–10 (Read text and commentary for Matthew 15:32–39.) Because many of the Jewish people eventually rejected Jesus as the Messiah, it is sometimes difficult to remember how many people followed after him during the earlier part of his ministry.

It is difficult to overestimate the transcendent appeal Jesus had for multitudes of the common people. Here we find four thousand men, plus an uncounted host of women and children, staying with him in a solitary area, without food or other necessities for three days; they are now faint from fasting and weary for want of beds and other normal home conveniences, yet they remain to hear every spoken word and rejoice in every gracious healing. Would they so have acted except for the inward assurance that here indeed, as they themselves had frankly avowed, was "the God of Israel"? (Matt. 15:31.) (DNTC 1:375.)

8:4 And his disciples answered him, From whence can a man satisfy these, *so great a multitude,* with bread, here in the wilderness? (JST; italics added.)

The disciples' question does not necessarily mean that they questioned the ability of Jesus.

Those speaking were the apostles who had participated in the feeding of the five thousand. They knew full well the miraculous creative powers of the Master whom they followed. The question as here put is rather an expression of their own inability to feed such a multitude with the scanty provisions at hand. We may suppose also that in their subservient position as followers of him who exceeds all men in power and might, they modestly and properly left to their Lord the decision as to what should be done. It is evident that Jesus did not deem it necessary to test their faith, as he had done before, by saying, "They need not depart; give ye them to eat" (Matt. 14:16); this time he simply asked what provisions were at hand and gave directions as to their distribution. (DNTC 1:375–76.)

8:7 And they had a few small fishes; and he blessed *them,* and commanded to set them also before *the people, that they should eat.* (JST; italics added.)

8:8 The Joseph Smith Translation uses "bread" in place of "meat." The Greek word often translated "meat" simply means "food." (See section 1, "Meat.")

8:10 The area identified here as "parts of Dalmanutha" is identified in Matthew 15:39 as the "coasts of Magdala." This area was evidently somewhere west of the Sea of Galilee, but its exact location now is not known. (See BD, "Dalmanutha.")

8:11–21 Read text and commentaries for Matthew 16:1–12. Read also Luke 12:54–57.

8:12 The Joseph Smith Translation adds additional information to this verse: "generation, *save the sign of the* *prophet Jonah; for as Jonah was three days and three nights in the whale's belly, so likewise shall the Son of Man be buried in the bowels of the earth."* (Italics added.)

8:16 And they reasoned among themselves, saying, *He hath said this, because we have no bread.* (JST; italics added.)

8:22–26 Compare Matthew 9:27–31.

This miracle is unique; it is the only recorded instance in which Jesus healed a person by stages. It may be that our Lord followed this course to strengthen the weak but growing faith of the blind man. It would appear that the successive instances of physical contact with Jesus had the effect of adding hope, assurance, and faith to the sightless one. Jesus personally (1) led the blind man by the hand out of the town, (2) applied his own saliva to the eyes of the sightless one, (3) performed the ordinance of laying on of hands, and (4) put his hands a second time upon the man's eyes.

Certainly the manner in which this healing took place teaches that men should seek the Lord's healing grace with all their strength and faith, though such is sufficient for a partial cure only, following the receipt of which, however, they may then gain the added assurance and faith to be made whole and well every whit. Men also are often healed of their spiritual maladies by degrees, step by step as they get their lives in harmony with the plans and purposes of Deity. (DNTC 1:379–80.)

8:23 "He asked him if he saw ought" could have been translated "and began to ask him: 'Do you see anything?'"

8:26 Some of the Greek texts do not contain the phrase "nor tell it to any in the town."

8:27–30 (Read text and commentaries for Matthew 16:13–20. Read also Luke 9:18–22.) The location of Caesarea Philippi can be determined on several maps in the Latter-day Saint edition of the King James Version of the Bible: 14 (grid E/2); 15 (grid E/1); 18 (grid B/4). (See BD, "Caesarea Philippi.")

8:29 The Joseph Smith Translation makes it clear that Peter knew that Christ was the Son of God: "Thou art the Christ, *the Son of the living God."* (Italics added.)

8:31–33 Read text and commentaries for Matthew 16:21–23. Read also Luke 9:21–22.

8:33 "For thou savourest not the things that be of God, but the things that be of men" have also been translated as "Your thoughts are men's thoughts, not God's"; "For you are not on the side of God, but of men"; and "You do not have in mind the things of God, but the things of men."

That Jesus "looked on his disciples" would suggest that Peter's statement was in the minds of all the apostles, for although the rebuke is directed toward Peter, it appears to be intended for all the others as well.

8:34–37 Read text and commentaries for Matthew 16:24–26. Read also Luke 9:23–25.

8:35 For whosoever will save his life, shall lose it; *or whosoever will save his life, shall be willing to lay it down for my sake; and if he is not willing to lay it down for my sake, he shall lose it.*

But whosoever shall *be willing* to lose his life for my sake, and the gospel's, the same shall save it. (JST; italics added.)

8:37 The Joseph Smith Translation adds the following verse after verse 37: "Therefore deny yourselves of these, and be not ashamed of me."

8:38 Read text and commentaries for Matthew 16:27–28. Read also Luke 9:26–27. (See section 1, "Resurrection.")

To gain salvation men must, among other things: (1) Deny themselves of all worldly lusts, and (2) Not be ashamed of Christ, of his gospel, and of his laws. Those who do not keep the commandments, because to do so would bring upon them the ridicule of the world, are by their course of disobedience signifying they are ashamed of Christ. A Latter-day Saint, for instance, who uses liquor or tobacco rather than face the jeers and contumely of associates is ashamed of Christ. (DNTC 1:396.)

The Joseph Smith Translation adds the following verses after verse 38:

And they shall not have part in that resurrection when he cometh.

For verily I say unto you, That he shall come; and he that layeth down his life for my sake and the gospel's shall come with him, and shall be clothed with his glory in the cloud, on the right hand of the Son of Man.

Elder Bruce R. McConkie has defined the "resurrection when he cometh":

The morning of the first resurrection, or resurrection of the just, or of life. At the Second Coming of our Lord the graves of those meriting a celestial kingdom "shall be opened; and they also shall be caught up to meet him in the midst of the pillar of heaven—They are Christ's, the first fruits." Thereafter those destined to inherit a terrestrial kingdom shall come forth, and finally, after the millennium, those entitled to a telestial inheritance and those who shall be cast out as sons of perdition shall come forth from their graves. (D&C 88:95–102.) (DNTC 1:396–97.)

Modern scripture also teaches that martyrs for the sake of Jesus Christ shall have "life eternal." (D&C 98:13.)

9:1 (Read text and commentaries for Matthew 16:27–28. Read also Mark 8:38; Luke 9:26–27.) In the Joseph

Smith Translation, this verse begins "And he said unto them *again* . . ." (Italics added.)

It is apparent that on a previous occasion, of which we have no present scriptural record, Jesus taught his disciples the truths about the doctrine of translation and promised that some of them would continue to live on earth until his Second Coming. John the Beloved is the only known one of those disciples who has continued to live without tasting death. (John 21:20–24.) Until the identity of any others is revealed, we have no way of knowing who they are or what mission they have been able to perform because of their translation. (DNTC 1:397.)

9:2–10 Read text and commentaries for Matthew 17:1–9. Read also Luke 9:28–36.

9:2 The Joseph Smith Translation contributes the following to this verse: "and John, *who asked him many questions concerning his sayings;* and *Jesus* . . ." (Italics added.)

9:3 See BD, "Fullers."

9:4 The Joseph Smith Translation reads, "with Moses, *or in other words, John the Baptist and Moses;* and . . ." (Italics added.)

It is not to be understood that John the Baptist was the Elias who appeared with Moses to confer keys and authority upon those who then held the Melchizedek Priesthood, which higher priesthood already embraced and included all of the authority and power John had held and exercised during his ministry. Rather, for some reason that remains unknown—because of the partial record of the proceedings—John played some other part in the glorious manifestations then vouchsafed to mortals. Perhaps he was there, as the last legal administrator under the Old Covenant, to symbolize that the law was fulfilled and all old things were done away, thus contrasting his position with that of Peter, James, and John who were then becoming the "first" legal administrators of the New Kingdom. (DNTC 1:404.)

(See section 1, "John the Baptist: On Mount of Transfiguration.")

9:6 Other translations of this verse are "He and the others were so frightened that he did not know what to say" and "For he did not know what to say, for they were exceedingly afraid."

9:8 And suddenly, when they had looked round about *with great astonishment,* they saw no man any more, save Jesus only with themselves. *And immediately they departed.* (JST; italics added.)

9:9 "He charged them" could have been translated "he expressly ordered them."

The comprehensiveness of the Lord's injunction, that until after His rising from the dead they tell no man of their experiences on the mount, prohibited them from informing even their fellows of the Twelve. Later, after the Lord had ascended to His glory, Peter testified to the Church of the wondrous experience, in this forceful way: "For we have not followed cunningly devised fables, when we made known unto you the power and coming of our Lord Jesus Christ, but were eyewitnesses of his majesty. For he received from God the Father honour and glory, when there came such a voice to him from the excellent glory, This is my beloved Son, in whom I am well pleased. And this voice which came from heaven we heard, when we were with him in the holy mount." (2 Pet. 1:16–18.) And John, reverently confessing before the world the divinity of the Word, the Son of God who had been made flesh to dwell among men, solemnly affirmed: "And we beheld his glory, the glory as of the only begotten of the Father, full of grace and truth." (John 1:14.) (JTC, p. 372.)

9:10 This is not the first time Peter, James, and John had heard Jesus teach of his coming death and resurrection, yet they still failed to catch the full significance of the teaching.

9:11–13 Read text and commentaries for Matthew 17:10–13.

9:12 "And be set at nought" could have been translated "and be treated as of no account."

"And restoreth all things" reads as "and prepareth all things; and teacheth you of the prophets" in the Joseph Smith Translation.

9:13 The Joseph Smith Translation adds the following to this verse: "and he bore record of me, and they received him not. Verily this was Elias."

The wording of this verse indicates that an earlier prophet had foretold that John the Baptist (as the Elias who would be the forerunner of Jesus) would be rejected by the Jews and killed for his testimony. This prophecy does not appear in the Old Testament.

9:14–29 Read text and commentaries for Matthew 17:14–21. Read also Luke 9:37–43.

9:15 "Saluted him" could have been translated "began to greet him."

Why were all the people greatly amazed when Jesus made his appearance? Obviously his coming was dramatic and striking in nature. Many have supposed, and it could well be, that some of the glory, which but a few hours before had shone forth from him on the Mount of Transfiguration, was still manifest. We know that such was the case with Moses, when that ancient prophet returned to Israel after communing with Deity for forty days upon the mountain. Indeed, "the skin of Moses' face shone" with such brilliance that he wore a veil while talking to the children of Israel. (Ex. 34:28–35.) (DNTC 1:410.)

9:17–18 The Joseph Smith Translation reads, "that hath a dumb spirit *that is a devil; and when he seizeth him,* he teareth *him; . . .*" (Italics added.)

9:20–23 And when *the man saw him, immediately he was torn by the spirit;* and he fell on the ground and wallowed, foaming.

And *Jesus* asked his father, How long *a time* is it since this came unto him? and *his father* said, *When* a child;

And ofttimes it hath cast him into the fire and into the *water,* to destroy him, but if thou canst, *I ask thee to* have compassion on us, and help us.

Jesus said unto him, If thou *wilt* believe all things *I shall say unto you, this is* possible to him that believeth. (JST; italics added.)

9:21 "Of a child" could have been translated "From childhood on." Another translation is "Ever since he was a child." The Joseph Smith Translation gives the answer of the father as "When a child."

9:22 The supplication of the agonized father for the benefit of his sorely afflicted son—"Have compassion on us, and help us" (Mark 9:22)— shows that he made the boy's case his own. In this we are reminded of the Canaanite woman who implored Jesus to have mercy on her, though her daughter was the afflicted one [Matt. 15:22]. In these cases, faith was exercised in behalf of the sufferers by others; and the same is true of the centurion who pleaded for his servant and whose faith was specially commended by Jesus [Matt. 8:5–10]; of Jairus whose daughter lay dead [Luke 8:41–42, 49–50]; and of many who brought their helpless kindred or friends to Christ and pleaded for them. . . . Faith to be healed is as truly a gift of God as is faith to heal; and, as the instances cited prove, faith may be exercised with effect in behalf of others. In connection with the ordinance of administering to the afflicted, by anointing with oil and the laying on of hands, as authoritatively established in the restored Church of Jesus Christ, the elders officiating should encourage the faith of all believers present, that such be exerted in behalf of the sufferer. In the case of infants and of persons who are unconscious, it is plainly useless to look for active manifestation of faith on their part, and the supporting faith of kindred and friends is all the more requisite. (JTC, p. 395.)

9:24 "I believe; help thou mine unbelief" could also have been translated "I have faith! Help me out where I need faith!"

To this qualifying expression "If thou canst do anything," which implied a measure of uncertainty as to the ability of the Master to grant what he asked, and this perhaps as in part a result of the failure of the apostles, Jesus replied: "If thou canst believe"; and added, "all things are possible to him that believeth." The man's understanding was enlightened; up to that moment he had thought that all depended upon Jesus; he now saw that the issue rested largely with himself. It is noteworthy that the Lord specified belief rather than faith as the condition essential to the case. The man was evidently trustful, and assuredly fervent in his hope that Jesus could help; but it is doubtful that he knew what faith really meant. He was receptive and eagerly teachable, however, and the Lord strengthened his feeble and uncertain belief. The encouraging explanation of the real need stimulated him to a more abounding trust. Weeping in an agony of hope he cried out: "Lord, I believe"; and then, realizing the darkness of error from which he was just beginning to emerge, he added penitently "help thou mine unbelief." (JTC, p. 380.)

(See section 1, "Faith.")

9:30–32 Read text and commentary for Matthew 17:22–23. Read also Luke 9:43–45.

9:30 "He would not that any man should know it" has also been translated "Jesus did not want anyone to know where he was."

The Joseph Smith Translation adds "privately" after "Galilee."

9:33–37 Read text and commentaries for Matthew 18:1–5. Read also Luke 9:46–48.

9:34 But they held their peace, *being afraid,* for by the way they had disputed among themselves, who was the greatest *among them.* (JST; italics added.)

9:35 Those who seek personal honors and glory rather than the welfare of Zion, and the triumph of the Lord's own purposes, are not chosen of God to be first, but by him they are cast out and made last and least of all. But those who put themselves last, and become the servants of all for the sake of Christ and the gospel, shall be accounted by him as the first, and they shall gain eternal life. (DNTC 1:415.)

9:37 Whosoever shall *humble himself like one of these* children, and receiveth me, *ye shall receive in my name.* And whosoever shall receive me, receiveth not me *only,* but him that sent me, *even the Father,* (JST; italics added.)

Similar teachings have been given by the Lord in this dispensation. (See D&C 39:5–6; 84:37–38.)

9:38–42 Read Luke 9:49–50.

On a previous occasion, Jesus taught that neither Satan nor his false ministers can cast out devils, for "Every kingdom divided against itself is brought to desolation . . . And if Satan cast out Satan, he is divided against himself." (Matt. 12:25–30.) Now he adds in plainness what was necessarily implied in his previous discourse that only those who follow him and are legal administrators in his kingdom can perform the miracle of casting out devils in his name. (DNTC 1:416.)

9:38 "Because he followeth not us" could have been translated "because he was not accompanying us."

He was not one of the Twelve to whom the express power had been given to cast out devils (Matt. 10:8); he was not one of the inner circle of disciples who traveled, ate, slept, and communed continually with the Master. Luke has it: "He followeth not *with* us"; that is, he is not one of our traveling companions. But from our Lord's reply it is evident that he was a member of the kingdom, a legal administrator who was acting in the authority of the priesthood and the power of faith. Either he was unknown to John who therefore erroneously supposed him to be without authority or else John falsely supposed that the power to cast out devils was limited to the Twelve and did not extend to all faithful priesthood holders. It is quite possible that the one casting out devils was a seventy. There is no New Testament record of the calling of the first quorum of seventy, but when Jesus (at a later day) called a second quorum of seventy into the ministry, he expressly gave them the power to cast out devils. (Luke 10:1–20.) (DNTC 1:417.)

9:39–40 The teachings of the Book of Mormon substantiate the teaching that only righteous persons who are keeping the commandments have the power to perform miracles: "There was not any man who could do a miracle in the name of Jesus save he were cleansed every whit from his iniquity." (3 Ne. 8:1.)

9:42–50 Read text and commentaries for Matthew 18:6–10. Read also Luke 17:1–2.

9:42 The Greek text indicates that an additional thought should be inserted after "millstone": "it would be finer for him if a millstone such as is turned by an ass were put around his neck." The idea is that the millstone is large.

9:43–48

King James Version	Joseph Smith Translation
43 And if thy hand offend thee, cut it off: it is better for thee to enter into life maimed, than having two hands to go into hell, into the fire that never shall be quenched:	40 Therefore, if thy hand offend thee, cut it off; or if thy brother offend thee and confess not and forsake not, he shall be cut off. It is better for thee to enter into life maimed, than having two hands, to go into hell.
	41 For it is better for thee to enter into life without thy brother, than for thee and thy brother to be cast into hell; into the fire that never shall be
44 Where their worm dieth not, and the fire is not quenched.	quenched, where their worm dieth not, and the fire is not quenched.

45 And if thy foot offend thee, cut it off: it is better for thee to enter halt into life, than having two feet to be cast into hell, into the fire that never shall be quenched.

46 Where their worm dieth not, and the fire is not quenched.

47 And if thine eye offend thee, pluck it out: it is better for thee to enter into the kingdom of God with one eye, than having two eyes to be cast into hell fire:

48 Where their worm dieth not, and the fire is not quenched.

42 And again, if thy foot offend thee, cut it off; for he that is thy standard, by whom thou walkest, if he become a transgressor, he shall be cut off.

43 It is better for thee, to enter halt into life, than having two feet to be cast into hell; into the fire that never shall be quenched.

44 Therefore, let every man stand or fall, by himself, and not for another; or not trusting another.

45 Seek unto my Father, and it shall be done in that very moment what ye shall ask, if ye ask in faith, believing that ye shall receive.

46 And if thine eye which seeth for thee, him that is appointed to watch over thee to show thee light, become a transgressor and offend thee, pluck him out.

47 It is better for thee to enter into the kingdom of God, with one eye, than having two eyes to be cast into hell fire.

48 For it is better that thyself should be saved, than to be cast into hell with thy brother, where their worm dieth not, and where the fire is not quenched.

9:48 "Worm" could have been translated "maggot."

9:49 As the flesh of the altar sacrifices had to be seasoned with salt, as a type of preservation from corruption, so also the soul must receive the saving salt of the gospel; and that salt must be pure and potent, not a dirty mixture of inherited prejudice and unauthorized tradition that has lost whatever saltness it may once have had. (JTC, p. 388.)

9:50 Every member of the Church shall be tested and tried in all things, to see whether he will abide in the covenant "even unto death" (D&C 98:14), regardless of the course taken by the other members of his family or of the Church. To gain salvation men must stand on their own feet in the gospel cause and be independent of the spiritual support of others. If some of the saints, who are themselves the salt of the earth, shall fall away, still all who inherit eternal life must remain true, having salt in themselves and enjoying peace one with another. (DNTC 1:421.)

The Joseph Smith Translation reads: "wherewith will ye season it? *(the sacrifice;)* . . ." (Italics added.)

10:1–12 Read text and commentaries for Matthew 19:1–12.

10:1 In the Joseph Smith Translation the last part of this verse reads, "and as he was accustomed to teach, he also taught them again."

10:2 "Tempting him" has been changed to "This they said, thinking to tempt him" in the Joseph Smith Translation.

10:4–12 "A bill of divorcement" could have been translated "a certificate [little book] of dismissal." The idea is that if a man and wife separate, they should legalize the divorce by getting a "writing" or "bill" of divorcement. If a man puts away ("casts out") his wife without giving her a bill of divorcement, and if she subsequently marries and has sexual relations with her new husband, then both she and her husband commit adultery. Thus, the injunction is for a man not to marry a woman who is only "put away" without a bill or writing of divorcement. (See section 1, "Divorce.")

10:13–16 Read text and commentaries for Matthew 19:13–15. Read also Luke 18:15–17. See 1 Nephi 12:7–10.

10:14 The Savior's statement could have been translated more literally "Let the young children come to me; do not try to stop them, for the kingdom of God belongs to suchlike ones."

This statement by Jesus says nothing whatsoever concerning the necessity of little children being baptized before they enter the "kingdom of God." The Book of Mormon also clearly and definitely teaches that little children need no baptism, for baptism is unto the remission of sins; little children cannot repent as they are not held accountable for their sins. (See Moroni 8:10–11; section 1, "Children: No Baptism," "Children: Inherit heaven.")

10:16 The blessing of children is still a practice in the true Church of Jesus Christ.

10:17–27 Read text and commentaries for Matthew 19:16–26. Read also Luke 18:18–27.

10:18 The Joseph Smith Translation changes the order of the words and the punctuation of the last part of this verse: "None is good but one, that is God."

10:19 The Greek word translated "kill" has the more precise meaning of "murder."

10:23 The Savior's statement could have been translated "How difficult a thing it will be for those with money to enter into the kingdom of God." The phrase "of God" is changed to "of my Father" in the Joseph Smith Translation.

10:27 The first part of this verse could have been translated "Looking straight at them, Jesus said, . . ."

And Jesus, looking upon them, *said,* With men *that trust in riches,* it is impossible; but not *impossible with men who trust in God and leave all for my sake, for with such all these things are possible.* (JST; italics added.)

10:28–31 Read text and commentaries for Matthew 19:27–30. Read also Matthew 20:1–16; Luke 18:28–30. See 1 Nephi 12:7–10.

The saints should not boast of their sacrifices for the gospel. Though Peter had forsaken all and was assured of rewards beyond measure as a consequence, yet Jesus rebuked him for putting himself forth as an example of one who had made sacrifices for the building up of the kingdom. (DNTC 1:558.)

10:31 But *there are many who make themselves first, that shall be last, and the last first.*
This he said, rebuking Peter; . . . (JST; italics added.)

10:32–34 Read text and commentaries for Matthew 20:17–19. Read also Luke 18:31–34.

10:34 "And the third day he shall rise again" could have been translated "but three days later [after three days] he will rise."

10:35–45 Read text and commentaries for Matthew 20:20–28.

10:39 In due course James and John and all the apostles, save Judas, drank of the Lord's cup and underwent his baptism—all suffered persecution and possibly even martyrdom, with the exception of John who was translated. Zebedee's son James was slain at Herod's command. (Acts 12:1–2.) (DNTC 1:566.)

(See section 1, "Cup, to drink of, of Christ.")

In spite of the rebuke but shortly before given Peter, that *"there are many who make themselves first, that shall be last,* and the last first" (I. V. Mark 10:30); and in apparent open disregard of the teaching just given in the Parable of the Laborers in the Vineyard, that all servants worthy of exaltation would be rewarded alike, each receiving his "penny" appointed— James and John, aided by their mother, now entreat Jesus for a promise that they will rank next to him in his eternal kingdom.

Tolerant of their human weaknesses, for they as yet have not gained the full and glorious vision of the gospel, Jesus thereupon teaches them how greatness in God's kingdom is gained. It is not the position occupied, but the service rendered; not the office held, but the call magnified; not the rank enjoyed, but the labors performed; not the pre-eminent station attained, but the spiritual diligence exhibited; not where one sits with reference to the King, but the love and obedience shown forth to him. (DNTC 1:565.)

10:40 "But it shall be given to them for whom it is prepared" could have been translated "but it belongs to those for whom it has been prepared."

And Jesus said unto them, Ye shall indeed drink of the cup that I drink of; and *be baptized* with the baptism that I am baptized *with;* but to sit on my right hand, and on my left hand, is not mine to give; but *they shall receive it for whom it is prepared.* (JST; italics added.)

Elder Bruce R. McConkie has commented on "not mine to give":

Certainly it is Christ's to give, for he has all power (Matt. 28:18) and all judgment is committed to the Son. (John 5:22.) Rather: "It is not mine to give as a matter of favoritism; it can be given only in accordance with justice. To sit on my right hand or on my left is not mine to give, except to them for whom it is prepared according to the Father's will, and the Father and I are one." (DNTC 1:566.)

10:42 The Joseph Smith Translation replaces "accounted" with "appointed."

10:45 Through his atoning sacrifice, Christ exercised his ransoming power in two ways: (1) All men are ransomed from the natural death in that they are resurrected and become immortal; and (2) "Many" are ransomed from spiritual death and are returned to the presence of God because they believe and obey the gospel law. (D&C 29:42–45.) (DNTC 1:566.)

10:46–52 (Read text and commentaries for Matthew 20:29–34. Read also Luke 18:35–43.) The repeated use by Bartimaeus of one of the sacred titles for the Messiah ("Son of David") indicates that he did accept Jesus as the Messiah. His faith was sufficient that Jesus could restore his sight. (See BD, "Bartimaeus," "Jericho." Jericho can be located in several of the maps included in the Latter-day Saint edition of the King James Version of the Bible, including map 9 [grid 5/D].)

10:48 The first part of this verse could have been translated "At this many began sternly telling him to be silent."

10:49 "Be of good comfort" could more literally have been translated "take courage."

10:52 "Made thee whole" could have been translated "made you well."

11:1–11 Read text and commentaries for Matthew 21:1–11. Read also Luke 19:29–40; John 12:12–19.

11:10 *That bringeth the kingdom of our father David;* Blessed is *he* that cometh in the name of the Lord. (JST; italics added.)

11:11 The Joseph Smith Translation states that Jesus "looked round about upon all things, and *blessed the disciples.*" (Italics added.)

Only Luke preserves for us the account of Jesus weeping over doomed Jerusalem. (Luke 19:41–44.) Mark says simply that he "looked round about upon all things." But then Mark says, as we learn from this more perfect account in the Inspired Version, that Jesus blessed his disciples. And what an enlightening addition this is to the scriptural account. Though Jerusalem, as a whole, was to be desolated and scourged as few cities have ever been, yet the faithful within her walls were to be saved, preserved, and blessed. (DNTC 1:579.)

11:12–14 Read text and commentaries for Matthew 21:18–22. Read also Mark 11:20–26.

And on the morrow, when they *came* from Bethany he was hungry; and seeing a fig tree afar off having leaves, he came *to it with his disciples; and as they supposed, he came to it to see if* he might find anything thereon.

And when he came to it, *there was nothing but leaves; for as yet the figs were not ripe.*

And Jesus *spake* and said unto it, No man eat fruit of thee hereafter, forever. And his disciples heard *him.* (JST; italics added.)

(See section 1, "Fig tree: Cursed.")

The leafy, fruitless tree was a symbol of Judaism, which loudly proclaimed itself as the only true religion of the age, and condescendingly invited all the world to come and partake of its rich ripe fruit; when in truth it was but an unnatural growth of leaves, with no fruit of the season, nor even an edible bulb held over from earlier years, for such as it had of former fruitage was dried to worthlessness and made repulsive in its worm-eaten decay. The religion of Israel had degenerated into an artificial religionism, which in pretentious show and empty profession outclassed the abominations of heathendom. As already pointed out in these pages, the fig tree was a favorite type in rabbinical representation of the Jewish race, and the Lord had before adopted the symbolism in the Parable of the Barren Fig Tree, that worthless growth which did but cumber the ground. (JTC, p. 527.)

11:15–19 Read text and commentaries for Matthew 21:12–17. Read also Luke 19:45–48.

11:16 This verse could have been translated more literally "And he would not let anyone carry a utensil through the temple."

11:17 The Savior's statement could have been translated "Is it not written, 'My house will be called a house of prayer for all the nations'? But you have made it a cave of robbers." (See commentary for Matt. 21:12–17.)

11:20–26 Read text and commentaries for Matthew 6:5–15; 21:18–22. Read also Mark 11:12–14. See 3 Nephi 13:10.

11:23 "But shall believe that those things which he saith shall come to pass" could have been translated "but has faith that what he says is going to occur, he will have it so."

11:25–26 Read commentaries for Matthew 6:5–15. Read also Luke 11:1–8. See 3 Nephi 13:5–15.

11:27–33 Read text and commentary for Matthew 21:23–27. Read also Luke 20:1–8.

11:32 But if we shall say, Of men; *we shall offend the people. Therefore* they feared the people; for all people *believed* John, that he was a prophet indeed. (JST; italics added.)

12:1–12 Read text and commentaries for Matthew 21:33–46. Read also Luke 20:9–19.

12:12 "Against them" could have been translated "with them in mind." Thus, the first part of this verse could have been translated "At that they began seeking how to seize him, but they feared the crowd, for they took note that he spoke the illustration [parable] with them in mind."

And now they were angry when they heard these words; and they sought to lay hold on him, but feared the people. (JST; italics added.)

12:13–17 Read text and commentaries for Matthew 22:15–22. Read also Luke 20:20–26.

12:15 "Why tempt ye me?" could have been translated "Why do you put me to the test?" (See commentary for Matt. 22:18.)

12:17 The Savior's statement could have been translated "Pay back the things of Caesar to Caesar, but the things of God to God."

12:18–27 Read text and commentaries for Matthew 22:23–33. Read also Luke 20:27–40.

12:24 This verse could have been translated more literally "Jesus said to them: 'Is not this why you are mistaken, your not knowing either the scriptures or the power of God?'"

And Jesus answering said unto them, *Ye do err therefore,* because ye know not, *and understand not* the Scriptures, neither the power of God. (JST; italics added.)

12:26 See BD, "Burning Bush."

12:27 "Ye therefore do greatly err" means "you are much mistaken."

He is not *therefore* the God of the dead, but the God of the living; *for he raiseth them up out of their graves.* Ye therefore . . ." (JST; italics added.)

How can there be a God unless there is a resurrection? Why would God create men and then let them vanish into nothingness? To be God he must be the God of something, and the dead are nothing; hence, there are no dead, "for all live unto him," "for he raiseth them up out of their graves." (DNTC 1:608.)

12:28–34 Read text and commentaries for Matthew 22:34–40.

12:34–37 Read text and commentary for Matthew 22:41–46. Read also Luke 20:41–44.

12:34 In the Joseph Smith Translation, the last part of this verse reads, "And no man after that durst ask him, *saying, Who art thou?*" (Italics added.)

12:37 This verse could have been translated more literally "David himself calls him 'Lord,' but how does it come that he is his son? And the great crowd was listening to him with pleasure."

The Joseph Smith Translation adds these words at the end of this verse: "but the high priest and the elders were offended at him."

12:38–40 Read text and commentaries for Matthew 23:1–22. Read also Luke 11:37–54; 20:45–47.

12:40 "These shall receive greater damnation" could have been translated "these will receive a heavier judgment."

12:41–44 Read Luke 21:1–4

In the accounts kept by the recording angels, figured out according to the arithmetic of heaven, entries are made in terms of quality rather than of quantity, and values are determined on the basis of capability and intent. The rich gave much yet kept back more; the widow's gift was her all. It was not the smallness of her offering that made it especially acceptable, but the spirit of sacrifice and devout intent with which she gave. On the books of the heavenly accountants that widow's contribution was entered as a munificent gift, surpassing in worth the largess of kings. "For if there be first a willing mind, it is accepted according to that a man hath, and not according to that he hath not." [2 Cor. 8:12.] (JTC, pp. 561–62.)

12:44 For all *the rich* did cast in of their abundance; but she *notwithstanding* her want, did cast in all that she had; *yea,* even all her living. (JST; italics added.)

13:1–2 Read text and commentaries for Matthew 24:1–2. Read also Luke 21:5–6. See D&C 45:15–21.

The Joseph Smith Translation adds a great deal to these verses:

And as Jesus went out of the temple, his disciples came to him for to hear him, saying, Master, show us concerning the buildings of the Temple.

And he said unto them, Behold ye these stones of the temple, and all this great work, and buildings of the temple?

Verily I say unto you, they shall be thrown down and left unto the Jews desolate.

And Jesus said unto them, See ye not all these things, and do ye not understand them?

Verily I say unto you, There shall not be left here upon this temple, one stone upon another, that shall not be thrown down.

And Jesus left them and went upon the mount of Olives.

13:3–6 Read text and commentaries for Matthew 24:3–5. Read also Luke 21:7–8.

13:3–4 And as he sat upon the mount of Olives, the disciples came unto him privately, saying,

Tell us, when shall these things be which thou hast said, concerning the destruction of the temple, and the Jews?

And what is the sign of thy coming, and of the end of the world, (or the destruction of the wicked, which is the end of the world?) (JST.)

13:7–8 Read text and commentaries for Matthew 24:6–8. Read also Luke 21:9–11.

13:7 The Joseph Smith Translation adds a great deal to this verse:

And ye also shall hear of wars, and rumors of wars; see that ye be not troubled; for all I have told you must come to pass, but the end is not yet.

Behold, I have told you before, wherefore if they shall say unto you, Behold, he is in the desert; go not forth; Behold, he is in the secret chambers; believe it not.

For as the light of the morning cometh out of the east, and shineth even unto the west, and covereth the whole earth, so shall also the coming of the Son of Man be.

And now I show unto you a parable. Behold, wheresoever the carcass is, there will the eagles be gathered together;

So likewise, shall mine elect be gathered from the four quarters of the earth.

And they shall hear of wars and rumors of wars. Behold I speak unto you for mine elect's sake.

13:8 "These are the beginnings of sorrows" could have been translated "these are a beginning of pangs of distress [birth pangs]."

13:9 (Read text and commentaries for Matthew 24:9. Read also Mark 13:11–13; Luke 21:12–19.) The Greek text indicates that "against" should be changed to "to." The final phrase in this verse would then read "for a witness to them."

13:10 Read text and commentaries for Matthew 24:14.

And *again this gospel of the kingdom shall be preached in all the world, for a witness unto* all nations, *and then shall the end come, or the destruction of the wicked.* (JST; italics added.)

13:11–13 Read text and commentaries for Matthew 24:9. Read also Mark 13:9; Luke 21:12–19.

13:13 Read text and commentaries for Matthew 24:10–13.

13:14–20 Read text and commentaries for Matthew 24:15–22. Read also Luke 17:31–37; 21:20–24.

When you *therefore* shall see the abomination of desolation, spoken of by Daniel the prophet *concerning the destruction of Jerusalem, then you shall stand in the holy place. (Whoso readeth let him* understand.)

Then let them *who* be in Judea flee into *the* mountains;

And let him who is on the housetop *flee, and not return* to take anything out of his house;

Neither let him who is in the field, *return* back *to take his clothes.*

And woe *unto* them who are with child, and *unto* them who give suck in those days.

Therefore pray ye *the Lord,* that your flight be not in the winter, *neither on the Sabbath day.*

For *then,* in those days, shall be *great tribulations on the Jews, and upon the inhabitants of Jerusalem;* such as was not *before sent upon Israel, of God, since the beginning of their kingdom, (for it is written their enemies shall scatter them,) until this time; no, nor ever shall be sent again upon Israel.*

All these things are the beginnings of sorrows.

And except *those days should be* shortened, *there should no flesh* be saved; but for the elect's sake, *according to the covenant, those days shall be shortened.*

Behold these things I have spoken unto you concerning the Jews. (JST; italics added.)

13:21–23 Read text and commentaries for Matthew 24:23–27. Read also Luke 17:22–25.

And then immediately after the tribulation of those days which shall come upon Jerusalem, if any man shall say unto you, Lo, here is Christ; or there; believe him not.

For in those days there shall also arise false Christs, and false prophets; and shall show *great* signs and wonders; *insomuch, that if possible, they shall deceive the very elect, who are the elect according to the covenant.*

Behold, I speak these things unto you, for the elect's sake.

Behold, I have told you before, wherefore if they shall say unto you, Behold, he is in the desert; go not forth; Behold, he is in the secret chambers; believe it not.

For as the light of the morning cometh out of the east, and shineth even unto the west, and covereth the whole earth, so shall also the coming of the Son of Man be.

And now I show unto you a parable. Behold, wheresoever the carcass is, there will the eagles be gathered together;

So likewise, shall mine elect be gathered from the four quarters of the earth.

And they shall hear of wars and rumors of wars. Behold, I speak unto you for mine elect's sake. (JST; italics added.)

13:22 "Seduce" could have been translated "lead astray."

13:23 This verse could have been translated more literally "You, then, watch out; I have told you all things beforehand."

13:24–27 Read text and commentary for Matthew 24:29–31. Read also Luke 21:25–28.

And immediately after the tribulation of those days, the sun shall be darkened, and the moon shall not give her light, and the stars shall fall from heaven, and the powers *of* heaven shall be shaken. . . .

And *they* shall see the Son of Man coming in the clouds *of heaven,* with power and great glory.

And whoso treasureth up my word shall not be deceived.

For the Son of Man shall come; and he shall send his angels *before him with the great sound of a trumpet,* and *they* shall gather together his elect from the four winds, from *one end* of heaven *to the other.* (JST; italics added.)

13:28–32 Read text and commentaries for Matthew 24:32–41. Read also Luke 21:29–33.

Verily I say unto you, This generation *in the which these things shall be shown forth,* shall not pass *away* till all *I have told you* shall be *fulfilled.*

Although the days will come that heaven and earth shall pass away, yet my words shall not pass away, *but all shall be fulfilled.*

And as I said before, After the tribulation of those days, and the powers of the heavens shall be shaken, then shall appear the sign of the Son of Man in heaven; and then shall all the tribes of the earth mourn; . . .

Now learn a parable of the fig tree. When *his branches are* yet tender, and putteth forth leaves, ye know that summer is *nigh at hand.*

So likewise, mine elect, when they shall see *all* these things, *they shall know that he is near,* even at the doors.

But of that day and hour *no one knoweth;* no, not the angels *of God in heaven, but my Father only.* (JST; italics added.)

13:29 The Greek text indicates that "it" should be replaced with "he." Thus, this verse could have been translated more literally "Likewise also you, when you see these things happening, know that he is near, at the doors."

13:32 (Read text and commentaries for Matthew 24:36–39. Read also Luke 17:26–30.) The Joseph Smith Translation drops "neither the Son," indicating that the Savior knows the time of his second coming.

13:33–37 (Read text and commentaries for Matthew 24:42–51. Read also Luke 12:35–48; 21:34–36.) Some students of the New Testament believe this particular story is contained only in Mark, while others feel that Jesus might be referring to incidents developed further in Matthew and Luke.

13:33 This verse could have been translated more literally "Keep looking, keep awake, for you do not know when the appointed time is."

13:36 This verse could have been translated more literally "When he arrives suddenly, he does not find you sleeping." "Sleeping" evidently refers to such things as inactivity in the Church, slothfulness in discharging one's duties, and lack of spiritual growth.

13:36–37 These two verses have been expanded into the following verses in the Joseph Smith Translation:

But as it was in the days of Noah, so it shall be also at the coming of the Son of Man; for it shall be with them as it was in the days which were before the flood.

Until the day that Noah entered into the ark, they were eating and drinking, marrying and giving in marriage, and knew not until the flood came and took them all away; so shall also the coming of the Son of Man be.

Then shall be fulfilled that which is written, That in the last days, two shall be in the field, one shall be taken and the other left.

Two shall be grinding at the mill; the one taken, and the other left.

And what I say unto one, I say unto all men.

Watch therefore, for ye know not at what hour your Lord doth come.

But know this, if the good man of the house had known in what watch the thief would come, he would have watched, and would not have suffered his house to have been broken up; but would have been ready.

Therefore, be ye also ready, for in such an hour as ye think not, the Son of Man cometh.

Who then is a faithful and wise servant, whom his lord hath made ruler over his household, to give them meat in due season?

Blessed is that servant whom his lord, when he cometh, shall find so doing.

And verily I say unto you, he shall make him ruler over all his goods.

But if that evil servant shall say in his heart, My lord delayeth his coming; and shall begin to smite his fellow servants, and to eat and drink with the drunken;

The lord of that servant shall come in a day when he looketh not for him, and in an hour that he is not aware of, and shall cut him asunder, and shall appoint him his portion with the hypocrites.

There shall be weeping and gnashing of teeth; and thus cometh the end.

13:37 "Watch" could also have been translated "keep on the watch [stay awake]."

14:1–2 Read text and commentaries for Matthew 26:1–5. Read also Luke 22:1–2.

14:1 The Joseph Smith Translation places the word "feast" with "unleavened bread" rather than with "passover."

14:2 But they said *among themselves, Let us not take him* on the feast day, lest there be an uproar among the people. (JST; italics added.)

14:3–9 Read text and commentaries for Matthew 26:6–13. Read also John 12:2–8.

14:3 (See section 1, "Spikenard.") The Joseph Smith Translation identifies the "he" as Jesus.

14:4 The Joseph Smith Translation makes it clear that the "some" who had indignation among themselves included "some among the disciples."

14:7 The Old Testament also indicates that "ye have the poor with you always": "For the poor shall never cease out of the land." (Deut. 15:11.)

14:8 She *has* done what she could, *and this which she has done unto me, shall be had in remembrance in generations to come,* wheresoever *my* gospel shall be preached, *for verily* she *has* come *beforehand* to anoint my body to the burying. (JST; italics added.)

14:10–11 Read text and commentaries for Matthew 26:14–16. Read also Luke 22:1–6.

14:10 Additional insight regarding Judas is given in the Joseph Smith Translation:

And he said unto Judas Iscariot, What thou doest, do quickly; but beware of innocent blood.

Nevertheless, Judas Iscariot, even one of the twelve, went unto the chief priests to betray Jesus unto them; for he turned away from him, and was offended because of his words.

14:11 And when *the chief priests* heard *of him* they were glad, and promised to give him money; and he sought how he might conveniently betray *Jesus*. (JST; italics added.)

14:12–17 Read text and commentaries for Matthew 26:17–20. Read also Luke 22:7–14.

14:18–21 Read text and commentaries for Matthew 26:21–25. Read also Luke 22:21–30; John 13:18–30.

14:22–25 Read text and commentaries for Matthew 26:26–29. Read also Luke 22:15–20.

14:22 The last clause in the Joseph Smith Translation reads: "Take *it, and* eat." (Italics added.) Then the Joseph Smith Translation adds the following very significant verse: "Behold, this is for you to do in remembrance of my body; for as oft as ye do this ye will remember this hour that I was with you."

"Take, eat: this is my body" could have been translated "Take it, this means my body." (See also commentary for Matt. 26:26.)

14:24 And he said unto them, This is *in remembrance of* my blood which is shed for many, *and the new testament which I give unto you; for of me, ye shall bear record unto all the world.*

And as oft as ye do this ordinance, ye will remember me in this hour that I was with you, and drank with you of this cup, even the last time in my ministry. (JST; italics added.)

14:25 Verily I say unto you, *Of this ye shall bear record; for* I will no more drink of the fruit of the vine *with you*, until that day that I drink it new in the kingdom of God.

And now they were grieved, and wept over him. (JST; italics added.)

14:26 Read text and commentaries for Matthew 26:30. Read also Luke 22:39; John 14:27–31. (See section 1, "Hymns.")

14:27–31 Read text and commentaries for Matthew 26:31–35. Read also Luke 22:31–38; John 13:36–38.

14:28 The Joseph Smith Translation adds the following verse after verse 28:

And he said unto Judas Iscariot, What thou doest, do quickly; but beware of innocent blood.

14:29 But Peter said unto *Jesus,* Although all men shall be offended *with thee,* yet *I will never be offended.* (JST; italics added.)

14:32–42 Read text and commentaries for Matthew 26:36–46. Read also Luke 22:40–46; John 18:1–2. See 2 Nephi 9:21–22; Mosiah 3:5–12; D&C 19:1–24. (See section 1, "Gethsemane.")

14:32–34 And they came to a place which was named Gethsemane, *which was a garden; and the disciples* began to be sore amazed, and to be very heavy, *and to complain in their hearts, wondering if this be the Messiah.*

And Jesus knowing their hearts, said to his disciples, Sit ye here, while I shall pray.

And he taketh with him, Peter, and James, and John, *and rebuked them, and said unto them,* My soul is exceeding sorrowful, even unto death; tarry ye here and watch. (JST; italics added.)

Gethsemane can be located on map 17 (grid D/2) of the Latter-day Saint edition of the King James Version of the Bible.

14:33 "Began to be sore amazed, and to be very heavy" could have been more literally translated "started to be stunned and to be sorely troubled." Other translations are "Distress and anguish came over him"; "he began to be deeply distressed and troubled"; and "began to be greatly distressed and troubled."

The Joseph Smith Translation makes it clear that the *disciples* (not Jesus) "began to be sore amazed, and to be very heavy, and to *complain in their hearts, wondering if this be the Messiah."* (Italics added.)

Even at this late hour because they had not yet received the gift of the Holy Ghost, the disciples wondered if Jesus was really the Messiah. Flashes of revelation had come in times past so certifying, but as yet they could not have available the constant companionship of that Holy Ghost whose mission it is to bear record of the Son. How important it is that men receive and enjoy the gift of the Holy Ghost. (DNTC 1:775.)

14:34 The Joseph Smith Translation states that Jesus "rebuked" Peter, James, and John and then said unto them, "My soul is exceeding sorrowful, even unto death."

Isaiah had prophesied that the Messiah would be "a man of sorrows." (Isa. 53:3–4.) Elder Bruce R. McConkie has stated that in the garden of Gethsemane Jesus bore "the agony and sorrow of the whole world. Sorrow is the child of sin, and as he took upon himself the sins of the world, he thereby bore the weight of the world's sorrows." (DNTC 1:775; see also D&C 19:16–20.)

14:36 See BD, "Abba." The Joseph Smith Translation

closes this verse: "nevertheless, not my will, but thine be done."

14:38 The Joseph Smith Translation indicates that it is the *disciples* (not Jesus) who say, "The spirit truly is ready, but the flesh is weak."

14:41 This verse could have been translated more literally "And he came the third time and said to them: 'At such a time as this you are sleeping and taking your rest! It is enough! The hour has come! Look! The Son of man is betrayed into the hands of sinners.'" It is evident from the context of the Greek text that in verse 41 Jesus is not commanding his disciples to "Sleep on now" inasmuch as he stated in verse 42, "Rise up, let us go."

The Joseph Smith Translation, however, indicates that the disciples did indeed sleep: *"And after they had finished their sleep,* he said, Rise up, let us go." (Italics added.)

14:43–52 Read text and commentaries for Matthew 26:47–56. Read also Luke 22:47–53; John 18:3–11.

14:47 The Joseph Smith Translation inserts this additional material after verse 47:

> But Jesus commanded him to return his sword, saying, He who taketh the sword shall perish with the sword. And he put forth his finger and healed the servant of the high priest.

Elder Bruce R. McConkie explains:

> Facing a frenzied mob, in the presence of a Roman band, and without reference to the faith of Malchus, Jesus restores to that servant his ear. Jesus was being arrested for "falsely" claiming to possess the power of God. Here, as in the past, however, he manifests that very power before them. One wonders what outpouring of divine power it would take to impress their sin-saturated souls with his divine status. (DNTC 1:782.)

14:48 Jesus' statement could have been translated "Did you come out with swords and clubs as against a robber to arrest me?"

14:50 *And the disciples, when they heard this saying,* all forsook him and fled. (JST; italics added.)

14:52 The Joseph Smith Translation ends this verse with "and saved himself out of their hands."

14:53–65 Read text and commentaries for Matthew 26:57–68. Read also Luke 22:54–65; John 18:13–24.

14:54 This first part of this verse could have been translated "But Peter, from a good distance, followed him as far as in the courtyard of the high priest."

14:56 "But their witness agreed not together" could have been translated "but their testimonies were not in agreement."

14:60 In the Joseph Smith Translation, the last question in this verse is worded "Knowest thou not what these witness against thee?"

14:64 "And they all condemned him to be guilty of death" could have been translated "They all condemned him to be liable to death."

14:66–72 Read text and commentaries for Matthew 26:69–75. Read also Luke 22:54–62; John 18:15–18, 25–27.

As pointed out in the commentaries of the Matthew texts, Peter denied *knowing Jesus* or being associated with Jesus; he did not deny that Jesus Christ was the Divine Son of God.

14:72 In the Joseph Smith Translation, the last sentence of this verse reads, "And he went out, and fell upon his face, and wept bitterly."

15:1 (Read text and commentaries for Matt. 27:1–2. Read also Luke 22:66–71; 23:1; John 18:28.) The Joseph Smith Translation indicates that the "whole council *condemned* him, and bound him." (Italics added.)

The following account of the judicial procedure of the Sanhedrin in capital cases is abridged from Schurer, who follows the Mishna. The members of the court sat in a semi-circle. A quorum of 23 was required. In front of them stood the two clerks of the court, of whom the one on the right hand recorded the votes for acquittal, and the one on the left hand the votes for condemnation. The "disciples of the wise" (pupils of the scribes) occupied three additional rows in front. It was required to hear the reasons for acquittal first (a regulation violated in the case of Jesus) and afterwards the reasons for condemnation. The "disciples of the wise" could speak, but only in favor of the prisoner. Acquittal could be pronounced on the day of the trial, but condemnation not till the following day (this regulation also was violated, though some suppose that there were two meetings, one on Thursday night, the other on Friday morning to render the proceedings technically legal). Each member stood to give his vote, and voting began with the youngest member. For acquittal a simple majority sufficed; for condemnation a majority of two was necessary. (*Dummelow*, p. 713.)

(See section 1, "Sanhedrin.")

15:2–5 Read text and commentaries for Matthew 27:11–14. Read also Luke 23:2–5; John 18:28–39.

15:2 In the Joseph Smith Translation, the Savior's reply is "I am, even as thou sayest."

15:6–15 Read text and commentaries for Matthew 27:15–26. Read also Luke 23:13–25; John 18:39–40.

15:6 "He released unto them one prisoner" could have been translated "he used to release to them one prisoner." The idea is that this was tradition. The Joseph Smith Translation reads, "Now *it was common at the feast,* for Pilate to release unto them one prisoner, whomsoever they desired." (Italics added.) (See section 1, "Barabbas.")

15:8 And the multitude, crying aloud, began to desire him to *deliver Jesus unto them*. (JST; italics added.)

15:10 This verse could have been translated "For he was aware that because of envy the chief priests had handed him over."

15:11 The following clause is added at the end of this verse in the Joseph Smith Translation: "as he had before done unto them."

15:13 And they cried out *again, Deliver him unto us to be crucified. Away with him*. Crucify him. (JST; italics added.)

15:16–21 Read text and commentaries for Matthew 27:27–32. Read also Luke 23:26; John 19:1–16.

15:16 "Praetorium" means "governor's court" or "judgment hall." Specifically, it is "the place where the praetor administered justice." (See BD, "Praetorium.")

15:17 "Platted" means "twined" or "braided." (See section 1, "Platted.")

15:21 See BD, "Alexander (1)."

15:22 (Read text and commentary for Matt. 27:33. Read also Luke 23:33; John 19:17.) The Joseph Smith Translation changes "skull" to "burial." (Golgotha can be located on map 17 (grid B/1) in the Latter-day Saint edition of the King James Version of the Bible; see section 1, "Golgotha.")

15:23 (Read text and commentary for Matt. 27:34.) "And they gave him to drink wine mingled with myrrh" could have been more literally translated "Here they tried to give him wine drugged with myrrh." The Greek then makes it clear that "He would not take it."

And they gave him to drink, *vinegar* mingled with *gall; and when he had tasted the vinegar, he would not drink*. (JST; italics added.)

15:24 Read text and commentaries for Matthew 27:35. Read also Luke 23:34; John 19:23–24.

15:25 Compare John 19:14.

15:26 Read text and commentaries for Matthew 27:36–37. Read also Luke 23:38; John 19:19–22.

And Pilate wrote his accusation and put it upon the cross, THE KING OF THE JEWS.
There were certain of the chief priests who stood by, that said unto Pilate, Write, that he said, I am the King of the Jews.
But Pilate said unto them, What I have written, I have written. (JST; italics added.)

(See section 1, "Written, what I have.")

15:27–28 (Read Matt. 27:38; Luke 23:32–33; John 19:18.) The crucifixion of Jesus between the two thieves fulfilled the prophecy of Isaiah: "And he was numbered with the transgressors." (Isa. 53:12.)

15:29–32 Read text and commentaries for Matthew 27:39–44. Read also Luke 23:35–43. See Helaman 14:20–27; 3 Nephi 8:5–22; 10:9.

15:29 "Railed on him" could have been translated "would speak abusively to him." Other translations are "hurled insults at him" and "derided him." Other possible meanings are "blasphemed" and "reproached." (See section 1, "Railed.")

15:32 "Reviled" could have been translated "reproached."

And one of them who was crucified with him, reviled him *also, saying, If thou art the Christ, save thyself and us.* (JST; italics added.)

15:33 Read text and commentary for Matthew 27:45. Read also Luke 23:44–45.

15:34–36 Read text and commentaries for Matthew 27:46–49. Read also John 19:28–29.

15:34 "Eloi" is found only in this verse. (See BD, "Eloi.") "Sabachthani" is a cry of distress found only here and in Matthew 27:46.

15:36 The Joseph Smith Translation makes it clear that those who said "Let him alone" were different people from those who offered him the vinegar: "And one ran and filled a sponge full of vinegar, and put it on a reed and gave him to drink; *others spake,* saying Let *him* alone; let us see whether Elias will come to take him down." (Italics added.)

15:37–38 Read text and commentaries for Matthew 27:50–51. Read also Luke 23:45–46; John 19:30.

15:39–41 Read text and commentaries for Matthew 27:54–56. Read also Luke 23:47–49.

15:40 The Joseph Smith Translation replaces the "less" with "younger."

15:42–46 Read Matthew 27:57–60; Luke 23:50–54; John 19:38–42. See BD, "Arimathaea," "Joseph of Arimathaea."

15:43 The possible location of the place Arimathea can be found on map 14 (grid C/5) of the Latter-day Saint edition of the King James Version of the Bible.

"An honourable counsellor" is frequently translated to indicate that Joseph of Arimathaea was "a reputable member of the Sanhedrin." (See BD, "Arimathaea.")

"Craved" could have been translated "requested," "begged," or "asked for."

15:44 In the Joseph Smith Translation, the first part of this verse reads, "And Pilate marvelled, *and asked him* if he were already dead." (Italics added.)

15:47 Read text and commentary for Matthew 27:61. Read also Luke 23:55–56.

16:1–8 Read text and commentaries for Matthew 28:1–10. Read also Luke 23:55–56; 24:1–11.

> *But* when they looked, they saw that the stone was rolled away, (for it was very great,) *and two angels sitting thereon, clothed in long white garments,* and they were affrighted.
> *But the angels said* unto them, Be not affrighted; ye seek Jesus of Nazareth, who was crucified; he is risen; he is not here; behold the place where they laid him;
> *And* go your way, tell his disciples and Peter, that he goeth before you into Galilee; there shall ye see him as he said unto you.
> *And they, entering into the sepulchre, saw the place where they laid Jesus.* (JST; italics added.)

Only Mark identified all the women who came with "sweet spices."

16:5–6 "Affrighted" could have been translated "astonished," "stunned," or "amazed."

The significance behind the words "He is risen" make them among the most important that have ever been uttered.

> "He is risen; he is not here." (Mark 16:6.) These words, eloquent in their simplicity, announced the most significant event of recorded history, the resurrection of the Lord Jesus—an event so extraordinary that even the Apostles, who had been most intimately associated with Jesus in his earthly ministry and who had been carefully taught of the coming event, had difficulty grasping the reality of its full significance. The first accounts which reached their ears "seemed to them as idle tales" (Luke

24:11) as well they might, for millions of men had lived and died before that day. In every hill and dale men's bodies mouldered in the dust, but until that first Easter morning not one had risen from the grave.

When we speak of Jesus being resurrected, we mean that his premortal spirit, which animated his mortal body from his birth in the manger until he died on the cross, reentered that body; and the two, his spirit body and his physical body, inseparably welded together, arose from the tomb an immortal soul.

Our belief is, and we so testify, that Jesus not only conquered death for himself and brought forth his own glorious resurrected body, but that in so doing he also brought about a universal resurrection. This was the end and purpose of the mission for which he was set apart and ordained in the great council in heaven, when he was chosen to be our Savior and Redeemer. (Marion G. Romney, *Ensign,* May 1982, p. 6.)

(See section 1, "Resurrection.")

16:9–11 Read John 20:11–18.

16:9 How much there is incident to the death, burial, and resurrection of our Lord which ennobles and exalts faithful women. They wept at the cross, sought to care for his wounded and lifeless body, and came to his tomb to weep and worship for their friend and Master. And so it is not strange that we find a woman, Mary of Magdala, chosen and singled out from all the disciples, even including the apostles, to be the first mortal to see and bow in the presence of a resurrected being. Mary, who had been healed of much and who loved much, saw the risen Christ! (DNTC 1:843.)

(See section 1, "Resurrection: Women at.")

16:11 See text and commentary for Luke 24:10–11 as to why the disciples and others had difficulty accepting the testimony of Mary Magdalene and other eyewitnesses concerning the resurrection of Jesus Christ.

16:12–13 Read text and commentaries for Luke 24:13–32.

16:13 "Residue" means "remainder."

16:14 Read Luke 24:36–44; John 20:19–21.

"Upbraided them" has also been translated "scolded them," "rebuked them," and "reproached them."

16:15–18 Read text and commentaries for Matthew 28:16–20. See also Mormon 9:22–24.

16:16 "Damned" could have been translated "condemned."

Both belief and baptism are essential to salvation; one without the other does not suffice. It is not enough to confess the Lord Jesus with the lips and stop there; nor does it suffice to be baptized, unless also there is resident in one's heart that sure knowledge that Jesus is Lord of all.

The salvation here involved is an inheritance in the celestial kingdom. As Nephi taught, Christ "commandeth all men that they must repent, and be baptized in his name, having perfect faith in the Holy One of Israel, or they cannot be saved in the kingdom of God." (2 Ne. 9:23.) To be damned is to be denied entrance to that glorious realm where God and Christ are. Baptism pertains to the celestial kingdom and to no other. Joseph Smith said: "A man may be saved, after the judgment, in the terrestrial kingdom, or in the telestial kingdom, but he can never see the celestial kingdom of God, without being born of water and the Spirit." (*Teachings* p. 12.) (DNTC 1:869.)

(See 3 Nephi 11:33–34; D&C 84:74; TG, "Baptism," "Baptism, Essential"; BD, "Baptism.")

16:17 This is an eternal, immutable, everlasting decree: *Signs shall follow them that believe*. When men believe the same gospel taught by Jesus and his apostles, signs and miracles follow; when they depart from this original, pure, and perfect Christianity, to some other system of religion, the promised signs are no longer found. Thus the presence or absence of signs becomes a means of identifying the true gospel, the same gospel had of old.

Aware that signs are no longer shown forth in the religions of the world, this plain statement of Jesus is explained away by such reasoning as this: "This gift of miracles was given in order to assist the diffusion of the gospel at the very first. When Christianity was firmly planted, the gift of miracles was withdrawn." (*Dummelow,* p. 733.) (DNTC 1:870–71.)

(See Mormon's statement on the relationship between faith and miracles in Moro. 7:35–38; section 1, "Signs.")

16:19–20 (Read text and commentary for Luke 24:50–53.) "He was received up into heaven" could have been translated "he was taken up to heaven."

Christ's Ascension is literal in the fullest and most complete sense of the word. He was a resurrected man, a personage of tabernacle who, though immortal, walked and talked and ate with his earthly friends. His Father has the same kind of a body, and the same character, perfections, and attributes. Heaven is a specific place, a planet where God dwells. The resurrected Lord ascended from the earth and went to the place where his Father is. As our latter-day revelation expresses it: He "ascended into heaven, to sit down on the right hand of the Father, to reign with almighty power according to the will of the Father." (D&C 20:24.)

As he went up, two angels stood by and said: "Ye men of Galilee, why stand ye gazing up into heaven? this same Jesus, which is taken up from you into heaven, shall so come in like manner as ye have seen him go into heaven." (Acts 1:11.)

This, then, is the message of the Ascension—that he who left shall come again; that the Lord who ascended "himself shall descend from heaven" (1 Thess. 4:16); and that when he comes, it shall be in the most literal sense of the word. He shall return as a Man; the same glorified and exalted personage who took leave from his former day disciples at

Bethany shall come again to his latter-day friends on Mount Zion, to be with them to "reign personally upon the earth" for a thousand years. (Tenth Article of Faith.)

"Even so, come, Lord Jesus." (Rev. 22:20.) (DNTC 1:872–73.)

(See section 1, "Ascension.")

LUKE

For background information on this book, see BD, "Gospels," "Harmony of the Gospels," and "Luke."

1:1–4 This is Luke's preface to his writings.

As I am a messenger of Jesus Christ, and knowing that many have taken in hand to set forth in order a declaration of those things which are most surely believed among us; . . . (JST; italics added.)

1:3 See BD, "Theophilus."

1:5–25 The account of the annunciation of the angel Gabriel (Noah) to Zacharias, recorded only in Luke, contains a wealth of information concerning the Jewish religion in those days. Additional helpful background information can be found in the Bible Dictionary. (See BD, "Aaron," "Altar," "Angels," "Elias," "Elisabeth," "Gabriel," "Herod," "Holy Ghost," "Incense," "Israel," "John the Baptist," "Judaea," "Lots, Casting of," "Prayer," "Priests," "Temple," "Zacharias.")

1:6 "Ordinances" means "righteous [legal] requirements."

1:7 "Stricken in years" means "advanced [well along] in years." Other translations are "very old" and "getting on in years."

1:8 In the Joseph Smith Translation, "course" is changed to "priesthood."

Though many of the Jews in the meridian of time were in a state of direful and awful apostasy, such darkness of mind and spirit was not universal. It did not envelope the whole nation. Elizabeth and Zacharias were righteous saints. Both were lineal descendants of Aaron, and Zacharias held the office of priest in the Aaronic Priesthood. (*Teachings,* pp. 272–73.) This lesser priesthood had continued in direct descent, without a break in the line, from Aaron to Zacharias and his son John the Baptist. (D&C 84:26–28.) (DNTC 1:78.)

1:9 In the Joseph Smith Translation, "custom" is changed to "law." (See BD, "Censer," "Incense.")

1:11–19 See BD, "Gabriel."

1:12 The Joseph Smith Translation replaces "him" with "angel."

1:16 "Turn" means "turn back." Thus, the Greek indicates that the children of Israel had left the Lord and were now to turn back to him.

1:17 This verse could have been translated "Also, he will go before him with Elijah's spirit and power, to turn back the hearts of fathers to children and the disobedient ones to the practical wisdom of righteous ones, to get ready for Jehovah a prepared people."

1:18 "Whereby shall I know this?" has also been translated "How shall I know if this is so?" and "How can I be sure of this?"

> The last words Zacharias had uttered prior to the infliction of dumbness were words of doubt and unbelief, words in which he had called for a sign as proof of authority of one who came from the presence of the Almighty; the words with which he broke his long silence were words of praise unto God in whom he had all assurance, words that were as a sign to all who heard, and the fame whereof spread throughout the region. (JTC, p. 79.)

1:20 (See text and commentary for Mark 7:37.) "In their season" could have been translated "in their appointed time."

1:26–38 The account of the annunciation to Mary is found only in Luke. (Read text and commentaries for Matt. 1:18–24. See BD, "Annunciation," "David," "Elisabeth," "Gabriel," "Galilee," "God," "Holy Ghost," "Jacob," "Jesus," "Lord," "Mary," "Nazareth.")

1:27 (Read text and commentaries for Matt. 1:18–24.) "Espoused" means "promised in marriage" or "betrothed."

1:28 Read text and commentaries for Matthew 1:23; 12:46–50.

> And the angel came in unto her and said, Hail, thou *virgin, who* art highly favored *of* the Lord. The Lord is with thee, *for thou art chosen and* blessed among women. (JST; italics added.)

> Mary was a virgin—"A virgin, most beautiful and fair above all other virgins" (1 Ne. 11:15)—until after the birth of our Lord. Then, for the first time, she was known by Joseph, her husband; and other children, both sons and daughters, were then born to her. (Matt. 13:55–56; Mark 6:3; Gal. 1:19.) She conceived and brought forth her Firstborn Son while yet a virgin because the Father of that child was an immortal personage. (DNTC 1:82.)

That Child to be born of Mary was begotten of Elohim, the Eternal Father, not in violation of natural law but in accordance with the higher manifestation thereof; and, the offspring from that association of supreme sanctity, celestial Sireship, and pure though mortal maternity, was of right to be called the "Son of the Highest." In His nature would be combined the powers of Godhood with the capacity and possibilities of mortality; and this through the ordinary operation of the fundamental law of heredity declared of God, demonstrated by science, and admitted by philosophy, that living beings shall propagate—after their kind. The Child Jesus was to inherit the physical, mental and spiritual traits, tendencies, and powers that characterized His parents—one immortal and glorified—God, the other human—woman. (JTC, p. 81.)

1:29 And when she saw *the angel,* she was troubled at his saying, and *pondered* in her mind what manner of salutation this should be. (JST; italics added.)

1:31 (See commentary for Matt. 1:21; section 1, "Jesus.") The name *Jesus* (also written *Jehoshua, Jeshua, Joshua,* or *Yeshua*) means "Jehovah is salvation."

1:32 See texts and commentaries for Matt. 12:23; 22:41–46.) *Son of David* was a sacred title used by the Jews to refer to the Messiah because of the numerous Old Testament prophecies that the Messiah would be of the loins of David. (See TG, "Jesus Christ, Davidic Descent of"; section 1, "Son of David.")

Our Lord was heir to David's throne in both the temporal and eternal sense of the word. Mary his literal mother and Joseph his foster father were descendants of David. Indeed, their lineage was in the royal house itself. "Had Judah been a free and independent nation, ruled by her rightful sovereign, Joseph the carpenter would have been her crowned king; and his lawful successor to the throne would have been Jesus of Nazareth, the King of the Jews." (*Talmage,* pp. 87, 90.) Thus Jesus was an heir to the throne of the temporal kingdom. But in a far greater sense, he is the Eternal King of Israel—the King whom they once served in all their ancient trials and tribulations, the King whom they shall serve again when the scattered remnants of Israel are gathered into one great millennial kingdom, with our Lord, the King, reigning personally upon the earth. (Ezek. 37:21–28; Tenth Article of Faith.) (DNTC 1:83–84.)

1:34–35 Not in the spirit of doubt such as had prompted Zacharias to ask for a sign, but through an earnest desire for information and explanation, Mary, conscious of her unmarried status and sure of her virgin condition, asked: "How shall this be, seeing I know not a man?" The answer to her natural and simple inquiry was the announcement of a miracle such as the world had never known—not a miracle in the sense of a happening contrary to nature's law, nevertheless a miracle through the operation of higher law, such as the human mind ordinarily fails to comprehend or regard as possible. Mary was informed that she would conceive and in time bring forth a Son, of whom no mortal man would be the father: — "And the angel answered and said unto her, The Holy Ghost shall come upon thee, and the power of the Highest shall overshadow thee: therefore also that holy thing which shall be born of thee shall be called the Son of God." (JTC, pp. 80–81.)

1:35 "That holy thing" is changed to "that holy child" in the Joseph Smith Translation.

1:36, 58 "Cousin" could have been more literally translated as "relative."

1:38 Mary's expression "be it unto me according to thy word" is a beautiful example of willingness to be obedient to the will of our Heavenly Father. The book of Moses in the Pearl of Great Price records a similar expression by Jesus in the pre-earthly existence: "Father, thy will be done, and the glory be thine forever." (Moses 4:2.)

1:39–56 The account of Mary's visit with Elisabeth is recorded only by Luke. It provides background on the births of John the Baptist and Jesus.

1:39 The exact location of the "city of Juda" where Elisabeth and Zacharias lived has not been determined. Tradition places their home in Ein Karem ("Spring of the Vineyard"), a village just west of Jerusalem. (See BD, "Hill country.")

1:40 "Saluted" means "greeted."

1:41 The scriptures do not make absolutely clear the exact time when the spirit enters the body before the birth of a child. This scripture, however, indicates that the spirit is in the body at least several months before birth:

> In this miraculous event the pattern is seen which a spirit follows in passing from his pre-existent first estate into mortality. The spirit enters the body at the time of quickening, months prior to the actual normal birth. The value and comfort attending a knowledge of this eternal truth is seen in connection with stillborn children. Since the spirit entered the body before birth, stillborn children will be resurrected and righteous parents shall enjoy their association in immortal glory. (MD, pp. 693–94.)

> The Book of Mormon account of Christ speaking to Nephi the grandson of Helaman and saying, "On the morrow come I into the world" (3 Ne. 1:13), is not intended to infer that the spirit does not enter the body until the moment of the actual birth. Rather this revelation to the Nephites was itself being conveyed in a miraculous and unusual way. Quite probably the one uttering the words was speaking in the first person as though he were Christ, in accordance with the law enabling others to act and speak for Deity on the principle of divine investiture of authority. (MD, p. 122.)

1:42 "Blessed art thou among women" is a Hebrew expression that indicates that Mary is being greeted as the most blessed of all women. Mary's elevated status is evident in the fact she was selected by our Heavenly Father to be the mother of his Only Begotten Son in the flesh.

1:43 In the Joseph Smith Translation, this verse begins, "And why is it, that this blessing is upon me, that the mother of my Lord should come to me?" Evidently the Holy Ghost had already borne witness to Elisabeth that Mary was to be the mother of the Son of God.

1:45 And blessed *art thou who* believed, for those things which were told *thee by the angel of the Lord, shall be fulfilled.* (JST; italics added.)

1:49 In the Joseph Smith Translation, the last clause of this verse is "and I will magnify his holy name."

1:53 The Joseph Smith Translation uses "but" rather than "and."

1:54 "Holpen" is changed to "helped" in the Joseph Smith Translation.

1:55 This verse ends the inspired response of Mary (the *Magnificat*) to the equally inspired greeting of Elisabeth.

Two psalms of praise, worship, thanksgiving, and prophecy were given by the Spirit, through especially chosen vessels, as the foundations were laid and announced for the ushering in of the great meridian gospel dispensation. While the Holy Ghost rested upon her, Mary responded to Elizabeth's inspired salutation by uttering the memorable words since adopted as part of the musical ritual of many churches under the Latin name, the *Magnificat*. Zacharias, similarly enlightened by the Spirit, enriched Christian literature and knowledge by speaking the so-called *Benedictus,* a song of praise over the birth and naming of his son, John the Baptist. Both psalms tie the traditions, teachings, and inspired declarations of the patriarchs and prophets of old into the new era of restoration that was commencing with the birth and ministry of our Lord and his forerunner. (DNTC 1:87.)

1:57–66 Some of the important points in Luke's account of the birth and naming of John are substantiated by modern scriptures, including D&C 27:7–8; 84:27.

Naming of children and circumcision of male members of the house of Israel took place on this [the eighth] day. In the case of John, he "was ordained by the angel of God at the time he was eight days old"—not to the Aaronic Priesthood, for such would come later, after his baptism and other preparation, but—"unto this power, to overthrow the kingdom of the Jews, and to make straight the way of the Lord before the face of his people, to prepare them for the coming of the Lord, in whose hand is given all power." (D&C 84:28.) That is, at this solemn eighth day ceremony, an angel, presumably Gabriel, gave the Lord's Elias the divine commission to serve as the greatest forerunner of all the ages. (DNTC 1:89.)

(See section 1, "John the Baptist"; BD, "Circumcision.")

1:62 And they made signs to his father, *and asked him* how he would have him called. (JST; italics added.)

1:64 In the Joseph Smith Translation, this verse ends ". . . and he *spake with his tongue,* and praised God." (Italics added.)

1:65 See BD, "Hill country."

1:67–79 Some elements of this prophecy of Zacharias are also in D&C 84:28.

1:69 The power of the Messiah has been spoken of by several of the Old Testament prophets and writers in the symbol of a "horn," the manifestation of the strength of the bull or wild ox. (See 1 Sam. 2:1, 10; 2 Sam. 22:3; Ps. 18:2; 92:10; 132:17; Ezek. 29:21.)

1:72–73 For additional background on the "holy covenant" and the "oath which he sware to our father Abraham," see Genesis 22:15–18, Abraham 2:10–11, and TG and BD, "Abraham, Covenant of."

1:75 The Greek word translated "holiness" has the basic meaning of "loyalty."

1:77 The Joseph Smith Translation makes it clear that baptism is necessary for a remission of sins: "by *baptism for* the remission of their sins." (Italics added.)

1:78 "Whereby the dayspring from on high hath visited us" has also been translated "when the day shall dawn upon us from on high."

Christ is the dayspring from on high, a figure of speech which has lost most of its force through translation, but which according to the original Greek word had two possible meanings: (1) That he was the *Branch* (Jer. 23:5–6, 33:15; Zech. 6:12); or (2) That he was the *Sun* or *Star of Israel.* Perhaps the meaning is similar to his own expression that he is the *bright and morning star.* (Rev. 22:16.) (DNTC 1:88.)

(See section 1, "Dayspring.")

1:80 This brief account of John's childhood is similar to the accounts of Jesus' childhood. (See Luke 2:40, 52.)

As is the case with his kinsman Jesus, the scriptures are virtually silent on the life and labors of John prior to his formal ministry, which commenced, according to Levitical law, when he was thirty years of age.

(Num. 4:3, 47.) We do know that "he was baptized while he was yet in his childhood" (D&C 84:28), meaning when he was eight years of age; that his parents were faithful and righteous people; that he "was a priest after his father, and held the keys of the Aaronic Priesthood, and was called of God to preach the Gospel of the kingdom of God" (*Teachings,* pp. 272–73); that he "waxed strong in spirit," that is, became a tower of spiritual strength; and that he was guided during his whole life by the Holy Ghost. It naturally follows that he was trained in obedience to the law of Moses, officiated in the Levitical ordinances and performances, was married (an almost mandatory social requirement among the Jews), and probably had children. (DNTC 1:89–90.)

(See section 1, "John the Baptist.")

2:1–7 This extremely valuable information on the birth of Jesus is provided almost solely by Luke. Background information on some of this material is available in 1 Nephi 11:18–20; Mosiah 3:5–8; Alma 7:10; Helaman 14:5–12; 3 Nephi 1:4–22.

2:1 "Taxed" could have been more literally translated "registered" or "enrolled." The idea is that a "decree" had gone out from Caesar Augustus that a census of the people should be taken.

The Joseph Smith Translation changes "the world" to "his empire." (See BD, "Augustus.")

2:2 See BD, "Cyrenius."

2:4 Bethlehem had been the prophesied place of the birth of the Messiah at least since the days of Micah. (See Micah 5:2.) The statement by Alma that the Messiah would be born "at Jerusalem, which is the *land* of our forefathers" probably has reference to the greater land area rather than the exact city, as Jerusalem and Bethlehem are only about six miles apart, and both were part of the inheritance given to the tribe of Judah when the land was divided among the tribes of Israel. (Josh. 15.)

2:5 According to the account in Matthew 1:24–25, Joseph and Mary were no longer "espoused" or betrothed, but they were now legally married.

2:6 This verse could have been translated "While they were there, the days came to the full for her to give birth."

2:7 Christmas is the traditional rather than the actual birthday of our Lord. As to the actual day and year, scholars generally are in such complete disagreement that reference to their various views does little more than multiply confusion and uncertainty. Authorities can be cited who contend his birth was during every year from B.C. 1 to B.C. 7. Perhaps most of them lean to the conjecture that it was in late 5 B.C. or early 4 B.C.

From the first sentence of the revelation given to Joseph Smith on the day the Church was organized in this dispensation, it appears that the latter-day kingdom formally came into being on the eighteen hundred and thirtieth anniversary of our Lord's birth. In other words, Christ was born April 6, B.C. 1. (D&C 20:1.) As pointed out by Elder James E. Talmage, the Book of Mormon accounts that the Messiah would come "six hundred years from the time that Lehi left Jerusalem" (3 Ne. 1:1; 1 Ne. 10:4), seem to corroborate this B.C. 1 birthdate. (DNTC 1:91.)

2:7 In the Joseph Smith Translation, the end of this verse reads, "because there was *none to give* room for them in the *inns*." (Italics added.)

Inns were square buildings, open inside, in which travelers commonly put up for the night; back parts of these erections were used as stables. Mary's condition probably required slow travel so that the inns were all filled upon their arrival in Bethlehem, necessitating their use of the stable part of one of them for shelter. It was the traveling hosts of Judah generally, not just an innkeeper or an isolated few persons, who withheld shelter from Joseph and Mary. Though her state was apparent, the other travelers—lacking in courtesy, compassion, and refinement—would not give way so she could be cared for more conveniently and commodiously. This rude rejection was but prelude to the coming day when these same people and their children after them would reject to their eternal sorrow the Lord who that night began mortality under the most lowly circumstances. (DNTC 1:91–92.)

2:8–20 This familiar and well-loved account of the witness to the shepherds and of their testimony to others is found only in Luke.

2:9 "They were sore afraid" could have been translated "they became very fearful."

2:11 The "city of David" is Bethlehem, the city of David's birth and boyhood. Later, after David became king, he made Jerusalem his capital, and it is also sometimes referred to as the city of David.

2:12 And this *is the way you* shall find the babe, *he is* wrapped in swaddling clothes, *and is* lying in a manger. (JST; italics added.)

"Swaddling clothes" are bands of cloth wrapped around newborn children.

2:13–14 See BD, "Music."

2:14 The Joseph Smith Translation uses "to" in place of "toward." Other possible renderings are "On earth peace among men of good will," "peace on earth for all those pleasing him," "peace upon earth among men of goodwill," and "peace to men who enjoy his favor."

A rather literal translation from the Greek is "Glory in the highest places to God and upon earth peace among men of good will."

Tidings of such import had never before been delivered by angel or received by man—good tidings of great joy, given to but few and those among the humblest of earth, but destined to spread to all people. There is sublime grandeur in the scene, as there is divine authorship in the message, and the climax is such as the mind of man could never have conceived—the sudden appearance of a multitude of the heavenly host, singing audibly to human ears the briefest, most consistent and most truly complete of all the songs of peace ever attuned by mortal or spirit choir. What a consummation to be wished—Peace on earth! But how can such come except through the maintenance of good will toward men? And through what means could glory to God in the highest be more effectively rendered? (JTC, pp. 93–94.)

2:18 "Wondered" could have been translated "marveled."

2:21 (Read commentaries for Matt. 1:25. See also 2 Ne. 25:19; Mosiah 3:8; Hel. 14:12; Moses 6:52.) The babe Jesus, who was now receiving circumcision according to the law, was the great pre-earthly Jehovah who had originally revealed the law to Abraham. (See BD, "Circumcision," "Abraham, Covenant of.")

2:22–38 The account of Mary and Joseph presenting the infant Jesus at the temple and performing "all things according to the law of the Lord" (v. 39) is recorded only by Luke.

2:22 Part of the law given through Moses to the Israelites in the wilderness and continued in force down through the centuries, related to the procedure prescribed for women after childbirth. [Lev. 12.] In compliance therewith, Mary remained in retirement forty days following the birth of her Son; then she and her husband brought the Boy for presentation before the Lord as prescribed for the male firstborn of every family. It is manifestly impossible that all such presentations could have taken place in the temple, for many Jews lived at great distances from Jerusalem; it was the rule, however, that parents should present their children in the temple when possible. Jesus was born within five or six miles from Jerusalem; He was accordingly taken to the temple for the ceremonial of redemption from the requirement applying to the firstborn of all Israelites except Levites. (JTC, p. 95.)

For forty days following the birth of a male child, eighty in the case of a female offspring, a mother in Israel remained in retirement. When this period, "the days of her purifying," were over, she brought to the priest a lamb for a burnt offering and either a young pigeon or a turtledove for a sin offering. If she could not afford both the lamb and the bird, then she was permitted to bring two pigeons or two turtledoves. (Lev. 12.) The modest temporal circumstances of Joseph and Mary are apparent from their presentation of the less costly sacrificial offering.

In the case of the firstborn male child, these sacrifices were part of a ceremonial of redemption which exempted the child from the burden of ministerial service which the Lord had laid instead upon the Levites. After the Lord slew the firstborn among the Egyptians (Ex. 12:29–30), he took in return as his own special servant the firstborn of each family in Israel. (Ex. 22:29.) Though the male Levites were later chosen to serve in the Priesthood instead of all the firstborn sons (Num. 8:14–18), the ceremonial requirement of ransoming or redeeming every such firstborn son was retained. (Ex. 13:2, 13; Num. 18:15.) (DNTC 1:99.)

2:25 "Just and devout" could have been translated "righteous and reverent."

Elder Bruce R. McConkie explains the idiom "consolation of Israel":

> An idiomatic expression meaning the Messianic age, the era in which King Messiah would come to bring comfort and solace to the people and to relieve their mental and physical distress. The Messiah himself, as the bearer and personification of these blessings, also may properly be called, the *Consolation of Israel*. (DNTC 1:100.)

2:32 "A light to lighten the Gentiles" could have been translated "a light for removing the veil [uncovering] from the nations." The essential meaning is that the blessings that come through the Messiah are for all people, Gentiles as well as Israel.

2:35 Yea, a *spear* shall pierce through *him to the wounding of thine* own soul also; that the thoughts of many hearts may be revealed. (JST; italics added.)

The spear that pierced the side of her Son at the crucifixion indeed wounded Mary's own soul. (See section 1, "Pierced by spear.")

2:36 In the Joseph Smith Translation, the last sentence reads, "She was of great age, and had lived with a husband *only* seven years, *whom she married in her youth*." (Italics added.)

The meaning of "great age" is made evident in the next verse, which indicates that Anna had lived "a widow" for "about fourscore and four years" (eighty-four years). Thus, ninety-one years would need to be added to the age of Anna at the time of her marriage to obtain her age at the time she saw the baby Jesus in the temple.

"Prophetess" does not refer to an office in the priesthood or to an office to which one is ordained or set apart; rather, it indicates that Anna had received a witness from the Holy Ghost that Jesus was the Christ. (See BD, "Anna.")

2:39–40 (Read texts and commentaries for Matt. 2:19–23.)

These two verses in Luke apparently cover the childhood of Jesus from the age of forty days (when he was presented in the temple) to twelve years (when he returned to the temple at the feast of the Passover). Luke 2:52 summarizes a later period of his life.

> [Jesus] came among men to experience all the natural conditions of mortality; He was born as truly a dependent, helpless babe as is any other child; His infancy was in all common features as the infancy of others; His boyhood was actual boyhood, His development was as necessary and as real as that of all children. Over His mind had fallen the veil of forgetfulness common to all who are born to earth, by which the remembrance of primeval existence is shut off. The Child grew, and with growth there came to Him expansion of mind, development of faculties, and progression in power and understanding. His advancement was from one grace to another, not from gracelessness to grace; from good to greater good, not from evil to good; from favor with God to greater favor, not from estrangement because of sin to reconciliation through repentance and propitiation. (JTC, pp. 111–12.)

(See section 1, "Jesus: Childhood of.")

2:40 The last clause in this verse could have been translated "and God's favor continued with him."

2:41–51 The interesting and informative episode of Jesus visiting the temple at the age of twelve at the time of the feast of the Passover is found only in the writings of Luke. (See BD, "Passover." Also, read text and commentaries for Matt. 26:17–20.)

2:42 "*Of* the feast," is changed in the Joseph Smith Translation to "*to* the feast."

> Under Jewish law, Jesus, now twelve, became "a son of the law"—one subject to its obligations. Now he rated a position in the congregation and stood forth as a recognized member of his home community. His religious and secular studies entered an advanced stage; his vocational preparations were intensified; and he could no longer be sold by his parents as a bond-servant.
>
> That he should now be taken to the annual passover celebration was a natural and expected thing; and that he should enter the temple courts, join the discussior groups, listen to the expositions of the rabbis, and ask and answer questions himself, was in perfect keeping with the customs of the day. The significance of his youthful appearance in the temple lies, not in the fact of its occurrence, but in the divine wisdom manifest by him in his conversation and in the testimony which he then bore of his own divinity. (DNTC 1:109–10.)

2:46 "Doctors" could have been more literally translated "teachers."

The Joseph Smith Translation makes a valuable contribution

to the last part of this verse: "and they [the doctors] were hearing *him,* and asking *him* questions." (Italics added.)

2:48 "Sorrowing" could also have been translated "in mental distress."

2:49 "Wist ye not that I must be about my Father's business" could have been translated "Did you not know that I must be doing the things of my father?" In the Joseph Smith Translation, Jesus answers, "*Why* is it that ye sought me? *Knew* ye not that I must be about my Father's business?" (Italics added.)

> Let us not say that there was unkind rebuke or unfilial reproof in the answer of this most dutiful of sons to His mother. His reply was to Mary a reminder of what she seems to have forgotten for the moment—the facts in the matter of her Son's paternity. She had used the words "thy father and I"; and her Son's response had brought anew to her mind the truth that Joseph was not the Boy's father. She appears to have been astonished that One so young should so thoroughly understand His position with respect to herself. He had made plain to her the inadvertent inaccuracy of her words; His Father had not been seeking Him; for was He not even at that moment in His Father's house, and particularly engaged in His Father's business, the very work to which His Father had appointed Him? (JTC, pp. 114–15.)

2:52 This one short verse covers approximately eighteen years of the most important life that has ever been lived or will ever be lived on this earth. Yet in those few words, Luke informs the world that Jesus developed in all the important aspects of life: "And Jesus increased in wisdom [intellectually] and stature [physically] and in favour with God [spiritually] and man [socially]. (See section 1, "Jesus: Childhood of.")

3:1–6 For further information about the prophecies and background of John the Baptist, read texts and commentaries for Matthew 3:1–6. Read also Mark 1:1–8; John 1:6–34. See 1 Nephi 10:7–10; D&C 35:4; 84:27–28.

3:1 "Tetrarch" means "district ruler." A tetrarch is the ruler of a fourth part of a country. (For additional background on the persons listed in this verse, read the appropriate entries in the Bible Dictionary. See section 1, "Abilene," "Tetrarch.")

3:2 The "word of God" rightfully came to John, as he was the ordained forerunner of the Messiah. (See Isa. 40:3–5; 1 Ne. 10:7–10; 11:27; D&C 84:26–28.)

John, at that time, was the only legal administrator in the affairs of the kingdom there was then on the earth. And holding the keys of power, the Jews had to obey his instructions or be damned, by their own law. (TPJS, p. 276.)

3:4–5 The Joseph Smith Translation adds the following between verses 4 and 5:

For behold, and lo, he shall come, as it is written in the book of the prophets, to take away the sins of the world, and to bring salvation unto the heathen nations, to gather together those who are lost, who are of the sheepfold of Israel;

Yea, even the dispersed and afflicted; and also to prepare the way, and make possible the preaching of the gospel unto the Gentiles;

And to be a light unto all who sit in darkness, unto the uttermost parts of the earth; to bring to pass the resurrection from the dead, and to ascend up on high, to dwell on the right hand of the Father.

Until the fulness of time, and the law and the testimony shall be sealed, and the keys of the kingdom shall be delivered up again unto the Father;

To administer justice unto all; to come down in judgment upon all, and to convince all the ungodly of their ungodly deeds, which they have committed; and all this in the day that he shall come.

The keys of the kingdom are the rights and powers of presidency; they consist of the authorization and obligation to preside over the Church (which is the kingdom of God on earth) and to regulate all of its affairs. In due course these keys were given to Peter, James, and John, and then to all the Twelve of that day. They were restored to Joseph Smith and his associates in this day and are now held by the living oracles of this dispensation. When the great gathering at Adam-ondi-Ahman takes place those who have held keys on earth will make accounting of their stewardships, Christ will take back the keys, and then the millennial era shall be ushered in, an era in which the rightful King of the kingdom shall reign personally upon the earth. Finally, there shall be a day when the salvation of man shall be completed, a day in which the keys shall be returned to the Father. Or, as Paul expresses it, "Then cometh the end, when he [Christ] shall have delivered up the kingdom to God, even the Father; when he shall have put down all rule and all authority and power." (1 Cor. 15:24; *Mormon Doctrine,* pp. 377–379.) (DNTC 1:116–17.)

(See section 1, "Keys of Kingdom.")

3:5 The Joseph Smith Translation of this verse begins, "*For it is a day of power; yea,* every valley . . ." (Italics added.) This, of course, is a reference to the Second Coming, when Jesus comes in power and glory.

3:7–18 Read text and commentaries for Matthew 3:7–12. Read also Mark 1:4–8; John 1:19–28.

3:7 The Joseph Smith Translation indicates that John was "crying against them [the multitude] with a loud voice."

3:8 Bring forth therefore fruits worthy of repentance, and begin not to say within yourselves, Abraham *is* our father; *we have kept the commandments of God, and none can inherit the promises but the children of Abraham;* for I say unto you, That God is able of these stones to raise up children unto Abraham. (JST; italics added.)

See commentary for Matthew 3:9.

John's hearers believed that they and their kindred only could provide seed for Abraham and that none could be saved except the literal seed of that ancient Patriarch. But John's stinging rebuke was that "Of these stony Gentiles, these dogs," these lowest of all creatures (in the Jewish mind), God is able "to raise up children unto Abraham." (*Teachings*, p. 319.) Our Lord's forerunner is teaching the principle of adoption: that Abraham is "the father of *all* them that believe" (Rom. 4:11), both Jew and Gentile; that through belief in Christ all men become "Abraham's seed, and heirs according to the promise" (Gal. 3:28–29); that all who believe the gospel shall be accounted as Abraham's seed and rise up and bless him "as their father." (Abra. 2:10.) (DNTC 1:120.)

3:9 "Is hewn down" is changed in the Joseph Smith Translation to "shall be hewn down."

3:12 See BD, "Publicans." Also, see commentary for Matthew 9:9.

3:13–14 The Joseph Smith Translation adds the following between verses 13 and 14:

For it is well known unto you, Theophilus, that after the manner of the Jews, and according to the custom of their law in receiving money into the treasury, that out of the abundance which was received, was appointed unto the poor, every man his portion;

And after this manner did the publicans also, wherefore John said unto them, Exact no more than that which is appointed you.

3:13 This verse could have been translated "He said to them: 'Do not demand anything more than the tax rate.'"

3:14 Jesus' statement could have been translated "Do not harass anybody or accuse anybody falsely, and be satisfied with your provisions."

3:17 "Fan" could have been translated "winnowing shovel [fork]." (See BD, "Fan.")

"Garner" means "granary," "barn," or "storehouse."

3:18 This verse could have been translated "Therefore he also gave many other exhortations and continued declaring good news to the people."

3:19–20 Read commentaries for Matthew 4:12. Read also Matthew 14:3–5; Mark 6:17–20.

3:21–22 Read commentaries for Matthew 3:13–17.

Read also Mark 1:9–11; John 1:32–34. See 1 Nephi 10:7–10; 2 Nephi 31:4–21.

3:21 The Joseph Smith Translation reads, "Jesus also *came unto John; and* being baptised *of him, . . .*" (Italics added.)

Luke is the only gospel writer who mentions the manifestation of the Holy Ghost and the voice of the Father.

Our Lord's baptism is one of the classical illustrations of the separate and distinct individualities who comprise the eternal Godhead. Jesus is present in mortality; the personage of the Holy Ghost is seen descending from heaven to be with him; and the voice of the Father is heard introducing his Son to the world. (DNTC 1:124.)

(See section 1, "Baptism: Of Jesus.")

3:23–38 For additional information on the genealogies of Jesus, see the texts and commentaries for Matthew 1:1–17.

These genealogical records of Matthew and Luke purport to give the lineage of Jesus, tracing it back from Joseph his foster father. Several discrepancies are apparent, but as Elder James E. Talmage points out, "such have been satisfactorily reconciled by the research of specialists in Jewish genealogy." Then he summarizes the known facts in this field in these words: "The consensus of judgment on the part of investigators is that Matthew's account is that of the royal lineage, establishing the order of sequence among the legal successors to the throne of David, while the account given by Luke is a personal pedigree, demonstrating descent from David without adherence to the line of legal succession to the throne through primogeniture or nearness of kin. Luke's record is regarded by many, however, as the pedigree of Mary, while Matthew's is accepted as that of Joseph. The all important fact to be remembered is that the Child promised by Gabriel to Mary, the virginal bride of Joseph, would be born in the royal line. A personal genealogy of Joseph was essentially that of Mary also, for they were cousins. Joseph is named as son of Jacob by Matthew, and as son of Heli by Luke; but Jacob and Heli were brothers, and it appears that one of the two was the father of Joseph and the other was the father of Mary and therefore father-in-law to Joseph. That Mary was of Davidic descent is plainly set forth in many scriptures; for since Jesus was to be born of Mary, yet was not begotten by Joseph, who was the reputed, and, according to the law of the Jews, the legal, father, the blood of David's posterity was given to the body of Jesus through Mary alone." (*Talmage,* pp. 83–87, 89–90.) (DNTC 1:94–95.)

3:23–24 And Jesus himself began to be about thirty years of age, *having lived with his father,* being, as was supposed *of the world,* the son of Joseph, *who was from the loins of* Heli,

Who was from the loins of Matthat, *who* was the son of Levi, *who was a descendant* of Melchi, *and* of Janna, *and* of Joseph. (JST; italics added.)

3:27 See BD, "Joanna."

3:29 See BD, "Eliezer."

3:38 *And* of Enos, *and* of Seth, *and* of Adam, *who was formed of* God, *and the first man upon the earth.* (JST; italics added.)

There were no so-called pre-Adamites. When Deity "formed man from the dust of the ground, and breathed into his nostrils the breath of life," that noble personage, thereafter to be named Adam, "became a living soul, the first flesh upon the earth, the first man also." (Moses 3:7; 1:34; 6:45; Abra. 1:3; D&C 84:16; 1 Ne. 5:11; 1 Cor. 15:45.) Adam was the first man from the standpoint of ancestry, lineage, pre-eminence, power, and position; he was the first flesh meaning the first mortal flesh. All things were first created in immortality, in a state devoid of death; then after Adam fell, the effects of his transgression passed upon the earth and all life thereon. (DNTC 1:95.)

That Adam "was the son of God" is discussed by Elder Bruce R. McConkie:

This statement, found also in Moses 6:22, has a deep and profound significance and also means what it says. Father Adam came, as indicated, to this sphere, gaining an immortal body, because death had not yet entered the world. (2 Ne. 2:22.) Jesus, on the other hand, was the Only Begotten in the flesh, meaning into a world of mortality where death already reigned. (DNTC 1:95.)

4:1–13 (Read texts and commentaries for Matt. 4:1–11. Read also Mark 1:12–13.) The Joseph Smith Translation makes valuable contributions to this account of the fasting and temptations of Jesus (italics added):

Verse 2: "*And after forty days, the devil came unto him, to tempt him.* And in those days . . ."

Verse 5: "And the *Spirit taketh* him up into a high mountain, *and he beheld* all . . ."

Verse 6: "And the devil *came unto him, and* said . . . I will give *them.*"

Verse 9: "And *the Spirit* brought him to Jerusalem . . . And *the devil came unto him, and* said . . ."

Jesus dwelt in mortality as a man. He was subject to all the passions, desires, appetites, and temptations that go with this mortal probation. To work out his own salvation, he had to overcome the flesh, bridle his passions, control his desires and appetites, and resist the tempting wiles of Lucifer. Thus he was called upon to "suffer temptations, the pain of body, hunger, thirst, and fatigue." (Mosiah 3:7; 15:5.) Though he dwelt in the flesh as the Son of God, "yet learned he obedience by the things which he suffered." (Heb. 5:8.)

True, he remained obedient and faithful in all things, and never at any time did sin gain power over him. Though he "was in all points tempted like as we are, yet [he remained] without sin." (Heb. 4:15.) But in accordance with the eternal laws of free agency he could have succumbed to temptation; he could have lost his own soul and failed in his divinely appointed mission. That he remained true to his trust, that he was faithful and obedient to the whole law, made him the great Exemplar, the light of the world, who could say to all men, "Follow thou me." (2 Ne. 31:10.) (DNTC 1:127–28.)

4:9 "Pinnacle" means "top corner," "extremity," or "wing."

4:12 The last part of Jesus' reply could have been more literally translated "you must not put Jehovah your God to the test."

4:14–15 Read text and commentaries for Matthew 4:12, 17. Read also Mark 1:14–15. Compare John 4:43– 46.

4:15 "Being glorified of all" could have been translated "being held in honor by all." The Joseph Smith Translation adds "who believed on his name" to the end of this verse.

What did Jesus teach? During his ministry did he just go around doing good, healing the sick, and proclaiming various ethical principles, which if accepted would raise men to a higher way of life? Such is the common sectarian view. In reality, Jesus taught the gospel of the kingdom of God. That is, he taught that the kingdom of God, which is the Church of Jesus Christ, had again been set up on the earth, and that it was the only true and living Church upon the face of the whole earth. He taught the gospel which means that he taught the terms and provisions of the plan of salvation. He taught that gospel which "embraces all of the laws, principles, doctrines, rites, ordinances, acts, powers, authorities, and keys necessary to save and exalt men in the highest heaven hereafter." (MD, pp. 305–6.)

4:16–30 It was allowable for the reader in the service of the Jewish synagog to make comments in explanation of what had been read; but to do so he must sit. When Jesus took His seat the people knew that He was about to expound the text, and "the eyes of all them that were in the synagogue were fastened on him." The scripture He had quoted was one recognized by all classes as specifically referring to the Messiah, for whose coming the nation waited. The first sentence of our Lord's commentary was startling; it involved no labored analysis, no scholastic interpretation, but a direct and unambiguous application: "This day is this scripture fulfilled in your ears." There was such graciousness in His words that all wondered, and they said, "Is not this Joseph's son?" (JTC, p. 179.)

(See BD, "Anointed One.")

4:17 See BD, "Esaias."

4:18 The phrase "to preach deliverance to the captives" is greatly clarified in D&C 138. Also Elder Bruce R. McConkie has commented on this phrase:

Isaiah says, "to proclaim liberty to the captives, and the opening of the prison to them that are bound." (Isa. 61:1.) Reference is here made, not to the freeing of mortal men from any imprisonment, but to the ministry of freedom and pardon which was prepared for the departed dead. Jesus' mission was not alone to those then living; he was also to carry the gospel, the glad tidings of salvation, to the spirits in prison. Those who had been "gathered together, as prisoners are gathered in the pit," those who had been "shut up in the prison," were, "after many days," to be visited by him who held the key for their release. (Isa. 24:22.)

While his crucified body lay in the tomb, Jesus "went and preached unto the spirits in prison" (1 Pet. 3:18–20; 4:6), announcing in their hearing that through baptism for the dead and other vicarious ordinances he had provided the means "which would enable us to redeem them out of their prison; for the prisoners shall go free." (D&C 128:19–25.) (DNTC 1:161.)

4:19 The proper, designated, approved, appointed, or accepted time, in the divine order of things, for a particular work to be done. Thus Isaiah, speaking of Messiah's coming, says that "in an acceptable time" he shall "say to the prisoners, Go forth." (Isa. 49:8–9.) Thus also Paul taught that his day was "a time accepted," a time when salvation had been made available to men. "Now is the accepted time," he wrote, "now is the day of salvation." (2 Cor. 6:2.) Accordingly, in using this expression, Jesus is saying, "This is the time and the day of Messiah's coming; this is the acceptable year; this is the time designated by the Father for his Only Begotten to minister among men, and I am he." (DNTC 1:161–62.)

4:20 "Fastened" could have been translated "intently fixed."

4:23 Elder Bruce R. McConkie has explained the proverb "Physician, heal thyself":

A common rabbinnical proverb, which as used here seems to mean: "You have performed miracles in Cana and Capernaum, but none here, and yet you are a native of Nazareth. Why can't we see a sign, some great exhibition of your purported power? Don't you know that charity begins at home, that unless the physician heals himself of his own diseases we cannot believe he has power to heal others?" (DNTC 1:162.)

4:25, 27 The two Old Testament prophets referred to are Elijah (Elias) and Elisha (Eliseus), both of whom were not well accepted by their own people but who brought great blessings to believing foreigners. (See BD, "Elijah," "Elias," "Elisha," "Eliseus.")

4:28–30 Elder James E. Talmage has commented on the reaction of the Nazarenes to the teachings of Jesus:

Then great was their wrath. Did He dare to class them with Gentiles and lepers? Were they to be likened unto despised unbelievers, and that too by the son of the village carpenter, who had grown from childhood in their community? Victims of diabolical rage, they seized the Lord and took Him to the brow of the hill on the slopes of which the town was built, determined to avenge their wounded feelings by hurling Him from the rocky cliffs. Thus early in His ministry did the forces of opposition attain murderous intensity. But our Lord's time to die had not yet come. The infuriated mob was powerless to go one step farther than their supposed victim would permit. "But he passing through the midst of them went his way." Whether they were overawed by the grace of His presence, silenced by the power of His words, or stayed by some more appalling intervention, we are not informed. He departed from the unbelieving Nazarenes, and thenceforth Nazareth was no longer His home. (JTC, pp. 180–81.)

4:31–32 Read text and commentaries for Matthew 4:13–16. Read also Mark 1:21–22 for further information on Jesus going to Capernaum.

4:31 The Greek word translated "sabbath days" is the plural of "sabbath." Thus, a more literal translation would be that Jesus "taught them on the sabbaths."

4:33–37 Read text and commentaries for Mark 1:21–28.

4:34 "Destroy us" does not refer to annihilation of the spirit, which is impossible, but probably to being prevented from influencing mortals.

4:37 Read text and commentaries for Matthew 4:23–25. Read also Mark 1:21–22, 29–39; Luke 4:42–44.

4:38–44 Read text and commentaries for Matthew 4:23–25; 8:14–17. Read also Mark 1:21–25, 29–39; Luke 4:37.

4:38–39 Read text and commentaries for Matthew 8:15–16. Read also Mark 1:29–31.

For verse 38, the Joseph Smith Translation begins, "And he arose, *and went* out of the synagogue," and ends, "for *to heal* her." (Italics added.)

4:40–44 Read text and commentaries for Matthew 4:23–25; 8:16–17. Read also Mark 1:32–34.

Though others before and since have preached the gospel and healed the sick, yet none ever wrought so ably and effectively as the man Jesus. "Never man spake like this man" (John 7:46), and never was the healing power of faith so abundantly attested as in his ministry.

Perhaps these very Galilean multitudes were the ones Nephi saw in vision more than six hundred years before. "I beheld the Lamb of God going forth among the children of men," he recorded. "And I beheld multitudes of people who were sick, and who were afflicted with all manner of diseases, and with devils and unclean spirits; . . . And they were healed by the power of the Lamb of God; and the devils and the unclean spirits were cast out." (1 Ne. 11:31.) (DNTC 1:171.)

(See section 1, "Healing.")

4:42–44 Read text and commentaries for Matthew 4:23–25. Read also Mark 1:21–22, 29–39; Luke 4:37.

4:42 (See commentary for Mark 6:31.) The Joseph Smith Translation uses "solitary" in place of "desert," and "desired" in place of "stayed."

4:44 The Greek word translated "Galilee" is really "Judea." Jesus evidently taught in synagogues other than those in the Galilee.

5:1–11 (Read text and commentaries for Matt. 4:18–22. Read also Mark 1:16–20.) The accounts in Matthew, Mark, and Luke do not agree in the precise details of the calling of these disciples. Elder Bruce R. McConkie has discussed the apparent discrepancies:

> From these abbreviated and fragmentary gospel accounts, it is difficult to reach a positive conclusion as to whether one or two calls are involved. Clearly Matthew and Mark are recording the same event, but Luke may have reference to a later and different occasion. Added details easily could harmonize the two seemingly different accounts and establish that they are records of one and the same event. Viewing the whole New Testament record as it now stands, however, it is not unreasonable to conclude that some of the disciples received as many as five separate calls to follow Jesus:
>
> (1) In Judea, John, Andrew, Simon, Peter, Philip, and Nathanael, seek out Jesus, receive assurance of his Messiahship, forsake all, and follow him. (John 1:35–51; I.V. John 1:42.)
>
> (2) In Galilee, Jesus walking, apparently alone, on the shores of the Sea of Galilee, finds Peter and Andrew as they fished in their ship; he calls them to follow him and promises to make them fishers of men. Later and at a distance he finds James and John as they mend their nets in another ship and calls them. These four, in groups of two, forsake all and follow him. Such is the account of Matthew and Mark.
>
> (3) At a seemingly later time, though also on the shores of the Sea of Galilee (as Luke records the account), Jesus finds two ships together; pressed by the multitude around him, he enters Simon's ship, preaches to the people, and performs the miracle of filling the net with fish; James and John come to Simon's assistance; Simon is told that his mission is to catch men; and again those involved forsake all and follow Jesus.
>
> (4) Five of the disciples mentioned in these calls—Peter, Andrew, James, John, Nathanael (Bartholomew)—are later called to the apostleship. (Matt. 10:1–4.)
>
> (5) Even after his resurrection, Jesus is still calling some of these same followers back to their appointed ministries. (John 21.) Indeed, it is not until after the day of Pentecost, when the full enjoyment of the gift of the Holy Ghost has come upon them, that the disciples forsake all in the full sense of never returning again to their temporal pursuits. (DNTC 1:165–66.)

5:1 The same body of water is variously called "lake of Gennesaret" (Luke 5:1), "sea of Galilee" (Matt. 2:18; 15:29;

Mark 1:16; 7:31; John 6:1), and "sea of Tiberias" (John 6:1; 21:1).

5:2 And saw two ships standing *on* the lake; but the fishermen were gone out of them, and were *wetting* their nets. (JST; italics added.)

5:4, 9 "Draught" means "catch" or "haul."

5:6 The Greek word translated "brake" indicates that the action is still in process. Thus, a more literal translation would have been "their nets began ripping [breaking] apart."

5:8 In the Joseph Smith Translation, this verse begins, "When Simon Peter saw the multitude of fishes, he fell down . . ."

Elder Bruce R. McConkie has commented on Peter's words "Depart from me; for I am a sinful man, O Lord":

> Peter's purpose was not to separate himself and his fortunes from those of his Lord. Rather, he was overwhelmed with the renewed realization that he was in Messiah's personal presence. It was as though he had said: "I am unworthy of this honor; a sinner such as I is not fit company for 'the King, the Lord of hosts' (Isa 6:5); depart from me that another more deserving may see thy countenance and behold thy person." (DNTC 1:166.)

5:9 This verse could have been more literally translated "For at the catch of fish which they took up astonishment overwhelmed him and all those with him."

5:12–16 Read text and commentaries for Matthew 8:1–4. Read also Mark 1:40–45.

5:14 In the Joseph Smith Translation, this verse begins, "And he charged him to tell no man; *but said unto him,* Go . . ." (Italics added.)

5:17–26 Read text and commentaries for Matthew 9:1–8. Read also Mark 2:1–12.

> From what Jesus said at the time he healed the man "sick with the palsy," it would seem that remittance of sins is the therapy which heals and that the two terms are synonymous. . . .
> In this instance there was a physical healing. Sometimes there is also a healing of the nervous system or of the mind. But *always the remittance of sins which attends divine forgiveness heals the spirit.* This accounts for the fact that in the scriptures conversion and healing are repeatedly associated. (Marion G. Romney, CR, Oct. 1963, pp. 24–25; italics added.)

5:17 The last clause could have been translated "And Jehovah's power was there for him to do healing."

5:19 In the Joseph Smith Translation, this verse begins, "And when they found that they could not bring him in for the multitude, they went . . ."

5:20 Now he saw their faith, and said unto the man, Thy sins are for-given thee. (JST.)

5:23 Does it require more power to forgive sins than to make the sick rise up and walk? (JST.)

5:24 But, that ye may know that the Son of Man hath power upon earth to forgive sins, *I said it. And he said unto the sick of the palsy,* I say unto thee, Arise, and take up thy couch, and go *unto thy* house. (JST; italics added.)

5:26 The first part of this verse could have been trans-lated "Then an ecstasy seized one and all, and they began to glorify God."

5:27–32 Read text and commentaries for Matthew 9:9–13. Read also Mark 2:13–17.

5:27 "A publican . . . sitting at the receipt of custom" could have been more literally translated "a tax collector . . . sitting at the tax office."

And after these things he went forth, and saw a publican, named Levi, sitting at the *place where they received* custom; and he said unto him, Follow me. (JST; italics added.)

(See section 1, "Matthew.")

5:33–39 Read text and commentaries for Matthew 9:14–17. Read also Mark 2:18–22.

5:36 (See commentaries for Matt. 9:16.) This statement could have been more literally translated "No one cuts a patch from a new outer garment; but if he does, then both the new patch tears away and the patch from the new gar-ment does not match the old."

And he spake also a parable unto them, *saying,* No man putteth a piece of new *cloth* upon an old *garment;* if *so,* then the new maketh a rent, and agreeth not with the old. (JST; italics added.)

5:37–38 (See text and commentary for Matt. 9:17.) "Bottles" should have been translated "waterskins" or "wineskins."

5:39 Probably Jesus made some statement to John's disciples and clinched it in their minds by using this one sentence parable. The sense and meaning is: "In following John, who was sent of my Father to prepare the way before me, you have conformed to the law of Moses. Now, however, a greater than Moses is here, even the Messiah, and as John taught, you must now follow him, even though it is difficult for you to "straightway" turn from your old teachings and accept the new." (DNTC 1:186.)

6:1–5 Read text and commentaries for Matthew 12:1–9. Read also Mark 2:23–28.

6:1 Most of the Greek texts do not differentiate between the second sabbath and the first sabbath. Rather, the texts simply indicate that "on a sabbath" Jesus passed through grainfields.

6:6–11 Read text and commentaries for Matthew 12:10–13. Read also Mark 3:1–6.

6:7 This verse could have been more literally translated "The scribes and the Pharisees were now watching him closely to see whether he would cure on the sabbath, in order to find some way to accuse him."

6:9 See section 1, "Sabbath."

6:12 This is only one of several accounts of Jesus going to pray alone. (See Matt. 14:23; 26:36; Luke 5:16; 9:28.) Another account of Jesus going "into a mountain" is in Mark 3:13.

6:13–16 Read text and commentaries for Matthew 10:1–4; Luke 5:1–11. Read also Mark 3:13–21. See 1 Nephi 13:24–26, 39–41; D&C 95:4.

6:13 (See commentary for Mark 3:14.) Elder Harold B. Lee has explained one of the special functions of an apostle:

> I was visiting with one of the missionaries some years ago when two missionaries came to me with what seemed to be a very difficult question, to them. A young Methodist minister had laughed at them when they had said that apostles were necessary today in order for a true church to be upon the earth. And they said the minister said: "Do you realize that when they met to choose one to fill the vacancy caused by the death of Judas, that they said it had to be one who companied with them and had been a witness of all things pertaining to the mission and resurrection of the Lord? How can you say you have apostles, if that be the measure of an apostle?" And so these young men said, "What shall we answer?" I said to them: "Go back and ask your minister friend two questions. First, how did the Apostle Paul gain what was necessary to be called an apostle? He didn't know the Lord; had no personal acquaintance. He hadn't accompanied the apostles. He hadn't been a witness of the ministry, nor the resurrection of the Lord. How did he gain his testimony sufficient to be an apostle? Now the second question you ask him: How does he know that all who are today apostles have not likewise received that witness?" I bear witness to you that those who hold the apostolic calling may, and do know of the reality of the mission of the Lord. ("Born of the Spirit," Address to Seminary and Institute Faculty, 26 June 1962.)

(See BD, "Apostle.")

6:15 "Zelotes" could have been translated more fully "the zealous one." (See BD, "Zelotes.")

6:17–26 Read text and commentaries for Matthew 5:1–12. See 3 Nephi 12:1–12.

6:17 Matthew records that this sermon was given on "a mountain." (Matt. 5:1.) Luke's reference to a plain could have meant a level place or a plateau up in the mountains.

6:19 The last part of this verse could have been more literally translated "because power was going out of him and healing them all."

6:20 In the Joseph Smith Translation, the last part of this verse reads, "Blessed are the poor; for theirs is the kingdom of God."

The Greek word translated "blessed" in these verses also means "happy."

6:23 The Joseph Smith Translation replaces "is" with "shall be."

6:24–26 (Read text and commentaries for Matt. 5:3–11.) Elder Bruce R. McConkie observes that the Beatitudes could have been written in a negative form:

> Opposite every blessing stands a curse; obedience brings the blessing, disobedience the curse. All men shall gain either the one or the other; there is no such thing as neutrality. Either men believe in Christ or they do not; either they obey his laws or they do not. All of the Beatitudes could be rewritten in the negative form to show the woes that result from taking a course opposite to that counseled by Jesus. (DNTC 1:217.)

(See section 1, "Beatitudes.")

6:27–35 (Read text and commentary for Matt. 5:43–47. See 3 Ne. 12:43–45.) This version of the Sermon on the Mount is not as complete as the corresponding materials in Matthew, and is given in a different order.

6:27 In the Joseph Smith Translation, this verse begins, "But I say unto you *who hear my words,* Love your enemies . . ." (Italics added.)

6:28 Bless them *who* curse you, and pray for them *who* despitefully use you *and persecute you.* (JST; italics added.)

6:29–30 (Read text and commentaries for Matt. 5:38–42. See 3 Ne. 12:33–42.) The last part of verse 29 could have been more literally translated "and from him that takes away your outer garment, do not withhold even the under garment."

> And unto him *who* smiteth thee on the cheek, offer also the other; *or, in other words, it is better to offer the other, than to revile again.* And him *who* taketh away thy *cloak,* forbid not to take thy coat also.
> *For it is better that thou suffer thine enemy to take these things, than to contend with him. Verily I say unto you, Your heavenly Father who seeth in secret, shall bring that wicked one into judgment.* (JST; italics added.)

Verse 30 begins with "Therefore," tying this verse to those immediately preceding it.

6:31 See text and commentary for Matthew 7:12 for other translations of this famous verse enunciating the Golden Rule.

6:32 For if ye love them *only who* love you, what *reward* have you? For sinners also *do even the same.* (JST; italics added.)

6:33 This verse is deleted from the Joseph Smith Translation, indicating that it may have been an unauthorized addition of an earlier scribe.

6:34 This verse could have been more literally translated "Also, if you lend [without interest] to those from whom you hope to receive, of what credit is it to you? Even sinners lend [without interest] to sinners that they may get back as much."

The Joseph Smith Translation replaces "thank" with "reward."

6:36 Read text and commentaries for Matthew 5:48. See 3 Nephi 12:48.

As the attainment of infinite perfection includes the acquisition of all of the attributes of godliness in their fulness, so a person who is perfect, as the Father is perfect, has also gained the same degree of mercy possessed by Deity. Similarly men are expected to be charitable, loving, honest, virtuous, upright, and clean, and to possess every godly attribute even as these are found in the being of the Father. (DNTC 1:231–32.)

6:37–42 Read text and commentaries for Matthew 7:1–5. See 3 Nephi 14:1–5.

6:39 (Read text and commentaries for Matthew 15:1–20. Read also Mark 7:1–23.) "Ditch" could also have been translated "pit," "well," or "cistern."

6:40 (Read text and commentaries for Matt. 10:16–31. Read also Luke 12:1–7; 12:11–12.) This verse could have been more literally translated "A pupil is not above his teacher, but everyone that is perfectly instructed will be like his teacher." The Greek word for *teacher* was quite consistently translated by the King James translators as *master.*

6:41–42 (Read text and commentaries for Matt. 7:1–5.) "Mote" could have been translated "chip" or "splinter," while "beam" means a large piece of timber.

(See section 1, "Mote.")

6:43–44 (Read text and commentaries for Matt. 7:15–20.

See 3 Ne. 14:15–20.) In verse 43, "corrupt" could also have been translated "rotten."

6:45 Read text and commentaries for Matthew 10:32–33; 12:31–37, 43–45. Read also Mark 3:28–30; Luke 11:24–26; 12:8–10.

6:46–49 Read text and commentaries for Matthew 7:24–29. Read also Luke 13:25–30. See 3 Nephi 14:21–27; D&C 11:16–25.

6:46 Read text and commentaries for Matthew 7:21–23. Read also Luke 13:25–30. See 3 Nephi 14:21–23.

6:49 The Greek text clearly indicates that "without a foundation" refers to the house rather than to the man. A more literal translation is, "is like a man who built a house upon the ground without a foundation."

7:1–10 Read text and commentaries for Matthew 8:5–13.

7:1 "In the audience of the people" could have been more literally translated "in the hearing of the people."

7:11–17 To raise the dead is to call back the spirit from the abode of departed spirits so that mortal life again continues for the person so raised. Men, in this sphere of their unending existence, are mortal beings, meaning that body and spirit are temporarily united. The natural or temporal death consists in the separation of body and spirit. That is, the life which is in the body departs, the body returns to the dust, and the spirit goes to a world of waiting spirits to await the day of resurrection. A resurrected personage is one for whom body and spirit are inseparably connected in immortality. A mortal person raised from the dead does not by that act gain immortality; rather, he becomes mortal a second time, must again die, and will finally be raised in immortality in the resurrection.

Various prophets have raised the dead, among them Elijah (1 Kings 17:17–24), Elisha (2 Kings 4:18–37), Peter (Acts 9:36–43), Paul (Acts 20:7–12), and Nephi, the disciple. (3 Ne. 7:18–20.) But none ever acted with such awesome majesty as the Lord Jesus, who, stopping the funeral cortege, said with simplicity: "Young man, I say unto thee, Arise." (DNTC 1:256.)

7:11–15 The Greek text does not indicate that it was a *man* who had died. Rather, as indicated in verse 14, the son of the widow was a "young man."

7:11 Several of the Greek texts indicate that this event "followed closely" the event recorded in the previous verses. These texts do not necessarily indicate that these events occurred "the day after." (See BD, "Nain.")

7:18–35 Read text and commentaries for Matthew 11:1–19. Read also Luke 16:16.

7:18 This verse could have been more literally translated "Now John's disciples reported to him about all these things."

7:23 And blessed are they who shall not be offended in me. (JST.)

7:28 Read text and commentaries for Matthew 11:11.

There is not a prophet who has borne greater or more important testimony of Jesus than that which fell from John's lips. Joseph Smith gave three reasons why John was considered one of the greatest prophets. "First. He was entrusted with a divine mission of preparing the way before the face of the Lord. Whoever had such a trust committed to him before or since? No man.

"Secondly. He was entrusted with the important mission, and it was required at his hands, to baptize the Son of Man. Whoever had the honor of doing that? Whoever had so great a privilege and glory? Whoever led the Son of God into the waters of baptism, and had the privilege of beholding the Holy Ghost descend in the form of a dove, or rather in the *sign* of the dove, in witness of that administration? . . .

"Thirdly. John, at that time, was the only legal administrator in the affairs of the kingdom there was then on earth. And holding the keys of power, the Jews had to obey his instructions or be damned, by their own law; and Christ himself fulfilled all righteousness in becoming obedient to the law which he had given to Moses on the mount, and thereby magnified it and made it honorable, instead of destroying it. The son of Zacharias wrested the keys, the kingdom, the power, the glory from the Jews, by the holy anointing and decree of heaven, and these three reasons constitute him the greatest prophet born of woman." (*Teachings,* pp. 275–276.) (DNTC 1:262–63.)

Whom did Jesus have reference to as being the least? Jesus was looked upon as having the least claim in God's kingdom, and [seemingly] was least entitled to their credulity as a prophet; as though he had said, "He that is considered the least among you is greater than John—that is I myself." (TPJS, p. 276.)

(See section 1, "John the Baptist: Greatest prophet.")
7:30 Read Mark 1:4.

For those who would gain salvation, baptism in water is mandatory. No accountable person can be saved without it. Such is the counsel and command of God. To suppose that water baptism is merely an outward sign of some inward grace, or that baptism of the Spirit without prior immersion in water, is all that Deity requires is the purest sectarian delusion. The very baptism by immersion for the remission of sins which John performed (followed, of course, by the baptism of the Spirit which Jesus administered) is the thing which the Almighty has commanded. (DNTC 1:263.)

7:36–50 Read Matthew 26:7–13; Mark 14:3–9.
(See section 1, "Baptism.")

7:37 The name of the woman who thus came to Christ, and whose repentance was so sincere as to bring to her grateful and contrite soul the assurance of remission, is not recorded. There is no evidence that she figures in any other incident recorded in scripture. By certain writers she has been represented as the Mary of Bethany who, shortly before Christ's betrayal, anointed the head of Jesus with spikenard; but the assumption of identity is wholly unfounded, and constitutes an unjustifiable reflection upon the earlier life of Mary, the devoted and loving sister of Martha and Lazarus. Equally wrong is the attempt made by others to identify this repentant and forgiven sinner with Mary Magdalene, no period of whose life was marked by the sin of unchastity so far as the scriptures aver. (JTC, pp. 263–64.)

8:1–3 See BD, "Joanna," "Mary Magdalene."

8:1 In the Joseph Smith Translation, this verse ends, "and the twelve *who were ordained of him,* were with him." (Italics added.)

8:2–3 See BD, "Joanna."

8:4 See Luke 8:9–10 below.

8:5–8 Read text and commentaries for Matthew 13:3–9, 18–23. Read also Mark 4:3–9, 14–20; Luke 8:11–15.

8:9–10 Read text and commentaries for Matthew 13:1–3, 10–17, 34–35. Read also Mark 4:1–2, 10–13, 33–34; Luke 8:4.

8:11–15 Read text and commentaries for Matthew 13:3–9, 18–23. Read also Mark 4:3–9, 14–20; Luke 8:5–8.

8:12 In the Joseph Smith Translation, this verse begins, "*That which fell* by the wayside are they who hear . . ." (Italics added.) Similar wording is used at the beginnings of verses 13, 14, and 15.

8:13 "In the time of temptation" could have been translated "in the season of testing."

8:15 But that *which fell* on the good ground are they, *who receive the word* in an honest and good heart, having heard the word, *keepeth what they hear,* and bring forth fruit with patience. (JST; italics added.)

8:16 (Read text and commentaries for Matt. 5:13–16. Read also Luke 11:33; 14:34–35. See 3 Ne. 12:13–16; D&C 101:39–40.)
"Candle" could have been translated "lamp."

No man who is a true minister, when he brings gospel light, covereth it with mystery and confusion (as in the case, for instance, with the sectarian creeds describing God), but he holds forth as much light before men as they are able to bear. (DNTC 1:291.)

8:17–18 Read text and commentaries for Mark 4:21–25.

8:17 This verse could have been more literally translated "For there is nothing hidden that will not become manifest, neither anything carefully concealed that will never become known and never come into the open." (See 2 Ne. 30:17–18; Ether 4:7–12.)

8:18 Take heed therefore how ye hear; for whosoever *receiveth,* to him shall be given; and whosoever *receiveth* not; from him shall be taken even that which he seemeth to have. (JST; italics added.)

8:19–21 Read text and commentaries for Matthew 12:46–50. Read also Mark 3:31–35; Luke 11:27–28.

8:19 In the Joseph Smith Translation this verse ends, "and could not *speak* to him for the *multitude."* (Italics added.)

8:20 In the Joseph Smith Translation, this verse begins, *"And some who stood by, said unto him,* Thy mother. . . " (Italics added.)

8:21 The Joseph Smith Translation replaces "these which" with "those who."

8:22–25 Read text and commentaries for Matthew 8:23–27. Read also Mark 4:35–41.

From this miraculous stilling of a tempest on the Sea of Galilee we learn several lessons:

(1) During his mortal probation, Jesus was subject to the same laws of health and physical conduct that apply to all mankind. Being physically exhausted, he slept; by labor he became weary; without food he hungered; without drink he thirsted. Sleeping calmly amid the raging billows of a tempest that threatened to sink the ship is certainly evidence of an unimpaired nervous system. It is clear that the mortal Jesus lived a normal, healthy, balanced life.

(2) The disciples knew Jesus had divine powers and could save them even from the raging tempest. Because of their fear they were themselves devoid of that confidence and assurance which would have enabled them to still the storm; yet, almost instinctively, they knew their Master could do what they hesitated to attempt, and so—as all men should when their own weak powers are ineffective—they turned for help to the fountain from which perfect help flows.

(3) Jesus, the Lord of nature and Creator of all things, had and freely exercised power over the creature of his creating. By his word, as he acted in the power of his Father, heaven, earth, and sea had their beginning. Now he spoke and winds and water obeyed.

(4) Deity intervenes in temporal things, even controlling and moderating the elements for the faithful. True, he makes the sun to shine and sends his rains upon the just and the unjust (Matt. 5:45), for all men have come to earth to receive the experiences and undergo the vicissitudes of

mortality. But he maintains special watch care over those who by obedience and righteousness become his especial friends. For them storms are stilled, barren soil becomes productive (Isa. 35), special needed rains fall and bounteous harvests mature (Lev. 26:3–5; Deut. 11:13–15; 28:11–12), climatic conditions of whole regions are changed, mountains are moved, and rivers are turned out of their courses. (Moses 6:34; 7:13–14.)

(5) As with almost all men in their divers walks, greater faith should have been evidenced by the disciples as their ship struggled in the surging waves of the Galilean sea. "O ye of little faith," and "Where is your faith?" were the Master's mild but pointed expressions of reproof.

(6) Implicit in Jesus' reproof of the weak faith of the disciples is the assurance that by faith they also could have commanded the elements and had them obey. By faith all things are possible, and when the Lord's servants rise in the full majesty of their callings, they have "power to command the waters." (D&C 61:27.) (DNTC 1:306–7.)

8:23 In the Joseph Smith Translation, this verse ends, "and they were filled with *fear,* and were in *danger.*" (Italics added.)

8:26–39 Read text and commentaries for Matthew 8:28–34; Mark 5:13. Read also Mark 5:1–20.

8:26 "Over against Galilee" means "on the side opposite Galilee." (See BD, "Gadara.")

8:27 And when *they* went forth to land, there met him out of the city a certain man, *who* had devils *for a* long time, and *he would* wear no clothes, neither abode in a house, but in the tombs. (JST; italics added.)

8:30 Elder Bruce R. McConkie has defined "the deep":

Into outer darkness, "into the lake of fire" (Rev. 20:14–15), prepared for the devil and his angels in eternity. (DNTC 1:314.)

8:31 The Joseph Smith Translation transposes verses 31 and 32 and inserts the following at the end of verse 31: "And he said unto them, Come out of the man."

8:32 The Joseph Smith Translation emphasizes "that he would suffer them to enter into *the swine.*"

"And he suffered them" could have been translated "And he gave them permission."

8:33 "Choked" could have been translated "drowned."

8:34 When they *who* fed *the swine* saw what was done, they fled, and went and told *the people* in the city and in the country. (JST; italics added.)

8:36 In the Joseph Smith Translation, this verse begins, "They also *who* saw *the miracle,* told them . . ." (Italics added.)

8:37 The Joseph Smith Translation makes it clear that "him" and "he" refer to Jesus. (See BD, "Gadara.")

8:40–56 Read text and commentaries for Matthew 9:18–26. Read also Mark 5:21–43.

8:43 This verse could have been more literally translated "And a woman, subject to a flow of blood for twelve years, who had not been able to get a cure from anyone, . . ."

8:44 "Stanched" means "stopped."

The Joseph Smith Translation identifies "him" as Jesus.

8:46 The Joseph Smith Translation reads "some one" rather than "somebody."

Joseph Smith, on March 14, 1843, wrote in his journal:

> Elder Jedediah M. Grant enquired of me the cause of my turning pale and losing strength last night while blessing children. I told him that I saw Lucifer would exert his influence to destroy the children that I was blessing, and *I strove with all the faith and spirit that I had to seal upon them a blessing that would secure their lives upon the earth; and so much virtue went out of me into the children, that I became weak,* from which I have not yet recovered; and I referred to the case of the woman touching the hem of the garment of Jesus. *The virtue referred to is the spirit of life; and a man who exercises great faith in administering to the sick, blessing little children, or confirming, is liable to become weakened.* (TPJS, pp. 280–81.)

(See text and commentaries for Mark 5:30; section 1, "Virtue.")

8:47 The first part of this verse could have been translated "Seeing that she had not escaped notice."

The Joseph Smith Translation reads, "And when the woman *found* that she was not hid . . ." (Italics added.)

8:50 "Believe only" has a much stronger meaning in the Greek, and could have been translated "exercise faith" or "put forth faith."

The Joseph Smith Translation begins this verse, "But Jesus heard him, and *he said unto the ruler of the synagogue,* Fear not . . ." (Italics added.)

8:54 When Peter raised Dorcas to life (Acts 9:36–42), he followed closely the pattern set by Jesus in this incident with the daughter of Jairus.

8:55 This verse could have been more literally translated "And her spirit returned, and she rose instantly, and he ordered something to be given her to eat."

9:1–6 Read text and commentaries for Matthew 9:35–38; 10:5–15. Read also Mark 6:6–13.

Men become true ministers of Christ, not by their own choice, not because they desire to preach the gospel, not because they choose to go to a divinity school, but because they are called of God. "Ye have not chosen me, but I have chosen you, and ordained you." (John 15:16.) Unless ministers receive power and authority from God, they do not have it; unless they receive the priesthood by the laying on of hands of those empowered so to act, they do not become legal administrators whose acts are binding on earth and in heaven.

"A man must be called of God, by prophecy, and by the laying on of hands, by those who are in authority to preach the Gospel and administer in the ordinances thereof." (Fifth Article of Faith.) To raise the dead, to cast out devils, to cure diseases, to heal the sick—such things take the power of God. Among those who have the power of God these miracles are performed; and where they are not performed, there the power of God is not. Professing ministers without this power are false ministers. (DNTC 1:328.)

9:3 A scrip is a leather pouch for food, or a leather wallet. Sometimes this word has been translated "traveling bag" or "beggar's bag." (See section 1, "Scrip.")

9:4 In the Joseph Smith Translation, this verse ends, "there abide *until ye* depart thence."

9:5 "Testimony" could also have been translated "witness."

9:7–9 Read text and commentaries for Matthew 14:1–12. Read also Mark 6:14–29.

9:7 A tetrarch is a ruler of a fourth part of a country. See commentary for Luke 3:1.

9:10–17 Read text and commentaries for Matthew 14:13–21. Read also Mark 6:30–44; John 6:1–14.

9:10, 12 In the Joseph Smith Translation, "desert" has been changed to "solitary."

9:10 The last sentence could have been translated "With that he took them along and withdrew to privacy into a city called Bethsaida."

9:12 (See commentaries for Matt. 14:13.) "Get victuals: for we are here in a desert place" could have been translated "find provisions, because out here we are in a lonely place."

9:13 (Read text and commentaries for Matt. 6:25–26; Mark 8:8.) In the Joseph Smith Translation, this verse ends, *"and* except we should go and buy meat, *we can provide no more food for all this multitude."* (Italics added.) The Greek word translated here as "meat" means "food." (See section 1, "Meat.")

9:16 Jesus blessed the loaves and fishes, not to cause them to multiply, but to set a pattern of thanksgiving for his disciples. (John 6:11.) In performing miracles it was not his wont to ask the Father to do the deed; rather, as evidence of his own power and divine Sonship, he spoke in his own name and heaven and earth obeyed his commands. In conformity with the pattern there set, it is proper for devout persons to give frequent thanks for their daily bread and to covenant to use the strength derived from it in righteous works. (DNTC 1:345.)

9:17 In the Joseph Smith Translation, this verse ends, "fragments which remained, twelve baskets."

9:18–22 Read text and commentaries for Matthew 16:13–20. Read also Mark 8:27–30.

9:18 And it came to pass, as he *went* alone *with his disciples to pray,* he asked them, saying, *Who* say the people that I am? (JST; italics added.)

Only Luke records the fact that Jesus and his disciples were alone praying when the question was asked that resulted in Peter's strong testimony.

9:19 In the Joseph Smith Translation, this verse begins, "They answering said, *Some say,* John the Baptist; but *others* say, Elias . . ." (Italics added.)

9:20 The Joseph Smith Translation records Peter's answer as "The Christ, *the Son* of God." (Italics added.)

9:21–22 Read text and commentaries for Matthew 16:21–23. Read also Mark 8:31–33.

9:21 The Joseph Smith Translation ends this verse, "tell no man *of him.*" (Italics added.)

9:23–25 Read text and commentaries for Matthew 16:24–26. Read also Mark 8:34–37.

9:24–25 For whosoever will save his life, *must be willing to* lose it *for my sake; and* whosoever will *be willing to* lose his life for my sake, the same shall save it.

For what *doth it profit a* man if he gain the whole world, and *yet he receive him not whom God hath ordained, and he lose his own soul, and he himself be a castaway?* (JST; italics added.)

Martyrdom is not an essential condition precedent to the attainment of eternal life. Men are judged according to their desires and the intents of their hearts as well as their works. Even though the dispensation of the meridian of time was one of martyrdom and slaughter of the saints, there were many who were able to escape these things. Through obedience to the gospel standards, their guarantee of attaining eternal life is equal to that of those who laid down their lives, because those who escaped the sword would have submitted to it rather than deny or forsake the gospel cause. In this latter-day dispensation relatively few have been called upon to lay down their lives in the gospel cause, but all saints are expected to be willing to do so if the necessity is laid upon them. (DNTC 1:394.)

9:26–27 Read text and commentaries for Matthew 16:27–28. Read also Mark 8:38 through 9:1.

9:26 In the Joseph Smith Translation, the end of this verse reads, "he shall come in his own *kingdom, clothed in the glory of his Father, with* the holy angels." (Italics added.)

9:27 *Verily,* I tell you of a truth, there *are* some standing here *who* shall not taste of death, *until* they see the kingdom of God *coming in power.* (JST; italics added.)

One of those who were standing there "who shall not taste of death" until the Second Coming was John the Beloved. (See John 21:21–24.)

9:28–36 Read text and commentaries for Matthew 17:1–9. Read also Mark 9:2–10.

9:29 In the Joseph Smith Translation, the ending of this verse reads, "his countenance was *changed,* and his raiment *became* white and *glittering.*" (Italics added.)

9:31 Who appeared in glory, and spake of his *death, and also his resurrection,* which he should accomplish at Jerusalem. (JST; italics added.)

9:32 Evidently this experience occupied the entire night, as they did not return to the other disciples until the next day. (See Luke 9:37.) This may explain why the three disciples with Jesus were "heavy with sleep."

9:33 In the Joseph Smith Translation, this verse begins, *"And after the two men departed from* him, Peter . . ." (Italics added.)

9:35 The quotation in this verse could have been more literally translated "This is my Son, the one that has been chosen. Listen to him."

9:36 In the Joseph Smith Translation, the second sentence in this verse begins, "And *these things* they kept close . . ." (Italics added.)

9:37–43 Read text and commentaries for Matthew 17:14–21. Read also Mark 9:14–29.

9:42 The Joseph Smith Translation reads, " . . . and tare him *again.*" (Italics added.)

9:43–45 Read text and commentary for Matthew 17:22–23. Read also Mark 9:30–32.

9:43 The first sentence in this verse could have been more literally translated "They all began to be astounded at the majestic power of God."

9:44 The Joseph Smith Translation reads "hearts" rather than "ears."

Elder James E. Talmage has commented on a possible reason why the disciples were having difficulty understanding these statements of Jesus:

> The thought of what the Lord's words might mean, even in its faintest outline, was terrifying to those devoted men; and their failure to comprehend was in part due to the fact that the human mind is loath to search deeply into anything it desires not to believe. (JTC, p. 382.)

9:46–48 Read text and commentaries for Matthew 18:1–5. Read also Mark 9:33–37.

9:47 In the Joseph Smith Translation, this verse ends, "and set him *in the midst.*" (Italics added.)

9:49–50 Read text and commentaries for Mark 9:38–40.

9:49 The Joseph Smith Translation indicates that John "spake" rather than "answered."

"We forbad him" could have been more literally translated "we tried to prevent him."

> **9:50** And Jesus said unto him, Forbid *not any;* for he *who* is not against us is for us. (JST; italics added.)

9:51–56 John also briefly mentions this trip, but does not indicate that Jesus went through Samaria. (See John 7:10.)

> **9:51** Jesus was leaving Galilee forever; his great Galilean ministry was ended. In Judea and Perea his voice would yet be heard, his mighty works seen. But the course of his life was toward the cross, and he was steadfast and immovable in his determination to follow this very course, one laid out for him by his Father. He had said of himself through the mouth of Isaiah, "I set my face like a flint, and I know that I shall not be ashamed." (Isa. 50:7.) Clearly, there was to be no turning back. (DNTC 1:439.)

> **9:53** *And the Samaritans would* not receive him, because his face was *turned* as though he would go to Jerusalem. (JST; italics added.)

> How easy it is to reject the truth, including the Son of God himself, when prejudice and false religious views darken the mind! In the early days of his ministry (as he traveled *away* from Jerusalem), many Samaritans had received Jesus gladly, hailing him as the promised Messiah (John 4:1–42), but now (as he was steadfastly determined to minister and

worship *in* Jerusalem), they refused even to let him eat and sleep in their village. If he were truly the Messiah, they reasoned, he would go to Mount Gerizim to worship, not to Jerusalem. (DNTC 1:439–40.)

9:54 And when his disciples, James and John, saw *that they would not receive him,* they said, Lord, wilt thou that we command fire to come down from heaven and consume them, even as Elias did? (JST; italics added.)

Though inharmonious with the true Spirit of Christ, this offer of James and John is neither so harsh or vindictive, nor so scripturally unrealistic, as it might seem. They knew that the God of Israel—the same Jesus in whose presence they then stood—had sent fire from heaven at Elijah's word to consume the enemies of that ancient prophet. (2 Kings 1.) They knew also that the same merciful God would destroy the wicked by fire at his Second Coming. (Mal. 4:1.) What they had yet to learn was that for their dispensation, under the conditions which then existed (and they are comparable today), the gospel message was to go forth with charity, patience, forbearance, and long-suffering. However, their offer to compensate for the rebuff suffered by their Master was a manifestation of rather majestic faith. Who but those thoroughly converted to the righteousness and ultimate triumph of their cause would expect Deity to send fire from heaven to defend and vindicate them? (DNTC 1:440.)

9:56 In going to another village when they were rejected in the first, Jesus was following the counsel he had given earlier to the disciples as recorded in Matthew 10:23.

9:57–62 Read text and commentaries for Matthew 8:18–22.

When men are called of God by the spirit of revelation, called in the omnipotent wisdom of him who knoweth all things, those calls take precedence over all conflicting interests. Missionaries so sent forth habitually forsake all personal and family obligations. Loved ones may pass away, but missionaries remain at their posts, preaching the kingdom of God. (DNTC 1:304.)

9:59 "Suffer" in this context means "permit."

9:60 The meaning of "Let the dead bury their dead" is that those who are spiritually dead may take care of burying those who are physically dead, or, in other words, attend to temporal matters. (See section 1, "Dead: Bury dead.")

9:62 "Fit" could have been translated "well fitted."

10:1–11 This call and commission to the seventies parallels the prior selection and sending forth of the Twelve; and well it should, for seventies also are especial witnesses of the Lord's name, chosen elders charged with the obligation to carry the message of salvation to the world. Like the Twelve, they hold the Melchizedek Priesthood and are ordained to be "traveling ministers," who "preach the gospel, . . . in all the world." (D&C 107:25, 97.)

"The seventies are called to be assistants to the Twelve Apostles," President Joseph F. Smith said. "Indeed, they are apostles of the Lord Jesus Christ, subject to the direction of the Twelve, and it is their duty to respond to the call of the Twelve, under the direction of the First Presidency of the Church, to preach the gospel to every creature, to every tongue and people under the heavens, to whom they may be sent." (*Gospel Doctrine,* 5th ed., p. 183.) (DNTC 1:431–32.)

[The Seventy] were not restrained, as the Twelve had been, from entering Samaritan towns or the lands of the Gentiles. This difference is consistent with the changed conditions, for now the prospective itinerary of Jesus would take Him into non-Jewish territory, where His fame had already spread; and furthermore, His plan provided for an extension of the gospel propaganda, which was to be ultimately world-wide. The narrow Jewish prejudice against Gentiles in general and Samaritans in particular was to be discountenanced; and proof of this intent could not be better given than by sending authorized ministers among those peoples. We must keep in mind the progressiveness of the Lord's work. At first the field of gospel preaching was confined to the land of Israel, but the beginning of its extension was inaugurated during our Lord's life, and was expressly enjoined upon the apostles after his resurrection. Duly instructed, the Seventy set out upon their mission. (JTC, pp. 426–27.)

10:7 In the Joseph Smith Translation, this verse begins, "And into *whatsoever house they receive you,* remain, eating and drinking . . ."

Elder Bruce R. McConkie has written concerning the clauses "the labourer is worthy of his hire" and "go not from house to house":

Those who give their full time to the ministry, who spend all their time serving the Church and their fellow men, must still eat, wear clothing, and find shelter from the elements. Such are entitled to be supported by those they serve. Similarly, when missionaries serve without purse or scrip, they are entitled to receive assistance from those among whom they minister. "Behold, I send you out to prove the world," the Lord says of them, "and the laborer is worthy of his hire. . . . Whoso receiveth you receiveth me; and the same will feed you, and clothe you, and give you money. And he who feeds you, or clothes you, or gives you money, shall in nowise lose his reward." (D&C 84:79, 89–90.) (DNTC 1:433.)

There is nothing mechanical or routine about proselyting procedures; it is not a matter of knocking on every door, but of seeking out the honest in heart; missionaries must have the Spirit to guide them in where they go so that receptive vessels may be found and filled with living water. (DNTC 1:433.)

10:12–15 Read text and commentaries for Matthew 11:20–24.

10:12–13 The Joseph Smith Translation of verse 12 reads "it shall be more tolerable in the *day of judgment* for Sodom . . ." (Italics added.)

The Joseph Smith Translation adds the following between verses 12 and 13: "Then began he to upbraid the people in every city wherein his mighty works were done, who received him not, saying, . . ."

10:13 The Joseph Smith Translation replaces "they had a great while ago repented" with "they would have repented."

10:14 The Joseph Smith Translation replaces "at the judgment" with "at the day of judgment."

10:16 This verse could have been more literally translated "He that listens to you listens to me [too]. And he that disregards you disregards me [too]. Moreover, he that disregards me disregards [also] him that sent me forth."

The Joseph Smith Translation adds the following preface to this verse: "And he said unto his disciples . . ."

10:17–20 This account of the return of the seventy is recorded only by Luke.

10:18 And he said unto them, *As lightning falleth from heaven, I beheld Satan also falling.* (JST; italics added. See Isa. 14:12.)

(See section 1, "Satan"; BD, "Lucifer.")

10:21–22 Read text and commentaries for Matthew 11:25–30.

10:21 The Joseph Smith Translation reads "thou hast hid these things from them *who think they are* wise and prudent, and hast revealed them unto babes . . ." (Italics added.)

Compared with the learned men of the time, such as the rabbis and scribes, whose knowledge served but to harden their hearts against the truth, these devoted servants were as babes in humility, trust, and faith. Such children were and are among the nobles of the kingdom. (JTC, p. 428.)

10:22 All things are delivered to me of my Father; and no man knoweth *that the Son is the Father, and the Father is the Son, but him* to whom the Son will reveal *it.* (JST; italics added.)

(See section 1, "Trinity, no.")

Not two personages, but one; not two beings in the express image of each other, but one being only who is both the Father and the Son. That is, Christ himself is the Father. "Behold, the mystery of godliness, how great is it!" (D&C 19:10.)

This doctrine that Christ is the Father, though seldom so well stated in the Bible, is abundantly and expressly taught in latter-day revelation. Many of the explanatory passages setting forth the doctrine are quoted or cited in the now famous document entitled, "The Father and The Son: A Doctrinal Exposition by The First Presidency and the Twelve," published in full, among other places, on pages 465 to 473 of the *Articles of Faith* by Elder James E. Talmage.

In the usual manner of speaking, the Father and the Son are two separate personages who are united as one in purpose and plan and in character and attributes. Christ is the Firstborn spirit offspring of the Father in preexistence, the Only Begotten in the flesh. But there are three specific scriptural senses in which Christ is spoken of and known as the Father:

(1) He is the Father in the sense of being the Creator and is thus referred to as "the Father of the heavens and of the earth, and all things that in them are." (Ether 4:7.)

(2) He is the Father of those who abide in his gospel. Faithful saints who receive him have power given them to become his sons. (D&C 39:4.) Those who are "spiritually begotten . . . are born of him"; they become "the children of Christ, his sons, and his daughters." (Mosiah 5:7.)

(3) He is the Father by divine investiture of authority. That is, the Father places his own name, power, authority, and Godship on the Son, and empowers him to act and speak in the first person as though he were the Father so that his words and acts become and are those of the Father. All things are truly delivered to him by his Father. (DNTC 1:467–68.)

10:23–24 These words which Jesus spoke "privately" to his disciples are recorded only by Luke. (For additional information on why Jesus taught in parables, read text and commentaries for Matt. 13:1–3, 10–17, 34–37. Read also Mark 4:1–2, 10–12, 33–34; Luke 8:4, 9–10.)

10:25–37 The famous parable of the Good Samaritan is contained only in Luke.

From the standpoint of weaving a plausible account of common happenings into a story that teaches a great spiritual truth, this is a perfect parable. The Jews esteemed themselves as a chosen race, superior to the religiously degenerate Samaritans whom they hated, whom they classified as foreigners, and whom they expressly refused to accept as neighbors. Between Jerusalem and Jericho lay a thief-infested highway that was often bathed in blood. Jericho itself was a city of priests and Levites. Wine, to cleanse wounds, and oil, as a salve to assuage their smarting, were the common remedies of the day. The two pence equaled two days' wages for a laborer and would have kept the injured man for several days. Indeed, so realistic is the story that it well may be a recitation of an actual happening well known to Jesus' hearers. (DNTC 1:471–72.)

10:25 The Greek word translated "lawyer" means "a certain man versed in the law."

We have seen that the Pharisees and their kind were constantly on the alert to annoy and if possible disconcert Jesus on questions of law and doctrine, and to provoke Him to some overt utterance or deed. It may be such an attempt that is recorded by Luke in immediate sequence to his account of the joyous return of the Seventy, for he tells us that the "certain lawyer," of whom he speaks, put a question to tempt Jesus. Viewing the questioner's motive with all possible charity, for the basal meaning of the verb which appears in our version of the Bible as "to tempt" is that of putting to test or trial and not necessarily and solely to allure into evil, though the element of entrapping or ensnaring is connoted, we may assume that he wished to test the knowledge and wisdom of the famous Teacher, probably for the purpose of embarrassing Him. Certainly his purpose was not that of sincere search for truth. (JTC, p. 429.)

10:27 The parable takes on additional meaning when it is understood that the meaning of the word *neighbor* had been narrowly defined by the Jews:

Among the sacred laws left on record by Moses was the command to "love thy neighbour as thyself." (Leviticus 19:18.) Centuries later, in laying down for the people narrow and uninspired interpretations of this command, the rabbis wrote: "We are not to contrive the death of the Gentiles, but if they are in any danger of death we are not bound to deliver them, e.g. if any of them fall into the sea you need not take him out, for such a one is not thy neighbour." (Dummelow, p. 751.) (LTJA, pp. 113–14.)

10:28 These simple words conveyed a rebuke, as the lawyer must have realized; they indicated the contrast between knowing and doing. Having thus failed in his plan to confound the Master, and probably realizing that he, a lawyer, had made no creditable display of his erudition by asking so simple a question and then answering it himself, he tamely sought to justify himself by inquiring further: "And who is my neighbour?" We may well be grateful for the lawyer's question; for it served to draw from the Master's inexhaustible store of wisdom one of His most appreciated parables. (JTC, pp. 429–30.)

10:31 In the Joseph Smith Translation, this verse ends, "he passed by on the other side *of the way.*" (Italics added.)

For further information on priests, who were then literal descendants of Aaron, see BD, "Priests."

10:32 And likewise a Levite, when he was at the place, came and looked *upon* him, and passed by on the other side *of the way; for they desired in their hearts that it might not be known that they had seen him.* (JST; italics added.)

(See BD, "Levites.")

10:33 See BD, "Samaritans." Also, read John 4:9.

10:35 "Host" could be translated more literally as "innkeeper." "Pence" is derived from the Greek *"denarii."*

The Joseph Smith Translation simply records that the

Samaritan "took *money,* and gave to the host." (Italics added.)

10:38–42 Only Luke records this interesting episode with Mary and Martha.

Mary and Martha were both faithful, devoted disciples of Jesus. Both knew he was the Son of God, Martha, in particular, so testifying when he raised their brother Lazarus from the dead. (John 11.) It appears that these sisters were on friendly, even intimate, terms with Jesus, that he visited them in Bethany from time to time, and that it was the privilege of Martha, at least to offer him the hospitality of her home.

Here we see Jesus dining in Martha's home. According to the social amenities of the day, Mary should have been assisting her sister in the serving and other details of the meal; instead, she sat at Jesus' feet feasting herself on the spiritual food which fell from his lips. From Martha's housewifely complaint and Jesus' mild reproof, we learn the principle that, though temporal food is essential to life, once a reasonable amount has been acquired, then spiritual matters should take precedence. Bread is essential to life, but man is not to live by bread alone. Food, clothing, and shelter are essential to mortal existence, but once these have been gained in reasonable degree, there is only "one thing" needful—and that is to partake of the spiritual food spread on the gospel table. (DNTC 1:472–73.)

11:1–5 Read text and commentaries for Matthew 6:5–15. Read also Mark 11:25–26. See 3 Nephi 13:5–15.

No doubt the apostles, being faithful Jews, were themselves men of prayer; yet as they watched Jesus in prayer, they were so humbled and impressed as to ask, when he had finished, "Lord, teach *us* to pray." Here he gave them a simple pattern, the same as had been given in the Sermon on the Mount. Perhaps even more helpful than the short sample itself were the pertinent guidelines and counsel he then gave them. (LTJA, p. 114.)

(See section 1, "Prayer.")

11:3 "Closets" could have been translated "private rooms."

11:4–5 And forgive us our sins; for we also forgive every one *who* is indebted to us. And *let* us not *be led unto* temptation; but deliver us from evil; *for thine is the kingdom and power. Amen.*

And he said unto them, Your heavenly Father will not fail to give unto you whatsoever ye ask of him. And he spake a parable, saying, . . . (JST; italics added.)

(See section 1, "Lord's Prayer.")

11:5–8 The interesting story of the Friend at Midnight is recounted only by Luke.

The parable is regarded by some as a difficult one to apply, since it deals with the selfish and comfort-loving element of human nature, and apparently uses this to symbolize God's deliberate delay. The explanation, however, is clear when the context is duly considered. The Lord's lesson was, that if man, with all his selfishness and disinclination to give, will nevertheless grant what his neighbor with proper purpose asks and continues to ask in spite of objection and temporary refusal, with assured certainty will God grant what is persistently asked in faith and with righteous intent. No parallelism lies between man's selfish refusal and God's wise and beneficent waiting. There must be a consciousness of real need for prayer, and real trust in God, to make prayer effective; and in mercy the Father sometimes delays the granting that the asking may be more fervent. But in the words of Jesus: "If ye then, being evil, know how to give good gifts unto your children: how much more shall your heavenly Father give the Holy Spirit to them that ask him?" (JTC, p. 435.)

11:9–13 Read text and commentaries for Matthew 7:7–12. See 3 Nephi 14:7–12.

11:9 This verse could have been more literally translated "Accordingly I say to you, Keep on asking, and it will be given you; keep on seeking, and you will find; keep on knocking, and it will be opened to you."

11:12 See BD, "Scorpion."

11:13 In the Joseph Smith Translation, the last part of this verse reads, "how much more shall your heavenly Father give *good gifts, through the* Holy Spirit, to them *who* ask him." (Italics added.)

11:14–23 Read text and commentaries for Matthew 9:27–34; 12:22–30. Read also Mark 3:22–27.

11:14–15 By casting out devils Jesus offered conclusive and irrefutable proof that he was the promised Messiah. This conclusion is evident from the following reasoning:

(1) Devils are not cast out except by the power of faith and the authority of the priesthood. Lucifer's ministers exercise the power to perform many miracles in imitation of those done by the Lord's authorized servants. But no one, acting pursuant to a delegation of authority from the devil, ever casts one of his kindred spirits out of the mortal tenement such spirit has unlawfully inhabited. Satan is not divided against himself anymore than angelic ministrants of the Lord are rebelling against each other. Hence, the fact that Jesus did in reality cast out devils, as was evident to the Pharisees and all the people, establishes that he operated in harmony with "the Spirit of God," and that "the kingdom of God," which is the true Church, had come forth again among men.

(2) Jesus bore frequent testimony that he was the Son of God, which testimony he would not have borne, if it had been untrue, because he had the Spirit of God with him, as evidenced by the fact that he cast out devils. In other words, if his testimony had been untrue, he could not have enjoyed the Spirit, for the Spirit will attest and seal only that which is true, and without the Spirit our Lord would have been without the power to cast out devils. But the fact that he did cast out devils, because he had the

Spirit, proves his harmony with the Father, through the Spirit, and therefore his witness of himself was true. (DNTC 1:268–69.)

(See section 1, "Devils: Power to cast out.")

11:16 Read text and commentaries for Matthew 10:34–42; 12:38–42. Read also Mark 9:41; Luke 11:29–32; 12:49–53.

11:17 In the Joseph Smith Translation, the last part of this verse reads, "and a house divided cannot stand, *but falleth."* (Italics added.)

11:18 If Satan also be divided against himself, how *can* his kingdom stand? *I say this,* because *you* say I cast out devils through Beelzebub. (JST; italics added.)

11:20 In the Joseph Smith Translation, the last clause in this verse reads, "the kingdom of God *has* come upon you." (Italics added.)

11:22 "Spoils" is changed to "goods" in the Joseph Smith Translation.

11:24–26 (Read text and commentaries for Matthew 12:43–45.) The Joseph Smith Translation uses "it" rather than "he" in referring to the "unclean spirit."

11:25 "It" is replaced by "the house" in the Joseph Smith Translation.

"Garnished" means "adorned"; sometimes it is translated "trimmed."

11:26 In the Joseph Smith Translation, the beginning and ending of this verse reads, "Then goeth *the evil spirit* . . . and the last *end* of that man is worse than the first." (Italics added.)

Does this mean that the man who has quit smoking or drinking or had sex pollutions finds life empty for a time? The things which engaged him and caught his fancy and occupied his thoughts are gone, *and better substitutions have not yet filled the void. This is Satan's opportunity.* The man makes a start but may find the loss of the yesterday's habits so great that he is enticed to return to his evil ways, and his lot thus becomes infinitely worsened. (MF, p. 172.)

11:27–28 Read text and commentaries for Matthew 12:46–50. Read also Mark 3:31–35; Luke 8:19–21.

11:28 *And* he said, Yea, *and* blessed are *all* they *who* hear the word of God, and keep it. (JST; italics added.)

Apparently the message that his mother and his brethren sought audience with Jesus caused another woman (undoubtedly herself a mother) to speak these words of praise for Mary. With them Jesus agreed. But then he taught that it is not motherhood of itself, but obedience to the word of God, that brings blessings. (DNTC 1:281.)

11:29–32 Read text and commentaries for Matthew 10:34–42; 12:38–42. Read also Mark 9:41; Luke 11:16; 12:49–53.

11:29 The Joseph Smith Translation uses "them" rather than "it."

11:32 In the Joseph Smith Translation, this verse begins, "The men of *Nineveh* shall rise up in the *day of* judgment with this generation; and shall condemn it." (Italics added.)

It shall be as though heathen and Gentile nations, those without the law and the light which Israel had, shall rise up in judgment against the chosen seed, whose opportunities to do right were far greater. The heathens of Nineveh repented when a man preached to them, but God's covenant race, the chosen of the whole earth, refused to repent when the very Son of God came among them. (DNTC 1:278.)

11:33–36 Read text and commentaries for Matthew 5:13–16 and 6:22–23. Read also Luke 8:16. See 3 Nephi 12:14–16; 13:22–23.

11:36 In the Joseph Smith Translation, the end of this verse reads, "as when the bright shining of a candle *lighteneth a room* and doth give the light *in all the room*." (Italics added.)

11:37–54 For other examples of Jesus denouncing hypocrisy, read text and commentaries for Matthew 23:1–36. Read also Mark 12:38–40; Luke 18:9–14; 20:45–47.

11:37–44 Read text and commentaries for Matthew 23:25–28.

11:40 "Ye fools" could have been translated "You unreasonable persons."

11:41 But *if ye would rather give* alms of such things as ye have; *and observe to do all things which I have commanded you, then would your inward parts be clean also.* (JST; italics added.)

11:42 (Read text and commentaries for Matt. 23:23–24.) In the Joseph Smith Translation, this verse begins, "But *I say unto you,* Woe *be* unto you, Pharisees!" (Italics added.)

"Herbs" could have been translated "vegetables."

11:45–48 Read text and commentaries for Matthew 23:29–33.

11:46 "Ye lawyers" could have been translated "you who are versed in the law."

11:47–49 Elder Spencer W. Kimball several years ago suggested there might be "modern-day sepulchre-builders" in the Church:

> Do you also build sepulchres for the dead prophets and tombs for those who have passed away long ago and disregard the living ones? (CR, Oct. 1949, p. 123.)

11:48 The first part of this verse could have been more literally translated "Certainly you are witnesses of the deeds of your forefathers and yet you give consent to them, because these killed the prophets."

11:49–51 Read text and commentaries for Matthew 23:34–36.

11:52–54 This material is contained only in the account by Luke.

11:52 Woe unto you, lawyers! *For* you have taken away the key of knowledge, *the fulness of the scriptures; ye enter* not in yourselves *into the kingdom;* and *those* who were entering in, ye hindered. (JST; italics added.)

> The devil wages war against the scriptures. He hates them, perverts their plain meanings, and destroys them when he can. He entices those who heed his temptings to delete and discard, to change and corrupt, to alter and amend, thus taking away the key which will aid in making men "wise unto salvation." (2 Tim. 3:15–17.)
>
> Accordingly, Jesus is here heaping wo upon those who have contaminated and destroyed scriptures which would have guided and enlightened the Jews. Nephi forsaw that the same treatment would be given to the writings of the apostles of Jesus (1 Ne. 13.) A comparison of the fore part of Genesis with the perfected version of the same material found in the Book of Moses illustrates what men have done to what God has said. Another comparison is Matt. 24 as found in the King James Version and in the Pearl of Great Price. The restored Book of Abraham, with its wealth of knowledge and gospel interpretation, is a sample of scripture that was wholly lost to the world. (DNTC 1:624–25.)

11:53 "The Pharisees began to urge him vehemently, and to provoke him to speak of many things" could have been more literally translated "the Pharisees started in to press upon him terribly and to ply him with questions about further things."

12:1–7 Read text and commentaries for Matthew 10:16–31. Read also Luke 6:40; 12:11–12.

12:1 "They trode one upon another" could have been translated "they were stepping on one another."

12:8–10 (Read text and commentaries for Matt. 10:32–33; 12:31–37, 43–45. Read also Mark 3:28–30; Luke 6:45; 11:24–26.) The Joseph Smith Translation adds two verses between verses 9 and 10 and contributes to a better understanding of verse 10:

> *Now his disciples knew that he said this, because they had spoken evil against him before the people; for they were afraid to confess him* before men.
>
> *And they reasoned among themselves, saying, He knoweth our hearts, and he speaketh to our condemnation, and we shall not be forgiven. But he answered them, and said unto them,*
>
> Whosoever shall speak a word against the Son of Man, *and repenteth*, it shall be forgiven him; but unto him *who* blasphemeth against the Holy Ghost, it shall not be forgiven *him*. (Italics added.)

12:11–12 Read text and commentaries for Matthew 10:16–31. Read also Luke 6:40; 12:1–7.

> **12:11** *And again I say unto you*, They *shall* bring you unto the synagogues, and *before* magistrates, and powers. *When they do this*, take ye no thought how, or what *things* ye shall answer, or what ye shall say; (JST; italics added.)

12:13–21 The parable of the Rich Fool is found only in Luke.

> The man's abundance had been accumulated through labor and thrift; neglected or poorly-tilled fields do not yield plentifully. He is not represented as one in possession of wealth not rightfully his own. His plans for the proper care of his fruits and goods were not of themselves evil, though he might have considered better ways of distributing his surplus, as for the relief of the needy. His sin was two-fold; first, he regarded his great store chiefly as the means of securing personal ease and sensuous indulgence; secondly, in his material prosperity he failed to acknowledge God, and even counted the years as his own. (JTC, p. 439.)

12:17–18 "Bestow" could have been more literally translated "gather." The idea is that the person wondered whether or not he would have room to gather (or store) his fruits. He was not concerned about whom he should give his fruits to.

> **12:21** So *shall it be with him who* layeth up treasure for himself, and is not rich toward God. (JST; italics added.)

Elder Bruce R. McConkie has explained the phrase "rich toward God":

Rich in the currency negotiable in the courts above; rich in eternal things; rich in the knowledge of the truth, in the possession of intelligence, in obedience to gospel law, in the possession of the characteristics and attributes of Deity, in all of the things which will continue to be enjoyed in eternity. (DNTC 1:474.)

12:22–32 Read text and commentaries for Matthew 6:25–34. Read also Luke 11:33–36; 16:9–13. See 3 Nephi 13:19–34.

12:23 This verse could have been more literally translated "For the soul is worth more than food and the body than clothing."

12:24 In the Joseph Smith Translation, the end of this verse reads, "*nevertheless,* God feedeth them. Are ye *not* better than the fowls?" (Italics added.)

12:25 "Stature" means "life-span." Thus, this verse might have to do with longevity rather than with height.

12:28 The Joseph Smith Translation ends this verse, "how much more will he *provide* for you, *if ye are not* of little faith." (Italics added.)

12:29 The last part of this verse could have been translated "quit being in anxious suspense."

12:30 The Joseph Smith Translation adds "who is in heaven" after "father," and then adds the following verse:

And ye are sent into them to be their ministers, and the labourer is worthy of his hire; for the law saith, That a man shall not muzzle the ox that treadeth out the corn.

12:31 In the Joseph Smith Translation, this verse begins, "*Therefore* seek ye *to bring forth* the kingdom of God . . ." (Italics added.)

12:33–34 Read text and commentaries for Matthew 6:19–24. Similar teachings are found in D&C 6:34; 29:5; 35:27.

12:33 In the Joseph Smith Translation, the beginning of this verse reads, "*This he spake unto his disciples, saying,* Sell that ye have and give alms; provide *not for* yourselves bags which wax old, *but rather provide* a treasure in the heavens . . ." (Italics added.)

"Provide not for yourselves bags which wax old" means that we are not to put our trust in purses that wear out and lose their earthly treasures.

12:35–48 (Read text and commentaries for Matthew

24:42–51; 25:1–13. Read also Mark 13:33–37; Luke 21:34–36.) Although this particular story is found only in Luke, the references mentioned deal with similar events. The account of Luke is greatly clarified by the numerous contributions of the Joseph Smith Translation (italics added):

Verse 35: " . . . and *have* your lights burning."

Verse 36: "That ye yourselves *may be* like unto men . . ."

Verse 37: *"Verily I say unto you, Blessed . . ."*

Verses 38 through 42:

For, behold, he cometh in the first watch of the night, and he shall also come in the second watch, and again he shall come in the third watch.

And verily I say unto you, He hath already come, as it is written of him; and again when he shall come in the second watch, or come in the third watch, blessed are those servants when he cometh, that he shall find so doing;

For the Lord of those servants shall gird himself, and make them to sit down to meat, and will come forth and serve them.

And now, verily I say these things unto you, that ye may know this, that the coming of the Lord is as a thief in the night.

And it is like unto a man who is an householder, who, if he watcheth not his goods, the thief cometh in an hour of which he is not aware, and taketh his goods, and divideth them among his fellows.

And they said among themselves, If the good man of the house had known what hour the thief would come, he would have watched, and not have suffered his house to be broken through, *and the loss of his goods.*

And he said unto them, Verily I say unto you, be ye therefore ready also; for the Son of Man cometh at an hour when ye think not.

Then Peter said unto him, Lord, *speaketh* thou this parable unto us, or unto all?

And the Lord said, I *speak unto those* whom the Lord shall make rulers over his household, to give *his children* their portion of meat in due season.

And they said, Who then is that faithful and wise servant?

And the Lord said unto them, It is that servant who watcheth, to impart his portion of meat in due season.

Verse 45: *"But the evil servant is he who is not found watching. And if that servant is not found watching, he will say in his heart,* My Lord delayeth his coming; and shall begin to beat the menservants, and *the* maidens, and to eat, and drink, and to be drunken."

Verse 46: "in sunder" is changed to "down."

Verse 47: "And that servant *who* knew his Lord's will, and prepared not *for his Lord's* coming, neither did . . ."

Verse 48 "But he that knew not *his Lord's will* . . ."

Inserted in the *Inspired Version* [JST] by revelation, these sayings of Jesus give a new and added concept to the teaching that men should watch, pray, and be ready for the Second Coming; they outline a concept which is not elsewhere set forth with the clarity and plainness here recorded. Interestingly, Dummelow came close to the very truth Jesus is here teaching when he speculated, as above quoted, that "Christ's return from the marriage feast . . . may mean his judgment of each individual soul at death."

All of the Lord's ministers, all of the members of his Church, and for that matter all men everywhere ('What I say unto one, I say unto all'), are counseled to await with righteous readiness the coming of the Lord. However, most men will die before he comes, and only those then living will rejoice or tremble, as the case may be, at his personal presence. But all who did prepare will be rewarded as though they had lived when he came, while the wicked will be "cut asunder" and appointed their "portion with the hypocrites" as surely as though they lived in the very day of dread and vengeance.

Thus, in effect, the Lord comes in every watch of the night, on every occasion when men are called to face death and judgment. The phrase, "He hath already come, as it is written of him," pointedly inserted in verse 42, is a witness that even then he ministered among mortal men and that they were judged by their acceptance or rejection of him. (DNTC 1:676–77.)

12:35–36 Read text and commentaries for Matthew 25:1–13. Read also D&C 45:56–59.

12:46 "Will cut him in sunder, and will appoint him his portion with the unbelievers" could have been more literally translated "will punish him with the greatest severity and assign him a part with the unfaithful ones."

12:49–53 Read text and commentaries for Matthew 10:34–42. Read also Mark 9:41; Luke 11:16, 29–32.

12:49 *For they are not well pleased with the Lord's doings; therefore* I am come to send fire on the earth; and what *is it to you, if I will that* it be already kindled? (JST; italics added.)

12:50 Translators have had difficulty agreeing on the exact interpretation of this verse. Elder Bruce R. McConkie has paraphrased this verse as follows:

But do not be perturbed, for even I have a baptism of blood and death to be baptized with, for my own familiar friend shall lift up his hand against me, one of my own official church family shall betray me; and what a burdensome pressure and responsibility rests upon me until I have accomplished this very mission and ordeal for which I came into the world. (DNTC 1:336.)

(See section 1, "Family members will not all accept.")

12:53 When honest truth seekers accept the gospel, they forsake the world and gain its hatred. The sword of persecution, of domestic dissension, and of family bitterness is often unsheathed by their closest relatives. Thousands of devout converts, in this dispensation alone, have been driven from their homes and denied their temporal inheritances, for accepting Joseph Smith and the pure, primitive gospel restored through his instrumentality. (DNTC 1:335.)

12:54–57 Read text and commentaries for Matthew 16:1–12. Read also Mark 8:11–21.

12:58–59 Read text and commentaries for Matthew 5:21–26. See 3 Nephi 12:21–30.

12:58 In the Joseph Smith Translation, this verse begins, "Why goest thou to thine adversary *for* a magistrate, when thou art in the way *with thine enemy?*" (Italics added.)

12:59 "Till thou hast paid the very last mite" could have been translated "until you pay over the last small coin of very little value."

13:1–5 No further information is provided in the scriptures on the loss of eighteen lives when "the tower of Siloam fell."

Does God send accidents, violent death, and other calamities upon individual men to punish them for their sins? Apparently there were those among Jesus' hearers who thought so. Accordingly, we find the Master expressly saying that those subject to the misfortunes here involved were not greater sinners than their fellows whose lives were spared.

True it is, as a general principle, that God sends disasters, calamities, plagues, and suffering upon the rebellious, and that he preserves and protects those who love and serve him. Such indeed were the very promises given to Israel—obedience would net them the preserving and protecting care of the Lord, disobedience would bring death, destruction, desolation, disaster, war, and a host of evils upon them. (Deut. 28; 30.)

But to say that particular individuals slain in war, killed in accidents, smitten with disease, stricken by plagues, or shorn of their property by natural calamities, have been singled out from among their fellows as especially deserving of such supposed retribution is wholly unwarranted. It is not man's prerogative to conclude in individual cases of suffering or accident that such has befallen a person as a just retribution for an ungodly course. (DNTC 1:475.)

13:1 The Joseph Smith Translation begins this account, "And there were present at that time, some who spake unto him of the Galileans . . ."

13:4 See BD, "Siloam."

13:6–9 A certain husbandman (God) had a fig tree (the Jewish remnant of Israel) planted in his vineyard (the world); and he came (in the meridian of time) and sought fruit thereon (faith, righteousness, good works, gifts of the Spirit), and found none. Then said he unto the dresser of his vineyard (the son of God), Behold, these three years (the period of

Jesus' ministry) I come seeking fruit on this fig tree, and find none; cut it down (destroy the Jewish nation as an organized kingdom); why cumbereth it the ground (why should it prevent the conversion of the world by occupying the ground and pre-empting the time of my servants)? And he (the Son of God) answering said unto him (God, the husbandman), Lord, let it alone this year also till I shall dig about it, and dung it (preach the gospel, raise the warning voice, show forth signs and wonders, organize the Church, and offer every opportunity for the conversion of the Jewish nation). And if it bear fruit, the tree is saved (the Jewish nation shall be preserved as such and its members gain salvation), and if not, after that thou shalt cut it down (destroy the Jews as a nation, make them a hiss and a byword, and scatter them among all nations). (DNTC 1:477.)

(See section 1, "Fig tree.")

13:6 The Joseph Smith Translation uses "husbandman" in place of "man."

13:7 "Why cumbereth it the ground" has also been translated "Why should it go on using up the soil."

13:9 And if it bear fruit, *the tree is saved,* and if not, after that thou shalt cut it down. *And many other parables spake he unto the people.* (JST; italics added.)

13:10–17 This is another incident of Jesus healing on the sabbath day. (See text and commentaries for Matt. 12:10–13.)

This particular healing is recorded in detail, not because of its miraculous nature, for many others equalled or surpassed it in this respect, but because it took place on the Sabbath day. See John 5:1–16. Out of the occurrences surrounding it we learn:

(1) For 18 years the woman had been bound by Satan with "a spirit of infirmity," presumably meaning that some mental or spiritual affliction attended her physical illness. Though Satan may rejoice in the afflictions—whether physical, mental, or spiritual—which befall mortal men, it is not to be assumed that he has power to impose them, except in isolated instances where people have complied with laws which permit such an imposition; otherwise, Satan would shackle all men with ills so drastic as to destroy them.

(2) Jesus appears to have sought out this woman and performed the miracle on his own initiate on the Sabbath to teach the principle that it is lawful to do good and work righteousness on that holy day.

(3) Though it was not always his habit so to do, in this instance he performed the healing by the laying on of hands, a physical performance which helps faith increase in the hearts of afflicted persons.

(4) False beliefs—as those relative to sabbath observance—lead to bigotry and place their adherents in a position where they deny and reject the pure mercies of God and become hypocrites.

(5) Every soul is honorable and deserving of dignified respect in the eyes of Deity. This woman, though decrepit and infirm, though shackled

with atrophied muscles and seemingly afflicted mentally and spiritually as well, was hailed by Jesus as a daughter of Abraham, a soul worthy of the blessings and mercies of Abraham's God. (DNTC 1:493–94.)

(See section 1, "Sabbath: Healing on.")

13:11 "Was bowed together, and could in no wise lift up herself" could have been translated "was bent double and was unable to raise herself up at all."

Behold, there was a woman *who* had a spirit of infirmity eighteen years, and was *bound* together, and could in no wise *straighten up*. (JST; italics added.)

13:14 "Answered" is replaced by "was filled" in the Joseph Smith Translation.

13:15 "Hypocrite" should be plural, according to the Greek text. Evidently, Jesus was referring to all of the people in the audience.

13:17 It was "his disciples" who rejoiced (rather than "all the people"), according to the Joseph Smith Translation.

13:18–19 Read text and commentaries for Matthew 13:31–32. Read also Mark 4:30–32.

13:18 "Whereunto shall I resemble it" could have been translated "to what shall I liken it" or "with what shall I compare it."

13:19 "Waxed" could have been translated "became."

13:20–21 Read text and commentaries for Matthew 13:33.

13:22–30 The discussion in these verses is primarily in response to the question, "Lord, are there few that be saved?"

Will few or many attain eternal life in the celestial kingdom? The answer, of great concern to all who seek salvation, depends upon what is meant by *few*. Few of what group? Of all persons born into the world? Of the portion of mankind who grow to a sufficient maturity to become accountable for their own sins? Or of the members of the Church who have covenanted in the waters of baptism to serve God and keep his command-ments in return for the promise of eternal salvation hereafter?

There are, of course, three kingdoms of glory to which resurrected per-sons will go—the celestial, terrestrial, and telestial. (1 Cor. 15:39–42; D&C 76.) Of these three, only the celestial is the kingdom of God; it is the kingdom reserved for the saints who obey the laws and ordinances of the gospel. Great hosts of persons will go to the other kingdoms and hence will not attain salvation in the full gospel sense.

From the spirit and letter of the Prophet's vision on the degrees of glory, it appears that great majority of accountable persons in the world will go to the telestial kingdom. He recorded in the revelation that the inhabitants of that lowest kingdom would be "as innumerable as the stars in the firmament of heaven, or as the sand upon the seashore." (D&C 76:109.)

On the other hand, speaking to accountable persons and of attainment of the celestial kingdom, Jesus said in the Sermon on the Mount; "Few there be that find it." (Matt. 7:14.) In other words, proportionately few of the earth's total accountable inhabitants will gain salvation. The overwhelming majority of them will go to lesser kingdoms and receive lower rewards.

Yet the total number who will gain salvation will be great and not small. John on one occasion saw in vision a group of exalted persons who exceeded 100,000,000 in number (Rev. 5:9–11) and on another occasion he beheld a group of saved persons which formed such a great multitude that "no man could number" them. (Rev. 7:9.)

Included among the celestial inhabitants will be all the children who die before they arrive at the years of accountability. (*Teachings,* p. 107.) Of this group President John Taylor said: "Without Adam's transgression those children could not have existed. Through the atonement they are placed in a state of salvation without any act of their own. These would embrace, according to the opinion of statisticians, more than one-half of the human family who can attribute their salvation only to the mediation and atonement of the Savior." (John Taylor, *Gospel Kingdom,* p. 119.)

As to members of the Church, many will gain salvation, many will not. For accountable persons to receive a celestial inheritance baptism coupled with personal righteousness is essential. For such persons to inherit eternal life in the celestial world, celestial marriage plus conformity to gospel law is required. Those members of the Church who act accordingly, will gain the rewards indicated; those who do not abide the laws involved will go to lesser inheritances in lower kingdoms and will not gain full salvation. (DNTC 1:495–96.)

13:23–24 Read text and commentaries for Matthew 7:13–14. See 3 Nephi 14:13–14.

And there said one unto him, Lord, are there few *only* that be saved? and he *answered him, and* said,

Strive to enter in at the *straight* gate; *for I say unto you, Many shall* seek to enter in, and shall not be able; *for the Lord shall not always strive with man.* (JST; italics added.)

Except during the brief hour of his personal ministry among men, the strivings of the Lord with men, to get them to believe, repent, and obey, are performed through his Spirit—the Spirit of Jesus Christ or Light of Christ. This is the Spirit that enlightens and guides all men and that leads them in paths of light and truth as long as they hearken to its voice. (D&C 84:44–48; 88:6–13; Moro. 7.) But when men rebel against truth and light, the Spirit withdraws its benign influence, "for my Spirit shall not always strive with man, saith the Lord of Hosts." (D&C 1:33.) (DNTC 1:496.)

13:24 "Strive to enter in at the strait gate" could have been translated "Exert yourselves vigorously to get in through the narrow door."

13:25–30 Read text and commentaries for Matthew 7:21–29. Read also Luke 6:46–49. See 3 Nephi 14:21–27; D&C 11:16–25.

13:25 *Therefore,* when once the *Lord of the kingdom* is risen up, and hath shut the door *of the kingdom, then* ye *shall* stand without, and knock at the door, saying, Lord, Lord, open unto us. *But the Lord* shall answer and say unto you, *I will not receive you, for ye* know not *from* whence ye are. (JST; italics added.)

13:27 The Joseph Smith Translation adds the word "from": "ye know not *from* whence ye are." (Italics added.)

13:28 The Joseph Smith Translation reads, "There shall be weeping and gnashing of teeth *among you* . . ." (Italics added.)

13:30 The Joseph Smith Translation adds a clause at the end of this verse: "and shall be saved therein." Elder Bruce R. McConkie has paraphrased this verse:

There are those Gentiles in all nations to whom the gospel is offered *last* who shall be saved ahead of you Jews to whom the word of God came *first,* and there are those among you who *first* had opportunity to hear the truth who shall be *last* as to honor, preference, and salvation hereafter. (DNTC 1:497.)

13:31–33 This material is found only in Luke.

13:31 The Joseph Smith Translation begins this verse: *"And as he was thus teaching,* there came *to him* certain of the Pharisees . . ."* (Italics added.)

"The same day" means "In that very hour."

13:32 "Fox" is replaced by "Herod" in the Joseph Smith Translation.

Elder Bruce R. McConkie has explained the clause "I shall be perfected":

Jesus was then perfect in the sense that he was without sin and was completely obedient to his Father's commands. But there was yet an eternal perfection for him to attain, the perfection spoken of in the command: "Be ye therefore perfect, even as your Father which is in heaven is perfect." (Matt. 5:48.) This future perfection, which would make him like his Father, was available to him only following his resurrection in connection with his receipt of "all power . . . in heaven and in earth." (Matt. 28:18; D&C 93:2–22.) (DNTC 1:498.)

13:33 What pointed irony is this! 'I shall not be killed by Herod here in Perea, for my work is not yet finished. But I shall go to Jerusalem, that great spiritual capital of the world, that city wherein ye think all religious light is centered. There, enveloped in the light that has become darkness, I shall be slain, not by pagan Herod, but by my own people.' (DNTC 1:498.)

The Joseph Smith Translation adds the following after verse 33: "This he spake, signifying of his death. And in this very hour he began to weep over Jerusalem, . . ."

13:34–35 Read text and commentaries for Matthew 23:37–39.

13:34 The Joseph Smith Translation ties this verse to the preceding verse by beginning it: "*Saying,* O Jerusalem, Jerusalem, *thou who* killest the prophets . . ." (Italics added.)

13:35 The Joseph Smith Translation adds significantly to this verse: "Ye shall not know me, *until ye have received from the hand of the Lord a just recompense for all your sins;* until the time come when ye shall say . . ." (Italics added.)

14:1–6 Although this specific incident of healing is contained only in the account by Luke, other healings by Jesus on the Sabbath are found in Matthew 12:1–15; Luke 13:10–17; John 5:1–16.

A possible reason for the propensity of Jesus to heal on the Sabbath has been proposed by Elder Bruce R. McConkie:

> Why did Jesus, again and again and again, seek occasion to exercise his healing powers on the Sabbath? Apparently this was one of his ways of keeping in the headlines. He was teaching the truths of salvation and inviting men to believe in him as the Son of God so that they might become heirs of eternal salvation. His miracles testified of his divine mission, and miraculous works wrought on the Sabbath would be known to more people, discussed in more synagogues, investigated by more truth seekers than those performed at any other time. (DNTC 1:499.)

(See section 1, "Sabbath: Healing on.")

14:5 The Savior's statement could have been translated more completely "Who of you, if his son or bull falls into a well, will not immediately pull him out on the sabbath day?"

14:7–11 This parable is found in this form only in Luke. The same principles are taught elsewhere in the scriptures, including Proverbs 25:6–7.

> **14:7** And he put forth a parable *unto them concerning those who* were bidden *to a wedding; for* he *knew* how they chose out the chief rooms, *and exalted themselves one above another; wherefore he spake* unto them, saying, . . . *(JST; italics added.)*

14:9 In the Joseph Smith Translation, this verse begins, "And he who bade thee, with him *who is more honorable, come . . .*" (Italics added.)

14:10 In the Joseph Smith Translation, the end of this verse reads, "then shalt thou have *honor of God,* in the presence of them *who* sit at meat with thee." (Italics added.)

"Worship" could have been more literally translated "honor," "glory," or "respect."

14:11 In a sense, Jesus here summarizes the whole plan and purpose of this mortal probation. It is to test men and see whether they will seek for worldly things—wealth, learning, honors, power—or whether they will flee from pride, humble themselves before God, and walk before him with an eye single to his glory. Without this basic Christian virtue of humility there is neither spiritual progression here nor eternal life hereafter. With it men are able to gain every godly attribute in this life and to qualify for full salvation in the mansions on high. "Be thou humble; and the Lord thy God shall lead thee by the hand and give thee answer to thy prayers." (D&C 112:10.) (DNTC 1:500.)

14:12–24 The Parable of the Great Supper, contained only in Luke, is somewhat similar to the Parable of the Marriage of the King's Son in Matthew 22:2–10.

Explication of the parable was left to the learned men to whom the story was addressed. Surely some of them would fathom its meaning, in part at least. *The covenant people, Israel, were the specially invited guests.* They had been bidden long enough aforetime, and by their own profession as the Lord's own had agreed to be partakers of the feast. When all was ready, on the appointed day, they were severally summoned by the Messenger who had been sent by the Father; He was even then in their midst. But the cares of riches, the allurement of material things, and the pleasures of social and domestic life had engrossed them and they prayed to be excused or irreverently declared they could not or would not come. *Then the gladsome invitation was to be carried to the Gentiles, who were looked upon as spiritually poor, maimed, halt, and blind.* And later, even the pagans beyond the walls, strangers in the gates of the holy city, would be bidden to the supper. These, surprised at the unexpected summons, would hesitate, until by gentle urging and effective assurance that they were really included among the bidden guests, they would feel themselves constrained or compelled to come. The possibility of some of the discourteous ones arriving later, after they had attended to their more absorbing affairs, is indicated in the Lord's closing words: "For I say unto you, That none of those men which were bidden shall taste of my supper." (JTC, p. 452; italics added.)

14:12 In the Joseph Smith Translation, this verse begins, "Then said he also *concerning* him *who* bade *to the wedding . . .*" (Italics added.)

14:23 "Go out into the highways and hedges" could have been more literally translated "Go out into the roads and the fenced-in places." The meaning is that the servant was being sent to the cultivated places.

14:25–33 This list of requirements for being a true disciple of Jesus is found only in Luke and is difficult to understand without the significant contributions of the Joseph Smith Translation.

14:25–26 *And when he had finished these sayings, he departed thence,* and there went great multitudes with him, and he turned and said unto them,

If any man come to me, and hate not his father, and mother, and wife, and children, and brethren, and sisters, *or husband,* yea and *their* own life also; *or in other words, is afraid to lay down their life for my sake,* cannot be my disciple. (JST; italics added.)

Not *hate* in the sense of intense aversion or abhorrence; such is contrary to the whole spirit and tenor of the gospel. Men are to love even their enemies, to say nothing of their own flesh and blood. (Matt. 5:43–48.) Rather, the sense and meaning of Jesus' present instruction is that true disciples have a duty toward God which takes precedence over any family or personal obligation. It is in thought content similar to the message previously given the Twelve: "He that loveth father or mother more than me is not worthy of me. and he that loveth son or daughter more than me is not worthy of me." (Matt. 10:37.) (DNTC 1:503.)

14:27 The Joseph Smith Translation adds, "Wherefore, settle this in your hearts, that ye will do the things which I shall teach, and command you."

14:28–33 That these verses pertain to converts to the Church is made clear in the addition to verse 30 in the Joseph Smith Translation: "And this he said, signifying there should not any man follow him, unless he was able to continue; saying . . ." The last word also ties the two consecutive parables together.

These two parables teach that converts should count the cost *before* joining the Church; that they should come into the kingdom only if they are prepared to make the sacrifices required; that they should go the whole way in the gospel cause, or stay out entirely; that they should "not . . . follow him, unless" they are "able to continue" in his word, to "do the things" which he teaches and commands.

Lukewarm saints are damned; unless they repent and become zealous the Lord promised to spue them out of his mouth. (Rev. 3:14–19.) Only the valiant gain celestial salvation; those saints "who are not valiant in the testimony of Jesus" can ascend no higher than the terrestrial world. (D&C 76:79.)

Those who are not able and determined to keep the commandments are better off outside the Church, "For of him unto whom much is given much is required; and he who sins against the greater light shall receive the greater condemnation." (D&C 82:3.) (DNTC 1:504.)

14:28 The Joseph Smith Translation ends this verse, "whether he have *money* to finish *his work?*" (Italics added.)

14:29 "Haply" is changed to "unhappily" in the Joseph Smith Translation. The Greek word thus translated has the element of uncertainty, and could have been translated "perhaps."

14:32 "He sendeth an ambassage" could have been translated "he will send a delegation."

14:34–35 Read text and commentaries for Matthew 5:13–16. Read also Luke 8:16; 11:33; 3 Nephi 12:13–16; D&C 101:39–40.

Then certain of them came to him, saying, Good Master, we have Moses and the prophets, and whosoever shall live by them, shall he not have life?

And Jesus answered, saying, Ye know not Moses, neither the prophets; for if ye had known them, ye would have believed on me; for to this intent they were written. For I am sent that ye might have life. Therefore I will liken it unto salt which is good;

But if the salt *has* lost *its savour,* wherewith shall it be seasoned?

It is neither fit for the land, not yet for the dung hill; men cast it out. He *who* hath ears to hear, let him hear. *These things he said, signifying that which was written, verily must all be fulfilled.* (JST; italics added.)

For nearly 1500 years righteous Israelites had sought salvation through conformity to the laws and ordinances revealed by Moses and the prophets. Now those among whom Jesus ministered erroneously assumed that the preaching of the ancients and the powers of past prophets were sufficient to give them a hope of eternal life. Hence they asked what was to them an obvious question: "Since we have the truths of salvation as revealed by Moses and the prophets, what need have we to hearken to you and your teachings about spiritual things?"

In reply, Jesus said in effect:

(1) "Ye do err, for ye neither know nor understand the teachings of Moses or the prophets. If ye understood their teachings, ye would believe in me, for all their teachings were given to prepare men for my coming and the salvation which I would bring."

(2) "Further, even assuming that ye believe Moses and the prophets, yet ye must turn to me, for 'salvation doth not come by the law alone' (Mosiah 13:28), for it is only in and through my atoning sacrifice that life and salvation come."

(3) "And now that I have come, the law of Moses has lost such saving power as it had; it has become as salt that has lost its savor and it cannot be

seasoned again; yea, the law is dead in me, and from henceforth it is not fit for anything except to be cast out. He who hath ears to hear, let him hear." (DNTC 1:506.)

15:1–7 Read text and commentaries for Matthew 18:11–14.

Sheep go where grass is. It seems apparent that the sheep in the parable was not lost through willful disobedience or careless neglect; it simply strayed away in search of greener pastures and soon was lost.

I ask you tonight, how did that sheep get lost? He was not rebellious. If you follow the comparison, the lamb was seeking its livelihood in a perfectly legitimate manner, but either stupidly, perhaps unconsciously, it followed the enticement of the field, the prospect of better grass until it got out beyond the fold and was lost.

So we have those in the Church, young men and young women, who wander away from the fold in perfectly legitimate ways. They are seeking success, success in business, success in their professions, and before long they become disinterested in Church and finally disconnected from the fold; they have lost track of what true success is, perhaps stupidly, perhaps unconsciously, in some cases, perhaps willingly. They are blind to what constitutes true success. (David O. McKay, CR, Apr. 1945, p. 120.)

15:1 The Joseph Smith Translation replaces "all" with "many."

15:5 The Joseph Smith Translation makes it clear that the shepherd did not leave the ninety and nine sheep *in* the wilderness; rather he left the ninety and nine to "*go into* the wilderness after that which is lost." (Italics added.)

15:8–10 In this case the thing lost was not in itself responsible. The one who had been trusted with that coin had, through carelessness or neglect, mislaid it or dropped it. There is a difference, and this is the one-third, which I think applies to us tonight. Our charge is not only coins, but living souls of children, youth, and adults. They are our charges. . . . Someone may be wandering because of the careless remark of a girl of her age in Mutual (and I have in mind a case), and the president of the Mutual lets her go, fails to follow her next Tuesday night and invite her to come. Another may be lost because of the inactivity of the Sunday School teacher, or the indifference of the Sunday School teacher who is satisfied with the fifteen people there that morning, instead of thinking of the fifteen who are wandering because of neglect. (David O. McKay, CR, Apr. 1945, pp. 121–22.)

15:11–32 The third parable is the prodigal son, the "younger son," we are told, so he was immature in his judgment. He was irking under the restraint, and he rather resented the father's careful guiding eye. He evidently longed for so-called freedom, wanted, so to speak, to try his wings. So he said, "Father, give me my portion, and I will go." The father gave him his portion, and out the lad went.

Here is a case of volition, here is choice, deliberate choice. Here is, in a way, rebellion against authority. And what did he do? He spent his means in riotous living, he wasted his portion with harlots. That is the way they are lost.

Youth who start out to indulge their appetites and passions are on the downward road to apostasy as sure as the sun rises in the east. I do not confine it to youth; any man or woman who starts out on that road of intemperance, of dissolute living will separate himself or herself from the fold as inevitably as darkness follows the day.

"My spirit shall not always strive with man" (Gen. 6:3), says the Lord. "My spirit will not dwell in an unclean tabernacle." He who tries to live a double life, who does live a double life in violation of his covenants, to quote one author, "is either a knave or a fool." Often he is both, because he himself is using his free agency to gratify his passions, to waste his substance in riotous living, to violate the covenants that he has made in the house of God.

In such cases there is little we can do but warn and plead until the recreant, as the prodigal son, at last "comes to himself." (David O. McKay, CR, Apr. 1945, pp. 122–23.)

Pharisees and scribes, to whom this masterpiece of illustrative incident was delivered, must have taken to themselves its personal application. They were typified by the elder son, laboriously attentive to routine, methodically plodding by rule and rote in the multifarious labors of the field, without interest except that of self, and all unwilling to welcome a repentant publican or a returned sinner. From all such they were estranged; such a one might be to the indulgent and forgiving Father, "this thy son," but never to them, a brother. They cared not who or how many were lost, so long as they were undisturbed in heirship and possession by the return of penitent prodigals. But the parable was not for them alone; it is a living perennial yielding the fruit of wholesome doctrine and soul-sustaining nourishment for all time. Not a word appears in condonation or excuse for the prodigal's sin; upon that the Father could not look with the least degree of allowance; but over that sinner's repentance and contrition of soul, God and the household of heaven rejoiced. (JTC, pp. 460–61.)

15:13 "Wasted his substance with riotous living" could have been translated "squandered his property by living a debauched life." The basic meaning is that he was a spendthrift and wasted his inheritance.

15:16 Other translations of this verse are:

He wished he could fill himself with the bean pods the pigs ate, but no one gave him anything to eat. (TEV.)

He longed to fill his stomach with the pods that the pigs were eating, but no one gave him anything. (NIV.)

(See BD, "Husks.")

15:17 "And when he came to himself" could have also been translated "When he finally came to his senses."

15:21 The Greek text indicates that the following sentence should be added at the end of this verse: "Make me as one of your hired men."

16:1–13 The Parable of the Unjust Steward is contained only in Luke, but some of the principles in the parable are found in Matthew 6:19–34; Luke 11:33–36; 12:22–32.

> It was not the steward's dishonesty that was extolled; his prudence and foresight were commended, however; for while he misapplied his master's substance, he gave relief to the debtors; and in so doing he did not exceed his legal powers, for he was still steward though he was morally guilty of malfeasance. The lesson may be summed up in this wise: Make such use of your wealth as shall insure your friends hereafter. Be diligent; for the day in which you can use your earthly riches will soon pass. Take a lesson from even the dishonest and the evil; if they are so prudent as to provide for the only future they think of, how much more should you, who believe in an eternal future, provide therefor! If you have not learned wisdom and prudence in the use of "unrighteous mammon," how can you be trusted with the more enduring riches? If you have not learned how to use properly the wealth of another, which has been committed to you as steward, how can you expect to be successful in the handling of great wealth should such be given you as your own? Emulate the unjust steward and the lovers of mammon, not in their dishonesty, stupidity, and miserly hoarding of the wealth that is at best but transitory, but in their zeal, forethought, and provision for the future. Moreover, let not wealth become your master; keep it to its place as a servant, for, "No servant can serve two masters: for either he will hate the one, and love the other; or else he will hold to the one, and despise the other. Ye cannot serve God and mammon." (JTC, p. 464.)

16:6–7 "Bill" could have been translated "written agreement."

16:9–13 Read text and commentaries for Matthew 6:19–34. Read also Luke 11:33–36; 12:22–32. See 3 Nephi 13:19–34.

16:9 (Read text and commentaries for Matt. 6:24–25.) "Mammon" is an Aramaic word meaning "riches." (See section 1, "Mammon.")

> In the Revised Version this verse reads: "And I say unto you, Make to yourself friends by means of the mammon of unrighteousness, that, when it shall fail, they may receive you into the eternal tabernacles." The sense and meaning is: "Ye saints of God, be as wise and prudent in spiritual things as the unjust steward was in worldly things. Use the things of this world—which are God's and with reference to which you are stewards—to feed the hungry, clothe the naked, and heal the sick, always remembering that when ye do any of these things unto the least of one of

these my brethren, ye do it unto me. By such a course, when your money is gone and your life is past, your friends in heaven will welcome you into eternal mansions of bliss." (DNTC 1:514–15.)

16:14–18 And they said unto him, We have the law, and the prophets; but as for this man we will not receive him to be our ruler; for he maketh himself to be a judge over us.

Then said Jesus unto them, The law and the prophets testify of me; yea, and all the prophets who have written, even until John, have foretold of these days.

Since that time, the kingdom of God is preached, and every man *who seeketh truth* presseth into it.

And it is easier for heaven and earth to pass, than *for* one tittle of the law to fail.

And why teach ye the law, and deny that which is written; and condemn him whom the Father hath sent to fulfill the law, that you might all be redeemed?

O fools! for you have said in your hearts, There is no God. And you pervert the right way; and the kingdom of heaven suffereth violence of you; and you persecute the meek; and in your violence you seek to destroy the kingdom; and ye take the children of the kingdom by force. Woe unto you, ye adulterers!

And they reviled him again, being angry for the saying, that they were adulterers.

But he continued, saying, Whosoever putteth away his wife, and marrieth another, committeth adultery; and whosoever marrieth her *who* is put away from her husband, committeth adultery. (JST; italics added.)

16:14 This verse could have been more literally translated "Now the Pharisees, who were money lovers, were listening to all these things, and they began to sneer at him." The Revised Version renders this verse: "And the Pharisees, who were lovers of money, heard all these things; and they scoffed at him."

16:15 Our Lord's reply to their words of derision was a further condemnation. They knew all the tricks of the business world, and could outdo the righteous steward in crafty manipulation; and yet so successfully could they justify themselves before man as to be outwardly honest and straightforward; furthermore, they made ostentatious display of a certain type of simplicity, plainness, and self-denial, in which external observances they asserted superiority over the luxury loving Sadducees; they had grown arrogantly proud of their humility, but God knew their hearts, and the traits and practices they most esteemed were an abomination in his sight. (JTC, p. 465.)

16:16 Read text and commentaries for Matthew 11:1–19. Read also Luke 7:18–35.

16:17 Read text and commentaries for Matthew 5:17–20. See 3 Nephi 12:17–20, 46–47.

Elder Bruce R. McConkie has explained the meaning of verses 16 and 17 as enlarged upon in the Joseph Smith Translation.

All of the divine teachings, revelations, visions, prophecies, miracles, and wonders of the past were considered by the Jews to have come through and because of the law and the prophets. Beginning with Adam, their father, the first man, the Lord God had sent prophets, at frequent and recurring intervals, to warn, teach, and guide his people. The whole body of their prophecies and inspired writings were known as the prophets. From the day of Moses, Israel had been under the law—the set of divine requirements and regulations which governed the chosen people in both temporal and spiritual matters.

With all this—the whole body of revealed knowledge about God and salvation and all things incident thereto—why, the Pharisees reasoned, was there a need for this Jesus and his teachings; what right did he have to rule and judge Israel.

The answer—"The law and the prophets testify of me. Yea, the whole purpose of the law was to teach Israel that I would come to redeem my people; all its requirements and performances were types and shadows of things to come; it was a schoolmaster to prepare Israel to receive me and my gospel. And as to the prophets, all 'who have prophesied ever since the world began' have testified of me, of my coming in the flesh, and of the redemption I would make for my people. (Mosiah 13:27–35.) Further: I am he who gave the law and in me it shall be fulfilled; not one tittle shall fail, but it shall all be fullfilled in me. (3 Ne. 12:17–19; 15:2–10.) Why do ye pretend to teach the law when ye condemn him whom the Father hath sent to fulfil it and to redeem you?" (DNTC 1:517–18.)

16:18 Read text and commentaries for Matthew 5:27–32. See 3 Nephi 12:31–32.

16:19–31 Verily I say unto you, I will liken you unto the rich man.

For there was a certain rich man, *who* was clothed in purple, and fine linen, and fared sumptuously every day. (JST; italics added.)

Wealth can save or damn men. In the *Parable of the Unjust Steward,* Jesus taught that unless men use their money wisely and in accordance with true principles, they cannot be saved in the kingdom of God. He now continues the same theme in the *Parable of Lazarus and the Rich Man* and, also, adds a flood of light relative to the state of the souls of men between death and the resurrection.

Riches as such will not send a man to hell, nor will poverty, without accompanying righteousness, assure him of the rest and peace of paradise. Jesus here describes a man of wealth and influence who was callous and indifferent to the known suffering of one of his fellow beings. Implicit in the account is the fact that Lazarus was poor in spirit, patient in suffering, had faith in God, and lived righteously. The rich man reveled in luxury, worldliness, selfishness, and unbelief; Lazarus found comfort in a life that would make him a companion of faithful Abraham.

The same doctrine, relative to riches and poverty, which the money-loving Pharisees were taught in a parable was given by the Lord to the saints in modern times in plain words. [D&C 56:16–20.] (DNTC 1:519.)

16:22 "Abraham's bosom" is the temporary abode of the righteous between death and resurrection. Alma refers to this place as "paradise" and describes some of the conditions there. (See Alma 40:11–14.)

16:23 "Hell," as used in this verse, refers to the temporary abode of wicked disembodied spirits awaiting the resurrection. Several other terms have been applied to this place, including spirit prison and outer darkness.

16:26 This "great gulf" between paradise and the spirit prison existed until the time of the resurrection of Jesus:

There was no intermingling by the spirits in paradise and hell until after Christ bridged the "great gulf" between these two spirit abodes. (Alma 40:11–14.) This he did while his body lay in the tomb of Joseph of Arimathea and his own disembodied spirit continued to minister to men in their spirit prison. (1 Pet. 3:18–21; 4:6; Joseph F. Smith, *Gospel Doctrine,* 5th ed., pp. 472–476.) [D&C 138.] "Until that day" the prisoners remained bound and the gospel was not preached to them. (Moses 7:37–39.) The hope of salvation for the dead was yet future.

But now, since our Lord has proclaimed "liberty to the captives, and the opening of the prison to them that are bound" (Isa. 61:1), the gospel is preached in all parts of the spirit world, repentance is granted to those who seek it, vicarious ordinances are administered in earthly temples, and there is a hope of salvation for the spirits of those men who would have received the gospel with all their hearts in this life had the opportunity come to them. (*Teachings,* p. 107.) At this time, as Joseph Smith explained it, "Hades, sheol, paradise, spirits in prison, are all one: it is a world of spirits." (*Teachings,* p. 310.) (DNTC 1:521–22.)

16:31 In the Joseph Smith Translation, the last clause reads, "though one *should rise* from the dead." (Italics added.)

Two great and eternal truths are here taught: (1) Deity chooses and sends his own agents and witnesses to mortal men to cry repentance and preach the gospel of salvation; unless men heed their message they are damned; and (2) Those who refuse to hear the living oracles sent to them in their day, and to believe the recorded teachings of the ancient prophets, would not be converted by a display of miracles that even included the raising of the dead.

Lazarus rose from the dead at Jesus' command and mingled again among men as a mortal being. Instead of being converted, many of the rebellious Jews sought to put him to death to prevent receptive persons from believing in Jesus and his divine power. (John 11:1–52; 12:10–11.) Our Lord himself rose from the dead in glorious immortality, appeared to many, and sent witnesses into all the world to testify of his resurrection and yet men did not believe. (DNTC 1:522.)

17:1–2 Read text and commentaries for Matthew 18:6–10. Read also Mark 9:42–50.

17:1 "Impossible" could have been translated "unavoidable."

17:3–4 Read text and commentaries for Matthew 18:15–22.

17:5–6 This brief example of faith is included only in the account by Luke. The *Lectures on Faith,* by the Prophet Joseph Smith, contain a great deal of information on this subject. These lectures teach that faith can be increased through several means:

1. Gaining a knowledge of God, that he actually exists and that he is our Heavenly Father.

2. Gaining a correct understanding of the character and attributes of God.

3. Learning the perfections of God and how we can strive for them.

4. Increasing in personal righteousness.

The Prophet Joseph Smith then indicates some of the results of an "increase in faith":

> When faith comes it brings its train of attendants with it—apostles, prophets, evangelists, pastors, teachers, gifts, wisdom, knowledge, miracles, healings, tongues, interpretation of tongues, etc. All these appear when faith appears on the earth, and disappear when it disappears from the earth; for these are the effects of faith, and always have, and always will, attend it. For where faith is, there will the knowledge of God be also, with all things which pertain thereto—revelations, visions, and dreams, as well as every necessary thing, in order that the possessors of faith may be perfected, and obtain salvation. (*Lectures on Faith,* pp. 70–71.)

(See section 1, "Faith.")

17:6 The Joseph Smith Translation replaces "sycamine" and "root" with "sycamore" and "roots."

17:7–10 This parable, included only by Luke, should be read in context of Jesus' reply to the request, "Lord, increase our faith." (JST.)

King Benjamin indicated that the Lord has a claim upon the services of his people, and that if we should serve him all the days of our lives with our souls "yet [we] would be unprofitable servants." (Mosiah 2:21–24.)

17:8 "And gird thyself" has also been translated "then put on your apron" and "make yourself tidy."

17:9 "Trow" means "suppose" or "think." Most Greek

manuscripts do not include words that could be translated "I trow not," thus no equivalent expressions are included in most modern translations.

17:10 "We have done that which was our duty to do" could have been more literally translated "What we have done is what we ought to have done." The Joseph Smith Translation reads, "We have done that which was no more than our duty to do."

17:11–19 This account is contained primarily in Luke.

> We are told that the grateful one was a Samaritan, from which we infer that some or all of the others were Jews. Pained over the lack of gratitude on the part of the nine, Jesus exclaimed: "Were there not ten cleansed? but where are the nine? There are not found that return to give glory to God, save this stranger." And to the cleansed Samaritan, still worshiping at His feet, the Lord said: "Arise, go thy way: thy faith hath made thee whole." Doubtless the nine who came not back were obedient to the strict letter of the Lord's command; for He had told them to go to the priests; but their lack of gratitude and their failure to acknowledge the power of God in their restoration stand in unfavorable contrast with the spirit of the one; and he was a Samaritan. The occurrence must have impressed the apostles as another evidence of acceptability and possible excellence on the part of aliens, to the disparagement of Jewish claims of superiority irrespective of merit. (JTC, p. 471.)

(See section 1, "Leper.")

17:12–13 That the lepers were "afar off" and had to "lift up their voices" (shout) indicates that they were living apart from the other people, as was prescribed by their laws and customs. (See Lev. 13:45–46.)

17:14–16 Their laws required them to show themselves to the priests in such instances. (See Lev. 13:49; 14:2–3.) Perhaps this was also a test of their faith, to see if they would obey the law.

17:20–21 These two important verses have been variously interpreted by New Testament scholars and students. One difficulty is the translation "within" for a Greek term that could have been better translated "among," inasmuch as this "you" is plural in the Greek. Thus, the last clause of verse 20 could have been translated "the kingdom of God is among you" or "the kingdom of God is in your midst." The Joseph Smith Translation reads: "the kingdom of God has already come unto you."

> One of the heresies which prevails in a large part of modern Christendom is the concept that Jesus did not organize a Church or set up a formal

kingdom through which salvation might be offered to men. This poorly translated verse is one of those used to support the erroneous concept that the kingdom of God is wholly spiritual; that it is made up of those who confess Jesus with their lips, regardless of what church affiliation they may have; that the kingdom of God is within every person in the sense that all have the potential of attaining the highest spiritual goals; and that baptism, the laying on of hands, celestial marriage, and other ordinances and laws are not essential to the attainment of salvation.

It is true that men have the inherent capacity to gain salvation in the celestial world; in a sense this power is within them; and so it might be said that the kingdom of God is within a person, if it is understood that such expression means that a person can gain that eternal world by obedience to the laws and ordinances of the gospel. But it is also true that Jesus did organize his Church and did give the keys of such kingdom to legal administrators on earth. (Matt. 16:13–19.)

Even the marginal reading in the King James Version changes the language here involved to read, 'The kingdom of God is in the midst of you,' meaning 'The Church is now organized in the midst of your society.' The Prophet's rendering of Jesus' thought, as such is recorded in the Inspired Version, is of course the best of all. Its essential meaning is: "The Church and kingdom has already been organized; it is here; it has come unto you: now enter the kingdom, obey its laws and be saved." (DNTC 1:540.)

Prophecies foretelling the events incident to the first and second comings of the Messiah were confused in the minds of the Jews. They falsely assumed that at his first coming he would come with an outward display of power which would overthrow and destroy all earthly kingdoms. Accordingly, basing their inquiry on a false premise, and with some apparent sarcasm, they demand an answer to this mocking question: "If thou art the promised Messiah, as you have repeatedly claimed to be, when will thy power be manifest, when will the Roman yoke be broken, when will the kingdom of God actually come?"

Jesus' reply is perfect. He simply goes back to basic principles, corrects their false understanding of the doctrine involved, and announces what the fact is. "You do err. This is my first appearance among men, and I came to work out the atoning sacrifice by which redemption comes. This time the kingdom of God cometh not with observation; there will be no great display of power and destruction. Men will not be able to say, Lo here! or, lo there! for all this is reserved for the Second Coming of the Son of Man. But as for this day and generation, the kingdom of God is my Church and it has already been organized and set up in your midst; it has already come unto you." (DNTC 1:539–40.)

17:22–25 Read text and commentaries for Matthew 24:23–27. Read also Mark 13:21–23.

17:22–24 And he said unto *his* disciples, The days will come, when *they will* desire to see one of the days of the Son of Man, and *they* shall not see it.

And *if* they shall say to you, See here! or, See there! Go not after them, nor follow them.

For as the light of the morning, that shineth out of the one part under heaven, *and lighteneth* to the other part under heaven; so shall also the Son of Man be in his day. (JST; italics added.)

17:25 The statement by Jesus that "first" he must "suffer many things, and be rejected of this generation" clearly indicates that the other events in his statement pertain to his *second* coming.

The Joseph Smith Translation use of "they" rather than the "ye" would also indicate this.

17:26–37 Much of the material in these verses is also contained in Matthew 24 and Mark 13, but sometimes in different sequences. (Read text and commentaries for Matt. 24:15–41. Also read Mark 13:14–23; Luke 21:20–24.)

17:26–30 (Read Matt. 24:36–39; Mark 13:22.) By comparing the events of his second coming to those of the "days of Noah" (v. 26) and the "days of Lot" (v. 28), Jesus is teaching about the destruction of the wicked and also of the dreadful nature of that time for the wicked; it will be for them essentially the same as it was for the wicked in Sodom when "it rained fire and brimstone from heaven" (v. 29).

17:31–33 (Read Matt. 24:15–22; Mark 13:14–20; Luke 21:20–24.) In the Joseph Smith Translation, verse 31 reads, *"the disciple* who shall be on the housetop . . ." (Italics added.)

17:34–37 (Read Matt. 24:40–41.) In verses 34–36, the Joseph Smith Translation does not indicate the sex of any of the "two" who shall be "in one bed," "grinding together," or "in the field." Also, most Greek texts do not indicate whether these persons are male, female, or both. Thus several other translations simply indicate "two people."

17:36–37 And they answered and said unto him, Where, Lord, *shall they be taken.*

And he said unto them, Wheresoever the body is *gathered; or, in other words, whithersoever the saints are gathered,* thither will the eagles be gathered together; *or, thither will the remainder be gathered together.*

This he spake, signifying the gathering of his saints; and of angels descending and gathering the remainder unto them; the one from the bed, the other from the grinding, and the other from the field, whithersoever he listeth.

For verily there shall be new heavens, and a new earth, wherein dwelleth righteousness.

And there shall be no unclean thing; for the earth becoming old, even as a garment, having waxed in corruption, wherefore it vanisheth away, and the footstool remaineth sanctified, cleansed from all sin. (JST; italics added.)

17:37 Read text and commentaries for Matthew 24:28.

18:1–8 This parable teaching the value of persistence in prayer is found only in Luke and has been called by two titles: the Parable of the Unjust Judge, and the Parable of the Importunate Widow. Somewhat similar teachings are found in D&C 101:81–92.

> The judge was of wicked character; he denied justice to the widow, who could obtain redress from none other. He was moved to action by the desire to escape the woman's importunity. Let us beware of the error of comparing his selfish action with the ways of God. Jesus did not indicate that as the wicked judge finally yielded to supplication so would God do; but He pointed out that if even such a being as this judge, who "feared not God, neither regarded man," would at last hear and grant the widow's plea, no one should doubt that God, the Just and Merciful, will hear and answer. The judge's obduracy, though wholly wicked on his part, may have been ultimately advantageous to the widow. Had she easily obtained redress she might have become again unwary, and perchance a worse adversary than the first might have oppressed her. The Lord's purpose in giving the parable is specifically stated; it was "to this end, that men ought always to pray, and not to faint." (JTC, p. 436.)

(See section 1, "Prayer.")

18:1 "Not to faint" could have been translated "not to give up."

18:2 "Neither regarded men" could have been translated "had no respect for man."

18:3 "Avenge me of mine adversary" has also been translated "Help me against my opponent," "Grant me justice against my adversary," and "Vindicate me against my adversary."

18:8 The Greek text indicates that "the'" should be inserted before "faith." The last sentence would then read, "Nevertheless when the Son of man cometh, shall he find the faith on the earth?" The question is whether or not *the* faith (the true Church) would be on the earth.

In the Joseph Smith Translation, the first sentence of this verse reads, "I tell you that he will *come, and when he does come,* he will avenge *his saints* speedily." (Italics added.)

18:9–14 We are expressly told that this parable was given for the benefit of certain ones who trusted in their self-righteousness as an assurance of justification before God. It was not addressed to the Pharisees nor to the publicans specifically. The two characters are types of widely separated classes. There may have been much of the Pharisaic spirit of self-complacency among the disciples and some of it even among the Twelve. . . . The parable is applicable to all men; its moral was summed up in a repetition of our Lord's words spoken in the house of the chief Pharisee: "For every one that exalteth himself shall be abased; and he that humbleth himself shall be exalted." (JTC, pp. 472–73.)

18:9 "Despised others" could have been more literally translated "considered the others as nothing."

18:10 See BD, "Pharisees," "Publicans."

18:11 That the Pharisee prayed "with himself" indicates that he was praying *for* himself and that his prayer was not with sufficient faith to achieve communion with God.

18:12 "Possess" could be more literally translated "acquire." The idea is that tithing should be paid on the increase each year, not on the total possessions at the end of each year. A more literal translation is "I give the tenth of all things I acquire."

18:15–17 Read text and commentaries for Matthew 19:13–15. Read also Mark 10:13–16.

18:16 "Suffer little children to come unto me, and forbid them not" could have been more literally translated "Let the young children come to me, and do not try to stop them." (See section 1, "Children: Inherit heaven.")

18:18–27 Read text and commentaries for Matthew 19:16–26. Read also Mark 10:17–27.

18:20 (See commentary for Matt. 5:21.) "Kill" could have been translated "murder."

18:23 "He was sorrowful" could have been more literally translated "he became deeply grieved."

18:25 (See text and commentary for Matt. 19:24.) "Through a needle's eye" has been interpreted by some scholars to refer to an entrance in the wall near the major gate of a walled city. However, the Greek text could be literally translated "through the aperture of a sewing needle."

18:26–27 And they *who* heard, said *unto him*. Who then can be saved?

And he said *unto them, It is* impossible *for them who trust in riches, to enter into the kingdom of God; but he who forsaketh the things which are of this world, it is* possible with God, *that he should enter in.* (JST; italics added.)

18:28–30 Read commentaries for Matthew 19:27–30. Read also Matthew 20:1–16; Mark 10:28–31. See 1 Nephi 12:7–10.

18:31–34 Read text and commentaries for Matthew 20:17–19. Read also Mark 10:32–34.

18:31 Jesus here reaffirms all of the Messianic prophecies contained in our present Old Testament, together with other statements "written by the prophets" that might not be included therein.

18:32 The Roman soldiers who carried out the scourging and crucifixion of Jesus would have been considered "Gentiles" by the Jews. Matthew contains a detailed account of how literally the words of Jesus were fulfilled. (See Matt. 27:26–31.)

"Spitefully entreated" could have been translated "treated insolently."

18:34 The Joseph Smith Translation replaces "knew" with "remembered."

Obviously the apostles knew what the words spoken meant, but with their as yet limited knowledge of the full purposes of Deity, they could not bring themselves to believe their accepted King would be crucified by sinful men. This inability to catch the vision of the atoning sacrifice until after the resurrection of Jesus stands out in pointed contrast to the fervent testimonies later born, a contrast which adds strength to the witness they were then to carry to the world. (DNTC 1:563.)

18:35–43 Read commentaries for Matthew 20:29–34. Read also Mark 10:46–52; Luke 19:1.

18:39 The first part of this verse could have been more literally translated "And those going in advance began to tell him sternly to keep quiet."

18:43 The Joseph Smith Translation replaces "people" with "disciples."

19:1 Read text and commentaries for Matthew 20:29–34; Mark 10:46–52; Luke 18:35–43.

19:2–10 The story of Zacchaeus is told only by Luke. Zacchaeus is obviously a Jew as his name is a variant of Zacharias with a Greek designation at the end. That he was particularly hated by other Jews is evident from his position as "chief among the publicans, and he was rich." The publicans were all employed by the hated Romans to collect despised taxes. The desire of Jesus to bring such persons to repentance and apply the mercy of forgiveness must have been a vivid lesson for all who saw and heard. (See BD, "Zacchaeus.")

19:3 "Press" could have been translated "crowd."

19:5 Jesus invites himself to meet with and teach Zacchaeus; he does not wait for an invitation. Similar procedures are followed by his representatives (missionaries) today.

19:7 The Joseph Smith Translation indicates that it was "the disciples" who murmured.

19:8 The Joseph Smith Translation replaces "false accusation" with "unjust means." Restitution is an integral part of repentance, and "fourfold" restitution for means unjustly taken would not have been unusual: "If a man shall steal an ox, or a sheep, and kill it, or sell it; he shall restore five oxen for an ox, and four sheep for a sheep." (Ex. 22:1.)

19:11–28 Jesus was enroute to Jerusalem for the last time. In about ten days he would die upon the cross, and to the Jews generally it would appear that he had failed to set up the promised Messianic kingdom. To correct the false concept that "the kingdom of God"—meaning the political kingdom, the kingdom which should rule all nations with King Messiah at its head, the millennial kingdom—"should immediately appear," Jesus gave the *Parable of the Pounds.* (DNTC 1:571.)

Christ is the nobleman; the far off country is heaven; the kingdom there to be given him is "all power . . . in heaven and in earth" (Matt. 28:18); and his promised return is the glorious Second Coming, when the literal and visible kingdom shall be set up on earth. The ten servants are the members of the Church to whom he has given physical, mental, and spiritual capacities (pounds) to be used in his service. Those designated as "citizens" are the other people in the world, those who are subject to him because he is the God of the whole earth, but who have not accepted his gospel and come into his fold as servants. The servants are commanded to labor in the vineyard on their Lord's errand until he returns. (DNTC 1:572.)

19:11 In the Joseph Smith Translation, the final clause reads, "because *the Jews* taught that the kingdom of God should immediately appear." (Italics added.)

19:13 "Occupy" means "Do business." "Occupy till I come" has also been translated "Trade with these till I come," "See what you can earn with this while I am gone," and "Put this money to work . . . until I come back."

19:14 "A message after him" could have been translated "a body of ambassadors after him." The Joseph Smith Translation reads, "a *messenger* after him." (Italics added.)

In his commentary on this verse, Farrar points out that it was not unusual in those days for a person to go somewhere else to receive a kingdom. Indeed, some of the current rulers in the land had gone to Rome in order to obtain their authority over the people:

"A nobleman going into a far country to receive a kingdom" would be utterly unintelligible, had we not fortunately known that this was done both by Archelaus and by Antipas. And in the case of Archelaus the Jews had actually sent to Augustus a deputation of fifty, to recount his cruelties and oppose his claims, which, though it failed at the time, was subsequently successful. Philipus defended the property of Archelaus, during his absence, from the encroachments of the Proconsul Sabinus. The magnificent palace which Archelaus had built at Jericho would naturally recall these circumstances to the mind of Jesus, and the parable is another striking example of the manner in which he utilized the most ordinary circumstances around him, and made them the bases of His highest teachings. It is also another unsuspected indication of the authenticity and truthfulness of the Gospels. (*Farrar,* p. 493, note, cited in JTC, p. 522.)

Elder Bruce R. McConkie has commented on the statement "We will not have this man to reign over us":

How literally this prophetic part of the parable was fulfilled! But a few days hence and the Jews would be proclaiming, "We have no king but Caesar," and "Write not, The King of the Jews; but that he said, I am King of the Jews." (John 19:15, 21.) Then after the Nobleman's ascension to heaven these same "citizens" would continue to exhibit violent hostility against his infant Church. (DNTC 1:572.)

19:17 The Joseph Smith Translation begins this verse, "And he said unto him, Well *done,* thou good servant . . ." (Italics added.)

19:23 "I might have required mine own with usury" could have been literally translated "I would have collected it with interest."

The Joseph Smith Translation replaces "required" with "received."

19:26 The Joseph Smith Translation reads, "For I say unto you, That unto every one *who occupieth,* shall be given; and from him *who occupieth* not, even that he hath *received* shall be taken away from him." (JST; italics added.)

19:29–40 Read text and commentaries for Matthew 21:1–11. Read also Mark 11:1–11; John 12:12–19.

19:36 This verse could have been more literally translated "As he moved along they kept spreading their outer garments on the road."

Only kings and conquerors received such an extraordinary token of respect as this. (2 Kings 9:13.) In every part of this triumphal entry to Jerusalem, Jesus seems not only to permit but to court the adulation and homage normally reserved for kings and great rulers. (DNTC 1:578.)

19:38 "Blessed be the King that cometh in the name of

the Lord" could have been more literally translated "Blessed is the One coming as the King in Jehovah's name."

19:39–40 Those acclaiming Jesus as Lord and God were disciples, believers, persons who had heard and understood the gospel message. In accepting and encouraging their reverential salutations, Jesus fulfilled the scripture and left a witness of his own divinity that would live in the hearts of true disciples ever after. (DNTC 1:579.)

19:41–44 Many of these details are recorded only by Luke.

19:41 It was the inhabitants of the city, not the beautiful buildings or the commanding view that the Savior saw through tear bedimmed eyes when he cried: "if thou hadst known . . . the things which belong unto thy peace! but now they are hid from thine eyes." (Luke 19:42.) He saw the people divided into conflicting and contending sects, each professing more holiness and righteousness than the other and all closing their eyes to the truth. There were the conservative Hebraic Jews, holding rigidly to the Mosaic law; there were the more liberal minded, Hellenistic Jews whose views had been modified by pagan philosophy; there were a few Essenes with their asceticism and rejection of the Aaronic Priesthood; there were the Sadducees with their lifeless and formal observance of the Sabbath, and their denial of the resurrection; and, finally, the Pharisees with their "ostentatious almsgiving," "broadened phylacteries," "greedy avarice," "haughty assertion of preeminence," "ill-concealed hypocrisy" which was often hidden under a venerable assumption of superior holiness. . . .

Such were the people whom the Son of Man saw when he stood twenty centuries ago on the Mount of Olives and "beheld the city and wept over it." (David O. McKay, CR, Oct. 1944, p. 78.)

(See section 1, "Jerusalem.")

19:42 Other translations of this verse are "Saying, If you only knew today what is needed for peace! But now you cannot see it!" and "Saying, Would that even today you knew the things that make for peace! But now they are hid from your eyes."

19:43 In the course of the siege, a wall was constructed about the entire city, thus fulfilling the Lord's prediction (Luke 19:43), "thine enemies shall cast a trench about thee," in which, by the admittedly better translation, "bank," or "palisade" should appear instead of "trench." In September A.D. 70 the city fell into the hands of the Romans; and its destruction was afterward made so thorough that its site was plowed up. Jerusalem was "trodden down of the Gentiles," and ever since has been under Gentile dominion, and so shall continue to be "until the times of the Gentiles be fulfilled." (Luke 21:24.) (JTC, p. 588.)

19:45–48 Read commentaries for Matthew 21:12–17. Read also Mark 11:15–19.

20:1–8 (Read text and commentary for Matt. 21:23–27. Read also Mark 11:27–33.) As on all other appropriate occasions, Jesus "preached the gospel" unto the people with evident power and authority, thus provoking the "chief priests and the scribes" to challenge his right to preach and to cast out the money changers in "their" temple.

20:9–19 Read text and commentaries for Matthew 21:33–46. Read also Mark 12:1–12.

20:10 "At the season" could have been more literally translated "in due season" or "at the appointed time."

The Joseph Smith Translation begins the verse, "And at the season of the harvest, he sent his servant to the husbandmen . . ."

20:13 "Respect" could have been translated "reverence."

20:16 "God forbid" means "May this thing never happen."

20:20–26 Read commentaries for Matthew 22:15–22. Read also Mark 12:13–17.

20:20 Another translation of this verse is "So they watched for the right time. They bribed some men to pretend they were sincere, and sent them to trap Jesus with questions, so they could hand him over to the authority and power of the Governor." (TEV.)

20:21 The Joseph Smith Translation replaces "acceptest" with "regardest."

20:22 "Tribute" could have been more literally translated "tax."

20:25 This statement could have been more literally translated "By all means, then, pay back Caesar's things to Caesar, but God's things to God."

20:26 Other translations of this verse are "They could not catch him in a thing there before the people, so they kept quiet, amazed at his answer" and "They were unable to trap him in what he had said there in public. And astonished by his answer, they became silent."

20:27–40 Read commentaries for Matthew 22:23–33. Read also Mark 12:18–27.

20:35 In the Joseph Smith Translation, "and the resurrection of the dead" reads "*through* resurrection from the dead." (Italics added.) This change indicates that the resurrection is not earned; it is provided to all mankind through the atonement of Jesus Christ.

20:38 "For all live unto him" means "for they are all living to him."

20:41–44 Read commentaries for Matthew 22:41–46. Read also Mark 12:34–37.

20:45–47 Read commentaries on Matthew 23:1–22. Read also Mark 12:38–40; Luke 11:37–54.

20:47 "The same shall receive greater damnation" could have been translated "these will receive a heavier judgment."

21:1–4 Read text and commentaries for Mark 12:41–44.

21:4 "Penury" means "poverty," "want," or "lack."

21:5–6 Read commentaries for Matthew 24:1–2. Read also Mark 13:1–2.

21:7–8 Read commentaries for Matthew 24:3–5. Read also Mark 13:3–6.

And *the disciples* asked him, saying, Master, when shall these things be? And what sign *wilt thou show,* when these things shall come to pass?

And he said, *The time draweth near, and therefore* take heed that ye be not deceived; for many shall come in my name, saying, I am Christ; go ye not therefore after them. (JST; italics added.)

21:9–11 Read commentaries for Matthew 24:6–8. Read also Mark 13:7–8.

21:9 "The end is not by and by" could have been translated "the end does not occur immediately."

The Joseph Smith Translation reads, "but this is not the end."

21:11 In the Joseph Smith Translation, the beginning of this verse reads, "But before all these things *shall come . . .*" (Italics added.)

21:12–19 Read commentary for Matthew 24:9. Read also Mark 13:9, 11–13.

21:12 The Joseph Smith Translation begins this verse, "But before all these *things shall come . . .*" (Italics added.)

21:14 "Meditate" is derived from a Greek word meaning "to rehearse beforehand."

The Joseph Smith Translation replaces "it" with "this."

21:14–15 These verses could have been more literally translated "Therefore settle it in your hearts not to rehearse beforehand how to make your defense, for I will give you a mouth and wisdom, which all your opposers together will not be able to resist or dispute."

21:17 The Joseph Smith Translation reads, "And ye shall be hated of all *the world* for my name's sake." (Italics added.)

21:18 See Alma 40:23 for an indication of the literalness of this promise at the time of the resurrection.

21:19 This verse could have been more literally translated "By endurance on your part you will acquire your souls." (See D&C 101:38.)

21:20–24 Read commentaries for Matthew 24:15–22. Read also Mark 13:14–20; Luke 17:31–37.

21:21 In the Joseph Smith Translation, the last clause of this verse reads, "and let not them *who* are in the countries, return to enter *into* the *city*." (Italics added.)

21:22 "For these be the days of vengeance" could have been translated "Because these are days for meting out justice."

21:24–25 *Now these things he spake unto them, concerning the destruction of Jerusalem. And then his disciples asked him, saying, Master, tell us concerning thy coming?*

And he answered them, and said, In the generation in which the times of the Gentiles *shall* be fulfilled, there shall be signs in the sun, and in the moon, and in the stars; and upon the earth distress of nations with perplexity, *like* the sea and the waves roaring. *The earth also shall be troubled, and the waters of the great deep;* . . . (JST; italics added.)

This present era, which is named, *the times of the Gentiles,* shall come to an end before our Lord returns in power and glory. Then, with his return, *the times of the Jews* shall begin; that is the era will commence in which the Jews shall accept the gospel and be blessed spiritually in an abundant way.

Within the meaning of these terms, all men are either Jews or Gentiles. The Jews are that portion of the house of Israel who inhabited Jerusalem and who were the remnant of the kingdom of Judah. (2 Ne. 30:4; 33:8.) All others were Gentiles, including the portion of Israel scattered among the Gentiles proper. (DNTC 1:656.)

21:25–28 Read commentaries for Matthew 24:29–31. Read also Mark 13:24–27; Luke 21:20–24.

21:28 In the Joseph Smith Translation, the end of this verse reads, "for *the day of* your redemption draweth nigh." (Italics added.)

21:29–33 Read commentaries for Matthew 24:32–41. Read also Mark 13:28–32.

21:32 Verily I say unto you, this generation, *the generation when the times of the Gentiles be fulfilled,* shall not pass away till all be fulfilled. (JST; italics added.)

21:34–38 Read text and commentaries for Matthew 24:42–51. Read also Mark 13:33–37; Luke 12:35–48.

21:34 This verse could have been more literally translated "But pay attention to yourselves that your hearts never become weighed down with overeating and heavy drinking and anxieties of life, and suddenly that day be instantly upon you." The word *surfeiting* has to do with intemperate eating and drinking, and the context indicates how unwise it is to place emphasis on carnal things rather than on spiritual things.

The Joseph Smith Translation directs these instructions particularly to the disciples: "*Let my disciples therefore* take heed to themselves, lest at any time *their* hearts be overcharged with surfeiting, and drunkenness, and cares of this life, and that day come upon *them* unawares." (Italics added.)

21:36 *And what I say unto one, I say unto all,* Watch ye therefore, and pray always, *and keep my commandments,* that ye may be *counted* worthy to escape all these things *which* shall come to pass, and to stand before the Son of Man *when he shall come clothed in the glory of his Father.* (JST; italics added.)

22:1–6 Read text and commentary for Matthew 26:14–16. Read also Mark 14:1–2, 10–11.

22:1–2 Read commentaries for Matthew 26:1–5. Read also Mark 14:1–2. In verse 2, the Joseph Smith Translation replaces "and" with "but" at the beginning of the last clause.

22:3 Did Satan literally occupy the body of Judas? Elder Bruce R. McConkie responds:

Perhaps, for Satan is a spirit man, a being who was born the offspring of God in the pre-existence, and who was cast out of heaven for rebellion. He and his spirit followers have power in some cases to enter the bodies of men; they are, also, sometimes cast out of these illegally entered habitations by the power of the priesthood. See Mark 1:21–28.

But if the body of Judas was not possessed literally by Satan, still this traitorous member of the Twelve was totally submissive to the will of the devil. (DNTC 1:701–2.)

22:3–6 Read text and commentary for Matthew 26:14–16. Read also Mark 14:10–11.

22:4 See BD, "Captain of the Temple."

22:6 This verse could have been more literally translated "So he consented, and he began to seek a good opportunity to betray him to them without a crowd around."

22:7–14 Read commentaries for Matthew 26:17–20. Read also Mark 14:12–17.

22:15–20 Read text and commentaries for Matthew 26:26–29. Read also Mark 14:22–25.

22:15 "With desire I have desired" could have been translated "I have greatly desired."

22:16 For I say unto you, I will not any more eat thereof, until it be fulfilled *which is written in the prophets concerning me. Then I will partake with you,* in the kingdom of God. (JST; italics added.)

22:19–20 This account of the sacrament of the Lord's supper makes it clear that the ordinance is "in remembrance of Jesus." (See section 1, "Sacrament.")

22:21–30 Read text and commentaries for Matthew 26:21–25. Read also Mark 14:18–21; John 13:18–30.

22:22 "Determined" could have been translated "decreed," "appointed," or "agreed upon."

22:24–30 Considering the prior teachings of Jesus and his long association with the Twelve, it seems a little strange that these favored few, who so measurably knew their Lord's will, would be contending about precedence at this late date. On an earlier occasion Jesus had resolved this issue for them; here he but paraphrases his prior teaching. Compare Matt. 20:20–28.

It may be, as Elder James E. Talmage suggests, that the muttering dispute among them was over "the order in which they should take their places at the table, over which triviality scribes and Pharisees as well as the Gentiles often quarreled." [JTC, p. 595.] In any event, out of it came again the pointed teaching that Christ and his ministers come to serve and not to receive adulation and honor from men. (DNTC 1:706.)

22:24 To do well those things which God ordained to be the common lot of all mankind is the truest greatness. To be a successful father or a successful mother is greater than to be a successful general or a successful statesman. One is universal and eternal greatness, the other is ephemeral. It is true that such secondary greatness may be added to that which we style commonplace; but when such secondary greatness is not added to that which is fundamental, it is merely an empty honor, and fades away from the common and universal good in life, even though it may find a place in the desultory pages of history. (GD, p. 285.)

22:26–27 But *it ought to be so with you;* but he *who* is greatest among you, let him be as the younger; and he *who* is chief, as he *who* doth serve.

For whether is he greater, *who* sitteth at meat, or he *who serveth? I am not as he who* sitteth at meat, but I am among you as he who serveth. (JST; italics added.)

22:28 This verse could have been more literally translated "However, you are the ones that have remained with me in my trials."

22:30 The Joseph Smith Translation inserts "twelve" before "thrones."

22:31–38 Read text and commentaries for Matthew 26:31–35. Read also Mark 14:27–31; John 13:36–38.

22:31 In the Joseph Smith Translation, the last clause reads, "that he may sift *the children of the kingdom* as wheat." (Italics added.)

> Satan wanted to tempt Peter beyond his power to resist; he wanted Peter, the chief apostle, to fall. Satan wanted to harvest the earth, to sift the saints as wheat, so that both wheat and tares would be garnered into his bin. This he would find easier to do were Peter not there to guide them. Hence, Jesus' special prayer that Peter's faith fail not; and hence the continuing prayers of the saints, always and ever, for the apostles and prophets who guide the Church. (DNTC 1:770.)

22:32 Many persons would assume that Peter was already converted because of his previous testimonies concerning the divinity of Jesus Christ. However, true conversion comes through the power of the Spirit:

> Conversion is more—far more—than merely changing one's belief from that which is false to that which is true; it is more than the acceptance of the verity of gospel truths, than the acquirement of a testimony. To convert is to change from one status to another, and gospel conversion consists in the transformation of man from his fallen and carnal state to a state of saintliness. . . .
>
> Peter is the classic example of how the power of conversion works on receptive souls. During our Lord's mortal ministry, Peter had a testimony, born of the Spirit, of the divinity of Christ and of the great plan of salvation which was in Christ. "Thou art the Christ, the Son of the living God," he said, as the Holy Ghost gave him utterance. (Matt. 16:13–19.) When others fell away, Peter stood forth with the apostolic assurance, "We believe and are sure that thou art that Christ, the Son of the living God." (John 6:69.) Peter knew, and his knowledge came by revelation.
>
> But Peter was not converted, because he had not become a new creature of the Holy Ghost. Rather, long after Peter had gained a testimony, and on the very night Jesus was arrested, he said to Peter: "When thou art converted, strengthen thy brethren." (Luke 22:32.) Immediately thereafter, and regardless of his testimony, Peter denied that he knew Christ. (Luke 22:54–62.) After the crucifixion, Peter went fishing, only to be called back to the ministry by the risen Lord. (John 21:1–17.) Finally on the day of Pentecost the promised spiritual endowment was received; Peter and all the faithful disciples became new creatures of the Holy Ghost; they were truly converted; and their subsequent achievements manifest the fixity of their conversions. (Acts 3; 4.) (MD, pp. 150–51.)

22:34 In this verse Jesus indicates that Peter will deny (disown) *knowing* Jesus. It is misleading to state that Peter denied Christ three times. Peter was not asked that night whether or not he believed that Jesus was the Christ; rather, the questions put to Peter had to do with his association with Jesus of Nazareth. Thus, it would be more accurate to say, "Peter denied knowing Jesus" or "Peter disowned Jesus." (See section 1, "Peter: Denial.")

22:36 In the Joseph Smith Translation, this verse begins, "Then said he unto them, I say unto you *again,* He *who* hath a purse, let him take it . . ." (Italics added.)

> Jesus here revokes the command previously given to go forth without purse or scrip. [See Matt. 10:9–10.] Conditions have changed; what was once required is no longer expedient—all of which shows the need of continuing revelation so the Lord's people will always know how to act in the circumstances confronting them at any given moment.
>
> When faced with persecution, do the Lord's ministers turn the other cheek or raise the sword in their own defense? Do they go forth supplying their own needs or do they rely for their daily wants upon the generosity of those among whom they minister? Who but God can answer such questions, for the answers depend on a full knowledge both of present conditions and on the future. Jesus counseled one course at one time and the opposite at another. There is, thus, no sure guide for the Lord's people except present day revelation. (DNTC 1:771.)

(See section 1, "Purse and scrip.")

22:37 "For the things concerning me have an end" could have been more literally translated "for that which concerns me is having an accomplishment."

That which "is written" is Isaiah 53:12, which indicates that the Messiah would be "numbered with the transgressors."

22:39 Read commentary for Matthew 26:30. Read also Mark 14:26; John 14:27–31.

"Wont" could have been translated "accustomed."

22:40–46 Read text and commentaries for Matthew 26:36–46; Mark 14:32–42. Read also John 18:1–2. See 2 Nephi 9:21–22; Mosiah 3:5–12; D&C 19:1–24.

> Jesus had to take away sin by the sacrifice of Himself. . . . And as He in His own person bore the sins of all, and atoned for them by the sacrifice of Himself, so there came upon Him the weight and agony of ages and generations, the indescribable agony consequent upon this great sacrificial atonement wherein He bore the sins of the world, and suffered in His own person the consequences of an eternal law of God broken by men. Hence His profound grief, His indescribable anguish, His overpowering torture, all experienced in the submission to the eternal fiat of Jehovah and the requirements of an inexorable law.
>
> The suffering of the Son of God was not simply the suffering of personal death; for in assuming the position that He did in making an atonement

for the sins of the world He bore the weight, the responsibility, and the burden of the sins of all men, which, to us, is incomprehensible. . . .

Groaning beneath this concentrated load, this intense, incomprehensible pressure, this terrible exaction of Divine Justice, from which feeble humanity shrank, and through the agony thus experienced sweating great drops of blood, He was led to exclaim, "Father, if it be possible, let this cup pass from me." He had wrestled with the superincumbent load in the wilderness, He had struggled against the powers of darkness that had been let loose upon him there; placed below all things, His mind surcharged with agony and pain, lonely and apparently helpless and forsaken, in his agony the blood oozed from His pores. (John Taylor, *The Mediation and Atonement,* pp. 149–50.)

(See section 1, "Gethsemane"; TG, "Jesus Christ," "Jesus Christ, Atonement through," "Jesus Christ, Lamb of God," "Jesus Christ, Mission of," "Jesus Christ, Redeemer," "Jesus Christ, Savior"; BD, "Atonement," "Christ," "Redemption.")

22:44 In the Joseph Smith Translation, the last clause reads, "and he sweat as it were great drops of blood falling down to the ground."

22:45 In the Joseph Smith Translation, this verse ends, "he found them sleeping; for they *were filled* with sorrow." (Italics added.)

"Sleeping for sorrow" could have been translated "slumbering for grief." (See commentary for Matt. 26:45–46.)

22:47–53 Read commentaries for Matthew 26:47–56. Read also Mark 14:43–52; John 18:3–11.

22:48 A more traitorous token could not have been chosen. Among the prophets of old, among the saints of that day, and even among the Jews, a kiss was a symbol of that love and fellowship which existed where pure religion was or should have been found. When the Lord sent Aaron to meet Moses, he found him "in the mount of God, and kissed him." (Ex. 4:27.) When Simon the Pharisee invited Jesus to a banquet but withheld the courtesy and respect due his guest, our Lord condemned him by saying, "Thou gavest me no kiss." (Luke 7:45.) Paul's counsel to the early brethren was, "Salute one another with an holy kiss." (Rom. 16:16.) Judas, thus, could have chosen no baser means of identifying Jesus than to plant on his face a traitor's kiss. Such act not only singled out his intended victim, but by the means chosen, desecrated every principle of true fellowship and brotherhood. (DNTC 1:781–82.)

(See section 1, "Kiss, sign of betrayal.")

22:54–65 Read text and commentaries for Matthew 26:57–75. Read also Mark 14:53–72; John 18:2, 13–27.

22:54–62 Read text and commentaries for Matthew 26:69–75. Read also Mark 14:66–72; John 18:15–18, 25–27.

22:55 "Hall" could have been translated "courtyard."

22:66–71 Read text and commentaries for Matthew 27:1–2. Read also Mark 15:1; Luke 23:1; John 18:28.

22:66 The council referred to is the Sanhedrin. (See BD, "Sanhedrin.")

22:67 As the Lord has indicated in modern revelation, whether he speaks to the people by his own voice, or by the voice of his servants, it is the same; the people still must be converted by the Spirit or they will not believe. (See D&C 1:38; 18:33–36.)

22:69 Another possible translation is "However, from now on the Son of man will be sitting at the powerful right hand of God."

22:70 When read in the context of the other gospel accounts, it is plain that Jesus is here affirming his divine Sonship. (See Matt. 26:64; Mark 14:62.)

22:71 This incident contains many ironies, not the least of which is that Jehovah was found guilty of blasphemy because he declared he was Jehovah!

23:1 Read commentaries for Matthew 27:1–2. Read also Mark 15:1; Luke 22:66–71; John 18:28.

23:2–5 Read text and commentaries for Matthew 27:11–14. Read also Mark 15:2–5; John 18:28–39.

23:2 "Perverting" could have been translated "subverting."

The members of the Sanhedrin who had previously accused Jesus of blasphemy (the most serious sin under their law) realized that Pilate would not consider blasphemy to be a crime, so they unhesitatingly accused Jesus of the most serious crime under Roman law—treason. Both of these charges allow the death penalty if the person is found guilty.

23:3 According to the Joseph Smith Translation, the answer of Jesus was, *"Yea,* thou sayest it." (Italics added.)

23:6–12 This detailed account of Jesus being taken before Herod is contained only in Luke.

Herod Antipas, the degenerate son of his infamous sire, Herod the Great, was at this time tetrarch of Galilee and Perea, and by popular usage, though without imperial sanction, was flatteringly called king. He it was who, in fulfillment of an unholy vow inspired by a woman's voluptuous blandishments, had ordered the murder of John the Baptist. He ruled as a Roman vassal, and professed to be orthodox in the observance of Judaism. He had come up to Jerusalem, in state, to keep the feast of the Passover. . . .

Whatever fear Herod had once felt regarding Jesus, whom he had superstitiously thought to be the reincarnation of his murdered victim, John the Baptist, was replaced by amused interest when he saw the far-famed Prophet of Galilee in bonds before him, attended by a Roman guard, and accompanied by ecclesiastical officials. Herod began to question the Prisoner; but Jesus remained silent. The chief priests and scribes vehemently voiced their accusations; but not a word was uttered by the Lord. Herod is the only character in history to whom Jesus is known to have applied a personal epithet of contempt. "Go ye and tell that fox" He once said to certain Pharisees who had come to Him with the story that Herod intended to kill Him. As far as we know, Herod is further distinguished as the only being who saw Christ face to face and spoke to Him, yet never heard His voice. For penitent sinners, weeping women, prattling children, for the scribes, the Pharisees, the Sadducees, the rabbis, for the perjured high priest and his obsequious and insolent underling, and for Pilate the pagan, Christ had words—of comfort or instruction, of warning or rebuke, of protest or denunciation—yet for Herod the fox He had but disdainful and kingly silence. Thoroughly piqued, Herod turned from insulting questions to acts of malignant derision. He and his men-at-arms made sport of the suffering Christ, "set him at nought and mocked him"; then in travesty they "arrayed him in a gorgeous robe and sent him again to Pilate." Herod had found nothing in Jesus to warrant condemnation. (JTC, pp. 635–36.)

(See section 1, "Herod.")

23:11 "Set him at nought, and mocked him" could have been translated "discredited him, and made fun of him."

23:13–25 Read text and commentaries for Matthew 27:15–30. Read also Mark 15:6–19; John 18:39–40; 19:1–16.

23:14 "As one that perverteth the people" could have been more literally translated "as one inciting the people to riot."

23:15 "Worthy of death" could have been translated "deserving of death." (See commentary for Matt. 26:66.)

23:16–25 Read Matthew 27:15–23; Mark 15:6–15; John 18:39–40.

23:22 "I have found no cause of death in him" could have been translated "I found nothing deserving of death in him." (See commentaries for Luke 23:15; Matt. 26:66.)

23:23 The first sentence could have been translated "At this they began to be urgent, with loud voices, demanding that he be impaled."

23:26 (Read text and commentaries for Matt. 27:27–32. Read also Mark 15:15–21; John 19:1–16.) Concerning Simon, the "Cyrenian," Elder Bruce R. McConkie has written:

From Mark's reference (Mark 15:21), and the possible reference of Paul (Rom. 16:13), to others of Simon's family, it is assumed that he was then or later became a Christian. The indication is he was born in Cyrene, North Africa, as part of the Jewish colony there. On this memorable day, apparently he had been working in the fields and was returning to the city. (DNTC 1:814.)

23:27–31 Although motherhood was the glory of every Jewish woman's life, yet in the terrible scenes which many of those there weeping would live to witness, barrenness would be accounted a blessing; for the childless would have fewer to weep over, and at least would be spared the horror of seeing their offspring die of starvation or by violence; for so dreadful would be that day that people would fain welcome the falling of the mountains upon them to end their sufferings. If Israel's oppressors could do what was then in process of doing to the "Green Tree," who bore the leafage of freedom and truth and offered the priceless fruit of life eternal, what would the powers of evil not do to the withered branches and dried trunk of apostate Judaism? (JTC, p. 654.)

23:27 "Which also bewailed and lamented him" could have been translated "who kept beating themselves in grief and bewailing him."

23:29 "Paps" means "breasts."

23:30 These words of Christ met with a painfully literal illustration when hundreds of the unhappy Jews at the siege of Jerusalem hid themselves in the darkest and vilest subterranean recesses, and when, besides those who were hunted out, no less than two thousand were killed by being buried under the ruins of their hiding places. (Farrar, p. 645; quoted in JTC, p. 667.)

23:31 *And if* these things *are done* in *the* green tree, what shall be done in the dry *tree?*

This he spake, signifying the scattering of Israel, and the desolation of the heathen, or in other words, the Gentiles. (JST; italics added.)

23:32–33 Read Matthew 27:38; Mark 15:27–28; John 19:18.

23:32–33, 39 A *malefactor* is a criminal, or wrongdoer, or an evildoer. (See section 1, "Malefactors.")

23:33 Read commentary for Matthew 27:33. Read also Mark 15:22; John 19:17. See BD, "Calvary."

23:34 Read text and commentaries for Matthew 27:35. Read also Mark 15:24; John 19:23–24.

Then said Jesus, Father, forgive them; for they know not what they do, (*Meaning the soldiers who crucified him.*) (JST; italics added.)

(See section 1, "Forgive: Them [the soldiers]," "Forgiveness.")

This first "word" from the cross [Luke 23:34] is equally as important for what it does not say as for what it does. It is not an utterance whereby anyone's sins are forgiven, but it is a petition asking for forgiveness in a particular and limited sense of the word. Jesus was the Son of God; as such he had power to forgive sins, a power which he had freely exercised in proper cases. See Matt. 9:2–8.

But no such power is exercised here. He does not say, "Thy sins be forgiven thee," as had been his wont on other occasion. Nor does he ask the Father to forgive the sins of those involved, in the sense of cleansing them from sin so as to qualify them for church membership or celestial inheritance. The law whereby such forgiveness is gained requires repentance and baptism. But he says, rather, "Father lay not this sin to their charge, for they are acting under orders, and those upon whom the full and real guilt rests are their rulers and the Jewish conspirators who caused me to be condemned. It is Caiaphas and Pilate who know I am innocent; these soldiers are just carrying out their orders."

Jesus did not, it should be noted, pray for Judas who betrayed him; for Caiaphas and the chief priests who conspired against him; for the false witnesses who perjured their souls before the Sanhedrin and in the judgment halls of Rome; for Pilate and Herod, either of whom could have freed him; nor for Lucifer whose power and persuasive ability underlay the whole wicked procedure. All these are left in the hands of Eternal Justice to be dealt with according to their works. Mercy cannot rob justice; the guilty do not go free simply because the righteous bring no railing accusation against them. (DNTC 1:818–19.)

23:35–43 Read text and commentaries for Matthew 27:39–44. Read also Mark 15:29–32.

23:36 Compare Matthew 27:34.

23:38 Read text and commentaries for Matthew 27:36–37. Read also Mark 15:26; John 19:19–22.

23:39 The Joseph Smith Translation changes "which were hanged" to "who was crucified with him."

23:43 The assumption that the gracious assurance given by Christ to the penitent sinner on the cross was a remission of the man's sins, and a passport into heaven, is wholly contrary to both the letter and spirit of scripture, reason, and justice. Confidence in the efficacy of death-bed professions and confessions on the basis of this incident is of the most insecure foundation. The crucified malefactor manifested both faith and repentance; his promised blessing was that he should that day hear the gospel preached in paradise; in the acceptance or rejection of the word of life he would be an agent unto himself. The requirement of obedience to the laws and ordinances of the gospel as an essential to salvation was not waived, suspended, or superseded in his case. (JTC, p. 677.)

(See BD, "Paradise.")

23:44–45 Read text and commentaries for Matthew 27:45–49. Read also Mark 15:33–36; John 19:28–29.

23:45–46 Read text and commentaries for Matthew 27:50–51. Read also Mark 15:37–38; John 19:30.

23:46 A more literal translation of the final words of Jesus could have been: "Father, into your hands I entrust my spirit." The Greek text then continues: "When he had said this, he expired [or died]."

Jesus was in complete control of the situation to the very end. Elder Bruce R. McConkie refers to his words "Father, into thy hands I commend my spirit" as "A perfect benediction for a perfect life, a benediction promised and foretold in a Messianic prophecy of olden time: 'Into thine hand I commit my spirit: thou has redeemed me, O Lord God of Truth.' (Ps. 31:5.)"

Jesus "gave up" his life; he did not lose it, and it was not taken from him against his will. As he had mentioned earlier in the writings of John, "No man taketh it from me, but I lay it down of myself." (John 10:17–18.)

(See section 1, "Death: Of Jesus.")

23:47–49 Read text and commentaries for Matthew 27:54–56. Read also Mark 15:39–41.

23:50–54 Read text and commentaries for Matthew 27:57–60. Read also Mark 15:42–46; John 19:38–42.

23:51 The Joseph Smith Translation begins this verse, "The same *day* had not consented . . ." (Italics added.)

23:55–56 Read text and commentaries for Matthew 27:61; 28:1–10. Read also Mark 15:47; 16:1–8; Luke 24:1–11.

24:1–11 Read text and commentaries for Matthew 28:1–10. Read also Mark 16:1–8; Luke 23:55–56.

24:1 The Joseph Smith Translation identifies *they* as "the women."

24:2–3 And they found the stone rolled away from the sepulchre, *and two angels standing by it in shining garments*.

And they entered *into the* sepulchre, *and not finding* the body of the Lord Jesus, they were much perplexed thereabout;

And were affrighted, and bowed down their faces to the earth. *But behold the angels said unto them,* Why seek ye the living among the dead? (JST; italics added.)

24:5 "Why seek ye the living among the dead?" could have been more literally translated "Why are you looking for the living One among the dead ones?"

24:6 On the third day there was a great earthquake. The stone was rolled back from the door of the tomb. Some of the women, among the most devoted of his followers, came to the place with spices "and found not the body of the Lord Jesus." (Luke 24:3.)

Angels appeared and said simply, "Why seek ye the living among the dead? He is not here, but is risen."

There is nothing in history to equal that dramatic announcement: "He is not here, but is risen." (Ezra Taft Benson, CR, Apr. 1964, p. 119.)

24:11 Mary Magdalene and the other women told the wonderful story of their several experiences to the disciples, but the brethren could not credit their words, which "seemed to them as idle tales, and they believed them not." After all that Christ had taught concerning His rising from the dead on that third day, the apostles were unable to accept the actuality of the occurrence; to their minds the resurrection was some mysterious and remote event, not a present possibility. There was neither precedent nor analogy for the stories these women told—of a dead person returning to life, with a body of flesh and bones, such as could be seen and felt—except the instances of the young man of Nain, the daughter of Jairus, and the beloved Lazarus of Bethany, between whose cases of restoration to a renewal of mortal life and the reported resurrection of Jesus they recognized essential differences. The grief and the sense of irreparable loss which had characterized the yesterday Sabbath, were replaced by profound perplexity and contending doubts on this first day of the week. But while the apostles hesitated to believe that Christ had actually risen, the women, less skeptical, more trustful, knew, for they had both seen Him and heard His voice, and some of them had touched His feet. (JTC, pp. 682–83.)

24:12 A more detailed account of this experience is given in John 20:1–10.

The Joseph Smith Translation of this verse begins, "Then arose Peter, and ran unto the sepulchre and *went in* . . ." (Italics added.)

24:13–32 Read text and commentaries for Matthew 28:11–15. Read also Mark 16:12–13.

Why did the risen Lord take this means of appearing to Cleopas and his companion (perhaps Luke, since it is he who records the account)? Was it to quote and interpret the Messianic prophecies "beginning at Moses and all the prophets"? Such could have been done under more effective circumstances, and for that matter, Luke does not even record the explanations given. Why did Jesus keep his identity hidden? Why walk and talk, perhaps for hours, along the dusty lanes of Palestine?

Obviously it was to show what a resurrected being is like. He was teaching the gospel as only he could, teaching a living sermon, a sermon that was to be climaxed shortly in an upper room in the presence of his apostles. See Luke 24:36–44.

Jesus walked down a Judean lane, walked for hours and taught the truths of the gospel, exactly as he had during three and a half years of his mortal ministry. So much did he seem like any other wayfaring teacher, in demeanor, in dress, in speech, in physical appearance, in conversation, that they did not recognize him as the Jesus whom they assumed was dead. "Abide with us," they said, as they would have done to Peter or John. "Come in and eat and sleep; you must be tired and hungry." They thought he was a mortal man. *Could anyone devise a more perfect way to teach what a resurrected being is like when his glory is retained within him?* Men are men whether mortal or immortal, and there need be no spiritualizing away of the reality of the resurrection, not after this Emmaus road episode. (DNTC 1:850.)

24:13 The distance of "about threescore furlongs" is approximately seven miles. The exact site of Emmaus has not been determined in modern times. (See BD, "Emmaus.")

24:16 This verse could have been more literally translated "But their eyes were kept from recognizing him."

The Joseph Smith Translation reads, "But their eyes were holden, *or covered,* that they *could* not know him." (Italics added.)

24:18 See BD, "Cleopas."

24:26 This verse could have been more literally translated "Was it not necessary for the Christ to suffer these things and to enter into his glory?"

24:29 "But they constrained him" has also been translated "but they held him back," "But they urged him strongly," and "but they pressed him to stay."

24:31 In the Joseph Smith Translation, the last clause in this verse reads, "and he *was taken up* out of their sight." (Italics added.)

There may have been something in the fervency of the blessing, or in the manner of breaking and distributing the bread, that revived memories of former days; or, possibly, they caught sight of the pierced hands; but, whatever the immediate cause, they looked upon their Guest, "and their eyes were opened, and they knew him; and he vanished out of their sight." (JTC, p. 686.)

24:33–35 Only Luke tells of the appearance of the resurrected Jesus to Simon Peter alone, although the incident is referred to in 1 Corinthians 15:3–8.

This is the sole mention made by the Gospel writers of Christ's personal appearance to Simon Peter on that day. The interview between the Lord and His once recreant but now repentant apostle must have been affecting in the extreme. Peter's remorseful penitence over his denial of Christ in the palace of the high priest was deep and pitiful; he may have doubted that ever again would the Master call him His servant; but hope must have been engendered through the message from the tomb brought by the women, in which the Lord sent greetings to the apostles, whom for the first time He designated as His brethren, and from this honorable and affectionate characterization Peter had not been excluded; moreover, the angel's commission to the women had given prominence to Peter by particular mention. To the repentant Peter came the Lord, doubtless with forgiveness and loving assurance. The apostle himself maintains a reverent silence respecting the visitation, but the fact thereof is attested by Paul as one of the definite proofs of the Lord's resurrection. (JTC, p. 687.)

But Jesus' appearance to Peter perhaps had additional significance. Earlier, during his mortal ministry, Jesus had announced that he would confer the "keys of the kingdom" upon Peter (Matthew 16:19). Peter, in conjunction with James and John, who would preside with him, received those keys on the Mount of Transfiguration (see Matthew 17:1–8; Luke 9:28–36), and thereafter "acted as the First Presidency of the Church in their day." (Smith, *Doctrines of Salvation,* 3:152.) Those keys "belong always unto the Presidency of the High Priesthood" (D&C 81:2), and can be exercised in their fulness on the earth by only *one man* at a time; and *that man* in the period just after Jesus ascended into heaven was Peter. It may have been, then, that Jesus' special appearance to Peter was associated in some way with the principle of keys. (LTJA, p. 200.)

24:34 The Joseph Smith Translation reads, "And they told what things *they saw and heard* in the way, and how he was known *to* them, in breaking bread." (Italics added.)

24:36–44 (Read also Mark 16:14; John 20:19–21.) Several important truths are affirmed in this incident, including that spirits have bodies that look like the bodies of physical men and women but are not bodies of flesh and bones, and that resurrected beings can eat the foods of this earth.

On the Emmaus road Jesus walked, talked, and appeared as a mortal man. Now he comes through the walls or roof of an enclosed room, thus showing another power and capacity of a resurrected body. Standing before his terrified and frightened disciples—and the group included the apostles, plus others (Luke 24:33)—he continued his "living sermon" on the resurrection by demonstrating further what a resurrected body was and how it operated.

The apostles and other disciples thought he was "a spirit," a misconception which, however, reveals what a spirit is. As Jesus stood before them he seemed in every respect to be a man. In other words a spirit is a man, an entity, a personage, not an ineffable nothingness pervading immensity. A spirit is what the Brother of Jared saw on the mountain when the yet unembodied Lord appeared and said: "This body, which ye now behold, is the body of my spirit; . . . and even as I appear unto thee to be in the spirit will I appear unto my people in the flesh." (Ether 3:16.)

Jesus then confirmed the disciples' belief that a spirit is a personage by showing how a resurrected body differs from a spirit body. He announced that his body was made of "flesh and bones" and invited all present to handle, feel, and learn of its corporeal nature. Then lest any feel later that their senses had been deceived, he asked for food and ate it before them, not to satisfy hunger, but to demonstrate that resurrected beings are tangible and can eat and digest food. See Luke 24:13–35.

When Paul adds to what is here revealed that the risen Lord is in "the express image of his" Father's "person" (Heb. 1:3), we have perfect Biblical confirmation of the revealed truth that "The Father has a body of flesh and bones as tangible as man's; the Son also." (D&C 130:22.) (DNTC 1:853.)

24:38 "Thoughts" could have been translated "doubts."

24:41 "Have ye here any meat?" could have been translated "Do you have something there to eat?"

24:45 This special spiritual endowment was a temporary gift. Scriptures are given and understood only by the power of the Holy Ghost. (2 Pet. 1:20–21.) The disciples would receive the ability to understand the scriptures in the full and continuing sense only after they gained the gift of the Holy Ghost on the day of Pentecost.

A similar thing to this happened also in the case of Joseph Smith and Oliver Cowdery. Following their baptism at the direction of John the Baptist, and before the Melchizedek Priesthood was restored so they could receive the gift of the Holy Ghost, the inspired account says: "We were filled with the Holy Ghost, and rejoiced in the God of our salvation. Our minds being now enlightened, we began to have the scriptures laid open to our understandings, and the true meaning and intention of their more mysterious passages revealed unto us in a manner which we never could attain to previously, nor ever before had thought of." (Jos. Smith 2:73–74.) But both the ancient and the modern disciples, in order to continue to enjoy the full guidance and endowment of the Spirit had to receive, in due course, the gift of the Holy Ghost. To a degree every sincere investigator begins to have his mind opened to the scriptures, as he seeks the truth even before baptism, but the great flood of enlightenment comes after the receipt of the companionship of the Holy Ghost. (DNTC 1:853–54.)

24:46 "Behoved" means "was proper for" or "was necessary for."

24:47 The admonition that "repentance and remission of sins should be preached in his name among all nations" indicates that Jesus and his gospel require more than "belief" as claimed by some modern "born again" Christians.

24:49 This account is contained only in Luke.

It is common in Christendom to suppose that Jesus here commanded his apostles to tarry in Jerusalem until the promised gift of the Holy Ghost was received, which gift would constitute an endowment of power from on high. Perhaps the statement can be so used, for certainly the disciples were marvelously and powerfully endowed when the Holy Spirit came into their lives on the day of Pentecost. (Acts 2.)

But from latter-day revelation we learn that the Lord had something more in mind in issuing this instruction. In this dispensation, after the elders had received the gift of the Holy Ghost and as early as January, 1831, the Lord began to reveal unto them that he had an endowment in store for the faithful (D&C 38:22; 43:16), "a blessing such as is not known among the children of men." (D&C 39:15.) In June, 1833, he said: "I gave unto you a commandment that you should build a house, in the which house I design to endow those whom I have chosen with power from on high; For this is the promise of the Father unto you; therefore I command you to tarry, even as mine apostles at Jerusalem." (D&C 95:8–9; 105:11–12, 18, 33.)

Thus the apostles—or any ministers or missionaries in any age—are not fully qualified to go forth, preach the gospel, and build up the kingdom, unless they have the gift of the Holy Ghost and also are endowed with power from on high, meaning have received certain knowledge, powers, and special blessings, normally given only in the Lord's Temple. (DNTC 1:859.)

24:50–53 Read text and commentary for Mark 16:19–20.

Worshipfully and with great joy the apostles returned to Jerusalem, there to await the coming of the Comforter. The Lord's ascension was accomplished; it was as truly a literal departure of a material Being as His resurrection had been an actual return of His spirit to His own corporeal body, theretofore dead. With the world abode and yet abides the glorious promise, that Jesus the Christ, the same Being who ascended from Olivet in His immortalized body of flesh and bones, shall return, descending from the heavens, in similarly material form and substance. (JTC, p. 697.)

JOHN

For background information on this book, see BD, "Gospels," "Harmony of the Gospels," "John, Gospel of," and "John."

1:1–5 This is John's introduction to his book.

In the beginning was the *gospel preached through the Son. And the gospel was the* word, and the word was with *the Son,* and *the Son was with God, and the Son was God.*

In him was *the gospel,* and the *gospel* was the *life, and the life was the* light of men;

And the light shineth in *the world,* and the *world perceiveth* it not. (JST; italics added.)

1:3 See D&C 93:6–9.

The passage is simple, precise and unambiguous. We may reasonably give to the phrase "In the beginning" the same meaning as attaches thereto in the first line of Genesis; and such signification must indicate a time antecedent to the earliest stages of human existence upon the earth. That the Word is Jesus Christ, who was with the Father in that beginning and who was Himself invested with the powers and rank of Godship, and that He came into the world and dwelt among men, are definitely affirmed. These statements are corroborated through a revelation given to Moses, in which he was permitted to see many of the creations of God, and to hear the voice of the Father with respect to the things that had been made: "And by the word of my power, have I created them, which is mine Only Begotten Son, who is full of grace and truth." [Moses 1:32–33.] (JTC, p. 10.)

1:4 "In him" could have been more literally translated "by means of him."

1:6–37 For additional information on the life and mission of John the Baptist, see text and commentaries for Matthew 3:1–6, Mark 1:1–8, Luke 3:1–6; 3:7–18. See also 1 Nephi 10:7–10; D&C 35:4; 84:27–28; 93:10–17.

1:7–10 The same came *into the world* for a witness, to bear witness of the light, *to bear record of the gospel through the Son, unto all,* that *through him men* might believe.

He was not that light, but *came* to bear witness of that light,

Which was the true light, which lighteth every man *who* cometh into the world;

Even the Son of God. He who was in the world, and the world was made by him, and the world knew him not. (JST; italics added.)

1:7 That John was "to bear record of the gospel through the Son, unto all" indicates that John was not only to bear witness that Jesus was the Son of God, but also was to testify that the gospel would be made efficacious through the life and teachings of the Son.

1:9 For further scriptural evidence that Jesus is "the true light, which lighteth every man who cometh into the world," see Moroni 7:12–19 and D&C 84:44–47.

1:11 Why was it at that time or why is it now that some will not receive him? No doubt they had expected something entirely different. They were looking for a leader in political and social reform and they had little interest in spiritual things. "The world was made by him, and the world knew him not." There are those today who pass him by without recognizing him. (Howard W. Hunter, CR, Oct. 1968, p. 141.)

1:13 In the Joseph Smith Translation, this verse begins, *"He was* born . . ." (Italics added.)

1:14 The Joseph Smith Translation deletes the parentheses and capitalizes the key words in the title "the Only Begotten of the Father." It begins this verse, "And the *same* word was made flesh . . ." (Italics added.)

1:15 "For he was before me" could have been translated "because he existed before me."

From latter-day revelation we learn that the material in the forepart of the gospel of John (the Apostle, Revelator, and Beloved Disciple) was written originally by John the Baptist. By revelation the Lord restored to Joseph Smith part of what John the Baptist had written and promised to reveal the balance when men became sufficiently faithful to warrant receiving it. (D&C 93:6–18.) Verse 15 of this passage is the key to the identity of the particular John spoken of. This verse should be compared with Matt. 3:16–17 to learn the identity of the writer.

Even without revelation, however, it should be evident that John the Baptist had something to do with the recording of events in the forepart of John's gospel, for some of the occurrences include his conversations with the Jews and a record of what he saw when our Lord was baptized—all of which matters would have been unknown to John the Apostle whose ministry began somewhat later than that of the Baptist's. There is little doubt but that the Beloved Disciple had before him the Baptist's account when he wrote his gospel. The latter John either copied or paraphrased what the earlier prophet of the same name had written. The only other possibility is that the Lord revealed to the gospel author the words that had been recorded by the earlier messenger who prepared the way before him. (DNTC 1:70–71.)

1:16–17 See D&C 93:12–14, 16–17.

For in the beginning was the Word, even the Son, who is made flesh, and sent unto us by the will of the Father. And as many as believe on his name shall receive of his fulness. And of his fulness have all we received, *even immortality and eternal life, through his grace.*

For the law was given *through* Moses, but *life* and truth came *through* Jesus Christ.

For the law was after a carnal commandment, to the administration of death; but the gospel was after the power of an endless life, through Jesus Christ, the Only Begotten Son who is in the bosom of the Father. (JST; italics added.)

To gain the *fulness of the Father* means to attain exaltation and godhood. This fulness consists of (1) all power, both in heaven and on earth, and (2) eternal increase or "a continuation of the seeds forever and ever." (D&C 132:19–24; *Mormon Doctrine,* pp. 275–276.) As is the case with all men, our Lord worked out his own salvation and exaltation. Having been made flesh, he continued in obedience to the whole law, until having overcome all things, he rose in the triumph of a glorious resurrection to receive, inherit, and possess all things, that is, to the "fulness of the glory of the Father." Having set the example himself, our Lord now proclaims: "If you keep my commandments you shall receive of his fulness and be glorified in me as I am in the Father." (D&C 93:20.)

Because the law of carnal commandments, as it prevailed from Moses to Christ, was administered by the Aaronic Priesthood, it was "the administration of death." That is, no one could gain the fulness of the Father by the Mosaic law alone. There is no celestial marriage without the Melchizedek Priesthood, and without celestial marriage and the consequent continuation of the family unit in eternity, men inherit what the Lord calls "the deaths." (D&C 132:25.) They do not have spirit children in the resurrection.

On the other hand, in the fulness of the gospel, as restored in the meridian of time by the Son, is found "the power of an endless life," meaning that through the Melchizedek Priesthood (which always accompanies the fulness of the gospel) men may gain endless life, or eternal life, or exaltation. In other words they may gain the fulness of the Father, which includes "eternal lives" as contrasted with "the deaths." To inherit "eternal lives" means to have eternal increase or spirit progeny forever. (D&C 132:15–32.) (DNTC 1:76.)

1:18 *And* no man hath seen God at any time, *except he hath borne record of the Son; for except it is through him no man can be saved.* (JST; italics added.)

As presently found in *the King James Version* this passage is one of the classical examples of scriptural mistranslation. The whole body of revealed truth bears record that Deity has been seen by man. What John actually taught was that the Father had never appeared to any man except for the purpose of introducing and bearing record of the Son. The joint appearance of the Father and the Son to Joseph Smith shows the pattern that has always been followed. (Jos. Smith 2:14–20.)

All things center in Christ. He is the God of Israel, the God of the Old Testament, the Advocate, Mediator, and Intercessor. Since the fall of Adam, all of the dealings of Deity with man have been through the Son. On occasions, however, in accordance with the principle of divine investiture of authority, the Son has and does speak in the first person as though he were the Father, because the Father has put his name on the Son. The visions of Moses as revealed anew to the Prophet in this day fall in this category. (Moses 1; *Mormon Doctrine,* pp. 24–25, 122, 355, 428–429.) (DNTC 1:77.)

1:19–28 Read text and commentaries for Matthew 3:7–12; Mark 1:4–5, 8; Luke 3:7–18.

1:20–21 And he confessed, and denied not *that he was Elias;* but confessed, *saying;* I am not the Christ.

And they asked him, *saying; How* art thou then Elias? And he *said,* I am not *that Elias who was to restore all things. And they* asked *him saying,* Art thou that prophet? And he answered, No. (JST; italics added.)

In the time of Jesus and John, the whole Jewish nation was stirred up with anxious expectation, awaiting the momentary appearance of the Messiah and his Elias. With great hosts from Jerusalem and all Judea flocking to John and accepting him as a prophet, and with the banks of the Jordan crowded with his baptized converts, it was natural for the leading Jews— members of the great Sanhedrin, whose obligation it was to test prophetic claims—to send priests and Levites to make detailed investigation. To their pointed questions, John gave bold and authoritative answers:

Art thou Elias? "Yes, I am Messiah's forerunner, his Elias; I have come in the spirit and power of Elias to prepare the way before him. I hold the Priesthood of Elias, the Aaronic Priesthood; I baptize with water only. He shall come in the power and authority of the Melchizedek Priesthood and baptize both with water and the Spirit. But, do not be confused, I am not that Elias who was to restore all things, for that Elias is the Messiah himself; he shall restore all things, even the fulness of the gospel which was had by Adam and Abraham and many of the prophets of old. He shall replace the lesser law of Moses with the high law of Christ." (*Mormon Doctrine,* pp. 203–206.)

Art thou that prophet like unto Moses whose coming is promised? See John 7:41. (Deut. 18:15–22.) "No; I am not that prophet, for that prophet is the promised Messiah himself. He it is who, coming after me, is preferred before me. Instead, I am the prophet whose coming Isaiah foretold (Isa. 40); I am the voice of one crying in the wilderness: Prepare ye the way of the Lord, who is the prophet of whom Moses spoke."

Art thou the Christ? "No; I am not the Christ; nor am I worthy to fill his place, or even to unloose the very latchet of his shoes. But I bear record of him; and he now standeth among you, and he is the Son of God." (DNTC 1:129–30.)

(See Section 1, "Elias: John is an.")

1:25 In the Joseph Smith Translation, this question is

worded, "Why baptizest thou then, if thou be not *the* Christ, nor Elias *who was to restore all things,* neither that prophet?" (Italics added.)

1:27 He it is *of whom I bear record. He is the prophet, even Elias,* who, coming after me, is preferred before me, whose shoe's latchet I am not worthy to unloose, *or whose place I am not able to fill; for he shall baptize, not only with water, but with fire, and with the Holy Ghost.* (JST; italics added.)

"Shoe's latchet" could have been more precisely translated "lace of the sandal."

1:28 The Joseph Smith Translation places this verse at the end of the account of the baptism of Jesus (that is, after verse 34) indicating that "Bethabara beyond Jordan" is where John was baptizing. (See BD, "Bethabara.")

1:29 Although this verse contains the first New Testament reference to Jesus as the "Lamb of God," the terms "Lamb" or "Lamb of God" are used many times in the Book of Mormon before the birth of Jesus Christ, including at least fifty-seven times between 1 Nephi 10:10 and 14:27.

How fitting for John—whose mission was to close the door on the past glory and worship of Israel, and to open it for the coming gospel and worship which was to be made available for all men of all races—to testify that Jesus was the Lamb of God! For four thousand years righteous men had sacrificed the firstlings of their flocks, lambs and other animals without spot or blemish, in similitude of the coming sacrifice of the Son of God. (Moses 5:5–8.) Now Deity's own Son, born of woman, grown to maturity and commencing his ministry, was soon to be slain as a Paschal Lamb to atone for the sins of the world. (DNTC 1:131.)

(See BD, "Lamb of God.")

1:30 In the Joseph Smith Translation, this verse begins, "And *John bare record of him unto the people, saying,* This is he . . ." (Italics added.)

1:31 The Joseph Smith Translation deletes "not," which would be consistent with the remainder of the testimony of John, inasmuch as he was testifying concerning that which he had already witnessed. (See commentary for John 1:33.)

1:32–34 For other materials pertaining to the baptism of Jesus by John, see text and commentaries for Matthew 3:13–17; Mark 1:9–11; Luke 3:21–22. See also 1 Nephi 10:7–10; 2 Nephi 31:4–21. (See section 1, "Dove: Sign of.")

1:32 And John bare record, saying, *When he was baptized of me,* I saw the Spirit descending from heaven like a dove, and it abode upon him. (JST; italics added.)

1:33 "Not" is deleted in the Joseph Smith Translation. This is consistent with the remainder of the testimony of John, who was testifying here of things he had both seen and heard. (See commentary for John 1:31.)

John's reference to "he that sent me" indicates that prophets must be sent of God to be legal administrators in the affairs of the kingdom of God.

1:35–37 Only one of these two disciples of John is identified by name: Andrew, the brother of Simon (Peter). Many students of the scriptures believe the other disciple may well have been John the Beloved who wrote this account but out of modesty might not have mentioned his own name. This would be consistent with the recounting of later events when he does not use his own name. (See John 13:23; 21:20–24.)

1:38–42 And he brought him to Jesus. And when Jesus beheld him, he said, Thou art Simon, the son of Jona, thou shalt be called Cephas, which is, by interpretation, *a seer, or* a stone. *And they were fishermen. And they straightway left all, and followed Jesus.* (JST; italics added.)

(See BD, "Cephas.")

1:43–51 These verses contain the account of the meetings with Philip and Nathanael.

1:44 *Bethsaida* means "house of fish" in Hebrew, an appropriate name for a town near the shore of the sea of Galilee and the home of such fishermen as Simon and Andrew.

The Joseph Smith Translation reads, "Philip was *at* Bethsaida" rather than "*of* Bethsaida."

1:45 When Philip stated that Jesus was he "of whom Moses in the law, and the prophets, did write," he was testifying that Jesus was the Messiah.

1:46 Nathanael's response, "Can there any good thing come out of Nazareth?" indicates the relatively bad reputation of Nazareth in those days. Just as Jesus chose to be born in a small village in humble circumstances, he evidently also chose to be reared in a village with no great reputation. (See BD, "Nathanael.")

1:47 "Guile" could have been translated as "deceit" or "fraud."

1:50 Our present New Testament account does not indicate which "greater things than these" may have been witnessed by Nathanael. Some scholars believe Nathanael may have been Bartholomew the apostle (Matt. 10:3), although the present evidence is inconclusive.

1:51 The sacred title "Son of Man" should always be capitalized and refers only to Jesus Christ, the Son of Man of Holiness (our Heavenly Father). (See Moses 6:57; 7:35; also, see text and commentary for Matt. 16:13; section 1, "Son of Man.")

"The Son of Man" was and is, specifically and exclusively, Jesus Christ. While as a matter of solemn certainty He was the only male human being from Adam down who was not the son of a mortal man, He used the title in a way to conclusively demonstrate that it was peculiarly and solely His own. It is plainly evident that the expression is fraught with a meaning beyond that conveyed by the words in common usage. The distinguishing appellation has been construed by many to indicate our Lord's humble station as a mortal, and to connote that He stood as the type of humanity, holding a particular and unique relationship to the entire human family. There is, however, a more profound significance attaching to the Lord's use of the title "The Son of Man"; and this lies in the fact that He knew His Father to be the one and only supremely exalted Man, whose Son Jesus was both in spirit and in body—the Firstborn among all the spirit—children of the Father, the Only Begotten in the flesh-and therefore, in a sense applicable to Himself alone, He was and is the Son of the "Man of Holiness," Elohim, the Eternal Father. In His distinctive titles of Sonship, Jesus expressed His spiritual and bodily descent from, and His filial submission to, that exalted Father. (JTC, pp. 142–43.)

2:1–11 The account of the "beginning of miracles . . . in Cana of Galilee" (verse 11) has been preserved only by John. (See section 1, "Miracles"; BD, "Cana of Galilee.")

2:1 In the Joseph Smith Translation, this verse begins, "And *on* the third day *of the week* . . ." (Italics added.)

2:4 Jesus *said* unto her, Woman, what *wilt thou* have *me* do *for* thee? *that will I do; for* mine hour is not yet come. (JST; italics added.)

The noun of address, "Woman," as applied by a son to his mother may sound to our ears somewhat harsh, if not disrespectful; but its use was really an expression of opposite import. To every son the mother ought to be pre-eminently the woman of women; She is the one woman in the world to whom the son owes his earthly existence; and though the title "Mother" belongs to every woman who has earned the honors of maternity, yet to no child is there more than one woman whom by natural right he can address by that title of respectful acknowledgment. When, in the last dread scenes of His mortal existence, Christ hung in dying agony upon the cross, He looked down upon the weeping Mary, His mother, and commended her to the care of the beloved apostle John, with the words: "Woman, behold thy son!" Can it be thought that in this supreme moment, our Lord's concern for the mother from whom He was about to be separated by death was associated with any emotion other than that of honor, tenderness and love? (JTC, pp. 144–45.)

2:6 A firkin is about nine gallons. Thus each of the six waterpots contained around 18 to 27 gallons of water, with the result that Jesus then created between 100 and 150 gallons of wine—a miracle showing that the wedding celebration was quite large. (LTJA, p. 29.)

2:9 The Joseph Smith Translation changes "ruler" to "governor," indicating this is the same person mentioned in verse 8. Other translations have been "master of ceremonies," "steward of the feast," and "master of the banquet."

"Knew not whence it was" means "he did not know where this wine had come from."

2:11 In the Joseph Smith Translation, this verse ends, "and the *faith* of his disciples *was strengthened* in him." (Italics added.)

First of the miraculous signs of his ministry, that is, the first of those intended for public knowledge, those designed as witnesses of the divine powers resident in him. He previously may well have performed other personal or private miracles. Indeed, Mary's appeal to him at the wedding celebration for aid carries an inference of her prior knowledge of his miraculous abilities. (DNTC 1:137.)

John's record of the marriage in Cana is fragmentary; it does not by any means tell the whole story. From what is recorded, however, we learn:

(1) Mary seemed to be the hostess at the marriage party, the one in charge, the one responsible for the entertainment of the guests. It was she who recognized the need for more wine, who sought to replenish the supply, who directed the servants to follow whatever instructions Jesus gave. Considering the customs of the day, it is a virtual certainty that one of Mary's children was being married.

(2) Jesus also had a close personal interest in and connection with the marriage and the subsequent festivities which attended it. He and apparently at least five of his disciples (John, Andrew, Peter, Philip, and Nathanael) were "called" to attend. Since the shortage of wine occurred near the close of the festivities, and since these commonly lasted from seven to fourteen days, it is apparent that Jesus' party was remaining for the entire celebration. Seemingly, also, he had some personal responsibility for entertaining the guests and felt an obligation to supply them with added refreshments.

(3) Participation by Jesus and his disciples in the marriage customs of that day places an endorsing stamp of divine approval upon the system of matrimony itself and also upon reasonable and modest display attending its solemnization.

(4) Jesus was no recluse, no hermit, no ascetic. He came eating and drinking, enjoying the natural, normal, and wholesome social intercourse of the day.

(5) By turning water into wine, he manifest during the early days of his ministry that he had power over temporal, physical matters.

(6) The faith of his disciples was strengthened in him.

(7) Obviously, also, it would be with this as with his subsequent miracles: when word of his miraculous powers was noised among the people, many would investigate, hear the proclamation of his Messiahship, listen to his teachings, believe his message of salvation, and become heirs of eternal life. (DNTC 1:135–36.)

2:12 This transitional verse between the miracle at Cana and the cleansing of the temple in Jerusalem could indicate the passage of considerable time.

"They continued there not many days" means "they stayed there a few days."

For further background on the brethren of Jesus (as contrasted with "his disciples"), see text and commentaries for Matthew 12:46–50.

2:13–17 The first cleansing of the temple by Jesus is preserved only by John. For information of his later experience with the money changers near the temple, see text and commentaries for Matthew 21:12–17.

2:13–14 See text and commentaries for Matthew 26:17–20, 26–29:

Ancient Israel in the day of Moses, was freed from temporal bondage in Egypt by the Lord Jehovah. To commemorate this deliverance, they were commanded to keep the Feast of the Passover. This feast was designed to bring two things to their remembrance: (1) That the angel of death passed over the houses and flocks of Israel, while slaying the firstborn among the men and beasts of the Egyptians; and (2) That Jehovah was their Deliverer, the same holy being who in due course would come into the world as King-Messiah to work out the infinite and eternal atonement.

All of the symbolisms of the feast centered around these two events. The feast (more so in the days of its inception than in the time of Jesus) was eaten in haste as though preparatory to flight; the sacrificial lamb was one without blemish, whose blood was shed, but whose bones were not broken; blood was sprinkled on the houses to be spared—all of which provided types and symbols for Messiah's coming mortal sacrifice. (Ex. 12.)

And now nearly a millennium and a half after Jehovah gave the Passover to Israel, he himself, tabernacled among men, was preparing to celebrate the feast, to fulfil the law given to Moses. (DNTC 1:704.)

2:14–16 The incident of Christ's forcible clearing of the temple is a contradiction of the traditional conception of Him as of One so gentle and unassertive in demeanor as to appear unmanly. Gentle He was, and patient under affliction, merciful and long-suffering in dealing with contrite sinners, yet stern and inflexible in the presence of hypocrisy, and unsparing in His denunciation of persistent evil-doers. His mood was adapted to the conditions to which He addressed Himself; tender words of encouragement or burning expletives of righteous indignation issued with equal fluency from His lips. His nature was no poetic conception of cherubic sweetness ever present, but that of a Man, with the emotions and passions essential to manhood and manliness. He, who often wept with compassion, at other times evinced in word and action the righteous anger of a God. But of all His passions, however gently they rippled or strongly surged, He was ever master. Contrast the gentle Jesus moved to hospitable service by the needs of a festal party in Cana, with the indignant Christ plying His whip, and amidst commotion and turmoil of His own making, driving cattle and men before Him as an unclean herd. (JTC, p. 158.)

As Jesus entered the outer courts of the temple, during the first Passover of his ministry, he beheld what he was to call three years later on a similar occasion, "a den of thieves." (Matt. 21:13.) Before him were stalls of oxen, pens of sheep, cages of doves and pigeons, with greedy hucksters offering them at exorbitant prices for sacrificial purposes. Crowded on every hand were the tables of the money-changers who, for a profit, changed the Roman and other coins into temple coins so that sacrificial animals could be purchased and the half shekel poll tax required at this season of the year might be paid. In righteous anger and with physical force he drove the apostate priesthood from their unhallowed merchandising enterprises.

This dramatic episode in the life of our Lord has been preserved to bear record:

(1) That the meek and lowly Nazarene was a man of action; a dynamic forceful character; a man of courage and physical strength; one whose soul filled with righteous indignation upon seeing the desecration of sacred things; one who responded zealously and vigorously in the cause of righteousness, though all men opposed him;

(2) That God was his Father; and

(3) That the temple was still his Father's house, though virtually all who worshiped there were walking in dark and direful apostasy. (DNTC 1:137–38.)

2:15 "A scourge of small cords" could have been translated "a whip of ropes."

2:17 The scripture that the "disciples remembered" is found in Psalm 69:9: "For the zeal of thine house hath eaten me up."

2:18–22 As Jesus has indicated elsewhere, it is "an evil and adulterous generation" that seeks for a sign. (See text and commentaries for Matt. 12:39; Mark 16:17.)

Blinded by their own craft, unwilling to acknowledge the Lord's authority, yet fearful of the possibility that they were opposing one who had the right to act, the perturbed officials found in the words of Jesus reference to the imposing temple of masonry within whose walls they stood. They took courage; this strange Galilean, who openly flouted their authority, spoke irreverently of their temple, the visible expression of the profession they so proudly flaunted in words—that they were children of the covenant, worshipers of the true and living God, and hence superior to all heathen and pagan peoples. With seeming indignation they rejoiced; "Forty and six years was this temple in building, and wilt thou rear it up in three days?" Though frustrated in their desire to arouse popular indignation against Jesus at this time, the Jews refused to forget or forgive His words. When afterward He stood an undefended prisoner, undergoing an illegal pretense of trial before a sin-impeached court, the blackest perjury uttered against Him was that of the false witnesses who testified: "We heard him say, I will destroy this temple that is made with hands, and within three days I will build another made without hands." And while He hung in mortal suffering, the scoffers who passed by the cross wagged their heads and taunted the dying Christ with "Ah, thou that destroyest the temple, and buildest it in three days, save thyself, and come down from the cross." Yet His words to the Jews who had demanded the credentials of a sign had no reference to the colossal Temple of Herod, but to the sanctuary of His own body, in which, more literally than in the man-built Holy of Holies, dwelt the ever living Spirit of the Eternal God. "The Father is in me" was His doctrine. (JTC, pp. 156–57.)

2:18 In the Joseph Smith Translation, this verse begins, "Then *spake* the Jews and said unto him . . ." (Italics added.)

2:19–21 On this and other occasions Jesus taught his own death and resurrection, and though disbelieving, the Jews knew what he was teaching and understood the meaning of the figurative expressions he used. Later, after his crucifixion, these same Jews, harking back to Jesus' teaching that he would be resurrected, told Pilate: "Sir, we remember that that deceiver said, while he was yet alive, After three days I will rise again." (Matt. 27:63.) Their testimony to the contrary at his trial was part of the conspiracy of perjury which led to his death. (Mark 14:58.) (DNTC 1:139.)

2:22 The Joseph Smith Translation changes "believed" to "remembered."

Only after the resurrection did the full and complete meaning of Jesus' announcement of his coming resurrection dawn upon his disciples. Then they remembered that the Lord Jehovah, the God of Israel himself, after his birth into mortality, was to die and be resurrected. They remembered that Isaiah had said of him: "He was cut off out of the land of the living: . . . He made his grave with the wicked, and with the rich in his death." (Isa. 53:8–9.) They remembered that the great Jehovah had said to Israel: "Thy dead men shall live, together with my dead body shall they arise." (Isa. 26:4, 19.) (DNTC 1:139.)

2:23–25 Only John records that many in Jerusalem at this Passover believed on Jesus "when they saw the miracles which he did."

2:24 The Joseph Smith Translation changes "men" to "things." The first part of this verse has been translated "But Jesus did not trust himself to them."

During his mortal life our Lord went from grace to grace and from truth to truth. He progressed from intelligence to intelligence until finally after the triumph of a glorious resurrection he gained all power, all knowledge, and all truth. It is only in this exalted and resurrected state that he came to a knowledge of all things in the ultimate and unlimited sense. (D&C 93:6–28.) However, in the course of his mortal probation, he knew all things in the sense that, having the constant companionship of that Spirit (the Holy Ghost) who does know all things, Jesus could and did receive revelation of all that was needed for his ministry from time to time. He knew all things in the sense that a knowledge of all things was constantly available to him.

In this same sense faithful saints are entitled to receive revelation from the Spirit, or in other words to "have the mind of Christ." (1 Cor. 2:16.) Those who gain their exaltation will, like Christ, be glorified in truth and light and know all things in the ultimate and absolute sense, meaning there will be no truth they do not know, no knowledge they have not mastered. (D&C 93:27–28.) (DNTC 1:139–40.)

3:1–18 This interview between the Pharisee Nicodemus, "a ruler of the Jews," and Jesus is recorded only by John.

The narrative of this interview between Nicodemus and the Christ constitutes one of our most instructive and precious scriptures relating to the absolute necessity of unreserved compliance with the laws and ordinances of the gospel, as the means indispensable to salvation. Faith in Jesus Christ as the Son of God, through whom alone men may gain eternal life; the forsaking of sin by resolute turning away from the gross darkness of evil to the saving light of righteousness; the unqualified requirement of a new birth through baptism in water, and this of necessity by the mode of immersion, since otherwise the figure of a birth would be meaningless; and the completion of the new birth through baptism by the Spirit—all these principles are taught herein in such simplicity and plainness as to make plausible no man's excuse for ignorance. (JTC, p. 162.)

To a limited extent this ruler of the Jews manifested faith in Christ, but as far as the New Testament record reveals, he never quite attained that state of valiant devotion which would classify him as a true disciple. This interview, at which presumably John and others were present, took place at night, away from the prying eyes of other members of the Sanhedrin. Later, when officers of that body were reporting upon their failure to take Jesus into custody, it was Nicodemus who queried his colleagues of the Sanhedrin by saying: "Doth our law judge any man, before it hear him, and know what he doeth?" (John 7:30–39, 50–53.) Still later we read of Nicodemus bringing a costly "mixture of myrrh and aloes" to use in preparing the body of the crucified Lord for burial. (John 19:38–42.) Whether he himself was ever born of water and of the Spirit remains unknown. (DNTC 1:141.)

(See BD, "Nicodemus.")

3:3 Several other scriptures refer to the necessity of a spiritual rebirth. (See Mosiah 3:19; 5:7; Alma 7:14;1 Pet.

2:2.) To Alma the younger the Lord said: "Marvel not that all mankind, yea, men and women, all nations, kindreds, tongues and people, must be born again; yea, born of God, changed from their carnal and fallen state, to a state of righteousness, being redeemed of God, becoming his sons and daughters; And thus they become new creatures; and unless they do this, they can in nowise inherit the kingdom of God." (Mosiah 27:24–29.)

3:3–5 The Greek words translated in verse 3 as "See" and in verse 5 as "enter" are different words. To "see" the kingdom of God is to receive a testimony of the gospel. To "enter" the kingdom of God is to have faith, repent, be baptized, and receive the gift of the Holy Ghost.

It is one thing to see the kingdom of God, and another thing to enter into it. We must have a change of heart to see the kingdom of God, and subscribe the articles of adoption to enter therein. (TPJS, p. 328.)

3:5 Read text and commentaries for Matthew 3:2; 6:10. See section 1, "Kingdom of Heaven or Kingdom of God."

The kingdom of God mentioned by the Savior in his conversation with Nicodemus points clearly to the fact that it is the celestial kingdom that is meant. This is also implied in the instructions given by our Savior to his apostles when he left them. They were to go into all the world and preach the gospel, all who accepted and were baptized should enter the celestial kingdom, but all others would be damned, or be assigned to one of the other kingdoms. (AGQ 5:147–48.)

3:9–21 A footnote in the Latter-day Saint edition of the King James Version reads: "The Greek construction suggests that verses 11–21 contain a direct quotation. This testimony of Jesus was given to a member of the Sanhedrin."

3:11 The plural pronouns "we" and "our" suggest that Jesus was also including the testimony and witness of the disciples in this statement.

3:12 That is: "If I have told you the simple, basic truths about being born again; if I have told you the first principles—faith, repentance, baptism, and the receipt of the Holy Ghost; and ye believe not; how shall ye either believe or understand if I tell you the 'wonders of eternity,' 'the hidden mysteries of my kingdom,' the 'things which eye has not seen, nor ear heard, nor yet entered into the heart of man'?" (DNTC 1:142.)

3:13 The Joseph Smith Translation of this verse begins, *"I tell you,* No man . . ." (Italics added.) Also, the sacred title "Son of Man" is capitalized in the Joseph Smith Translation.

One of the "heavenly things," of which Jesus bore record, was that he, the Messiah who had come down from heaven, was the Son of Man of Holiness who is in heaven. (Moses 6:57.) Like Nicodemus, almost the whole so-called Christian world, as yet unable to understand even "earthly things," rejects the full and literal meaning of this divine testimony. (DNTC 1:143.)

3:14–15 Numbers 21:4–9 is the initial reference to the serpent Moses raised up in the wilderness. However, the symbol is also emphasized in the Book of Mormon (see Hel. 8:13–15), and some LDS scholars believe this symbol is the basis for one of the names given by the early native Americans to the God who came out of the sky like a bird but who had been lifted up like the serpent—Quetzalcoatl, the "bird serpent."

3:16 Elder Bruce R. McConkie has identified this verse as "perhaps the most famous and powerful single verse of scripture ever uttered."

It summarizes the whole plan of salvation, tying together the Father, the Son, his atoning sacrifice, that belief in him which presupposes righteous works, and ultimate eternal exaltation for the faithful.

Similarly, our Lord "so loved the world that he gave his own life, that as many as would believe might become the sons of God." (D&C 34:3.) . . . Only begotten in the flesh . . . in mortality. This designation of our Lord signifies that he was begotten by Man of Holiness as literally as any mortal father begets a son. The natural processes of procreation were involved; Jesus was begotten by his Father as literally as he was conceived by his mother. (DNTC 1:144.)

3:18 He *who* believeth on him is not condemned; but he *who* believeth not is condemned already, because he hath not believed *on* the name of the Only Begotten Son of God, *which before was preached by the mouth of the holy prophets; for they testified of me.* (JST; italics added.)

The Joseph Smith Translation indicates that this testimony was definitely given by Jesus and is not simply an observation by John, as some scholars have assumed.

3:21 The last part of this verse is expanded into a full verse in the Joseph Smith Translation: "And he who obeyeth the truth, the works which he doeth they are of God."

3:22 The Greek text makes it clear that Jesus was doing some of the baptizing with his disciples. This would agree with the substance of verse 26 and with the Joseph Smith Translation of John 4:2. (See commentary for John 4:1–2; section 1, "Baptism: Jesus practiced.")

3:23–24 That John was baptizing in a place "because

there was much water there" would indicate that he was definitely baptizing by immersion, as "much water" is not needed for the false practices of sprinkling and pouring. (See BD, "Aenon," "Salim.")

3:25–26 The ministries of Jesus and John overlapped. Both were now preaching and baptizing. John's baptisms were in water only, after which his disciples were told (as John the apostle and Andrew had been) to follow Jesus who would baptize them with fire and the Holy Ghost. Jesus' baptisms were also in water unto repentance, but then he added the promise that in due course his converts would be baptized by the Spirit. Further, John, who had once baptized to cleanse, purify, and prepare a people for a Messiah who was to come, now was baptizing into the kingdom set up by the Holy One of Israel who had come. However, according to the apostate Jewish traditions, the purifying power of baptism was needed only for Gentile proselytes; those of the seed of Abraham claimed exemption from its cleansing power and substituted various ritualistic cleansing ordinances of their own. (Mark 7:1–8.)

It is not unnatural that these diverse views should arouse questions "between some of John's disciples and the Jews about purifying," and that those disciples should come to John to inquire about Jesus and the baptizing being done by him and his disciples. In answer John preached one of the greatest sermons ever delivered on the divinity of Christ and the obligation resting upon all men to accept him as the Son of God if they would be saved. Few if any prophets have ever preached stronger doctrine or testified more powerfully to the divinity of their Lord than did the Lord's own forerunner on this occasion. Verses 27–36 contain a brief digest of his inspired utterances. (DNTC 1:146–47.)

3:26 (See text and commentaries for John 3:22 and 4:1–2.) In the Joseph Smith Translation, this verse ends, "the same baptizeth, and *he receiveth of all people who* come unto him." (Italics added.)

3:27–36 This inspiring testimony by John the Baptist has been preserved only in the writings of John. In it, John explains somewhat concerning his lesser role as a forerunner of the greater One who is Jesus.

3:29 In this symbolism, Jesus would be the Bridegroom, the chosen covenant people the bride, and John the "friend of the bridegroom."

3:32 In the Joseph Smith Translation, the last clause reads, "and *but few men* receive his testimony." (Italics added.)

3:33 This verse could have been translated "He that has accepted his witness has put his seal to it that God is true." The Revised Standard Version reads: "he who receives his testimony sets his seal to this, that God is true."

3:34 For he whom God hath sent, speaketh the words of God; for God giveth *him* not the Spirit by measure, *for he dwelleth in him, even the fulness.* (JST; italics added.)

3:36 *And* he *who* believeth on the Son hath everlasting life; and *shall receive of his fulness. But* he *who* believeth not the Son, shall not *receive of his fulness; for* the wrath of God *is upon* him. (JST; italics added.)

4:1–3 For other information relating to Jesus leaving Judea and going to the Galilee, see text and commentaries for Matthew 4:13–16. Read also Mark 1:14; Luke 4:14–15; John 4:43–46.

4:1–2 *When therefore the Pharisees had heard that Jesus made and baptized more disciples than John,*
They sought more diligently some means that they might put him to death; for many received John as a prophet, but they believed not on Jesus.
Now the Lord knew this, though *he* himself baptized not *so many as* his disciples;
For he suffered them for an example, preferring one another. (JST; italics added.)

(See section 1, "Baptism: Jesus practiced.")

These verses prove that Jesus baptized others, and they substantiate similar statements in John 3:22, 26.

The statement that "Jesus made and baptized more disciples than John" should not be interpreted to mean that Jesus baptized more *people* than John. Verse 3 of the Joseph Smith Translation makes it clear that Jesus did not baptize as many people as his disciples, but does not compare his baptisms with the number of baptisms performed by John.

Also, the statement in verse 2 of the Joseph Smith Translation that "many received John as a prophet" should not be interpreted to mean that they accepted him in the full sense; otherwise, they would have accepted Jesus as the Messiah. They accepted John as a prophet in much the same way as many Christians today accept the prophets of old but do not always follow their teachings.

4:4–30 These verses contain the only account of Jesus' visit with a woman of Samaria at Jacob's Well.

4:4 In the Joseph Smith Translation, this verse reads, "And *said unto his disciples, I* must needs go through Samaria." (Italics added.)

4:6 Here we view one of the most human scenes of the Master's whole ministry. The Lord of heaven, who created and controls all things, having made clay his tabernacle, is physically tired, weary, hungry, and thirsty, following his long journey from Judea. He who had power to draw food and drink from the elements, who could have transported himself at will to any location, sought rest and refreshments at Jacob's well. In all things he was subjecting himself to the proper experiences of mortality. (DNTC 1:151.)

4:8 "Meat" means "food." (See text and commentaries for Matt. 6:25–26; Mark 8:8; Luke 9:13; section 1, "Meat.")

4:9 In the Joseph Smith Translation, this verse begins, "*Wherefore he being alone,* the woman of Samaria said unto him . . ." (Italics added.)

Why the Jews had "no dealings with the Samaritans" is explained in the commentaries for Luke 17:11–19. Also, Elder Bruce R. McConkie has written:

> When the Ten Tribes were transported to Assyria more than seven centuries before the Christian Era, Samaria was repeopled by heathen colonists from other Assyrian provinces. These pagan peoples, intermixing somewhat with scattered remnants of Israel, founded the race of despised and hated Samaritans of Jesus' day. As a nation, they claimed Jacob as their father and maintained they were inheritors of the blessings of the chosen seed. Their religion, partially pagan in nature, accepted the Pentateuch, but rejected the prophets and the psalms. In the day of Jesus they were friendly to Herod and Rome, but bitter toward the Jews, a feeling fully reciprocated by their Jewish kindred. (DNTC 1:151.)

4:10 How graphically Jesus uses the simple truths of everyday life to teach the eternal spiritual realities of his gospel! For the thirsty and choking traveler in a desert wilderness to find water, is to find life, to find an escape from agonizing death; similarly, the weary pilgrim traveling through the wilderness of mortality saves himself eternally by drinking from the wells of living water found in the gospel.

Living water is the words of eternal life, the message of salvation, the truths about God and his kingdom; it is the doctrines of the gospel. Those who thirst are invited to come unto Christ and drink. (John 7:37–38.) Where there are prophets of God, there will be found rivers of living water, wells filled with eternal truths, springs bubbling forth their life-giving draughts that save from spiritual death. "Unto him that keepeth my commandments," the Lord says, "I will give the mysteries of my kingdom, and the same shall be in him a well of living water, springing up unto everlasting life." (D&C 63:23.) (DNTC 1:151–52.)

4:13 The Joseph Smith Translation replaces "water" with "well." This seems to be consistent with the "well of water" in verse 14.

4:14 The Greek word translated "well" in this verse is not the same word so translated in verses 11 and 12. A more correct translation is "spring" or "fountain."

4:20 The Samaritan woman was referring to Mount Gerizim when she said, "Our fathers worshipped in this mountain." The Samaritans who live in modern Nablus at the foot of Mount Gerizim still conduct some of their Passover services on this mount. (See BD, "Gerizim.")

4:22 "Ye worship ye know not what" might also be applied to many so-called Christians today who refer to the nature of God as a "mystery."

In the Joseph Smith Translation, the last clause in this verse reads, "*and* salvation is of the Jews." (Italics added.)

> Though in that day most of the Jews were in a state of apostasy, yet they did have the prophetic writings and the psalms, in which the knowledge about God was recorded. They had a reasonable knowledge of the nature and kind of Being Deity is. Further, salvation was to be offered to all men through the Jews, because they were the ones who preserved the scriptures and the recorded truths of salvation; and most importantly, Messiah himself, in whom salvation centers, was a Jew. (DNTC 1:153.)

This verse could have been more literally translated "You worship what you do not know; we worship what we know, because salvation originates with the Jews."

4:24 *For unto such hath God promised his Spirit.* And they *who* worship him, must worship in spirit and in truth. (JST; italics added.)

> What marvels of mischief one mistranslated phrase has done! Jesus never, never, never said, "God is a Spirit," but rather that God had promised his Spirit unto those who worshiped him in Spirit and in truth. Yet, falsely supposing our Lord to be the author of this statement, the whole sectarian world has turned to it, more than any other single passage, to find support for their false creeds.
>
> There is a sense in which it might be said, without impropriety, that God is a Spirit. He is most assuredly not a spirit in the sense in which the creeds speak, in the sense that he is an ethereal nothingness which fills the immensity of space and is everywhere and nowhere in particular present. But when it is remembered that a spirit is a personage, an entity, a living personality whose body is made of more pure and refined substance than the temporal bodies of men; and when it is remembered that such spirits live in pre-existence, come to earth to gain temporary physical bodies, are separated from those bodies by the natural death, with the assurance that eventually body and spirit will be inseparably connected again in resurrected immortality; and when it is remembered, further, that God himself is an exalted, perfected, glorified, resurrected Man; then it might truly be said that God is a spirit. He is a Spirit Personage, a Personage with a body of flesh and bones. (D&C 130:22.) He is a Spirit in the same sense that all men are spirits, and in the sense that all men eventually will have resurrected or spiritual bodies as contrasted with their present natural or mortal bodies. (1 Cor. 15:42–50; D&C 88:25–28.) (DNTC 1:153.)

4:25–26 Unable or unwilling to understand Christ's meaning, the woman sought to terminate the lesson by a remark that probably was to her but casual: "I know that Messias cometh, which is called Christ:

when he is come, he will tell us all things." Then, to her profound amazement, Jesus rejoined with the awe-inspiring declaration: "I that speak unto thee am he." The language was unequivocal, the assertion one that required no elucidation. The woman must regard Him thereafter as either an impostor or the Messiah. She left her pitcher at the well, and hastening to the town told of her experience, saying: "Come, see a man, which told me all things that ever I did: is not this the Christ?" (JTC, p. 175.)

Jesus was his own chief witness; again, and again, and again—both in figurative language known to and understood by his hearers, and in plain, unequivocal utterances as here—he proclaimed himself as the Messiah, the King of Israel, the Son of God, the Redeemer of the world. It is a strange thing that there are people in the world today who accept him as the greatest moral teacher of the ages and yet reject his divine Sonship. How could he be a great moral teacher, if he taught and lived a lie, if he openly proclaimed himself as the Only Begotten in the flesh without in fact being such? (DNTC 1:154.)

(See section 1, "Messiah.")

4:27 The initial statement in this verse could have been translated "Now at this point his disciples arrived."

4:29 The Joseph Smith Translation changes "all things that ever I did" to "all things that I have ever done."

4:31–38 These verses contain the account of Jesus speaking to his disciples about missionary work.

4:31 The Joseph Smith Translation changes "while" to "time."

4:33 "Ought" is printed in italics, indicating that it did not appear in the Greek manuscript used by the King James translators.

4:34 Though weary and hungry Jesus' first concern was to plant the seeds of salvation in the hearts of the approaching multitude. Similarly, those sent forth by him to preach the gospel, who have the spirit of their calling, are so imbued with divine zeal that they scarcely take time to eat or rest as they herald the message of salvation to the world. (DNTC 1:156.)

4:37 "That saying" referred to by Jesus is not found in our present Old Testament. Evidently Paul was also acquainted with the ancient scripture, now unknown, when he wrote: "I have planted, Apollos watered; but God gave the increase." (1 Cor. 3:6.)

4:38 The Joseph Smith Translation changes "other men laboured" to "the prophets have labored." Jesus is indicating to his disciples that they are building on the foundations established by the earlier prophets.

4:39–42 These verses recount Jesus' ministry among the Samaritans.

4:39 In the Joseph Smith Translation, the last clause of this verse reads, "He told me all that *I have ever done*." (Italics added.)

4:42 The irony of the situation is that many of the Samaritans who were hated of the Jews and were not allowed to worship in Jerusalem came to know that Jesus was "indeed the Christ, the Saviour of the world," whereas many of the self-righteous Jews at Jerusalem rejected him and later demanded his crucifixion.

4:43–46 Read text and commentaries for Matthew 4:13–16. Read also Mark 1:14; Luke 4:14–15; John 4:3.

4:46–54 Jesus was still in the vicinity of Cana when he gave the command that the son should be healed, and immediately some twenty miles distant the healing took place. This is a good example that the power of faith is not limited by distance. (See section 1, "Healing.")

4:52 "The hour when he began to amend" could have been translated "the hour in which he began to recover."

4:53 In the Joseph Smith Translation, this verse begins, "So the father knew that *his son was healed* in the same hour . . ."

4:54 This *being* the second miracle *which* Jesus *had done* when he *had* come out of Judea into Galilee. (JST; italics added.)

The Joseph Smith Translation makes it clear that Jesus had not performed only two miracles up to this time. John 2:23–25 mentions miracles performed by Jesus in Jerusalem, and evidently the report of these miracles prompted the nobleman to seek out Jesus and enlist his power.

5:1 John does not make clear exactly which feast was being celebrated by the Jews at this time.

If, according to the traditional view, this was a Passover feast, then the active ministry of Jesus lasted three and a half years; *if,* as some scholars have speculated, it was the Feast of Purim, which takes place about a month before the Passover, then our Lord's ministry was a year less. (DNTC 1:188.)

5:2–16 These verses recount the healing at the pool of Bethesda.

5:2 "Porches" has also been translated "arches," "porticoes," and "colonnades."

5:4 No doubt the pool of Bethesda was a mineral spring whose waters had some curative virtue. But any notion that an angel came down and troubled the waters, so that the first person thereafter entering them would be healed, was pure superstition. Healing miracles are not wrought in any such manner. If we had the account as John originally wrote it, it would probably contain an explanation that the part supposedly played by an angel was merely a superstitious legend comparable to some that have since been devised by some churches of Christendom. (DNTC 1:188.)

(See BD, "Bethesda.")

5:6 The Joseph Smith Translation changes "in that case" to "afflicted."

Seemingly Jesus deliberately sought out a man worthy to be healed so that he might exercise his curative powers on the Sabbath day. The interest and animosity resulting from this Sabbath miracle were such that our Lord gained an attentive, though largely disbelieving congregation of hearers, for what is perhaps his greatest recorded sermon of the relationship of the Father and the Son. (DNTC 1:188.)

5:8 "Bed" has also been translated "mat."

5:9 In the Joseph Smith Translation, the last clause reads, "and it was on the Sabbath day." For other reactions to the healings of Jesus performed on the Sabbath, see text and commentaries for Matthew 12:10–13; Luke 13:10–17; 14:1–6.

The Scribes had elaborated from the command of Moses, a vast array of prohibitions and injunctions, covering the whole of social, individual, and public life, and carried it to the extreme of ridiculous caricature. Lengthened rules were prescribed as to the kinds of knots which might legally be tied on the Sabbath. The camel-driver's knot and the sailor's were unlawful, and it was equally illegal to tie or to loose them. A knot which could be untied with one hand might be undone. A shoe or sandal, a woman's cup, a wine or oil-skin, or a flesh-pot might be tied. A pitcher at a spring might be tied to the body-sash, but not with a cord. . . .

To kindle or extinguish a fire on the Sabbath was a great desecration of the day, nor was even sickness allowed to violate Rabbinical rules. It was forbidden to give an emetic on the Sabbath—to set a broken bone, or put back a dislocated joint, though some Rabbis, more liberal, held that whatever endangered life made the Sabbath law void, "for the commands were given to Israel only that they might live by them." One who was buried under ruins on the Sabbath, might be dug for and taken out, if alive, but, if dead, he was to be left where he was, till the Sabbath was over. (Geike, ch. 38, quoted in JTC, pp. 215–16.)

5:13 The Joseph Smith Translation changes "wist" to "knew."

This verse could have been more literally translated "But the healed man did not know who he [Jesus] was, for Jesus had turned aside, there being a crowd in the place."

5:15–16 The man went and told the rulers who it was that had healed him. This he may have done with a desire to honor and glorify the Giver of his boon; we are not justified in ascribing to him any unworthy purpose, though by his act he was instrumental in augmenting the persecution of his Lord. So intense was the hatred of the priestly faction that the rulers sought a means of putting Jesus to death, under the specious pretense of His being a Sabbath-breaker. We may well ask for what act they could possibly have hoped to convict Him, even under the strictest application of their rules. There was no proscription against speaking on the Sabbath; and Jesus had but spoken to heal. He had not carried the man's bed, nor had He attempted even the lightest physical labor. By their own interpretation of the law they had no case against Him. (JTC, p. 208.)

5:17–24 In these verses, Jesus explains the relationship of the Father and the Son.

5:17 Jesus reaffirmed that God's work must go forth even on the Sabbath. The injunction against work has to do with temporal, earthly pursuits ("ye shall do no *servile* work therein." [Lev. 23:8; italics added]), not to the Lord's work.

5:18 Though the Father is greater than the Son and takes precedence over him, yet the Son is equal with the Father in the sense that the Father has given all things into the hands of the Son, and that the Son has attained all power, all wisdom, all knowledge, all truth, and the fulness of all of the attributes of godliness. (D&C 93:6–26.) In this same sense all men who gain exaltation shall "receive their inheritance and be made equal with" the Father and the Son. (D&C 88:107; 93:27–34.) (DNTC 1:191.)

5:19–20 What did Jesus do? Why; I do the things I saw my Father do when worlds came rolling into existence. My Father worked out his kingdom with fear and trembling, and I must do the same; and when I get my kingdom, I shall present it to my Father, so that he may obtain kingdom upon kingdom, and it will exalt him in glory. He will then take a higher exaltation, and I will take his place, and thereby become exalted myself. So that Jesus treads in the tracks of his Father, and inherits what God did before; and God is thus glorified and exalted in the salvation and exaltation of all his children. It is plain beyond disputation, and you thus learn some of the first principles of the Gospel, about which so much hath been said. (TPJS, pp. 347–48.)

5:19 Jesus is not independent of the Father, is not his rival, and does not act except in conformity with the Father's will. The Son has all power because the Father has bestowed it upon him. So it is with all righteous men; none ever act independent of Deity; rather, their power and authority comes from and is centered in the Almighty. (DNTC 1:192.)

5:20 The "greater things" yet to be shown are such things as the Atonement, including the Resurrection, the Second Coming, and the Judgment.

5:21 "Quickeneth" means "to cause to make alive." It could refer to the life that would come again after either physical or spiritual death.

5:22 The Judgment will be by the will and justice of the Father but under the direction of the Son.

5:25–30 These informative, but to some people confusing, statements of Jesus concerning his future work among the dead are found only in John. However, additional information may be obtained by reading Isaiah 24:22; 42:7; 61:1; 1 Peter 3:18–21; 4:6; D&C 138; Moses 7:37–39; Abraham 2:10–11. These are all consistent with the teaching of Jesus that "God is not the God of the dead, but of the living." (Matt. 22:32.)

5:25 "They that hear shall live" could also have been translated "those who will give heed will live." 1 Peter 4:6 indicates that when the dead have the gospel preached to them they will "be judged according to men in the flesh, but live according to God in the spirit."

5:26 As an immortal, exalted, and resurrected being—one whose body and spirit are inseparably connected, one who cannot die—the Father has life in himself, life that is unending, eternal, everlasting. In him the power to live forever dwells independently. Because Jesus is literally his son, his offspring, the fruit of his body, he has inherited from his Father the power of immortality, the power to live forever, the power to unite body and spirit again in a resurrected state, he having voluntarily permitted them to be separated as an essential part of working out the infinite and eternal atonement. (DNTC 1:194–95.)

5:28–29 Jesus said that *all* "that are in the graves shall hear his voice and shall come forth." Thus, the gospel will be preached to *everyone* in the spirit world. Also, *everyone* will be resurrected from the dead. As Paul later recorded, "As in Adam all die, even so in Christ shall all be made alive." (1 Cor. 15:22.) Even the sons of perdition will come forth in the resurrection.

This enunciation of the resurrection, so plainly made that the most unlettered could understand, must have offended any Sadducees present, for they emphatically denied the actuality of the resurrection. The universality of a resurrection is here unquestionably affirmed; not only the righteous but even those who merit condemnation are to come forth from their graves in their bodies of flesh and bones. (JTC, p. 210.)

While working on the translation of the Bible, Joseph Smith and Sidney Rigdon were meditating upon verse 29 when they received the vision of the three degrees of glory that was later recorded as the seventy-sixth section of the Doctrine and Covenants.

5:29–30 The Joseph Smith Translation gives these two verses as follows:

And shall come forth; they *who* have done good, *in* the resurrection of *the just;* and they *who* have done evil, *in* the resurrection of *the unjust.*

And shall all be judged of the Son of Man. For as I hear, I judge, and my judgment is just;

For I can of mine own self do nothing; because I seek not *my* own will, but the will of the Father *who* hath sent me. (Italics added.)

Resurrection of life, the first resurrection. Those coming forth in the morning of this resurrection do so with celestial bodies and shall inherit a celestial glory; these are they who are Christ's the firstfruits. Those coming forth in the afternoon of this resurrection do so with terrestrial bodies and consequently shall inherit that kingdom; they are described as being Christ's at this coming. All who have been resurrected so far have received celestial bodies; the coming forth of terrestrial beings does not commence until after the Second Coming. (D&C 76:50–80; 88:95–99.)

Resurrection of damnation, the second resurrection. In this day of sorrow and remorse the bodies and spirits of the rest of mankind will be inseparably connected in immortality. At the end of the millennium, and in the morning of this second resurrection, those shall come forth who merit telestial bodies, and they shall be rewarded accordingly. Finally, in the afternoon of the second resurrection, those who "remain filthy still," those who having been raised in immortality are judged and found wholly wanting, those whom we call sons of perditions, shall be cast out with Lucifer and his angels to suffer the vengeance of eternal fire forever. (D&C 76:25–49, 81–113; 88:101–102; 2 Ne. 9:14–16.) (DNTC 1:196–97.)

5:30 Independent action on the part of the Son is impossible; his power comes from the Father, according to the laws ordained by the Father. The Son has become and is a god because of obedience to the laws of the Father, and he is now so completely one with the Father that everything he thinks, says, and does is precisely what the Father would do under the same circumstances. . . .

That judgment which grows out of the fact of resurrection will be automatic, meaning that it will operate according to law, and all men will receive exactly what they merit, neither adding to nor diminishing from. Power of judgment will rest with the Son, but he will exercise it in accordance with the laws ordained by the Father; hence, "my judgment is just." (DNTC 1:197.)

5:31–38 These verses contain Jesus' teachings about witnesses.

5:31 *Therefore* if I bear witness of myself, *yet* my witness is true. (JST; italics added.)

This verse could have been more literally translated "If I alone bear witness about myself, my witness is not true."

If Jesus was the only witness of his Messiahship, then, according to the law of witnesses (see 2 Cor. 13:1), his hearers were not required to accept it. However, as indicated in the next verse, he has other witnesses of his divinity.

5:32 *For I am not alone,* there is another *who* beareth witness of me, and I know that the *testimony* which he *giveth* of me is true. (JST; italics added.)

5:34 *And he received* not *his* testimony *of* man, but *of God, and ye yourselves say that he is a prophet, therefore ye ought to receive his testi-mony.* These things I say that ye might be saved. (JST; italics added.)

5:36 In the Joseph Smith Translation, this verse begins, "But I have a greater witness than *the testimony* of John . . ." (Italics added.)

Who bears testimony that Jesus is indeed the Christ?

(1) Jesus himself, repeatedly, bluntly, plainly, over and over again testi-fied of his own divine Sonship;

(2) His Father by his own voice out of heaven, by personally coming to earth to introduce the Son, and by sending the Holy Ghost to speak to the spirits of the contrite;

(3) The Holy Ghost, the Spirit member of the Godhead, whose mission is to bear record of the Father and the Son;

(4) The works performed by Jesus in his mortal ministry, including his miracles, teachings, resurrection, and atoning sacrifice which made immor-tality and eternal life a reality;

(5) Prophets and apostles of all ages—Moses, John, Peter, Nephi, Joseph Smith, the elders of Israel, a great host which no man can number; and

(6) The scriptures and recorded revelations of the past and present. (DNTC 1:198–99.)

5:37 In the Joseph Smith Translation, the last sentence of this verse reads, "*And verily I testify unto you,* that ye have never heard his voice at any time, nor seen his shape." (Italics added.)

Here Jesus clearly witnesses that his Father has shape, contrary to many dogmas of modern Christianity, which declare that God is "without body, parts, or passions."

5:38 This verse could have been more literally translated "And you do not have his word remaining in you, because the very one whom he dispatched you do not believe."

The Joseph Smith Translation begins this verse with "for" rather than "and."

5:39 Elsewhere Jesus had indicated that the fullness of the scriptures constituted the key to knowledge. (See text and commentaries for Luke 11:53.) Here, as in other places, he instructed a careful and diligent search of the scriptures. (See also text and commentaries for Matt. 24:30–31.)

Since we cannot "live by [the words which] proceedeth forth from the mouth of God" unless we know what they are, it is imperative that we study them. This the Lord has directed us to do.

As the Jews disputed with Jesus because he said that God was his Father, he pointedly responded: "Search the scriptures; for in them ye think ye have eternal life: and they are they which testify of me." (John 5:39.)

In the Lord's preface to his Book of Commandments, he said: "Search these commandments, for they are true and faithful, and the prophecies and promises which are in them shall all be fulfilled." (D&C 1:37.)

We are under divine instruction to "teach the principles of [the] gospel, which are in the Bible and the Book of Mormon." (D&C 42:12.) This we cannot do unless we know what they are. (Marion G. Romney, CR, Apr. 1973, p. 117.)

5:40–47 These verses contain Jesus' teachings about honoring the Father and the Son.

5:40 And ye will not come to me that ye might have life, *lest ye should honour me*. (JST; italics added.)

What petty jealousies keep men from receiving gospel blessings! They will not accept the prophets sent of God, lest in doing so they thereby certify to the greatness and honor of the prophet-servant sent to minister to them. They reject the Son himself, lest in hearkening to his voice, they should honor him in the eyes of the people. What does it detract from one person because another is honored? Rightly viewed, is there not enough honor and to spare in God's kingdom for all who will receive it? (DNTC 1:201.)

5:41 No honor that man could bestow upon Jesus, "the Creator of the heavens and the earth and all things which in them are" could possibly add to the honor he already has and the honor he shares with the Father. Yet all we need do to share that honor is to keep their commandments, which we will do if we truly love God and our neighbors.

5:44 This verse could have been more literally translated "How can you believe, when you are accepting glory from one another and you are not seeking the glory that is from the only God?"

In the Joseph Smith Translation, this verse begins, "How can ye believe, who *seek* honor one of another . . ." (Italics added.)

5:45 In the Joseph Smith Translation, this verse ends, "there is Moses who accuseth you, in whom ye trust."

5:46–47 The same concepts are taught by Nephi in the Book of Mormon: "Believe in Christ and deny him not, for by denying him ye also deny the prophets and the law." (2 Ne. 25:28.)

6:1–14 Read text and commentaries for Matthew 14:13–21; Mark 6:30–44; Luke 9:10–17.

6:1 In this one verse the same body of water is referred to as "the sea of Galilee" and "sea of Tiberias." It is also called "the lake of Gennesaret." (Luke 5:1.)

6:5–14 As to the miracle itself, human knowledge is powerless to explain. Though wrought on so great a scale, it is no more nor less inexplicable than any other of the Lord's miraculous works. It was a manifestation of creative power, by which material elements were organized and compounded to serve a present and pressing need. The broken but unused portion exceeded in bulk and weight the whole of the original little store. Our Lord's direction to gather up the fragments was an impressive object-lesson against waste; and it may have been to afford such lesson that an excess was supplied. The fare was simple, yet nourishing, wholesome and satisfying. Barley bread and fish constituted the usual food of the poorer classes of the region. The conversion of water into wine at Cana was a qualitative transmutation; the feeding of the multitude involved a quantitative increase; who can say that one, or which, of these miracles of provision was the more wonderful? (JTC, pp. 334–35.)

(See section 1, "Miracles: Fed 5,000"; BD, "Barley.")

6:12 In the Joseph Smith Translation, this verse begins, "When they *had eaten and were satisfied . . .*" (Italics added.)

Elder Bruce R. McConkie has commented on the statement "Gather up the fragments that remain, that nothing be lost":

An object lesson in economy and the wise use of the temporal bounties so graciously bestowed by an omnipotent Deity. True the Incarnate Creator had but to speak and food and all needful things would be immediately at hand. But waste is sin. And his grace and compassion having been manifest, now the Twelve must make wise use of the excess food he had provided. (DNTC 1:345.)

6:15 Many of the Jews of Jesus' time were caught up in a feverish expectation for an imminent appearance of their longawaited Messiah. The oppressive hand of Roman domination grew heavier day by day. It was only natural, therefore, that they thought they saw in Jesus the fulfillment of their earthly hopes and dreams. Did he not possess miraculous powers? Had he not changed ordinary water into wine, raised the dead, healed the sick, and turned a few loaves of bread and fish into sufficient food to feed more than five thousand people? Could he not turn those same powers against Rome and free the Jews from foreign subjugation?

"The multitude, now fed and filled, gave some consideration to the miracle. In Jesus, by whom so great a work had been wrought, they recognized One having superhuman powers. 'This is of a truth the prophet that should come into the world,' said they—the Prophet whose coming had been foretold by Moses and who should be like unto himself. Even as Israel had been miraculously fed during the time of Moses, so now was bread provided in the desert by this new Prophet. In their enthusiasm the people proposed to proclaim Him king, and forcibly compel Him to become their leader. Such was their gross conception of Messianic supremacy." (Talmage, *Jesus the Christ,* p. 335.) (LTJA, p. 90.)

6:16–21 Read text and commentaries for Matthew 14:22–23; Mark 6:45–52.

6:18 This verse could have been translated "Also, the sea began to be stirred up because a strong wind was blowing."

6:19 A furlong ("furrow long") is one hundred and twenty paces, or about one-eighth of a mile. Thus, the distance of "about five and twenty or thirty furlongs" would be approximately three and a half miles.

6:22–27 Other texts and commentaries concerned with the period immediately following the experience of Jesus walking on the waters of the sea of Galilee are Matthew 14:34–36 and Mark 6:53–56.

6:25 In the Joseph Smith Translation, this verse ends, "Rabbi, *how* camest thou hither?" (Italics added.)

The word *rabbi* which literally means "my great one," was a term of highest respect among the ancient Jews. The local rabbi in any given village was one of the most educated men in the area, generally a graduate of a recognized rabbinical school, and one designated to teach the people. Jesus' followers appear to have felt that he was such a graduate, likely because he showed so much learning. A rabbi literally devoted himself to serving the common people by teaching them in their synagogues, by administering to their wants and needs by charitable means, and by continuing study and application of the law of Moses (Torah) as he understood it. (LTJA, p. 90.)

(See section 1, "Rabbi.")

6:26–27 The ending of Jesus' answer reads as follows in the Joseph Smith Translation: "Ye seek me, not because ye *desire to keep my sayings, neither* because ye saw the miracles, but because ye did eat of the loaves and were filled. Labor not for that meat which perisheth, but for that meat which endureth unto everlasting life, which the Son of *Man hath power to* give unto you; for him hath God the Father sealed." (Italics added.)

"For him hath God the Father sealed" could have been translated "for upon this One the Father, even God, has put his seal [of approval]."

6:28–59 This masterful discourse on the Bread of Life is contained only in the account of John. Jesus, who pronounced himself as the "Bread of Life," was born in Bethlehem, the name of which in Hebrew means "House of Bread."

Elder James E. Talmage has shown the relationship of this sermon to the dialogue that immediately preceded it:

> The Master's rebuke was followed by admonition and instruction: "Labour not for the meat which perisheth, but for the meat which endureth unto everlasting life, which the Son of man shall give unto you: for him hath God the Father sealed." This contrast between material and spiritual food they could not entirely fail to understand, and some of them asked what they should do to serve God, as Jesus required. The answer was: "This is the work of God, that ye believe on him whom he hath sent." That Jesus was referring to Himself none could doubt; and straightway they demanded of Him further evidence of His divine commission; they would see greater signs. The miracle of the loaves and fishes was nearly a day old; and its impressiveness as evidence of Messianic attributes was waning. Moses had fed their fathers with manna in the desert, they said; and plainly they regarded a continued daily supply as a greater gift than a single meal of bread and fish, however much the latter may have been appreciated in the exigency of hunger. Moreover, the manna was heavenly food; whereas the bread He had given them was of earth, and only common barley bread at that. He must show them greater signs, and give them richer provender, before they would accept Him as the One whom they at first had taken Him to be and whom He now declared Himself to be. (JTC, pp. 339–40.)

6:30–31 These verses have been paraphrased by Elder Bruce R. McConkie:

> They said therefore unto him, We cannot accept your claim of divine Sonship unless you show us some great sign. True, you fed five thousand and more of us yesterday near Bethsaida with five loaves and two fishes, but surely you won't claim that as proof of the exalted claim to divinity which you now make. Why Moses, who was a man and not a god, fed millions of our fathers daily for forty years with manna from heaven. His miracle far exceeded yours of yesterday. Surely, if you are the Son of God, as you say, you will do some great work so we may believe on thee. Yea, we challenge your claim of divinity by asking, What miraculous work dost thou do? (DNTC 1:353.)

(See BD, "Manna.")

6:37 "I will in no wise cast out" means "I will by no means drive away."

6:40 In the Joseph Smith Translation, this verse ends, "and I will raise him up *in the resurrection of the just* at the last day." (Italics added.) Elder Bruce R. McConkie has paraphrased this verse:

And this also is the will of the Father who sent me, that everyone who receiveth me as the Son of God, and who believeth that I am the Christ, and who obeyeth the laws and ordinances of my gospel, enduring in righteousness to the end, shall have everlasting life; yea, it is his will that all such shall come forth in the resurrection of the just, raised in immortality and unto eternal life. (DNTC 1:354.)

6:44 No man can come *unto* me, except *he doeth the will of my* Father *who* hath sent me. *And this is the will of him who hath sent me, that he receive the Son; for the Father beareth record of him; and he who receiveth the testimony, and doeth the will of him who sent me,* I will raise up *in the resurrection of the just.* (JST; italics added.)

6:48–51 Elder Bruce R. McConkie has paraphrased these verses to provide background for the rest of this sermon:

I am the bread of everlasting life, even that spiritual bread of which men must eat to gain everlasting life. This spiritual bread is that which cometh down from heaven, that a man may eat thereof and not die spiritually, which spiritual death is to be cast out of the presence of the Lord and to die as pertaining to things of righteousness. True, your fathers did eat manna in the wilderness, but they are dead, for this manna satisfied their temporal hunger only; it was not that spiritual bread of which men may eat and gain spiritual or eternal life. But I am the living bread, even the Son of God who came down from the Father in heaven. If any man shall eat of this spiritual bread, he shall live forever in that, being born again, he shall be spiritually alive in this world and inherit eternal life, which is spiritual life in the presence of the Father, in the world to come. And to eat the living bread is to accept me as the Son of God and to obey my commandments. And this living bread, which I shall give unto all who believe in me and obey my law, is my own flesh, in that it shall be because of my atoning sacrifice and temporal death that men shall have power to eat of the living bread and gain eternal life. Therefore say I unto you, I will give my flesh for the life of the world. (DNTC 1:356–57.)

6:52–58 There was little excuse for the Jews pretending to understand that our Lord meant an actual eating and drinking of His material flesh and blood. The utterances to which they objected were far more readily understood by them than they are by us on first reading; for the representation of the law and of truth in general as bread, and the acceptance thereof as a process of eating and drinking, were figures in everyday use by the rabbis of that time. Their failure to comprehend the symbolism of Christ's doctrine was an act of will, not the natural consequence of innocent ignorance. To eat the flesh and drink the blood of Christ was and is to believe in and accept Him as the literal Son of God and Savior of the world, and to obey His commandments. By these means only may the Spirit of God become an abiding part of man's individual being, even as the substance of the food he eats is assimilated with the tissues of his body.

It is not sufficing to accept the precepts of Christ as we may adopt the doctrines of scientists, philosophers, and savants, however great the wisdom of these sages may be; for such acceptance is by mental assent or deliberate exercise of will, and has relation to the doctrine only as independent of the author. The teachings of Jesus Christ endure because of their intrinsic worth; and many men respect His aphorisms, proverbs, parables, and His profoundly philosophical precepts, who yet reject Him as the Son of God, the Only Begotten in the flesh, the God-Man in whom were united the attributes of Deity with those of humanity, the chosen and foreordained Redeemer of mankind, through whom alone may salvation be attained. But the figure used by Jesus—that of eating His flesh and drinking His blood as typical of unqualified and absolute acceptance of Himself as the Savior of men, is of superlative import; for thereby are affirmed the divinity of His Person, and the fact of His preexistent and eternal Godship. The sacrament of the Lord's supper, established by the Savior on the night of His betrayal, perpetuates the symbolism of eating His flesh and drinking His blood, by the partaking of bread and wine in remembrance of Him. Acceptance of Jesus as the Christ implies obedience to the laws and ordinances of His gospel; for to profess the One and refuse the other is but to convict ourselves of inconsistency, insincerity, and hypocrisy. (JTC, pp. 342–43.)

6:52 "The Jews therefore strove among themselves" means "Therefore the Jews began contending with one another."

6:53–54 In the Joseph Smith Translation, the end of verse 54 reads, "I will raise him up *in the resurrection of the just* at the last day." (Italics added.)

> In substance and effect Jesus then said to the Jews:
> "Solemnly and soberly I say unto you, Except ye eat the flesh of the Son of God, and drink his blood, by accepting me and my mission and obeying my gospel, ye have no spiritual life in you, but rather are spiritually dead and are not born again.
> "Whoso eateth my flesh, and drinketh my blood—by accepting me, keeping my commandments, and enduring unto the end—shall have eternal life; and I will raise him up in the resurrection of the just to an inheritance of exaltation in my Father's kingdom." (DNTC 1:359.)

In these words about eating his flesh and drinking his blood, Jesus reaches the climax of his great discourse on the Bread of Life. Since he is the Bread of Life (meaning the Son of God), which came down from the Father, and since men must eat this spiritual bread in order to gain salvation, it follows that eternal life is gained only by eating the flesh and drinking the blood of the Son of God, or in other words, eternal life is gained only by accepting Jesus as the Christ and keeping his commandments.

To eat the flesh and drink the blood of the Son of God is, first, to accept him in the most literal and full sense, with no reservation whatever, as the personal offspring in the flesh of the Eternal Father; and, secondly, it is to keep the commandments of the Son by accepting his gospel, joining his Church, and enduring in obedience and righteousness unto the end. Those who by this course eat his flesh and drink his blood shall have eternal life, meaning exaltation in the highest heaven of the celestial world. Speaking of ancient Israel, for instance, Paul says: They *"did all eat the same spiritual meat; And did all drink the same spiritual drink: for they drank of that spiritual Rock that followed them: and that Rock was Christ."* (1 Cor. 10:3–4.) (DNTC 1:358.)

6:60–65 Why did Jesus select this particular time to stress a teaching many of "his disciples" felt was "an hard saying"?

By the simple expedient of teaching strong doctrine to the hosts who followed him, Jesus was able to separate the chaff from the wheat and choose out those who were worthy of membership in his earthly kingdom. Before entering the synagogue in Capernaum to preach his great discourse on the Bread of Life, Jesus was at the height of his popularity. Great multitudes of the common people followed him gladly; more than five thousand sympathizers had just sought to take him by force and make him king. For some two and a half years he had traveled, preached, and taught throughout all Palestine. At his command disciples had gone forth teaching his doctrine and testifying that he was the promised Messiah. All men knew of his message and miracles; his doctrine was discussed in every synagogue; his gospel was heralded from the housetops. The seeds, so profusely planted, had sprouted and grown; and now the time had arrived to begin to separate the chaff from the wheat, to test the faith of his disciples, to learn who, following him at all hazards, were worthy of him. Unable to believe and accept his strong and plain assertions about eating his flesh and drinking his blood, even many classified as disciples fell away. And this process of sifting, trial, and testing was to continue with increasing intensity for the final climactic year of his mortal ministry.

This testing and shifting process has ever been part of the Lord's system. Man have been placed on earth to be tried and tested, "to see if they will do all things whatsoever the Lord their God shall command them." (Abra. 3:25.) After they accept the gospel and join the Church, this testing process continues, indeed, is often intensified. "I have decreed in my heart, saith the Lord, that I will prove you in all things, whether you will abide in my covenant, even unto death, that you may be found worthy. For if ye will not abide in my covenant ye are not worthy of me." (D&C 98:14–15.) (DNTC 1:361–62.)

6:65 And he said, Therefore said I unto you, that no man can come unto me, except *he doeth the will of* my Father *who hath sent me.* (JST; italics added.)

6:66–71 [The sermon on the Bread of Life as recorded by John] is highly spiritual, and contains references about Christ as the "Bread of

Life," *which His followers could not believe.* They could not comprehend what He was saying, and many of them walked away. . . . The twelve . . . slightly glimpsed the spiritual significance of that sermon. . . . Those apostles had that day the power and privilege of making a choice—*whether they would walk with those who were impressed only with the physical favors, advantages, which nature could give, or whether their gifts [would] heed to the spiritual in man. . . .* Such a decision may determine whether one responds to the call of one's soul to rise, or yields to the tendency to grovel . . . The disciples of Jesus glimpsed a light that would enlighten their souls spiritually as the sun replaces darkness with beams of light. But *there are few persons who see that Light* or even believe in the fuller life, and *often after glimpsing it, they turn away to the grosser and more sordid* things. (David O. McKay, "Whither Shall We Go?" *Speeches of the Year,* 1961, pp. 2–4; italics added.)

7:1 "In Jewry" actually reads in the Greek text "in Judea" and is so worded in most modern translations.

7:2–9 Read text and commentary for Matthew 12:46–50.

A testimony of the divinity of Christ and of the saving power of his gospel is not bestowed automatically because of family relationship. It comes only by personal obedience to those eternal laws upon which its receipt is predicted. In nearly all ages there have been prophets and righteous men whose sons and daughters have forsaken the faith of their fathers and have chosen to walk after the manner of the world.

Frequent special reference is made to the sons of Joseph and Mary as the "brethren" of Jesus, though in fact they were his half brothers. (Matt. 12:46; 13:55; John 2:12; Acts 1:14; 1 Cor. 9:5.) Though they were reared in the same household and came under the benign influence of Joseph and Mary, though they were aware of the teachings, ministry, and miracles of Jesus himself, yet these his close relatives had not so far accepted him as the Messiah. However, all of them, apparently, were converted later (Acts 1:14); one of them, identified by Paul as "James the Lord's brother" (Gal. 1:19), was to minister in the holy apostleship; and yet another, Judas, who calls himself, "Jude, the . . . brother of James" (Jude 1), wrote the epistle of Jude. (DNTC 1:437.)

(See section 1, "Brethren of the Lord.")

7:3 The Joseph Smith Translation inserts "there" so that the verse ends "that thy disciples *there* also may see the works that thou doest." (Italics added.)

7:8 By stating that he was not going to the feast *yet,* Jesus indicated that he indeed intended to go later but at a time and under conditions of his own choosing. Thus he "abode still" (remained) in Galilee for a while longer. In the Joseph Smith Translation, verse 9 ends, "He *continued* still in Galilee." (Italics added.)

7:10 (Read Luke 9:51–56.) In the Joseph Smith Translation, this verse begins, "But *after* his brethren were gone up . . ." (Italics added.)

Students of the New Testament have disagreed concerning the meaning of "as it were in secret." Some believe this means Jesus made the trip alone; others say he went only with his chosen twelve disciples; still others believe that he avoided going with one of the large caravans of people who would be going to Jerusalem for the Feast of Tabernacles. Also, he may have gone by a route that was not commonly traveled.

7:11–13 Apparently the hatred and persecution of Jesus was so great that even some of his closest disciples were afraid to speak "openly of him."

7:13 Today's English Version translates this verse "But no one talked about him openly, because they were afraid of the Jewish authorities."

7:14–24 The first part of His discourse is not recorded, but its scriptural soundness is intimated in the surprise of the Jewish teachers, who asked among themselves: "How knoweth this man letters, having never learned?" He was no graduate of their schools; He had never sat at the feet of their rabbis; He had not been officially accredited by them nor licensed to teach. Whence came His wisdom, before which all their academic attainments were as nothing? Jesus answered their troubled queries, saying: "My doctrine is not mine, but his that sent me. If any man will do his will, he shall know of the doctrine, whether it be of God, or whether I speak of myself." His Teacher, greater even than Himself, was the Eternal Father, whose will He proclaimed. The test proposed to determine the truth of His doctrine was in every way fair, and withal simple; anyone who would earnestly seek to do the will of the Father should know of himself whether Jesus spoke truth or error. (JTC, p. 400.)

7:16 The Father, not the Son, is the Author of the plan of salvation. This plan embodies the Father's doctrine, the Father's laws, the Father's gospel. He ordained and announced the whole plan of creation, redemption, salvation, and exaltation, and he chose one of his spirit offspring to be born into the world as his Son to work out the infinite and eternal atonement— all in accordance with his will. The laws which must be obeyed to gain salvation are spoken of as the gospel of Jesus Christ because our Lord himself conformed to them perfectly, adopted them as his own, taught them in the power of his Father, and worked out the atoning sacrifice, by means of which they gained full force and validity. (DNTC 1:441–42.)

7:17 In searching the record as it is given to us by men who associated daily with the Lord, we find that upon one occasion men who were listening to him cried out against him. They opposed his works, as men today oppose him. And one voice cried out and said in effect, "How do we know that what you tell us is true? How do we know that your profession of being the Son of God is true." And Jesus answered him in just a simple way (and note the test): *"If any man will do* his will, he shall know of the doctrine, whether it be *of God, or whether I speak of myself."* (John 7:17. Italics added.)

That test is most sound. It is most philosophical. It is the most simple test to give knowledge to an individual of which the human mind can conceive. *Doing* a thing, *introducing it into your very being,* will convince you whether it is good or whether it is bad. You may not be able to convince me of that which you know, but *you know it because you have lived it.* That is the test that the Savior gave to those men when they asked him how they should know whether the doctrine was of God or whether it was of man. (David O. McKay, CR, Oct. 1966, p. 136.)

7:22–23 In referring to the fact that the Jews were permitted to circumcise on the Sabbath day but not to do any healings, Jesus emphasized that their traditions had become more important and binding to them than the scriptures ("the law of Moses").

This colloquy between Jesus and his detractors is a perfect illustration of the damning power of false doctrine. Here we find an account of the Jews rejecting their Messiah, spurning his gospel, and even conspiring to slay him—all because his ministerial acts ran counter to their false traditions. They had circumscribed the law of sabbath observance with a host of ritualistic restrictions; Jesus violated these; therefore, he could not be the Messiah.

Nor is it any different with professing religionists today. Their false traditions say that revelation and prophecy ceased with the death of the ancient apostles; Joseph Smith comes among them wearing the prophetic mantle, thus running counter to all their preconceived notions; therefore, he could not be a prophet. (DNTC 1:442.)

7:24 Judge not according to *your traditions,* but judge righteous judgment. (JST; italics added.)

7:25–31 These verses contain the people's reactions to Jesus' teachings.

7:27 The following footnote on this verse is contained in the Jerusalem Bible: "Although the prophecy that the Messiah would be born in Bethlehem was well known, it was commonly believed that he would appear suddenly from some secret place."

7:30 That some leaders of the Jews "sought to take" Jesus as soon as he had finished his statement indicates that they clearly understood that he had claimed to be the Son of God; thus, they were ready to bring him to trial for blasphemy. However, "his hour was not yet come."

7:32–39 The unrepentant Jews would not be able to follow Jesus when he returned to his Father because no unclean thing can enter there. In John 14:1–3 he tells his faithful followers, "Where I am, there ye may be also."

7:37–39 In the majesty of his own eternal might, the Lord Jehovah had proclaimed to ancient Israel: "I will pour water upon him that is thirsty, and floods upon the dry ground: I will pour my spirit upon thy seed, and my blessing upon thine offspring." (Isa. 44:3.) "Ho, every one that thirsteth, come ye to the waters." (Isa. 55:1.)

Now the same Eternal One, tabernacled in the flesh, ministering as the Lord Jesus unto the seed and offspring of them of old, proclaimed his willingness to give the Holy Ghost to men so that floods of living water might be poured out upon them. His solemn invitation, "If any man thirst, let him come unto me, and drink," was a plain and open claim of Messiahship. In making it he identified himself as the very Jehovah who had promised drink to the thirsty through an outpouring of the Spirit. After such a pronouncement his hearers were faced with two choices: Either he was a blasphemer worthy of death, or he was in fact the God of Israel.

For the publicizing of such a sobering and transcendent doctrine Jesus chose one of the most solemn and dramatic moments of Jewish worship. On each of the eight days of the feast of Tabernacles, as most authorities agree, it was the custom, for the priest as part of the temple service, to take water in golden vessels from the stream of Siloam, which flowed under the temple-mountain, and pour it upon the altar. Then the words of Isaiah were sung: "With joy shall ye draw water out of the wells of salvation." (Isa. 12:3.) And it was at this very moment of religious climax that Jesus stepped forth and offered draughts of living refreshment which would satisfy the deepest spiritual cravings of the thirsty soul. (DNTC 1:445–46.)

7:38 "Out of his belly shall flow rivers of living water" is not found in the Old Testament, although Isaiah wrote, "I will pour water upon him that is thirsty. . . . . I will pour my spirit upon thy seed." (Isa. 44:3; see also 55:1; 58:11.) If "out of his belly" means "out of his inner heart" or "out of his inmost soul," then verse 39 might indicate that the gift of the Holy Ghost, given to true believers who are baptized, could be the "rivers of living water" that flow to others.

7:39 (But this spake he of the Spirit, which they that believe on him should receive; for the Holy Ghost was *promised unto them who believe, after that* Jesus was glorified.) (JST; italics added.)

In this instance John is explaining two things about the Holy Ghost: (1) That it is by the power of the Holy Ghost that rivers of living water flow forth from the true disciples to all who will drink of them; and (2) That the actual enjoyment of the gift of the Holy Ghost by the disciples is yet future; the promise has been made that they shall have the coveted companionship; but the fulfilment of the promise is not to be realized until after Jesus returns to the Father in resurrected glory. The fact that the enjoyment of the gift or companionship of the Holy Ghost was yet future did not mean that the disciples had not on occasions and from time to time received revelation and guidance from that member of the Godhead. The testimonies previously borne by them were born of the Spirit. (See Matt. 16:17.) (DNTC 1:447.)

(See section 1, "Holy Ghost.")

7:40–44 This "division among the people" brought forth the revealing comments that the people knew the Christ would come "of the seed of David" and "out of the town of Bethlehem." (See text and commentaries for Matthew 12:23; 22:41–46; Luke 1:32; 2:4.) The major question remaining was "Shall Christ come out of Galilee?" Isaiah had foretold that "the land of Zebulun and the land of Naphtali" would receive a special blessing (Isa. 9:1), and Matthew felt that when Jesus moved into the Galilee this fulfilled Isaiah's words. (See text and commentaries for Matt. 4:13–16.)

One wonders—in the midst of all the miracles and inquiry into his claimed Messiahship—why these religionists did not search out the fact that our Lord was both a Galilean and a Judean, that he came both from Nazareth and Bethlehem. But such a failure to investigate and learn the facts is ever the child of prejudice. In a similar sense one wonders why professing modern Christians—seeing the fruits of the ministry of Joseph Smith—do not make attentive and intelligent inquiry into the claims surrounding his divine mission. (DNTC 1:448–49.)

7:40–41 The distinction between "The Prophet" (v. 40) and "the Christ" indicates that the people believed they were to be two separate persons:

One of the great Messianic prophecies foretold that when Christ was raised up, he would come as a prophet like unto Moses. (Deut. 18:15–19; Acts 3:22–23; Jos. Smith 2:40; 3 Ne. 20:23.) *The Prophet* was to be *the Christ*. But in their darkened spiritual state some of the Jews attending the feast had come to view this prophet as a forerunner of the Messiah rather than as the Messiah himself. (DNTC 1:448.)

7:45–53 Even though "the officers" of the chief priests and Pharisees were duly impressed with the teachings of Jesus ("Never man spake like this man"), this did not keep them from seeking judgment against him. Only Nicodemus appears to have spoken in his favor.

Concerning the question put by Nicodemus ("Doth our law judge any man, before it hear him, and know what he doeth?"), Elder Bruce R. McConkie, trained in the law himself, has observed:

How right Nicodemus was, as his fellow Sanhedrinists well knew, for their whole system of jurisprudence was built around the revealed injunctions: (1) That men should not raise a false report, nor join with the wicked as unrighteous witnesses (Ex. 23:1); (2) That the judges in Israel were to hear the causes of the people before deciding them, and then they were to judge righteously (Deut. 1:16); (3) That issues could be decided only upon the prior, formal testimony of two or three competent witnesses. (Deut. 19:15.) (DNTC 1:449.)

8:1–11 The account of the woman caught in adultery is recorded only by John.

8:3 In the Joseph Smith Translation, this verse ends, "in the midst *of the people*." (Italics added.)

8:5 Old Testament scriptures that mention death by stoning as the penalty for betrothed or married persons guilty of adultery include Exodus 20:14; Leviticus 20:10; Deuteronomy 13:9–10; 17:2–7; 22:13–22; Ezekiel 16:35–43. The law also prescribed that the two or more official witnesses whose testimony resulted in the conviction were to cast the first stones. (Deut. 13:9; 17:7; see also BD, "Adultery.")

8:6 "Tempting" has also been translated as "trap" and as "test."

Elder Bruce R. McConkie has explained how the scribes and the Pharisees were "tempting" Jesus:

In bringing this adulteress to Jesus, the scribes and Pharisees were laying this trap for the Master: (1) If he *agreed* with Moses that she should be stoned, he would both (a) arouse the ire of the people generally by seeming to advocate the reinstitution of a penalty which did not have popular support, and (b) run counter to the prevailing civil law by prescribing what Rome proscribed. (2) If he *disagreed* with Moses and advocated anything less than death by stoning, he would be accused of perverting the law, and of advocating disrespect of and departure from the hallowed practices of the past. (DNTC 1:450–51.)

8:9–11 And they which heard it, being convicted by their own conscience, went out one by one, beginning at the eldest, even unto the last; and Jesus was left alone, and the woman standing in the midst *of the temple*.

When Jesus had *raised* up himself, and saw none *of her accusers, and* the woman *standing,* he said unto her, Woman, where are those thine accusers? hath no man condemned thee?

She said, No man, Lord. And Jesus said unto her, Neither do I condemn thee; go, and sin no more. *And the woman glorified God from that hour, and believed on his name.* (JST; italics added.)

"Neither do I condemn thee" should not be construed to mean that the woman was completely pardoned or forgiven:

Did the Lord forgive the woman? Could he forgive her? There seems to be no evidence of forgiveness. His command to her was, "Go, and sin no more." He was directing the sinful woman to go her way, *abandon her evil life, commit no more sin, transform her life.* He was saying, Go, woman, and start your repentance; and he was indicating to her the beginning step—to *abandon her transgressions.* (MF, p. 165.)

Could this woman gain forgiveness of so gross a crime as adultery? Certainly. Through faith, repentance, baptism, and continued obedience, it was within her power to become clean and spotless before the Lord and a worthy candidate for his celestial presence. Repentant persons have power to cleanse themselves even from so evil a thing as sex immorality. (1 Cor. 6:9–11; 3 Ne. 30.) That such seemingly was the course taken by this woman is inferred from the Inspired Version statement that she believed in Christ and glorified God from that very hour. (DNTC 1:451.)

If Jesus were to stand by and be asked to judge those whom we accuse and should say to us, "He that is without sin among you, let him first cast a stone at her," and then should stoop and write in the sand, how many of us would feel to steal away ashamed, convicted in our own conscience? How sound is his counsel! (N. Eldon Tanner, CR, Apr. 1972, p. 57.)

8:12–20 Jesus' statement "I am the light of the world" and his subsequent teachings on this witness of himself and the Father's witness of him are found in detail only in John.

Elder Bruce R. McConkie has noted the appropriateness of Jesus teaching these things near the temple:

It appears to have been our Lord's deliberate design to dramatize the great truths relative to himself by associating them with the religious and social practices then prevailing. It was, for instance, while drinking at Jacob's well with the woman of Samaria (John 4:6–15), and again while the priests carried water in golden vessels from the pool Siloam during the Feast of Tabernacles (John 7:37–39), that he chose to speak of *living water.* It was after miraculously providing loaves and fishes for the hungering thousands, that he proclaimed himself as the *living bread* sent down from heaven. (John 6.) And so now, apparently while the great golden lamp-stands in the temple were blazing forth their light as part of the festivities of the Feast of Tabernacles, he took occasion to associate himself with the Messianic prophecies by announcing, *"I am the light of the world."*

His hearers well knew that their Messiah should stand as a light to all men; that is, they knew that he as the very source of light and truth, would stand forth as a light, an example, a dispenser of truth; they knew that his would be the mission to mark the course and light the way which all men should travel. (3 Ne. 15:9; 18:16, 24.) Messianic prophecies given to their fathers promised that he would be "a light to the Gentiles" (Isa. 49:6), a light piercing the darkness of error and unbelief. (Isa. 60:1–3.) Jesus' application of these prophecies to his own person was a clear proclamation of his own Messiahship and was so understood by his hearers. (DNTC 1:452–53.)

8:19 "Where is thy Father?" was an obvious challenge to Jesus to produce more evidence that he was indeed the Son of God.

8:21–30 These words Jesus spake "in the treasury, as he taught in the temple" are recorded only by John.

Jesus was soon to return to his Father in heaven. "No unclean thing can enter" into the presence of our Heavenly Father, so these unrepentant people could not follow Jesus there. (See 3 Ne. 27:19–20.)

8:25–28 The question "Who art thou?" indicates that the Pharisees still were not willing to receive Jesus as the Messiah, but wanted him to make the claim clearly so they could bring him to trial for blasphemy. In referring to himself by the sacred title "Son of Man," Jesus again proclaimed his divine nature.

8:31–59 These strong teachings, recorded only by John, reveal the weakness of many of the traditions of the Pharisees as contrasted with the teachings in their scriptures.

8:32 Elder Bruce R. McConkie has interpreted the foregoing expression to mean that we shall be made "free from the damning power of false doctrine; free from the bondage of appetite and lust; free from the shackles of sin; from every evil and corrupt influence and from every restraining and curtailing power; free to go on to the unlimited freedom enjoyed in its fulness only by exalted beings." (DNTC 1:456–57.) (LTJA, p. 108.)

8:33–34 Elder James E. Talmage has commented on the saying "the truth shall make you free," relating it to the response of the Pharisees:

At these words, so rich in blessing, so full of comfort for the believing soul, the people were stirred to angry demonstrations; their Jewish temper was immediately ablaze. To promise them freedom was to imply that they were not already free. "We be Abraham's seed, and were never in bondage to any man: how sayest thou, Ye shall be made free?" In their unbridled fanaticism they had forgotten the bondage of Egypt, the captivity of Babylon, and were oblivious of their existing state of vassalage to Rome. To say that Israel had never been in bondage was not only to convict themselves of falsehood but to stultify themselves wretchedly.

Jesus made it clear that He had not referred to freedom in its physical or political sense alone, though to this conception their false disavowal had been directed; the liberty He proclaimed was spiritual liberty; the grievous bondage from which He would deliver them was the serfdom of sin. (JTC, p. 409.)

8:37–40 Jesus made it clear that although the Pharisees might be of Abraham's seed physically, they were not spiritually his children, for they did not the works of Abraham.

For nearly 2,000 years all of Israel had clung tenaciously to God's promise to Abraham: "I will establish my covenant between me and thee and thy seed after thee in their generations for an everlasting covenant, to be a God unto thee, and to thy seed after thee." (Gen. 17:7.) Also: "And in thy seed shall all the nations of the earth be blessed." (Gen. 22:18.) Now these unbelieving Jews, a remnant of the seed of faithful Abraham, glorying in their Abrahamic descent, contended with Jesus about their assumed preferential status as the "seed" of that ancient patriarch.

To understand this discussion between Jesus and his Jewish detractors, it must be remembered that men are born in various families, nations, and races as a direct result of their pre-existent life. (Deut. 32:7–8; Acts 17:26.) Many choice spirits from preexistence are sent in selected families. This enables them to undergo their mortal probations under circumstances where the gospel and its blessings will be more readily available to them.

Abraham gained the promise from the Lord that his descendants, his "literal seed, . . . the seed of the body," would be natural heirs to all of "the blessings of the Gospel." (Abra. 2:11.) His seed were to be "lawful heirs, according to the flesh," because of their "lineage." (D&C 86:8–11.) Accordingly, since Abraham's day, the Lord has sent a host of righteous spirits through that favored lineage.

Further, Abraham also gained the divine assurance that all those who thereafter received the gospel, no matter what their literal lineage, should be "accounted" his seed and should rise up and bless him as their father. (Abra. 2:10.) By adoption such converts would "become . . . the seed of Abraham." (D&C 84:34.) Conversely, and in this spiritual sense, such of the literal seed of Abraham as rejected the gospel light would be cut off from the house of their fathers and be denied an eternal inheritance with Israel and Abraham. "For they are not all Israel, which are of Israel," as Paul explained it. "Neither, because they are the seed of Abraham, are they all children: . . . That is, They which are the children of the flesh, these are not the children of God: but the children of the promise are counted for the seed." (Rom. 9:6–8.)

Thus there are two distinct meanings of the expression, "seed of Abraham": (1) There are his literal descendants who have sprung from his loins and who by virtue of their favored family status are natural heirs of the same blessings which Abraham himself enjoyed; and (2) There are those (including adopted members of the family) who become the "seed of Abraham" in the full spiritual sense by conformity to the same gospel principles which Abraham obeyed. In this spiritual sense, the disobedient literal descendants of Abraham, being "children of the flesh," are not "accounted" as Abraham's seed, but are cut off from the blessings of the gospel. (DNTC 1:458–60.)

(See BD, "Abraham, Covenant of.")

8:38 Jesus was contrasting the two "fathers" we may

choose to obey: "my Father" (our Heavenly Father) and "your father" (the devil). (See v. 44.)

8:43 In the Joseph Smith Translation, this verse ends, "ye cannot *bear* my word." (Italics added.)

8:44 The devil was a "murderer from the beginning" because he influenced Cain to kill Abel and because he sought to destroy the truth. (See Alma 39:6; Ether 8:15; D&C 76:25–27; Moses 5:18–25.)

"When he speaketh a lie, he speaketh of his own" could have been more literally translated "When he speaks the lie, he speaks according to his own disposition."

8:46 The first question in this verse has been translated "Which of you convicts me of sin?" and "Which one of you can prove that I am guilty of sin?"

8:47 The Joseph Smith Translation replaces "heareth" and "hear" with "receiveth" and "receive."

8:48 Read text and commentaries for Luke 17:11–19 and John 4:9 for further background on the term *Samaritan*.

> They had before called Him a Galilean; that appellative was but mildly depreciatory, and moreover was a truthful designation according to their knowledge; but the epithet "Samaritan" was inspired by hate, and by its application they meant to disown Him as a Jew. (JTC, p. 411.)

> The inhabitants of Samaria were a mixed people, in whom the blood of Israel was mingled with that of the Assyrians and other nations; and one cause of the animosity existing between them and their neighbors both on the north and the south was the Samaritans' claim for recognition as Israelites; it was their boast that Jacob was their father; but this the Jews denied. The Samaritans had a version of the Pentateuch, which they revered as the law, but they rejected all the prophetical writings of what is now the Old Testament, because they considered themselves treated with insufficient respect therein.

> To the orthodox Jew of the time a Samaritan was more unclean than a Gentile of any other nationality. It is interesting to note the extreme and even absurd restrictions then in force in the matter of regulating unavoidable relations between the two peoples. The testimony of a Samaritan could not be heard before a Jewish tribunal. For a Jew to eat food prepared by a Samaritan was at one time regarded by rabbinical authority as an offense as great as that of eating the flesh of swine. While it was admitted that produce from a field in Samaria was not unclean, inasmuch as it sprang directly from the soil, such produce became unclean if subjected to any treatment at Samaritan hands. Thus, grapes and grain might be purchased from Samaritans, but neither wine nor flour manufactured therefrom by Samaritan labor. On one occasion the epithet "Samaritan" was hurled at Christ as an intended insult. "Say we not well that thou art a Samaritan, and hast a devil." (JTC, pp. 172–73.)

8:51–52 The Lord has said in this dispensation, "And it shall come to pass that *those that die in me shall not taste of death,* for it shall be sweet unto them; And they that die not in me, wo unto them, for their death is bitter." (D&C 42:46–47; italics added.)

The statement in verse 51 has been translated in the New English Bible as "he shall never know what it is to die."

Another meaning is, of course, that those who follow the Savior will not die the spiritual death that is the consequence of sin.

8:53 "Whom makest thou thyself?" could have been more literally translated "Who do you claim to be?"

8:56 Jesus' statement "Your father Abraham rejoiced to see my day" indicates that at one time the Old Testament may have contained teachings similar to those in Abraham 2:6–11, where we learn that Jehovah appeared to Abraham and gave him many promises concerning the gospel and the priesthood.

This verse could have been more literally translated "Abraham your father rejoiced greatly in the prospect of seeing my day, and he saw it and rejoiced."

8:57 Jesus did not say he had seen Abraham, but rather that Abraham had seen him and his day, thus making himself greater than the foremost patriarch of the Jewish nation. But the Jews, in an apparent attempt to subtract honor from him in whose presence they then stood, twisted our Lord's statement to mean that he had looked back and seen the day of Abraham. (DNTC 1:463.)

8:58 "Before Abraham was, I am" could have been translated "Before Abraham came into existence, I have been." However, some Latter-day Saint authorities have indicated that a more correct rendering is "Before Abraham, was I AM."

This was an unequivocal and unambiguous declaration of our Lord's eternal Godship. By the awful title I AM He had made Himself known to Moses and thereafter was so known in Israel. . . . It is the equivalent of "Yahveh," or "Jahveh," now rendered "Jehovah," and signifies "The Self-existent One," "The Eternal," "The First and the Last." Jewish traditionalism forbade the utterance of the sacred Name; yet Jesus claimed it as His own. In an orgy of self-righteous indignation, the Jews seized upon the stones that lay in the unfinished courts, and would have crushed their Lord, but the hour of His death had not yet come, and unseen of them He passed through the crowd and departed from the temple.

His seniority to Abraham plainly referred to the status of each in the antemortal or preexistent state; Jesus was as literally the Firstborn in the spirit world, as He was the Only Begotten in the flesh. Christ is as truly the Elder Brother of Abraham and Adam as of the last-born child of the earth. (JTC, pp. 411–12.)

9:1–41 This account of the healing by Jesus of a man who "was blind from his birth" is contained only in John. The entire chapter forms a complete whole.

9:2 The intriguing question "Who did sin, this man, or his parents, that he was born blind?" indicates that the disciples believed in a pre-earthly existence and that it was possible to sin in the pre-earthly existence.

Apparently the Jews had some understanding of the doctrine of pre-existence. Among their righteous forbears it had been taught plainly as a basic gospel truth. (Moses 3:4–9; 4:1–4; 6:51; Abra. 3:22–28.) Such scriptures as were then available to them however, contained only passing allusions to it. (Num. 16:22; Isa. 14:12–20; Jer. 1:5.) But it was a doctrine implicit in the whole plan of salvation as such was known to and understood by them. They had, for instance, no more occasion to prove the ante-mortal existence of spirits than they did to prove God was a personal Being. Both truths were assumed; concepts to the contrary were heresies which gained prevalence in later ages.

Jesus' disciples—probably as a direct result of his teachings—knew and believed that men were the spirit children of God in the pre-existence and that in such prior estate they were subject to law and endowed with agency. Otherwise they never would have asked nor would there have been any sense or reason to a question which is predicated upon the assumption that men can sin before they are born into mortality. (DNTC 1:480.)

(See section 1, "Blindness.")

9:4 I must work the works of him that sent me, while *I am with you; the time* cometh when *I shall have finished my work, then I go unto the Father.* (JST; italics added.)

The Book of Mormon also teaches that "a night" will come "when no man can work": "After this day of life, which is given us to prepare for eternity, behold, if we do not improve our time while in this life, then cometh the night of darkness wherein there can be no labor performed." (Alma 34:33.)

9:6 It is not clear exactly why Jesus "anointed the eyes of the blind man with the clay"; he had not followed this practice in other healings. (See texts and commentaries for Matt. 4:24; Luke 4:40–44; John 4:46–54.) Some scholars have thought Jesus may have anointed the blind man's eyes to strengthen his faith.

9:7 By this act of giving sight to a blind beggar Jesus, in a dramatic and irrefutable manner, proclaimed himself as: (1) The Light of the World; and (2) The very Son of God. Incident to its performance he also: Confirmed the disciples' belief in pre-existence; rejected the belief of some that physical handicaps result from ante-mortal sin; taught that his own work was assigned him by the Father; reaffirmed that he stands in judgment upon the world; and taught that rejection of light and truth bring condemnation. (DNTC 1:479.)

9:13 And they brought him *who had been blind* to the Pharisees. (JST; italics added.)

9:14 For further background on the reactions of the apostate religious leaders to healings performed on the Sabbath, see texts and commentaries for Matthew 12:10–13; Luke 13:10–17; 14:1–6.

9:16 The Pharisees who accused Jesus of breaking the Sabbath in performing this healing were in fact acknowledging that the healing had taken place. However, whether or not the Sabbath had been properly kept was not the real issue:

The real problem bothering the Pharisees was not whether it was proper for Jesus to heal on the Sabbath day. Nor did it concern them whether or not Jesus was truly the Messiah. The Pharisees felt that their very existence as interpreters of the Mosaic Law was threatened. They demanded that every Jew conform his life to a harsh set of ritual rules and laws, the breaking of which would make him unclean and, therefore, unacceptable to God

In contrast, Jesus taught that God's laws were based on love; that obedience brought freedom, happiness, and fulfillment. The essence of Christ's teachings shed the light of truth upon those false and burdensome philosophies which kept men in the darkness of disbelief, ignorance, and sin. See John 9:39. Jesus clearly set forth the path by which men could achieve salvation and offered a choice: remain as you are, or transform your life and follow me. It was as though Jesus had said this:

"I am come into the world to sit in judgment upon all men, to divide them into two camps by their acceptance or rejection of my word. Those who are spiritually blind have their eyes opened through obedience to my gospel and shall see the things of the Spirit. Those who think they can see in the spiritual realm, but who do not accept me and my gospel shall remain in darkness and be made blind to the true spiritual realities." (McConkie, DNTC 1:482.) (LTJA, p. 109.)

9:22 "He should be put out of the synagogue" is the equivalent of "he should be excommunicated from the Church."

9:27 He answered them, I have told you already, and ye did not *believe;* wherefore would *you believe if I should tell you* again? *and would you* be his disciples? (JST; italics added.)

9:29 The Joseph Smith Translation changes "fellow" to "man."

Concerning the thinking behind the statement "We know that God spake unto Moses; as for this man we know not from whence he is," Elder Bruce R. McConkie has observed:

> From age to age disbelieving persons fall back on the same shaky notions to justify themselves from rejecting light and truth. In modern times they say, in effect, "We know that God spake unto Jesus, and unto Peter, James and John; but as for this Joseph Smith, we know not from whence he is." To which one whose eyes have been opened spiritually might aptly reply: "Why herein is a marvelous thing, that ye know not whether Joseph Smith was sent of God, and yet he hath communed with God, received revelation upon revelation, translated the Book of Mormon, performed many miracles, set up again the kingdom of God on earth, and organized a Church which is fast becoming a world power and to which hundreds of thousands of the elect are gathering from all parts of the earth. Now we know that God heareth not sinners: but if any be a worshiper of God, and doeth his will, him he heareth. Since the world began was it not heard that any man could do the mighty works performed in this dispensation unless God was with him. If Joseph Smith were not of God, his fraudulent claims would have been uncovered long ago and his work come to naught." (DNTC 1:481.)

9:32 "Since the world began" could have been more literally translated "From of old."

The Joseph Smith Translation adds "except he be of God" at the end of this verse.

9:34 The accusation of the Pharisees that Jesus was "born in sins" could indicate they also understood the doctrine of a pre-earthly existence. (See text and commentary for John 9:2.)

9:35 The Greek text indicates that this statement could have been worded "Are you putting faith in the Son of Man?"

9:38 "Lord, I believe" could have been more literally translated "I do put faith in him, Lord."

9:39–41 Elder Bruce R. McConkie has paraphrased and commented on these verses:

> "I am come into the world to sit in judgment upon all men, to divide them into two camps by their acceptance or rejection of my word. Those who are spiritually blind have their eyes opened through obedience to my gospel and shall see the things of the Spirit. Those who think they can see in the spiritual realm, but who do not accept me and my gospel shall remain in darkness and be made blind to the true spiritual realities."
>
> "He who sins against the greater light shall receive the greater condemnation." (D&C 82:3.) "Where there is no law . . . there is no condemnation."

(2 Ne. 9:25.) Modern sectarians, to whom the message of the restoration is presented, are in this same state of blindness and sin. They have the scriptures before them; they study the gospel doctrines contained in them; they are concerned about religion in general; and then they hear the latter-day elders, speaking as those having authority, present the message of salvation—and yet they choose to remain in the churches of the day rather than accept the fulness of revealed truth. If they were blind, knowing none of these things, they would be under no condemnation for rejecting the light; but when the truth is offered to them and they reject it, claiming to have the light already, they are under condemnation, for their sin remaineth. (DNTC 1:482.)

10:1–16 Among the pastoral people of Palestine, service as a pastor or shepherd was one of the most honorable and respected vocations. Accordingly, many of the prophets had used the shepherd's vocation as a basis for teaching great spiritual truths and as a means of foretelling the coming of the Messiah, who would be the Good Shepherd. By means of this allegory of the shepherd and the sheepfold Jesus bears record of his own divinity and specifies how his true shepherds should deal in the spiritual pastures of the gospel. (DNTC 1:483–84.)

The shepherd in Palestine lived a lonely life and was noted for his faithfulness and protection to his sheep. At night the sheep would be brought into an enclosure called a sheepfold which had high walls to keep anything or anyone from getting in. At the top of the walls were placed thorns which prevented wolves from leaping into the enclosure. Proper entrance was at the door only. (John 10:1.)

Often several flocks were brought into one fold and one shepherd, called a porter, would stand guard at the door during the night while the others would go home to rest. When they would return in the morning, they would be recognized by the doorkeeper, allowed to enter, and each call his own flock and lead them forth to pasture. (John 10:2–3.) The shepherd provided the food for the sheep.

The shepherd walked ahead of his sheep and led them. The sheep knew the shepherd and trusted in him and would not follow a stranger. (John 10:4–5.) He generally had a name for each sheep and each knew its own name and would come when called. If a stranger called, the sheep became nervous and startled and would not obey the voice of the stranger, for they knew their master's voice. (John 10:3–4, 27.)

The true shepherd, the owner of the sheep, was willing to give his life for the sheep if need be. Sometimes a leopard or panther, when driven by hunger, would leap over the walls of the fold and into the midst of the frightened sheep. Then was the time when the nerve and heart of the shepherd was tried. A hireling, one who did not own the sheep, might at such a crisis flee from the danger and shrink from the duties of the shepherd. (John 10:11–13.) Unwatched, the hireling might not put the welfare of the sheep foremost in his life. Hirelings had been known to sell sheep and then pocket the money and account for the loss by saying that wolves came and destroyed the sheep. When this is applied to the gospel, it is seen what a "hireling" might do with the care of human souls. But the true shepherd's chief concern was the welfare of the sheep. (John 21:1–17.)

Even the shepherd's clothing was designed to aid him in his care of the sheep. The shepherd's coat generally had a large pocket inside, suitable for carrying a weak or wounded lamb to safety. Isaiah made reference to this pocket when he ascribed to Christ the role of shepherd. (Isaiah 40:10–11.)

Jesus' station as the Good Shepherd is complete in every detail. He is the door of the fold, by which we must enter. There is none other. (John 10:9.) He is not a hireling but is the true shepherd of human souls, and "we are not our own" (1 Corinthians 6:19–20), but he has purchased us with his precious blood. (1 Corinthians 7:23; 1 Peter 1:18–19; 2 Peter 2:1; Acts 20:28.) The shepherd provided the pasture on which the sheep feed. Jesus has given us his word. We are warned against the doctrines of men. Only the "pasture" that the Lord provides is proper food for his sheep, and no man can be saved in ignorance of his word or without his revelations. The true sheep know his voice. The true Shepherd knows and owns his sheep and he calls them. We thus take upon us the name of Christ, for he owns us; we are his sheep; and, if we have his name, we can enter "by the door." (Robert J. Matthews, *The Parables of Jesus,* pp. 75–76.)

10:3 "Porter" has also been translated "gatekeeper," "door-keeper," and "watchman."

10:4–5 Peter also used the imagery of the shepherd and of the sheep:

Feed the flock of God which is among you, taking the oversight thereof, not by constraint, but willingly; not for filthy lucre, but of a ready mind; Neither as being lords over God's heritage, but being ensamples to the flock. And when the chief Shepherd shall appear, ye shall receive a crown of glory that fadeth not away. (1 Pet. 5:1–4.)

10:7 The Joseph Smith Translation replaces "sheep" with "sheepfold."

10:8 In the Joseph Smith Translation, this verse begins, "All that ever came before me *who testified not of me* are thieves and robbers . . ." (Italics added.)

"To him give all the prophets witness." (Acts 10:43.) There never was a prophet of God in any age who did not testify of Christ and his mission. Any professing prophet, teacher, pastor, shepherd, minister, or priest, in any age, who is not in fact called of God and who does not bear witness of Christ is a false prophet, or as Jesus here says a thief and a robber. (DNTC 1:484–85.)

10:10 "Robber" could have been translated "plunderer." The latter translation is more consistent with the context, inasmuch as a "thief" and a "robber" are essentially the same, but there could be a substantial difference between a "thief" and a "plunderer."

10:11 "I am the Messiah, the Redeemer, the Son of God." All Israel knew their Messiah would be the great Shepherd, the Teacher, who as the Lord God incarnate, would make his sheep to lie down in green pastures, would lead them beside still waters, would restore their souls and lead them in the paths of righteousness for his name's sake, and who in the end would cause them to dwell in the house of the Lord forever. (Ps. 23.)

All Israel knew also that Isaiah had prophesied: "Behold, the Lord God will come with strong hand, and his arm shall rule for him: behold, his reward is with him, and his work before him. He shall feed his flock like a shepherd: he shall gather the lambs with his arm, and carry them in his bosom, and shall gently lead those that are with young." (Isa. 40:10–11.)

And now One ministered among them who said: "I am he!" (DNTC 1:485.)

10:12–13 The Joseph Smith Translation changes the beginning of each of these verses (italics added):
Verse 12: "*And the shepherd is not as a* hireling . . ."
Verse 13: "*But he who is a hireling* fleeth . . ."

Never has been written or spoken a stronger arraignment of false pastors, unauthorized teachers, self-seeking hirelings who teach for pelf and divine for dollars, deceivers who pose as shepherds yet avoid the door and climb over "some other way," prophets in the devil's employ, who to achieve their master's purpose, hesitate not to robe themselves in the garments of assumed sanctity, and appear in sheep's clothing, while inwardly they are ravening wolves. (JTC, pp. 417–18.)

10:14 The Joseph Smith Translation transposes versed 13 and 14 of the King James text, and begins verse 13 "*For I am the good shepherd* . . ." (Italics added.)

10:16 "They shall hear my voice; and there shall be one fold" could have been translated "they will listen to my voice, and they will become one flock."

The "other sheep" here referred to constituted the separated flock or remnant of the house of Joseph, who, six centuries prior to the birth of Christ, had been miraculously detached from the Jewish fold in Palestine, and had been taken beyond the great deep to the American continent. When to them the resurrected Christ appeared He thus spake: "And verily, I say unto you, that ye are they of whom I said, other sheep I have which are not of this fold; them also I must bring, and they shall hear my voice; and there shall be one fold, and one shepherd." [3 Ne. 15:21.] The Jews had vaguely understood Christ's reference to other sheep as meaning in some obscure way, the Gentile nations; and because of their unbelief and consequent inability to rightly comprehend, Jesus had withheld any plainer exposition of His meaning, for so, He informed the Nephites, had the Father directed. "This much did the Father command me," He explained, "that I should tell unto them, That other sheep I have, which are not of this fold; them also I must bring, and they shall hear my voice; and there shall be one fold, and one shepherd." On the same occasion the Lord declared that there were yet other sheep, those of the Lost, or Ten, Tribes, to whom He was then about to go, and who would eventually be brought forth from their place of exile, and become part of the one blessed fold under the governance of the one supreme Shepherd and King. [3 Ne. 16:1–5.] (JTC, p. 419.)

10:17–21 Jesus had no father of the flesh, that is who was mortal and subject to death. Our Eternal Father to whom we pray is the Father of the body of Jesus Christ and from his Father he inherited life and death was always subject to him. He had the power to lay down his life, because he was the Son of Mary who was like us, mortal, and he had the power to take his life up again for that power was in him. In his teachings to the Jews and his disciples he frequently told them of this power and of his mission. (AGQ 1:33.)

10:19–21 The division among the Jews regarding Jesus was so deep and bitter that nearly his every teaching and act widened the gap between the believers and the unbelievers.

10:22–39 Nearly two hundred years before the public ministry of Jesus began, Antiochus Epiphanes, a Selucidian king who controlled Palestine, attempted to destroy Judaism by compelling his subjects to accept the Greek culture. In a show of utter contempt for the Jewish faith, Antiochus sacrificed a pig (the filthiest of animals, according to the Jews) upon a small Greek altar built for the occasion within the temple confines. Following this, Antiochus prohibited all religious ordinances enjoined by the law of Moses and ordered the burning of all known copies of the Jewish law. Finally, he ordered that heathen altars be constructed throughout Palestine and that the Jews worship the heathen gods or suffer death. This suppression of the Jewish religion precipitated what is known as the Maccabean revolution.

Judas Maccabaeus, together with his four brothers, gathered about him a number of devout Jews who refused to honor the demands of Antiochus. They formed a guerrilla army and waged relentless war against the troops employed by Antiochus to enforce his religious policies. Eventually, the Maccabees seized control of Jerusalem. Judas then proceeded to purify the temple (which for three years had been used to make offerings to Zeus) and restore the worship of Jehovah. *The Feast of Dedication, sometimes called the Feast of Lights, or Hanukkah, was inaugurated to celebrate the recovery and rededication of the Jewish temple.* The feast takes place in the month of Chislev, corresponding to portions of our months of November and December, and lasts for eight days. It is marked by elaborate meals, special synagogue services, and extra illumination in all homes. Hence its title, "Feast of Lights." (LTJA, p. 118.)

10:23 "Solomon's porch" is generally considered to be the portico on the east side of the temple that was supposed to

be part of the original temple built by Solomon and preserved in the reconstructions of Zerubabbel and of Herod.
(See BD, "Solomon's Porch.")

10:27 Why do some persons believe in Christ and his saving truths
while others do not? Why is it easier for some to believe all of the gospel
truths than for others? There is only one rational explanation why selected
sheep hearken more readily to the Master's voice; it is the fact that men
developed different talents in pre-existence. Spirits sent to inhabit some
mortal bodies developed talents for spirituality, for recognizing the truth, for
believing spiritual realities while yet in pre-existence; others did not. Many
of the offspring of Deity, having excelled in spiritual attainments in pre-
existence, are born as members of the house of Israel in this life. (Deut.
32:7–9.) (DNTC 1:490.)

10:30 The Father and the Son are "one" in many ways:
witness, testimony, teachings, doings, goals, purposes,
ideals, attributes, powers. However, they are not *one* in
personality:

> The [Joseph Smith Translation] gives for John 10:30: "I and the Father
> are one" instead of "I and my Father are one." By "the Father" the Jews
> rightly understood the Eternal Father, God. In the original Greek "one"
> appears in the neuter gender, and therefore expresses oneness in attributes,
> power, or purpose, and not a oneness of personality which would have
> required the masculine form. (JTC, p. 500.)

10:31–33 "Blasphemy consists in either or both of the following:
1. Speaking irreverently, evilly, abusively, or scurrilously against God or
sacred things; or 2. Speaking profanely or falsely about Deity." (*Mormon
Doctrine,* p. 85.) In its most criminal and corrupt form it consists in claiming
falsely to be God or the Son of God. Thus Jesus would have been guilty of
the most terrible of all blasphemous crimes if his claim to divine Sonship
had been false. Death by stoning was the penalty of blasphemy in ancient
Israel. (Lev. 24:16.) (DNTC 1:490–91.)

10:34–35 Though "there is none other God but one" for men on this
earth to worship, yet "there be gods many, and lords many" throughout the
infinite expanse of eternity. (1 Cor. 8:4–7.) That is, there are many exalted,
perfected, glorified personages who reign as gods over their own dominions.
John saw 144,000 of them standing with Christ upon Mount Zion, all "having his Father's name written in their foreheads" (Rev. 14:1), which is to say
that they were gods and were so identified by wearing crowns so stating.
Indeed, to each person who overcomes and gains exaltation, Christ has
promised: "I will write upon him the name of my God," and he shall "sit
with me in my throne, even as I also overcame, and am set down with my
Father in his throne." (Rev. 3:12, 21.)

Joseph Smith said: "Every man who reigns in celestial glory is a god
to his dominions." (*Teachings,* p. 374.) All exalted persons "are gods,
even the sons of God." (D&C 76:58.) Through obedience to the whole
gospel law, including celestial marriage, they attain the "fulness of the

glory of the Father" (D&C 93:6–28) and "a continuation of the seeds forever and ever. Then shall they be gods, because they have no end; therefore shall they be from everlasting to everlasting, because they continue; then shall they be above all, because all things are subject unto them. Then shall they be gods, because they have all power, and the angels are subject unto them." (D&C 132:19–20.)

But to us there is but one God, who is Elohim, and one Lord, who is the Lord Jehovah; the Holy Ghost acts as their minister; and these three are one Godhead, or as it is more graphically expressed, one God. Thus we find the Psalmist, whom Jesus quoted, saying: "God standeth in the congregation of the mighty; he judgeth among the gods. . . . I have said, ye are gods; and all of you are children of the most High." (Ps. 82:1, 6.) (DNTC 1:491.)

10:36 In verse 24 the Jews had challenged Jesus to "tell us plainly" whether he professed to be the Son of God. His statement in verse 36 makes it clear that he had claimed to be the Son of God and that the Jews had to acknowledge that he had so claimed. (See section 1, "Son of God.")

10:37 This is the same sort of logic that Nephi uses to establish the truth of the Book of Mormon. "Believe in Christ," he says to those who read that book, "and if ye believe not in these words believe in Christ. And if ye shall believe in Christ ye will believe in these words, for they are the words of Christ, and he hath given them unto me; and they teach all men that they should do good." (2 Ne. 33:10.)

Similarly, and in effect, Jesus said: "ye say ye do not believe in me; very well, then believe in the works which I do, for ye cannot deny they have come by divine power; and if ye accept the works, then ye shall believe in me also, for I could not do the works alone; they came by the power of the Father." (DNTC 1:492.)

10:38 This verse could have been more literally translated "But if I am doing them, even though you do not believe me, believe the works, in order that you may come to know and may continue knowing that the Father is in union with me and I am in union with the Father."

10:39–41 The exact spot to which Jesus retired is not made clear in our present scriptures, although it is generally understood that he went to the "other side of the Jordan":

Once again the Jews sought to take Jesus by force but did not succeed, because the time for his death and atoning sacrifice had not yet arrived. Instead, Jesus "went away again beyond Jordan into the place where John at first baptized; and there he abode." (John 10:40.) This area beyond Jordan was known as Perea, a word which literally means "the land beyond." Elder Talmage writes: "The duration of this sojourn in Perea is nowhere recorded in our scriptures. It could not have lasted more than a few weeks at most. Possibly some of the discourses, instructions, and parables already treated as following the Lord's departure from

Jerusalem after the Feast of Tabernacles in the preceding autumn, may chronologically belong to this interval. From this retreat of comparative quiet, Jesus returned to Judea in response to an earnest appeal from some whom He loved. He left the Bethany of Perea for the Judean Bethany, where dwelt Martha and Mary." (Talmage, *Jesus the Christ*, p. 490.) (LTJA, p. 118.)

11:1–46 This dramatic account of Jesus raising Lazarus from the dead is recorded only in John.

At least twice before Jesus had raised the dead, but neither time under such dramatic circumstances or with such a display of divine power as was evidenced in the case of Lazarus. The daughter of Jairus had been called back to mortality in a matter of hours and before her body had been prepared for burial (Luke 8:41–42, 49–56), and the widow's son in Nain had lived and breathed again after most of the burial preparations were complete and while the corpse was being carried to the grave. (Luke 7:11–17.) In neither of these instances had Jesus courted any especial publicity, and in the case of Jairus' daughter he had even enjoined secrecy on the part of those who witnessed the miracle.

But with "our friend Lazarus" it was different. Jesus with full knowledge of Lazarus' sickness, did nothing to prevent his death; allowed his body to be prepared for burial; waited until the funeral was over and the entombment accomplished; permitted four days to pass so that the processes of decomposition would be well under way; tested the faith of Mary and Martha to the utmost; came to the rock-barred tomb under circumstances which attracted many sceptics and unbelievers; conducted himself in every respect as though he were courting publicity; and then—using the prerogative of Deity to give life or death according to his own will—commanded: "Lazarus, come forth."

Why this studied buildup, this centering of attention upon one of the mightiest miracles of his ministry? Two reasons in particular stand out. (1) As our Lord neared the climax of his mortal ministry, he was again bearing testimony, in a way that could not be refuted, of his Messiahship, of his divine Sonship, of the fact that he was in very deed the literal Son of God; and (2) He was setting the stage, so as to dramatize for all time, one of his greatest teachings: That he was the resurrection and the life, that immortality and eternal life came by him, and that those who believed and obeyed his words should never die spiritually. (DNTC 1:530–31.)

11:1–2 Now a certain man was sick, *whose name was Lazarus, of the town of Bethany;*

And Mary, his sister, who anointed the Lord with ointment and wiped his feet with her hair, *lived with her sister Martha, in whose house her brother Lazarus was sick.* (JST; italics added.)

11:4 Jesus' statement could have been translated "This sickness is not with death as its object, but is for the glory of God, in order that the Son of God may be glorified through it."

The Joseph Smith Translation of this verse begins "And when Jesus heard *he was sick* . . ." (Italics added.)

11:6 *And Jesus tarried two days, after he heard that Lazarus was sick, in the same place where he was.* (JST; italics added.)

Jesus and his intimate disciples were in Perea, at least twenty-five miles from Bethany. During the two days, before starting for Bethany, it appears that the Master performed a sabbath healing (Luke 14:1–6), discoursed on sacrifice (Luke 14:25–33), taught that the law and the prophets bore record of him (Luke 16:14–18), talked of faith (Luke 17:5–6), and gave a series of parables—the *Parable of the Wedding Guests* (Luke 14:7–11), of the *Great Supper* (Luke 14:12–24), of the *Lost Sheep* (Luke 15:3–7), of the *Lost Coin* (Luke 15:8–10), of the *Prodigal Son* (Luke 15:11–32), of the *Unjust Steward* (Luke 16:1–13), of *Lazarus and the Rich Man* (Luke 16:19–31), and of the *Unprofitable Servant* (Luke 17:1–10.) (DNTC 1:531.)

11:9–10 Elder Bruce R. McConkie has paraphrased these verses:

Certainly Jesus would go to Judea in spite of the threats of death that faced him there. "Though it be the eleventh hour of my life, yet there are twelve hours in the day, and during that designated period, I shall do the work appointed me without stumbling or faltering. This is the time given me to do my work. I cannot wait for the night when perchance the opposition will die down. He that shirks his responsibilities and puts off his labors until the night shall stumble in the darkness and fail in his work." (DNTC 1:531.)

11:12 "Do well" could have been translated "Get well" or "be saved."

11:16 Then said Thomas, which is called Didymus, unto his fellow disciples, Let us also go, that we may die with him; *for they feared lest the Jews should take Jesus and put him to death, for as yet they did not understand the power of God.* (JST; italics added.)

Didymus means "a twin." Although Thomas is often remembered as the apostle who insisted on feeling the resurrected body of Jesus before believing in the resurrection, here he showed his courage and devotion by being willing to die with the Lord.

11:17 And when Jesus came to Bethany, to Martha's house, Lazarus had already been in the grave four days. (JST.)

On the very probable assumption that the journey from Bethany in Judea to the place where Jesus was, in Perea, would require one day, Lazarus must have died on the day of the messenger's departure; for this day and the two days that elapsed before Jesus started toward Judea, and the day required for the return, would no more than cover the four days specified. It was and still is the custom in Palestine as in other oriental countries to bury on the day of death.

It was the popular belief that on the fourth day after death the spirit had finally departed from the vicinity of the corpse, and that thereafter decomposition proceeded unhindered. This may explain Martha's impulsive though gentle objection to having the tomb of her brother opened four days after his death. (John 11:39). It is possible that the consent of the next of kin was required for the lawful opening of a grave. Both Martha and Mary were present, and in the presence of many witnesses assented to the opening of the tomb in which their brother lay. (JTC, pp. 500–501.)

11:18 "About fifteen furlongs" is a little less than two miles. Because Bethany was so close to Jerusalem, it was relatively easy for friends and officials to come and mourn with Mary and Martha.

11:21 "My brother had not died" could have been more literally translated "my brother would not have died."

11:25–26 "He that believeth in me, though he were dead, yet shall he live" could have been translated "he that exercises faith in me, even though he dies, will come to life."

Jesus, in effect, is saying to Martha: "I am he through whom immortality and eternal life come. He that believes in me and obeys my gospel, though he die the natural death, yet through me he shall gain both immortality and eternal life. And whosoever is spiritually alive, having been born again so as to have the companionship of the Holy Ghost, and who thereafter endures in righteousness to the end, shall never die; that is, he shall have spiritual life in this world and eternal life in the world to come." (DNTC 1:532.)

11:29 In the Joseph Smith Translation, this verse begins, "As soon as *Mary* heard that *Jesus was come* . . ." (Italics added.)

11:31 This verse could have been more literally translated "Therefore the Jews that were with her in the house and that were consoling her, on seeing Mary rise quickly and go out, followed her, supposing [thinking] that she was going to the memorial tomb to weep there."

11:33 The marginal readings for "he groaned in the spirit" (John 11:33) and "again groaning in himself" (v. 38), as given in the revised version, are "was moved with indignation in the spirit" and "being moved with indignation in himself." All philological authorities agree that the words in the original Greek express sorrowful indignation, or as some aver, anger, and not alone a sympathetic emotion of grief. Any indignation the Lord may have felt, as intimated in verse 33, may be attributed to disapproval of the customary wailing over death, which as vented by the

Jews on this occasion, profaned the real and soulful grief of Martha and Mary; and His indignation, expressed by groaning as mentioned in verse 38, may have been due to the carping criticism uttered by some of the Jews as recorded in verse 37. (JTC, p. 501.)

11:39– 44 The procedure throughout was characterized by deep solemnity and by the entire absence of every element of unnecessary display. Jesus, who when miles away and without any ordinary means of receiving the information knew that Lazarus was dead, doubtless could have found the tomb; yet He inquired: "Where have ye laid him?" He who could still the waves of the sea by a word could have miraculously effected the removal of the stone that sealed the mouth of the sepulchre; yet He said: "Take ye away the stone." He who could reunite spirit and body could have loosened without hands the cerements by which the reanimated Lazarus was bound; yet He said: "Loose him, and let him go." All that human agency could do was left to man. In no instance do we find that Christ used unnecessarily the superhuman powers of His Godship; the divine energy was never wasted. (JTC, p. 495.)

11:45 The raising of Lazarus stands as the third recorded instance of restoration to life by Jesus. In each the miracle resulted in a resumption of mortal existence, and was in no sense a resurrection from death to immortality. In the raising of the daughter of Jairus, the spirit was recalled to its tenement within the hour of its quitting; the raising of the widow's son is an instance of restoration when the corpse was ready for the grave; the crowning miracle of the three was the calling of a spirit to reenter its body days after death, and when, by natural processes the corpse would be already in the early stages of decomposition. Lazarus was raised from the dead, not simply to assuage the grief of mourning relatives; myriads have had to mourn over death, and so myriads more shall have to do. One of the Lord's purposes was that of demonstrating the actuality of the power of God as shown forth in the works of Jesus the Christ, and Lazarus was the accepted subject of the manifestation. (JTC, pp. 495–96.)

11:47–53 These verses recount the reactions of members of the Sanhedrin, preserved only in the writings of John.

11:47 The Joseph Smith Translation changes "What do we?" to "What shall we do?"

According to the Greek text, the council referred to in this verse is the Sanhedrin.

11:47– 48 What a testimony this is to the effect and verity of our Lord's miracles. None could explain them away. None could escape the very evident conclusion that they were performed by the power of God. None could justifiably attribute unrighteousness to him who performed them, for even the most spiritually untutored knew "that God heareth not sinners." (John 9:31.)

The miracles proved Jesus' claim to divine Sonship. Either they must cease or this Galilean must be accepted as the Messiah. To these sin-saturated souls who comprised the Sanhedrin, there was but one solution:

Stop the miracles by slaying him who performed them. Such a course, they rationalized, was proper and justified, for it would avoid that tumult among the people which would bring on them further Roman restrictions. (DNTC 1:534–35.)

11:49–52 Caiaphas, the high priest mentioned by name, in a few short days would preside over the council that condemned Jesus to death. (See text and commentaries for Matt. 26:57–68. For further information on Caiaphas, read text and commentaries for Matt. 26:3; John 18:12–14. See section 1, "Caiaphas"; BD, "Caiaphas.")

John's statement that Caiaphas was high priest "that same year" must not be construed as meaning that the office of high priest was of a single year's tenure. Under Jewish law the presiding priest, who was known as the high priest, would remain in office indefinitely; but the Roman government had arrogated to itself the appointive power as applying to this office; and frequent changes were made. This Caiaphas, whose full name was Josephus Caiaphas, was high priest under Roman appointment during a period of eleven years. To such appointments the Jews had to submit, though they often recognized as the high priest under their law, some other than the "civil high priest" appointed by Roman authority. Thus we find both Annas and Caiaphas exercising the authority of the office at the time of our Lord's arrest and later. (John 18:13, 24; Acts 4:6; compare Luke 3:2.) Farrar (p. 484, note) says: "Some have seen an open irony in the expression of St. John (11:49) that Caiaphas was high priest 'that same year,' as though the Jews had got into this contemptuous way of speaking during the rapid succession of priests—mere phantoms set up and displaced by the Roman fiat—who had in recent years succeeded each other. There must have been at least five living high priests, and ex-high priests at this council—Annas, Ismael Ben Phabi, Eleazar Ben Haman, Simon Ben Kamhith, and Caiaphas, who had gained his elevation by bribery." (JTC, p. 501.)

Caiaphas, the high priest, cut short the discussion by saying: "Ye know nothing at all." This sweeping assertion of ignorance was most likely addressed to the Pharisees of the Sanhedrin; Caiaphas was a Sadducee. His next utterance was of greater significance than he realized: "Nor consider that it is expedient for us, that one man should die for the people, and that the whole nation perish not." John solemnly avers that Caiaphas spake not of himself, but by the spirit of prophecy, which, in spite of his implied unworthiness, came upon him by virtue of his office, and that thus: "He prophesied that Jesus should die for that nation; and not for that nation only, but that also he should gather together in one the children of God that were scattered abroad." But a few years after Christ had been put to death, for the salvation of the Jews and of all other nations, the very calamities which Caiaphas and the Sanhedrin had hoped to avert befell in full measure; the hierarchy was overthrown, the temple destroyed, Jerusalem demolished and the nation disrupted. (JTC, p. 498.)

11:54 See BD, "Ephraim, a city."

11:55–57 These verses show the speculation of the Jews as to whether or not Jesus would come to the feast. This information is contained only in John.

11:55 Instructions on ceremonial cleansings that should precede the celebration of the Passover are found in 2 Chronicles 30:15–20.

11:56 In the Joseph Smith Translation, the last two questions read, "What think ye *of Jesus? Will he* not come to the feast?" (Italics added.)

11:57 "He should shew it, that they might take him" could have been more literally translated "he should disclose it, in order that they might seize him."

In the Joseph Smith Translation, the end of this verse reads, "if any man knew where he *was,* he should *show them,* that they might take him." (Italics added.)

12:1–11 Some of the specific information concerning these incidents in Bethany "six days before the passover" are mentioned only by John, although many scholars feel the anointing of Jesus by the woman in the house of "Simon the leper" (see Matt. 26:6–13; Mark 14:3–9) is the same as mentioned in John.

12:2–8 Read text and commentaries for Matthew 26:6–13; Mark 14:3–9.

12:6 "Had the bag, and bare what was put therein" could have been more literally translated "had the money box and used to carry off the monies put in it." Other translations are "he carried the money bag and would help himself from it"; "as keeper of the money bag, he used to help himself to what was put into it"; and "as he had the money box he used to take what was put into it."

12:7 Then said Jesus, Let her alone; *for she hath preserved this ointment until now, that she might anoint me in token of my burial.* (JST; italics added.)

We are left without certain information as to whether Mary knew that within a few days her beloved Lord would be in the tomb. She may have been so informed in view of the hallowed intimacy between Jesus and the family; or she may have gathered from the remarks of Christ to the apostles that the sacrifice of His life was impending; or perhaps by inspired intuition she was impelled to render the loving tribute by which her memory has been enshrined in the hearts of all who know and love the Christ. John has preserved to us this remark of Jesus in the rebuke called forth by the grumbling Iscariot: "Let her alone; against the day of my burying hath she kept this"; and Mark's version is likewise suggestive of definite and solemn purpose on Mary's part: "She is come aforehand to anoint my body to the burying." (JTC, p. 513.)

12:12–19 Read text and commentaries for Matthew 21:1–11; Mark 11:1–11; Luke 19:29–40.

12:13 This incident forms the basis of Palm Sunday, celebrated by many Christians the Sunday before Easter Sunday.

Amid shouts of praise and pleas for salvation and deliverance, we see the disciples strewing our Lord's course with palm branches in token of victory and triumph. This whole dramatic scene prefigures that yet future assembly when "a great multitude," which no man can number, "of all nations, and kindreds, and people, and tongues," shall stand "before the throne, and before the Lamb, clothed in white robes, and palms in their hands," crying with a loud voice, "Salvation to our God which sitteth upon the throne and unto the Lamb." (Rev. 7:9–10.) (DNTC 1:578.)

12:14 And Jesus, when he had *sent two of his disciples and got* a young ass, sat thereon; as it is written, . . . (JST; italics added.)

12:15 The scripture being quoted here is Zechariah 9:9. One reason Jesus permitted the people to pay him this honor was so that words of the prophets might be fulfilled. (See section 1, "Triumphant entry.")

12:16 This verse could have been more literally translated "These things his disciples took no note of at first, but when Jesus became glorified, then they called to mind that these things were written respecting him and that they did these things to him."

The full significance of the memorable events of this day could only be understood by the power of the Spirit. Thus it was not until the gift of the Holy Ghost came on the day of Pentecost that the deep meaning of King Messiah's triumphal entry into the capital-for-the-moment of his earthly kingdom became apparent. (DNTC 1:579.)

12:19 "Perceive ye how ye prevail nothing?" has also been translated "You see, we are not succeeding at all!" and "See, this is getting us nowhere."

12:20–26 These teachings of Jesus to "certain Greeks" (probably Gentile proselytes to Judaism) are found only in John.

To them Jesus testified that the hour of His death was near at hand, the hour in which "the Son of man should be glorified." They were surprised and pained by the Lord's words, and possibly they inquired as to the necessity of such a sacrifice. Jesus explained by citing a striking illustration drawn from nature: "Verily, verily, I say unto you, Except a corn of wheat fall into the ground and die, it abideth alone: but if it die, it bringeth forth much fruit." The simile is an apt one, and at once impressively simple and beautiful. A farmer who neglects or refuses to cast his wheat into the earth, because he wants to keep it, can have no increase; but if he sow the wheat in good rich soil, each living grain may multiply itself many fold, though of necessity the seed must be sacrificed in the process. So, said the Lord, "He that loveth his life shall lose it; and he that hateth his life in this world shall keep it unto life eternal." The Master's meaning is clear; he that loves his life so well that he will not imperil it, or, if need be, give it up, in the service of God, shall forfeit his opportunity to win the bounteous increase of eternal life; while he who esteems the call of God as so greatly superior to life that his love of life is as hatred in comparison, shall find the life he freely yields or is willing to yield, though for the time being it disappear like the grain buried in the soil; and he shall rejoice in the bounty of eternal development. If such be true of every man's existence, how transcendently so was it of the life of Him who came to die that men may live? Therefore was it necessary that He die, as He had said He was about to do; but His death, far from being life lost, was to be life glorified. (JTC, pp. 518–19.)

12:23 For additional information on the sacred title "Son of Man" see text and commentary for Matthew 16:13.

12:24 "It abideth alone" could have been translated "it remains just one."

Just as one kernel ("corn") of wheat can reproduce manyfold, so the death of Jesus and his subsequent resurrection will produce "much fruit." As Paul was to exclaim later, "For as in Adam all die, even so in Christ shall all be made alive." (1 Cor. 15:22.)

12:25 Read text and commentary for Matthew 10:39.

12:26 After the testimony of the Scriptures on this point, the assurance is given by the Holy Ghost, bearing witness to those who obey Him, that Christ Himself has assuredly risen from the dead; and if He has risen from the dead, He will, by His power, bring all men to stand before Him: for if He has risen from the dead the bands of the temporal death are broken that the grave has no victory. If then, the grave has no victory, *those who keep the sayings of Jesus and obey His teachings have not only a promise of a resurrection from the dead, but an assurance of being admitted into His glorious kingdom; for, He Himself says, "Where I am there also shall my servant be"* (see John xii). (HC 2:19; italics added.)

This is the doctrine of exaltation. Christ our Lord overcame all things and ascended into heaven to sit on the throne of his Father. (Rev. 3:21.) Those who are to be with Christ must of necessity inherit the same glory and kingdom and indeed become "like him." (1 John 3:2.) "Ye shall sit down in the kingdom of my Father; . . . and ye shall be even as I am, and

I am even as the Father; and the Father and I are one." (3 Ne. 28:10.) What greater honor could the Father bestow upon anyone than this? (DNTC 1:629.)

12:27–36 Only John has written in detail the prayer of Jesus to his Father, the Father's response, and Jesus' subsequent teachings.

12:27–30 In the Gospel of John is related a parallel experience in the Master's ministry showing how, out of a multitude, only a few — or none — may hear God when he speaks.

Only the Master, apparently, knew that God had spoken. So often today, men and women are living so far apart from things spiritual that when the Lord is speaking to their physical hearing, to their minds with no audible sound, or to them through his authorized servants who, when directed by the Spirit, are as his own voice, they hear only a noise as did they at Jerusalem. Likewise, they received no inspired wisdom, nor inward assurance, that the mind of the Lord has spoken through his prophet leaders. (Harold B. Lee, CR, Oct. 1966, pp. 115–16.)

12:27 Jesus came into the world to bring about the Atonement, including the Resurrection; thus the significance of his statement "For this cause came I unto this hour."

12:31 "Prince" could have been more literally translated "ruler."

The "prince of this world" is clearly Satan, who will be cast out when his world is finally judged and found wanting. "Now [in the time of Jesus] is the judgment of this world" in that the world had to decide whether or not it would accept Jesus.

12:32 See 3 Nephi 27:14–15.

12:34 Of course the scriptures said Christ and his kingdom should abide forever (Isa. 9:7; Ezek. 37:25; and Dan. 7:14, among many others); and so shall it be commencing in the millennial day when "the kingdoms of this world are become the kingdoms of our Lord, and of his Christ; and he shall reign for ever and ever." (Rev. 11:15.)

But the scriptures also said that King-Messiah "was wounded for our transgressions, . . . bruised for our iniquities," "brought as a lamb to the slaughter," and *"cut off out of the land of the living."* They said, *"he made his grave with the wicked, and with the rich in his death"* (Isa. 53); that he, "the Lord Jehovah" would "swallow up death in victory," and bring to pass the resurrection of all men. Indeed, it was the great Jehovah himself who had said to their fathers: "Thy dead men shall live, *together with my dead body shall they arise."* (Isa. 25:8; 26:4, 19.)

There was no occasion for Jesus' captious critics either to have or to feign ignorance of the true and mortal ministry of their Messiah. (DNTC 1:631.)

12:35–36 Read text and commentaries for John 8:12–20.

12:37–43 These verses help to verify some of the great Messianic passages from Isaiah. (See Isa. 53.)

Concerning the fact the people would not receive the "report" of Jesus nor be converted through his miracles, Elder Bruce R. McConkie has observed:

Are there those today who think: "Had I seen the miracles of Jesus, I would have believed in him"? What causes men to believe? Do miracles create faith?

All things operate according to law. (D&C 88:13, 36.) Blessings flow from obedience, curses from disobedience. (D&C 130:20–21; 132:5.) The law of faith provides that if men do certain things, they will gain faith; otherwise, they will not. See Luke 17:5–6.

One of the terms and conditions of the law of faith is: If there is faith, there will be miracles. "These signs shall follow them that believe." (Mark 16:17.) "He that hath faith in me to be healed, and is not appointed unto death, shall be healed. He who hath faith to see shall see. He who hath faith to hear shall hear. The lame who hath faith to leap shall leap." (D&C 42:48–51.)

But the converse is not true. There is no provision in the law of faith that miracles will create faith. Signs *follow;* they do not precede. It is true that someone who has seen a sign may thereafter do the things which will enable him to gain faith, but it is not the miracle as such which begets the faith; it is obedience to that law upon which its receipt is predicated. Thus Moroni writes: "Ye receive no witness until *after* the trial of your faith. . . . For if there be no faith among the children of men God can do no miracle among them; wherefore he showed not himself until *after* their faith. . . . And neither at any time hath any wrought miracles until *after* their faith; wherefore they *first* believed in the Son of God." (Ether 12:6–18.) (DNTC 1:632–33.)

12:43 This verse could have been more literally translated "For they loved the glory of men more than even the glory of God."

12:44–50 Some of these summary statements by Jesus as he prepared for his final passover as a mortal are found only in John.

12:44 Elder Bruce R. McConkie has paraphrased this verse:

"He who believes I am the Son of God, believes not only in my divine mission, but also in my Father who sent me." This pronouncement is both simple logic and revealed truth. It is not possible to believe that Christ is the Son of God without believing that God is the Father of Christ. There cannot be a Father without a Son, nor a Son without a Father. Thus Jesus says, "He that receiveth me receiveth my Father" (D&C 84:37); the two cannot be separated. They are both divine and holy beings, or neither is. (DNTC 1:634.)

12:46 "Abide" could also have been translated "remain."

12:49–50 Again, Jesus emphasized that not only had he spoken of his divinity, but also the Father, who commanded Jesus what he should say.

13:1–17 This account of Jesus washing the apostles' feet is found only in John.

Washing of feet is a gospel ordinance; it is a holy and sacred rite, one performed by the saints in the seclusion of their temple sanctuaries. It is not done before the world or for worldly people. For his day and dispensation Jesus instituted it in the upper room at the time of the Last Supper. (DNTC 1:708.)

Our Lord did two things in the performance of this ordinance: 1. He fulfilled the old law given to Moses; and 2. He instituted a sacred ordinance which should be performed by legal administrators among his true disciples from that day forward.

As part of the restoration of all things, the ordinance of washing of feet has been restored in the dispensation of the fulness of times. In keeping with the standard pattern of revealing principles and practices line upon line and precept upon precept, the Lord revealed his will concerning the washing of feet little by little until the full knowledge of the endowment and all temple ordinances had been given. (MD, pp. 829–30.)

13:1 Jesus knew the time had come to bring about the Atonement, and he loved his fellowmen enough to endure suffering and even death. (See D&C 19:16–19.)

13:2 Read text and commentary for Luke 22:3.

13:7 Jesus' statement could have been translated "What I am doing you do not understand at present, but after [later] you will understand these things."

13:8 In the Joseph Smith Translation, this verse begins, "Peter saith unto him, Thou *needest not* to wash my feet." (Italics added.)

13:10 Jesus saith to him, He that *has washed his hands and his head,* needeth not save to wash his feet, but is clean every whit; and ye are clean, but not all. *Now this was the custom of the Jews under their law; wherefore Jesus did this that the law might be fulfilled.* (JST; italics added.)

13:13–14 "Master" could have been more literally translated "Teacher." (See commentary for Luke 6:40.)

13:16 See text and commentary for Luke 6:40.

13:18–30 Read text and commentaries for Matthew 26:21–25; Luke 22:21–30. Read also Mark 14:18–21.

13:18 The scripture quoted here is Psalm 41:9:

King David, whose throne the Son of David inherited, while engaged in civil war in Israel, wrote the Forty-first Psalm. In it he declaimed his betrayal by the traitor Ahithopel in these words: "Mine own familiar friend, in whom I trusted, which did eat of my bread, hath lifted up his heel against me." (Ps. 41:9.) Interestingly, when Absalom failed to follow Ahithopel's counsel, that traitor, as though his name were Judas, went and hanged himself. (2 Sam. 15:10–12; 17.)

Now we find Jesus quoting David's words and ascribing to them Messianic import, a meaning which was of course intended from the beginning. These words thus become a classical illustration of *how* Messianic prophecies were often given and of *why* they can be interpreted only by the power of the Holy Ghost. (DNTC 1:715.)

Judas was a spiritual pygmy from the beginning; as an unrepentant thief, he did not at any time possess apostolic stature. Yet he had his agency; he was free to choose his own course. "All mankind," and there are no exceptions, "may be saved, by obedience to the laws and ordinances of the Gospel." (Third Article of Faith.) Judas was no different in this respect than any other man. He could have chosen the course of righteousness; he had sufficient spiritual capacity to work out his salvation with fear and trembling before the Lord. And Jesus knew both the spiritual nothingness of Judas and the elections which that poor soul would make where his own salvation was concerned. (DNTC 1:714–15.)

(See section 1, "Judas.")

13:19 In the Joseph Smith translation, the end of this verse reads, "ye may believe that I am *the Christ*." (Italics added.)

13:20 Read text and commentaries for Matthew 10:40–41.

13:26–27, 30 "Sop" means "morsel," "mouthful," or "crumb." (See section 1, "Sop.")

In areas of the world where table utensils are not used at mealtime, it is common practice to place both broth and meat in a dish in the center of the table. Thin pieces of bread, often shaped to make a spoon, are used to extract both meat and broth from their repository. The bread thus dipped becomes a "sop." It is a mark of great honor for two friends to dip from the same sop-dish and an even greater mark of respect for one to dip for a friend and present the sop to him. Thus it was that Judas attempted to feign his love and loyalty for Jesus at the Passover meal by dipping his hand in the same dish with him. (See Matthew 26:23.) John reports that it was Jesus who dipped the sop for Judas and then handed it to him with the words, "That thou doest, do quickly." (John 13:27.) (LTJA, p. 160.)

13:26 Jesus may have answered John in a whisper or low voice, for the other disciples apparently either did not hear or did not understand. (See vv. 28–29.)

13:27 "That thou doest, do quickly" could have been translated "What you are doing, get done more quickly." Other translations are "As soon as Judas took the bread, Satan went into him. Jesus said to him, 'Hurry and do what you must!'" and "As soon as Judas took the bread, Satan entered into him."

As to whether or not Satan actually entered the body of Judas on this occasion, read text and commentaries for Luke 22:3.

13:31–35 These statements of Jesus are recorded only by John.

13:31 The prophet Joseph Smith has helped explain how the "Son of Man" is glorified "and God is glorified in him":

> What did Jesus do? Why; I do the things I saw my Father do when worlds came rolling into existence. My Father worked out his kingdom with fear and trembling, and I must do the same; and when I get my kingdom, I shall present it to my Father, so that he may obtain kingdom upon kingdom, and *it will exalt him in glory.* He will then take a higher exaltation, and I will take his place, and thereby become exalted myself. So that Jesus treads in the tracks of his Father, and inherits what God did before; and *God is thus glorified and exalted in the salvation and exaltation of all his children.* (TPJS, pp. 347–48; see also D&C 132:29–31.)

> **13:34** Yes, and an old commandment too; a commandment both old and new, a commandment that commences now and yet is everlasting; a commandment that is new each time it is revealed, but is old because it has always been in force. John, who here preserves this saying of our Savior, amplified and explained it in his own writings. Speaking of the "love of God," he said: "Brethren, I write no new commandment unto you, but an old commandment, which ye had from the beginning." And then speaking also of the same thing he says: "Again, a new commandment I write unto you." (1 John 2:1–8.)
>
> This gospel manner of naming the same thing as being both new and old is nowhere better illustrated than in the designation, "the new and everlasting covenant." The gospel is the everlasting covenant, the covenant of salvation which God always has and always will make with men, but it is a new covenant each time it is revealed. The gospel we have today is new to the world for this era; it is old because it was had anciently; it is everlasting because it is the same from age to age and from eternity to eternity. (DNTC 1:726.)

(See section 1, "Love, gospel of.")

> **13:35** It has been aptly observed that while many of the world's great religious leaders taught the principle of love, Jesus is the only one who could truly say, "Follow me," for he alone not only taught the principle but exemplified it. And we are to love one another as he has loved us. "By this," he says, "shall all men know that ye are my disciples, if ye have love one to another." (John 13:35.) (LTJA, p. 162.)

13:36–38 Read text and commentaries for Matthew 26:31–35; Mark 14:27–31; Luke 22:31–38.

13:36 "Thou shalt follow me afterwards" may have had reference not only to the fact that Peter must die but also the manner of Peter's death. According to tradition, Peter was crucified by the Romans, but unlike his Master, Peter was crucified head downward. (See also John 21:18–19.)

13:38 "Denied" could have been more literally translated "disowned." (See text and commentaries for Matt. 10:33; 26:34–35.)

14:1–4 These far-reaching words of Jesus have been preserved only by John.

14:2 "Mansions" has also been translated "abodes," "homes," "rooms," and "dwelling places."

> My text is on the resurrection of the dead, which you will find in the 14th chapter of John—"In my Father's house are many mansions." It should be—"In my Father's kingdom are many kingdoms," in order that ye may be heirs of God and joint-heirs with me....
>
> There are mansions for those who obey a celestial law, and there are other mansions for those who come short of the law, every man in his own order. (TPJS, p. 366.)

14:3 In the Joseph Smith Translation, this verse begins, "And *when* I go, *I will* prepare a place for you, *and* come again. . . ." (Italics added.)

14:5–11 These teachings of Jesus are recorded only in John.

14:6 "But by me" could have been translated "except through me."

> No man who has ever lived—neither Jew nor Gentile, pagan nor Christian, saint nor sinner—can come unto the Father (and thereby be saved) until he accepts Christ, believes and obeys his laws, and walks in the way he has appointed. He is the Savior of all men; unto him every knee shall bow and every tongue confess; his is the only name whereby salvation comes; and his laws apply to all, both in and out of the Christian community. "I am the Lord thy God; and I give unto you this commandment—that no man shall come unto the Father but by me or by my word, which is my law, saith the Lord." (D&C 132:12.) (DNTC 1:730.)

(See BD, "Amen.")

14:7–11 The Son appears and is in all respects like his Father; and conversely, the Father looks and acts and is in all respects like the Son. Their physical appearance is the same, both possess the attributes of godliness in their fulness and perfection; each would do and say precisely the same thing under the same circumstances. (*Mormon Doctrine,* pp. 294–295.) Hence the enigmatic and epigrammatic statement: "He that hath seen me hath seen the Father."

Thus, *God was in Christ manifesting himself to the world*—a gracious and condescending thing for the Eternal Father to do, for thereby men could come to know him and to gain that eternal life which such knowledge brings. (DNTC 1:731.)

(See section 1, "Trinity, no.")

14:10 "Believest thou not that I am in the the Father, and the Father in me?" could have been more literally translated "Do you not believe that I am in union with the Father and the Father is in union with me?"

14:11 The first part of this verse could have been more literally translated "Believe me that I am in union with the Father and the Father is in union with me."

14:12–14 All these sayings put together give as clear an account of the state of the glorified saints as language could give—the works that Jesus had done they were to do, and greater works than those which he had done among them should they do, and that because he went to the Father. He does not say that they should do these works in time; but they should do greater works, because he went to the Father. He says in the 24th verse [of the 17th chapter of John]: "Father, I will that they also, whom thou hast given me, be with me where I am; that they may behold my glory." These sayings, taken in connection, make it very plain that the greater works which those that believed on his name were to do were to be done in eternity, where he was going and where they should behold his glory. (*Lectures on Faith*, pp. 64–66.)

(See section 1, "Faith.")

14:13–14 Similar thoughts on the importance of praying in faith are found in the teachings of Jesus as recorded in the Book of Mormon, with the explanation that the thing requested should be right (3 Ne. 18:20) and good (Moro. 7:26).

Elder James E. Talmage believed this is the first time the Savior directed his disciples to pray "in his name":

For the first time the Lord directed His disciples to pray in His name to the Father, and assurance of success in righteous supplication was given in these words: "And whatsoever ye shall ask in my name, that will I do, that the Father may be glorified in the Son. If ye shall ask any thing in my name, I will do it." The name of Jesus Christ was to be thenceforth the divinely established talisman by which the powers of heaven could be invoked to operate in any righteous undertaking. (JTC, p. 602–3.)

14:15–26 These statements about the two Comforters climax and crown the teachings of the Son of God. We have no record of anything he ever said which can so completely withdraw the curtain of eternity and open to the faithful a vision of the glories of God. Based on love, born of obedience, Jesus promises the saints that they can have, here and now in this life, the following:

(1) The gift and constant companionship of the Holy Ghost; the comfort and peace which it is the function of that Holy Spirit to bestow; the revelation and the sanctifying power which alone will prepare men for the companionship of gods and angels hereafter;

(2) Personal visitations from the Second Comforter, the Lord Jesus Christ himself, the resurrected and perfected being who dwells with his Father in the mansions on high; and

(3) God the Father—mark it well Phillip!—shall visit man in person, take up his abode with him, as it were, and reveal to him all the hidden mysteries of his kingdom.

Joseph Smith, as the Holy Ghost poured light and revelation into his soul, said this about the two Comforters: "There are two Comforters spoken of. One is the Holy Ghost, the same as given on the day of Pentecost, and that all Saints receive after faith, repentance, and baptism. This first Comforter or Holy Ghost has no other effect than pure intelligence. It is more powerful in expanding the mind, enlightening the understanding, and storing the intellect with present knowledge, of a man who is of the literal seed of Abraham, than one that is a Gentile, though it may not have half as much visible effect upon the body; for as the Holy Ghost falls upon one of the literal seed of Abraham, it is calm and serene; and his whole soul and body are only exercised by the pure spirit of intelligence; while the effect of the Holy Ghost upon a Gentile, is to purge out the old blood, and make him actually of the seed of Abraham. That man that has none of the blood of Abraham (naturally) must have a new creation by the Holy Ghost. In such a case, there may be more of a powerful effect upon the body, and visible to the eye, than upon an Israelite, while the Israelite at first might be far before the Gentile in pure intelligence.

"The other Comforter spoken of is a subject of great interest, and perhaps understood by few of this generation. After a person has faith in Christ, repents of his sins, and is baptized for the remission of his sins and receives the Holy Ghost (by the laying on of hands), which is the first Comforter, then let him continue to humble himself before God, hungering and thirsting after righteousness, and living by every word of God, and the Lord will soon say unto him, Son, thou shalt be exalted. When the Lord has thoroughly proved him, and finds that the man is determined to serve him at all hazards, then the man will find his calling and his election made sure, then it will be his privilege to receive the other Comforter, which the Lord hath promised the saints, as is recorded in the testimony of St. John, in the 14th chapter, from the 12th to the 27th verses. Note the 16, 17, 18, 21, 23 verses. . . .

"Now what is this other Comforter. It is no more nor less than the Lord Jesus Christ himself; and this is the sum and substance of the whole matter; that when any man obtains this last Comforter, he will have the personage of Jesus Christ to attend him, or appear unto him from time to time, and even he will manifest the Father unto him, and they will take up their abode with him, and the visions of the heavens will be opened unto him, and the Lord will teach him face to face, and he may have perfect knowledge of the mysteries of the kingdom of God; and this is the state and place the ancient saints arrived at when they had such glorious visions—Isaiah, Ezekiel, John upon the Isle of Patmos, St. Paul in the three heavens, and all the saints who held communion with the general assembly and Church of the First Born." (*Teachings,* pp. 149–151.) (DNTC 1:735–36.)

(See section 1, "Holy Ghost.")

14:15 See text and commentaries for Matthew 5:43–47; 22:37–40; John 13:34.

Love of God is thus measured in terms of service and obedience. Jesus says: "Now this is the commandment: Repent, all ye ends of the earth, and come unto me and be baptized in my name, that ye may be sanctified by the reception of the Holy Ghost, that ye may stand spotless before me at the last day." (3 Ne. 27:20.) Consider in this connection those who cry, Lord, Lord, professing their love for him with their lips, while remaining outside his Church—do such really love him?

He commands his saints to pay their tithes and offerings, to seek the attributes of godliness, to keep themselves morally clean, to serve in the kingdom and testify of the divinity of his great latter-day work. How great is the love of those who fail or who fall short? (DNTC 1:736–37.)

14:16 "Comforter" could have been translated "helper." The other Comforter or Helper referred to here is the Holy Ghost. (See BD, "Comforter.")

14:17 The "Spirit of truth" in this verse is the "other Comforter" mentioned in the preceding verse, or the Holy Ghost.

"The Holy Ghost has not a body of flesh and bones, but is a personage of Spirit. Were it not so, the Holy Ghost could not dwell in us. A man may receive the Holy Ghost, and it may descend upon him and not tarry with him." (D&C 130:22–23.) The Holy Ghost as a personage does not inhabit the bodies of mortal men, but that member of the Godhead dwells in a man in the sense that his promptings, the whisperings of the Spirit, find lodgment in the human soul. When the Holy Spirit speaks to the spirit in man, the Holy Ghost is thereby dwelling in man, for the truths that man then gives forth are those which have come from the Holy Ghost. "Therefore it is given to abide in you; the record of heaven; the Comforter; the peaceable things of immortal glory; the truth of all things; that which quickeneth all things, which maketh alive all things; that which knoweth all things, and hath all power according to wisdom, mercy, truth, justice, and judgment." (Moses 6:61.) (DNTC 1:738.)

14:18 "Comfortless" could also have been translated "as orphans" or "bereaved." That Jesus Christ does indeed "come to" the faithful is verified by other scriptures. (See D&C 93:1; Ether 3:19–20.)

14:20 This verse could have been more literally translated "In that day you will know that I am in union with my Father and you are in union with me and I am in union with you."

14:22 In the Joseph Smith Translation, the beginning of this verse is punctuated as follows: "Judas saith unto him, (not Iscariot,) Lord . . ."

14:26 See commentary for John 14:1–6.

The disciples of Jesus did not receive the gift of the Holy Ghost while he was with them. The reason for this, in part at least, was due to the fact that they had with them to guide and teach them the second member of the Godhead, even Jesus himself. While he was with them there was no occasion for them to have the companionship of the Holy Ghost. Before the Savior left them, he promised to send them the Comforter, or Holy Ghost. (AGQ 2:159.)

Elder Bruce R. McConkie has commented on "He shall teach you all things":

All things? Yes, all things; and all things means all things. "And by the power of the Holy Ghost ye may know the truth of all things." (Moro. 10:5.) The revealed word says God knows all things and has all truth, which means there is nothing he does not know and no truth he does not possess. Consequently, now or hereafter, in time or eternity, the Holy Ghost shall teach all things to deserving and eligible students. (DNTC 1:741.)

14:27 These inspiring words on peace have elicited many commentaries, including the following by Elder McConkie:

Not the salutation, "Peace be with you," which was common among the Jews; not merely the absence of war; not an enforced or voluntary armistice between armed belligerents; not worldly peace. Rather, an inner peace born of a sure conviction of the divinity of the Lord's earthly kingdom; a peace which carries an assurance of a better world to come; a peace that dwells in the souls of men though they may be in the midst of war and turmoil. (DNTC 1:742.)

14:28–29 The Savior again emphasizes to his disciples that he must go again to the Father (after his resurrection) but then he will return again to them. Thus, they indeed had cause to "rejoice."

14:29 Jesus emphasized that one of the purposes of prophecy is "that, when it is come to pass, ye might believe."

14:30–31 Hereafter I will not talk much with you; for the prince of *darkness, who is of* this world, cometh, *but hath no power over me, but he hath power over you.*

And I tell you these things, that ye may know that I love the Father; and as the Father gave me commandment, even so I do. Arise, let us go hence. (JST; italics added.)

14:30 "For the prince of this world cometh, and hath

nothing in me" could have been translated "for the ruler of the world is coming, and he has no hold on me."

So powerful was he in the Master's day that the Master referred to Satan as "the prince of this world," but he added, 'the prince of this world cometh, and hath nothing in me.' (John 14:30.) We must be able to say, though the power is evil on every side, "As for me and my house, we shall serve the God of this land." The prince of this world is coming to tempt every one of us, and the only ones who will stand through these evil days are those who have founded their houses upon the rock, as the Master said: when the storms descended and the winds blew and the rains came and beat upon the house, it fell not because it was founded upon the rock. That is what the Lord is trying to say to us today. (Harold B. Lee, *British Area Conference Report,* Aug. 1971, p. 135.)

15:1–11 In superb allegory the Lord thus proceeded to illustrate the vital relationship between the apostles and himself, and between himself and the Father, by the figure of a vinegrower, a vine, and its branches. . . . A grander analogy is not to be found in the world's literature. Those ordained servants of the Lord were as helpless and useless without him as is a bough severed from the tree. As the branch is made fruitful only by virtue of the nourishing sap it receives from the rooted trunk, and if cut away or broken off withers, dries, and becomes utterly worthless except as fuel for the burning, so those men, though ordained to the Holy Apostleship, would find themselves strong and fruitful in good works, only as they remained in steadfast communion with the Lord. Without Christ what were they, but unschooled Galileans, some of them fishermen, one a publican, the rest of undistinguished attainments, and all of them weak mortals? As branches of the Vine they were at that hour clean and healthful, through the instructions and authoritative ordinances with which they had been blessed, and by the reverent obedience they had manifested. (JTC, pp. 604–6.)

Members of the Church are like the branches and leaves on a great tree. They are on the tree, but that alone does not save them. If they do not receive the nourishment and sustaining power that comes from Christ, who is the trunk (whose sustaining power is carried to them by the Holy Ghost only as they make themselves worthy to receive it), then they wither and fall away like dry leaves. Of this, President John Taylor said: "As a Saint you say, 'I think I understand my duty, and I am doing very well.' That may be so. You see the little twig: it is green; it flourishes and is the very picture of life. It bears its part and proportion in the tree, and is connected with the stem, branches, and root. But could the tree live without it? Yes, it could. It need not boast itself and get uplifted and say, 'How green I am! and how I flourish! and what a healthy position I am in! How well I am doing! and I am in my proper place and am doing right.' But could you do without the root? No: you bear your proper part and position in the tree. Just so with this people. When they are doing their part—when they are magnifying their calling, living their religion, and walking in obedience to the Spirit of the Lord, they have a portion of his Spirit given to them to profit withal. And while they are humble, faithful, diligent, and observe the laws and commandments of God, they stand in their proper position on the tree: they are flourishing; the buds, blossoms, leaves, and everything about them are all right, and they form a part and parcel of the tree." (John Taylor in JD 6:108.) (LTJA, p. 167.)

15:4 "Abide in me" could have been translated "Remain in union with me."

15:8 Jesus amplified, to three of the Nephite Twelve, the promise here given to his Old World special witnesses: "Ye have desired that ye might bring the souls of men unto me, while the world shall stand," he said unto them. "And for this cause ye shall have fulness of joy; and ye shall sit down in the kingdom of my Father; yes, your joy shall be full, even as the Father hath given me fulness of joy; and ye shall be even as I am, and I am even as the Father; and the Father and I are one." (3 Ne. 28:9–10.)

This promise, in principle, is available to all saints, for "Men are, that they might have joy" (2 Ne. 2:25), and that God who is no respecter of persons desires to reward all his children with the choicest blessings of time and eternity. (DNTC 1:747.)

15:12–17 These teachings of Jesus to his "friends," the disciples, are found only in John.

15:12–13 See text and commentaries for Matthew 5:43–47; 22:37–40; John 13:34.

15:14 Friends of the Lord, what a salutation this is! Our Lord's friends are those who, having overcome all things, having kept his commandments to the full, having made their callings and elections sure, are the ones he will call to dwell and associate with him in glorious exaltation.

This same gladsome salutation has been given to men in this dispensation also. To selected elders of his latter-day kingdom came these words from his mouth: "As I said unto mine apostles, even so I say unto you, for you are mine apostles, even God's high priests; ye are they whom my Father hath given me; ye are my friends, . . . for from henceforth I shall call you friends." (D&C 84:63, 77.) Also: "Verily, I say unto my servant Joseph Smith, Jun., or in other words, I will call you friends, for you are my friends, and ye shall have an inheritance with me—I called you servants for the world's sake, and ye are their servants for my sake." (D&C 93:45–46.) (DNTC 1:747–48.)

15:15 Elder Bruce R. McConkie has commented on "All things that I have heard of my Father I have made known to you":

This statement, undoubtedly part of a digested and summarized account of Jesus' statements to his friends, must be interpreted and understood along with the statement he was shortly to make about saying many additional things to them. (John 16:12–15.) The meaning is: "I have told you and will tell you all things I have heard from my Father which you are able to bear at this time. When you receive the enlightening power of the Holy Ghost, then, through him as my revealer and witness, I shall have many more things to teach you." (DNTC 1:748.)

15:16 God's ministers are ordained. They have the holy priesthood conferred upon them and are ordained by the laying on of hands to officiate in specific offices and callings. Priesthood is the power and authority of God delegated to man on earth to act in all things for the salvation of men; it is divided into two orders—Aaronic and Melchizedek. These apostles had been chosen by revelation and ordained by Jesus to their high and holy ministry in the Melchizedek Order. And as it is with them, so it is with all true representatives of the Lord, for Paul said: "No man taketh this honour unto himself, but he that is called of God, as was Aaron." (Heb. 5:4.) Unless the Lord's ministers actually have this authority from the Lord they cannot cast out devils, heal the sick, confer the Holy Ghost, perform a baptism that will be recognized in heaven, or do any of the host of things reserved for performance by legal administrators in the Lord's earthly kingdom. (DNTC 1:748–49.)

(See section 1, "Ordained.")

15:18–27 Opposition of the world is one of the chief identifying characteristics of true religion. Worldly people always resent and resist the higher way of life manifest through the gospel. "Adultery, fornication, uncleanness, lasciviousness, idolatry, witchcraft, hatred, variance, emulations, wrath, strife, seditions, heresies, envyings, murders, drunkenness, revellings, and such like" are of the world. (Gal. 5:19–21.) Those who live after the manner of the world follow after these things. When true Christians seek to ban alcoholic beverages, to prohibit gambling, to curtail recreation and commercialism on the Sabbath, to prevent the publication of lewd and pornographic materials, to abolish war, or to do any of a host of things which run counter to the appetites and passions of carnal people, then the battles break out anew. (DNTC 1:750.)

15:18–19 "World" as used in these verses refers to the social conditions among the people who live on the earth, not to the earth or planet itself. Thus the "end of the world" refers to "the end of worldliness" or "the destruction of the wicked." (See text and commentaries for Matt. 13:39–43, 49; 24:3–5, 23–27, 51. See also Mosiah 3:19; Alma 42:10; 1 John 2:15–17; James 4:4; JS-M 1:24.)

15:20–21 See D&C 122:5–8.

15:22–25 The Jews to whom Jesus taught the gospel had "no cloke for their sin" because they had rejected the added light and truth he had brought to them. (See D&C 82:3–4; read text and commentaries for John 9:39–41.)

15:22 "Cloke" could also have been translated "pretext" or "excuse."

15:25 The scripture quoted here is Psalm 69:4. This is another example of a Messianic prophecy that can be interpreted only through the power of the Holy Ghost. (Read text and commentaries for John 13:18.)

15:26 One of the major functions of the Holy Ghost is to testify of both the Father and the Son. (Read also 3 Ne. 11:32–36.)

16:1–4 Jesus' observation that "the time cometh, that whosoever killeth you will think that he doeth God service" has elicited the following comment from Elder Bruce R. McConkie:

> Sincerity has almost nothing to do with gaining salvation. Men who slay the saints can be just as sincere as those who thus become martyrs. Men can believe so devoutly in falsehood that they will even lay down their own lives for it. What does it matter that those who killed the prophets, either ancient or modern, thought they did God service? The thing that counts is truth, pure God-given truth. (DNTC 1:752.)

16:5–15 This information about Jesus leaving and then sending the Comforter is found only in John.

16:5 "None of you asketh me, Whither goest thou?" seems almost an invitation for the disciples to ask for further information. The promise is that we should "ask, seek, knock" to learn additional truths, and when we fail to follow these simple admonitions we may fail to obtain the additional truths. (Read also 3 Ne. 15:16–24.)

16:7–8 These verses could have been more literally translated "Nevertheless, I am telling you the truth. It is for your benefit I am going away. For if I do not go away, the helper will by no means come to you; but if I do go my way, I will send him to you. And when that one arrives he will give the world convincing evidence concerning sin and concerning righteousness and concerning judgment."

> Just as Jesus and the Father are so much alike in appearance, and so completely united in doctrine and in all the attributes of godliness, that he who has seen one has in effect seen the other, so there is a similar unity between Jesus and the Holy Ghost. They are one in that they both would say and do the same thing under the same circumstances. Hence, as long as Jesus was with the disciples in person, there was not the full need for them to have the constant companionship of the Spirit that there would be after Jesus left. The disciples had on occassions felt the promptings of the Spirit. Peter, for one, had received a revelation from the Father, given by the power of the Holy Ghost, certifying that Jesus was "the Christ, the Son of the living God." (Matt. 16:16.) But the enjoyment of the gift of the

Holy Ghost, that is the actual and continuing companionship of that holy being, was yet future.

Earlier Jesus had said he would ask the Father to send the Holy Ghost. (John 14:16, 26.) Now he says he will do it himself. Both statements are descriptive of the fact. The Holy Ghost is the third member of the Godhead and as such does the bidding of both the Father and the Son. (DNTC 1:753–54.)

(See section 1, "Holy Ghost.")

16:8 "Reprove" has also been translated "convince," "prove," and "show." The meaning is to prove that a person is wrong, or to convict him.

16:9–11 These are difficult verses which have come to us in such a condensed and abridged form as to make interpretation difficult. The seeming meaning is: "When you receive the companionship of the Spirit, so that you speak forth what he reveals to you, then your teachings will convict the world of sin, and of righteousness, and of judgment. The world will be convicted of *sin* for rejecting me, for not believing your Spirit-inspired testimony that I am the Son of God through whom salvation comes. They will be convicted for rejecting your testimony of my *righteousness* — for supposing I am a blasphemer, a deceiver, and an imposter — when in fact I have gone to my Father, a thing I could not do unless my works were true and righteous altogether. They will be convicted of false *judgment* for rejecting your testimony against the religions of the day, and for choosing instead to follow Satan, the prince of this world, who himself, with all his religious philosophies, will be judged and found wanting." (DNTC 1:754.)

16:10 The Joseph Smith Translation changes "ye" to "they," referring to those who will be reproved because of their sins.

16:12 The things of God cannot be fully understood without the Holy Ghost, and the disciples did not receive the right of the permanent companionship of the Holy Ghost until the day of Pentecost. (See Acts 2:1–4; 1 Cor. 2:11–16.)

16:13 This promise is made to the saints, not to the world. Jesus had just told them that the world could not receive the Holy Ghost, meaning the gift or the companionship of that member of the Godhead. (John 14:17.) Now our Lord is saying that the saints can have that companionship, and through it can come to a knowledge of all things. People outside the Church can and do receive revelation from the Holy Ghost telling them of the divinity of the Lord's work. It is in this way that sincere investigators get to know that the Book of Mormon is true, for instance. And if they, then, come into the Church and receive the gift of the Holy Ghost by the laying on of hands, they have made available to them the constant companionship of the Holy Spirit. Then the promise of Moroni can be fulfilled: "And by the power of the Holy Ghost ye may know the truth of all things." (Moro. 10:4–5.) (DNTC 1:754–55.)

16:14 Read text and commentaries for John 13:31.

16:15 That men can be joint-heirs with Jesus Christ is also taught in D&C 84:38.

16:16–33 During these closing hours of his mortal life, Jesus gently and with increasing plainness renews his teachings that he shall die and be resurrected. He is approaching the high point of his ministry, the hour when he shall take upon himself the sins of the world, when he shall suffer himself to be crucified, when he shall come forth in glorious immortality to minister briefly among mortal men, and shall ascend to everlasting exaltation at the right hand of his Father.

Jesus' coming separation from his beloved disciples is to be brief. They shall witness his death; place his body in the tomb; be absent while he visits the spirits in paradise; and then the third day he shall rise again to appear and minister once more to them. They shall sorrow because of the separation, rejoice at the reunion; they shall lament at his death, feel exultation at his resurrection—all of which is a type and shadow of how, for all men, the sorrow and separation of death is swallowed up in the joy of the resurrection. (DNTC 1:758.)

16:18 "We cannot tell what he saith" could have been translated "we do not know what he is talking about."

16:21 The first part of this verse could have been translated "A woman, when she is giving birth, has grief, because her hour has arrived."

16:23 In the Joseph Smith Translation, the first sentence of this verse is expanded: "And in that day ye shall ask me nothing *but it shall be done unto you.*" (Italics added.)

16:24 Since the divine law in all ages called for men to pray to the Father in the name of Christ, why had Jesus awaited this hour to institute the age-old system among his disciples? Perhaps it is a situation similar to that which is involved in receiving the gift of the Holy Ghost; as long as Jesus was with the disciples they did not enjoy the *full manifestations* of the Holy Ghost. (John 16:7.) Perhaps as long as Jesus was personally with them many of their petitions were addressed directly to him rather than to the Father. Such was the course followed by the Nephites when the resurrected and glorified Lord ministered among them. They prayed directly to him and not to the Father. (DNTC 1:758.)

16:25 "Proverbs" has also been translated "parables," "figures," and "metaphors." (See text and commentaries for Matt. 13:1–3, 10–17, 34–35; Mark 4:1–2, 10–13, 33–34. Read also Luke 8:4, 9–10.)

16:28 This is one of many verses that show that Jesus and the Father are separate and distinct beings. (Read text and commentaries for Matt. 3:16–17; Luke 10:22; John 14:7–11.)

16:30 Other translations of this verse are:

Now we know that you know all things, and need none to question you; by this we believe that you came from God. (RSV.)

Now we can see that you know all things and that you do not even need to have anyone ask you questions. This makes us believe that you came from God. (NIV.)

The basic idea is that Jesus knew the thoughts of the people.

16:33 There is a great difference between the kind of peace that Jesus spoke of and the world around us. We live in a wicked world, a world gone crazy with wanton indulgence and crime. Each day the news bears tragic record of wars, natural disasters, terror, and the frustrated efforts of mankind to avert or respond intelligently to the disasters. In spite of all this, Jesus has promised his followers that they may have peace in this world. Read John 16:33. Compare Philippians 4:7.

And Jesus' promise is real, for those who obey his commandments do feel his influence and comfort in their hearts, and they are not afraid. In the face of every threatening peril, they can pray to God and he will answer them by the "still small voice" of the Holy Spirit, and speak peace to their souls. (LTJA, p. 168.)

17:1–26 This magnificent "high priestly" or "intercessory" prayer is found only in John.

With a perfect understanding of his mission and that the time of his atonement was "at hand," Jesus concluded the teaching portion of his ministry with a prayer—a prayer which has sometimes been referred to as the high-priestly or great intercessory prayer. (See John 17.) These designations are not inappropriate, for, as we shall see, Jesus, our Great High Priest, first offered himself as an offering; then, as Mediator, he interceded on behalf of worthy members of his kingdom. The pattern for this had been established in ancient Israel.

Once each year, the presiding high priest in ancient Israel entered into the holy of holies, the most sacred place within the tabernacle. There he would perform certain rites in connection with the Day of Atonement, a day set aside for national humiliation and contrition. Having bathed himself and dressed in white linen, he would present before the lord a young bullock and two young goats as sin offerings, and a ram as a burnt offering in behalf of his sins and those of the people. The high priest's role was that of a mediator, or one who interceded with the Lord in behalf of the people. His role, of course, was but a type of the type of the great mediating role of the Savior in our behalf. Thus, when Jesus pleaded to the Father for all those who believed on him, he did so as our Intercessor, or Great High Priest.

The prayer he offered on this occasion had three distinct parts: In the first part (see John 17:1–3), Jesus offered himself as the great sacrifice. His hour had come. The next part of the prayer (see John 17:4–19) was a reverent report to the Father of his mortal mission. In the last part (see

John 17:20–26) of his prayer, Jesus interceded not only for the eleven apostles present, but for all who shall believe on Jesus "through their word," in order that all would come to a perfect unity, which unity invested Christ in them as Christ is in the Father. Thus all would be perfect in unity, and the world would believe that the Father had sent his Son. (LTJA, p. 171.)

17:3 As used in the scriptures, *eternal life* is the name given to the kind of life that our Eternal Father lives. The word *eternal,* as used in the name *eternal life,* is a noun and not an adjective. It is one of the formal names of Deity (Moses 1:3; 7:35; D&C 19:11) and has been chosen by him as the particular name to identify the kind of life that he lives. He being God, the life he lives is God's life; and his name (in the noun sense) being Eternal, the kind of life he lives is eternal life. Thus: *God's life is eternal life; eternal life is God's life—*the expressions are synonymous.

Accordingly, eternal life is not a name that has reference only to the unending duration of a future life; immortality is to live forever in the resurrected state, and by the grace of God all men will gain this unending continuance of life. But only those who obey the fulness of the gospel law will inherit eternal life. (D&C 29:43–44.) It is "the greatest of all the gifts of God" (D&C 14:7), for it is the kind, status, type, and quality of life that God himself enjoys. Thus those who gain eternal life receive exaltation; they are sons of God, joint-heirs with Christ, members of the Church of the Firstborn; they overcome all things, have all power, and receive the fulness of the Father. They are gods. (MD, p. 237.)

It is one thing to know about God and another to know him. We know about him when we learn that he is a personal being in whose image man is created; when we learn that the Son is in the express image of his Father's person; when we learn that both the Father and the Son possess certain specified attributes and powers. But we know them, in the sense of gaining eternal life, when we enjoy and experience the same things they do. To know God is to think what he thinks, to feel what he feels, to have the power he possesses, to comprehend the truths he understands, and to do what he does. Those who know God become like him, and have his kind of life, which is eternal life. (DNTC 1:762.)

(See section 1, "Eternal life, what to gain.")

17:6–8 For similar lofty thoughts by Jesus pertaining to those whom he has called out of the world and who have been faithful to him, see 3 Nephi 19:20–22.

17:9–10 The resurrected Jesus Christ used similar phraseology in praying for his chosen disciples among the righteous Lehites. (See 3 Ne. 19:28–29.)

17:11 If the disciples are to become one, even as the Father and the Son are one, the oneness referred to could not refer to a oneness of substance as claimed in the apostate creeds of some so-called Christian churches. (See text and commentaries for Matt. 3:16–17; Luke 10:22; John 14:7–11.)

17:12 Judas . . . was probably not a son of perdition in the sense of one who is damned forever, but in the sense that he was a son or follower of Satan in this life. See Matt. 26:21–25. (DNTC 1:765.)

(See section 1, "Judas: Son of perdition?")

17:13 "That they might have my joy fulfilled in themselves" could have been translated "that they may have my joy in themselves to the full."

17:20–26 "Be one!" Such is God's eternal command to his people. "Be one; and if ye are not one ye are not mine." (D&C 38:27.) If and when perfect unity exists among the saints, they accomplish the Lord's purposes on the earth and gain their own exaltation in the life to come. . . .

Those who live the perfect law of unity "become the sons of God, even one in me as I am one in the Father, as the Father is one in me, that we may be one." (D&C 35:2.) To Adam the Lord said: "Behold, thou art one in me, a son of God; and thus may all become my sons." (Moses 6:68.) (DNTC 1:766–67.)

17:21 This verse could have been more literally translated "In order that they may all be one, just as you, Father, are in union with me and I am in union with you, that they also may be in union with us, in order that the world may believe that you sent me forth."

18:1–2 For additional information concerning what occurred after Jesus "went forth . . . over the brook Cedron" and entered into the Garden of Gethsemane, read text and commentaries for Matthew 26:36–46; Mark 14:32–42; Luke 22:40–46. See also 2 Nephi 9:21–22; Mosiah 3:5–12; D&C 19:1–24. (See BD, "Cedron.")

18:2 "For Jesus ofttimes resorted thither with his disciples" could have been translated "because Jesus had many times met there with his disciples."

18:3–11 For further information pertaining to the betrayal and arrest of Jesus, read text and commentaries for Matthew 26:47–56; Mark 14:43–52; Luke 22:47–53.

Judas guided a small army well supplied with weapons. A band consisted of some six hundred Roman soldiers with a tribune at their head. The Roman overlords were taking no chance on an uproar during the week of the Passover. Accompanying the soldiers was a "great multitude," perhaps thousands in number. This was no secret arrest, no private kidnapping; all Jerusalem would be aware of the taking into custody of the city's most noted inhabitant. Probably Judas would have led the entire "army" to the site of the Upper Room and not finding Jesus and the disciples would have guided them on to Gethsemane, for "Judas . . . knew the place: for Jesus ofttimes resorted thither with his disciples." (DNTC 1:781.)

18:5, 7 The Greek words translated here "Jesus of Nazareth" read "Jesus the Nazarene."

18:10–11 Further details on this incident involving Peter are found in Matthew 26:51–55; Mark 14:47–49; Luke 22:49–53.

18:12 Other accounts of the arrest of Jesus include additional information concerning the fact that some of the disciples fled at this time. (See Matt. 26:50, 56; Mark 14:46, 50–52.) The identification of some of those who arrested Jesus ("the band and the captain and officers of the Jews") indicate that this was a formal arrest, organized with sufficient forces to prevent any uprising among the people who might be present at that time of the night.

18:13–24 For additional information pertaining to the trial of Jesus before the "high priest" and his associates, read text and commentaries for Matthew 26:57–68; Mark 14:53–65; Luke 22:54–65.

Only John mentions that Jesus was taken before "Annas first." This has led some scholars to conclude that the subsequent events took place before Caiaphas, who is mentioned in the same verse and in the succeeding verse.

(See section 1, "Caiaphas"; BD, "Annas.")

Two reasons are offered for concluding that the events here involved occurred before Caiaphas. (1) After reciting what took place John says, "Now Annas had sent him bound unto Caiaphas the high priest." (V. 24.) Both Dummelow and Jamieson, however, explain that the correct translation is, "Annas, therefore, sent him bound unto Caiaphas," thus making it a happening which took place after the interrogation rather than before. (*Dummelow*, p. 805; *Jamieson*, p. 91.) (2) Edersheim's argument is: "For as, according to the three synoptic Gospels, the palace of the high priest Caiaphas was the scene of Peter's denial, the account of it in the fourth Gospel must refer to the same locality, and not to the palace of Annas." (Edersheim, cited, *Talmage*, pp. 643–644.) Both Dummelow and Jamieson answer this by explaining that Annas and Caiaphas lived in different parts of the same building and that the same court served them both. (*Jamieson*, p. 162; *Dummelow*, p. 805.) Thus the great probability is that Jesus was in fact examined and smitten in the presence of Annas before he was taken to Caiaphas. There would seem to be no other reason for John to make special mention that Jesus was taken before Annas unless something there occurred which was important to his narrative. (DNTC 1:783–84.)

18:13 The high priest Annas is mentioned by name only four times in the Bible: Luke 3:2; John 18:13, 24; Acts 4:6 John identifies Annas as the "father in law to Caiaphas" who was also a high priest.

Cyrenius . . . deprived Joazar of the high priesthood . . . and he appointed Ananus, the son of Seth, to be high priest. . . . [Valerius Gratus] deprived Ananus of the high priesthood, and appointed Ismael, the son of Phabi, to be high-priest. He also deprived him in a little time, and ordained Eleazar, the son of Ananus, who had been high-priest before, to be high-priest: which office, when he had held for a year, Gratus deprived him of it, and gave the high-priesthood to Simon, the son of Camithus; and, when he had possessed that dignity no longer than a year, Joseph Caiaphas was made his successor. When Gratus had done those things, he went back to Rome, after he had tarried in Judea eleven years, when Pontius Pilate came as his successor. (Josephus, *Antiquities of the Jews*, 18.2.1–2.)

Joseph Caiaphas was high priest between the years A.D. 18–36, but Annas continued to exercise much religious and political control over the Jews as either substitute for the high priest, president of the Sanhedrin, or chief examining judge. Annas' wealth was immense; and it derived, in part, at least, from the sale of materials used in the temple sacrifices. (See Hastings, *Dictionary of the Bible*, s.v. "Annas"; Smith, *Dictionary of the Bible*, rev. ed., s.v. "Annas.") Joseph Caiaphas was the Jewish high priest under Tiberius (see Matthew 26:3, 57; John 11:49; 18:13, 14, 24, 28; and Acts 4:6) and was appointed to the office of high priest by Valerius Gratus. (See Smith, *Dictionary*, s.v. "Caiaphas.") In John 18:13 we read that Joseph Caiaphas was the son-in-law of Annas. (LTJA, p. 181.)

18:15–18 These verses, with verses 25–27, contain John's account of Peter's denial that he knew Jesus. (Read text and commentaries for Matt. 26:69–75; Mark 14:66–72; Luke 22:54–62.)

18:20 "Whither the Jews always resort" has also been translated "where all the Jews come together."

18:22–23 "Answerest thou the high priest so?" could have been more literally translated "Is that the way you answer the chief priest?"

That Jesus maintained his equanimity and submissiveness even under the provocation of a blow dealt by a brutish underling in the presence of the high priest, is confirmatory of our Lord's affirmation that he had "overcome the world" (John 16:33). One cannot read the passage without comparing, perhaps involuntarily, the divine submissiveness of Jesus on this occasion, with the wholly natural and human indignation of Paul under somewhat similar conditions at a later time (Acts 23:1–5). The high priest Ananias, displeased at Paul's remarks, ordered someone who stood by to smite him on the mouth. Paul broke forth in angry protest: "God shall smite thee, thou whited wall: for sittest thou to judge me after the law, and commandest me to be smitten contrary to the law?" Afterward he apologized, saying that he knew not that it was the high priest who had given the command that he be smitten. (JTC, p. 644.)

18:23 Jesus' answer could have been translated "If I spoke wrongly, bear witness concerning the wrong; but if rightly, why do you hit me?"

18:25–27 (See John 18:15–18; read text and commentaries for Matt. 26:69–75; Mark 14:66–72; Luke 22:54–62.) It is important to remember that Peter did not deny that Jesus was the Messiah; Peter denied *knowing* Jesus of Nazareth.

18:28–39 For further information on the trial before Pilate, read text and commentaries for Matthew 27:11–14; Mark 15:2–5; Luke 23:2–5.

Jesus had been convicted of blasphemy by the Sanhedrin, a Jewish but not Roman crime. So when Pilate asked, "What is the charge against this man?" their designs were temporarily thwarted. They were seeking a Roman execution for a Jewish death sentence, a thing Pilate could have approved. But now it appeared Pilate was taking original jurisdiction and wanted to try the case over again. They replied, probably through Caiaphas as spokesman: "We have already tried him; he is guilty; we come to you to endorse our sentence and order the execution." Pilate replies: "If it is a Jewish crime and not a Roman, Judge him according to your law." Their answer: "We cannot put a man to death; you must do that." This was not true; they could have executed Jesus by stoning if Pilate had approved their death sentence. But such an execution would have caused a riot among the people; Jesus had many followers in Jerusalem; and their conspiracy called for a Roman execution, one that could not be questioned by the people. The effect of their plan would be, as John says, to fulfill Jesus' saying that he would be crucified. The Jews stoned their victims to death; Rome crucified hers; and both Divine Providence and Satan's mortal helpers were now combining to assure the decreed type of death.

Knowing now that they have failed to gain a Roman crucifixion for the Jewish capital offense of blasphemy, they immediately change their charge to high treason, with three counts in their indictment: He is guilty of sedition by stirring up the whole nation; of forbidding to give tribute to Caesar; and of assuming the royal title. (DNTC 1:800–801.)

18:28 The Greek word translated "judgment hall" is translated "praetorium" in Mark 15:16. Another possible translation is "governor's palace." (See text and commentaries for Matt. 27:1–2; Mark 15:1; Luke 22:66–71; 23:1; section 1, "Praetorium.")

18:29 Roman governor or procurator of Judea, Samaria, and Idumea, [Pilate] resided normally at Caesarea on the Mediterranean seashore, but had come to Jerusalem during the Passover to help keep order. Appointed in 26 A.D. he served for ten years. "He was then summoned to Rome to answer certain charges made against him, and was banished to Vienna in Gaul, where he is said to have committed suicide." (*Dummelow,* p. 715.) (DNTC 1:800.)

For further background on this Roman official, read text and commentaries for Matthew 27:24–25.

18:30 See commentary for Luke 23:32–33, 39 on "malefactor."

18:31 John the apostle intimates in this last remark a determination on the part of the Jews to have Jesus put to death not only by Roman sanction but by Roman executioners; for, as we readily may see, had Pilate approved the death sentence and handed the Prisoner over to the Jews for its infliction, Jesus would have been stoned, in accordance with the Hebrew penalty for blasphemy; whereas the Lord had plainly foretold that His death would be by crucifixion, which was a Roman method of execution, but one never practiced by the Jews. Furthermore, if Jesus had been put to death by the Jewish rulers, even with governmental sanction, an insurrection among the people might have resulted, for there were many who believed on Him. The crafty hierarchs were determined to bring about His death under Roman condemnation. (JTC, pp. 632–33.)

18:36 "But now is my kingdom not from hence" could have been translated "but, as it is, my kingdom is not from this source."

18:38 The position in the sentence of the Greek word translated "again" makes possible two interpretations of the last sentence: "And when he had said this, he went out again unto the Jews" or "And after saying this again, he went out to the Jews."

Pilate's question "What is truth?" has elicited many commentaries, including these thoughts by Elder Bruce R. McConkie:

The issue is not so much what-is-truth in the sense of separating truth from error, and thereby being able to know with finality that any specific doctrine or principle is an eternal reality. Hence we find the revealed definition of truth saying: "And truth is knowledge of things as they are, and as they were, and as they are to come. (D&C 93:24.)

Truth, thus, in a purely abstract sense is the thing which actually is. But truth, in the sense of separating it from error or untruth, is the knowledge which men have of what actually is. To illustrate, the fact that there is a God is a truth in the abstract sense because it is a verity that actually is. But the knowledge that God is a personal being in whose image man is created, and not a congeries of laws operating throughout the universe, is the ultimate and specific answer to the question what-is-truth where Deity is concerned. (DNTC 1:802.)

18:39–40 For additional information on the custom that a prisoner should be released "at the passover" and on the selection of Barabbas, read text and commentaries for Matthew 27:15–26; Mark 15:6–15; Luke 23:13–25.

19:1–16 For additional information on the trial of Jesus before Pilate, read text and commentaries for Matthew 27:27–32; Mark 15:15–21; Luke 23:26.

19:4 Jesus is innocent. Pilate knew it; Herod knew it; Caiaphas knew it; the Sanhedrin knew it; the mob-multitude knew it—and Satan knew it. Yet he is to be pronounced guilty and sentenced to death. (DNTC 1:809.)

19:5 Pilate seems to have counted on the pitiful sight of the scourged and bleeding Christ to soften the hearts of the maddened Jews. But the effect failed. Think of the awful fact—a heathen, a pagan, who knew not God, pleading with the priests and people of Israel for the life of their Lord and King! (JTC, p. 639.)

19:7–11 Jesus' sentence by the Sanhedrin was for blasphemy, a Jewish crime; Pilate's sentence was for sedition, a Roman offense. Now that our Lord's death has been ordered, the Jews seek to make it appear that Pilate has endorsed their Jewish death decree. Their mention of "the Son of God" increases Pilate's fears for having ordered an unjust execution. He asks, "Are you a man or a demigod?" Jesus disdains to answer. Pilate is piqued and boasts of his power to save or destroy Jesus. Then our Lord becomes the Judge and places Pilate before the judgment bar: "Against me you have only such power as Divine Providence permits; your sentence is unjust, but Caiaphas who delivered me to thee has the greater sin for as a Jew he knows of my divine origin." (DNTC 1:809.)

19:9 "Whence art thou?" could have been translated "Where are you from?"

19:12 This clinched the matter. Any complaint to Caesar that Pontius Pilate was anything but ruthless in destroying claimants to kingly office was the last thing the Roman procurator wanted. The Jews had given Pilate a selfish interest in the death of the Man whose life they sought. Pilate was prepared, reluctantly, to let his prior death decree be enforced. (DNTC 1:809–10.)

19:13 "Gabbatha" means more literally "the stone pavement."

19:15 Even so was it and was to be. The people who had by covenant accepted Jehovah as their King, now rejected Him in Person, and acknowledged no sovereign but Caesar. Caesar's subjects and serfs have they been through all the centuries since. Pitiable is the state of man or nation who in heart and spirit will have no king but Caesar! (JTC, p. 641.)

19:17 The Joseph Smith Translation replaces "skull" with "burial." (Read text and commentaries for Matt. 27:33; Mark 15:22. Read also Luke 23:33.)

19:18 Read text and commentaries for Mark 15:27–28; Luke 23:32–33. Read also Matthew 27:38.

19:19–22 Read text and commentaries for Matthew 27:36–37; Mark 15:26. Read also Luke 23:38.

Pilate's action in so wording the title, and his blunt refusal to permit an alteration, may have been an intended rebuff to the Jewish officials who had forced him against his judgment and will to condemn Jesus; possibly, however, the demeanor of the submissive Prisoner, and His avowal of Kingship above all royalty of earth had impressed the mind if not the heart of the pagan governor with a conviction of Christ's unique superiority and of His inherent right of dominion; but, whatever the purpose behind the writing, the inscription stands in history as testimony of a heathen's consideration in contrast with Israel's ruthless rejection of Israel's King. (JTC, p. 657.)

In Hebrew, Greek, and Latin—as though to symbolize the fact that here was a message for all nations and tongues—Pilate bore a written testimony of the divine Sonship of our Lord, a testimony which he obdurately refused to change, a testimony which is true and so stands everlastingly. (DNTC 1:817.)

19:23–24 Read text and commentaries for Matthew 27:35; Luke 23:34; Read also Mark 15:24.

19:23 "Made four parts" means "divided them into four parts [or shares]."

19:24 "Vesture" could have been translated "apparel."

19:25–27 With supreme solicitude, and though he himself was in agony on the cross, Jesus places his mother in the care and keeping of John. From the choice of John to perform this Christian service, we may infer several things:

(1) Mary, probably now about sixty years of age, needed a home and temporal sustenance. While Jesus had been among them, he would have been watchful to see that his mother had what she needed temporally and spiritually; with his leaving John was to assume this responsibility.

(2) Joseph, her husband, is obviously dead and her other sons, not yet converted to the Church, would not have provided the household of faith in which to care for the tender feelings of one who had conversed with Gabriel, borne God's Son in her womb, and seen him crucified by wicked men.

(3) John, beloved and chosen among the disciples, had the facilities and means to care for her. From his acquaintance with the high priest (John 18:15), and his detailed knowledge of Jesus' ministry in Jerusalem, it appears John had a home there. Such could have been the place where Jesus himself stayed when in that city. (DNTC 1:826.)

19:28–29 Read text and commentaries for Matthew 27:46–49; Mark 15:34–36. The scripture fulfilled here is Psalm 69:21.

19:29 "Upon hyssop" could have been more literally translated "upon a hyssop stalk."

Now there was a vessel full of vinegar, *mingled with gall,* and they filled a *sponge* with *it,* and put upon hyssop, and put to his mouth. (JST; italics added.)

(See BD, "Hyssop," "Myrrh.")

19:30 Read text and commentaries for Matthew 27:50–51; Mark 15:37–38; Luke 23:45–46.

19:31–33 It was now late in the afternoon; at sunset the Sabbath would begin. That approaching Sabbath was held to be more than ordinarily sacred for it was a high day, in that it was the weekly Sabbath and a paschal holy day. The Jewish officials, who had not hesitated to slay their Lord, were horrified at the thought of men left hanging on crosses on such a day, for thereby the land would be defiled; so these scrupulous rulers went to Pilate and begged that Jesus and the two malefactors be summarily dispatched by the brutal Roman method of breaking their legs, the shock of which violent treatment had been found to be promptly fatal to the crucified. The governor gave his consent, and the soldiers broke the limbs of the two thieves with cudgels. Jesus, however, was found to be already dead, so they broke not His bones. Christ, the great Passover sacrifice, of whom all altar victims had been but suggestive prototypes, died through violence yet without a bone of His body being broken, as was a prescribed condition of the slain paschal lambs. (JTC, pp. 663–64.)

19:34–37 Several prophecies concerning the Messiah are fulfilled in these verses; as examples, read Exodus 12:46, Numbers 9:12, Psalm 34:20.

In speaking of his Second Coming, Christ said through the mouth of Zechariah, "They shall look upon me whom they have pierced." (Zech. 12:10.) This Messianic utterance shall find fulfillment in the appearance of the resurrected Lord to the descendants of his ancient covenant people when he returns in glory. They will then say: "What are these wounds in thine hands and in thy feet?" His reply: "These wounds are the wounds with which I was wounded in the house of my friends. I am he who was lifted up. I am Jesus that was crucified. I am the Son of God." (D&C 45:51–52; Zech. 13:6.)

That the spear wound was of major proportion, one that would have slain him had he not already voluntarily given up his life, is evident from his statement made to the Nephites after his resurrection, "Thrust your hands into my side." (3 Ne. 11:14.) (DNTC 1:835.)

(See section 1, "Pierced by spear.")

19:34 John, who was eye witness to the water and blood gushing from Jesus' side after his spirit had left his body, later wrote of being "born of God" through the atonement in these words: "Whatsoever is born of God overcometh the world. . . . Who is he that overcometh the world, but he that believeth that Jesus is the Son of God? This is he that came by water and blood. And it is the Spirit that beareth witness, because the Spirit is truth. . . . And there are three that bear witness in earth, the spirit, and the water, and the blood." (1 John 5:1–8.) (DNTC 1:835; see Moses 6:59.)

While, as stated in the text, the yielding up of life was voluntary on the part of Jesus Christ, for He had life in Himself and no man could take His life except as He willed to allow it to be taken, (John 1:4; 5:26; 10:15–18) there was of necessity a direct physical cause of dissolution. As stated also the crucified sometimes lived for days upon the cross, and death resulted, not from the infliction of mortal wounds, but from internal congestion, inflammations, organic disturbances, and consequent exhaustion of vital energy. Jesus, though weakened by long torture during the preceding night and early morning, by the shock of the crucifixion itself, as also by intense mental agony, and particularly through spiritual suffering such as no other man has ever endured, manifested surprising vigor, both of mind and body, to the last. The strong, loud utterance, immediately following which He bowed His head and "gave up the ghost," when considered in connection with other recorded details, points to a physical rupture of the heart as the direct cause of death. If the soldier's spear was thrust into the left side of the Lord's body and actually penetrated the heart, the outrush of "blood and water" observed by John is further evidence of a cardiac rupture; for it is known that in rare instances of death resulting from a breaking of any part of the wall of the heart, blood accumulates within the pericardium, and there undergoes a change by which the corpuscles separate as a partially clotted mass from the almost colorless, watery serum. Similar accumulations of clotted corpuscles and serum occur within the pleura. Dr. Abercrombie of Edinburgh, as cited by Deems (*Light of the Nations,* p. 682), "gives a case of the sudden death of a man aged seventy-seven years, owing to a rupture of the heart. In his case 'the cavities of the pleura contained *about three pounds of fluid,* but the lungs were sound.'" Deems also cites the following instance: "Dr. Elliotson relates the case of a woman who died suddenly. 'On opening the body the pericardium was found distended with *clear serum,* and a very large coagulum of blood, which had escaped through a spontaneous rupture of the aorta near its origin, without any other morbid appearance.' Many cases might be cited, but these suffice." For detailed treatment of the subject the student may be referred to Dr. Wm. Stroud's work *On the Physical Cause of the Death of Christ.* Great mental stress, poignant emotion either of grief or joy, and intense spiritual struggle are among the recognized causes of heart rupture.

The present writer believes that the Lord Jesus died of a broken heart. The psalmist sang in dolorous measure according to his inspired prevision of the Lord's passion: "Reproach hath broken my heart; and I am full of heaviness: and I looked for some to take pity, but there was none; and for comforters, but I found none. They gave me also gall for my meat; and in my thirst they gave me vinegar to drink." (Psalm 69:20, 21; see also 22:14.) (JTC, pp. 668–69.)

19:38–42 Additional information on the claiming of Jesus' body by Joseph of Arimathaea and of the burial in the

tomb is found in the text and commentaries for Matthew 27:57–60; Mark 15:42–46; Luke 23:50–54.

19:38 "Pilate gave him leave" has also been translated "Pilate gave permission" and "Pilate told him he could have the body."

20:1–10 (Read Luke 24:12.) Portions of these accounts of early appearances of the resurrected Jesus Christ are also found in the other gospels. However, the account of the visit of Peter and "the other disciple" to the empty tomb is given in much greater detail by John, lending credence to the belief that John was that "other disciple."

20:1 The Joseph Smith Translation adds to the end of this verse "and two angels sitting thereon."

That "it was yet dark" when Mary Magdalene visited the tomb and found it empty indicates that the resurrection took place sometime before sunrise on "the first day of the week."

> Because Jesus came forth from the grave on the first day of the week, to commemorate that day and to keep in remembrance the glorious reality of the resurrection, the ancient apostles, as guided by the Spirit, changed the Sabbath to Sunday. That this change had divine approval we know from latter-day revelation, in which Deity speaks of "the Lord's day" as such and sets forth what should and should not be done on that day. (D&C 59:9–17.) (DNTC 1:841.)

(See section 1, "Three days will rise.")

20:11–18 Mark gave an abbreviated account of this meeting of Mary Magdalene with the resurrected Jesus Christ. (See Mark 16:9–11.)

20:14 "Knew not that it was Jesus" could have been translated "did not discern that it was Jesus."

20:17 "Touch" has frequently been translated "hold." This usage is substantiated by the Joseph Smith Translation, which reads "Hold me not."

> One may wonder why Jesus had forbidden Mary Magdalene to touch Him, and then, so soon after, had permitted other women to hold Him by the feet as they bowed in reverence. We may assume that Mary's emotional approach had been prompted more by a feeling of personal yet holy affection than by an impulse of devotional worship such as the other women evinced. Though the resurrected Christ manifested the same friendly and intimate regard as He had shown in the mortal state toward those with whom He had been closely associated, He was no longer one of them in the literal sense. There was about Him a divine dignity that forbade close personal familiarity. To Mary Magdalene Christ had said: "Touch me not; for I am not yet ascended to my Father." If the second clause was spoken in explanation of the first, we have to infer that no

human hand was to be permitted to touch the Lord's resurrected and immortalized body until after He had presented Himself to the Father. It appears reasonable and probable that between Mary's impulsive attempt to touch the Lord, and the action of the other women who held Him by the feet as they bowed in worshipful reverence, Christ did ascend to the Father, and that later He returned to earth to continue His ministry in the resurrected state. (JTC, p. 682.)

Elder Bruce R. McConkie sees significance in the careful wording of Jesus on this occasion: "I ascend unto *my* Father, and *your* Father; and to *my* God, and *your* God." (Italics added.)

Such careful choice of words was in keeping with his invarying custom of maintaining a distinction between himself and other men. He was the Son of God, literally; other men had mortal fathers. Thus, for instance, he was careful to say. "I ascend unto my Father, and your Father; and to my God and your God" (John 20:17), not unto *our Father* and *our God*." (DNTC 1:413.)

20:19–23 Other accounts of this visit of the resurrected Jesus Christ to ten of the apostles are Mark 16:14 and Luke 24:36–44. Portions of these accounts may also pertain to his appearance a week later when Thomas was also present.

20:19 "The doors were shut" means "the doors were locked." (See v. 26.)

20:22 Baptism divides into two parts—immersion in water and immersion in the Spirit. "I indeed baptize you with water unto repentance," proclaimed John, the Lord's forerunner, "but he that cometh after me is mightier than I, whose shoes I am not worthy to bear: he shall baptize you with the Holy Ghost, and with fire." (Matt. 3:11.)

From the time of John to this hour when the resurrected Lord stood before his apostolic witnesses, the only legally performed baptisms had been in water, with the promise in each instance of a future baptism of fire. Now the time was at hand to perform the ordinance which would entitle the saints to receive the baptism of fire. And so Jesus "breathed on them," which probably means that he laid his hands upon them as he uttered the decree: "Receive the Holy Ghost." (DNTC 1:856–57.)

(See section 1, "Baptism: of Spirit.")

20:23 God only can forgive sins; Jesus exercised this power during his ministry to show he was God. Priesthood is the power and authority of God delegated to man on earth to act in all things for the salvation of men. And so we now find Jesus authorizing the apostles to use their priesthood, which is the power of God, to retain and remit sins. Obviously they cannot do so except in those cases where Christ himself would have so acted had he been present performing this ministerial service.

Revelation from the Lord is always required to retain or remit sins. Since God is the one who must cleanse and purify a human soul, the use of his priestly powers to do so must be authorized and approved by him, and this approval comes by revelation from his Holy Spirit. In many cases in this dispensation the Lord by revelation announced that the sins of certain persons were forgiven. (D&C 60:7; 61:2; 62:3; 64:3.) Accordingly, if by revelation he should tell his apostles to act for him, using his power which is priesthood, and to thus retain or remit sins, they would do so, and their acts would in effect be his. See Matt. 16:13–20; 17:1–9; 18:18.

This same apostolic power is always found in the true Church, and hence we find the Lord saying to Joseph Smith: "I have conferred upon you the keys and power of the priesthood, . . . and whosoever sins you remit on earth shall be remitted eternally in the heavens; and whosoever sins you retain on earth shall be retained in heaven." (D&C 132:45–46.) (DNTC 1:857–58.)

(See section 1, "Forgiveness.")

20:24–29 Thomas apparently did not understand or believe that Jesus had come forth with a literal, tangible body of flesh and bones, one that could be felt and handled, one that bore the nail marks and carried the spear wound, one that ate food and outwardly was almost akin to a mortal body. Obviously he had heard the testimony of Mary Magdalene and the other women, of Peter, and of all the apostles. It is not to be supposed that he doubted the resurrection as such, but rather the literal and corporeal nature of it. Hence his rash assertion about feeling the nail prints and thrusting his hand into the Lord's side.

His skepticism is almost the perfect pattern for even the religiously inclined of modern Christendom, people who profess belief in Christ's resurrection and yet suppose he has become some kind of spiritual person or essence who does not continue to live as a corporeal entity. The case of Thomas shows why the Lord went to such great lengths on the Emmaus road and in the upper room to show beyond peradventure of doubt exactly what his body was like. And so rather than point the finger of scorn at Thomas we might do well to look carefully at the modern disbelief in that holy being who with his Father reigns as a Holy Man in the heavens above. (DNTC 1:860.)

20:26 Elder James E. Talmage has commented on the construction "after eight days":

A week later, for so the Jewish designation, "after eight days," is to be understood, therefore on the next Sunday, which day of the week afterward came to be known to the Church as the "Lord's Day" and to be observed as the Sabbath in place of Saturday, the Mosaic Sabbath, the disciples were again assembled, and Thomas was with them. The meeting was held within closed and, presumably, guarded doors, for there was danger of interference by the Jewish officers. (JTC, p. 690.)

20:30–31 (Read text and commentaries for John 21:25.) John's intent in writing his gospel is explained beautifully in verse 31: "that ye might believe that Jesus is the Christ, the Son of God."

21:1–14 The account of the resurrected Christ to seven

apostles on the shore of the "sea of Tiberias" is found only in John. (Read text and commentaries for Matt. 4:18; Luke 5:1.)

21:5–7 The incident of following the command to cast their net on the other side, which resulted immediately in a large catch of fish, must have triggered the memories of John and Peter of an earlier experience with Jesus that now assisted them to recognize the resurrected Lord. (Read Luke 5:1–11.)

21:8 "Two hundred cubits" is the about three hundred feet.

21:11 "And for all there were so many, yet was not the net broken" could have been translated "although there were so many the net did not burst."

21:14 This is the third time they have seen him as a group. It is his seventh, perhaps eighth, known appearance. He came first to Mary Magdalene; then to the other women; then to Cleopas and his companion on the Emmaus road; thereafter to Peter alone; perhaps somewhere during this time to James, his brother; and twice to the apostles in the upper room. He has yet to appear on the Mount in Galilee, which probably is the occasion when he came to "above five hundred brethren at once'" (1 Cor. 15:5–7); he has yet to spend the balance of the first forty days of his resurrected life ministering to and teaching them (Acts 1:3); and finally in their presence he has yet to ascend to eternal glory. And of course there may have been appearances without number of which there is no New Testament record. He of course ministered among the Nephites on the American continent and among the Lost Tribes of Israel in an unspecified land. (3 Ne.) (DNTC 1:862.)

(See section 1, "Resurrected being: Appearances of Jesus as.")

21:15–19 The Greek text adds considerably to an understanding of these verses. The English texts indicate that the Savior asked Peter essentially the same question three times. However, the Greek verb of the third question asks for a higher degree of commitment than the verb used earlier. Also, although the English texts use "feed" all three times in the response of the Savior, the Greek text uses the word for "shepherding" in verse 16. Thus, the Savior was not asking the same question each time, nor were his responses identical.

This is a very important question for each one of us. May I ask each of you, "Do you love the Lord?" The answer almost without exception would be, "Yes." . . .

We show and prove our love by *feeding the lambs and the sheep*. There are over three billion people on the earth today, and at the present rate of teaching, over two and a half billion of God's children will never be taught the gospel of Jesus Christ. What if you were to live on this earth and never had a chance to hear and be taught the true way of life?

Our task is great. Teachers are needed. Every member of this Church that has a testimony and is converted is urgently needed. The lambs and the sheep are hungry for the bread of life, for the gospel of Jesus Christ. We can show our love by following the prophet of God, "by every member being a missionary" to bring one or more souls into the Church each year. (Bernard P. Brockbank, CR, Oct. 1963, pp. 66.)

Now Peter, still not fully converted, for such must await the Spirit's descent on Pentecost, is called upon to erase the three averrals that he knew not the Man, by thrice asserting his love for the risen Lord. That he was singled out from the seven apostles there assembled is an added evidence that he was chief among them. The question, "Lovest thou me more than these?" was one of deep import, for Peter, the senior apostle of God on earth, had gone fishing; that is, instead of devoting himself, with all his means and energy to the ministry, he had gone off after temporal things. Our Lord now calls him back and asks: "Lovest thou me more than these one hundred and fifty-three fish, more than the things of this world?" And the commands, "Feed my lambs. . . . Feed my sheep," are announced as tests for Peter and for all Christ's ministers, tests which measure how much the elders of the kingdom love their Lord. (DNTC 1:863.)

21:18 This verse could have been more literally translated "Most truly I say to you, When you were younger, you used to gird yourself and walk about where you wanted. But when you grow old you will stretch out your hands and another [man] will gird you and bear you where you do not wish."

21:19 "Thou shalt follow me," our Lord said to Peter on that recent day when the chief apostle pledged, "I will lay down my life for thy sake," (John 13:36–38.) How literally the Master then spoke, and how fully Peter is to do as he offered, he now learns. He is to be crucified, a thing which John in this passage assumes to be known to his readers. Peter's arms are to be stretched forth upon the cross, the executioner shall gird him with the loin-cloth which criminals wear when crucified, and he shall be carried where he would not, that is to his execution. (2 Pet. 1:14–15.) (DNTC 1:863–64.)

21:20–24 These revealing words of the resurrected Jesus Christ concerning the future of John the Beloved have been preserved only by John, and have been greatly misunderstood by many New Testament students and scholars.

"There be some standing here," Jesus said about the time Peter gave his famous testimony of our Lord's divine Sonship, "which shall not taste of death, till they see the Son of man coming in his kingdom." (Matt. 16:28.) John is the only one of these of whom we have any knowledge.

On this present occasion, Peter having learned of his own future martyrdom, desires to know what awaits John. The answer: "He is to tarry in the flesh until I come in my glory at the end of the world."

John's own account of his translation was revealed anew in this day in these words: [Read D&C 7:1–8.]

It is interesting to note that in the gospel account John specifies that he was promised that he should tarry until the Second Coming and not that he should escape death. From the account of the translation of the Three Nephite disciples we learn that this is exactly what takes place. A change is wrought in their bodies so they cannot die at this time, but when the Lord comes again they "shall be changed in the twinkling of an eye from mortality to immortality," and thus they "shall never taste of death." (3 Ne. 28:1–10, 36–40.) They will be like a person who lives during the millennium. Of such the revelation says: "It is appointed to him to die at the age of man. Wherefore, children shall grow up until they become old; old men shall die; but they shall not sleep in the dust, but they shall be changed in the twinkling of an eye." (D&C 63:50–51.) Thus they shall die, in the sense indicated, but they shall not "taste of death." In this respect it is profitable to note the language used by the Lord with reference to the death of the righteous: "And it shall come to pass that those that die in me shall not taste of death, for it shall be sweet unto them." (D&C 42:46.) (DNTC 1:864–65.)

(See section 1, "Translated.")

21:25 The expression that "even the world itself could not contain the books" should not be interpreted to mean that the earth would not be large enough to hold the books. Rather, the "worldliness" of the people is such that they ("the world") could not understand nor appreciate fully the additional words of Jesus, even if they should be written.

Elder James E. Talmage saw the closing testimony of John as essentially the close of the apostolic period during the meridian of time:

> The final ministry of John marked the close of the apostolic administration in the Primitive Church. His fellow apostles had gone to their rest, most of them having entered through the gates of martyrdom, and although it was his special privilege to tarry in the flesh until the Lord's advent in glory, he was not to continue his service as an acknowledged minister, known to and accepted by the Church. Even while many of the apostles lived and labored, the seed of apostasy had taken root in the Church and had grown with the rankness of pernicious weeds. This condition had been predicted, both by Old Testament prophets and by the Lord Jesus. The apostles also spake in plain prediction of the growth of the apostasy all too grievously apparent to them as then in progress. Personal manifestations of the Lord Jesus to mortals appear to have ceased with the passing of the apostles of old, and were not again witnessed until the dawn of the Dispensation of the Fulness of Times. (JTC, pp. 717–18.)

BIBLIOGRAPHY

Dummelow, J. R., ed. *A Commentary on the Whole Bible*. New York: Macmillan, 1943.

The Holy Scriptures, ("An Inspired Revision of the Authorized Version, by Joseph Smith, Jr.") Independence, Mo.: Herald Publishing House, 1974.

Journal of Discourses. 26 vols. London: Latter-day Saints' Book Depot, 1854–86.

Kimball, Spencer W. *The Miracle of Forgiveness*. Salt Lake City: Bookcraft, 1969.

McConkie, Bruce R. *Doctrinal New Testament Commentary*. 3 vols. Salt Lake City: Bookcraft, 1965–73.

———. *Mormon Doctrine*. Salt Lake City: Bookcraft, 1966.

Smith, Joseph. *History of The Church of Jesus Christ of Latter-day Saints*. 7 vols. 2nd ed. rev. Edited by B. H. Roberts. Salt Lake City: The Church of Jesus Christ of Latter-day Saints, 1932–51.

———. *Lectures on Faith*. Compiled by N. B. Lundwall. Salt Lake City: N. B. Lundwall, n.d.

———. *Teachings of the Prophet Joseph Smith*. Selected by Joseph Fielding Smith. Salt Lake City: Deseret Book Company, 1938.

Smith, Joseph F. *Gospel Doctrine*. 5th ed. Salt Lake City: Deseret Book Company, 1938.

Smith, Joseph Fielding. *Answers to Gospel Questions*. 5 vols. Compiled by Joseph Fielding Smith Jr. Salt Lake City: Deseret Book Company, 1957–66.

———. *Doctrines of Salvation*. 3 vols. Compiled by Bruce R. McConkie. Salt Lake City: Bookcraft, 1954–56.

———. *The Way to Perfection*. Salt Lake City: Deseret Book, 1975.

Talmage, James E. *The Articles of Faith*. 12th ed. Salt Lake City: The Church of Jesus Christ of Latter-day Saints, 1924.

———. *Jesus the Christ*. 3rd ed. Salt Lake City: The Church of Jesus Christ of Latter-day Saints, 1916.

Taylor, John. *The Mediation and Atonement*. Salt Lake City: Deseret News Company, 1882.

INDEX